The Anti-Rent Era
in New York Law and Politics,
1839-1865

Studies in Legal History

Published by the University of North Carolina Press
in association with the American Society for Legal History

Thomas A. Green and Hendrik Hartog, editors

THE Anti-Rent

ERA IN NEW YORK LAW AND POLITICS

1839-1865

Charles W. McCurdy

THE UNIVERSITY OF NORTH CAROLINA PRESS   CHAPEL HILL & LONDON

Publication of this book has been aided by generous grants
from the L. J. Skaggs and Mary C. Skaggs Foundation
and the University of Virginia School of Law.

Designed by April Leidig-Higgins
Set in Monotype Bulmer by Keystone Typesetting, Inc.
Manufactured in the United States of America

The paper in this book meets the guidelines for permanence
and durability of the Committee on Production Guidelines
for Book Longevity of the Council on Library Resources.

Library of Congress Cataloging-in-Publication Data
McCurdy, Charles W., 1948–
The anti-rent era in New York law and politics, 1839–1865 /
by Charles W. McCurdy.
p. cm. (Studies in legal history) Includes index.
ISBN 0-8078-2590-5 (cloth : alk. paper)
1. Landlord and tenant—New York (State)—History.
2. Rent strikes—New York (State)—History. 3. Law and
politics. I. Title. II. Series.
KFN5145.M33 2001   346.74704'344 dc21   00-030263

05 04 03 02 01   5 4 3 2 1

For Sharon

Contents

Tables and Maps

Preface

The most spectacular tenant rebellion in United States history began on the 726,000-acre Manor of Rensselaerwyck in 1839 and gradually engulfed the other great estates of eastern New York. At its height in 1845, the uprising involved approximately 10,000 tenant families in eleven counties with a total of 1.8 million acres under lease for lives or forever. An archaic legal form, unique to the Hudson-Mohawk region, lay at the root of the revolt. Lawyers called it a "lease in fee." Tenant farmers had other words for the contractual relation this legal form established and sustained. They described themselves as a people enmeshed in "feudal servitude interminable," an "unhallowed bondage" that amounted to "voluntary slavery." Emancipation was their goal. The rent strike was the instrument they chose to unify their communities and dramatize their plight for the general public.

Tenant resistance to rent collections vexed landlords and embroiled New York politics for more than a decade. Armed bands of anti-renters intimidated sheriffs who tried to serve process and terrorized neighbors who subverted the cause by word or deed. Three people were killed. Although state governors sent the militia into Anti-Rent counties three times between 1839 and 1845, the tenant agitation always resumed after the troops departed. Landlord responses to the rent strike varied from county to county and over time. On the Manor of Rensselaerwyck, the proprietors offered to sell their interest in tenant farms before the strike began. Their tenants, however, claimed that the terms were unacceptable. As the Anti-Rent movement grew larger and its threat to rights of property and contract more alarming, the Van Rensselaers dug in their heels and refused to compromise. The majority of landlords went the other way. Dozens of great proprietors with no intention of selling changed their minds in the face of Anti-Rent resistance and hostile public opinion. They eventually accepted offers, proposed from the outset by the Anti-Rent associations, that converted covenants for rents and services into mortgages. Most tenant families bought their farms during the late 1840s and early 1850s. But the rent strike on the Manor of Rensselaerwyck did not come to an end until 1865, when state militiamen returned with orders from New York's highest court and crushed the last pocket of tenant resistance. Many manor families lost their homes; many others remained mired in "voluntary slavery." Liability for perpetual rent is attached to scattered parcels of real estate in eastern New York to this day.

The amazing thing about the Anti-Rent story is that nobody defended the lease in fee after the rent strike began. Four consecutive state governors condemned it, one legislative committee after another denounced it, a generation of appellate judges hated it, and virtually all the organs of public opinion scorned it. Even the forty or fifty landlords with a vested interest in the rent system came to regard it as an anachronism that ought to be extinguished. Yet the lease in fee survived. It survived a succession of ingenious land reform proposals drafted at the behest of renowned New York governors. It survived a constitutional convention that outlawed the lease in fee in future agreements but did nothing for the thousands of families constrained by existing contracts that ran forever. And it survived more than a decade of litigation in which the state judiciary recast New York's law of real property yet declined to slay a legal form that had been spared by the political process.

Much of what we know—or think we know—about politics and law in the 1840s makes the outcome of the Anti-Rent agitation seem surprising. Historians of the Second Party System have shown that Whig and Democratic leaders sought to win elections by posing as champions of republican values, framing distinctive agendas for government action, and portraying the opposition as antirepublican or aristocratic. Competition between the two parties generated astonishingly high rates of voter turnout. Because every ballot counted in such a competitive political order, each party organization had an incentive to reach out for any big bloc of voters whose particular grievances could be accommodated within the party's more general public philosophy. Anti-renters were a logical target of opportunity on both counts. Tenants outnumbered their landlords by a ratio of 1,000:1, and the Anti-Rent associations bid for public support with appeals to republican values from the beginning.

Viewed from the perspective of mid-nineteenth-century law, the survival of the lease in fee seems equally puzzling. Since the publication of Willard Hurst's pathbreaking *Law and the Conditions of Freedom in the Nineteenth-Century United States* forty years ago, legal historians have repeatedly shown how contract principles, property rules, and constitutional doctrines facilitated the dramatic changes we now call "the market revolution." Judges and legislators not only conceived of law as an instrument of policy but, in Hurst's words, "valued change more than stability and valued stability most often where it helped create a framework for change." The idea of progress permeated the legal system; as a result, whole domains of law tended to favor "dynamic rather than static property, property in motion or at risk rather than property secure and at rest." Anti-Rent complaints about the lease in fee, a paradigmatic form of static property, made it a logical candidate for extinction. Lawyers associated with both the Whig and Democratic parties claimed that manorial tenures impaired the tenants' ability to obtain credit and adjust to new market conditions, frustrated the adoption of improved agricultural techniques, and impoverished the farmers and villagers of the Hudson-Mohawk region. Yet the lease in fee was not suppressed by statute, by New York's bellwether constitutional convention of 1846, or by judicial decision. Even private bargaining in the shadow of public opinion failed on the Manor of Rensselaerwyck. Explaining this paradox at the borderland of American legal and political history is the principal purpose of this book.

The structure of the book is straightforward. The first chapter accounts for the emergence of the lease in fee as a problem in New York public life; the last two describe how it ceased to be regarded as a problem that required a public solution. The intervening chapters proceed chronologically. Each recounts the struggle for land reform against the backdrop of other issues—banking, internal improvements, public and private debts, labor radicalism, slavery—that not only competed for the attention of lawmakers but also influenced their response to Anti-Rent petitions and proposals. Four main themes are elaborated as the story unfolds. The first is the changing conditions of law that set limits on government's competence to disturb the property and contract rights of landlords. The second is the role of lawyers in integrating legal theory and party ideology as they tried to formulate land reform programs capable of passing constitutional muster. The third is the changing conditions of politics that either prevented party leaders from mobilizing their own people behind a land reform measure or encouraged members of the opposition to prevent the enactment of decisive land reform legislation. The fourth is the manifold ways in which the discourse of lawyers and politicians at the state capital constantly reconfigured the matrix of action on the ground. My focus throughout is the law-making process, the strategic behavior of private adversaries, and the ways both were shaped by legal doctrine and partisan politics in a federal system.

This enterprise requires a new approach to integrating legal and political history. Most accounts of social movements, including the standard histories of the Anti-Rent era, emphasize the resulting effects on law and politics. At the heart of such studies—good, bad, and indifferent—is a presumption that the legal system and the party system respond to "social forces." In the strongest formulations, law and politics act as mirrors that reflect the demands placed upon them. This book, in contrast, considers the effects of law and politics on a social movement. It treats the legal system and the party system as forces in their own right and shows how each, sometimes separately though more often in combination, channeled action and shaped the formation of agendas by public and private actors alike. Integrating legal and political history in this way requires attention to the distinctive logics, the distinctive cultures, of law and party politics. It requires attention to the role of lawyers in bridging the two. And it requires attention to the configurative effects of all these things on the "social forces" that figure so prominently in conventional studies of American reform movements.

What follows, then, is an account of the relationship between law and politics within the context of one evolving event. The book does not argue a single thesis. Jurisprudential imperatives and partisan imperatives converged to check the drive for land reform in different ways at different moments in time. Throughout the Anti-Rent era, however, there was constant tension between legal constraints and political opportunities on the one hand, and political constraints and legal opportunities on the other. By writing a synchronic narrative that highlights the mutual penetration of legal doctrine and partisan politics, I hope to engage both legal historians inclined to regard most studies of politics as a wasteland (one election campaign after another) and political historians inclined to regard most studies of law in much the same way (one judicial decision after another). Some readers may decide to reconsider their assumptions about how the nineteenth-century "polity of courts and parties" operated and how it affected social policy. I also like to think that telling the Anti-Rent story fulfills an important purpose of humanistic scholarship. By showing how law and politics frustrated the achievement of something everyone wanted to achieve, this book may help us to think in useful ways about the ideas and institutions that diminished the promise of democracy in the American past.

I am grateful for the encouragement, support, and patience of a great many people and institutions. Acknowledgment is owed first to the University of Virginia. A year of leave from teaching in the College of Arts and Sciences got me going. Subsequent summer grants from the Virginia Law School Foundation, courtesy of Dean Robert Scott, enabled me to complete and then revise the manuscript. Generous colleagues in the Department of History and the School of Law sustained my labor year after year. Michael Holt, Joseph Kett, Barry Cushman, and G. Edward White read the entire manuscript, and all made valuable suggestions. Edward Ayers, Brian Balogh, Stephen Innes, Michael Klarman, John Harrison, and Lillian BeVier read and commented on a chapter or more. Two senior colleagues, Robert Cross and William Harbaugh, read early drafts of the first several chapters and encouraged me to push on when I considered throwing in the towel. My debt to them is everlasting. So is my debt to an entire generation of Virginia graduate students. Helping them frame seminar papers, theses, and dissertations gradually broadened my own sense of what a legal historian could do and how it could be done to reach a larger audience. Their influence is discernible on every page.

The contributions of people and institutions beyond Charlottesville have scarcely been less important. Harry Scheiber, Michael Parrish, and Roy Ritchie taught me the historian's craft at the University of California, San Diego. My legal education was guided by Stanton Wheeler, director in the early 1970s of the pathbreaking Russell Sage Program in Law and Social Science at the Yale Law School. Research grants from the University of Wisconsin Legal History Program, the Institute for Humane Studies, and the John Simon Guggenheim Memorial Foundation supported inquiries from which this book germinated. Colleagues in Jurisprudence and Social Policy at Berkeley, where I taught as Visiting Professor of Law in 1995, provided a stimulating environment for research and writing. Publication was made possible by the American Society for Legal History and the University of North Carolina Press. Robert W. Gordon supplied the press with an exceptionally thorough reader's report; the conclusion, framed in response to his gentle complaints about my first ending, owes much to his wise counsel. Dirk Hartog, Tom Green, Lew Bateman, and Brian MacDonald provided the kind of encouragement and editorial assistance every author hopes for.

Charles Joseph and Rebecca May McCurdy are as responsible as anyone for this volume. Their birth in 1986 prompted me to set aside another, seemingly bigger project in favor of one I could finish before they started high school. I barely made it. Watching them grow under the tutelage of their summer companions, beloved cousins Theresa and Christine Fagan, was much more rewarding than watching the pile of pages grow on my desk. Dave Farrer and Harry Scheiber remonstrated against the decision to lock Stephen Field in the filing cabinet yet supported this endeavor in more ways than I can ever repay. Sharon, my wife and best friend, favored the Anti-Rent story from the beginning. For a dedication, however, she preferred to wait for the other one "because it has California in it." Images of the Hempseys, McCurdys, and Moshers who gather periodically in San Diego, Irvine, or Pismo Beach, and of the steadfast friends who descend on Holden Beach every August, kept me from honoring Sharon's request. None of them would understand how this book could possibly be dedicated to anyone else.

April 2000

The Anti-Rent Era
in New York Law and Politics,
1839-1865

1

Governor Seward and the Manor of Rensselaerwyck

On July 4, 1839, angry tenant farmers on New York's oldest estate assembled in the Albany County village of Berne to adopt a declaration of independence from their landlord. Nobody counted heads that afternoon. But 3,063 families leased farms on the 726,000-acre Manor of Rensselaerwyck, and all of them had cause to complain. Manor contracts required an annual rent for every 100 acres ranging from ten to fourteen bushels of wheat, delivered to the landlord and ready for milling. All mill sites and mines were reserved, together with all rights necessary and proper to make them available to the Van Rensselaer family or its agents. Mills might be built, cropland or pasture flooded, and roads laid out on the tenant's premises without payment of compensation. There were also feudal dues. Every year farmstead heads owed a day's labor with horse and wagon and were bound to deliver "four fat fowl" on rent day, though manor custom allowed the labor to be commuted at the rate of two dollars per year and the fowl at fifty cents. Fines on alienation, called quarter sales, were more significant. Leases on Rensselaerwyck ran forever and vested an estate of inheritance in each tenant. If the holder of a perpetual lease conveyed his farm to a stranger, however, one-fourth of the purchase money (under most indentures) or an extra year's rent (under the rest) went to the proprietor or "patroon." Every indenture enumerated remedies for breach of this or any other covenant. Among them was the landlord's right to reenter the premises and repossess not only the land but also any improvements—houses, barns, fences, growing crops—annexed to the land. Taken together, proclaimed the Independence Day mass meeting at Berne, these contractual provisions amounted to "voluntary slavery." The time had come to avow "that we can no longer endure the infamy of tamely entailing upon future generations such wretchedness and unhallowed bondage as inevitably awaits them if we any longer submit ourselves to be thus unjustly, unrighteously, inhumanly oppressed and imposed upon." So began the longest rent strike in United States history.[1]

The legal relation that the tenants vowed to throw off had existed for a very long time. From the outset of colonization, Kiliaen Van Rensselaer, "patroon on the North River of New Netherland" by virtue of a grant from the Dutch government in 1629, maintained a proprietary interest in his entire domain "above and below Fort Orange, on both sides of the river." Every inhabitant owed the patroon fealty; shipping on the Hudson had to display "colony of Rensselaerswyck" colors as it approached the settlement. The first patroon ran the enterprise from Amsterdam. Van Rensselaer, like English counterparts who drew up blueprints for Maryland and the Carolinas, embedded visions of great wealth in legal forms that ill suited a New World environment he never saw. Feudal schemes collapsed in one North American colony after another during the seventeenth century. But the land system on Van Rensselaer's fiefdom endured because it fit the designs of other powerful men following the English conquest of New Netherland in 1664.[2]

Colonial governors appointed by the Duke of York (later King James II) not only confirmed the Van Rensselaer family's land title but used the Dutch patroonship, reconstructed into an English manor, as a prototype for units of local administration. Governors Richard Nicolls (1664–68), Francis Lovelace (1668–73), and Thomas Dongan (1682–88) created eight additional manors and an equal number of independent patents. Two like-minded successors, Benjamin Fletcher (1692–98) and Viscount Cornbury (1701–8), established five more manors and a score of great patents. These ranged in size from tiny Gardner's Island at the east end of Long Island to the huge Hardenbergh Patent, which covered most of present-day Delaware, Greene, Sullivan, and Ulster counties. "This whole province," one New York official complained in 1698, "is given away to about thirty persons in effect." Although the administrative functions of the manors atrophied or were divested and granted to county governments during the eighteenth century, New York's improvident land policy sustained a distinctive form of tenure. With few exceptions, the great proprietors agreed that land should never be alienated in fee simple. Leases for lives were available on Livingston Manor, parts of the Hardenbergh Patent, and the Mohawk country patents owned by George Clarke. Perpetual leases on the Rensselaerwyck model prevailed almost everywhere else. "The Hudson River," Richard Hofstadter wrote in *America at 1750*, "was like a dagger cutting a swath of land monopoly and aristocratic domination between New England and the colonies to the south and west." By most accounts this was precisely what Nicolls, Lovelace, Dongan, Fletcher, and Cornbury—all career men in the English army—had hoped to achieve.[3]

Challenges to the rent system came from several directions in the eighteenth century. Cadwallader Colden, a New York civil servant, regularly fired off letters to superiors in London urging the necessity of land reform; John Tabor Kempe,

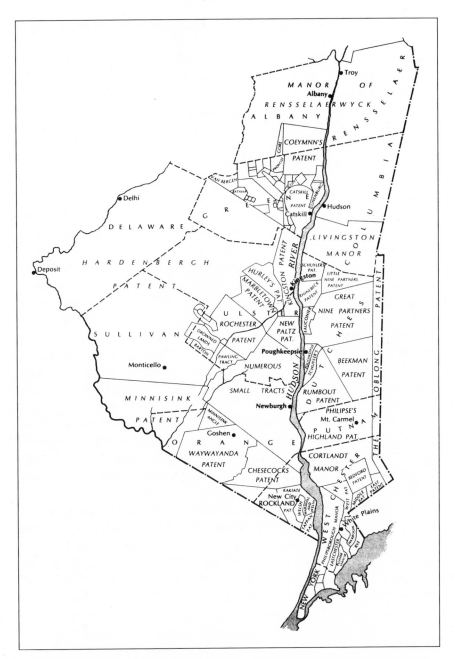

MAP 1. Hudson River Valley Manors and Patents, c. 1750 (Julius Goebel Jr. and Joseph H. Smith, *The Law Practice of Alexander Hamilton: Documents and Commentary*, 5 vols. [New York: Columbia University Press, 1964–81], 3:7. Reprinted with permission.)

a provincial lawyer, toyed with the idea of litigation to contest the validity of great-proprietor titles. In theory, at least, many of the land grants were voidable because the annexed conditions, requiring settlement of a specified number of families within a prescribed number of years, had not been fulfilled in the allotted time. The most significant challenge to the landlords, however, came from the 6,000 tenant farmers. Spectacular uprisings engulfed Livingston Manor, Courtlandt Manor, the Beekman Patent, and Phillipse's Highland Patent in 1766. Violent resistance to rent collections on Livingston Manor flared up again in 1777. Fifteen years after England acknowledged American independence, Governor John Jay summoned the militia to put down a tenant rebellion on Claverack, the 200,000-acre Columbia County estate that had once been a part of Rensselaerwyck. The insurrections evoked some subtle changes in the landlord-tenant relation. But government authorities, acting sometimes in the name of the king and sometimes in the name of the people, crushed every attempt to contest the proprietors' rights of property or subvert the tenants' obligation of contract.[4]

The farmers on Rensselaerwyck had little reason to expect a different result as they launched their rent strike in the summer of 1839. And part of the historic pattern was repeated. On December 10, Governor William H. Seward called up the militia to suppress the violence portended by the Independence Day rally in Albany County. Seward coupled that action, however, with something no previous governor had ever dreamed of doing. He pronounced the contracts in force on the Manor of Rensselaerwyck "oppressive, antirepublican and degrading," and he promised to work for land reform when the state legislature convened a month later. "It cannot be denied," Seward said, "that [the tenants'] complaints are well grounded, and that legislative intervention in their behalf is required, not only upon considerations of justice and equality, but by sound and enlightened policy."[5]

Governor Seward's decision to champion the tenant cause had a momentous effect on New York law and politics. Once manorial tenures had been defined as a public problem that required a public solution, Anti-Rent agitation continued until every possible means of extinguishing "voluntary slavery" by force of law had been exhausted. This chapter recounts the circumstances that brought Seward and the tenants of Rensselaerwyck to such a fateful rendezvous.

A Whig in the State House

In November 1838, eight months before the Rensselaerwyck tenants issued the "Anti-Renters' Declaration of Independence," New Yorkers cast ballots for governor, lieutenant governor, and members of the state legislature. Intense competition between the rival Whig and Democratic parties brought a record

83 percent of the state's eligible voters to the polls, and the Whigs achieved a
stunning victory. William H. Seward, a thirty-seven-year-old lawyer and former
state senator, defeated Governor William L. Marcy, the three-term Democratic
incumbent. Whig candidates also won 81 of the 128 assembly races. Only the
state senate, one-fourth of which turned over each year, remained in Democratic hands. Thurlow Weed, the "dictator" of the Whig Party and Seward's
partner in politics since 1824, led the cheers. "It is like the overthrow of
Robespierre and the Reign of Terror in France," he wrote in his *Albany Evening
Journal* on November 16. "The people, worn-out and exhausted with wrong
and aggression, have risen—as men sometimes will rise—and in their strength
have struck down their oppressors!"[6]

Weed's rhetoric might have been overblown, but 1838 did mark a political
revolution. For thirteen years Governor Marcy and his associates in the "Albany
Regency" had run the state government while Martin Van Buren, builder of the
Democratic Party in New York, performed on the national stage as senator,
secretary of state, minister to England, vice-president, and, since March 1837,
as president. The Democrats had come to power as the friends of the people,
and Andrew Jackson's popular war against the Bank of the United States had
kept them in office. Shortly after his inauguration, however, President Van
Buren proposed a measure that rankled some members of his own party. In
response to the suspension of specie payments during the Panic of 1837, he
urged Congress to take United States funds out of the state banks, which
"thr[ew] them into active employment as bank capital," and deposit them
instead in an Independent Treasury. Two prominent New York Democrats led
the successful opposition in Congress; the Van Buren men waged the 1838
campaign in New York as a referendum on the president's policy in Washington. Regency veteran John A. Dix, author of the Democratic address to the
voters, defined the election as a contest between "the democracy and the
aristocracy," between the people and "the enemies of republicanism." Democrats insisted that it would determine "whether the money power or the democracy shall rule." But this time they were defeated. "The result will be felt like an
electric shock throughout the Union," Weed exclaimed. "Here all was to be lost
or won. And here, in Van Buren's own state, and in defiance of his legions of
office-holders, a victory has been achieved which terminates the misrule of
demagogues and despots."[7]

Governor Marcy blamed his defeat on Van Buren's pursuit of the Independent Treasury. The impending "separation of bank and state" had generated
fears of another credit crisis just as commercial activity started to recover from
the Panic of 1837. Bankers and merchants who previously voted Democratic
had massed against him. "The election was conducted chiefly with reference to
the policy of the federal government," Marcy lamented. "If we had nothing but

our own policy to vindicate I cannot bring myself to doubt that we should have had a different result." As they prepared to leave office, however, the lame-duck Democrats took comfort in the assumption that they would soon be back. The victorious Whigs "are not united by any common bond of principle," wrote Edwin Croswell, editor of the Regency's flagship newspaper, on November 16. "They are bloated with their present accidental success; they only agree upon one point, and that is opposition to the Democratic Party." Millard Fillmore, a Whig congressman from Buffalo, admitted as much. He described his party as a "heterogeneous mass of old National Republicans and revolting Jackson men; Masons and Antimasons; abolitionists and proslavery men; bank men and antibank men with all the lesser fragments that have been, from time to time, thrown off from the great political wheel in its violent revolutions." Croswell insisted that "a party composed of such a compound . . . cannot remain together long enough to keep the state."[8]

Weed and Seward aimed to prove the Democrats wrong. Both had been born in eastern New York yet made their initial mark in the west, Weed as a Rochester newspaperman and Seward in Auburn as law partner of Judge Elijah Miller and later as general counsel for the Holland Land Company. Weed aspired to be the party boss he had become. Seward entered politics because, as he told his wife in 1833, "enthusiasm for the right and ambition for personal distinction are passions of which I cannot divest myself." Together the tall, flamboyant journalist and the short, bookish lawyer had made the transition from "the friends of John Quincy Adams" in 1824, to Antimasonry in 1828, and to Whiggery in 1834. Years of opposition to "Van Burenism" had honed their political skills and prepared them to govern. Weed had become a shrewd tactician; Seward had developed a rare ability in prose or speech to evoke idealism in the hearts and minds of the people. But the big job that loomed before them fell primarily on Seward's shoulders. The new governor had to articulate a public philosophy that appealed to all elements of the diverse Whig coalition, and he had to rally the legislature around an agenda for state action that would consolidate and ramify the party's strength. "A fearful responsibility is upon you," Weed wrote Seward from Albany on November 9. "God grant you the light necessary to guide you safely through."[9]

Seward took the oath of office on January 1, 1839. He performed his first official duty, delivery of a message to the state legislature, later the same day. There had never been a governor's message anything like it. Seward wrapped his remarks on the state of the state and the measures that would make things better, traditional topics in the genre, around a philosophical discourse on "the great responsibilities of the age." He spoke about the duty of Americans "to illustrate the peacefulness, the efficiency, the beneficence, and the wisdom of republican institutions." He addressed "our obligations to promote the happiness of the people, to multiply and raise their social enjoyments," and to cultivate "the improving spirit that pervades our country and animates our citizens." Above all, he set forth a vision of the promise of American life and the state government's role in its fulfillment that inspired his Whig supporters, shocked the Democratic leadership, and laid the foundation for new lines of partisan division in subsequent campaigns.[10]

"This generation," Seward said, "is ordained to reach, on this continent, a higher standard of social perfection than it has ever yet attained," and from American striving "will proceed the spirit which shall renovate the world." The republican form of government made pursuit of "these sublime purposes" possible. Self-government impelled deliberation on the public good by the people themselves, Seward explained, and "the light of the human intellect increases in brilliancy" through political participation. In a republic the "energies" of the people "break through the restraints of power and prejudice" monarchy had sustained for centuries; "the democratic principle" made the "passions" of the people "more equable and humane." American citizens understood that individual liberty and public responsibility went hand in hand, that "the law of improvement" applied to all institutions of social and political life. "Despotism denies this," Seward observed. "It holds that institutions are complete, and that laws are wise because they are old. It maintains that error is sanctified by prescription, and compels the submission which renders it invulnerable." But "a different principle prevails in America" because its political institutions had been established for the people as well as by the people.[11]

Seward's emphasis on what he called "the agency of institutions of self-government" marked him as a progressive politician determined to explode the image of Whiggery as the party of slavish devotion to "the aristocracy." He embraced democracy with alacrity, yet turned Democratic ideology on its head. President Van Buren's war on "the money power" was predicated on the assumption that the banking system posed a threat to the liberty and independence of plain, honest, republican citizens. Pumping public money into privately operated banks, Democrats argued, clothed "irresponsible sovereignties" with power to divest the people's economic independence and thus to destroy the rock upon which republican institutions were built. Regency stalwart Silas Wright declared that in such a regime "the people must be content to fatten upon the humble boons which corporate wealth shall in mercy grant, whether those boons shall be presented in the unmitigated form of an irredeemable paper currency, or the more severe aspect of menial service, in a manufactory, or upon a manor." For Democrats, as Marvin Meyers has said, "when government governed least, society—made of the right republican materials— would realize its own natural moral discipline." Seward, in contrast, claimed that republican citizens were made, not born, and government had a duty to shape the social condition of the people.[12]

Government promotion of internal improvements was the duty foremost in

Seward's mind as the state legislature's 1839 session began. "Thirteen years' experience," he told the assembled lawmakers, "has proved the inadequacy of all our thoroughfares for the transportation of persons and property between the frontier and tide-waters." Since the death of Governor De Witt Clinton, whose "comprehensive views" and "magnanimous efforts" produced the Erie Canal, the dominant Albany Regency had adhered to a "narrow policy" of internal improvement. The pay-as-you-go approach trumpeted by Democrats meant that the unfinished Genesee Valley and Black River canals, as well as railroads capable of bringing all New York households into the market economy, had become "rival enterprises, each by the operation of local jealousies hindering and delaying the others." Seward proposed a bold new departure. He contended that state-owned canals and privately owned railroads should be considered "as parts of one system," and he urged the legislature to accelerate progress on the public works by authorizing the Canal Board and the state's railroad corporations to borrow $4 million a year for the next decade. Government had an obligation, he said, "to equalize the advantages of internal improvement." The state's credit had never been stronger, capital markets had rebounded from the Panic of 1837, and "the enterprise of our people is resuming suspended employments in every department of social industry." Each $500,000 increment of revenue from canal tolls, Seward pointed out, would pay the interest on another $10 million of debt. As a result, "taxation for purposes of internal improvement is happily unnecessary as it would be unequal and oppressive."[13]

The effect of Seward's audacious recommendation, maybe even its purpose, was to superimpose party discipline upon a process long governed by the struggle for local advantage. Democrats decried the governor's "visionary theories." Edwin Croswell, editor of the *Albany Argus*, claimed that Seward's "extravagant" idea of extending internal improvements "through every valley and over every hill" would destroy the state credit and eventually require "a direct tax on the labor and the land of those who get their bread by the sweat of their faces." In the governor's message, he wrote on January 24, 1839, "the ancient doctrine of Federalism is revived that 'a public debt is a public blessing.'" Croswell, a lifetime advocate of government spending for internal improvement, put a new slogan on the masthead of the Regency organ: "For a Prudent and Impartial System of Internal Improvements, Against a Forty Million Dollar Debt." Democratic radicals took a stronger stand against Seward's program. Samuel Young, an influential state senator, and William Cullen Bryant, editor of the *New York Evening Post*, claimed that the legislature had no business appropriating money for canals and railroads under any circumstances. In their view, "the only legitimate function of government is the protection of individual rights."[14]

Democratic opposition was decisive in 1839. Before the legislature adjourned on May 7, the Democratic senate had killed every internal-improvement bill passed by the Whig assembly. Seward and Weed expressed disappointment that, in the latter's words, "all the various works so important to the people and the state have been stayed." Yet the result actually thrilled them. It defined the Whig Party as the friend, the Democratic Party as the foe, of internal improvements. It supplied Whig candidates with a popular state issue that consolidated the party in New York and dovetailed with existing partisan divisions on national policy. At both levels of government Whiggery became the party of commerce and credit, the party of progress, the party of collective striving by a republican body politic for economic growth and the equalization of opportunity. Getting control of the state senate was the next objective, and Whigs believed that they had concocted a winning issue. "If the Empire State is disposed to go back into its shell—if the people want no more canals and railroads," Weed remarked in an *Evening Journal* editorial as the legislature's 1839 session came to end, "they will attach themselves to the Van Buren car, re-elect his followers," and join in the Democratic chorus of " 'Perish Commerce! Perish Credit!' "[15]

Seward's program for the Whig Party assumed that individual New Yorkers, whether artisans or farmers, possessed the freedom necessary to take advantage of internal improvements and a robust credit system. That the Empire State was home to thousands of farmers who lacked enough freedom to exploit new opportunities never crossed his mind until a tenant rebellion erupted later in 1839. The rebellion would prove nasty, brutish, and long. But the chain of events that triggered it began innocently. Stephen Van Rensselaer III, senior major general in the New York militia, chancellor of the state university, president of the Canal Board, and eighth patroon of the Manor of Rensselaerwyck, died on January 28, 1839. Seward announced the "mournful event" to the state legislature two days later; the assembled lawmakers adjourned for the funeral and resolved to wear badges of mourning for thirty days afterward. The governor's special message spoke of "the universal esteem which he has secured by the blamelessness and benevolence of his life." For once Croswell did not disagree. "In all the qualities that constitute the gentleman and ennoble the human character," he remarked in the *Argus*, "Stephen Van Rensselaer may be said to have been preeminent." President Van Buren called him "that good and true gentleman," and Whig merchant Philip Hone said "few men were more extensively known and loved." The residents of Albany showed as much after the funeral on February 1. More than a thousand people joined the procession of state officials and other dignitaries that followed the hearse carrying Van Rensselaer from the North Dutch Church to the family burial ground at Watervliet. None of them imagined that a tenant uprising would soon be a consequence of his renowned benevolence or that land reform would appear on the Whig agenda in 1840.[16]

The Patroon's Domain

"To be an aristocrat," Robert R. Palmer once observed, "it is not enough to think of oneself as such, it is necessary to be thought so by others." Stephen Van Rensselaer III never had a problem on either score. His father and mother, the former Catherine Livingston, announced his birth in 1764 with canon fire at Watervliet, the seat of Rensselaerwyck and site of a newly constructed mansion "so much finer and grander and more gorgeous than any other house of the age that it had the effect of a palace." The manor's tenant families, which numbered about 275 and lived within two or three miles of the Hudson River, paraded to the big house bearing gifts for the patroon's heir. More substantial presents poured in from members of the Beekman, Livingston, Schuyler, and Van Cortlandt families, each of which had been linked with one another and with the Van Rensselaers by strategic marriages. The infant attracted all this attention for good reason. As the first son, Stephen Van Rensselaer III stood to inherit the estate that had been in his family's hands since 1629.[17]

Colossal size was Rensselaerwyck's most striking characteristic. A patent issued in 1685 transformed the Dutch patroonship into an English manor and vested in the Van Rensselaers a domain that stretched twenty-four miles along the Hudson and ran twenty-four miles back into the country on both sides of the river. Yet the vast bulk of Rensselaerwyck remained wilderness at the birth of Stephen Van Rensselaer III in 1764. His seventeenth-century forebears had been merchants rather than land developers; they made fortunes in the fur trade until it declined in the 1690s. The patroons of the early eighteenth century preferred the life of the sedentary rentier to the life of the entrepreneur. Only eighty-two tenant families lived on Rensselaerwyck as late as 1712, and William Livingston reported that Jeremiah Van Rensselaer (1705–45), the fifth patroon, was "scarce ever worth a groat in cash . . . [and] murdered his days with gamesters and debauchers." Van Rensselaer's father, Stephen II, had ambitious plans for the manor but very little opportunity to effect them. He died at age twenty-seven in 1769.[18]

The coming of the American Revolution interrupted attempts to develop the manor for fifteen years. More pressing things preoccupied Philip Livingston and Abraham Ten Broeck, the executors of the Van Rensselaer estate. Livingston, young Van Rensselaer's grandfather, sat in the Continental Congress and signed the Declaration of Independence. Ten Broeck, his uncle, served in the state legislature and as an officer in George Washington's army. Their devotion to the patriot cause did keep Rensselaerwyck intact. Loyalist proprietors were not so fortunate. Confiscation acts swept the rent system from Westchester County through much of Dutchess County; about two-thirds of the new owners previously worked the manor farms as tenants. The Revolution not only shook up the land system in eastern New York but ensured the planting of fee-simple holdings in the west. In the Act Concerning Tenures, passed in 1787, the legislature provided that the tenure of lands granted in the name of the people "shall be and remain allodial, and not feudal." All of New York State west of Fort Stanwix (Rome), which the tribes of the Six Nations ceded to the state government between 1784 and 1800, was peopled by settlers with mortgages rather than leases for lives or forever. In a number of ways, then, Revolutionary republicanism diluted the concentration of landownership that had sustained manorial tenures for more than a century. When Stephen Van Rensselaer III turned twenty-one and took possession of the family land in 1785, the 5 million acres of real estate for sale in northern and western New York dwarfed the un-improved land offered for lease on both sides of the Hudson, along the east and west branches of the Delaware, and in scattered parts of the Mohawk country.[19]

Developing the manor became the first project in Van Rensselaer's long and active life. He "stood in one sense between the present and the past; between two distinct and even opposite orders of things," his friend Daniel Dewey Barnard wrote. "He was a thorough republican, in a republican state, and yet he bore to his death, by common courtesy and consent—never claimed but always conceded—the hereditary title which had anciently attached to the inheritance to which he had been born." Van Rensselaer may not have claimed the title of patroon, but he always acted the part. The celebration of his twenty-first birth-day on November 1, 1785, "was reminiscent of feudal times." People came to Watervliet from all over eastern New York to feast on the roasted beef, drink from the barrels of liquor, and acclaim the new patroon. At sunset Ten Broeck mounted a platform built for the occasion; he presented Van Rensselaer with ninety-five contracts, each one representing a new tenant family that had settled on the manor since 1769. The uncertainties spawned by the Revolution, Ten Broeck explained, had prompted the executors to negotiate leases for years, all but one of which expired on that very day. As Van Rensselaer stepped forward to take possession of the estate and welcome the new tenant families, nobody in the crowd had any doubts about the terms he would offer. The manor policy of grants in perpetuity, with covenants and conditions that preserved a Van Rensselaer interest in the land, was about to be resumed.[20]

Good fortune enabled Van Rensselaer to people the manor under "anti-republican" contracts at the dawn of the republican era. The great migration of New England farmers into upstate New York began just as he took possession of the estate. For two decades, every February day saw 500 families huddled on sleighs arrive in Albany. Most of them merely passed through on the way west. But the period's steady increase in wheat prices and Rensselaerwyck's prox-imity to the market induced many to settle on the manor. The population of New York State jumped from 340,120 in 1790 to 589,051 in 1810; New York

City, which grew at approximately the same rate, became the biggest city in North America. Still, Rensselaerwyck grew faster. The patroon's tenants numbered about 600 on his twenty-first birthday. By 1812 the manor had become home to more than 3,000 families working farms that averaged 142 acres.[21]

Van Rensselaer attributed his success to generous terms. "No hired lands, in this or any other state," he boasted on a promotional broadside posted around Albany in 1789, "are let on such favorable terms to the tenants as my lands are." The claim had something to it. Settlers paid no rent for the first seven years, and a good farmer could clear ten acres each year. The annual rent of fourteen bushels of wheat per hundred acres amounted to the average yield of a single acre cultivated for the first time. And the price of wheat, driven by steady European demand, kept surging. The profitable wagoning distance for wheat doubled to over 100 miles between 1772 and 1819; farmers who lived close to deepwater ports like Albany earned the highest incomes. Most tenant families prospered while the boom lasted. The shrewdest Yankee settlers mined the soil, saved their money, sold out to newcomers, and joined the procession into the new west. Others dug in. People who had entered the land for nothing grew attached to the farms their labor made and to the vibrant communities that sprang up all over Rensselaerwyck.[22]

The patroon grew richer. Manor stores supplied merchandise to the tenants, manor gristmills processed the tenants' grain, and manor sawmills supplied materials for tenant homes and barns as well as lumber for export. Profits from rents, trade, and milling tolls not only were intertwined but had a multiplier effect on earnings. Every farmer induced to settle on the estate increased Van Rensselaer's take from each phase of his integrated operation. Tenant turnover swelled his income too. Fines on alienation for eight contiguous farms in Sand Lake Township, Rensselaer County, yielded $5,237 between 1790 and 1830. One farm changed hands six times and the quarter sales totaled $1,166. Contemporaries took it for granted that Van Rensselaer was the richest man in America; a British traveler who passed through Albany in 1818 estimated his wealth at $7 million.[23]

Then the bubble burst. Wheat prices declined so steeply following the Panic of 1819 that, as Van Rensselaer confessed to the Board of Agriculture, planting grain could no longer "repay the labor expended on its production." Rents in arrear on Rensselaerwyck doubled between 1814 and 1823; the patroon responded the same way other creditors with continuing relationships responded during troughs in the business cycle. He took what little the tenants' could pay, carried unpaid balances and accrued interest on the books, and waited patiently for the rising tide of prosperity that would raise all boats. But the recovery never came. The completion of the Erie Canal in 1825 brought a flood of wheat into eastern markets from the West. "Produced on virgin land that was subject to little or no taxation," Paul Wallace Gates wrote in *The Farmer's Age*, "this western wheat demoralized farmers in the older communities, who were already struggling with declining fertility, low yields, parasitic infestations, increasing costs, and declining prices." By the mid-1830s, when wheat prices soared again, Rensselaerwyck farmers already had lost their battles with soil exhaustion, the Hessian fly, and western competition. Nobody on the manor even tried to grow winter wheat; irregular sales of livestock generated the only cash farmers saw. Ambitious forms of readjustment, such as dairying, required credit that manor tenants had no way of obtaining. They could not borrow money from the patroon while their rents remained unpaid or from mortgage companies as long as Van Rensselaer held reserved interests in their farms. With each passing year, the rents in arrear luxuriated and the irrationality of the rent system became more apparent to patroon and tenant alike.[24]

Van Rensselaer wrestled with what he had wrought during the last decade of his life. He was a tireless promoter of the Erie Canal and served as president of the Canal Board from 1825 until death in 1839. Yet the transportation revolution diminished the income of the tenants on his estate. In 1820 he helped establish the New York Board of Agriculture, an organization dedicated to the dissemination of improved agricultural techniques. Yet the form of land tenure on Rensselaerwyck prevented his tenants from adopting the readjustment strategies advocated by agricultural reformers. In 1824 he endowed the college at Troy that became Rensselaer Polytechnic Institute; its mission, in his words, was "instructing the sons and daughters of farmers and mechanics" in the "application of science to common purposes of life." Yet very few of his increasingly desperate tenants had the means to educate their children there. Van Rensselaer recognized the contradictions between his roles as community builder and land developer, public benefactor and manor proprietor. Dealing with them was another matter. He could not bring himself either to give up his family's interest in tenant farms or to sully his reputation for "blamelessness and benevolence" by taking legal action against tenants in default of their contractual obligations. When he died on January 26, 1839, only the clerks in the manor office knew how bad the situation had become. Rents in arrear amounted to more than $400,000.[25]

The terms of Van Rensselaer's will, probated on April 10, 1839, were awaited with great interest by people on the manor. By long indulgence the patroon had allowed them to believe that back rents would be forgiven upon his death. Van Rensselaer possessed more than enough money to fulfill his tenants' dreams, but he had a wife and ten children with equally high expectations. To his second wife Cornelia he bequeathed a life estate in the family mansion and an annuity of $4,000 per year. Two sons, Stephen Van Rensselaer IV and his half brother William Paterson Van Rensselaer, split the 726,000-acre manor that the

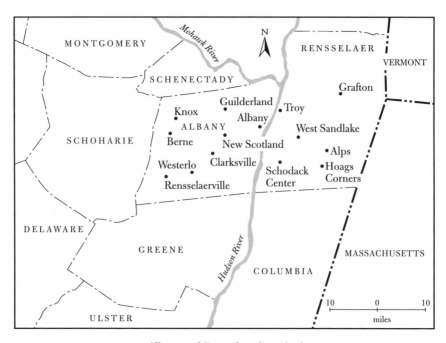

MAP 2. Albany and Rensselaer Counties in 1839

family had controlled for two centuries. Stephen took title for himself, his heirs, and his assignees to all "lands, tenements, hereditaments and real estate with the rents, issues, and profits thereof, situate in the Manor of Rensselaerwyck, on the west side of the Hudson River" in Albany County. About half of Stephen's land had been leased in perpetuity to 1,397 tenant families; the rest, some of it still covered with first-growth forest, vested in him absolutely. The estate William inherited on the east side of the river was about the same size. It spanned all of Rensselaer County, except the northern tier of townships, from the Hudson to the Massachusetts line. He became entitled to "the rents, issues and profits" generated by 1,666 tenant families on 202,100 acres and a slightly smaller amount of wild land. Eight other children divided most of Van Rensselaer's other assets—city lots and commercial buildings in Albany and Manhattan, land in Hamilton and St. Lawrence counties, bank stocks and New York securities worth close to $1 million.[26]

Stephen Van Rensselaer III also had liabilities when he commissioned his will. Rather than remitting the accumulated back rents, as his tenants anticipated, the patroon bequeathed them in trust to be collected and applied on his own debts. Van Rensselaer's will admonished the trustees—Daniel Dewey Barnard, Jacob T. B. Van Vechten, and James Stevenson—to collect the rents in arrear "with all reasonable indulgence to the persons . . . indebted to me, who are poor or otherwise unfortunate." But the trustees could not possibly exercise as much forbearance as the late patroon customarily had and still fulfill their assigned task. In mid-April, when accountants compiled Van Rensselaer's sundry debts, the total stood at $311,000.[27] It was doubtful whether all the personal property owned by the manor's 3,063 families could fetch such a sum at sheriff's sales. The debts of Stephen Van Rensselaer III had to be paid all the same. In effect, his will called for the systematic impoverishment of people whose loyalty, even devotion, he had cultivated assiduously for more than fifty years.

The trustees revolted against their impossible situation before the manor tenants learned about theirs. Daniel Dewey Barnard, an Albany lawyer and Whig congressman, understood that executing the duty thrust upon him by the will would be to commit political suicide. Barnard had some bargaining leverage too. Stephen Van Rensselaer III owed him $35,580 at the time of his death, making him the estate's largest creditor. What soon crystallized was a significant agreement which William Paterson Van Rensselaer came up from Manhattan to sign on May 28. The agreement released Barnard, Van Vechten, and Stevenson from their obligations by providing for a division of the $311,000 debt "into two nearly equal parts," one of which was to be paid by Stephen Van Rensselaer IV and the other by his half brother William. Each proprietor took responsibility for collecting back rents from his own tenants.[28]

William P. Van Rensselaer, already a rich man in his own right, paid off some creditors assigned to him and staved off the others. He wanted no trouble with the tenants in Rensselaer County and, for the moment at least, continued to carry the back rents just as his father had before him. Stephen Van Rensselaer IV was apparently in a less liquid position. The money owed to Barnard was assigned to him; Barnard agreed to take a mortgage on the Albany County half of the manor, thus reducing Stephen's immediate liabilities by 25 percent. Still, the new proprietor insisted on recovering the rents in arrear. He did not even wait for the agreement with the trustees to be signed. Stephen notified Albany County tenants about his intention to collect the back rents early in May, telling them to pay what they owed before the sheriff arrived with writs of *fieri facias* that would mean the attachment and ultimately the forced sale of their livestock, tack, farm implements, and growing crops.[29]

The notices sent out by Stephen Van Rensselaer IV caused a furor in Albany County. Tenant families were disappointed to learn that the late patroon had not forgiven the back rents; they were shocked to learn that his son expected immediate payment. "The manor," Barnard recalled some years later, "was instantly alive with a general stir."[30] At mass meetings in five townships—Berne, Knox, New Scotland, Rensselaerville, and Westerlo—the assembled tenants quickly reached a consensus on a course of action. First, Van Rensselaer had to be persuaded to accept less than the full amount they owed. Second, he had to renegotiate the existing leases. Finally, he had to agree to sell his interest in their farms at a principal sum, which, invested at 7 percent interest, would yield the value of the annual rents in perpetuity. The third demand seemed especially promising to the tenant assemblies. If every family's existing obligations were converted into a mortgage, all would obtain the same sort of breathing space that Van Rensselaer had secured for himself in the agreement with his half brother and Barnard. Such a deal would also transform a manorial form of tenure into an allodial one. The tenants wanted above all to be free from their overlord.

A committee of representatives from the five towns carried the tenant demands to the manor office on May 22. Van Rensselaer refused to talk with the delegates, but the new patroon did agree to consider a written statement of their proposals. The resulting document, framed that afternoon at Dunbar's tavern, began with a recitation of the tenants' grievances. "The enormous price put upon wheat above what it formerly was when the leases were originally given," Lawrence Van Deusen wrote for the committee, "makes it extremely difficult for many of the tenants to support their families and pay their rents." In 1790, "at which time wheat could be raised in abundance," it sold for 75¢ per bushel "at the extreme." Between 1835 and 1838, in contrast, the price of wheat fluctuated between $1.50 and $2.25 per bushel. Yet producing wheat had been "physically impossible" in Albany County for a great many years. Because the contracts in force on Rensselaerwyck required payment of rents in wheat at the market price, the tenants' annual obligations had more than doubled at the very time their land had grown less productive. What is more, the contracts limited their options. The patroon's reservation of water rights prevented them from building sawmills; they could not even sell their farms and go west without forfeiting a quarter of the purchase money.[31]

Van Deusen and his colleagues proposed that the existing leases be "abolished" and new ones given in which the rents would be based on the varying fertility of the farms rather than the market price of wheat. Under the new scheme, some tenants would pay a dollar per bushel of wheat and others as little as 63¢. They also asked the new patroon to waive the back rents "in whole, or at all events in equal proportion to the stipulations to be entered into for future rents," and they insisted that the quarter sale, water rights, and mineral reservations be surrendered. The tenant delegates saved their fundamental demand for last. Van Rensselaer must agree to sell out his interest in each farm, "at any future time, for such sum as the [annual] interest thereof will amount to the amount of rent on each lot now to be fixed."

Stephen Van Rensselaer IV sent the Anti-Rent leaders his answer on May 29, twenty-four hours after signing the agreement with his half brother William and the executors of his father's estate. His letter began with a reminder that "your ancestors or yourselves, who are tenants, accepted leases with a full knowledge of the kind and amount of rent to be paid, and of the reservations and conditions to which the land was subject; and it was [a] matter of agreement, the nature of which was fully understood at the time the same was made." What the tenant delegates now proposed, Van Rensselaer wrote, "is that I shall depreciate my income more than one half, and yield up reservations, which constitute part of my property, and all without any consideration or compensation therefor." The very idea was preposterous. Under no circumstances would he renegotiate the existing contracts.

Yet the new proprietor, unlike his father, was willing to sell his interests in tenant farms. Stephen Van Rensselaer IV was forty-eight years old. He had very little money and no hope of restoring the manorial economy that had collapsed in 1819. But the sale terms his tenants proposed were unacceptable. Their offer would bring him only $2.50 an acre. Van Rensselaer replied that he would sell all his interests for $5 an acre in any farm excepting those below the brow of the Helderberg Mountains—that is, in the townships of Bethlehem, Guilderland, New Scotland, and Watervliet. "The lands below the hill cannot be included" in the general offer, he explained, because "the land [is] generally nearer market and more valuable." Those tenants would have to pay more. Van Rensselaer linked his willingness to sell, however, with the one thing few tenants could afford to do. "It must be expressly understood," he wrote, "that all arrears of rent must be paid before I will release the covenants of rent [and] quarter sales." His first priority was to wring some instant cash out of the manor population. Preventing him from succeeding became the first tactical objective of the Anti-Rent movement.[32]

At the Independence Day rally in Berne the assembled tenants called Van Rensselaer's reply to their proposals "an outrage upon the laws of humanity," and they announced their intention to resist "an unconditional submission to the will of one man, elevated by an aristocratic law, emanating from a foreign monarchy." But issuing the "Anti-Renters' Declaration of Independence" did not prevent tenant leaders from retreating a bit from the demands set forth on May 22. The manifesto adopted on July 4 expressed their willingness to have the rent on all qualities of land commuted to $1 per bushel; they agreed to pay the back rents at the same rate. Both concessions eliminated any difference in treatment between the tenant families who resided above and below "the hill." One function of the revised proposal, then, was to forge the solidarity required to effect the eradication of "voluntary slavery." The concluding resolution adopted at the Independence Day meeting restated the tenants' principal demand with precision: "The privilege at any future time hereafter of buying the soil for a sum of money that the interest thereof at seven percent, will amount to a sum equal to the value of the wheat on each and any lot at said $1 per bushel."

Until the proprietor agreed to sell all his interests in every farm on those terms, the tenants pledged "each unto the other our fortunes and our sacred honor even to the last extremity in protecting our rights and property from being wantonly and unjustly forced from us." The series of civil disorders known ever since as the Helderberg War showed that they meant it.[33]

The Helderberg War

County sheriffs, charged by law with responsibility for serving landlord writs, felt the effects of the "Anti-Renters' Declaration of Independence" before anyone else. Amos Adams, undersheriff of Albany County, got the tenant message on August 28, 1839. "I went to see Isaac Hungerford on his farm" near Rensselaerville, Adams reported in a deposition taken two days later; "he asked me if I had others to serve." The deputy replied that had writs of *fieri facias*, returnable to the New York Supreme Court, for scores of people in the Helderberg townships of Berne, Knox, Rensselaerville, and Westerlo. "Hungerford then said I had better go home and be in some other business; he said we have pledged ourselves that no officer shall travel through here to serve process for the patroon; he said we have made up our minds to die, and we are ready to die in the cause of resisting any officer that should come there on the patroon's business." Hungerford brandished "a large jack-knife" as he spoke. He and some neighbors amplified the threat when the undersheriff stopped for the night at a local tavern. The anti-renters broke into the stable, tore the wheels from Adams's wagon, cut up his harness, and sheared his horse's mane and tail.[34]

Sheriff Michael Artcher received a comparable warning two weeks later. "I understand you are calculating to soon make your electors a visit in your official capacity, in favor of the tenants' monarch," a New Scotland anti-renter wrote him on September 9. "As the tenants were so friendly as to elect you to the office of sheriff, gratitude would say they ought to inform you of the perilous tour you are about commencing." Van Rensselaer tenants were through "pray[ing] to their landlord like children to a parent," the missive explained. "The tenants have organized themselves into a body, and resolved not to pay any more rents until they can be redressed of their grievances. . . . If you come out in your official capacity, you come against a great strength, and I would not pledge for your safe return."[35]

Artcher apparently took the threat seriously. On September 15, he hired an independent contractor, "an active and fearless young man" named Daniel Leonard, to serve process in favor of Stephen Van Rensselaer IV. Next day Leonard rode into the Helderbergs with a saddlebag full of writs; his first day of work proved to be his last. Leonard stopped at the Berne farm of Paul Vincent early that morning. Vincent made no trouble, but he dispatched "his boy" to warn other tenants that "one of the patroon's men was out serving papers." As Leonard proceeded down the road, he heard horns blowing in every direction. Vincent rode by at a gallop moments later, yelling "if I wanted to save my life I must make tracks, as quick as possible, for home." Still, Leonard pressed on to the farm of James Leggett. "I told him I had a paper for him and offered it to him," Leonard reported in a deposition. "He said it was a Van Rensselaer paper . . . and ordered me off his land." Leonard threw down the writ but retrieved it when Leggett told his son to get his gun. Both men followed the special deputy down the road, calling him "a scoundrel, traitor, rascal and villain" and declaring that they would "shoot a man in minute that came on such business." Leonard promised to deliver no more process and started back to Albany.

Leonard stopped in the village of Berne "to get refreshments and rest." Shortly after arriving, he noticed Vincent and Leggett amid a gathering crowd. "The mail stage . . . came along," the process server later testified; "I went to the door and told them I wanted to go with the mail." But he had been seen. One member of the mob shoved Leonard away from the coach. Another announced that every Van Rensselaer writ must be burned. "They got a tar barrel, set fire to it; they then took hold of me, led me out to the tar barrel . . . and told me they would spare my life if I burned them." When the special deputy met that demand, others followed. The anti-renters required him to buy a round of drinks. Then, sufficiently invigorated, they carried Leonard to each of the farms where he already had served writs and compelled him to burn them as well. "From there they took me to Lawrence's tavern on the Delaware turnpike; they required me treat again." Leonard bought two more rounds. After each one, they ignited another tar barrel and boisterously debated whether to tar and feather him. Nightfall approached before the Anti-Rent mob, having "hurrahed frequently during the day" and called Leonard "their prisoner," finally let him go.[36]

Lawyers for the Van Rensselaer family soon presented Sheriff Artcher with another batch of writs, and he made three halfhearted attempts to do his duty. In early October, Artcher and three deputies got as far as Clarksville, about sixteen miles west of downtown Albany, where they were stopped by 70 to 100 men tending a tar barrel in the middle of the road. The sheriff "commanded and enjoined them to give way and let him pass, which they absolutely refused to do," and the posse turned back "without having served any process, not having force enough to overcome the resistance." Artcher tried again on November 27. This time he and his deputies encountered a force of 300; the anti-renters seized their horses and turned them toward Albany. "A large portion" of the crowd followed the sheriff's party for eight miles on the road back to the city, "blowing their horns and vociferously crying out 'down with the rent.'"[37]

Artcher's last foray into the Helderbergs became the butt of parodies in the local press. On November 29 he summoned a *posse comitatus*—the power of the county. About 700 inhabitants of Albany, including former Governor William Marcy and John Van Buren, the twenty-nine-year-old son of President Van Buren, answered the call and marched out of town on December 2. None of them had been issued a gun; they straggled back to Albany that evening after meeting a screaming, club-wielding mob, "variously estimated at from fifteen to eighteen hundred, who entirely blocked the road" outside Reidsville. "[I] did not deem it discreet or advisable," Artcher reported to Governor Seward on December 4, "to attempt to put the posse (chiefly and almost wholly unarmed) against the force opposed." He preferred to thrust the problem of serving process into the governor's lap.[38]

Seward understood Artcher's impulse to apply for military assistance. The sheriff had to stand for reelection in 1840, and Albany County contained 1,397 tenant families—about 2,000 eligible voters—in "unhallowed bondage" to one person. Claiming that the Anti-Rent resistance could not be suppressed by local authorities enabled Artcher, a Democrat, to pass political responsibility up the chain of law-enforcement command. The sheriff's gambit also put the Whig governor in an awkward position from which there was no easy escape. Seward could neither neglect his duty to uphold the law nor infuriate Anti-Rent voters without putting himself and his party in political jeopardy. Just one month earlier Whig candidates had won seven of the ten senate seats up for grabs, three of them in the third (Albany) district. The Whig triumph finally gave Seward the working majority in both houses necessary to enact his internal-improvement program and command the state patronage. Thurlow Weed had raised $8,000 from New York City bankers and lawyers for the third-district contest; "the Albany Regency," he exulted when the results came in, "are overthrown and utterly routed in this their very den!" But the three senate candidates won by an average majority of only 133 votes. Seward and Weed cringed at the thought of forfeiting the tenant vote in 1840 and making Albany County a Democratic stronghold once again.[39]

While the governor and "the dictator" fretted, the New York body politic finally learned what the Helderberg War was all about. On December 6, the Albany newspapers published a letter "To the Public" from Stephen Van Rensselaer IV. He included transcripts of the May 22 tenant proposal, his own reply dated a week later, and the "Anti-Renters' Declaration of Independence." Casparus F. Pruyn, a manor agent across the river in Rensselaer County, reported that the patroon's statement "has had a wonderful effect in Albany . . . [and] has united all classes in his favor." Pruyn misread public opinion. "All classes" deplored the Anti-Rent violence, but commentators tended to express sympathy for the tenants and blame the uprising on the management style of the late patroon. William Cullen Bryant, the urbane Democrat who edited the *New York Evening Post*, set forth a typical interpretation of the excitement on the manor. "The heir of the Van Rensselaer estate has strict law on his side," he wrote, "and we hope that they who have hitherto resisted will see the propriety of submitting peaceably to the law." Bryant insisted that there was "hardship in the case of the tenants" all the same. "Their late landlord, the excellent and amiable Stephen Van Rensselaer," had allowed unpaid rents to build up, "many of them extending back, it is said, through a period of twelve or eighteen years." As a result, many of the tenants "imagined" that the rents in arrear would be canceled in his will. But this had not been done. "It was certainly a great error either that these rents were not regularly collected or else remitted at the time," Bryant concluded. "The effect has been, that the tenants of the manor, from being a peaceable and contented population, are all at once transformed into a set of men armed and organized to resist the process of law."[40]

Seward had an incentive to probe more deeply beneath the surface of events. His reading of the documents released by Stephen Van Rensselaer IV suggested that the tenants had not been contented so much as mollified by the late patroon's paternalism. The conditions and covenants in every lease had prevented the farmers from obtaining credit and adjusting to new market conditions; the patroon's forbearing approach to rent collection had covered up the resulting economic distress and social discontent. At the root of the Anti-Rent disorders, then, lay the form of land tenure on Rensselaerwyck. An interview or two with Henry G. Wheaton, a newly elected Whig assemblyman and counsel for the Albany County tenants, reinforced Seward's impression. Although the governor was not yet prepared to call manorial tenures "oppressive, antirepublican and degrading," adjectives which he still used almost exclusively to describe the measures sponsored by the Democratic Party, he finally responded decisively to the county sheriff's request for military assistance.[41]

On December 10, six days after Sheriff Artcher's application, Seward announced that militia units from Montgomery County and New York City had been summoned "to maintain the supremacy of the laws." The battalions, he said, were ready to move at two hours' notice with 500 and 1,500 men respectively. "But before actually employing the said military force," Seward declared, "it appears to me proper to issue this my proclamation as a further effort to avoid that extremity." He implored the anti-renters "to reflect upon the nature and consequences" of their lawless acts and urged them to remember that organized resistance to legal process "is insurrection, and that if death ensue the penalties of treason and murder are incurred." He held out an olive branch as well. After admonishing the tenants on strike that "the only lawful means to obtain relief from any injuries or redress of any grievances of which they complain are by application to the courts of justice and to the legislature," he promised "every facility which the executive department can afford in bringing their complaints before the legislature." Seward promised Assemblyman Wheaton more. He told him that he intended to ask for legislation designed to extinguish the archaic system of land tenure still in effect on Rensselaerwyck.[42]

Wheaton and his law partner, Azor Taber, carried the news of Seward's intentions to the Helderberg townships on the very day the governor issued his proclamation. "Several citizens . . . have assured us that all resistance to the sheriff . . . will be immediately withdrawn," they reported to Seward on December 11. A coda followed: "We hasten to communicate this intelligence to your excellency, that such measures may be adopted as in your opinion the public good may require." The civil disorders known as the Helderberg War thus ended. Weed's *Evening Journal* praised the governor for having taken "the right and wise course" and urged the tenants to begin framing petitions for the legislature's consideration. But one public voice struck a discordant note as peace returned to Albany County. It belonged to Edwin Croswell, Democratic Party wheelhorse and editor of the *Argus*. His lead editorial on December 13 pointed out that the Constitution of the United States prohibited state legislation impairing the obligation of contracts. "We trust we shall not be accused of incendiarism," Croswell remarked, "if we ask what can the legislature do? Can it interfere with contracts? Can it 'redress' the 'complaints' of the tenants? And if so, how? Will his excellency or the *Evening Journal* condescend to inform us?" Seward had no idea how to answer Croswell's daunting questions, but the essential first step seemed clear. He had to learn something about the legal foundation of social relations on Rensselaerwyck.[43]

Land Law and the Law of the Land

Reading a standard Rensselaerwyck contract for the first time, as Governor Seward did in December 1839, was a disorienting experience. Patroons had referred to people on the manor as their tenants for 200 years; the tenants always had called the Van Rensselaers their landlords. Yet the contracts under which settlers took possession of the land were not leases. They were grants in fee, and the grantees became owners of the soil. Every indenture recited that the "proprietor of the Manor of Rensselaerwyck . . . doth grant, bargain, sell, remise, reléase, and confirm" a designated "piece or parcel of land" for a consideration of five shillings, "to him in hand paid," and also in consideration of "the yearly rents, covenants and conditions, hereinafter contained." The latter included the annual rents payable forever in fowl and bushels of wheat, the personal service requirements, the reservation of water and mineral rights, the restraints on alienation, and the promise to "well and duly discharge and pay all taxes, charges, and assessments" levied by state or local governments.

Every indenture also reserved a right in the proprietor, "his heirs and assignees, or any of them," to reenter the land and thus "to have again, repossess and enjoy . . . their former estate" upon the breach of any condition or covenant. Many of these conditions and covenants, though lawful in a lease, were illegal or just plain impossible in a conveyance of the fee. Seward was an able attorney, "an expert conveyancer," with a substantial real-estate practice in western New York. Still, he had never seen anything like the indentures on Rensselaerwyck. They upset all he had been taught and rendered futile his usual methods of thought.[44]

Consider, first, the presumption that manor farmers were tenants of the Van Rensselaers. Nineteenth-century lawyers had trouble grasping the idea that a grant of land forever might be understood as a lease. At common law, the distinguishing feature of a lease was the landlord's retention of ownership while conveying his right of possession to a tenant for a fixed term. The legal interest remaining in the landlord, called a reversion, was alienable during life and descendible at death; the interest vested in the tenant was also alienable and inheritable unless restricted by an express covenant in the indenture. Conditions and covenants that "touch[ed] and concern[ed] the land" ran with the land because successors in interest to the landlord and successors in interest to the tenant, though strangers to the original contract, had privity of estate. One party had the reversion and the other possession until the term stipulated in the lease expired.[45] But the contracts on Rensselaerwyck had no term. Only a right of reentry, not a reversion, remained in the proprietor and his heirs or assignees. This seemed easy enough to explain. In every indenture the patroon purported to convey the fee. Stephen Van Rensselaer III must have been a grantor rather than a landlord.

Other difficulties emerged, however, if the relation between the parties on Rensselaerwyck were defined as one between a grantor and the owners of the soil. The common law did not favor the reservation of rents in fee-simple conveyances. One form of such a fee-farm rent, called a rent charge, James Kent observed in 1826, "is where the rent is created by deed, and the fee granted." In conveyances of this sort, which were rare in England and virtually unknown in the United States, no reversion remained in the grantor and an action of eject-ment for nonpayment of rent could not be maintained absent a clause in the contract reserving a right of reentry. Yet the insertion of a reentry clause, as on Rensselaerwyck, did not resolve all the enforcement problems arising from the rent-charge relation.[46]

At common law, the grantor who reserved a rent charge could not transfer his right of reentry to a third party. Conditions and covenants annexed to con-veyances of the fee, Kent reported, "can only be reserved for the benefit of the grantor and his heirs; a stranger cannot take advantage of them." It was doubtful, moreover, whether the burden of covenants in such grants ran with the land. William Rawle, author of the first American treatise on covenants, confidently stated that they did not. "If the owner of land granted it in fee, reserving to himself a rent which the grantee covenanted to pay," he wrote, "though the covenant was to be performed out of the land, yet the assignee of the covenantor would hold the land discharged from its liability." Thomas Platt, author of the standard English treatise, used more guarded language. "Sometimes indeed it occurs," he pointed out in 1829, "that on a conveyance . . . the purchaser covenants to pay a rent-charge thereon to the vendor and his heirs, but in this case, the covenant, it appears, will not run with the lands in the hands of an assignee." Another commentator put it this way: "Upon the whole, there appears to be no authority for saying that the burden of a covenant will run with land in any case, except that of landlord and tenant."[47]

Early nineteenth-century jurists discerned a formal explanation for the bar on assignment of rent charges. The grantor who reserved a rent charge retained no reversion in the land; he and the grantee had privity of contract but not privity of estate. Rent-charge covenants, in other words, seemed to be personal (between the contracting parties) rather than real (attached to the land). It followed that the legal obligation to fulfill promises that burdened the land became unenforceable once the grantee's interest had been transferred to a stranger. But the intention of the parties on Rensselaerwyck had been otherwise. Van Rensselaer indentures expressly provided that liability for all conditions and covenants, including rents, attached to the grantee's heirs and assignees in perpetuity; the indentures expressly empowered the patroon's heirs and assignees to enforce them. As a matter of legal form, the contracts in force on Rensselaerwyck were grants in fee. In effect, however, they vested the grantor with the legal rights of landlords. The relation between the parties, it appeared, could be described only with an oxymoron. It must be a "lease in fee."

The restraints on alienation in every Van Rensselaer indenture perplexed the nineteenth-century legal mind for much the same reason. Here, too, the distinction between leases and grants in fee was ordinarily of great importance. "A condition annexed to a conveyance in fee, or by devise, that the purchaser or devisee should not alien, is unlawful and void," Kent wrote in his *Commentaries on American Law*. "The restraint is admitted in leases for life or years, but it is incompatible with the absolute right appertaining to an estate in tail or in fee."[48] Nineteenth-century lawyers accounted for the distinction with ease. Restraints on alienation in leases protected the landlord's reversion; stipulations against assignment and subletting gave landlords control over the people in possession of their property. Grantors in fee, on the other hand, had no reversion to protect. Thus the validity of the quarter-sale conditions in force on Rensselaerwyck depended on how legal relations on the manor were conceptualized.

On this question, however, the New York Supreme Court had spoken. In *Jackson* ex dem. *Lewis & Wife v. Schutz*, decided in 1820, the court not only upheld restraints on alienation in a grant in fee but also tried to explain why thousands of New York farmers could be regarded as both tenants and owners of the soil. This one remarkable case made it possible for Seward to grasp, though not to appreciate, the lease in fee.

At issue in *Schutz* was an action of ejectment for a farm on the 21,766-acre Rhinebeck Patent in Dutchess County. The plaintiffs were Morgan Lewis and his wife Gertrude, daughter of Robert R. Livingston of Clermont and the former Margaret Beekman. Gertrude's great-grandfather, Henry Beekman, had acquired Rhinebeck by grant from Governor Benjamin Fletcher in 1697; her grandfather had peopled the patent in the eighteenth century under indentures comparable with those used on Rensselaerwyck. Beekman's policy was to convey the fee in consideration of a perpetual yearly rent of "eighteen bushels of good merchantable winter wheat" and one day's labor "with a wagon, sled or plough, and an able man to drive, with horses or oxen." Every contract reserved a right of reentry for breach of any covenant or condition. One of them prohibited alienation of the premises without giving the Rhinebeck proprietor a preemptive right to meet any offer; it also required payment of 10 percent of the purchase money should the proprietor decline to buy the farm at the market price. The Lewises continued to use Beekman's conveyance forms after Gertrude acquired her mother's interest in Rhinebeck by a deed dated January 5, 1790. They filed this action when one of their tenants, who had taken possession of a farm under the standard contract in 1805, sold it seven years later for $1,150 without offering them the required preemption or paying them one-tenth of the purchase price.[49]

The arguments of counsel in *Schutz* were as significant as the opinion of the court. Thomas J. Oakley for the defendant flatly stated that the restraints on alienation could not be enforced. "Here is a grant to a man and his heirs and assign[ee]s forever, without any reservation of any part of the interest, to create a reversion," he asserted. "According to our law and the principles and spirit of our government, this must be deemed a fee simple, or the highest estate in law," and Oakley cited a long string of English authorities attesting to the illegality of restraints on alienation in fee-simple conveyances. James Emmot, counsel for the plaintiffs, claimed that Oakley's argument rested on two false premises. First, the indenture at issue, though in form a grant in fee, did not convey an estate in fee simple because "the whole interest of the grantor" had not been transferred to the grantee. The indenture plainly showed that "the parties intended to establish the relationship of landlord and tenant between them." Second, the English authorities on whom Oakley relied had no bearing on the case. The land law of New York and the land law of England, Emmot contended, diverged at a crucial point. Quia Emptores, a statute passed by Parliament and accepted by King Edward I in 1290, had destroyed legal relations of the sort that prevailed on the Rhinebeck Patent, Rensselaerwyck, and other great estates in eastern New York. "But the statute Quia Emptores," Emmot insisted, "never was in force in this state."[50]

Every nineteenth-century American lawyer knew something about the ancient statute on which Emmot's argument pivoted. In William Blackstone's *Commentaries on the Laws of England*, a basic text, readers learned that the commodification of land and the fee-simple estate, or freehold, were among the consequences of Quia Emptores. For 200 years following the Norman Conquest of 1066, Blackstone reported, the feudal tenant's holding (called his fee) could not be sold without his lord's consent. But the act of 1290 authorized every "freeman" to sell the fee "at his pleasure," provided that the buyer "shall hold the same of the chief lord of the same fee, by such service and customs as . . . [the vendor] held before." Quia Emptores thus established the principle of free alienation and forbade subinfeudation—the creation of new feudal obligations among buyers and sellers of land. It also undermined feudalism in England. Frequent conveyances severed the personal ties between lords and their tenants in fee. The right of alienation encouraged the English "freeman" to think of himself as the owner of his land. And the reserved "services and customs," which ultimately grew payable in money, became nominal through centuries of inflation and were gradually extinguished.[51]

Blackstone, writing in the 1760s, provided lawyers with more than an account of how Quia Emptores fostered the growth of commercial society in England. He addressed the technical questions at the heart of cases like *Schutz*. The act of 1290, Blackstone pointed out, brought an end to the creation of new manors. This was a necessary result of the prohibition on subinfeudation in conveyances of the fee. "All manors existing at this day must have existed as early as Edward the First," he wrote, "for it is essential to a manor, that there be tenants who hold of the lord and . . . no tenant of a common lord since the statute Quia Emptores could create any new tenants to hold of himself." Furthermore, the act wiped out a form of fee-farm rent known as rent service. "Rent service is so called," Blackstone explained "because it has some corporeal service incident to it. . . . For, if a tenant holds his land by fealty and ten shillings rent, or by the service of ploughing the lord's land and five shillings rent, these pecuniary rents, being connected with personal services, are therefore called rent-service." Unlike the grantor who reserved a rent charge and retained "no future interest or reversion expectant in the land," the grantor who reserved a rent service maintained a landlord-tenant relation with the grantee. Such a relation amounted to a lease in fee. After subinfeudation had been prohibited, however, grants in fee that reserved a rent service to the grantor could no longer be made. In Britain the lease in fee survived only in Scotland where Quia Emptores did not apply.[52]

History and legal theory supported Emmot's claim that Quia Emptores "was never in force" in New York. King Charles II's charter to his brother James, the Duke of York, in 1664 did not expressly waive the ancient statute, as did the 1681 charter to William Penn. But New York had been conquered from the Dutch. In seventeenth-century English law and practice, an act of Parliament applied to conquered lands only when Parliament named the colony in the statute or the colonial legislature adopted the statute of its own accord. Quia Emptores had not entered New York law through either procedure. What is more, nobody had presumed that the act applied. Governors of colonial New York deliberately created manors; their grantees blithely subinfeudated the land. According to Emmot, the relation between the parties on the Rhinebeck Patent made sense only as "a *rent service*, which always creates a tenure." The personal service and "fat fowl" requirements in every indenture confirmed this irresistible conclusion. On Rhinebeck and Rensselaerwyck, as in early medieval England, the function of such covenants was to establish bonds of fealty that denoted a privity of estate between landlords and their tenants in fee.[53]

Chief Justice Ambrose Spencer endorsed Emmot's theory with enthusiasm. It explained almost everything that required explanation. Grantors without reversions could be landlords, owners of the soil mere tenants, because the relationship between them was a rent service rather than a rent charge. "We never supposed," Spencer remarked during oral argument in the *Schutz* case, "that the statute of Quia Emptores existed here." But one thing gave the chief justice pause. In 1787 the New York legislature had passed an Act Concerning Tenures, "the language of which," Spencer pointed out, "is taken from the English statutes." What, then, were the effects of the 1787 act?[54]

Emmot anticipated the question. He conceded that the American Revolution and the ensuing establishment of republican institutions had changed the land law in two important ways. The people of New York, as constituent sovereign, succeeded to the king's prerogatives as paramount lord of the soil in 1776, and the Act Concerning Tenures prohibited leases in fee on land conveyed by the state government. But the 1787 statute did not disturb the rights of proprietors who owned land under British grants prior to the Revolution. "The framers of the act," Emmot asserted, "supposed that the feudal tenures did exist here." Thus the statute included a saving clause; it stipulated that "this act . . . shall not take away, nor be construed to take away or discharge any rents certain or other services . . . due or to grow due to any mesne lord, or other private person." Furthermore, nothing in the statute affected the right of pre-1776 proprietors to reserve a rent service in subsequent contracts with willing tenants. The system established following the Revolution, in other words, recognized two distinct forms of land tenure. One was to be and remain allodial because it arose from grants by the people of New York State. The other retained its feudal character because tenants in fee held, not of the people, but of private proprietors whose rights had vested under grants from the British crown.[55]

Emmot's argument impressed Chief Justice Spencer and his four associates—Jonas Platt, William W. Van Ness, John Woodworth, and Joseph C. Yates. All five justices agreed that the Rhinebeck Patent indenture was "a lease in fee," and they rejected as "without foundation" the notion that such conveyances could vest fee-simple estates in the tenants. But Emmot's construction of Quia Emptores and the Act Concerning Tenures had a downside. It meant that a form of landholding Parliament had strangled half a millennium earlier still existed in New York State. It meant that in one respect, at least, republican New York was more feudal than monarchical England. None of the justices were inclined either to make such a confession or to repudiate Emmot's general theory of New York land law. In their judgment, however, the restraints on alienation at issue in *Schutz* could be sustained without calling the relation between the parties a rent service. The alternative rationale derived from a modern principle rather than an antiquated tenure. It derived from freedom of contract.[56]

Justice Platt, a prominent Federalist, spoke for the court in *Schutz* and put a new face on the perpetual lease with restraints on alienation. The operation required two moves. First, Platt reinterpreted the history of the land law. Before the enactment of Quia Emptores, he reported, the tenant in fee could not transfer the land without the "express license" of his lord. According to Platt, "the object of the statute was to reverse the old rule so that the right of alienation was made incident to the grant . . . unless"—and here he made freedom of contract a thirteenth-century principle—"the parties qualified that right by an express stipulation." Absolute restraints on alienation thus became void. But neither Quia Emptores nor the New York statute enacted in 1787, said Platt, purported to forbid partial restraints: "The parties have a right to bargain as they please." Platt's second move came easier. The preemption and tenth-sale conditions in every Rhinebeck Patent indenture, he said, "formed an essential part of the consideration for the grant, and we may reasonably presume that from a regard to these covenants, the stipulated rents are lower than would otherwise have been agreed on." And the market arguably worked as the court supposed. The defendant in *Schutz* had paid a rent "of about $27 a year" for a farm that he sold for $1,150. As Platt sized up the situation, then, it did not matter whether the proprietor had a reversion in the land. Nor did it matter whether the indenture created a rent service or a rent charge. The parties on Rhinebeck had "a right to bargain as they please," the resulting contract was not unreasonable, and the proprietor's right to reenter upon breach of any condition or covenant followed as a matter of course.[57]

The decision in *Schutz* was not surprising. Thousands of comparable contracts governed social relations in eastern New York, and it figured that the judges would conjure up a way to sustain them. By leaving the Quia Emptores question open and declining to say whether the lease in fee had established a rent service or a rent charge, however, the court complicated the politics of land reform in New York State. Legislators would have to aim at a target having an uncertain legal foundation. Chancellor Kent was no land reformer, but *Schutz* vexed even him. His *Commentaries on American Law* classified the various types of estates in land with loving particularity. And the lease in fee fit none of them. Although he dutifully summarized the New York court's holding, Kent endorsed neither Platt's freedom-of-contract theory nor Emmot's feudal-tenure theory. Perhaps he deemed it odd that such diametrically opposed premises could yield the same result. "A restraint upon alienation in cases of leases in perpetuity, with a reservation of rent, and with covenants and conditions annexed," Kent said, "is tolerated and held valid in law." He did not attempt to explain why this was so.[58]

Governor Seward had a stronger reaction to *Schutz* when he first encountered the case in December 1839. In his view, the theories elaborated at the bar and in the opinion of the court made a powerful case for land reform. Emmot's feudal-tenure theory astonished him. Whatever its merits as a matter of law, its "antirepublican" implications could not be tolerated. If the relation between the parties on the Manor of Rensselaerwyck were indeed a rent service, Van Rensselaer tenants owed fealty to a superior lord and therefore lacked the independence required for republican citizenship. "Voluntary slavery" described their situation precisely. Justice Platt's freedom-of-contract theory astonished him for a different reason. Seward had found a report that condemned fines on alienation in the *Assembly Journal* for 1812; the report's authors were Ambrose Spencer, William W. Van Ness, and John Woodworth—three of the five judges who decided *Schutz* eight years later. "It cannot be pretended that in setting the terms of the lease, the landlord took a lower rent on the contingency that his tenant would change his mind and become disposed to part with his lease," the justices of 1820 said in 1812. "If it should be objected that tenants enter into such kind of stipulations voluntarily, and that every man should be left free to contract in such manner as he pleases, we answer that the public is bound to protect and guard individuals from oppression." Spencer, Van Ness, and Woodworth said these things as ad hoc commissioners, not as appellate judges, and their report failed to stimulate legislative action against fines on alienation. Still, Seward believed that the claims they made so forcefully in 1812 exploded the court's reasoning in *Schutz*. The relation between the parties on Rensselaerwyck, however defined in law, was "oppressive, antirepublican and degrading."[59]

Making a case for land reform was easier than showing how manorial tenures could be abolished. Whether understood as a rent service or a rent charge, the prevailing legal relation on Rensselaerwyck was clearly a contractual one; the Constitution forbade legislation impairing the obligation of contracts. These facts supplied the foundation for the daunting questions Edwin Croswell fired at Seward and Weed on December 13, 1839. "The *Albany Argus* is quite right in one thing it says on this subject," remarked a Whig newspaper in New York City several days later. "It is very ridiculous to suppose that the legislature can do anything between these parties. We should really like to know what any human legislature can do, while the Constitution of the United States is considered in force." What is more, the principle underlying the Contract Clause had become a cultural norm, not merely a juristic one, during the early nineteenth century. Only a handful of New Yorkers disputed the general idea that a deal should be a deal in the absence of force or fraud; people took it for granted that the settled expectations of contracting parties should not be upset by retrospective legislation. If the legislature did enact a law that disturbed existing contractual obligations, however, courts could be expected to strike down the offending statute. Gulian C. Verplanck, one of New York's most distinguished Whig jurists and statesmen, wrote in 1838 that "this provision of our federal Constitution and the series of wise and salutary decisions under it . . . form the most important safeguard of the rights of industry and labor possessed by the American citizen."[60]

Seward knew what he was up against, but the obstacles did not faze him. Two things fortified his confidence. First, other kinds of legal relations that once seemed natural had come to be seen as intolerable, and the state legislature had found ways to extinguish them. Chattel slavery had been abolished in New York; so had imprisonment for debt. Second, the Whig conception of executive power absolved him of all responsibility for explaining how manorial tenures might be abolished. His party originated in objections to the "usurpations" of Andrew Jackson, the "despot" in the White House who had vetoed the bill rechartering the Bank of the United States and removed the government deposits in violation of an act of Congress. Whigs not only decried those encroachments on legislative power but also revived a central strand of eighteenth-century "Real Whig" thought. The separation of powers, as Whigs understood the principle, comprehended legislative autonomy in the making of public law; it barred the exertion of executive influence at every stage of deliberation and decision. For Whigs, then, wrestling with ways and means of accomplishing public purposes belonged exclusively to the legislative department. Presidents and governors rightfully participated in law making only at the beginning and end of the process. They presented an agenda worthy of the legislature's consideration at the outset of each session, and they transformed bills into law by signing the measures mandated by a majority of the people's representatives.[61]

Maxims of Whig constitutionalism freed Seward from one difficult task yet saddled him with another. He had to make such a persuasive case for land reform in his second annual message, scheduled for delivery on January 7, 1840, that the legislature would undertake a thorough reconnaissance of the legal terrain and identify an appropriate means of extinguishing the lease in fee on Rensselaerwyck. The self-evident validity of tenant complaints about the rent system sustained his hope of success. So did the November election results. When the legislature's 1840 session began in January, both houses would have a Whig majority for the first time.

2

Whig Reconnaissance

Since 1821 the New York Constitution has provided that the governor "shall communicate by message to the legislature, at every session, the condition of the State, and recommend such matters to them as he shall judge expedient."[1] For much of the nineteenth century, the governor's effectiveness as party leader turned on his performance of this duty. Both houses of the legislature organized committees to consider the executive's recommendations. Hearings were conducted and measures produced before debate began on the bills or resolutions reported out of committee. But governors did not aim their remarks at Albany insiders only. Every major newspaper in the state printed the message verbatim; people talked about it and read about it for weeks afterward. No instrument at the chief executive's command was more important in shaping public opinion, and no governor wielded it better than William H. Seward.

Seward's 1840 message was very long. The *Argus* pronounced it, with no sense of exaggeration, "quite the most formidable in that respect of any ever presented to a state legislature." Its vast proportions reflected Seward's many purposes. Eighteen forty was a presidential year, and the "Democratic Whig National Convention," which met at Harrisburg, Pennsylvania, on December 4, 1839, had selected a ticket of William Henry Harrison and John Tyler—Tippecanoe and Tyler too—but had adjourned amid the ballyhoo without offering a platform or issuing an address. Seward provided what his party's national convention did not. Working from the premise that the state of the state was "indissolubly connected with" national affairs, he blasted the Democratic Party's devotion to negative government and called for decisive action by Congress to stabilize the currency, stimulate investment, and provide funds for internal improvements administered by the states. Seward also elaborated a full agenda for the New York legislature. He wanted the state to go forward with the enlargement of the Erie Canal and construction on the new "auxiliary or lateral works," the Genesee Valley and Black River canals. He favored government loans to railroad corporations. He hoped the life of the geological survey would be extended, "confidently anticipat[ing] that it will not only develop the material resources of the state, but will secure to agriculture its rightful consideration and influence." He thought "the alienation of land should be facilitated" by legislation requiring all liens and encumbrances to be recorded in the county where the land was situated. And he advocated "some measure" designed to abolish the manorial tenures that "are regarded as inconsistent with existing institutions, and have become odious to those who hold under them."[2]

The message had many purposes but one public philosophy. Seward regarded government, national and state, as an agent of change. He associated progress with the growth of commerce, the diffusion of virtue, and the reform of institutions in conformity with "the humane spirit of the age." Above all, he believed that moral progress went hand in hand with material advancement. Internal improvements, for example, brought all sorts of wonderful social returns. Transport development opened new markets and fostered an increasingly efficient division of labor. It encouraged more and more people to exercise the personal habits—hard work, temperance, frugality, discipline—that enabled them to capitalize on the new economic opportunities. It facilitated the circulation of information, widened horizons, and made people more hopeful for the future. "The principle of internal improvement derives its existence from the generous impulses of the Revolutionary age," Seward said. The enactment of measures for "overcoming physical obstructions to trade and commerce" and for "furnishing to each region, as far as reasonably practicable, facilities of access to [New York City,] the great commercial emporium of the Union," he proclaimed, "is not only the right but the bounden duty of the legislature."[3]

Seward's case for land reform sounded many of the same themes. Relations between landlord and tenant "by which mines and hydraulic privileges, rents payable in kind, personal services, and quarter sales are reserved," he contended, "are unfavorable to agricultural improvement, inconsistent with the prosperity of the districts where they exist, and opposed to sound policy and the genius of our institutions." These obstacles to moral and material progress, like the physical barriers that government breached with internal improvements, the legislature had a "bounden duty" to overcome. "While full force is allowed to the circumstances that the tenants entered voluntarily into such stipulations," Seward declared, "the state has always recognized its obligation to promote the general welfare and guard individuals against oppression. The legislature has the same power over the remedies upon contracts between landlord and tenant as over all other forms of legal redress."[4]

These remarks left one thing unclear. Judicial decisions stretching back to 1802 had indeed established the legislature's competence to regulate "remedies on contracts." The Supreme Court had upheld the abolition of imprisonment for debt on that ground. It did so, however, because statutes withdrawing the

creditor's remedy did not impair the debtor's contractual obligation. "The right
to imprison," Justice Joseph Story declared for a unanimous Court in *Beers v.
Haughton* (1835), "constitutes no part of the contract, and a discharge of the
party from imprisonment does not impair the obligation of contract, but leaves
it in full force against his property and effects." Seward's call for land reform
envisioned something altogether different. He asked the legislature to "assimilate the tenures in question to those which experience has proved to be more
accordant with the principles of republican government." How this might be accomplished without running afoul of the Contract Clause remained a mystery.[5]

The gap between the end to be accomplished and the means Seward mentioned did not completely overshadow the governor's justification for state
action. Uniting land reform with the Whig public philosophy shaped the legislative process in two important ways. The first was manifest. Seward's message
designated the abolition of manorial tenures as a party objective; he compelled
Whig leaders in the legislature to achieve the goal or explain why it could not be
done. The second, though less apparent, was at least as significant. In Whig
discourse the idea of progress figured more prominently than the sense of
injustice and the exercise of governmental powers for collective purposes out-
weighed the defense of individuals against oppression. The rhetorical thrust of
"The Anti-Renters' Declaration of Independence" ran the other way. In effect,
then, Seward translated tenant demands into terms the legislature's Whig majority would find more congenial. He could do nothing more to link the prospect for land reform with the prospects of the Whig Party.

Public Purposes in Party Dialogue

The bulk of Seward's message concentrated on the "derangement of commerce," the manifold signs of depression, that worried all Americans in 1840.
Economic distress had frustrated more than one statesman's ambitious plans for
constructive action, and Seward was determined to avoid the common fate. He
felt unlucky all the same. Just one year earlier he had exulted in the "pass[ing]
away" of all the "gloom which gathered over our country" after the Panic of
1837. But the recovery could not be sustained. Low cotton prices in the fall of
1839 triggered massive exports of specie to settle accounts with English creditors; the result was another liquidity crisis. Banks curtailed their circulation.
Interest rates soared as the money market tightened. Stocks and bonds fell in the
effort to convert them into cash. On October 9 the Philadelphia banks, spearheaded by the Bank of the United States (reorganized in 1836 as a Pennsylvania
corporation), suspended specie payments. Banks in the South and West followed suit within a week.[6]

The financial crisis put enormous pressure on the nation's largest debtors, the state governments. In 1839 the several states had outstanding long-term obligations amounting to more than $170 million; of this sum $60.2 million had been issued for canal construction, $42.8 million for railroads, and $6.6 million for turnpikes. Only in Ohio, however, had the state legislature provided for direct taxation in support of public works. Within weeks of suspension the financial press began to talk darkly about defaults on interest payments by Pennsylvania, Maryland, Michigan, Indiana, and Illinois. These reports proved premature, but there was no denying the fact that many states already stood at what one observer called "the brink of repudiation and lasting disgrace."[7]

Seward blamed "the general embarrassment" on twelve years of Democratic misrule in Washington. Andrew Jackson had hobbled interstate exchange by destroying the United States Bank, "disturbed the general confidence" of capitalists by removing the government deposits, and shrunk the money stock at a critical moment by requiring specie in all transactions with the General Land Office. Martin Van Buren, brought face-to-face with the "disastrous consequences" of his predecessor's policies, had stayed the course after the Panic of 1837. Rather than putting the public money to work for public purposes, Van Buren asked Congress for an Independent Treasury that would completely divorce the national government from the banking system. Van Buren and his minions even opposed Henry Clay's distribution bill, an "eminently enlightened, just and equal" plan for using federal dollars to finance (or refinance) internal improvements in the heavily indebted states. The weight of Democratic Party dogma, manifested in "neglect of the national government's appropriate and important functions," had become too great for the economy to bear. "Every effort to rise has been followed by greater depression," Seward complained. It was time for a change.[8]

The governor's commentary on the depression and its causes was more than an endorsement of the Harrison-Tyler ticket. His assessment of the national situation also provided a new line of defense for the Whig agenda at Albany. In 1839 Seward had asked the legislature to accelerate transport development by authorizing the Canal Board and New York railroad corporations to borrow $4 million a year for the next decade. This could be done, he had insisted, without raising taxes or impairing the state credit. Democrats had disagreed. Denouncing the governor's recommendations as "extravagant," "reckless," even "mad," the Democratic majority in the state senate had killed one assembly bill that would have authorized $1.25 million for new construction on the canal system and ten others that would have provided a total of $3.39 million for loans to railroad corporations. Voters removed the political obstacle to Seward's program in the election of 1839. But the crash presented other obstacles. The financial crisis made New York bonds "a perfect drug on the foreign markets," exploding Seward's assumption that $40 million could be borrowed in ten annual installments at an interest of 5 percent. Hard times reduced traffic on the Erie Canal, shattering Seward's premise that constantly increasing tolls could extinguish the state debt without taxation. Democrats congratulated themselves for having saved the public credit from certain ruin in 1839, and they called for retrenchment in 1840.[9]

Seward still wanted to go forward. He made two moves to justify government borrowing for internal improvements in 1840. First, he pushed responsibility for dealing with the depression upward through the federal system. Because national economic policy had distorted the financial markets and deranged internal commerce, national authorities had an obligation to make things right. It would make no sense at all, Seward argued, for the (Whig) state government to cease doing things it should be doing for the people of New York because the (Democratic) national government had ceased doing things it should be doing for the people of the United States. The crisis called for reform at Washington, not retrenchment in Albany. Second, Seward downplayed the effects of the depression and tried to defuse the "imaginary" alarm. He made only one concession. New issues of government bonds, he recommended, should "be so limited that the interest on the whole debt of the state shall at no time exceed its surplus revenues." Seward insisted that "the adoption of this principle would place our credit upon the most impregnable ground." At a time when revenues already were declining, however, this vaunted "principle" made no provision whatever for paying the principal.[10]

The governor's disquisition on internal improvements left Democrats aghast. Holding up visions of great things to be accomplished without pointing out the means of achieving them was not statesmanship. It was demagoguery. For Democrats, the very idea of increasing the state debt seemed so rash, so irrational, that Whig talk about economic development and the diffusion of opportunity sounded more hollow than ever. Seward's adherence to a "comprehensive and magnanimous" policy of government spending made sense only in terms of political advantage. Until William Henry Harrison got elected, charged William Cullen Bryant's *Evening Post*, "the money of the people will be scattered about with as loose a hand as a poulterer throws corn to his chickens." But corn-barrel politics could not go on forever, and "the Junto" of Seward and Weed knew it. Nevertheless, they were prepared to blink away "the utter impracticability" of new bond issues and risk the possibility that New York would be "reduced to a level with Pennsylvania," where new taxes had just been levied to service the state debt, in order to carry the Empire State for the Whig ticket in November. Democrats deplored the motive. At the same time, they showed grudging respect for the Whig strategy. "The message was designed as an electioneering paper," Edwin Croswell remarked in the *Argus*, "and in that point of view only it does credit to the combined faculties of the Junto."[11]

Democrats reacted to Seward's call for land reform in much the same way. On January 10, 1840, when Whig managers in the upper house brought to the floor a series of resolutions referring various topics in the message to standing and special committees, the last resolution in the series, authorizing a select committee to investigate "the manor difficulties" in light of the governor's recommendation, drew more Democratic fire than all the others combined. Samuel L. Edwards, a longtime Van Buren lieutenant, immediately moved to amend the resolution so as to refer the matter instead to Attorney General Willis Hall, "with instructions to report whether any relief can be constitutionally granted by the legislature, and if in his opinion such relief can be granted, then to report a bill for that purpose." Senator Edwards confessed that he did not expect Hall to produce anything of value, for "the legislature is powerless in respect to the conditions of leases which have assumed the forms of solemn contracts." Yet he also talked about how "much time and labor will be saved" if the legislature worked through the executive branch rather than an investigative committee. The objective buried in Edwards's motion was clear enough. Democrats wanted to flush out Seward. They wanted him to present a plan and defend its constitutionality or have the goal articulated in his message exposed as rank demagoguery. Edwards and others regarded the one as an impossibility; Democrats wanted to establish the other before New Yorkers went to the polls in the fall. An investigation of "the manor difficulties" by senate committee might never end, allowing the Whigs to pose as champions of the oppressed tenants until long after the November election.[12]

Samuel Young, a radical Democrat, spoke at length in support of the Edwards amendment. "I wish the power did exist, to wipe off every vestige of leasehold property in the state," he proclaimed. "I know it is unfavorable to improvement—in riding through a tract of country thus held, I can mark the difference between its appearance and where the cultivator is the independent lord of the soil." But Young insisted that the tenants should not be misled. "Most men, not being lawyers, will understand the governor's language as an intimation that the legislature can interfere with the *tenure* of the leases," he asserted. The inference, however, was unwarranted. "The remedy for the enforcement of the contract is indeed within our reach; but the conditions, the terms, the word and letter of the contract, we can no more change than we can take the seal off a bond." Any attempt to do so would violate the Contract Clause of the Constitution. The entire matter was "so plain and so firmly settled" in American constitutional law, Young added, that Seward's call for legislation to abolish manorial tenures "could not have been sincere."[13]

Alonzo Paige, for thirteen years reporter for the New York Court of Chancery and the senate's most respected lawyer, endorsed Young's construction of the Contract Clause. So did Daniel S. Dickinson, a self-proclaimed conservative Democrat who rarely saw eye to eye with Young. "If the language of the governor means anything," Dickinson asserted, "it clearly means to hold encouragement to the tenants that the legislature can modify the terms of their leases." The objective was understandable, for the indentures in force on Rensselaerwyck were "relics of barbarism, incompatible with the institutions of a free people and the spirit of the age." But the gulf between ends and means seemed unbridgeable. "It is very clear that the *remedies* to enforce the leases can be altered," he declared. Yet complaints about the manner of enforcement had not triggered the Helderberg War. "It was the onerous, oppressive, and degrading conditions of the leases which the tenants desired to shake off." The question at issue, "whatever the motives of his excellency in making this extraordinary recommendation," was whether the Constitution prohibited legislation impairing contracts between landlords and their tenants. Dickinson thought it did. "Neither the governor, after suggesting there is a remedy [for the tenants' grievances], nor his friends, should complain that it is proposed to submit this question to the highest law enforcement officer of the state—the friend and constitutional advisor of his excellency, to point out what the remedy is, and wherein these *tenures* can be modified."[14]

None of the Whig senators wanted to argue the law with Young, Paige, and Dickinson. As long as discussion stayed in the familiar channels of Contract Clause doctrine, where Seward's message put it, effective rebuttal was unlikely to materialize in floor debate. Even if the Democrats were right, however, no Whig could support the Edwards amendment. It envisioned the very sort of executive participation in the legislative process that Whig doctrine forbade. The only Whig to speak at any length was Mitchell Sanford; he rose to defend the governor's character, insisting that he had known Seward "too long and too well to believe him guilty of insincerity." After the proposed committee submitted its report, Sanford added, there would be ample "time for gentlemen to take the alarm as to violation of contracts." What alarmed Democrats, however, was not the production of an unconstitutional bill so much as the political opportunism they detected in Seward's message. "In all that has been said," Young thundered in exasperation, "no senator has yet contradicted the doctrine I stated at the outset—that the legislature has no power to change the condition of these leases. . . . Since, then, none of the governor's friends here are acquainted with his contemplated measure of relief," was not "the direct and obviously proper course" to refer the matter to Attorney General Hall, "through whom the executive plan could be officially communicated?" The Whigs furnished no answers. But they had the votes. Senator Edwards's amendment was rejected, seventeen Whigs to twelve Democrats, and the resolution authorizing a committee investigation passed without a roll call.[15]

Next morning the lower house organized a comparable committee without any fuss at all. The speaker promptly named William A. Duer Jr., a tall, "rather athletic" newcomer from Oswego, to chair the Select Committee. Duer was a brilliant young lawyer from a family of distinguished attorneys. His father sat on the New York Supreme Court before resigning in 1829 to accept the presidency of Columbia College; he was the author of *A Course of Lectures on the Constitutional Jurisprudence of the United States* (1839), a highly regarded text. Young Duer's uncle, John Duer, had been Seward's law teacher. He was best known for his work on the New York *Revised Statutes*, a major landmark in the development of American property law compiled in 1828. John Duer and his fellow commissioners instituted a great many reforms in the land law designed, as they put it, "to abolish all technical rules and distinctions, having no relation to the essential nature of property and the means of its beneficial enjoyment, but which derived from the feudal system [and] rest solely upon feudal reasons." The *Revised Statutes* streamlined conveyancing, modified the common law doctrine barring noncitizens from owning real property, and tightened the English rule against perpetuities. Future interests in land became invalid if they suspended the power of alienation for more than two lives in being. The sundry reforms of 1828 expressed what Lawrence Friedman has called the "one dominant aim of [nineteenth-century] land law reform: to keep the land market open and mobile."[16]

Seward's message challenged the state legislature to devise a method of extending the same policy to the Manor of Rensselaerwyck. By choosing thirty-six-year-old William A. Duer Jr. to chair the assembly committee, the Whig leadership may have relied on the talents of his eminent kinsmen as much as his own. If anyone could conjure up a way to "assimilate the tenures in question to those . . . more accordant with the principles of republican government, . . . without the violation of contracts," the Duers could. As it turned out, young Duer did not disappoint his party.

The Wheaton Bill

Henry G. Wheaton, a Whig assemblyman from Albany County and counsel for the tenants on the Manor of Rensselaerwyck, posed the only challenge to the Duer Committee's mandate. Wheaton, thirty-four, had graduated from Union College and studied law in the office of Samuel Stevens, a lawyer for the Van Rensselaer family, before he married "an attractive young lady, descended from one of the oldest and most wealthy families in Albany," and emerged as a promising lawyer and politician. The anti-renters became his clients because they were his constituents. Wheaton had played a pivotal role in negotiating the Helderberg War armistice, time and again reassuring Albany County tenants that Governor Seward could be trusted to fulfill his pledge of assistance once the legislature convened. But a committee investigation was not the sort of action he had envisioned. Wheaton distrusted the process for the same reason Democrats did. Unlike the Democrats, however, he believed that manorial tenures could indeed be extinguished, albeit indirectly, by tinkering with the remedies available to landlords. Wheaton's proposal, incorporated into a bill introduced on January 16, contained two simple provisions. The first abolished the remedy of distress if the rent was not payable in cash; the second took away the remedy of ejectment if a tenant, upon sale of the premises, failed to pay his landlord the one-quarter share of the purchase money specified in every indenture.[17]

Wheaton's objective, though not apparent on the face on the bill, was clear between the lines. He wanted to give Stephen Van Rensselaer IV an added incentive to renegotiate the contracts in force on the manor. The terms Wheaton had in mind were those the anti-renters of Albany County had proposed, and the new patroon had rejected, during the summer of 1839: (1) commutation of the wheat rent to a money rent payable at the rate of $1.00 for each bushel of wheat stipulated in the existing indentures; (2) remission of all rents in arrear on the same terms; (3) surrender of all "feudal" claims on the tenants, including the personal service requirements and quarter-sale reservations; and (4) acknowledgment of every tenant's right to buy out the landlord's entire interest in the premises, at any time, for $2.50 an acre. Wheaton, like his clients, regarded the final demand as the fundamental one. The others either provided short-term relief for the immediate crisis or buttressed the tenants' bargaining position on the principal demand.

The first section of Wheaton's bill addressed the Anti-Rent demand for new contracts with rents payable in cash. He proposed to enhance their bargaining position by abolishing the right of landlords to collect unpaid wheat rents by distress. New York law provided that when rent was due and unpaid, the landlord needed only to notify the sheriff of the arrear, whereupon the sheriff might enter the premises and "distrain," or seize, any goods or chattels found there. A sheriff's sale followed the summary seizure; the proceeds satisfied the unpaid rent. In his *Commentaries on American Law* (1826), James Kent traced the right to distrain back to medieval England and located its source in the quest for an effective way "to compel [every tenant] to perform his feudal obligations." This "summary remedy," he pointed out, "is applicable to no other contracts for the payment of money than those between the landlord and tenant." Still, Kent claimed that "the growth and prosperity of our cities" depended on the distress sale. "It is that speedy and effectual security which encourages moneyed men to employ their capital in useful and elegant improvements," he explained. "If they were driven in every case to the slow process of a suit at law for their rent, it would lead to vexatious and countless lawsuits, and be, in many respects, detrimental to the public welfare." Wheaton built the first section of his bill on Kent's "sound policy" presumptions. He believed that the Van Rensselaers would prefer to collect money rents with the right to distrain rather than wheat rents without it.[18]

The second section was far more draconian. It prohibited the ejectment of any tenant for breach of his contract's quarter-sale provisions. If a tenant sold the premises, his obligation to pay the stipulated portion of the purchase money would remain unimpaired. But ejectment was the only remedy conferred by New York law for violation of leasehold conditions other than payment of rent. Upon passage of the bill, then, two messages would be conveyed to the Van Rensselaer family. One would be obvious. As a practical matter, the quarter-sale reservations, being unenforceable, would no longer exist; landlords could not expect to be compensated for them in buyout agreements with tenants. The other message would be more subtle. If the bill were enacted, the second section would establish principles of legislative competence susceptible to further, almost infinite ramification. The same power that enabled the legislature to divest landlords of all remedies for breach of quarter-sale covenants might also be invoked to divest them of all remedies for breach of other contract terms, including payment of rent. In effect, Wheaton proposed a government-sponsored war of attrition against manorial tenures. The Van Rensselaer family must either accept new deals on terms approximating those offered by Albany County anti-renters in 1839, or risk harder bargains later in the face of repeated government intervention on the tenants' behalf.

Among the many virtues Wheaton saw in his bill, two stood out. Although designed to bring the patroons to their knees, the measure did not disturb the existing structure of legal rights enjoyed by landlords in other settings— specifically, the apartment-building owners of New York City and other urban places. Recovery of unpaid rent by distress was deemed such an extraordinary remedy by 1840 that several state legislatures had abolished it altogether. But Wheaton did not urge New York to follow suit. His bill divested the right to distrain only when the rent was not payable in cash, thereby forestalling any opposition from urban landlords who regarded the remedy as an invaluable one. Subsequent government forays might be framed in the same way. If the Van Rensselaer family remained intransigent after the enactment of the Wheaton bill, an act abolishing ejectment for nonpayment of wheat rents could be passed during the legislature's next session. Landlords who collected rents in cash would not be affected. The most attractive feature of the Wheaton bill, however, was its congruence with Governor Seward's message. The leader of the Whig Party in New York had emphasized that "the legislature has the same power over the remedies upon contracts between landlord and tenant as over all other forms of legal redress." Wheaton proposed to exercise that very power to attain the goal Seward had set forth: "assimilat[ion] of the tenures in question to those which experience has proved to be more accordant with the principles of republican government, and more conducive to the general prosperity, and the peace and harmony of society." Samuel Young, Alonzo Paige, and Daniel S. Dickinson had said it could not be done. Wheaton's bill showed how it could.[19]

The Wheaton bill reached the assembly floor on February 7. After the Albany County lawmaker described its provisions, William A. Duer Jr. rose to speak. "The subject matter of this bill," he said, "is now before a Select Committee." He threatened to "ask a discharge, and surrender the whole matter" if discussion of the bill were allowed to "anticipate the deliberations" of his own committee. Wheaton was quick to reply. "The portion of the [governor's] message referred to the Select Committee relates exclusively to the difficulties between Mr. Van Rensselaer and his tenants," he asserted. "This bill is a general law, modifying the remedy in certain cases, and applies to other counties than this." Duer, angry now, claimed that Wheaton was being disingenuous. "Nobody can doubt that these provisions as to quarter sales and rent payable in other things than money, have any application whatever unless it is to this case," he insisted. "They would never have been thought of but for the difficulties in [Albany County]." Floor debate on Wheaton's proposal, Duer concluded, would be "equivalent to an intimation that the house does not want the advice of the Select Committee on this subject, or has no confidence in its ability to advise in the matter."[20]

Derick Sibley, a Whig from Monroe County, settled the dispute with aplomb. "It is true," he remarked, that Wheaton's measure was "a general one" and would apply wherever conditions comparable with those on Rensselaerwyck prevailed. Because "those cases are very rare," however, he agreed with Duer "that the house cannot, without disrespect to the Select Committee, undertake now to forestall them." Sibley moved that the bill be referred to Duer's committee; the house so ordered by a voice vote. Six weeks later Duer filed his report.[21]

Land Reform and Whig Constitutionalism

The report of the Duer Committee is a remarkable document that merits the kind of attention legal historians have long lavished on judicial opinions. It began with an assessment of the committee's task and the legitimate scope of its concerns. Petitions from tenants on Rensselaerwyck, "signed by a very large number of persons," had been referred along with Governor Seward's message and the Wheaton bill; Duer took them up first. The petitions alleged that many of the original settlers, "being very poor and illiterate," had been induced to enter the land by misrepresentations as to the nature of the indentures that would be granted. Agents of Stephen Van Rensselaer III had told new settlers, the petitioners claimed, that all conditions and covenants recited in the agreements "were mere matters of form, and never intended to be enforced." Several affidavits in proof of these charges had been submitted to the committee along with the petitions. The tenant petitioners also pointed out that circumstances had changed since the 1785–1810 period, when the vast bulk of the contracts had been signed. Land once capable of raising good wheat crops no longer did; meanwhile, wheat had doubled in price. Consequently their rents had become "onerous and oppressive."[22]

At the root of the specific complaints recited by the tenants lay an unarticulated theory of the legislative function. The petitioners assumed that whenever inequality of knowledge or bargaining power resulted in unconscionably harsh contracts, either through oral representations bordering on fraud at the outset or through changing circumstances that rendered improvident agreements more oppressive over time, the legislature might step in and provide relief. In effect, they conceived the legislative branch as the organ of the people that dispensed justice through parliamentary processes. Duer was quick to reject the assumptions implicit in the tenant petitions. "With respect to the suggestions of fraud in procuring the leases, and the hardship and inequality of the bargains," he wrote, "these circumstances either afford grounds of relief, if they can be substantiated, in courts of justice, in which case legislative interference is uncalled for; or else, if under existing laws there is no remedy, it is clearly improper to depart from the general laws to legislate for these particular cases." Embedded in this statement were two maxims of nineteenth-century jurisprudence that structured legislative consideration of Anti-Rent petitions throughout the 1840s. Both flowed from American ideas about the separation of powers, and each merits some attention.[23]

The first maxim addressed the legislature's competence to do something about allegations of fraud and unconscionability supported by affidavits of particular tenants. These allegations, said Duer, must be directed to "courts of justice." Duer did not explain why this was so, but his assumptions were plain. Some of the people who signed perpetual leases with Stephen Van Rensselaer III might have been told that particular contract terms, such as the quarter-sale reservation, were "mere matters of form" that would never be enforced. Yet the tenant petitioners did not claim—indeed, they could not claim—that every contract on Rensselaerwyck was tainted with fraud. The same thing was true, though to a lesser extent, with respect to tenant allegations of unconscionability. For Duer, as for most nineteenth-century American lawyers, rights to equitable relief necessarily hinged on the unique character of particular transactions; they turned, specifically, on particular records of fraud or unconscionability built by individual suitors. But legislatures characteristically dealt with matters of common concern and addressed them with general laws. With the exception of petitions for divorce, which jeopardized contractual relations involving a uniquely compelling state interest, legislatures had long since renounced jurisdiction over petitions for relief unless acts of government, or government officials, were implicated. The first maxim implicit in Duer's reply to the tenant petitions, then, might be stated as follows: courts of equity are equipped to adjudicate particular complaints of injustice arising from private contracts, legislatures are not.[24]

Duer recognized that directing the tenants of Rensselaerwyck to courts of equity was unlikely to assist more than a handful of them. The defense of unconscionability against the enforcement of hard bargains had all but disappeared from the state's equity jurisprudence since *Seymour v. Delancey* (1824), where New York's highest court had renounced the judiciary's "arbitrary power [of] interfering with the contracts of individuals and sporting with their vested rights." Courts of equity continued to treat inadequacy of consideration as possible evidence of fraud; but exploitative contract terms, unsupported by additional evidence of unfair dealing, seldom triggered judicial relief. Each party to a contract, Kent wrote in his *Commentaries*, "judges for himself, and relies confidently, and perhaps presumptuously, upon the sufficiency of his own knowledge, skill, and diligence." Courts had no authority to deny one party the fruits of "his superior knowledge" and they certainly could "not go the romantic length of giving indemnity against the consequences of indolence and folly, or a careless indifference to the ordinary and accessible means of information." Francis Bohlen neatly summarized the liberal moral philosophy that infused nineteenth-century contract law: "The common law makes no pretence of being a social reformer, and does not profess to reduce all persons to an absolutely equal position by eliminating all natural advantages, but rather, recognizing society as it is, considers social inequalities as the natural inevitable tactical advantages of those lucky enough to possess them."[25]

The people who framed the tenant petitions apparently understood the contours of New York contract law in 1840, and they asked the legislature for relief because none was available in courts of justice. But here they were throttled by Duer's second maxim: "If under existing laws there is no remedy, it is clearly improper to depart from the general laws to legislate for these particular cases." The impropriety flowed from the distinction between judicial and legislative power in the American constitutional order. Courts adjudicated controversies involving particular claims and conduct under the standing law; legislatures enacted statutes establishing general rules for the resolution of such controversies in the future. It followed that a statute purporting to benefit one person by disturbing another's vested right—a right "to do certain actions, or possess certain things" under the standing law—was by definition a judicial act. Any legislature that passed such an act left its orbit in the system of separated

tenant's goods and chattels. This right, stipulated in the contract itself, the bill proposed to take away. "It is true [that] there is a well settled distinction between laws which impair the obligation of a contract, and laws which merely affect the remedy," wrote Duer. "But this distinction, it is conceived, applies to cases where the law gives the remedy, and not to cases where the parties themselves have entered into a stipulation, in the nature of a remedy, for the purpose of securing the performance of the principal obligation." The relationship between the payment of rent and the right to distrain in Rensselaerwyck contracts was essentially the same as the relationship between the payment of interest and the right to foreclose in mortgage contracts. In both situations the parties had agreed to "secondary contracts," the object of which was to secure a remedy for the performance of the principal obligation. Yet nobody supposed that the legislature had the authority to enact laws forbidding the foreclosure of mortgages; the Contract Clause had been designed to bar legislation of that very kind. "It is therefore the opinion of your committee," said Duer, "that the first section of the bill referred to, taking away the remedy by distress, would, as far as the leases in question are concerned, be inoperative, as contrary to the Constitution of the United States."[30]

The second section of the bill, taking away the remedy of ejectment for violation of quarter-sale covenants, was not liable to the same objection. The remedy Wheaton proposed to divest had been conferred by law; it had not been stipulated in the contracts. "But the difficulty," Duer remarked, "is that there is no other remedy in the law, whereby the landlord may recover possession, than by this very action of ejectment, proposed by the bill to be taken away; nor is any other remedy given by the bill." If the legislature enacted this provision, "the landlord would have a right of reentry, a right of possession but there would be no means whatever, by which the right could be enforced. He would have a right without a remedy, an abstraction, a shadow, while the tenant, without right, would retain, under protection of the law, the actual use and enjoyment of the property." Wheaton recognized this "difficulty" and regarded it as the chief strength of his bill. But Duer and his committee thought it impaired the obligation of contracts. The Supreme Court had invoked the right-remedy distinction to sustain laws abolishing imprisonment for debt because creditors retained other means of action against defaulting borrowers. Wheaton's bill, in contrast, was anchored on the premise that the right-remedy distinction might be mobilized to nullify the command of the Constitution. "There is an obvious distinction between . . . taking away any particular remedy, so that another is left or a new one given, and wholly extinguishing all remedies, so that no redress whatever is left," wrote Duer. "Between taking away a right and all remedy to enforce a right, there is practically no difference."[31]

Duer offered these constitutional objections to Wheaton's bill with some diffidence. The "secondary contract" doctrine he invoked in analyzing the bill's first section was apparently his own creation, and the limitation he annexed to the right-remedy distinction was grounded in dictum and commentary only. The Supreme Court had not yet struck down a state law because it left one party to a contract without an effective remedy for the other's breach. Even if the Wheaton bill were constitutional, however, Duer believed it should not be enacted for "other weighty reasons." Each amounted to a partial critique that supplied another pillar upon which Duer built the Select Committee's total critique of Wheaton's solution to "the manor difficulties."

One of Duer's "weighty reasons" was rather ironic. It hinged on the equal-rights principle, the touchstone of Democratic opposition to Whig positions on banking and tariff legislation. William Leggett, "the prince of the Locofocos," stated the principle forthrightly in 1836: "The only safeguard against oppression is a system of legislation which leaves to all the free exercise of their talents and industry, within the limits of the GENERAL LAW, and which, on no pretence of public good, bestows on any particular class of industry, or any particular body of men, rights or privileges not equally enjoyed by the great aggregate of the body politic." Leggett, whose creed Whigs repeatedly called "disorganizing," focused on legislative discrimination in grants of rights or privileges. Duer invoked the equal-rights principle to condemn legislative discrimination in the denial of them. The first section of Wheaton's bill, he pointed out, would abolish the right to distrain only when the overdue rent was not payable in cash. Yet wheat rents were neither harmful to society nor necessarily exploitative to lessees. Adam Smith and other economists had long approved them, Duer pointed out, "especially in long leases, as more stable in value than rents payable in money." The action of ejectment, which the second section of Wheaton's bill proposed to bar in certain instances, was equally unobjectionable on general principles. "If the remedies by distress for rent, and of ejectment to recover the possession of land are, as remedies, oppressive or otherwise objectionable," Duer asserted, "they should be taken away or modified, not in these only but in all other cases."[32]

It is unlikely that Duer's heart was in this incantation of the equal-rights creed. He invoked it to make a second point. The only possible reason for Wheaton's impulse to "discriminate" between wheat rents and money rents, as well as between ejectment for nonperformance of quarter-sale covenants and ejectment for violation of other agreements secured by real estate, lay in the assumption "that the passage of this bill would produce such a change in the situation of the parties as would lead to a settlement" on tenant terms. The very idea of using law for such a purpose outraged Duer. He refused to concede it would work. "The same cause that would tend to reduce the demands of the landlord," Duer asserted, "would have the probable effect of increasing those of the tenants." Rather than evoking a settlement, the enactment of such legislation might generate additional civil disorders and perhaps bloodshed on a large scale. What really frightened him, however, was the possibility that Wheaton's scheme might work very well indeed.[33]

Embedded in the Wheaton bill were two linked premises that Duer regarded as threats to the very existence of democratic capitalism in America. The first was manifest. "It is proposed," Duer declared, "to strike at the contract through the remedy; to do indirectly that which it is out of our power to do directly; to evade the Constitution; to pass a law which courts cannot pronounce void, only because they cannot with certainty reach our motives; finally, to take property from one man and give it to another." The second, implicit in the bill and openly avowed by its author, was the notion that law could be legitimately mobilized as an instrument of class warfare. In Duer's judgment, Wheaton's method and motive clashed not only with "the science of legislation" but also with the foundations of democracy. "It has always been objected to our form of government, that its tendency is to render property insecure," Duer declared. "In all countries, our own not excepted, the great mass labor for a subsistence, more or less comfortable, while a few live in luxury and ease. Hence it has been argued, that where the power was in the hands of the many, the wealth of the few could not be safe. Experience, so far in our government, has shown that these fears are groundless, and that property has more to dread from monarchs and nobles than from the people." But now Wheaton proposed an alarming new departure. He aimed to seize the property of landlords and give it to their tenants; he aimed to prove that the wealth of the few was indeed unsafe when legislative power was in the hands of the many.[34]

The seeds of Duer's own approach to land reform were scattered throughout his critiques of the tenant petitions and the Wheaton bill. The legislature could not provide equitable relief for tenants who held land under "onerous and oppressive" contracts, but it could act to advance vital public interests. Among the concerns of "the community at large" was the suppression of legal relations that reduced productivity and inhibited the luxuriation of an "industrious and intelligent population." The legislature could not pass laws impairing the obligation of contracts. Nor could it divest parties of all remedies for breach of contract. "But is there not a distinction," Duer asked, "between legislation that acts upon and has reference only to the rights of the parties to a contract, and an interposition on the part of the state, by virtue of its sovereign power for the interest of the people?" Duer regarded this distinction, like the others drawn in the course of his report, as an obvious one. It led to still another question, the answer to which solved the riddle Governor Seward had thrust upon the legislature in January: "When contracts embrace something contrary to the policy of the state, something though lawful when entered into, which is found upon experience to tend to immorality, or to be in any way detrimental to the public interest, may not the state interpose for the public good, and drawing to itself, *upon just compensation*, the property of the creditor in the contract, release the debtor from its obligation?" Duer's answer, of course, was yes. The "manor difficulties" were rooted in land tenures having all the incidents of a "species of perpetuity." The public had an interest in extinguishing them; it followed that the situation on Rensselaerwyck might be resolved by the exercise of New York's eminent domain power.[35]

Duer conceded that using the eminent domain power to "assimilate" manorial tenures into New York's "republican" land system would not be entirely free of constitutional difficulties. The operative language in the state constitution was "private property shall not be taken for public use without just compensation." This text, said Duer, could be read in two ways. It "admits of a narrow construction, which would deprive the legislature of all power . . . [to take] property unless strictly speaking [what government took] was for the use of the state or public." Read narrowly, in other words, the taking clause would permit expropriation for public works such as government buildings and the Erie Canal. The general public used both as a matter of right and not merely as a favor. But it would bar takings if the legislature purported to devote the property taken to a use that the general public could not possibly enjoy. Exponents of strict construction thus focused on the text; the phrase "for public use," they insisted, meant precisely what it said. Duer was quick to add that the taking clause also admitted of a broad construction. From this perspective, he explained, the words "for public use" were "synonymous with, for public purposes, for the public good, and do not imply that the property taken shall be occupied or possessed by the public or the state." Exponents of broad construction were clearly uncomfortable with textual analysis. But they had a trump card. In their judgment, the New York Constitution's language had to be read in light of American ideas about the separation of powers. Weighty questions of public policy were involved in every use of the eminent domain power; consequently the legislative department, not the judicial, should determine the circumstances that justified its exercise.[36]

With considerable satisfaction, Duer reported that a broad construction of the eminent domain power prevailed not only in New York but throughout the Union. The leading case was *Beekman v. Saratoga & Schenectady Railroad Co.* (1831). At issue there was a provision in the company's charter authorizing it to take private property for a right-of-way on which railroad track might be laid. Chancellor Reuben Walworth declined to enjoin an ensuing taking, and Duer not only quoted but italicized the court's opinion in his 1840 report:

> The right of eminent domain does not . . . imply a right in the sovereign power to take the property of one citizen and transfer it to another, even

for a full compensation, where the public interest will be in no way promoted by such transfer. . . . *But if the public interest can be in any way promoted* by the taking of private property, it must rest *in the wisdom of the legislature* to determine whether the benefit to the public will be of sufficient importance to render it expedient for them to exercise the right of eminent domain, and to authorize an interference with the private rights of individuals for that purpose.

Walworth reasserted the same view in *Bloodgood v. Mohawk & Hudson Railroad Co.* (1837), where New York's highest court confirmed the legislature's authority to clothe railroad corporations with the state's eminent domain power.[37]

Duer professed "the highest respect" for lawyers inclined to read the taking clause narrowly. In his judgment, however, the question had been settled. "The exercise of the power has been sanctioned repeatedly by the courts of different states, where the benefits flowing therefrom have been strictly local, as to drain swamps, to bring water to cities and villages, and even to take land for a mill site," he reported. Clearly, then, "to make the 'use' 'public,' within the meaning of the constitution, it is not requisite that the whole community be directly interested therein." Duer also believed that the question had been settled correctly. An act of the legislature expropriating the Van Rensselaer family's interest in tenant farms would not throw open the land for the use of all New Yorkers. But the public benefits, though diffuse, would be substantial. "It is as much for the public use or the public good that the tenures by which land is held be so regulated as to promote agricultural improvement and enterprise, as that highways and canals should be constructed," Duer concluded. "It seems to your committee that it could not have been intended by the employment of the word 'use' [in the New York Constitution] to deprive the legislature of a power so essential."[38]

The Making of the Manor Commission

The eminent domain argument framed by the Duer Committee was so plausible that one wonders why nobody thought of it before. One reason, perhaps, was the magnitude of the contemplated task. Nineteenth-century Americans associated eminent domain with public works. But the cost of land acquisition for canals and railroads was small potatoes compared with the undertaking Duer envisioned. Rensselaerwyck contained 3,063 farms on 436,000 acres. In 1839 the tenants had demanded the right to extinguish the landlord's interest in the land at $2.50 per acre on the theory that such an amount, invested at 7 percent interest, would provide the Van Rensselaer family with an annual income equal to the perpetual rents. If government commissioners fixed the value of the rents at the same figure, which Stephen Van Rensselaer IV had rejected as too low, the state treasury would have to come up with $1,090,000. And that would mark only the beginning. The tenants had also declared that the landlord's quarter-sale reservations and other "feudal rights" were so oppressive, so contrary to the spirit of the age, they had no duty to pay for them in a final settlement. Duer's report disagreed. Liquidating the quarter-sale covenants, which the Van Rensselaers had long agreed to do at $30 per farm, would require another $95,000. The resulting figure of $1.2 million, conservatively estimated, would not include the value of water and mineral rights reserved in every indenture, the 3,063 personal service agreements payable at $2 per year, and the rents in arrear. Huge as it was, moreover, Rensselaerwyck constituted only about a third of the manor district.

It was one thing for the Duer Committee to contend that "the state [might] interpose for the public good, drawing to itself, upon just compensation, the property of the creditor in the contract to release the debtor from its obligation." It was something else to face the whopping price tag incident to the eradication of manorial tenures through the eminent domain power. When Duer came up with the idea, he took it for granted that the tenants would foot the bill just as railroad corporations paid for every parcel of land taken along their rights-of-way. But the manor tenants, like the entrepreneurs who organized railroad companies, had a dearth of fluid capital. It was unlikely that an eminent domain scheme could be implemented without a loan of the state's credit. The legislature would have to create an agency authorized to hold a mortgage on each tenant's farm until the government loan, advanced to extinguish the landlord's interest in the premises, had been repaid. Long-term payment schedules and other terms would have to be fixed and then enforced. Implicit in Duer's legal argument, in other words, was one of the most expensive, most complicated exercises of the eminent domain power in Anglo-American history.

Duer and his four associates on the committee, all of them Whigs, must have considered the cost and logistics of effecting such a scheme. As their discussion progressed, however, it must have become increasingly clear that they were playing with political dynamite. Following Seward's lead, Duer had assembled a very persuasive argument linking land reform with transport development and both with the spirit of improvement. But the state credit already had been stretched to the breaking point—beyond it, Democrats claimed—by deficit financing of canal and railroad construction. The state debt, which amounted to less than $8 million in 1837, stood at $18 million three years later. European investment bankers who gobbled up New York bonds at a 22 percent premium in 1833 would underwrite them only at a 22 percent discount in 1840. How far could "the great cause of improvement," facilitated by massive state expenditures, be carried? Could the Whig Party, already under Democratic fire for its "extravagance," sustain another worthy yet very expensive program? The questions were so daunting that the Duer Committee was reluctant even to broach them.[39]

The report finessed all the tough questions. "Your committee have determined not to recommend at this time any measure of legislation, in execution of the views and opinions which they have expressed," Duer wrote. "It appears to them, that in a matter so interesting and important, the state may as well act as mediator, before, as a final resort, she has recourse to her [eminent domain] power." Duer introduced an appropriate bill on the same day his committee reported. It provided for the appointment of two commissioners, nominated by the governor and compensated at a sum "not exceeding three dollars per day," and charged them to "effect a settlement of the disputes existing between the landlords and tenants of the Manor of Rensselaerwyck" and to "ascertain the just and fair value" of the Van Rensselaer family's entire interest in the tenant farms. The commissioners were to "report fully to the next legislature, of their action with reference to the duties imposed upon them by this act."[40]

Duer's report, submitted to the assembly on March 23, had something for everyone who counted. It contained a persuasive legal theory, establishing with clarity and force the legislature's formal authority to extinguish manorial tenures upon payment of just compensation to the landlords. The report resolved the ambiguities in Governor Seward's message, met the constitutional challenges invoked so confidently by Democrats, and accomplished both with an argument that was consonant with Whig principles. It also supplied Henry Wheaton with the bargaining leverage he sought for his tenant constituency. Duer's bill made it "the duty" of the commissioners to ascertain the value of the Van Rensselaer family's rights in the farms, a first step in any condemnation proceeding; the Select Committee's report spoke forthrightly about recourse to the eminent domain power "as a final resort." Wheaton believed that the legislature's threat would enable him to wrest a favorable settlement from the Van Rensselaers. "Its effects," he proclaimed on the house floor early in May, "will be to allay the excitement now existing and to bring about an adjustment of their difficulties to the satisfaction of all parties." Finally, the committee had conjured up a way to achieve all these things with a measure that reinforced voter identification of the Whig Party with "the great cause of improvement," yet cost taxpayers virtually nothing.[41]

Complaints about the Duer Committee's handiwork came from predictable sources. Casparus F. Pruyn, the Van Rensselaer family's agent across the Hudson in Rensselaer County, condemned the report's "agrarian" legal theory. "The Whigs seem greater Locofocos than the New York [City] Locos," he wrote William P. Van Rensselaer on March 24. Assemblyman James I. Roosevelt, one of those very radical Democrats, had nothing to say about Duer's eminent domain argument. But he did characterize the bill "as one designed to create new officers to perambulate the manor and do service for the 'hard cider' cause . . . at the public expense." In the senate, Democrats patted themselves on the back for having foreseen this result since January. Alonzo Paige called the bill an "entirely useless," "altogether illusory" gesture. "The commissioners will not even have the power of arbitrators under existing laws," he said. "The committee has blinked the question, and in effect denied the prayer of the petitioners." Daniel S. Dickinson insisted that the bill, "instead of [the] peace-offering" Whigs promoted, was "a cheat-offering" because it spent the money of taxpayers for a futile purpose.[42]

Democratic lawmakers scored some debating points, but they changed no minds. Only four Whigs broke party ranks and voted against the Duer bill in the assembly. It passed 54-49. The Whig majority held firm in the senate, and Governor Seward signed the bill into law on May 13. A batch of internal improvement measures also got Seward's signature before the legislature adjourned the next day. One statute authorized the Canal Board to borrow $2.5 million for the Erie Canal enlargement and another $3 million for construction on the lateral-canal projects. Eight railroad corporations divided more than $1 million in new government loans. All of these acts engendered dogged Democratic opposition and passed by narrow majorities. The resulting increase in the state debt, which reached the $20 million mark early in 1841, compromised the Manor Commission's bargaining position in ways that Seward, Duer, and other Whig leaders should have anticipated. As the state debt mounted and Democratic objections to the Whig Party's spending programs grew more compelling, Van Rensselaer lawyers had reason to regard the eminent domain argument as so much bluff and bluster.[43]

The commissioners did not "perambulate" Rensselaerwyck for the "hard cider cause" that fall, as the Democrats feared. Seward immediately named two eminent New Yorkers, William Kent and Gideon Lee, but both declined to serve. Not until late July did Seward manage to staff the Manor Commission with Gary V. Sacket, a farmer from Seneca Falls, and New York City attorney Hugh Maxwell. The commissioners invited "all persons concerned" to an August 11 meeting in downtown Albany, where Sacket and Maxwell announced their intention "to proceed to the several towns within the manor" in December. At that time, they told the anti-renters who crowded the room, the Manor Commission would "afford them a full opportunity of being heard" and supervise the election of tenant delegates to negotiate with the Van Rensselaers at a mediation session in January. Delay did not discourage Anti-Rent leaders. Government intervention resulted in a stay on rent collections that kept writ-bearing deputy sheriffs out of the Helderberg townships. The very existence of the Manor Commission sustained the rent strike.[44]

Election day brought a Whig landslide. William Henry Harrison carried New York by 13,000 votes and walloped Van Buren in the electoral college, 234 to 60. Seward was returned to the statehouse and another Whig majority to the state legislature. Whigs also captured a majority in the House of Representatives (133 Whigs, 102 Democrats, 6 "Independents"); the newly elected state legislatures soon gave them control of the Senate (28 Whigs to 22 Democrats). Thurlow Weed reveled in the results. "I think of going to Washington by your train," he wrote Congressman Francis Granger, in Canandaigua for the recess, on November 9. "It is the first time that I ever wanted to see the Capitol."[45]

More people than ever before were looking toward Washington in the fall of 1840. Voter turnout across the nation reached unprecedented heights, jumping from 57.8 percent in 1836 to 80.2 percent in 1840. New voters cast an incredible 37.5 percent of the ballots; three-fifths of the 900,000 first-time voters went for Harrison. Whig leaders attracted them by presenting the party's traditional program in a new, more popular format. State and local party organizations competed with one another in organizing great rallies, vast encampments, "*acres of men!*" The crowds drank barrels of hard cider and sang entertaining songs:

> What has caused the great commotion, motion, motion
> All our country through?
> It is the ball a rolling on, on
> For Tippecanoe and Tyler too—Tippecanoe and Tyler too.
> And with them we'll beat little Van, Van, Van
> Van is a used up man . . .

Horace Greeley published a collection of campaign ditties in the *Log Cabin Song Book* (1840). "People like the swing of the music," he told Weed. "After a song or two they are more ready to listen to the orators." Exactly so. Frivolity nurtured a sense of solidarity, which Whig stump speakers reinforced with vivid recitations of the common hardships borne by the depression. And the hardships made political participation meaningful. "Men wish to see ground for better hope," said Daniel Webster, describing the crux of the Whig Party's appeal to the voters. "General Harrison's election will bring this confidence and this hope of a better time."[46]

Tenants on the Manor of Rensselaerwyck, excited about the Whig Party's reconnaissance of land reform in 1840, entertained a quite different "hope of a better time" that fall. Anti-renters looked toward Albany, not Washington, for relief from the conditions that oppressed them. But the two levels of government did not operate independently in the era of the Second Party System. Whig ideology posited a web of fiscal interdependence that linked state policies to national ones and subordinated the former to the latter. Far more than anti-renters anticipated, the capacity of the Whig majority in the New York legislature to do something about manorial tenures was connected to the ability of the Whig majority in Congress to do something about the depression.

3

The Politics of Evasion

Governor Seward's third annual message, delivered to the legislature on January 6, 1841, contrasted sharply with the previous two. "Instead of being thickly peppered with brisk and confident recommendations of plans and measures as were his last messages," remarked William Cullen Bryant, "the present one makes few suggestions of the kind, and such as it makes are offered in a timorous and hesitating manner, and carefully guarded with apologies and qualifications." Seward even suggested that appropriations for internal improvements be made with "moderation and economy." The problem was money. New York had an empty treasury and credit had not been as tight for a generation. Yet the money crunch got worse before it got better. Early in February the Bank of the United States closed its doors for good; the sudden fall in stock prices caused one Wall Street investment house to collapse and left others "shivering in the wind." The panic "makes it impossible for anyone to support an increased debt," the president of New York's largest trust company told Gulian C. Verplanck, chairman of the state senate's Finance Committee. Seward's man on the Canal Board agreed. "It seems to me that it is important to let the storm blow over . . . before bringing in any bills appropriating monies for our public works," Samuel B. Ruggles wrote Verplanck on February 11. "We shall go farther in 1842 by going prudently in 1841."[1]

Ruggles expected to "go farther in 1842" with federal funds. Seward did too. Both expected the first fruits of William Henry Harrison's stunning victory to come in the form of legislation distributing the net receipts from public land sales among the states according to their federal representation. Seward devoted the last 5,000 words of his 1841 message to "this great measure." He claimed that when New York and other states possessing western lands ceded them to the United States "with the magnanimity characteristic of the Revolutionary period," they did so "as a basis for the redemption of the funded debts of the Union." The terms of cession, as Seward and other Whigs read them, merely authorized the national government to hold the public domain "as a trustee" and implied an equitable reversion to the states upon discharge of the national debt in 1833.[2]

Seward's theory of the public domain had profound ramifications for economic policy in the federal system. It suggested, first, that Congress violated a sacred trust by using receipts from land sales to fund national programs or pay federal employees. "The revenues derived from imposts and upon imported merchandise," declared Seward, "are or ought always to be, adequate to the ordinary expenses of the [United States] government." The argument for distribution, in other words, was an argument for a higher tariff. It was also an argument for maintaining active state governments without increasing direct taxes on persons or property. In Seward's view, the American constitutional order contained a significant flaw. "The states have reserved the chief responsibilities and powers of legislation for the public welfare," he told the New York legislature, "but have yielded to the general government an undue proportion of the taxes." Distribution would restore balance to the federal system by providing state governments with sufficient means to perform the great public purposes thrust upon them.[3]

What the Whig governors liked best about distribution, of course, was the revenue. Seward estimated that New York's share in the first year alone would be "nearly six hundred thousand dollars," and he rhapsodized about the value of its share over the long haul. "After such an accession to our revenues the various enterprises of internal improvements would no longer be rivals, prosecuted against the influence of local jealousies and alarms of taxation," he declared. "It would be in our power, not only to extend our system of improvement but also to increase in various other ways the general happiness." Seward compiled an imposing list of public projects that had been slighted because of the "cold and calculating charity we are now obliged to practice" but would have to be deferred no longer. He did not include compensated abolition of manorial tenures. In 1840 the legislature had resolved to invoke its eminent domain power only as a "final resort," and it would have been impolitic for the governor to anticipate the failure of the Manor Commission's mediation.[4]

Seward had another reason to avoid discussion of "the manor difficulties" in his 1841 message. Relying on federal dollars to finance land reform and the public works reduced his leverage on the Van Rensselaer family. Because the newly elected Congress was not scheduled to convene until December, months after the Manor Commission had to lay its report before the state legislature, Seward refrained from promising the tenants something he might be unable to deliver. He remained optimistic all the same. While the state government waited for money from Washington, however, Seward confronted one crisis after another. Stephen Van Rensselaer IV tried to resume rent collections in March; the anti-renters were quick to revive their resistance. Other forces beyond Seward's control fractured Whig Party discipline in the legislature and caused the state credit to plummet. In the fall of 1841, New York Whigs patched up their differences and established a temporary truce in the Anti-Rent war. But land reform disappeared from the Whig agenda. Neither Seward nor his party renounced the public's interest in extinguishing manorial tenures. As the state's changing political and financial situation made an eminent domain law increasingly "inexpedient," however, Whig leaders allowed the recommendations of the Duer Committee to disappear quietly from public view.[5] They practiced a politics of evasion.

Portents of Failure

Very few of the Whig legislators who convened in Albany on January 5, 1841, were comfortable with the prospect of marking time until Congress supplied new money for their favorite projects. Yet they could afford to wait. Impending bankruptcy confronted state governments in Pennsylvania and Maryland, in the Old Northwest, and in the band of cotton-belt states stretching from Alabama to Arkansas. During the boom of the mid-1830s those jurisdictions had run up such massive debts relative to revenues that the crash of 1839 reduced them to issuing new bonds in order to pay interest on the old. In the summer of 1840, however, European investment bankers, citing saturated markets and concerns about the solvency of American state governments, suddenly refused to underwrite new issues of their securities at any price. No state defaulted in 1840. Financial officers met scheduled interest payments by liquidating state assets such as land and corporate stocks or by looting trust funds set up for schools and other public purposes. Lawmakers in Pennsylvania and Illinois reluctantly levied new property taxes. Throughout the South and West, however, ordinary government expenses were funded primarily with unconventional loans from state-chartered banks that had suspended specie payments in 1839. State agencies conveyed currently unsalable bonds ("assets") to commercial banks that paid out currently unredeemable bank notes ("liabilities") to government employees, suppliers, and building contractors. People understood that bootstrap finance of this sort could not carry the overextended states through 1841. Without "the powers of Midas," an Ohio canal commissioner remarked in November 1840, it would be difficult "to keep things going."[6]

Henry Clay, leader of the Whig Party in Congress, thought he had the Midas touch. The election of William Henry Harrison, he asserted in December 1840, marked "a great civil revolution." Harrison had promised to defer to Congress on matters of domestic policy, and Clay could hardly wait to start "healing the wounds and building up the prosperity of the country." He bragged that he had "a perfect Bank in my head." He insisted that distribution would rescue the state governments "greatly in debt, at a loss even to raise means to pay the interest upon their bonds." And he presumed that Congress could balance the budget with federal borrowing coupled, perhaps, with "the imposition of duties on the free articles" enumerated in the Compromise Tariff of 1833.[7]

Clay also argued incessantly for a special session of Congress to enact the Whig program. His case, broadcast by the *National Intelligencer* on February 5, 1841, anticipated George Norris's case for what became the Twentieth Amendment (1933). In Clay's view, the Constitution's provisions for a regime change were antirepublican. It made no sense, he insisted, to have the people vote against the existing administration and thus demand "a change of policy— a change in the measures of government" in November of one year, yet compel them to wait until December of the following year for the newly elected Congress to assemble and "carry out their will." Only the president's authority to summon Congress for a special session could mitigate the difficulty, and Clay urged Harrison to act "at the earliest convenient and practicable day" following his inauguration on March 3. "The effect of postponing any action by the next Congress until the day fixed by the Constitution," he contended, "will be to prolong Mr. Van Buren's administration twelve or eighteen months after its constitutional termination." The *Washington Globe*, principal organ of Jacksonian Democracy, described Clay's case more succinctly: "An extraordinary session is necessary [so] that the bill for distributing the public lands may be rushed through with a hard cider hurrah."[8]

Thurlow Weed's *Evening Journal* elaborated a number of "insuperable objections" to Clay's call for a special session. At the root of them all, however, were fears that Whig unity, sustained by a common foe and hard cider during the campaign, could not be maintained in Congress. Whig divisions—between old National Republicans and old Antimasons, between easterners and westerners, between strict and broad constructionists of the Constitution—might harden rather than soften if exposed prematurely, immobilizing the congressional party in the face of the depression. A great many Whig managers in the New England and South Atlantic states shared Weed's view. But in the West, where capital was more scarce and the solvency of state governments more precarious, Whig leaders feared delay more than division. President Harrison did too. Weed "anxiously" fell into step. "We trust that the Whig majority of Congress will rise above the petty jealousies, temporizing expedients, and sectional antipathies that have too often prevailed in the halls of the Capitol," the *Evening Journal* announced on March 22. When the special session convened in May, the fate of the nation and party alike would depend on "a close and perfect union among the Whig members."[9]

The hopes and fears that animated the debate over a special session of Congress also shaped the prospects for land reform at Albany. Decisive action against manorial tenures by New York authorities, like virtually all state projects for improvement and reform in 1841, hinged on new money from Washington. And the enactment of new measures by Congress required a unified Whig party. Among the issues that threatened to divide the New York Whigs, however, was land reform. Governor Seward had committed himself to the abolition of manorial tenures, and the Duer Committee had identified a way to do it. Henry G. Wheaton, one of Albany County's three Whig assemblymen, had spoken to tenant groups up and down the Manor of Rensselaerwyck, explaining how an eminent domain law might be implemented. But the targets of all this activity, Stephen Van Rensselaer IV and his half brother William P. Van Rensselaer, were also Whigs. Teunis Van Vechten and Samuel Stevens, counsel for the proprietors and for the estate, respectively, had been active members of the Whig Party from its inception. Daniel Dewey Barnard, Albany's two-term Whig congressman and a longtime friend of the Van Rensselaer family, held a $35,000 mortgage on the Albany County half of the manor. He was also the acknowledged leader of the party's small band of old-guard conservatives in New York State.[10]

Seward and Barnard maintained an uneasy association from their first meeting in the early 1830s. The governor had come to his Whiggery through Antimasonry, a mass movement that celebrated political democracy and ferociously attacked "licensed monopolies" and other bastions of "aristocratic privilege" in the name of equality. Seward regarded the doctrine of political equality as the touchstone of republican government. The defining characteristic of the Whig Party was, in his view, that "it seeks to establish perfect equality of political rights; but it levels upward, not downward, by education and benignant legislation." Barnard, on the other hand, had come to his Whiggery through the Federalist Party; he still clung to what Louis Hartz aptly described as a "grim Harringtonian theory of class conflict." For Barnard, political equality was a condition to be opposed or feared, not encouraged, and he believed that all talk of leveling posed very real threats to the virtue, civility, and refinement that flowed from aggregations of private property. In his view, the defining characteristic of the Whig Party was its unrelenting opposition to attacks on property rights by political majorities.[11]

The two versions of the Whig mission did not necessarily conflict. Seward respected vested rights; Barnard favored government spending for internal improvements, education, and other "benignant" purposes. Both believed that the fate of the nation hung on the enactment of Henry Clay's agenda for the special session of Congress. But their different political ideas, not to mention their different interests, generated different responses to the clamor for land reform on Rensselaerwyck. At the heart of Barnard's conservatism was a classical republican mode of thought. He took it for granted that only free and independent men made responsible citizens, that property and power had to go together. He also understood that suffrage restriction was just one method of fulfilling those classical maxims. Agrarianism—the forcible redistribution of property to maintain a free and independent citizenry—was another. Preserving republican forms had figured as a justification for Tiberius Gracchus's agrarian law in the late Roman Republic (133 B.C.), for James Harrington's comparable scheme in the influential *Commonwealth of Oceana* (1656), and for Thomas Paine's redistributive proposals in *Agrarian Justice* (1797). Orestes Brownson, a lightening rod for Whig attacks on Democratic radicalism, worked from the same premises. "A Locofoco," he wrote in January 1841, "is a Jeffersonian Democrat, who having realized political equality, passed through one phase of the revolution, now passes on to another, and attempts the realization of social equality, so that the actual condition of men in society shall be in harmony with their acknowledged rights as citizens." Barnard lamented the failure of his Federalist forebears to stave off the first "phase of the revolution," and he regarded the Whig Party as the first line of defense against the second. Seward hit an exposed nerve, then, by describing manorial tenures as "antirepublican" and calling for their abolition. Barnard bristled at the very idea of legislation designed to expropriate the proprietors of the oldest estate in New York.[12]

Yet Barnard did not denounce Seward's stance on the manor question in 1840. Nor did Stevens, Van Vechten, or the Van Rensselaers. John A. King, the eldest son of Federalist wheelhorse Rufus King and proprietor of the 17,000-acre Blenheim Patent, a Schoharie County estate peopled by several hundred tenants in fee, was one of four Whig assemblymen to vote against the Duer bill. But he said nothing in debate. Neither King nor the landlord lawyers were prepared to jeopardize Whig unity during the presidential campaign. Nevertheless, all of them regarded Duer's eminent domain scheme as rank agrarianism and thought the Manor Commission had no business interfering with inviolable contracts between landlords and their tenants. They believed that the Van Rensselaers owed their party only the most perfunctory cooperation with the government commissioners, followed by a decisive reassertion of their legal right to collect overdue rents.[13]

Tenant leaders were equally intransigent as they awaited the arrival of the government commissioners in the winter of 1840–41. They hoped for the best, yet prepared for the worst. When farmers in the township of New Scotland, Albany County, held their mass meeting in mid-December, they did not merely elect delegates to the January mediation session. They also resolved against paying more "tribute to Caesar," declaring that "we will use all laudable exertions in ridding ourselves of this yoke of oppression" and calling upon all "fellow heirs in bondage" to join their struggle. Tenant assemblies in the Helderberg towns—Knox, Berne, Westerlo, and Rensselaerville—passed com-

parable resolutions. The rent strike would continue if government intervention failed.[14]

Seward did not appreciate all the confrontational talk. Negotiations that
broke down in acrimony were the stuff of his nightmares. It would mean
another Helderberg War. It would mean a personal defeat, a divided party at a
turning point in the nation's history, and civil disorders that made a mockery of
Whig homilies on government's duty to harmonize social interests. In more
sanguine moments Seward thought the Manor Commission might fulfill its
responsibility "to effect a settlement." But he was prepared to accept delay. If
landlords and tenants could be kept talking until Congress enacted the Whig
economic program, Seward believed that conservative resistance to an eminent
domain law might be overcome. A statute of the sort Duer, Wheaton, and
Seward envisioned would not just compensate the proprietors. It would mean a
great deal more money than anything the Van Rensselaers could expect to get
by negotiating with the anti-renters. The men Seward appointed to the Manor
Commission, however, proved unable even to stall effectively. Their performance could not have been more inept.

The Debacle in Albany

Commissioners Hugh Maxwell and Gary V. Sacket construed their duties
under the "act to provide for the settlement of the disputes existing between the
landlords and tenants of the Manor of Rensselaerwyck" in the narrowest possible way. The statute spoke in terms of "the landlords," plural, vesting the Manor
Commission with jurisdiction over William P. Van Rensselaer and his tenants in
Rensselaer County as well as Stephen Van Rensselaer IV and his tenants in
Albany County. But the commissioners visited only "several western towns
within the manor, where difficulties existed," and ignored the Van Rensselaer
family's other tenants, all of whom held their land under the same "obnoxious"
terms as their more rebellious brethren in the Helderberg highlands. Maxwell
and Sacket thus defined their task in terms of pacification, not land reform.
They also entertained a very narrow conception of their duty to mediate the
dispute and "effect a settlement." The commissioners did not even orchestrate
negotiations, let alone cajole or threaten the parties. In their view, mediation
involved nothing more than bringing tenant delegates and landlord lawyers
together at a single place at a stated time.[15]

The late January session in Albany was a farce. Teunis Van Vechten, counsel
for the Van Rensselaer family, arrived at the meeting with a written proposal,
which Maxwell and Sacket dutifully printed in their subsequent report to the
legislature. The terms were only slightly more generous than those Stephen Van
Rensselaer IV had offered prior to the Helderberg War in 1839. Tenants in the

four western townships—Rensselaerville, Westerlo, Berne, and Knox—could extinguish the landlord's interest in their farms for $4 per acre, "payable with one-fifth of the purchase price in hand and four equal annual installments with lawful interest, to be paid annually; to be secured by a bond and mortgage on such premises." Van Vechten emphasized that tenants in New Scotland, Guilderland, and other manor communities could not take advantage of this general offer. They would have to negotiate special buyout contracts at the manor office. The qualified scope of the Van Rensselaer offer suggested that the proprietors regarded $4 per acre as a rock-bottom price. Tenants with farms closer to the Hudson River, or across it in Rensselaer County, would have to pay more. Another qualification in the offer directly affected the tenant delegates at the meeting. Van Vechten pointed out that the proprietors would not sell their interest in any farm until the back rents had been paid in full. "Mr. Van Vechten then retired," the commissioners reported, "to give the tenants an opportunity to reply."[16]

The tenant leaders did not deliberate very long. They proposed that every family in possession of the land have "the privilege" of buying out the Van Rensselaers for a sum that, invested at 7 percent interest, would amount to the annual rent payable in perpetuity. In other words, the tenants stood fast on their 1839 position. They refused to pay for the abolition of personal service, quarter-sale, waterpower, and other "feudal" reservations. They also refused to allow the Van Rensselaers to benefit from increases in the value of the land occasioned by their own improvements or by externalities such as improved transportation facilities and population growth in nearby urban markets. The upshot of the tenant position, of course, was a far lower price than that quoted by Van Vechten. Commissioners Maxwell and Sacket calculated it at $2 per acre. (Interest rates had been driven upward by the spiraling state debt since 1839, when a tenant offer framed on the same theory would have brought the Van Rensselaers $2.50 per acre.) But the delegates from the Helderberg townships were not looking out for their own interests alone. By insisting as a matter of principle that the Van Rensselaer family must relinquish its interest in the farms on terms that provided compensation for the lost rents only, the Helderberg delegates expressed their solidarity with the rest of the manor population. Implicit in the tenant counteroffer was the idea that there could be but one equitable price, effective everywhere on Rensselaerwyck, for the eradication of manorial tenures.[17]

The tenant delegates said nothing about the back rents at the January meeting. Perhaps they were prepared to compromise their 1839 position on that issue in the course of bargaining. But the Manor Commission conducted no negotiations. Van Vechten did not return to the room; the meeting simply adjourned once the tenant delegates had submitted their counteroffer. Nor did the commissioners subsequently attempt "to ascertain the just and fair value of the rights of water, mines and quarter sales possessed" by the Van Rensselaer family, as the statute mandated. "Opinions will vary as to such matters, according to the enterprise or views of individuals," they wrote in their report to the legislature. "The value of the water rights, like the value of anything else, may be ascertained when by enterprise and practical results, proper data can be furnished." Maxwell and Sacket obviously did not understand the valuation process as a preliminary step toward an exercise of the state's eminent domain power. Stephen Van Rensselaer IV did. On February 5, 1841, one of his agents wrote Andrew Lansing, manager of the manor office in Albany County, to report that he had completed a description of the patroon's water privileges and an estimate of their value along Ten-Mile Creek in Rensselaerville, "as he informed me that you requested me to do." If the commissioners had taken their valuation duties seriously, the Van Rensselaers would have been prepared to contest their figures.[18]

The commissioners were ready to write a report as soon as the tenant delegates left town. Maxwell and Sacket, like every public official who addressed the matter during the 1840s, had "no hesitation in declaring their conviction that tenures of the kind existing on the Manor of Rensselaerwyck, are in every way unfortunate in their operation upon the tenants individually, and upon the general condition of the country. They are incongruous with the general laws, institutions, customs and habits of the people of this state." Despite their own "earnest desire" to make things right, however, nothing had been accomplished. Sacket finished a draft of the Manor Commission's report during the first week in February and delivered his handwritten manuscript to Governor Seward. Impatient to go home, he stopped by Seward's office and left a note. "I do not call on you this morning hearing that you are not in condition to see anyone on business," he wrote. "And under the belief that it will not be in your power for some days yet to finish the report now under your supervision, I have reluctantly come to the conclusion to leave for home tomorrow morning and return again at such time as you shall be enabled to say the report is ready. Or can I authorize you to sign it in my absence?" Sacket did not return to Albany during the legislature's 1841 session. Maxwell later made some revisions at Seward's request; the assembly received the Manor Commission's report on April 23, too late in the session for an appropriate legislative response.[19]

Seward had ten weeks to avoid this embarrassing denouement. What the governor did while the Manor Commission report remained under his "supervision" cannot be determined from the surviving evidence. But it is unlikely that he did nothing at all. Seward must have been encouraged by Stephen Van Rensselaer's offer to finance the sale of his interest, over five years secured by bond and mortgage, in the four western townships of Albany County. If that offer were extended to the entire manor and an agreement on terms could be reached, the "antirepublican" tenures on Rensselaerwyck could be extinguished without cost to the state. Seward undoubtedly huddled with Van Vechten and Wheaton, insisting that their failure to negotiate a settlement was likely to engender civil disorders that would be bad for everyone on the manor and very bad for the Whig Party. Whatever plea the governor made, however, it came to nothing.

Attempts to collect rent resumed in mid-March. "The Helderbergers, whose conquest was attempted last year, have again resorted to resistance, but in a new fashion," the *Evening Post* reported. "When the sheriff comes upon the ground, to sell their goods, they quietly suffer him to take his way. The goods are of course levied upon and exposed for public sale. Crowds of the tenants flock around, and the eagerness of their competition in running up the bids would throw a Pearl Street auctioneer into raptures." The bidding continued "from morning until night, without reaching a conclusion," said the correspondent. "It is a peaceful way of carrying on the war, which is likely to exhaust the patience of the patroon." Seward doubted this upbeat conclusion. But he could not prevent the escalation of landlord-tenant hostilities. Sending a special message to the legislature that described the Manor Commission's failure and called for an eminent domain law, the "last resort" promoted by the Duer Committee, would have been fruitless. New York law required immediate payment when government took property for public use, and the state treasury was empty. Besides, Seward did not have the votes. The conservatives in his own party could not be persuaded to swallow the compensated emancipation of manor tenants, and the Whig majority in the state senate could accomplish nothing without their support. The fate of Mark Sibley's bill "to extend the exemption of household furniture and working tools from distress for rent, and sale under execution" illustrated the point.[20]

Sibley, a Whig from Canandaigua, introduced the bill on January 23, 1841, and he accurately described it as "an extension of this state's ancient policy of withdrawing certain property from liability to seizure" for debts. Statutes enacted in 1788, 1815, and 1824 allowed every householder to hold free from execution or distress all spinning wheels and looms, ten sheep and their fleeces, one cow, two swine, necessary cooking utensils, wearing apparel and bedding for six, one table, six chairs, six knives and forks, stoves kept for use in a dwelling, and enough fuel to fire a stove for sixty days. Sibley's bill was framed on the theory "that the existing exemptions are too restricted." In a report for the Senate Judiciary Committee, he contended that the apartment dweller's "cherished garniture" and the young bride's "precious wedding gifts" merited the same sort of protection as the yeoman's livestock and his wife's loom. Rather than attempting to compile another "list of privileged property," adapted to the circumstances of life in 1841, Sibley proposed that every householder be authorized to designate exempt items of personal property valued at $150, "in addition to the articles now exempt by law from distress for rent, or levy and sale under execution."[21]

The very considerations of "sound public policy" and "regard to the wants and exigencies of the poor" that generated the existing exemption laws, Sibley insisted, justified their extension. "Extreme poverty discourages effort and represses the manly ambition of the willing debtor to apply his labor to the payment of his debts and the bettering of his condition," he explained. "By extending suitable protection, the law, instead of depressing, becomes an agent of improving and elevating the citizen; it acknowledges his social dignity and value, inspires his self-respect, stimulates his ambition, and [by] . . . encouraging him to hope for ultimate success, it animates the effort to secure it." Sibley thus appealed to the same principles that had evoked Seward's description of manorial tenures as "oppressive, antirepublican, and degrading" in 1840. The bill to extend the exemptions for debtors was designed to enhance the productive effort of New Yorkers and endow them with a larger measure of dignity.[22]

The press immediately hailed the Sibley bill. Weed's *Evening Journal* not only supported the measure with daily editorials but also reprinted nearly a dozen favorable notices from other Whig newspapers around the state. Even some Democratic prints backed the bill, although they tended to supplant Sibley's emphasis on the public interest in private contracts with appeals to equal rights. Putting "the poor and worthy householder" on a closer par with "the wealthy stockholder," who "furnished his mansion . . . with debts contracted in the name of the corporation" yet remained immune to subsequent seizure by the principle of limited liability, proclaimed the *Argus*, was the "imperative duty" of every member in the legislature's Democratic minority. Editors from both parties also clarified a matter Sibley and his associates on the Judiciary Committee had taken for granted. Although the bill was intended to have a retrospective effect, providing immediate relief to debtors driven from pillar to post by "the fluctuations of the times," its constitutionality seemed beyond question. The proposed legislation merely regulated the creditor's remedy. It would impair the obligation of contracts in the same way and for much the same reason as laws abolishing imprisonment for debt.[23]

Yet the bill's modest redistributive consequences outraged a handful of Whig conservatives in the upper house. "This doctrine, which has lately come into vogue, of protecting property from its rightful owners by legislation, is a dangerous and mischievous one," Erastus Root thundered when the debate began. "The law to abolish imprisonment for debt is sufficiently mischievous in its operation, without trying another experiment, vastly to increase the evils that already exist." Martin Lee, a Whig from Washington County, agreed. For several weeks he denounced the bill each time it got to the floor. Lee was imperious, unyielding, and finally triumphant. On the last day of the 1841 session, he moved for an adjournment to prevent a vote on the bill; the motion carried 13-11. Nine Whigs joined Lee and only five voted with Sibley. Eight senators, half of them Whigs, already had gone home.[24]

Senator Lee's case against the exemption bill deserved a better cause. "If we would make the poor man independent and elevate his standing in society," he said on May 6, "we must do it by moral and intellectual culture." Attempting to uplift the masses with legislation was "sheer quackery." Besides, he added, "to pass this bill would be an encouragement of what I can call no more appropriate name than a moral theft. We enable a man to get possession of his neighbor's property, and then turn around and defy him to collect his just dues." Lee shifted his focus from moral principle to legal principle on the following day; holding the line against agrarianism became his main theme. "Gentlemen had better add a provision to this bill for a division of all property," he declared. "The arguments urged in its favor would apply with equal force in favor of unlimited agrarianism." Should the legislature authorize a modest debtors' exemption in 1841, he insisted in his final speech on the bill, it would only invite measures "to carry additional exemptions from $150 to $1000" in subsequent sessions. "Why not at once bring in the millennium of agrarianism, and thus elevate the poor at once to the level of their purse-proud superiors in the world's comforts? The same false principles that support the policy of this bill will support that golden measure of equalization." What a legislator who conjured up the specter of agrarianism to defeat a $150 exemption bill would have said about the Duer Committee's "last resort," if Seward had mustered the temerity to recommend eminent domain legislation in 1841, must be left to the imagination.[25]

The 1841 session, which the *Evening Journal* pronounced "as inglorious to the legislature as it is disastrous to the people," thus ended with nothing for "the poor but honest" debtors, whose votes Weed had cultivated for the Whig Party, and nothing for the 3,063 tenants of Rensselaerwyck. Constitutional difficulties had not barred effective governmental action. The legislature's competence to pass Sibley's exemption bill seemed so clear that nobody had invoked the Contract Clause in debate. And its authority to extinguish the lease in fee, though much in doubt early in 1840, had been confirmed by the Duer Committee. Seward and Weed could point to all sorts of crosscutting fiscal and ideological pressures that frustrated their attempts to rally the party behind these measures. They could also claim that land reform and debtors' exemptions had merely been postponed. Instead, they chose to focus on the obstinacy of the conservative Whigs.[26]

Weed complained that conservatives like Lee were unable to distinguish "sudden innovations . . . that might seriously affect vested rights," which every Whig opposed, from "safe and moderate change that may do away with all prescriptive abuses." In a republican polity, he argued, legislators had a duty to balance security of possession against the public's interest in a free, independent, hopeful population of citizens. But too many Whigs still clung to a Federalist vision of society in which government took care of the rich and the rich took care of the poor. In Weed's judgment, their knee-jerk hostility to every measure that would put "the protecting aegis of the law around the rights and happiness of the lower classes" jeopardized the very existence of republican government. "What produced the convulsions that shook the Roman Commonwealth to its center during the civil and servile wars prior to Julius Caesar?" he asked on April 26. "Was it not that the iron heel of the aristocracy had crushed the spirit of the Roman people and by the destruction of everything like free labor reduced the Roman citizen to the condition of a pauper fed from the public granaries? In vain that citizen was appealed to, in the hour of danger, to defend his hearth and household goods! He had no hearth—no household goods to defend!"[27]

Dogmatic conservatism had always rankled Weed. His quarrel with the conservatives became especially intense in 1841, however, because they seemed to be calling all the shots. Stephen Van Rensselaer IV and Daniel Dewey Barnard had decided when deputy sheriffs bearing distress warrants should return to rural Albany County; Senator Lee had decided whether the debt-exemption bill should come to a vote. Weed understood that property rights justified the one kind of power and parliamentary practice the other. Nevertheless, he resented the fact that people with reactionary ideas and interests in "antirepublican" forms of property—people who were out of step with the Whig majority— had managed to control events. Seward shared Weed's frustration. As he reflected on the disappointments of the legislature's 1841 session, however, Seward began to consider the possibility that people like Weed and himself, not the conservatives, deviated from mainstream Whiggery. He also decided to leave public life upon the expiration of his term. "My principles are too liberal, too philanthropic, if it not be vain to say so, for my party," Seward wrote Christopher Morgan, a Whig friend in Washington for the special session of Congress, on June 10. "All that can now be worthy of my ambition is to leave the state better for my having been here, and to entitle myself to a favorable judgment in history."[28]

Anti-Rent Revived

Anti-renters responded swiftly to the Manor Commission's ineptitude. On April 28, 1841, five days after the legislature sent the commissioners' report to the printer, they assembled in Berne and adopted a new manifesto:[29]

Whereas the Declaration of American Independence affirms that all men are created equal, and endowed by their Creator with certain inalienable rights, among which are life, liberty, and the pursuit of happiness; and whereas the Constitution of the United States guarantees to the several states republican forms of government: Therefore, *Resolved*, That . . . the holding of so large a territory of land by one man, as claimed by the patroon of the colony of Rensselaerwyck, is in direct violation of that sacred declaration upon which American independence has been so long proudly maintained, and repugnant to that section of the United States Constitution which guarantees to each and every state of the Union, republican forms of government. *Resolved*, That we petition the next Congress for a redress of grievances. *Resolved*, That the Anti-Rent inhabitants of the county of Albany go into a ten year contest with the patroon of the colony of Rensselaerwyck, or until a redress of grievances be obtained.

The adoption of these resolutions marked more than the tenants' determination to resume the Helderberg War. It also signified their disenchantment with the Whig Party.

Governor Seward had spoken eloquently about "ancient leases" as public wrongs. He had emphasized government's duty to promote the spirit of improvement, to secure the peace and harmony of society, to effect the public good. But he had achieved nothing. Tenants on Rensselaerwyck still felt unjustly oppressed; they still felt the "wretchedness and unhallowed bondage" of perpetual rent. Long before the Manor Commission disbanded and the rent collectors reappeared, moreover, tenants recognized that they suffered the wrongs of manorial tenures directly, whereas some ill-defined, diffuse public felt them only indirectly, if at all. Anti-renters concluded that Whig talk about the public interest failed to describe the tenants' situation let alone remedy it. Only the language of natural rights and republican liberty seemed to express their grievances and aspirations in a suitable way.

James Watson Webb's *Courier and Enquirer*, principal organ of New York's conservative Whigs, poured venom on the Anti-Rent manifesto. "It is worse than the doctrines of Brownson, and almost low enough for Skidmoreism," he asserted. Webb's analogues had been notorious in Whig circles for years. Thomas Skidmore, cofounder of the New York Working Men's Party and author of *The Rights of Man to Property! Being a Proposition to Make It Equal among the Adults of the Present Generation* (1829), was the era's leading apostle of a thoroughgoing agrarian law. Orestes Brownson, the urbane editor of the *Boston Quarterly Review*, wrote an equally famous article in 1840 that endorsed the abolition of inheritance as a way "to elevate the laboring classes, so that . . . each man shall be free and independent." Both assumed that republican government was grounded on a wide distribution of property. Both believed that mixing labor with land to create new value was the only justifiable source of ownership. And both claimed that their redistributive schemes were in accordance with natural right. The tenant manifesto adopted at Berne, like the agrarian writings of Skidmore and Brownson, fused strands of thought from Harrington and Locke, Jefferson and Paine, into a configuration that denied the legitimacy of certain vested rights. But the *Courier and Enquirer* linked agrarianism with Anti-Rentism to disparage it, not to probe the nature and sources of the tenants' ideology. "It is a little mortifying," said Webb, "to find that the enlightened state of New York—the empire member of the Union, as she certainly is or ought to be in population, enterprise, commerce, manufactures and intelligence, can muster within her borders, any number of citizens dark enough in intellect and debased enough in the knowledge necessary to keep people out of the fire, to entertain such notions as these."[30]

At least the anti-renters evoked a reaction from Webb. Congress simply ignored the tenant petition. The same fate befell another 1841 petition, submitted by some constituents of John Quincy Adams, that declared African American slavery inconsistent with the Guarantee Clause. Both petitions were regarded as mere curiosities, in part because they relied so heavily on the phrase "republican form of government" in Article IV, section 4, of the Constitution. When yoked to the verb "guarantee," the text seemed to rule out interpretations of the very sort advanced by anti-renters and radical abolitionists. James Madison, writing in *The Federalist*, pointed out that the authority of the national government "extends no further than to a *guaranty* of a republican form of government, which supposes a pre-existing government of the form which is to be guaranteed. As long, therefore, as the existing republican forms are continued by the States, they are guaranteed by the federal Constitution." It followed that rights in land or slaves, vested by state law under "existing republican forms" in 1789, were immune to attack under cover of the Guarantee Clause. Nor was that all. Read with the Domestic Violence Clause, which follows it in Article IV, the Guarantee Clause clothed national authorities with the power to suppress what Madison called "illicit combinations for purposes of violence." The standard illustration in the treatise literature was the national government's duty, on application of state officials, to put down slave rebellions. Ironically, the third Anti-Rent resolution, pledging the tenants to a "ten year contest" with Stephen Van Rensselaer IV, heralded comparable uprisings by the "voluntary slaves" of Albany County.[31]

The argument in the Berne Manifesto, however outlandish it seemed to lawyers and unsympathetic commentators like Webb, had an inner logic that made it impervious to legalistic objections. Anti-Rent leaders did not conceive of rights as trumps enforceable in courts of law so much as descriptions of the right. They appealed to the Declaration of Independence because natural law provided an acknowledged standard for evaluating the righteousness of human law; they invoked the Guarantee Clause because manorial tenures seemed so clearly, so self-evidently, "antirepublican." That sort of talk might have been designed, as Daniel Rodgers has said of similar antebellum manifestos, "to cover the agitator's legal and practical nakedness [and] the novelty of his claims." Yet anti-renters fully expected to make their case in the court of public opinion. The most important audience for the Berne Manifesto, however, was the tenant farmers of Rensselaerwyck. Because the language of natural rights and republican government had been the language of the American Revolution, Anti-Rent agitators used it to provide the striking farmers with a justification for resistance that connected their struggle with the glorious cause of the Revolutionary fathers.[32]

New forms of resistance reinforced the connection. Beginning in April 1841, farmers and their sons disguised themselves as Indians, in emulation of the Boston Tea Party, before breaking up distress sales at Berne and Rensselaerville. On one occasion the "Indians" formed a silent ring around the assembled buyers while the sheriff solicited bids on items seized for payment of overdue rent. Nobody made an offer. On another a purchaser came up from Albany—a Van Rensselaer "hireling," it was said—and bid on a horse only to beat a hasty retreat after the "Indians" rolled him down a hillside. Going to distress sales to watch the spectacle soon became a popular pastime. New York law required sheriffs to "give five days' public notice of the sale of the goods and chattels so distrained, by affixing such notice on a conspicuous part of the demised premises, and also in two public places in the town." Country people gathered from miles around each time a sale was advertised; the entrance of the local tribe, "dressed in all the simplicity of nature, with bow and knife, amusing the assembled people with feats of agility . . . hardly credible," was greeted with cheers and applause. Sometimes the crowd called for the "snake around," a war dance in which a single line of chanting braves imitated the writhings of a monster reptile. But always the "Indians" remained focused on the task at hand. Tenants painted their faces, put on "skins and other grotesque dresses," and set up "mighty war whoops" because their vaunted independence from "the patroon of the colony of Rensselaerwyck" could be maintained only by preventing the collection of rents. The tactics certainly impressed Amos Adams, the newly elected Whig sheriff of Albany County. "I would give fifty dollars," he reportedly wailed during one unsuccessful distress sale, "if the patroon himself could but just witness what my eyes now behold."[33]

Sheriff Adams mustered a show of force on September 9, 1841. "Early this morning, our streets were alive with the bustle of military preparations for a descent on the Helderbergs," the *Albany Argus* reported. "Not less than four of our uniform companies, under the requisition of the sheriff, were on the ground in front of the City Hall, at 7 o'clock, each company numbering about 40 muskets, and fully equipped for service." The target for this "pretty formidable corps" was the farm of Jacob H. Martin, located about twelve miles west of the city. Personal property belonging to Martin had been advertised for sale that day, and Sheriff Adams had vowed to collect the overdue rent. With such an overwhelming force in the field, few observers expected trouble. The *Argus*, for example, assumed "that the sheriff will find a wide berth in the rebellious region, and return without even having seen an 'Indian.' " The assumption was wrong.[34]

An "immense concourse," made up of perhaps two hundred "Indians" and as many "lookers-on," awaited the arrival of Sheriff Adams and his posse at the Martin farm. The items advertised for sale—livestock, tack, implements, and tools—had already been removed from the premises and hidden elsewhere in the neighborhood. Only "a wagon load of rye" remained in Martin's barn; some forty men and boys, all unarmed, had taken up positions inside. The crowd outside began yelling the moment Sheriff Adams and his troops came into view. Rocks were thrown at the Albany Republican Artillery, the first unit in the line of march. "It was with great difficulty," reported one witness, "that Captain Bayeaux restrained his men from firing at once upon the rioters." The hostile crowd angered Sheriff Adams. Fury turned to rage, however, when he learned that nothing bidders had come up from Albany to buy could be found.

The sheriff, powerless to conduct the scheduled distress sale, enforced his authority instead by ordering the troops to drive the "Indians" from the barn and seize the store of grain. The ensuing fray lasted just a few minutes. Two platoons under the command of Captain Bayeaux advanced through the barn door with fixed bayonets; most of the "Indians" retreated "helter skelter" toward a rear exit. Jacob Martin stood his ground and an undisguised bystander, George Chesebrough, apparently did not move fast enough. Both sustained flesh wounds from the "bristling bayonets." (Each was later tried for assault and battery on an officer and for "riot and affray." Chesebrough was acquitted; the *Evening Journal* reported that the evidence against Martin was overwhelming, "but notwithstanding this the jury were out 18 or 20 hours before they could agree.") With the grain secured and loaded, Sheriff Adams and his posse departed for Albany much as they had arrived, amid a flurry of yells, hisses, groans, and stones. "The Helderberg troubles open badly," Governor Seward wrote his wife on September 10. "Despite the ridicule heaped upon them, [the anti-renters] will attract notice, and blood will yet flow in a cause that has, thus far, moved only derision."[35]

Reflection on the incident at Jacob Martin's farm had just begun when a band of "Indians" ambushed Deputy Sheriff Bill Snyder near Rensselaerville on September 20. When he still had not returned the next morning, Sheriff Adams sent out a posse to look for him. The search party found the deputy's battered hat, his shredded writs, and signs of a scuffle. But they were unable to find Snyder. News of his disappearance electrified Albany. Talk of kidnapping, even murder, surged through the city until the lawman straggled out of the woods uninjured early on September 22. He told a harrowing story of capture, of threats against his life, and of escape while being, in the words of the *Evening Journal*, "pursued and fired at, but not hit." The farmers scoffed at the deputy's tale and celebrated an entirely different version of the incident in "The End of Bill Snyder," the best-known Anti-Rent ballad:[36]

> The moon was shining silver bright;
> The sheriff came in the dead of night;
> High on a hill sat an Indian true,
> And on his horn, this blast he blew—
>   Keep out of the way—big Bill Snyder—
>   We'll tar your coat and feather your hide, Sir!
> The Indians gathered at the sound,
> Bill cocked his pistol—looked around—
> Their painted faces, by the moon,
> He saw, and heard that same old tune—
>   Keep out of the way, &c.
> "Legs! Do your duty now," says Bill,
> "There's a thousand Indians on the hill—
> When they catch tories they tar their coats,
> And feather their hides, and I hear the notes"—
>   Keep out of the way, &c.
> He ran, and he ran, til he reached the wood,
> And there, with horror, still he stood;
> For he saw a savage, tall and grim,
> And he heard a horn, not a rod from him;
>   Keep out of the way, &c.
> And he thought he heard the sound of a gun,
> And he cried, in his fright, "Oh! my race is run!
> Better had it been, had I never been born,
> Than to come within the sound of that tin horn;"
>   Keep out of the way, &c.
> And the news flew round, and gained belief,
> That Bill was murdered by an Indian chief;
> And no one mourned that Bill was slain,
> But the horn sounded on, again and again—
>   Keep out the way—big Bill Snyder—
>   We'll tar your coat and feather your hide, Sir!

The ballad celebrated "The End of Bill Snyder" for good reason. The deputy's foray into the Helderbergs in September 1841 marked Albany County's last attempt to collect rent from a Van Rensselaer tenant for nearly three years. "Indian" activity, being defensive, also ceased. Stephen Van Rensselaer IV and his lawyers had turned on the resistance with distress warrants in the spring; they turned it off by halting legal action in the fall. Albany County officials welcomed the end of the patroon's offensive. They were concerned not only about the safety of Sheriff Adams and his deputies but also about the cost of enforcing Van Rensselaer's legal rights. "This affair is a county matter," the *Argus* pointed out as the ill-starred expedition to Jacob Martin's farm marched out of town, "and the expense . . . (if the war is as protracted and costly as before) will be no joke for the tax-ridden citizens of Albany." The cessation of hostilities was also popular with local militiamen. "The sympathies of the great majority are enlisted in favor of the oppressed tenants," wrote one veteran of the assault on Martin's barn. "This vile remnant of feudalism, so utterly opposed to the spirit of our institutions, is looked upon by all as rank oppression . . . and all unite in execrating the man, who because forsooth he has law on his side, spurns all offers of compromise." But the decision to suspend distress actions was not made for the citizen-taxpayers and citizen-soldiers of Albany. Van Rensselaer did it for the Whig Party.[37]

The Compromise of 1841

Stephen Van Rensselaer IV needed the cooperation of Daniel Dewey Barnard, his largest creditor, in order to forgo further pursuit of the overdue rents. But the two men, apparently in collaboration with Seward and Weed, readily reached an accord. Deescalating the Helderberg War might even have been Congressman Barnard's idea. He had returned to Albany from Washington in a somber mood on September 20, the very day Bill Snyder disappeared. The special session of Congress, called by President Harrison in March to enact the Whig program for recovery and relief, had ended disastrously. Harrison had died before the session began on May 31; John Tyler, a Virginia strict constructionist, had refused to acknowledge Congress's primacy in the formulation of domestic policy. Tyler had supported repeal of the Independent Treasury Act and the enactment of a national bankruptcy law. He had also signed the Land Act of 1841, which authorized preemption by settlers at the minimum price of $1.25 per acre and provided for the distribution of land-sale receipts among the states on the basis of federal representation. On August 16, however, Tyler had vetoed Henry Clay's bank bill, prompting Barnard to write his sister that the "accidental president" had brought the Whig Party to "the point . . . of breaking to pieces." The "point" every Whig feared yet none proved able to avert had come with a second bank veto just hours before Congress adjourned on September 10. All of the cabinet, save Secretary of State Daniel Webster, had resigned in protest the next day. When Barnard's wife complained that he had grown "pale and thin" over the course of the special session, she also described the deteriorating condition of the Whig Party that had routed the Democracy in 1840.[38]

The Whig debacle in Washington magnified the party's difficulties in the several states. Whig governors and state legislators, many of whom had been pulled into office on Harrison's coattails, had relied from the beginning of the depression on a political strategy that put responsibility for relief on the Congress. Time and again they had told voters that prosperity would be restored by a national bank and the distribution of public land receipts among the states, linked perhaps with a higher tariff to pay for it all. While they awaited federal action, Whig state legislatures had adopted one stopgap measure after another. As the special session of Congress wore on, however, it became increasingly apparent that distribution, the most promising source of new revenue for state governments, would not amount to much in the immediate future. Public land sales, like all forms of commercial activity, were way down. In the second quarter of 1841 the General Land Office reported receipts of $313,000, a pittance in comparison to the record $8,423,000 collected in the second quarter of 1836. New York's first-year share in the distributed funds was only $95,436.[39] Thus the proposed national bank became the centerpiece of the party's program. In Whig theory, at least, it could monetize a larger national debt, refinance the crushing state debts, help the faltering state banks resume specie payments, and inject new money into the credit-starved stream of commerce. But President Tyler refused to let all this happen, leaving Whig state officials with no solution for the financial crisis that loomed before them.

The situation was especially desperate in the states with big debts to the south and west of New York. Arkansas, Indiana, and Mississippi defaulted before Congress adjourned on September 10; the political fallout frightened Whigs everywhere. In Indiana, where voters went to the polls shortly after Tyler's first veto, a Whig majority of fifty-five in the state assembly was transformed into a Democratic majority. The Mississippi campaign attracted even more attention. Governor Alexander McNutt, a Democrat, had argued in January 1841 that a big chunk of the state debt, having been incurred in violation of state law, should be repudiated. The Whig legislature had responded with resolutions condemning the insinuation that Mississippi would violate its plighted faith; but the Whigs, clinging to the promise of relief from Washington, had also resisted a tax hike. When the second bank veto came down in September, Whig pundits grimly predicted a Democratic victory in the November election, followed by an act of repudiation that would mean disgrace and dishonor not just for Mississippi but, in the eyes of Europeans, for all the American states.[40]

New York's financial situation, though not so desperate as that of some states, was nonetheless serious when Barnard returned from Washington. The state-subsidized railroads and the Canal Board had dumped New York securities on the market through midsummer, driving their value progressively lower. When 6 percent bonds could no longer be sold at eighty cents on the dollar, the Canal Board had kept things going with short-term bank loans at higher interest rates. By the end of September interest on the "temporary" loans was costing the government nearly $300,000 a month and the Canal Board still owed contractors on the public works nearly $1 million. Meanwhile, two railroad companies that obtained government loans totaling $515,700 in 1840 had defaulted, and their assets had been liquidated at foreclosure sales. The Catskill & Canajoharie had fetched only $11,600 for the state treasury, the Ithaca & Owego just $4,500.[41]

The disarray in Whig internal improvement policy was compounded by the disorders on Rensselaerwyck. Responding to the assault on Deputy Sheriff Snyder with force would be expensive and extremely unpopular. It would also be very embarrassing for Seward. Unlike so many matters that vexed the Whig Party in 1841, however, the "Indian" question was subject to the control of New York officeholders. Barnard could take the pressure off the tenants and restore peace to the manor; Seward could take land reform off his agenda and restore peace of mind to the conservative Whigs. Neither move required a public explanation. Stephen Van Rensselaer IV did not have to disavow his property rights, and Seward did not have to disavow his hostility to manorial tenures. Both could simply exercise forbearance until the governor's term ended the following year. And so the deal was struck. Barnard granted Van Rensselaer a respite from his contractual obligations, Van Rensselaer suspended distress actions on the manor, and Seward abandoned the tenant cause.[42]

The Whig state convention, held in Syracuse on October 6 and 7, produced no surprises. Barnard, Duer, and Millard Fillmore delivered the principal orations. David Graham, a conservative New York City lawyer, framed the resolutions. Weed and John A. King collaborated on the address to the voters, a long restatement of the party's "cardinal doctrines" written for publication in the Whig press. Every speaker and writer praised the manifold achievements of the Seward administration, lauded Congress for its "distinguished and efficient exertions" during the special session, and bemoaned President Tyler's departures from established Whig principles. The address held that "we have a right to hope and expect, that the president will look again, and with more care, and better judgment and conclusions, into the important subjects on which he and Congress have differed." The resolutions mentioned the Mississippi campaign, linked "the opposition party" with the repudiation of debts, and insisted that significant Democratic gains in the state legislature would be a calamity. None of the Whig documents breathed a word about land reform or the recent disorders on Rensselaerwyck. A sense of impending defeat pervaded the convention all the same. And the defeat came. The Whig vote was some 52,000 less than the year before; the Democrats not only won control of the senate but rolled up an astonishing majority of 95-33 in the lower house. Seward pronounced the result "a disastrous overthrow of the Whig party in this state."[43]

New York Whigs had company in their misery. Democrats also recaptured the state legislatures in Alabama, Maine, Georgia, Maryland, Ohio, Pennsylvania, and Mississippi. In Michigan, a Harrison state in 1840, the Democrats elected the governor, a majority in the senate, and all but one member of the lower house. The winter's financial news was just as bad. Illinois, Maryland, and Michigan defaulted in January; Pennsylvania soon followed. In those four states and in Indiana the Democratic legislatures passed pious resolutions promising to resume payments on their bonds as soon as conditions permitted. On February 26, 1842, however, the governor of Mississippi approved the legislature's repudiation of a substantial portion of the state debt. For years afterward, it was dangerous to identify oneself as an American in London or Amsterdam.[44]

The elections of 1841 and their immediate aftermath provided an ironic conclusion to a tumultuous year in American political history. It began with promises of relief for the strapped state governments and the oppressed tenants of Rensselaerwyck. It ended with seven states in default of their contractual obligations and more than a thousand tenants still in default of theirs. Yet none could be sued. The defaulting states enjoyed immunity under the Eleventh Amendment,[45] the striking tenants under a secret agreement between their Whig champion and their Whig enemies. Anti-renters naturally interpreted their deliverance from Sheriff Adams and his deputies as a vindication of the "Indian" resistance. All over the manor that winter, boisterous tenant assemblies belted out "The End of Bill Snyder" with the same enthusiasm Whig conclaves had sung "Van, Van Is a Used Up Man" in 1840. They also circulated petitions for relief. In 1842 the state legislature would be in the hands of Van Buren's friends for the first time since the rent strike began.

4

The Trouble with Democrats

The magnitude of the Democracy's victory surprised the party leadership. As the astonishing returns rolled in, however, Democratic pundits experienced no difficulty in accounting for what the *Argus* called "the revolution of 1841." From the onset of the depression, Democrats had insisted that it arose "out of causes upon which legislation can have no power." Massive expenditures for internal improvements, made possible by heavy European investment in state securities, fueled the boom of the 1830s; when the influx of foreign capital stopped, the supply of money fell and prices declined proportionately. For Democrats, it was axiomatic that "the establishment of a national bank will prove as ineffectual to counteract this effect . . . as if Congress were to attempt to legislate for staying the ebb and flow of the tide on the east coast." But the Whigs had been so intent on restoring "all the odious schemes of Federalism of the Hamilton school" that they had refused to give the people an honest appraisal of the depression's cause. Whig designs "had been covered up by coon skins and concealed by cider barrels" during the 1840 campaign. Once the Whig Party's intentions had been "fully avowed" in Congress, however, "the condemnation of the people followed as a matter of course." "In this election," proclaimed Edwin Croswell, "we have a distinct manifestation of '*the sober second thought of the people, never wrong and always efficient*.' " The maxim's author was Martin Van Buren.[1]

Democrats claimed that the rout of the Whigs vindicated Van Buren, but they maintained a state-centered strategy for returning him to the White House in 1844. Unlike the Whigs, who relied on the national government to reconstruct state financial systems and "increase in various other ways the general happiness," Jacksonians preferred to work from the bottom up. "It is an unfortunate feature in the political organization of the United States, that federal interests are allowed to absorb so much attention," remarked William Cullen Bryant on the eve of the 1841 election. "It is to the state government that [the people] must look for their municipal laws, for an administration of justice, and the guarantees of the largest freedom. It is the state government which has the disposal of the vital questions related to the banking system, internal improvement schemes, legal reforms, and individual rights. . . . One state, administered on Democratic principles, would speedily regenerate the politics of nearly all the others." Bryant had a great many ideas, grounded on "a liberal faith," for reforming New York institutions in ways that would benefit the state's own inhabitants and make the Empire State a model for the imitation of people in other jurisdictions. All of them, ranging from the abolition of capital punishment to repeal of the usury laws, involved limitations on the power of government.[2]

New York Democrats did not think of state government, as Louis D. Brandeis did nearly a century later, in terms of "a laboratory" for undertaking "novel social and economic experiments without risk to the rest of the country." Bryant, Croswell, and others believed that Democratic principles were universally true, not contingent on circumstances. They regarded the party's control of the state legislature as an opportunity for moral leadership, and their objective was to release "the best energies of society." The Democracy's "liberal faith" certainly had no place for manorial tenures. In 1839 Bryant called the archaic leases in force on Rensselaerwyck "an embarrassment," and he rejoiced that New York's curse had not taken root in the West. Daniel S. Dickinson, the Democratic nominee for lieutenant governor in 1842, used more evocative language in the aftermath of the first Helderberg War, describing manorial tenures as "relics of barbarism, incompatible with the institutions of a free people and the spirit of the age." Throughout the Whig ascendancy, however, Democrats greeted tenant petitions for state action with a face of flint. Time and again they blasted Governor Seward for making promises that the legislature had no power to fulfill. As the Anti-Rent leadership circulated tenant petitions in the winter of 1841–42, they could only hope that Democrats would sing a different tune when in control of the legislature.[3]

The hope had some foundation. As long as political responsibility lay with the Whigs, Democrats made a party affair of every Whig bill and ascribed vile motives to every Whig maneuver. Democratic legislators aimed, above all, to embarrass and ultimately defeat their political enemies; the ritualistic routine of partisanship minimized serious Democratic study of Whig policy initiatives. There was no evidence to suggest that Democrats had even read the Duer Report, let alone conducted an energetic search for other solutions to the manor question. Anti-renters meant to change that, but they enjoyed very little success. Abolishing the lease in fee required state action of a sort that was difficult to square with the Democracy's commitment to negative liberalism. "The true political science," Dickinson asserted in 1843, "teaches . . . that it is the legitimate province of government to protect its citizens in the enjoyment of their industry, but not to attempt the vain and idle experiment of accumulating for them; that all power or advantage conferred by legislation upon one, is taken from another, or from the mass, and is productive of inequality and injustice."[4]

Anti-renters paid attention to Democratic talk about the legitimate scope of government's responsibility for public and private wrongs during the legislature's eventful 1842 session. Tenant leaders got a firm grip on their trouble with Democrats, modified their arguments, and even retained a lawyer who drafted a bill tailored to Jacksonian sensibilities. Meanwhile, the number of tenants on strike grew much larger. So did the political costs of denying petitions for government action against "voluntary slavery." At the end of 1843 anti-renters had reason to think that land reform was imminent.

Whig "Fallacies"—Democratic Solutions

In his final annual message, delivered to the legislature on January 4, 1842, Governor Seward dodged the issues that had divided Whigs the previous year. His message contained only one reference to manorial tenures. The sheriff of Albany County, he pointed out, "has encountered many and novel difficulties . . . in executing civil process." Seward said nothing at all about extending debtors' exemptions from distress for rent and sale under execution. But he was anxious to maintain government sponsorship of internal improvements as a core element of the Whig creed, and he implored the Democratic legislature to stay the course on canal construction and railroad aid. "Our established policy," Seward said, "invades no rights, and . . . contributes to ameliorate the condition of society and establish the sway of democratic power."[5]

Seward did not ignore the gravity of New York's "embarrassing financial situation." In his view, however, the problem stemmed from forces outside the state government's control. When Mississippi moved toward repudiation and six other states defaulted, European investors shunned even the securities of the Empire State. "Hesitation by one state," Seward told the legislature, "brought distrust upon all." Because the problem was national in scope, he insisted, "the general government has seemed to me to present the only suitable and adequate agency" for dealing with the state debt crisis. The lawmakers were already familiar with Seward's plan. Shortly after the election he had written a public letter to Secretary of War John C. Spencer pointing out that the Constitution clothed Congress "with the responsibilities of maintaining a post office, and of providing for the national defense, not to speak of its responsibilities in regard to the regulation of internal trade and commerce." The discharge of those duties entailed the use of transport facilities built with state funds; consequently Seward suggested that the national government "come to the relief of the states by purchasing the perpetual enjoyment of the right to use such public thoroughfares." Yet President Tyler wanted no part of such a scheme. In December

1841, he promised to veto any legislation having "the slightest approach to an assumption by this government of the debts of the states."[6]

Democrats took the governor's message for what it was—a wistful restatement of Whig principles that had been buried with William Henry Harrison, not a constructive program for addressing New York's immediate financial problems. Before the Democratic legislature took matters into its own hands, however, the caucus thought one of its number should answer Seward's main points and display the Democracy's superior wisdom. The nod went to Michael Hoffman, a fifty-five-year-old attorney from Herkimer who had more than fifteen years' experience in New York public life. Hoffman was a tall, spare man with a slight stoop that was said to lend "dignity to his mien." Bryant characterized him as "quick-sighted, fearless, indomitable," and, most important of all, "a democrat of the radical school—of that school which trusts the people, which seeks to confine the functions of government to the fewest objects, and to keep political questions as far as may be unconnected with private interests." He also had a sardonic sense of humor. "Seward is for *equality* [alright]," Hoffman remarked in reference to the governor's $200,000 personal debt, "he wants every man, woman, child, bank, city, [and] state to owe as deeply as he does." Although known more for his "patience and diligence as a committeeman" than for his oratory, Hoffman delivered the speech of his life beginning on January 14, 1842. He spoke for two days, holding the rapt attention of the legislature and, through transcripts in the Democratic press, the people, with what the *Argus* called a "clear and unanswerable exposition of the 'real financial condition of the state' and of the fallacies of those who attempt to escape from [it]."[7]

Hoffman declared that he knew "no language of reprobation or reproach too severe" for Seward's stubborn adherence to the same old spend-but-not-tax philosophy that had propelled the state debt from $11.9 million to $26.8 million in three years. "To borrow all, spend all, and pay nothing" was to "rush into the condition of Pennsylvania, Maryland, Illinois, Indiana, Michigan" and to "reach the same end—the same disgrace." It was also to drive the economy into deeper depression. For nearly two years, Hoffman explained, capital markets had been so "overloaded" with securities that each new government loan had pushed the value of New York bonds still lower. The resulting "cramps in the stock market" affected everybody because the Free Banking Act of 1838 pegged circulating bank notes to government bonds on deposit with the comptroller. When the market for state stock was strong, as in 1838–39, the banking community's principal asset grew in value, and credit was easy. When government bonds dipped below par and continued to decline, however, responsible bankers had no choice but to curtail their loans. "The state has eviscerated the banks largely," Hoffman proclaimed. "In every city, and village, everything is 'tight,' in the technical language of financiers—tight to the state—tight to every class of citizens. Long loans have become impossible." Yet the process might be reversed. "The public officers should have been now in the market buying state stocks," Hoffman asserted. Open market operations would restore the state credit, buoy the value of bank reserves, create "lendable funds for productive industry," and quicken the pace of business. All the government had to do was stop borrowing and start taxing. Astonishingly, Seward had "urged—urged—urged" precisely the opposite course, one that would carry the Empire State "to the fatal verge of ruin."[8]

Hoffman had still stronger words for Seward's reliance on "projects of universal relief" from the United States. Appropriations for the War Department ("The God of War, with all his thunders, is to be invoked to sustain the credit of the states!") and receipts from public land sales, he asserted, "are not the ways and means of states and statesmen, but of desperation." Each scheme entailed "the sale of our rights." The federal dollars used to fund state debts, Hoffman pointed out, had to be generated by redistributive government action. Protective tariffs built up the wealth of factory owners at the expense of consumers who paid "artificially high prices" for manufactured goods; distribution "robbed" settlers who connected their labor to the "virgin west" only to see their purchase money "carted off," not to defray legitimate expenses of the General Land Office, but to enable the "old states" and their creditors "to plunder the public treasury of the United States." Both policies struck unequally at "a man's right to his property, to the avails of his labor, [which] . . . he claims and holds as sacred as anything under heaven." And both belied Seward's contention that his party's "established policy" on internal improvements "invade[d] no rights." In Hoffman's judgment, that was the Whig leader's most preposterous claim of all.[9]

The two-day attack on Seward's "persevering folly, fatuity, and fanaticism" galvanized public support for the Democracy's own battery of measures for the 1842 session. First in time and importance was the famous Stop and Tax Act, which Hoffman reported out of his Ways and Means Committee on March 7 and Seward reluctantly signed into law on March 29. The act provided for the suspension of all canal construction, except that essential to navigation or "necessary to preserve the work already done from destruction by ice or floods." It also provided for a one-mill property tax. Every dollar generated by the tax and an amount from canal tolls "at least equal to one third of the interest of the canal debt remaining unpaid" were "sacredly" pledged to debt retirement. Next came a resolution, supported by an elaborate report written by Assemblyman John Cramer, a protégé of Samuel Young, "that our senators in Congress be instructed, and our representatives be requested, to vote for an immediate repeal of the act to appropriate the proceeds of the public lands, passed at the extra session" in 1841. The assembly endorsed it by a strict party division on April 7; the senate followed suit four days later. Cramer's resolution evoked furious debate in both houses, but the question soon lost its saliency. On August 30, President Tyler signed the Little Tariff, raising rates high enough to trigger the suspension of distribution. The only payment to New York was less than 15 percent of the amount Seward had forecast in his 1841 message.[10]

The remarkable Democratic unity that propelled the Stop and Tax Act and the Cramer resolution through the legislature broke down when the assembly took up the "People's Resolution," a constitutional amendment designed to prevent a recurrence of the state debt crisis. Framed and introduced by Arphaxed Loomis, a Herkimer associate of Hoffman's, the resolution proposed that "the constitution of the state be so amended, that every law authorizing the borrowing of money . . . shall specify the object for which the money shall be appropriated; and that every such law shall embrace no more than one such object, which shall be singly and specifically stated; that no such law shall take effect until it shall be distinctly submitted to the people at the next general election, and be approved by a majority of the votes cast for and against it." Loomis's sponsor speech, delivered in the assembly chamber on March 16, had been rehearsed many times since 1837, when he first proposed the People's Resolution at the Herkimer County Democratic Convention and the *Mohawk Courier* put it on the masthead of its editorial page. Time had made his arguments for a popular check on government borrowing seem increasingly compelling.[11]

At the heart of the problem, said Loomis, was "a want of responsibility on the part of the representatives of the people." Few lawmakers could resist constituent pressures for government spending on a canal or railroad through their own districts; representatives of each "local or sectional interest" invariably forged "combinations" with the representatives of others. The doctrine of "equalization of benefits," expounded by Seward beginning in 1839, merely formalized the logrolling process and enforced it with party discipline. But the people were immune to the pressures that compromised the civic virtue of their representatives. The very idea of "combinations among the people to subvert and prostrate their own interests," Loomis asserted, "is an absurdity." In his judgment, the People's Resolution provided an "eminently democratic" cure for a congenital sickness of representative government. "It is for the want of a provision like this in the constitution of our state and in those of other states," he concluded, "that this confederacy, this great and beautiful experiment of republican government, now finds itself, individually and collectively, on the verge of bankruptcy, discredit and dishonor."[12]

Loomis's proposed amendment caused an uproar in the New York Democracy. Democratic assemblymen with districts along the Erie Canal, the unfinished "feeder" canals, and the New York & Erie Railroad regarded the

People's Resolution as a kiss of death. Standing for reelection on the Stop and
Tax Act, which suspended construction temporarily, would be hard enough.
Defeating Whig opponents on a platform that was likely to result in the aban-
donment of internal improvements by state government would be virtually
impossible. Yet the representatives of various local interests were in no position
to invoke threatened projects, or the fate of the Democratic Party in the canal
counties, as grounds for their opposition to the People's Resolution. Discourse
of that sort would merely buttress Loomis's argument. Conservative Democrats
felt compelled to fight principle with principle and conjure up good republican
objections to Loomis's "eminently democratic" scheme. The result was an
important debate, carried on at a fairly high degree of abstraction, that revealed
a variety of Democratic sensibilities on the propriety of constitutional change,
the relationship between public and private obligations, even the nature and
scope of government's duty to establish justice. While the Whig members, in
Weed's words, "wisely kept out of the ring," Democrats elaborated constitutional ideas that were as pertinent to the manor question as to the state
debt crisis.[13]

Bargain Theory in the Jacksonian Persuasion

John W. Tamblin, a Democrat whose Jefferson County district straddled the
unfinished Black River Canal, led the conservative assault on the People's
Resolution. Adoption of Loomis's constitutional amendment, he declared on
March 23, "will open the door for the introduction of an illimitable number of
amendments of a kindred character. Every new legislative abuse, or supposed
abuse . . . will, with equal importunity and equal reason, claim a new amendment of the constitution." But the "whole power" of constitutional restrictions
on legislative authority, he said, "consists in the veneration and respect" people
accorded to "great general principles, or rules of universally acknowledged
validity and justice." Loading the constitution with "minor principles" would
degrade it to "the dignity of a common statute." And once "the magic power" of
the constitution had been dissipated, no "barrier between lawless power and
the people" would remain "and the government will be nothing more nor less
than a majority despotism." If the doctrines embedded in the People's Resolution were right, Tamblin concluded, "then Jefferson, Madison, and all the
Revolutionary statesmen and patriots" had been wrong about the first principles of republican government.[14]

John A. Dix, a longtime Van Buren confidant, got the floor next and delivered a thoughtful rejoinder on the "great question of constitutional principle."
Of all the powers of government in a free society, he said, only the power to
borrow money "casts upon future generations burdens of debt, which are often

accompanied with no corresponding benefit," thus compelling some people to labor for others without reward. The "inevitable consequence" was an outraged citizenry that declaimed against the "injustice" of it all. Repudiation, on the other hand, could never be countenanced. "How can it be expected that individuals will scrupulously fulfill their contracts if governments shall openly violate theirs?" Dix asked. "I know of no just distinction between public and private morality. What is honest in individuals, and in classes of individuals, is honest in a state; and what is dishonest in the one is equally so in the other." Dix claimed that adoption of the People's Resolution would strengthen the sense of public responsibility and reinforce the connection between governmental and personal obligations. In his view, moreover, Tamblin had misstated Jefferson's opinion. Dix clinched the point by reading the house a letter to John Taylor of Caroline, written in 1798, in which Jefferson endorsed the idea of constitutional limitations on the power to borrow money.[15]

Trumping his adversary satisfied Dix. He did not trace Jefferson's view back to a more famous text, the 1789 letter to Madison setting forth the principle that "the earth belongs in usufruct to the living." Samuel Young, a leading radical Democrat, did so with alacrity. In a widely noticed pamphlet on "the mad career of public debt," Young pointed out that "the great apostle of American liberty uttered his most impressive admonitions against this destructive course; and demonstrated, by unanswerable arguments, its gross injustice and outrage upon the inalienable rights of mankind." Yet the Whigs had "openly trampled" on Jefferson's precept. Their "meretricious impudence" not only aggravated the depression but violated the first principle of republican self-government: "Instead of leaving posterity free to pursue happiness, they have attempted to appropriate their inalienable rights, and to throw the manacles of slavery around them."[16]

Although Dix wanted to invoke Jefferson's authority on the propriety of a specific constitutional amendment, the related notion that "the earth belongs in usufruct to the living" did not suit his purposes. The People's Resolution was designed to check improvident borrowing, not to set a one-generation limit on the duration of public obligations. The proposed amendment was also designed to stifle supposed justifications for repudiation, something that loose talk about "the manacles of slavery" and "the inalienable rights of mankind" tended to keep alive. Dix had no quarrel with Jefferson's bold proposition as a moral directive. But he endorsed the People's Resolution because it promised to shape the future without impairing legal obligations incurred in the past. "It is the great merit of our institutions that, as defects become apparent in them, it is in the power of the people to apply the proper correctives," Dix asserted near the close of his long speech. "If they cannot wholly remedy the evils of the past, they may at least provide safeguards for the future."[17]

Two weeks of sporadic debate followed the Tamblin-Dix exchange before the assemblymen voted on Loomis's constitutional amendment. Fifty-five Democrats said "aye," nineteen others joined thirty Whigs in the "nay" column. But twenty-one Democrats refused to vote at all. Thus the measure was lost for want of a majority of all members *elected* to each house, as required by the amendment provision of the New York Constitution. Expressions of regret that "the game of stock issues and debt is not yet played out" filled the Democratic press. Few observers, however, were surprised by the result. Loomis had argued that the People's Resolution was necessary because combinations of local interests tended to triumph over the public good in the legislative process, and the very combination that the amendment aimed to destroy worked to prevent its adoption. One conclusion seemed inescapable, though no Democrat openly said so until 1843. Limitations on the legislature's power to create debt could be effected only by a constitutional convention.[18]

The radical Democracy never let go of the argument for the People's Resolution. Their very pertinacity suggests why Democrats tended to sympathize with the anti-renters yet had never been responsive to tenant petitions. For Jacksonians, the principal duty of government officials—legislative, executive, and judicial—was to secure the rights of the people. Threats to liberty and equality pervaded the body politic. But the forms of injustice Democrats chose to battle in the people's behalf did not spring from market processes. They arose from collective acts of government that, in the Jacksonian mind, arbitrarily redistributed wealth and opportunity. Democrats attributed such legislation to the machinations of "the rich and the powerful," its primary beneficiaries; party leaders dedicated themselves to the destruction of "artificial" restrictions on the voluntary actions of a free people. For more than a decade, Jacksonians had attacked special charters for banking corporations, the protective principle in tariff legislation, and other public policies with a tendency, as Theodore Sedgwick put it, "to empty one pocket and fill another." They had also applauded when President Van Buren declared in 1837 that measures designed to provide "relief" in hard times would produce justifiable "complaints of neglect, partiality, injustice, and oppression." The party's watchword, Van Buren said, must be "the less government interferes with private pursuits the better."[19]

Democratic opposition to state financing of internal improvements had a more recent vintage. As it became increasingly clear that the public works could not be financed out of annual canal revenues, however, the threat of unequal taxation triggered conventional Jacksonian doctrine. Hoffman, Loomis, and others argued that it was unjust to take property from the people of one region in order to build transport facilities for the enjoyment of people in other regions. Dix and Young decried government programs that, in Young's vivid phrase, "endeavored to appropriate the toil of subsequent generations to glut the hungry cravings of this." For most Democrats, the optimal solution for such oppression was the People's Resolution. It would enable the people to give direct consent to the contracts that bound them collectively, making the process of creating public obligations more like the process of creating private ones. In the Democratic mind, market relations were not just more "natural" than "artificial" state action. Bargain theory also provided an appropriate standard for reforming the constitutional order. Only with great difficulty, then, could the Democratic public philosophy be accommodated to private wrongs arising from oppressive contractual obligations. Yet the advocates of debtor-protection legislation and the Anti-Rent activists on Rensselaerwyck asked Democratic lawmakers to do precisely that during the 1842 session. Significantly, the former succeeded but the latter did not.

Debtors and Tenants before the Legislature

Twenty-four hours after the New York legislature's 1842 session began, Senator Henry W. Strong, a Democrat from Troy, gave notice of his intention to introduce "An act to extend the exemption of household furniture and working tools from distress for rent, and sale under execution." The first section of the measure, which Strong reported out of the Judiciary Committee on March 16, was identical to the Sibley bill that had given Whigs so much grief the year before. It provided that "in addition to the articles now exempt by law from distress for rent, or levy and sale under execution," debtors might claim an exemption for additional "household furniture and working tools" valued up to $150. Strong's justification for the measure, however, differed from that proffered by his Whig predecessor. Sibley had spoken of the public's interest in contractual arrangements and emphasized government's duty to provide "relief" for worthy debtors in periods of economic distress. Each of those justifications ran against the grain of Jacksonian doctrine; Strong relied instead on a rationale that fused custom and the equal-rights principle.[20]

The committee report comprised nineteen printed pages, fourteen of which reprinted the exemption statutes on the books of every state and territory in the Union. In Strong's capable hands, the documentary evidence told a compelling story. No two states, he pointed out, had identical statutes. New York exempted cooking utensils but Pennsylvania did not. Yet Pennsylvania exempted "any quantity of meat not exceeding two hundred pounds, twenty bushels of potatoes, ten bushels of grain, or the meal made therefrom," whereas New York exempted none of those things. In every state, however, a great many specified items of personal property could not be seized by landlords or judgment creditors. The very universality of such disparate statutes indicated that exemption laws must be regarded as "one of the legitimate fruits of civilization."[21]

Strong conceded that in theory such protective legislation might be "termed a robbery" under color of law. But the fact remained that exemption laws, though seemingly inconsistent with "strict justice," reflected the "humanity" of "modern times" and, through long usage, had become part of the nation's common law. In no jurisdiction, moreover, were these "liberal" statutes prospective only. Strong noted that their retrospective character had often been attributed to "the distinction between the *obligation* of a contract, and the *remedy* to enforce it," which, he said, "is so well understood that it is scarcely necessary to advert to it." But the earliest exemption laws antedated the right-remedy distinction in Contract Clause jurisprudence and arguably shaped its very creation. The "true source" of retrospectivity in such legislation, Strong argued, lay in the unwillingness of its architects to "console themselves with the reflection, that, although they were restricted by the customs of barbarous ages, and must go down to the grave without improvement or melioration, they *were* empowered to pass laws which would benefit posterity." Exemption laws were best understood, then, as universally acknowledged exceptions to the general rule forbidding governmental interference with existing contractual obligations.[22]

The bill to extend the exemption law, Strong insisted, had an altogether different foundation. Enlightenment "principles of humanity and justice," which spawned the existing legislation, might not justify further inroads on the rights of creditors. But the principle of equal rights did. "The exemption of ten sheep, now allowed in the statute, is ordinarily of no avail to a mechanic, because he neither cultivates nor occupies a farm," Strong observed. Similarly, "the exemption of a mechanic's tools, to the amount of $25, according the existing law, is a mockery to the unfortunate farmer, whose hoe and plough and harrow can be swept from him by the inflexible and unequal mandate of the present law." General legislation that exempted all forms of property up to a fixed value, rather than specified articles only, would eradicate the "inequality" arising from the "variant occupations, habits, wants and conditions" of New York families. This was good Democratic doctrine, and the *Argus* declared that "the reasoning of the report on this point is forcible, and we think unanswerable." In "practical operation," Croswell wrote in an enthusiastic editorial, "the bill introduced by Mr. Strong would be rather an *equalization* of the law than an *extension* of it. . . . It is not therefore so much a favor to poor debtors generally, as a measure of equal justice to portions of them." In point of fact, the bill accommodated both purposes. But it could not be characterized as a "relief" measure. The second section of Strong's bill provided that "this act shall take effect on the first day of May next."[23]

Strong's artfully framed bill evoked none of the impassioned talk of agrarianism that had killed Sibley's measure in 1841. Its provision for delayed implementation satisfied short-term lenders and urban landlords, most of whom could recover on existing contracts and require higher interest or rents in new deals before the act went into effect. Only the Hudson Valley landlords would be hit really hard. Leases for lives or in perpetuity could not be renegotiated to take account of the landlord's greater risk; since few tenants owned personal property worth more than $150, the act would effectively put an end to distress sales like those that had generated "Indian" activity the previous summer. Yet nobody mentioned this effect as Strong's bill progressed through the legislature. On March 31 the senate defeated one amendment that would have given the act a prospective operation and another, offered by a Whig from Buffalo, that would have renamed the measure "An act to oppress the poor by depriving them of credit." Later the same day, the upper house passed the bill by a vote of 19-10. It would have died, however, without backing from a half-dozen progressive Whigs. Five Democrats supported the motion to make the bill inapplicable "to any debts contracted previous to the time when this act shall take effect," and the same five lawmakers said "nay" on the final vote. In their judgment, government had no business disturbing vested rights even to "equalize" the benefits of existing legislation. The roll call in the assembly was also close; one-third of the Democrats, including Hoffman and Loomis, voted against the measure. It passed 47-39. Governor Seward signed the bill into law on April 11, 1842.[24]

Nobody tried to make a comparable case for land reform in 1842, but the manor question could not be evaded altogether. Petitions for redress of grievances poured into the assembly from the Helderberg towns beginning on January 31. Another petition arrived late in February from tenants on the 50,000-acre Scott Patent in Schoharie County. Contracts on the latter estate, owned by the descendants of John Livingston, required a higher wheat rent than on Rensselaerwyck. In addition, the Scott Patent indentures conveyed the land for two lives rather than in perpetuity. At the expiration of each lease the Livingstons had the option of ousting the tenant's family and retaining all improvements on the farm. Very few people who signed indentures in the 1780–1800 period were still alive; the sons of Schoharie knew that as soon as their fathers died they faced loss of their homes or, with the landlord's consent, renewal of agreements that would "enslave" their families for another two generations. Both contingencies enraged them. Tenants on the Scott Patent, like the tenants on Rensselaerwyck, wanted to own the farms their forebears had carved out of the wilderness. But the Livingston family's interest in the land was not for sale.[25]

The tenant petitions were referred to the Judiciary Committee, chaired by Arphaxed Loomis. The author of the People's Resolution freely confessed his annoyance with the assignment. "We find ourselves embarrassed" by this "difficult and delicate subject," he told the house on March 3, and "have no particular desire to report on it." Loomis had cause to be reticent. He was sympathetic to the Anti-Rent complaints, opposed to government intervention, and at a loss as to how such conflicting attitudes might be conveyed to the petitioners. The crux of Loomis's difficulty was the contractual relationship between the tenants and their overlords.

Manorial tenures had been created by the voluntary acts of free people, and every settler on Rensselaerwyck and the Scott Patent had consented to the stipulated terms before entering the land. Yet the common law maxim *volenti non fit injuria* (no injury is done to one who consents) no longer fit the facts. Very few of the petitioners had been parties to the contracts at issue; most had merely inherited family farms. Because the tenants were nominally free to terminate the legal relation established by their fathers, consent might be inferred from their decision to remain on the land. But such an inference was implausible in view of the quarter-sale conditions in force on Rensselaerwyck and the landlord's reversionary interest in tenant improvements on the Scott Patent. Each time a farm changed hands, the landlords seized the value added by tenant labor. What made Loomis's predicament so "embarrassing," then, was the striking similarity between the complaints recited in the Anti-Rent petitions and the complaints about public debt that Democrats recited in the People's Resolution debate. In effect, the tenants asked their lawmakers to operationalize Jefferson's precept that "the earth belongs in usufruct to the living."[26]

As Loomis struggled with the "delicate" problem of framing a suitable reply, he readily identified two distinctions between the public-debt question and the manor question. One distinction focused on the prospectivity norm in legislation. Loomis, Dix, and other advocates of the People's Resolution had repeatedly emphasized government's duty to learn from past mistakes and provide safeguards for the future. But a prospective land reform act—prohibiting leases of agricultural land for more than twenty years, for example, in future contracts between landlords and tenants—would not help the petitioners. The existing leases on Rensselaerwyck ran forever; tenants on the Scott Patent forfeited all property rights in the farms when their leases expired. "Whether laws ought to be passed preventing the future creation of estates of this character," Loomis reported, "is a question not raised by the petitioners, and could not affect their condition." Only retrospective legislation, disturbing prior contractual obligations, could relieve the tenant complaints. And the Contract Clause of the Constitution barred such legislation.[27]

Loomis was comfortable with the conclusion that nothing could be done, for it dovetailed neatly with his presumption that government had no responsibility to act. The presumption flowed from a second distinction between the public-debt and manor questions. When government policy saddled taxpayers with oppressive contractual obligations for internal improvements, Loomis believed that the legislature had a duty to prevent it from happening again. But the evils of manorial tenures arose from improvident private contracts, not from state action. Loomis, like most Democrats, was quick to acknowledge the legislature's responsibility for curing evils that government produced yet remained hesitant to identify public interests in the private dealings of a free people.

The gist of an appropriate committee report, denying relief to the petitioners, had formed in Loomis's mind by the end of March. His principal objective was to minimize the Democratic Party's moral and political responsibility for the plight of the tenants. Above all, he did not want to say anything that might drive the nominally Democratic tenants of Albany and Schoharie counties into the Whig fold. But no justification that might be perceived as hardhearted was required. Because the Contract Clause negated the legislature's capacity to remedy tenant grievances, nothing more had to be said. When the Judiciary Committee finally took up the tenant petition in early April, however, George Simmons, a Whig assemblyman from Essex County, upset Loomis's initial calculations. Simmons reminded his Democratic colleagues that the assembly had grappled with the manor question in 1840. Two very able Whig lawyers, Henry Wheaton and William A. Duer Jr., had thoroughly explored Contract Clause limitations on state action. And each had devised a way to extinguish manorial tenures without violating the Constitution. Wheaton, relying on the right-remedy distinction in Contract Clause jurisprudence, had proposed to besiege the landlords with laws that took away their remedies against defaulting tenants. Duer had resisted that approach because it would effectively take property from one person and give it to another; he suggested, instead, direct action under the eminent domain power. Simmons told Loomis that, in his judgment, Duer had been right about the problems with Wheaton's scheme. But the debtor-exemption bill, which the senate had just passed, was arguably vulnerable to the same objection. As for the eminent domain idea, Simmons said as he brandished a copy of the Duer Report, it was fraught with practical difficulties but its constitutionality seemed beyond reproach.[28]

Loomis apparently read the Duer Report that evening. It was an unnerving experience. Compensated emancipation of the tenants seemed like a just and reasonable, even ingenious, solution to the vexatious manor question. Acting on that perception, however, threatened to unravel the Democratic Party's approach to recovery and reform. Loomis did not see how an eminent domain scheme could succeed without government financing of the very sort that the Stop and Tax Act had suspended and the People's Resolution purported to abate in the future. For Loomis, moreover, the Democracy's state debt policies were grounded on a bedrock principle. His People's Resolution proclaimed that the legislature had no rightful authority to borrow money for purposes that a majority of the voters would not endorse in a statewide referendum. And if the taxpayers of New York City and Buffalo had a right to prevent the use of their property for construction of the Black River Canal, they also had a right to prevent the appropriation of tax dollars for extinguishing manorial tenures in the Hudson Valley. The social benefits that would flow from a compensated land reform act, as projected by the Duer Report, were certainly substantial. In Loomis's view, however, they were just too local to justify a massive loan of purchase money by the state government. Reaching this conclusion was easy. What unnerved him was the prospect of communicating it to the tenant petitioners.

Two forms of explanation occurred to Loomis, but neither was satisfactory. His committee might focus on the fiscal ramifications of an eminent domain program and inform the petitioners that decisive action against manorial tenures would undermine the legislature's strenuous efforts to restore the state credit. Yet a lecture on the necessity for retrenchment was the last thing oppressed tenants wanted to hear from their representatives, and it would only add more fuel to a movement that already had spread from Albany County to Schoharie. Alternatively, his committee might focus on the scope of the eminent domain power in the American constitutional order. Shifting the analysis from the powers to borrow and spend to the power to take had some logic, for it could plausibly be argued that the latter was narrower than the former. In 1842 the New York Constitution contained no express limitations on the legislature's power to borrow or spend, but it authorized takings of private property upon just compensation for "public use" only. A narrow definition of "public use"— confining the exercise of eminent domain to property that the public might actually use as a matter of right—fit snugly with Loomis's strict-construction, negative-government proclivities. Yet his committee could not tell the petitioners that well-settled principles of constitutional law barred government intervention in their behalf. As long as *Beekman v. Saratoga & Schenectady Railroad Co.* (1831) remained good law, the broad conception of the eminent domain power trumpeted by the Duer Report would have ample support in New York jurisprudence. To take notice of an eminent domain option, then, was to compromise Loomis's principal objective. He wanted to make the Constitution, not the Democratic Party, responsible for the committee's adverse report on the tenant petitions.

Simmons, the lone Whig on the Judiciary Committee, counted on Loomis's dilemma. In the end, however, Loomis decided to pretend that it did not exist. The committee's majority report, which the assembly received on April 9, contained only two brief paragraphs. In the first one Loomis insisted that the Contract Clause posed "an insuperable barrier" to land reform of the kind requested by Anti-Rent petitioners. He mentioned neither the eminent domain power nor the legislature's authority to regulate landlord remedies against tenants who failed to perform their contractual obligations. Loomis aimed to shut off discussion of state action, not reopen it. His second paragraph supplied a sugarcoating for the first. "The committee . . . keenly feel the disadvantages, not to say degradation, resulting from these tenures," he wrote. "Happily, however, time will cure the evil. Such estates, under our system of laws of inheritance, and under the all-pervading influence of our institutions, will in a few years be gradually worn away, and these lands will finally be held in fee as in other sections of the state." Loomis might have believed what he said. The assumption that the abolition of primogeniture would break up large estates, thus "be[ing] the means of preserving that equality of condition which so eminently distinguishes us," had figured prominently in American discourse for three generations. Alexis de Tocqueville summarized the conventional wisdom in *Democracy in America* (1835): "When the legislator has once regulated the law of inheritance, he may rest from his labor. The machine once put in motion will go on for ages, and advance, as if self-guided, towards a point indicated beforehand."[29]

Modern scholarship has repeatedly shown that Tocqueville, in the words of Stanley N. Katz, "overestimate[d] both the theoretical and actual impact of republican laws of inheritance upon nineteenth-century American society."[30] Loomis made the same mistake. Since the abolition of primogeniture by the New York legislature in 1782, ownership of the Scott Patent in Schoharie County already had been divided among the heirs of John Livingston. Yet the Livingstons and their spouses, none of whom lived on the estate, retained their interest in the land as a matter of course. They understood what Loomis refused to concede. Owning a share of a Hudson Valley manor or patent was a *rentier* dream. The tenants absorbed all maintenance costs and paid any taxes; the quarter-sale conditions tended to forestall turnover and provided landlords with a bounty when conveyances did occur. Although no investment of labor or capital was required, trust and estate lawyers in Manhattan or Albany mailed a fat check every year. Only two things threatened their sweet repose. One was "Indian" activity of the sort that had frustrated rent collections on Rensselaerwyck in 1841. The other was government intervention of the sort Loomis tried so hard to suffocate.

Simmons's minority report, though more candid than Loomis's for the majority, also discouraged the tenant petitioners. He readily admitted that "in the progress of society here, under our free and republican institutions, this species of lease property is constantly growing more repugnant to the popular feelings." But the state government could not respond to those feelings in an effective way. Simmons acknowledged that the legislature had the power, "in all cases, to take private property for the public good, by paying a just compensation." An eminent domain law, however, would not "conduce to the interests of the petitioners" for the foreseeable future. Government loans to effect land reform were out of the question; because the credit crisis had throttled mortgage lending by banks and other financial intermediaries, manor tenants would have no way to pay "the full and just compensation to be rendered by the state to the landlords." Simmons, writing from a Whig perspective, thus reached a conclusion with which even Loomis could concur. Both reports admonished anti-renters that land reform was a dead issue.[31]

Anti-Rent activists refused to heed the message. All were impressed, not by the Judiciary Committee's conclusions, but by the circumspect way its spokesmen expressed them. Loomis and Simmons did not even mention the power to regulate landlord remedies against defaulting tenants. Yet the legislature had passed Henry Strong's retrospective debtor-exemption bill with alacrity. The approach to the eminent domain power in the Judiciary Committee reports was equally remarkable. Loomis said nothing about it; Simmons left the door ajar for the enactment of compensated emancipation at a more propitious moment. Yet neither lawmaker had hesitated before voting in favor of a bill that chartered the Goshen and Albany Railroad Company, a projected feeder for the newly completed Boston and Albany, and vested it with authority to take private property at administered prices for its right-of-way. The route of the Goshen and Albany cut a swath through Rensselaerwyck and required condemnation of landlord interests, as well as tenant interests, in the affected portion of the estate. "Let a purse-pampered aristocrat or some company knock at the door, and they are at once admitted," complained one anti-renter. "We want you, they say, to grant us a privilege to run a railroad from Boston to Albany. Oh, yes, yes, this is constitutional—the hole in the Constitution is large enough to throw a bull through." When oppressed tenants made a comparable request, however, "the hole in the Constitution" shrank and "the door" to legislative assistance got slammed.[32]

Perceptive anti-renters understood that the trouble with Democrats did not stem from a slavish devotion to monied interests. It arose, instead, from an obsession with government debt and other public wrongs that clouded Democratic perceptions of the manor question and obscured their vision of appropriate ways to establish justice in the Hudson Valley. Loomis offered the tenants sympathy and supine legalism. What anti-renters demanded was an Enlightenment spirit, attributed by Strong to the architects of debtor-exemption laws, that would inspire the people's representatives to shun any tendency to "console themselves with the reflection, that, although they were restricted by the customs of barbarous ages, and must go down to the grave without improvement or melioration, they *were* empowered to pass laws which would benefit posterity." Nobody doubted the Democracy's capacity for steadfast crusades against vested wrongs. As the legislature's 1842 session came to an end, the Anti-Rent leadership tried to think of new ways of tapping that capacity, of directing the Democratic Party's long-standing hostility toward privilege and corruption against the Van Rensselaers and other great landlords. Keeping the land reform issue alive required nothing less.

While tenant leaders plotted their next move, the Schoharie rank and file took to the warpath. On April 23, 1842, less than two weeks after the legislature adjourned, an armed band of "Indians" seized the Livingston family agent, "put him in personal jeopardy, extorted promises from him, and subjected him to some personal indignity." Three days later, Governor Seward issued a proclamation giving notice that, in his words, "all the powers of the laws will be exercised to prevent the recurrence of such unlawful transactions, and to bring to condign punishment those who have offended, or shall hereafter offend in that manner." The appearance of "tumultuous bodies of disguised and armed men" in a second leasehold county shocked "all friends of law and order" in Albany. It also generated a widespread fear that "this quasi civil war" might engulf Rensselaerwyck once again, "and thus render a resort to more stringent measures necessary." Hoffman harbored an altogether different kind of fear that spring. "There is but one serious danger in this business," he wrote Azariah Flagg, "and that is that the landlords may join with the tenants to cast on the state, in the shape of a debt, their rents against tenants maddened by their dead feudalism."[33]

Anti-Rent Transformed

Michael Hoffman's apprehension was a Democratic phantom, and concerns about renewed tenant violence gradually dissipated during the quiet summer of 1842. There were no further reports of "Indian outrages" anywhere in the Hudson Valley for two years. Accounting for what one scholar has called the "temporary lull in Anti-Rent violence" is a speculative enterprise. William C. Bouck, a colorless Democrat, succeeded Seward as governor on January 1, 1843, thereby releasing the Van Rensselaers from their promise to suspend distress sales. Yet the suspension continued. Beginning in May 1842, the heirs of John Livingston followed the same policy of forbearance in Schoharie; John A. King, the New York City proprietor of the Blenheim Patent, a 17,000-acre estate adjacent to the Livingston's, did not summon the sheriff when his tenants organized a rent strike early in 1843. As deputy sheriffs bearing distress warrants disappeared from the countryside, so did the "Indians." The landlords' forbearance might have stemmed from a paternal regard for the depression-borne troubles of their tenants. But the ramifications of Henry Strong's debtor-exemption law provide a more likely explanation.[34]

Shortly after the legislature adjourned in mid-April, Whig mercantile interests organized a concerted campaign to repeal the exemption law before it went into effect on May 1, 1843. Petitions were circulated at party meetings all over the state; Erastus Root paraded them before the senate in August, when the legislature convened in a special session for the purpose of dividing the state into congressional districts pursuant to the 1840 census. Strong strenuously resisted "entering into discussion upon extraneous matters at this session," and the Democratic members followed his lead. Day after day for two weeks, the senate tabled petitions for repeal and bills for repeal on a party division. The merchants redoubled their efforts that fall and bombarded the legislature with 7,127 petitions during the 1843 session. They also secured the new Democratic governor's support. "According to my impressions," Bouck declared in his first annual message, "this act in all its provisions, has not met with general favor. . . . All laws which interfere with the relations between debtor and creditor, by impairing the obligation of contracts, have a demoralizing influence upon the people, and seldom, if ever, prove beneficial, even to those for whose benefit they were professedly made."[35]

The Van Rensselaers and the Livingstons kept a low profile while the debtor-exemption question remained in doubt. Nobody had more to gain from repeal than they did, and the great proprietors understood that the movement had a chance of succeeding as long as debate focused on the cost and availability of credit. Tumultuous distress sales, marked by "Indian" resistance and perhaps militia action to overcome it, could only hurt the cause. But the landlords came to regret their forbearance. Senator Strong averted action on the repeal petitions with a second brilliant report, followed by a series of skillful parliamentary maneuvers in the waning days of the 1843 session. And once the statute went into effect, the remedy of distress for rent became worthless on the great estates. New York law did authorize landlords to eject a tenant from the premises for unpaid rent. Moreover, it authorized them to recover costs from ousted tenants and to reclaim double rents for so long a time as tenants "willfully hold over any lands or tenements" after a thirty-day notice had been given. In the Hudson Valley context, however, the remedy of ejectment was not very serviceable. Landlords wanted rents, not possession of land that new entrants would refuse to lease for lives or in perpetuity. Not surprisingly, the Van Rensselaers and their colleagues in Schoharie temporarily sat on their hands while their tenants engaged in what Daniel Dewey Barnard, invoking the negative image of unpaid state debts in the West and South, called "practical repudiation of debts, in the shape of rents."[36]

The long lull in "Indian" resistance brought an end to newspaper coverage of tenant activity, and most New Yorkers presumed that the problem had been resolved. But the inhabitants of Rensselaerwyck, including its two proprietors, knew better. As the cold war on the manor entered its fifth year, the rent strike spread and intensified. Anti-renters organized William P. Van Rensselaer's previously quiescent tenants in 1843. At year's end the newly established Anti-Rent Association of the County of Rensselaer claimed 4,000 members, nearly double the number of Albany County tenants who had committed themselves to a "ten-year contest" with Stephen Van Rensselaer IV in 1841. The spectacularly successful membership drive shifted the movement's center of gravity from the Helderberg townships on the west side of the Hudson to Rensselaer County on the east. It also pumped more money into the common cause. Every head of household contributed two cents an acre to his association's treasury in lieu of paying rent.[37]

In 1843, at least, appropriations from the Anti-Rent "war chests" bought legal advice rather than massive amounts of calico for the "Indian" auxiliaries. An executive committee of association officers—Smith A. Boughton and Burton Thomas from Rensselaer, Lawrence Van Deusen and Hugh Scott from Albany—was determined to avoid repetition of previous disappointments at the hands of the state legislature. Only specific proposals for government action, not petitions that merely recited grievances and prayed for relief, could forestall the evasive tactics that the Judiciary Committee had used to bury the manor question in 1842. Boughton and his colleagues wanted the hired lawyers to write a land reform bill, framed in the requisite legal terminology and endorsed by the membership, which they could defend before the legislature on constitutional as well as moral grounds. An appropriate bill, entitled "An Act Concerning Tenures by Lease," had been drafted but not yet endorsed by the association members when the legislature adjourned in 1843.

The dramatic changes in the movement's size, structure, and operation were fueled by new evidence that seemed to confirm old suspicions about the Van Rensselaer land title. Sometime in 1842 an enterprising Anti-Rent attorney paid a visit to the secretary of state's office and asked to see the New York government's copy of the British patent for Rensselaerwyck. Two documents were produced from the official records. The first was a 1685 patent bearing the signature of Governor Thomas Dongan. It conveyed the manor in the name of King James II to Kiliaen Van Rensselaer, son of Johannes, and Kiliaen Van Rensselaer, son of Jeremias, "in trust" for "the right heirs and assignees" of their common grandfather and namesake, the first patroon, who had established the colony of Rensselaerwyck under a 1629 charter from the Dutch government. The second was a confirmatory patent, dated 1704 and issued by Viscount Cornbury in the name of Queen Anne. It dissolved the trust established in 1685 and vested the manor absolutely in Kiliaen Van Rensselaer, son of Jeremias, "his heirs and assignees forever." The grounds for this action were stated in the 1704 document, which recited that Kiliaen Van Rensselaer, son of Johannes, had died without issue in 1687, "whereby" Kiliaen Van Rensselaer, son of Jeremias, "became solely seised and possessed" of the estate. With the assistance of a Van Rensselaer genealogy, the Anti-Rent investigator readily determined that the current proprietors claimed title to the manor by descent from Kiliaen Van Rensselaer, son of Jeremias, the survivor of the two trustees named in the 1685 patent. But a comparison of the genealogy with the provisions of the patents also suggested that Stephen Van Rensselaer IV and his half brother William did not have a valid title to the manor.[38]

This electrifying conclusion appeared to follow logically from the fact that the first patroon had more than the two sons, Johannes and Jeremias, mentioned by name in the British patents. Jan Baptist Van Rensselaer, director of the family's operations in America between 1651 and 1658, when he returned to Holland for good, was believed to be the first patroon's eldest son. And he, too, had sired an heir named Kiliaen. The 1685 patent did not convey the Manor of Rensselaerwyck directly to Kiliaen, son of Jan Baptist, to whom and whose heirs the estate would descend according to the common law rule of primogeniture, but to Kiliaen, son of Johannes, and to Kiliaen, son of Jeremias, in trust for the "right heirs and assignees" of the first patroon. As a matter of law, however, it seemed clear that Kiliaen, son of Jan Baptist, was the right heir for whom the trust estate had been created in the 1685 patent. Yet the 1704 confirmatory patent did not even mention Kiliaen, son of Jan Baptist, let alone account for the liquidation of the rights vested in him and his race by the 1685 grant. The Anti-Rent lawyer had no reason to doubt the 1704 recital concerning the death without issue of Kiliaen, son of Johannes. But the fact remained that in the absence of a release from Kiliaen, son of Jan Baptist, the Kiliaen in possession still held the manor in trust for his cousin, the true heir of their grandfather.

Anti-renters jumped to the conclusion that Kiliaen, son of Jeremias, had covered up the very existence of the cousin who really mattered and thus secured the confirmatory patent by fraud and corruption. The seal on the 1704 patent, purportedly conferred in the name of Queen Anne, seemed to confirm the presumption of rascality. It had been broken in three places; when the Anti-Rent investigator carefully reassembled the pieces, the seal contained the names of William and Mary. Mary had died in 1694, William in 1701. "It is indeed curious," declared one manor militant, "that these sovereigns should rise after they had been dead and interred three years and execute a document." Two things seemed clear whatever the machinations that put Stephen Van Rensselaer IV and his half brother William in a position to inherit the manor in 1839. The 1704 patent was invalid because it vested title in a mere trustee without the express consent of the first patroon's "right heirs and assignees." And the 1685 patent was voidable because neither Kiliaen, son of Jan Baptist, nor any heir from his line of Van Rensselaers had ever emigrated from Holland, petitioned for British citizenship, and taken possession of the estate. At common law, aliens could not hold legal title to land.[39]

This early version of the argument against the Van Rensselaer title, though plausible on its face, was anchored on a false premise. Primogeniture did not supplant the Dutch custom of partible inheritance following the British conquest of New Netherland in 1664. The articles of capitulation expressly provided that the Dutch settlers might "enjoy their own customs concerning their inheritances." The first patroon had died without a will in 1643; when the 1685 patent conveyed the manor in trust to the two Kiliaens, twelve family members—not just one—had an equitable interest in the estate. The argument was also anchored on a false presumption. Because the 1704 confirmatory patent did not mention Kiliaen, son of Jan Baptist, anti-renters concluded that Kiliaen, son of Jeremias, had fraudulently cut off his cousin. In point of fact, the surviving trustee had negotiated a settlement with all the Dutch heirs in 1695. When the confirmatory patent issued in 1704, only Jeremias Van Rensselaer's six surviving children retained shares of the manor.[40]

These revelations, which occurred in the spring of 1844, exploded the initial version of the argument. But they also provided the foundations for another version. In the reconstituted argument, the 1685 patent was valid but the 1704 patent was not. It purported to vest title in only one of the six shareholders, violating the terms of the trust established in 1685. In 1844 there was no evidence—and none has been exhumed since—that all of Kiliaen's five siblings had agreed to release their interests in the manor. One month after the 1704 patent issued, Kiliaen conveyed to one brother, Hendrick, the 200,000-acre "lower manor" at Claverack in what is now Columbia County as quid pro quo for Hendrick's relinquishment of all rights to Rensselaerwyck. If Kiliaen struck comparable deals with his other two brothers and his two sisters, Maria Schuyler and Anna Nicolls, the records did not survive the ages. In the summer of 1844 a Staten Island shipmaster named William Sill, a lineal descendant of Anna Nicolls, and Jeremiah Schuyler of Ballston Spa stepped forward to reclaim their "rightful" interests in the manor under the 1685 patent. It was also reported that both wanted to vote their shares in favor of the buyout terms proposed by the Helderberg tenants since 1839.[41]

The first version of the title argument was good enough to cause a sensation among the manor's 3,063 tenant families. It comported with their republican ideology, and it renewed their hopes for an end to "feudal servitude interminable" through the legal process. Previous petitions to the legislature, stressing the "onerous and oppressive" terms of the leases and pronouncing their perpetual character "inconsistent with the spirit of our republican institutions," had evoked sympathy but no relief. Shifting the focus to the Van Rensselaers' defective title might turn the tide. Among those who thought so was Smith Boughton, a country doctor from the Rensselaer village of Alps and founder of the county's Anti-Rent association. A native of the Helderbergs, Boughton learned details of the title argument from boyhood companions who had been part of the movement for years. "I could not stand idle," he later wrote, "and see thousands deprived of their natural and, as I conceived, social and legal rights." As he carried news of the patroon's fraudulent title to William P. Van Rensselaer's tenants in 1843, Boughton "develop[ed] an eloquence he never knew he had" and persuaded all but a handful of them to go on strike. Anti-Rent orators who recited the argument at mass meetings in Albany County addressed people long since committed to the cause. But there, too, the message rekindled the tenants' expectations of legislative intervention and kept their enthusiasm at fever pitch.[42]

By the end of the year very few inhabitants of the manor believed that the proprietors had a valid title. When an anti-renter was prosecuted for cutting timber and carrying it away from the wild lands of William P. Van Rensselaer in February 1844, the Rensselaer County trial court had "great difficulty" impaneling a jury. "Nearly all of the list were challenged by the district attorney, on the ground of being members of the Anti-Rent Association, or, of having expressed opinions against the title of the patroon to the Manor of Rensselaerwyck," reported a correspondent for the *Argus*. "Similar objections were successfully argued to a large number of talesmen, summoned by the sheriff *de circumstantibus.*" In retrospect, the wonder is not that the court experienced "great difficulty" in impaneling a jury so much as that one willing to convict eventually got selected.[43]

While Boughton and his friends across the Hudson rallied the tenants, lawyers retained by the Anti-Rent associations hammered out a strategy for the legislature's 1844 session. By the spring of 1843 they had drafted a bill. The proposed Act Concerning Tenures by Lease contained two sections:

> Section 1. In all cases when lands are held for a longer term than twenty years by lease, conditioned for the payment of annual rent to persons who claim to derive title from the British government, such persons claiming such annual rent shall establish the validity of such grant before any of the conditions of such lease shall be enforced by law.

> Section 2. Any person holding lands by lease, in perpetuity, subject to the payment of annual rent and other covenants and conditions, may have the cash value of such rents, covenants and conditions ascertained by the appraisal of three disinterested persons to be appointed by —— and on the payment or tender of such sum, so appraised, shall hold such lands allodial.

Legal ideas expounded in recent sessions of the state legislature provided a foundation for both provisions.[44]

The crucial first section would compel the Van Rensselaers to prove the validity of their title before resuming rent collections on the manor. Landlords had no such duty at common law. The very acts of accepting a lease and taking possession under it constituted an acknowledgment by the tenant of the landlord's title.[45] Anti-renters understood the policy of the common law doctrine, but they had good reason to believe that the Manor of Rensselaerwyck posed a special case. If the inhabitants of two counties had long been deceived and humbugged, defrauded and oppressed by a defective claim of title, it seemed crazy to allow the Van Rensselaers to take advantage of their own wrong in perpetuity. What could be more outrageous, Anti-Rent orators asked, than a rule of law that permitted the "pretended proprietors" to invoke oppressive, antirepublican leases as sufficient evidence of title to enforce those very agreements? Compelling them to prove the validity of their British patents was a matter of simple justice, and the legislature's competence to abrogate the common law rule seemed unquestionable. The first section of the Act Concerning Tenures by Lease, like the debtor-exemption law enacted in 1842, would affect the creditor's remedy only. The tenantry's contractual obligations would remain undisturbed. Rent collections might be resumed and the quarter-sale conditions enforced as soon as the Van Rensselaers established a legal interest in the land possessed by manor families.

The framers of the proposed Act Concerning Tenures by Lease were prudent men. If the Van Rensselaers somehow managed to prove the validity of their title, the second section would enable tenants to extinguish their landlords' interest in their farms through the eminent domain power. The idea and justification for this measure came, of course, from the Duer Report of 1840. And it was artfully drawn. The proposed legislation did not envision a single, dramatic act of compensated expropriation whereby the state, in Duer's words, "draws to itself" the last vestiges of feudalism for the public good. That conception of the eminent domain power had fostered assumptions about government financing and a huge accretion to the state debt that a great many Whigs, not to mention the Democrats, had instinctively resisted. The lawyers retained by the Anti-Rent leadership in 1843 tried to suppress those assumptions; they did so by calling for enabling legislation, the implementation of which would cost the state nothing.

The second section of the proposed Act Concerning Tenures by Lease, like the mill acts in force throughout much of the Union, simply described a set of circumstances that authorized one person to take the property of another upon payment of just compensation. The eminent domain process would be triggered by individual tenant petitioners, not state officials, each of whom would have to make immediate payment for "the cash value of [all] rents, covenants and conditions ascertained by the appraisal of three disinterested persons." It might take years to complete the eradication of manorial tenures under the proposed statute. But the Erie Canal had not been built in a day. If the legislature enacted the Act Concerning Tenures by Lease, the people of New York could anticipate gradual and rapid progress, without violence or an increase in the state debt, toward achievement of a great public purpose.[46]

The proposed legislation delighted Boughton and other leaders of the Anti-Rent associations. It capitalized on new evidence that cast doubt on the validity of the Van Rensselaers' title. It supplied an eminent domain safety net that might be invoked if the anticipated title litigation failed. And it met every fiscal and constitutional objection that had been raised to previous proposals for extinguishing manorial tenures. The proposed Act Concerning Tenures by Lease also accommodated the needs of Schoharie anti-renters. They had read the terms of the Scott Patent, granted by King George III in 1770, and determined that the Livingstons, in the words of their 1844 petition to the legislature, "are not the true and legal owners or inheritors of the soil!" The grant required the proprietors to settle a specified number of families and put a specified number of acres into cultivation within three years; otherwise the grant "shall cease and be absolutely void," with the land reverting to the British crown "as if this present grant had not been made." Yet it was a matter of public record that none of the conditions annexed to the grant had been fulfilled in the allotted time.[47]

This argument, like the more complex one against the Van Rensselaer title, had momentous implications for the movement's trouble with Democrats. Anti-renters were now prepared to show that government acts tinged with fraud, not merely a batch of private contracts, had enabled their landlords to monopolize the soil and foist an oppressive form of tenure upon its settlers. Privilege, corruption, oppression—Democratic watchwords for nearly a generation—could be wiped out by enacting a single, well-conceived statute. With a presidential election in the offing, it seemed impossible that the overwhelmingly Democratic legislature would decline to do the right thing and earn the everlasting gratitude of several thousand tenant families in eastern New York.

Boughton, Van Deusen, and others took the Act Concerning Tenures by Lease to the membership in the summer of 1843, asking the tenants to sign petitions imploring the legislature to enact the bill. From the Rensselaer County hamlet of Hoags Corners to the Albany County village of Berne, voting-age men lined up to endorse the plan at mass meetings surging with excitement. The 6,000 signatories had every reason to be confident. Their rent strike had nullified the Van Rensselaers' interest in the land for two years or more, and their own associations had devised a way for the legislature to finish the job. What neither the tenants nor their leaders knew was that the courts already had diminished the chances for enactment of the Act Concerning Tenures by Lease.

Two landmark decisions handed down in 1843, one by the Supreme Court of the United States and the other by the New York Supreme Court, transformed the configuration of constitutional law that had fixed the boundaries of political discourse on the manor question since 1840. Landlord-tenant relations were not at issue in either case. But the federal decision compromised the legal theory that sustained the bill's first section, and the New York decision subverted the legal theory that sustained the bill's second section.

5

Depression-Era Constitutionalism

Almost every index of economic activity plunged to a record low in 1842. Wholesale prices and the volume of bank loans continued their downward slide for the third consecutive year. Railroad stocks fell to less than half the value that prevailed in 1839. Construction all but ceased on transport facilities, manufactories, and housing—the most visible manifestations of the mid-1830s boom. Real-estate values collapsed, especially in the West. Land in Chicago retained only 14 percent of its market value just six years earlier; Bessie Pierce's study of the city's newspapers led her to conclude that "practically all of the leading business men of 1836 were either bankrupt or greatly impoverished by 1842." Hundreds of cotton-belt planters packed up their slaves and fled to the Republic of Texas, where judgment creditors could not reach them. Arthur H. Cole, an unusually perceptive economic historian, wrote that the trough of 1842 must have been "the more depressing by the reason of its slow arrival . . . [and] must have seemed to the merchants of the day torpor itself when compared with the feverish activity of 1836."[1]

The economy's long downward slide had a pronounced effect on public policy. When the Whig Party failed to enact its recovery program during the special session of Congress in 1841, Democrats had an alternative course of action at the ready. Its foundation was hard money. Aiming their salvos at state legislatures in the South and West, where banking corporations had suspended specie payments in violation of contractual obligations to noteholders imposed by their charters, Democratic publicists called for the annihilation of note-issuing banks. "Require the immediate redemption, in gold and silver, of the notes banks have now in circulation," Orestes Brownson thundered in early 1841. Decisive action by the state legislatures, which breathed life into the offending institutions in the first place, would shut down the suspended banks and "restore the currency to the constitutional standard" of gold and silver. Brownson conceded that "this . . . bold measure," standing alone, might "caus[e] great suffering." In Chicago, for example, most people were both debtor and creditor; with the suspension of specie payments, the value of bank notes fell with the price level and local business continued as long as nobody insisted on payment in specie. Destroying the banks would disturb the resulting equilibrium by eliminating the circulating medium. But this effect, Brownson argued, might be mitigated. "Why not require the creditor, in the case of all debts contracted prior to the change, and estimated in a depreciated paper currency, to deduct this percent from the nominal amount claimed? This would be just to both parties, requiring the debtor to pay only the amount of value he had stipulated to pay, and giving the creditor all the value he ever had a right to demand." Bank reform might be safely achieved, then, by coupling it with retrospective legislation for debtor relief.[2]

Other Democratic journalists were quick to endorse Brownson's scheme for closing down the state banks that had suspended specie payments in 1839. "Admitting the charter of [each] bank to have been a contract," William Cullen Bryant explained in March 1841, "it is evident that the conditions of it are broken by the refusal to redeem its obligations in coin. The stoppage of payment is *ipso facto* a forfeiture of privilege. . . . It is guilty, in the language of the common law, of a *non user* or rather *misuser* of its franchises, and is no longer recognized by the community, and cannot expect to be recognized by the law, as such an institution as its charter designed to create." Francis Preston Blair, editor of the *Washington Globe*, addressed Democrats in more forthright terms. "One of the most sacred duties which now devolves with more force than ever upon the Democratic Party," he wrote several months later, "is the task of bank reform—immediate, thorough, and permanent reform. Immediate resumption is the first thing; no future suspensions is the second thing; and subordination to law and morals, the third and lasting thing."[3]

Yet many eastern Democrats withheld support for the debt-valuation laws advocated by Brownson. In their judgment, the Democracy could not insist that bankers fulfill one kind of legal obligation while permitting merchants and farmers to escape another. Besides, debt-valuation laws would impose an unequal hardship on New York financiers with interests in the West. New Yorkers had to pay the full amount of local debts in specie, or bank notes redeemable in specie on demand, yet the proposed legislation would impair their right to reciprocal treatment from western debtors. The enactment of debtor-relief legislation, Bryant remarked, would make a mockery of the question every Democrat should be posing to the voters: "Are we to have one code of morals for banking companies and another for the people?"[4]

Democratic legislators in the South and West were less circumspect than Bryant and like-minded easterners. Mississippi, Arkansas, Illinois, and Indiana—also the first states to default on public debts—took Brownson's "medicine" for the depression in the winter of 1840–41. The Mississippi legislature enacted one statute that compelled banks to resume specie payments by the end of the year or forfeit their charters. On the same day, it passed another that forbade sales on execution or foreclosure unless two-thirds of the appraised value, as determined by "three persons, entirely disinterested and unconnected [to the parties], either by consanguinity or affinity," had been bid for the property. Arkansas lawmakers promptly enacted comparable legislation; Illinois and Indiana passed retrospective valuation and redemption laws in 1841 but dragged their feet on the bank question until 1842. In that banner year for the implementation of Brownson's "bold" recommendations, legislatures with newly elected Democratic majorities mandated resumption and supplied debtor relief in Virginia, Pennsylvania, Ohio, Michigan, and Alabama. Virginia's two-thirds valuation law, the archetype 1842 statute, provided that the act was to go into force on January 1, 1843, unless the state banks resumed specie payments in the interim. Banks in the Old Dominion managed to resume in September 1842. But only eight survived in Pennsylvania, ten in Ohio, and one each in Michigan and Alabama. Meanwhile, the debtor-relief statutes, popularly known as "stay laws," went into effect in eight states. John M. Berrien, the formidable Whig senator from Georgia, called them "the finishing blow to American credit abroad."[5]

The policies established by state governments in the South and West formed a pattern that outraged people in the East. "All those moral and legal obligations which formed the basis of credit have been swept away," lamented *Hunt's Merchants' Magazine* in March 1843. "A merchant cannot trust a western dealer, because the state laws give him no protection. The capitalist cannot repose confidence in banks, because . . . upwards of sixty banks have failed, sinking $132,363,800 of capital. He cannot trust states, because the same principles which induced the passage of stay laws disposed the people to resist taxation."[6] What was to be done? As some indexes of economic activity began to inch upward in 1843, two parallel movements for reconstructing the American political economy took shape. The first, led by conservative Whigs, focused on the enhancement of judicial power in order to check the depredations of Democratic state legislatures. The second, led by radical Democrats, looked to the reform of state constitutions in order to curtail the Whig penchant for borrowing money, chartering privileged corporations, and otherwise impairing the principle of equal rights. In many states, Democrats tended to resist the one movement and Whigs the other. In New York, however, Democrats spearheaded both drives. Jacksonian judges and lawyers aimed to translate their party's political ideology, with its broad conception of public wrongs and narrow conception of public responsibility for private contracts, into effective constitutional limitations on state legislatures. The effort had one consequence that nobody took into account. It changed the legal and political environment for land reform in New York State.

Tightening the Right-Remedy Distinction

John Marshall embarked the Supreme Court down a long and slippery slope in *Sturgis v. Crowinshield* (1819), where he proclaimed that "the distinction between the obligation of a contract and the remedy given by the legislature to enforce that obligation . . . exists in the nature of things." The impulse to frame such a distinction was understandable. "To punish honest insolvency by imprisonment for life, and to make this a constitutional principle," Marshall declared, "would be an excess of inhumanity which will not readily be imputed to the illustrious patriots who framed our Constitution, nor to the people who adopted it." Yet Marshall also presumed that the Founders conceived of the Contract Clause as a bar to stay laws (temporarily suspending the creditor's right to an execution or foreclosure) and commodity payment acts (authorizing payment of debts with goods at a value fixed by law). The enactment of such legislation during the Confederation era, he wrote in his *Life of George Washington*, was contrary to "the principles of moral justice, and of sound policy." Fortunately, Marshall added, the adoption of the Contract Clause "impressed upon that portion of society which had looked to the government for relief from embarrassment, that personal exertions alone could free them from difficulties; and an increased degree of industry and economy was the natural consequence of this opinion."[7]

The fact remained that the statutes Marshall condemned in his biography of Washington did not dissolve the debtor's obligation. Stay laws and commodity payment acts merely impaired the creditor's remedy. Thus the distinction laid down in the *Sturgis* case threatened to negate vested rights in the very situations that generated the constitutional prohibition. Marshall and his associates acknowledged the problem and discussed it repeatedly. In case after case, however, the Court stated that "it is unnecessary, on the present occasion, to attempt to draw, with precision, the line between the right and the remedy." The long awaited occasion came in *Bronson v. Kinzie* (1843). There a 7-1 majority ruled, for the first time, that retrospective state legislation purporting to regulate remedies on executory contracts also impaired their obligation.[8]

At issue in *Bronson v. Kinzie* was the validity of two Illinois statutes enacted in 1841. The first prohibited judicial sales on execution or foreclosure unless two-thirds of the appraised value, as determined by "three householders of the proper county," had been bid for the property. The second permitted mortgagors to redeem property sold on foreclosure by repaying the purchase money with interest during the subsequent year. Both statutes expressly provided for retrospective application. Arthur Bronson, the plaintiff, was described by one contemporary as "the closest, most penurious rich man in New York." A heavy investor in western land, Bronson had extended his far-flung operations into "the Kinzie addition" on Chicago's north side in 1833. Bronson's difficulties with the defendant began when he loaned Kinzie $4,000 so that the Chicago developer could save property from another creditor. As collateral, the New Yorker accepted a mortgage on two unencumbered lots in Chicago plus Kinzie's half interest in the Lake House Hotel, reputedly the city's finest. The note carried an annual interest of 12 percent and stipulated that, upon default, Bronson could sell the property at a "strict foreclosure"—an auction sale without any possibility of redemption. In 1841 Bronson filed a bill to foreclose the mortgage in the United States Circuit Court for the District of Illinois. Kinzie invoked the state's stay laws as a bar to execution of the contract's "strict foreclosure" provision, triggering consideration of the important Contract Clause question. The case reached the Supreme Court on a certificate of division from the judges below.[9]

Chief Justice Roger Taney spoke for the Court. He began by restating the established, though incoherent, distinction between the obligation of a contract and its remedy. "Undoubtedly a state may regulate at pleasure the modes of proceeding in its courts in relation to past contracts as well as future," Taney asserted. Legislation abolishing imprisonment for debt and "shorten[ing] the period of time within which claims shall be barred by the statute of limitations" already had been sustained on that ground. Retrospective exemption laws, he added in a sentence that must have pleased Henry Strong and the New York Democracy, were governed by the same principle: "Whatever belongs merely to the remedy may be altered according to the will of the state, provided the alteration does not impair the obligation of the contract." Taney conceded that the Illinois legislation at issue was also remedial "in form" and did not purport to dissolve the debtor's obligation. In the Court's judgment, however, the statutes did "not act merely on the remedy, but directly upon the contract itself, and . . . engraft[ed] upon it new conditions injurious and unjust to the mortgagee." Valuation laws and redemption acts, in other words, were not among the state regulations "properly belonging to the remedy." Unlike statutes of limitation and exemption acts, which "every civilized community" gave a retrospective operation on grounds of "policy and humanity," the Illinois laws were "injurious and unjust."[10]

Chief Justice Taney's opinion stated a conclusion, not a principled standard of constitutional interpretation. *Bronson* stood for the proposition that the Court knew violations of the Contract Clause when it saw them; vicious legislation cloaked "in the form of a remedy" could not withstand judicial scrutiny. Justice John McLean, dissenting, professed to be shocked by the majority's willingness to consider the reasonableness of state laws that impaired the remedies of creditors. "Where shall this judicial discretion find a limit?" he asked. McLean thought "every contract is entered into with a supposed knowledge by the parties, that the lawmaking power may modify the remedy." To depart "from this rule of construction," he exclaimed, was to make American constitutional law "depend upon the arbitrary decision of the courts."[11]

Taney anticipated McLean's objections, and he answered them with aplomb. "It is difficult, perhaps, to draw a line that would be applicable in all cases between legitimate alterations of the remedy and provisions which, in the form of remedy, impair the right," he remarked. But if the right-remedy distinction existed "in the nature of things," as John Marshall said, judicial discretion did too. Taney put it this way:

> It is manifest that the obligation of the contract, and the rights of a party under it, may, in effect, be destroyed by denying a remedy altogether; or may be seriously impaired by burdening the proceedings with new conditions and restrictions, so as to make the remedy hardly worth pursuing. And no one, we presume, would say that there is any substantial difference between a retrospective law declaring a particular contract or class of contracts to be abrogated and void, and one which took away all remedy to enforce them, or encumbered it with conditions that rendered it useless or impracticable to pursue it.

To adopt McLean's "rule of construction," then, would be to make a "great and useful" provision of the Constitution "illusive and nugatory; mere words of form, affording no protection, and producing no practical result." Such an outcome had to be resisted.[12]

The decision in *Bronson v. Kinzie* evoked a storm of protest in the West. In New York, however, the Court's ruling was greeted with what one observer, exaggerating only slightly, termed "universal satisfaction." Horace Greeley's *Tribune* called the decision "just" in an editorial that taunted Democrats for supporting stay laws in the West while decrying them in the East. Bryant's *Evening Post* not only spoke warmly about "the healthy influence which [the Court's holding] will exert on the community" but also reminded the Whigs "that this bold, fearless, and really conservative opinion proceeds from judges, every one of which was appointed under those awfully agrarian Locofoco administrations of Andrew Jackson and Martin Van Buren." Edwin Croswell proclaimed that "the reign of honesty and law" had been restored. "Legislative interference with private contracts can no longer be of avail," crowed the *Argus*. "This has been the vice of the last six years. It will now be checked."[13]

William A. Duer Jr., back in Oswego practicing law, must have been among the more avid readers of the *Bronson* opinions. In 1840 he had denounced the Wheaton bill on the ground that unchecked amplification of the legislature's power over landlord remedies would render the Contract Clause "utterly without force or value." The *Bronson* decision thus vindicated and comforted him. There was an important difference, however, between the reasoning in Duer's report and Taney's opinion for the Court. Duer attempted to tame the trouble-some right-remedy distinction with rules of constitutional construction. One of them—the notion that "the distinction . . . applies to cases where the law gives the remedy, and not to cases where the parties themselves have entered into a stipulation, in the nature of a remedy, for the purpose of securing the perfor-mance of the principal obligation"—might have been invoked in *Bronson*. Taney did not explain why the Court spurned this line of argument. But it is clear why Duer resisted the doctrine of reasonableness, which *Bronson* estab-lished, in 1840. The discretion Taney claimed for the judiciary under the Contract Clause would have undermined Duer's assertion that the legislature, not the courts, must determine whether public exigencies justified an exercise of the eminent domain power. *Taylor v. Porter* (1843), the second great decision in that banner year for vested rights, did that very thing. There the New York Supreme Court not only held that the judicial department had the final say on the propriety of eminent domain takings but also grounded its decision, for the first time in a widely noticed opinion, on the state constitution's due process clause.[14]

Due Process and the Eminent Domain Power

Unlike the *Bronson* case, which involved a highly charged controversy affecting the stay laws of eight states, *Taylor v. Porter* stemmed from a petty squabble between neighboring landowners in Saratoga County, New York. The plaintiff's farm abutted a public highway; his neighbor to the rear, hemmed in by adjoin-ing landowners on all sides, had no access to the road and could not persuade Taylor to sell him an easement. A New York statute, enacted in 1772, supplied the defendant with a remedy. It authorized landowners who desired access to a public highway across a neighbor's property to petition the highway commis-sioners "of any town, for a private road." The act provided that whenever such an application had been filed, "twelve disinterested freeholders of the town" were to be summoned "on a day certain; of which day, notice shall be given to the owner or occupant" of the land to be taken. At the ensuing hearing the twelve freeholders were "to view the lands," determine whether "such road is necessary," and fix the compensation that "shall be paid by the person applying for the road." The act also stipulated that "every such private road, when so laid out, shall be for the use of such applicant, his heirs and assign[ee]s; but not to be converted to any other use or purpose, than that of a road." Porter set the requisite procedures into motion on May 18, 1840. Ten months later, "twelve disinterested freeholders" authorized the local highway commissioners to lay out a road 545 feet long and three rods wide across Taylor's land. But Taylor refused the compensation tendered and sued for trespass when construction began. Porter invoked the Private Road Act as justification for the trespass; Taylor argued that the law was unconstitutional.[15]

It took gall to claim that the legislature had exceeded its powers in the Private Road Act. The statute had been on the books for seventy years, and nobody had breathed a doubt about its constitutionality. Justifications for the act abounded. The core ideas of civic republicanism provided one line of defense. None of the essential duties of citizenship—serving on juries and in the militia, participating in the affairs of the polis as voter and officeholder, even working on the public highways for the common good—could be performed by free-holders who could not leave their own land without trespassing on their neighbor's. Principles of positive liberalism, which Duer had elaborated in defense of the state's power to expropriate the Van Rensselaers, provided an equally compelling rationale for the Private Road Act. The public interest in developing resources, increasing the volume of transactions, and cultivating human capital could not possibly be effected if landowners lacked access to the market. In *Beekman v. Saratoga & Schenectady Railroad Co.* (1831), moreover, Chancellor Reuben Walworth had proclaimed that "if the public interest can be in any way promoted by the taking of private property, it must rest with the wisdom of the legislature to determine whether the benefit to the public will be of sufficient importance to render it expedient for them to exercise the right of eminent domain."[16]

Chief Justice Samuel Nelson, a conservative Democrat, said all these things and more in *Taylor v. Porter*. "The universal opinion heretofore," he remarked, "has been that the law authorizing the laying out of private roads stands upon the same principle with the law in respect to highways; and that all these improvements, if not equally necessary, are at least so much a matter of public concern as to justify the full exercise of the right of eminent domain." But Nelson spoke in dissent. Two other Democrats, Justices Greene Bronson and Esek Cowen, struck down the act. In their judgment, recent experience proved that "the universal opinion heretofore" had been far too sanguine about the capacity of state legislatures to exercise their discretion within acceptable bounds. Evidence of the disposition to use law as an instrument of "theft and robbery," Bronson asserted in *Stone v. Green* (1842), was everywhere at hand. The stay laws enacted in a great many states constituted only one manifestation of "that lax morality in relation to the payment of debts which is now beginning to disgrace sovereign states, as well as individuals and private corporations." The rent strike in Albany and Rensselaer counties, which Bronson did not mention, was another. Although the Private Road Act of 1772 could scarcely be blamed on what he called the "demoralizing tendency of the times," its underlying principle had been invoked by the Duer Committee as justification for a massive redistribution of property rights. The decision in *Taylor v. Porter* was designed to scotch all such schemes. Bronson encapsulated the gist of the court's holding in a single sentence: "When one man wants the property of another, I mean to say that the legislature cannot aid him in making the acquisition."[17]

The structure of Justice Bronson's majority opinion was as pathbreaking as the holding. He began by conceding that "the right to take private property for *public* purposes is one of the inherent attributes of sovereignty, and exists in every independent government." Yet the very terms of the Private Road Act suggested that the legislature had not contemplated a public purpose. "The road is paid for and owned by the applicant," he pointed out. "The public has not title to, nor interest in it. No citizen has a right to use the road as he does the public highway." A less talented judge than Bronson might have concluded his opinion here. The state constitution authorized compensated takings for "public use" only; because the Private Road Act did not contemplate public use of the premises, it was unconstitutional. But this line of reasoning played into the hands of people like Walworth, Nelson, and Duer. By what right, they would ask, did the court substitute its judgment for the legislature's as to what exigencies justified an exercise of the eminent domain power?[18]

Bronson avoided this troublesome question, temporarily at least, by simply denying the assumption that the Private Road Act could be conceived as an eminent domain law. The statute provided compensation for property taken and thus had one earmark of an eminent domain measure. But eminent domain was, by definition, the power to take property for public use; calling the Private Road Act an exercise of that power could not make it one. This move enabled Bronson to characterize the statute for what, in his judgment, it really was: "The property of A. is taken, without his permission, and transferred to B." Two questions of his own followed: "Has the legislature any power to say it may be done? . . . Where, then, shall we find a delegation of power to the legislature to take the property of A. and give it to B., either with or without compensation?" Pursuit of these questions led him to an inquiry about the nature and scope of legislative power in the American constitutional order.[19]

Justice Bronson's inquiry amounted to a brief civics lesson. "Under our form of government the legislature is not supreme," he said. "It is only one of the organs of that absolute sovereignty which resides in the whole body of the people." The doctrine of popular sovereignty, institutionalized in New York through ratification of a written constitution framed in convention, derived from the notion that legitimate government arose only from a compact among the people themselves. And "security of life, liberty and property," Bronson was quick to add, "lies at the foundation of the social compact." In his *Second Treatise of Government* (1689), John Locke linked constitutional compacts and rights of property in an argument every American lawyer knew: "The supreme power cannot take from any man part of his property without his own consent;

for the preservation of property being the end of government and that for which men enter into society, it necessarily supposes and requires that the people should have property, without which they must be supposed to lose that, by entering into society, which was the end for which they entered into it—too gross an absurdity for any man to own."[20]

Bronson claimed that only one clause of the New York Constitution could be invoked to justify the Private Road Act. "That," he said, "is the first section of the first article, where the people have declared that 'the legislative power of this state shall be vested in a senate and assembly.'" But "to say that this grant of 'legislative power' includes the right to attack private property is equivalent to saying that the people have delegated to their servants the power of defeating one of the great ends for which the government was established." It followed for Bronson, as it had for a great many appellate judges in the early republic, that legislative power was necessarily subject to implied limitations. "If there was not one word of qualification in the whole instrument," he asserted, "I should [still] feel great difficulty in bringing myself to the conclusion that the clause under consideration had clothed the legislature with despotic power; and such is the extent of their authority if they can take the property of A., either with or without compensation, and give it to B."[21]

The doctrine of implied limitations was not dispositive in *Taylor v. Porter*. Justice Cowen, whose vote Bronson needed to strike down the Private Road Act, resisted the idea that "the foundation of the social compact" could be enforced by the judicial department. "Strong expressions may be found in the books against legislative interference with vested rights," he declared in 1841; "but it is not conceivable that, after allowing the few restrictions to be found in the federal and State constitutions, any further bounds can be set to legislative power." In Cowen's judgment, moreover, the question was no longer an open one in New York jurisprudence. Gulian C. Verplanck, speaking for the state's highest court in 1838, had flatly stated that judicial interposition could not limit "the omnipotence of the legislative power . . . except so far as the express words of a written constitution give that authority." Neither Cowen nor Verplanck was inclined to disparage natural rights. But both jurists discerned the soft spot in implied limitations theory. When the people of New York created "the legislative power," they had excluded the judiciary from any share in its exercise. Yet court decisions negating statutes "as contrary to the first principles of natural right" clearly involved judicial participation in the shaping of legislation. Statutes challenged as contrary to "the express words of a written constitution" stood on a different footing. The people of New York had coupled their grant of "the legislative power" with a list of restrictions on its exercise; Cowen and Verplanck took it for granted that a statute was voidable if it conflicted with the express will of the sovereign people.[22]

Justice Bronson had little difficulty accommodating Cowen's views in *Taylor v. Porter*. He simply found a textual basis for the doctrine of implied limitations. The validity of the Private Road Act "does not necessarily turn on the section granting legislative power," Bronson asserted. "The people have added negative words, which should put the matter at rest." One provision of the state constitution, adopted in 1777, declares, "No member of this state shall be disfranchised, or deprived of any of the rights or privileges secured to any citizen thereof, unless by the law of the land, or the judgment of his peers." Another, added to the same section in 1821, provides, "No person shall be deprived of life, liberty, or property, without due process of law." Both constitutional limitations, Bronson pointed out, derived from Magna Carta and its subsequent reenactments by Parliament; in Sir Edward Coke's *Second Institute of the Laws of England* (1642), the phrases "law of the land" and "due process of law" were linked to the common law and said to possess interchangeable meanings. Bronson confessed that no jurist or commentator had ever elaborated those meanings with any precision. But he was quite certain that "the law of the land" could not possibly comprehend a statute that "compel[s] any man to sell his land or his goods, or any interest in them, to his neighbor, when the property is not to be applied to public use."[23]

Justice Bronson reached this conclusion in much the same way Chief Justice Taney arrived at his in *Bronson v. Kinzie*. "The words 'by the law of the land,' as here used, do not mean a statute passed for the purpose of working a wrong," he said. "That construction would render the restriction absolutely nugatory, and turn this part of the constitution into mere nonsense. The people would be made to say to the two houses: 'You shall be vested with the legislative power of this state; but no one shall be disfranchised, or deprived of any of the rights or privileges of a citizen, unless you pass a statute for that purpose'; in other words, 'You shall not do the wrong, unless you choose to do it.'" On the basis of a recent North Carolina decision, recommended as "replete with sound constitutional doctrines" in the 1840 edition of Kent's *Commentaries*, Bronson said the "law of the land" clause "seems to mean, that no member of the state shall be disfranchised, or deprived of any of his rights or privileges, unless the matter shall be adjudged against him upon trial according to the course of the common law." Bronson spoke with more confidence about the due process principle: It "cannot mean less than a prosecution or suit instituted and conducted according to the prescribed forms and solemnities for ascertaining guilt, or determining the title to property." Because life and liberty, as well as property, secured "protection against legislative encroachment" from this clause of the state constitution, Bronson observed, "if the legislature can take the property of A. and transfer it to B., they can take A. himself, and either shut him up in prison, or put him to death."[24]

Once he had established that "none of these things can be done by mere legislation," Bronson returned to his point of departure—the scope of the eminent domain power. "Of course, I shall not be understood as saying that a trial and judgment are necessary in exercising the right of eminent domain," he said. "When private property is taken for public use, the only restriction is, that just compensation shall be made to the owner." The Private Road Act, however, could not be sustained on that ground even though compensation had been tendered. It took property for a private use; calling it an eminent domain measure did not make it one. This had been Bronson's major premise from the outset. But now he was prepared to refute the claim that, in Chancellor Walworth's words, "it must rest with the wisdom of the legislature to determine whether the benefit to the public will be of sufficient importance to render it expedient for them to exercise the right of eminent domain." Every act involving "the transfer of one man's property to another without the consent of the owner, and although compensation is made," said Bronson, was subject to judicial review. "There must be due process of law." Protecting private rights, in other words, required judicial review of public purposes professed by the legislature. This is the stuff of substantive due process.[25]

The majority opinions in *Taylor v. Porter* and *Bronson v. Kinzie* were cut from the same bolt of cloth. In each instance the judiciary tackled a stubborn problem in constitutional law that pitted a fundamental principle (legislatures cannot take property for private use or impair contractual obligations) against an established rival principle (legislatures can define public purposes and regulate contract remedies). In each instance the rival principle threatened to swallow the fundamental one. And in each instance the opinion of the court expressed what Edward S. Corwin called "a feeling . . . that to leave the legislature free to pass arbitrary or harsh laws . . . [would be] to yield the substance while contending for the shadow."[26]

Neither opinion fixed a clear boundary between the conflicting principles at hand. Justice Bronson did not explain how public uses might be distinguished from private ones in subsequent controversies; Chief Justice Taney did not explain how the Court might thereafter distinguish between statutes "properly belonging to the remedy" and legislation that impaired the obligation of contracts "by burdening the proceedings with new conditions and restrictions, so as to make the remedy hardly worth pursuing." Yet both decisions had a galvanizing effect on legal thought and political practice. On the hustings and on the floor of state legislatures, lawyer-politicians immediately began to hurl "the rule" of *Taylor v. Porter* or *Bronson v. Kinzie* at opponents whose proposals even squinted in the direction of "theft and robbery" through the legislative process. Every reform movement that envisioned a modest redistribution of property rights was affected. In New York, at least, the first casualty turned out

to be the Act Concerning Tenures by Lease framed for the Anti-Rent associations in the spring of 1843.

Judicial Review in a Democracy

The vested rights decisions of 1843, like ambitious exercises of judicial power
before and since, evoked thoughtful criticism. Chief Justice Samuel Nelson,
dissenting in *Taylor v. Porter*, complained that reviewing the legitimacy of
compensated takings clothed judges with the incongruous authority to ascertain "the public interest or welfare." Justice John McLean, dissenting in *Bronson v. Kinzie*, complained that assessing the reasonableness of laws affecting
creditor remedies meant the subjection of legislation to "the arbitrary decision
of the courts." John Bannister Gibson, chief justice of the Pennsylvania Supreme Court, amplified the voices of McLean and Nelson. By what right, he
asked, did appointed judges strike down statutes framed by lawmakers depu-
tized directly by the people to effect the public good? Judicial review of legislation, Gibson insisted, violated the principle of democracy as well as the principle of coequal government departments.[27]

Gibson elaborated his case against "judicial usurpation" in *Chadwick v.
Moore* (1844), a constitutional challenge to the Pennsylvania stay law enacted
two years earlier. "This statute was evidently produced by the emergency
which arose from collapse of the credit system," he wrote for a unanimous
court. "Is such an exercise of the [legislature's] sound discretion . . . so unreasonable as materially to impair the remedy, and amount to a denial of the right?"
Gibson thought not. "To hold that a state legislature is incompetent to relieve
the public from the pressure of sudden distress by arresting a general sacrifice
of property by the machinery of the law, would invalidate many statutes whose
constitutionality has hitherto been unsuspected." Two such statutes were mentioned. "Laws imposing military service on apprentices, or dissolving the contract of marriage for causes not declared at the time of its solemnization, have
not been resisted," he declared. "And practical contemporaneous usage goes far
to settle a question of [constitutional] construction."[28]

The Pennsylvania court's deference to the legislature's "sound discretion" in
the stay-law case had a counterpart in eminent domain law. Nelson, dissenting
in the New York private-road case, invoked Gibson's opinion in *Harvey v.
Thomas* (1840) as a persuasive authority on the subject. At issue was an 1832
statute authorizing coal operators to take private property, upon payment of just
compensation fixed by six "public viewers," as a right-of-way for "lateral railroads" designed to carry anthracite from the mines to the public works and on
to market. Gibson, speaking for the court, gave two reasons for rejecting the
constitutional challenge to the act. The first evinced his notorious penchant for

textual fundamentalism. Pennsylvania's constitution did not contain a provision that specifically prohibited takings for private use; furthermore, it required the payment of just compensation only when the legislature mandated the expropriation of property for public use. "It is true," Gibson said, that the legislature had "usually, perhaps always," coupled the authority of private parties to take with a duty to compensate. "But this has been done from a sense of justice, and not of constitutional obligation." Gibson's second reason underscored his belief in a positive state. "The end to be attained by this lateral railroad law is the public prosperity," he declared. "Pennsylvania has an incalculable interest in her coal mines," and the state legislature had often invoked "public utility" as a justification for delegating the eminent domain power to incorporated railroad and navigation-improvement companies. "It surely will not be imagined," Gibson concluded, "that a privilege constitutionally given to an artificial person, would be less constitutionally given to a natural one."[29]

The self-denying approach to judicial review Gibson exemplified in *Chadwick v. Moore* and *Harvey v. Thomas* might have caught on under different circumstances. But state politics in the depression era, driven by the Democratic Party's hard-money crusade and "the revulsion against internal improvements," squeezed his faith in the positive state between Democratic and Whig assumptions about the legislative process. Whig jurists grew increasingly vigilant for legislation that seemed to rob the few for the supposed benefit of the many. Democratic jurists, especially in the East, acted more decisively on their perception of legislatures as annexes of the marketplace where interest groups conspired to rob the many for the benefit of the few. Gibson's textual fundamentalism fared no better. The "demoralizing tendency of the times," manifested in what one commentator called "the diabolical work of arraying one portion of the community against another, the poor against the rich, the laborer with his hands against the laborer with the head," pushed bench and bar toward more expansive conceptions of the judicial function. Even in the West, courts took their cues from Taney rather than Gibson and struck down stay laws beginning in 1845. The reaction to *Harvey v. Thomas* was more portentous.[30]

In July 1843 the *American Law Magazine*, "the oracle of Philadelphia lawyers," carried a thirty-page article entitled "The Security of Private Property." Peter S. DuPonceau, an eminent Whig legal scholar, wrote it to assail the Pennsylvania court's "truly alarming" decision in *Harvey v. Thomas*. Chief Justice Gibson, said DuPonceau, was just wrong when he claimed that the Pennsylvania Constitution contained no "express disaffirmance" of takings for a private use. In point of fact, "there exists a disaffirmance of it, clear, positive and unequivocal." DuPonceau then quoted the due process principle, first in Latin from the Magna Carta, then in English from Coke's *Second Institute*, and finally from the Pennsylvania Declaration of Rights. "Fortunately," he added,

Chief Justice Gibson's "broad positions . . . are not sustained by the current of American decisions." What followed was a scissors-and-paste compilation of quotations, virtually all of them obiter dictum, from the law reports of the several states. DuPonceau's article contained no references to *Taylor v. Porter*, the one case directly on point. It had not yet been reported. Justices Bronson and Cowen, the architects of substantive due process in New York, must have been delighted with the piece all the same. DuPonceau provided independent support for their logic and their method. He also distilled the central meaning of the revamped vested rights jurisprudence in New York and the nation: "The reader of this article will lay it aside with the reflection that the liberty of the republican states of America will owe their perpetuity to their courts, executing the supreme will of the people against acts of tyranny and oppression, whether proceeding from the executive or the legislature."[31]

Theodore Sedgwick Jr., one of the New York Democracy's more trenchant commentators on law and politics, consolidated the new dispensation in *A Treatise on the Rules which Govern the Interpretation and Application of Statutory and Constitutional Law* (1857). In his view, sporadic criticism of decisions like *Taylor v. Porter* and *Bronson v. Kinzie* stemmed from "a want of clear perception as to the true nature of law; or, in other words, a want of accurate notions as to the boundary line which, under our system, divides the legislative and judicial powers." Sedgwick's attack on the arguments of Gibson, McLean, and Nelson began with a question: "Is an act depriving one man of his property for the benefit of another a *law*?" The separation of powers, "a leading idea in the American mind at the time of the Revolution," precluded an affirmative answer. "What distinguishes a judicial from a legislative act," Sedgwick explained, "is, that the one is a determination of what the existing law is in relation to some particular thing already done or happened, while the other is a predetermination of what the law shall be for the regulation and government of all future cases falling under its provision." When legislatures claimed authority to divest an interest in property already acquired, as they did with the Private Road Act in New York and the stay laws in Illinois, they "trench[ed] on the functions of legal tribunals." By definition such acts were not laws but "enactments really of a judicial nature." For Sedgwick, then, it was perverse to say that *Taylor v. Porter* sanctioned judicial control of the legislature's rightful discretion to define public purposes. "It does no such thing," he insisted. Legislatures left their assigned sphere in the constitutional order every time they interfered with vested rights; consequently they had no discretion to be usurped.[32]

Sedgwick conceded that American courts often permitted legislatures to abridge vested rights. Restrictions on "the full enjoyment of private property" came in so many different forms, protected so many different public interests, and disturbed vested rights in so many different ways that he made no attempt to classify the statutes or to digest the pertinent case law. Sedgwick also confessed that "the whole subject" of vested rights jurisprudence "must be considered as in a state of very unsatisfactory uncertainty." The source of the problem was easy to identify. "On the one hand," he remarked, "any interference with rights acquired under existing laws is a positive evil and injury; while on the other, to deny to the legislature power to make such changes as the social or political condition requires, would reduce us to a state of Chinese stagnation and immobility; and would be absurdly inconsistent with the condition of our country and the character of our people." Nevertheless, Sedgwick expressed confidence in the judiciary's capacity to expel the "incongruities" that pervaded vested rights jurisprudence in the American states. As courts got more and more experience in the application of existing standards, they would gradually develop an array of consistent rules.[33]

Sedgwick's treatise, the nation's first intensive study of state constitutional law, was more than a decade in the making and incorporated ideas that he had been expounding for twenty years. "The acquisition of property raises the lower classes [and] the diffusion of property humbles the upper," he wrote in 1837. "Those laws which most sacredly guarantee and most rigidly enforce the right which a man has to the fruits of his labor, are not merely incentives to industry—they are the surest bulwarks of freedom." But in 1843, when *Taylor v. Porter* and *Bronson v. Kinzie* came down, Sedgwick had more patience with charges of "judicial usurpation" than he would a decade later. Lingering doubts about the legitimacy of judicial review in a polity bottomed on popular sovereignty prompted him to propose another way to protect vested rights against legislative attack. Judicial glosses on vague constitutional texts like due process, Sedgwick told a huge throng in Manhattan's Broadway Tabernacle on August 15, 1843, should be translated into increasingly precise limitations on legislative power by constitutional conventions held at twenty-year intervals. This solution did more than accommodate the criticism of Gibson, McLean, Nelson, and others. It offered the Anti-Rent associations a forum more authoritative than the state legislature to press their case for land reform.[34]

In 1843 Sedgwick believed that periodic constitutional reform had two distinct advantages over broad-gauged judicial review. First, state constitutions would become repositories of the nation's political experience. Lessons drawn from controversies over private roads and stay laws at one point in time, for example, might be constitutionalized for the ages in specific textual provisions. Thus one section of the New York Constitution might be amended to provide that "private property shall not be taken for private use, nor shall private property be taken for use by the public without payment of just compensation." Another might provide that "contractual obligations shall not be impaired; although the legislature may regulate the remedies available to the parties in relation to past contracts as well as future ones, stay laws and all other retrospective legislation that materially diminish creditor remedies are prohibited." Second, the resulting limitations on legislative majorities not only would be imposed by the people themselves but also would be ramified and reaffirmed by each succeeding generation of the constituent sovereign. The judicial department would remain the people's first line of defense against government's unconstitutional acts. As written constitutions grew more and more precise, however, the scope of judicial discretion would contract. Mechanical application of specific constitutional limitations, rather than interpretation of general principles like due process, would become the norm in constitutional adjudication. Popular sovereignty and judicial protection for vested rights of property could thus be fully harmonized in the American constitutional order.

Sedgwick merely alluded to these possibilities in his speech at the Broadway Tabernacle. But two younger New York City attorneys, John Bigelow and Elisha P. Hurlbut, elaborated the argument during the summer of 1843. Bigelow, Sedgwick's former law clerk, called for more precise textual protection of vested rights in the *Democratic Review*; Hurlbut, Bigelow's roommate, echoed him in a series of essays for the *Evening Post*. Both complained that, as Bigelow put it, "a man's rights over his own property, are not properly or even decently respected" in the existing constitutional order, because "his land may be taken from him, and his houses torn down, to gratify an unprincipled lust of gain, without any pretence of public necessity." And both protested that, in Hurlbut's words, "the provision in the Constitution of the United States which enjoins a state from passing any law impairing the obligation of contracts, does not come up to our requirement, since that provision is construed not to reach laws which merely affect the remedy." Neither noticed the recent decisions in *Taylor v. Porter* and *Bronson v. Kinzie*. Their approach to constitutional change made such rulings quite dispensable. "Experience has proved it necessary to guard against legislative encroachments by adopting a constitutional code," Hurlbut wrote. "Among other things, the [state] constitution ought to prohibit the legislature from contracting debts without the direct consent of the people through the ballot boxes; from delegating the power of eminent domain to corporations in the manner heretofore practiced; from changing the remedies for the enforcement of rights to any such extent as in the least to impair the right itself; from granting special charters; from conferring special privileges; from granting bounties to particular pursuits; and from interfering with private business."[35]

Hurlbut restated his main point in *Essays on Human Rights and Their Political Guaranties* (1845), essentially a compilation of the articles he wrote two years earlier. "It is triffling with mankind to declare by the constitution that they shall not be deprived of their rights 'unless by the law of the land,'" he insisted, "since it is by law or its mode of administration that most rights are sacrificed." In his view, however, the problem admitted of an easy solution. "A proper constitution must . . . enter into detail—and every year of a nation's experience will enlarge its specification of abuses." Bigelow said much the same thing in his widely noticed 1843 article for the *Democratic Review*. "Constitutional guarantees against the encroachments of the legislative power," he wrote, "are the cogs which the people have fixed upon the machinery of legislation, to prevent its return to the often-rejected absurdities of the past." Because a written constitution "is intended to operate both as a guarantee against encroachment by the legislature upon the rights of the people, and against the political caprices of the people themselves," it followed that "the constitution will require periodical inspection, and comparatively frequent repairs." On this subject, as on so many others, Bigelow added, Thomas Jefferson had it right: "We have always felt that when Mr. Jefferson proposed that every American constitution should be subjected to a periodical revision, once in every twenty years, he had a very correct and philosophical idea of the longevity of all political admonitions, as well as a just sense of the progress of political science among a free people."[36]

An extraordinarily large audience grappled with the arguments advanced in Sedgwick's speech on August 15, 1843, and in the writings of Bigelow and Hurlbut during the months that followed. But the excitement did not stem from their solution to the "countermajoritarian difficulty" in constitutional law. What attracted so much attention was the general proposition they laid before the people of New York. Sedgwick, Bigelow, and Hurlbut spoke for the State Association for Constitutional Reform, an organization established by radical Democrats to generate public support for a resolution of the legislature that, subject to popular ratification, would result in a constitutional convention.

The Logic of Constitutional Reform

The movement for a convention to revise the New York Constitution grew out of Democratic divisions on the internal-improvement question. In 1842 the New York Democracy united behind the Stop and Tax Act that curtailed further expenditures on public works, imposed a direct tax on real property, and pledged a portion of the canal revenues as a sinking fund for payment of the state debt. Its enactment on March 29, 1842, immediately restored confidence in the New York financial system. State bonds carrying 7 percent interest sold at par early in June; 6 percent bonds reached par in September. New York banks, their reserves buoyed by the rising market for government securities, soon eased credit and injected new money into the stream of commerce. The depression was not yet over. But conditions improved even in the canal counties, and

Democrats were quick to claim credit for having saved New York from the battery of repudiation, suspension, and stay laws that had deranged the economies of so many other states. In the election of 1842 voters supplied a ringing endorsement of the Stop and Tax policy. William C. Bouck, the Democratic candidate for governor, carried forty-three out of fifty-nine counties and rolled up a majority four times larger than Seward's in 1840. One reason the Stop and Tax Act proved so popular, however, was its ambiguity. Democratic differences on the "true meaning" of the statute, muted during the 1842 campaign, got thoroughly aired when the legislature convened in January. The upshot was the famous Barnburner-Hunker split in the New York Democracy.[37]

Governor Bouck, a former member of the Canal Board, stated the Stop and Tax gospel according to conservative Democrats in his first annual message, transmitted to the legislature on January 3, 1843. "The general prosperity of the country should assume a more favorable aspect" during the new year, he reported. Government receipts from canal tolls, which had fallen steeply since 1840, would be "favorably affect[ed]" and might even rebound to predepression levels as interregional trade revived. Bouck's bullish forecast had important policy ramifications. The Stop and Tax Act pledged to debt retirement every dollar generated by the property tax and an amount from canal tolls "at least equal to one third of the interest of the canal debt remaining unpaid." But what if the anticipated rise in canal receipts generated a surplus? Did the Stop and Tax Act authorize the use of surplus funds on suspended construction projects? Bouck thought so, and he urged the legislature to provide in advance for that happy day. "I am convinced that the completion of the unfinished work . . . [on the Erie Canal enlargement] would be essentially useful, and some of it may be indispensably necessary," Bouck proclaimed. "The speedy completion of the Black River Canal . . . and the Genessee Valley Canal . . . is doubtless anxiously desired by the friends of these improvements. I do not feel that I should faithfully discharge my duty did I not recommend for your careful consideration these portions of the public works."[38]

Bouck's message stunned the New York Democracy. Many observers thought it was inconceivable that a Democrat could broach the idea of new government spending, however qualified by admonitions about moving with "great caution," just nine months after a majority of the party's assemblymen had voted in favor of the People's Resolution, providing for an amendment to the New York Constitution that would require popular ratification of every law affecting the state debt. Martin Van Buren, writing to William Marcy on January 13, 1843, spoke darkly about "a ruinous schism in our ranks," and Marcy agreed that the party would remain in peril until the governor "put himself right" on the canal question. But the "open profligacy" portended in Bouck's message did not surprise Michael Hoffman. On June 30, 1842, he had written a disconsolate letter to Azariah Flagg, predicting that "the Democratic Party is to be hoaxed in part and in part circumvented, into the nomination of Colonel Bouck." "If successful," he added, the result was bound to be another round of "state expenditure and that perfect bankruptcy, misery, ruin, depravity, and disgrace . . . of which the Southwest and West afford an instructive example." Hoffman understood the short-term calculations of party managers. Nominating a person whose record held out the promise of renewed construction on the public works might enable Democrats to survive Whig competition along the canal routes in western New York. What the party managers failed to appreciate, however, were the long-term costs of playing politics with the state debt.[39]

During the summer of 1842, Hoffman told everyone who would listen that internal-improvement legislation had always unified the Whigs and divided the Democrats. Every project funded by a government loan tended to create another Whig stronghold, and this was true whether or not the bill got support from logrolling Democrats responsive to local interests. If public works helped the Whigs and hurt the Democrats, Hoffman argued, it made political sense to constitutionalize the issue. Enactment of the People's Resolution would remove questions involving government spending from the caldron of partisanship and thrust them upon the people at large. It would simultaneously establish justice and benefit the Democratic Party. But the measure would have no chance in a Bouck regime. "If we are to have further loans and additional debts, I go for a convention and a new constitution," he wrote Flagg following Bouck's nomination. "Monopoly may hiss and locality may yell, but a convention of the people must be called to sit in judgment on the past and command the future."[40]

On the internal-improvements question, the legislature's 1843 session ended in a stalemate. The radicals bottled up one bill to assist the ailing New York and Erie Railroad Company and another, especially favored by Bouck, to spend $500,000 on the lateral canals. Meanwhile, the conservatives killed the People's Resolution with Whig support. William McMurray, a New York City Democrat, did manage to get the proposed constitutional amendment, along with a hard-hitting committee report, to the floor on April 1. "It was from unjust taxation that our forefathers were impelled to throw off the British yoke," McMurray wrote; "but not more oppressive or unequal were British impositions than that system which taxes a man in one section of the state for improvements made in another, not only without benefit to him, but frequently to his direct or consequent injury." In his view, even the phrase internal improvement was a misnomer: "It should rather be called, as it really is, robbery and plunder, inflicted by the strong arm of a bandit government upon the weak, miserable abject and defenseless victims, not of its fostering care, but of its peculation and avarice." Yet the People's Resolution did not come to a vote; shortly after the legislature adjourned, the *Evening Post* endorsed "a plan in agitation" for a constitutional convention. "The improvement party, if not closely watched, will make its appearance stronger in the next legislature than it was in the last," Bryant explained. "We shall be compelled to struggle with them, session after session, at the risk of being overcome by the influences of the lobbies, unless we put an end to the dispute by an amendment of the constitution."[41]

The "agitation" was very well organized. For nine weeks beginning on June 1, 1843, the *Evening Post* periodically announced, with increasing fanfare over time, the formation of county-level associations for constitutional reform throughout the state. Early in August the State Association for Constitutional Reform emerged with Hoffman as its president. "Immense meetings" were held in New York City on August 15 and in Albany on November 21. Smaller rallies occurred in the interim at other scattered locales. As the movement gathered momentum, its objectives proliferated. "To what should the reformation extend?" Hoffman asked in a published letter, dated July 31, to the New York City association; he answered, "to all ascertained abuses." Ten specific objectives followed:

1. [The convention] must retrench expenditure, reform useless offices and make the revenue equal in a short and reasonable period, to the payment of the whole of the public debt, secure that revenue from destruction or diversion by the legislative power, and make it certain that soon the people shall be freed from debt and taxation for it.

2. It must limit the legislative power over debt and expenditure as stringently, at least, as is proposed in the People's Resolution. . . .

3. It must secure the common school . . . and other trust funds from conversion or destruction by the legislative power.

4. It must make all bankers issuing paper money individually responsible for all demands against them, their corporations, or associations.

5. It must fix safe and certain limits to the powers of all municipal bodies to create debts. . . .

6. It must secure the citizen against special legislation and the grant of exclusive privileges, whereby the favored few are authorized by law to devour the many, and by all the ways and means known to experience oblige delegated power in its legislation to regard that law of nature and command of God, which declares that "he that will not work shall not eat."

7. It must limit the officers of government to functions strictly governmental, and to the smallest number, that for a moderate compensation can discharge the duty well, and refer their appointment, as far as practicable, to the people and to the bodies the nearest and most dependent on and responsible to them.

8. It must strip the legislative and executive as far as practicable of the appointing power.

9. It must divest the legislature of all judicial power, and provide courts of law and equity with original and appellate jurisdiction to be held by Judges to be elected by the people for a reasonable term of years. These courts of the people must have power to decide all constitutional questions, and thus maintain the limits set by the constitution on delegated power. . . .

10. My last position is, that the constitution should provide for a convention of the people at least once in *twenty* years—to correct errors, reform abuses, and make all needful improvements more effectually to secure *the equal natural rights of every man.*

Hoffman's "last position" was as significant as his emphasis suggested. The state constitution that went into force in 1822 prescribed a method for amendment by successive legislatures, followed by popular ratification at the polls. But it did not expressly provide for subsequent conventions of the people. Thus Jefferson's maxim that "each generation . . . has . . . a right to choose for itself the form of government it believes the most productive of its happiness" did not merely shape the reformers' objectives. It also supplied a rationale for attaining them by a method unknown to the positive law.[42]

The bulk of Hoffman's professed objectives evinced the radical Democracy's aversion to public debt, special privilege, and the corruption incident to the "spoils system." He proposed to constitutionalize the principles of "equal rights" and direct democracy "as far as practicable." The ninth plank looked to an enhancement of judicial review as a necessary complement to the system. "Divest[ing] the legislature of all judicial power" meant abolishing the New York Court for the Correction of Errors. Established in 1821, the state's highest court consisted of the chancellor, the three justices of the supreme court, and every member of the senate. It sat twice each year to pass on judgments of law and decrees in equity, including those involving constitutional challenges to statutes that the senators had framed in their capacity as legislators. Hoffman regarded the institution as an abomination. So did Sedgwick. "You have no constitution. The State of New York exists without one," he told the crowd at the Broadway Tabernacle on August 15. "The fundamental idea of a constitution is, that it is an instrument in which the people impose restrictions and limits on the legislature, and which that legislature cannot transcend without a direct appeal to the people themselves. No such state of things exists with us, simply because the legislature (or one branch of it) is the highest branch of our judiciary, and passes on the constitutionality of its own acts." For Sedgwick, as for Hoffman, only independent "courts of the people" could be trusted to maintain the limits on delegated power. "The Court of Errors," Sedgwick insisted, "derives its existence from the English House of Lords, it is the relic of a colonial prejudice, and had better be abolished with the other badges of colonial servitude."[43]

The core ideas of New York's constitutional reformers remained unchanged, then, even as the movement's focus shifted from getting the People's Resolution out of the legislature and before the constituent sovereign to securing what Bigelow called "a substantial and comprehensive constitutional reform." Every argument for each particular reform ultimately turned on the closely linked concepts of natural rights and popular sovereignty. When government put rights in jeopardy, the people had the right to demand more appropriate constitutional forms. Nothing like the Dorr War, "the drama which has so lately been played" in Rhode Island, said Sedgwick, should be "re-enact[ed] on the theatre of New York." The state legislature had a duty in 1844 to do precisely what it did in 1820: pass a resolution, by simple majority in each house, authorizing a referendum at the next general election on the question, "convention" or "no convention."[44]

In retrospect, the agenda for constitutional reform omitted an obvious item. Hoffman and the *Evening Post* crowd spoke forthrightly about securing the rights of the people "against all fraud, injustice, oppression, and force," yet did not target manorial tenures for extinction. The lease in fee certainly fit Sedgwick's description of the Court of Errors—"a relic of a colonial prejudice"— and very few radical Democrats were inclined to disagree with the Anti-Rent claim that manorial tenures, like New York's archaic high court, "had better be abolished with the other badges of colonial servitude." In the summer of 1843, however, the manors and great patents of eastern New York had been quiet for more than a year. Nobody knew that the Anti-Rent wars were about to resume with greater fury than ever before. Tenant leaders missed their cue too. When the State Association for Constitutional Reform held its Albany mass meeting on November 21, Smith Boughton and Lawrence Van Deusen, presidents of the Anti-Rent associations in the counties of Rensselaer and Albany, respectively, did not attend. They had a different agenda for 1844. The proposed Act Concerning Tenures by Lease, drafted earlier in the year, already had been endorsed by the rank and file. Boughton and Van Deusen planned to lay it, along with the tenant petitions, before the state legislature in January.

The settled Anti-Rent strategy was rather ironic. The vested rights decisions of 1843 had all but exploded the constitutional theory embedded in the proposed law. Yet the movement for a constitutional convention provided an opportunity to negate the implications of the New York Supreme Court's ruling in *Taylor v. Porter*. If section two of the Anti-Rent bill, authorizing the exercise of eminent domain powers to extinguish manorial tenures, were placed in the very text of the state constitution, the judicial department could not disturb its implementation. In the American constitutional order, only the Constitution of the United States established principles of law that outranked the convictions of each state's constituent sovereign. And in *Barron v. Baltimore* (1833) the Supreme Court, speaking through Chief Justice Marshall, had held that the Fifth Amendment provisions of due process, public use, and just compensation "must be understood as restraining the power of the general government, not as applicable to the States."[45]

Beginning in 1845, some land reformers did identify a convention of the people as the necessary and proper forum for extinguishing the lease in fee. They were as adept as the radical Democrats at manipulating "first principles" derived from natural law and popular sovereignty. But the logic of hitching the Anti-Rent movement to the call for a constitutional convention was temporarily obscured by the dramatic events of 1844. In the spring, Democratic lawmakers invoked *Bronson v. Kinzie* and *Taylor v. Porter* to pillory the proposed Anti-Rent legislation. Shortly afterward, the New York Supreme Court gutted the Exemption Act of 1842 that had brought peace to the Manor of Rensselaerwyck and the great patents of Schoharie County. Impatient landlords made new attempts to break the rent strikes; "Indian" attacks on law enforcement officials followed. Meanwhile, the state's Democratic and Whig party managers grappled with President John Tyler's decision to put the annexation of Texas on the national agenda. The impending presidential election shaped both developments, and the strategy of Anti-Rent leaders changed as the conditions of New York politics changed. After tailoring the Act Concerning Tenures by Lease to Democratic sensibilities, the embattled tenants ended up forging a new alliance with the Whigs.

6

Signs of War

On December 9, 1843, the lead editorial in William Cullen Bryant's *Evening Post* endorsed Martin Van Buren for the presidency. In many respects the editorial was unremarkable. Enough state conventions already had declared for Van Buren to assure a majority at the Democratic National Convention, scheduled for Baltimore on May 27, 1844, and even the Whigs expected to run against him. The *Evening Post* editorial was significant all the same. After beating the drums for a constitutional convention throughout the summer and fall, Bryant acknowledged that the presidency mattered more. As John Bigelow later confessed, the New York radicals "postponed" the agitation in 1844 for fear of "embarrass[ing] the then approaching presidential canvass with a measure which might have periled a result towards which the Democracy of the state were then looking with legitimate feelings of hope and pride."[1]

The quest for unity, if not harmony, within the New York Democracy animated conservatives as well as radicals. It pervaded Governor William C. Bouck's message to the legislature on January 2, 1844. On the two most divisive questions, constitutional reform and government spending for internal improvements, the governor took "a cautious middle course between the extremes of the two sections of his own party." Bouck considered constitutional reform first. Following a paean to the American genius for constitutionalism, he adhered to the conservative position "that the fundamental law should not be frequently changed, nor for light or transient causes." He also resisted the radicals' penchant for invoking the New York convention of 1821 as a precedent that ought to be followed in every succeeding generation. "It was a defect in the constitution of 1777, that it contained no provision for its amendment," Bouck observed. "This created the necessity for the convention of 1821, as the only mode of making amendments, which had been demanded by the people." Because the state's organic law now provided a means for revision by successive legislatures, subject to ratification by the people, he thought the procedure prescribed in the text of the constitution should be obeyed. After throwing cold

water on the call for a convention, however, Bouck endorsed the idea of check-
ing the legislature's power to borrow money with a constitutional amendment.[2]

Governor Bouck tried to be equally accommodating on the canal question.
In 1844, unlike the previous year, he painstakingly distinguished the conservative Democrat approach to government spending from "the spirit of wild speculation and extravagance" that had prevailed during the Whig ascendancy.
Bouck lauded "the wise policy" embodied in the Stop and Tax Act of 1842 and
declared that "the means of doing anything more at this time, than making all
needful repairs, and keeping the canals in a good navigable condition," could
not be obtained without increasing taxes or contracting new debt. "The former
I deem highly inexpedient," he added, "and the latter entirely inadmissible."
Yet the governor had no intention of abandoning his friends in the conservative
ranks. He pointed out that the Stop and Tax Act expressly authorized the use of
canal toll receipts, less an amount equal to one-third of the remaining interest on
the state debt, for repair of existing facilities. "Where new structures are so
nearly finished, that it would cost less to complete them than to keep in repair
the old ones they were designed to supersede," Bouck declared, "they should,
in my judgment, be put in a condition to be used." Consequently he recommended "that the Canal Board be authorized to complete such new works, as in
their opinion, can be done with better economy, than to sustain those designed
to be superseded."[3]

Bouck's conciliatory message set the tone for the legislature's 1844 session.
Assemblyman Horatio Seymour, the Utica conservative who chaired the Canal
Committee, reported out a bill in conformity with the governor's recommendation on April 23. A handful of radicals complained that the broad construction
of "repairs" embedded in the bill would provide "an entering wedge in the
encouragement of promiscuous canal extension." But the ensuing debate was
not acrimonious. The bill contained a "saving clause," which Seymour astutely
put in the bill's last section, providing that "nothing in this act shall be construed to authorize an expenditure of more than one hundred and fifty thousand dollars." This pittance bought so much goodwill for the Democracy in
western New York that even Hoffman did not vote against the bill, though he
did not vote for it. Bouck signed the "Act to provide for the preservation of
certain public works" into law on May 6. Meanwhile, the legislature approved
five constitutional amendments. One constitutionalized the Stop and Tax Act;
another, modeled on the People's Resolution, barred the legislature from incur-
ring any debts, "singly or in the aggregate, at any time, exceed[ing] one million
dollars," without the consent of the voters at a general election. The other three
amendments provided for a larger, more efficient judicial system but kept the
state senate at its apex. Democrats who opposed the People's Resolution cheerfully voted for all five amendments. They had reason to believe that the pro-

posed restriction on the legislature's borrowing power could not possibly get the required two-thirds majority in both houses during 1845.[4]

Only two gaffes marred the Democratic Party's president-making performance. One of them occurred upon the legislature's adjournment. Erastus Corning, chairman of the committee to frame the Democracy's traditional address to the voters, insisted on declaring that Bouck had "adhered with fidelity to the sound policy which has ever characterized Democratic administrations, and advanced the state in a career of prosperity and honor." Twenty-one radicals, including Hoffman and Henry W. Strong, refused to sign the address because it effectively endorsed Bouck's bid for renomination. Augustus Hand believed that the tiff portended division and defeat at the polls. "Confidence seems now all gone," he wrote Van Buren. "Our best men despair." Hand overreacted. Two former state governors, William L. Marcy and William H. Seward, had a much better understanding of "the presidential game," and both described the session's essential dynamic before it even began. "Those who oppose the governor have a strong motive for electing Van Buren to the presidency and would restrain themselves until that matter was concluded," Marcy confided to his diary on September 12, 1843. "Those who support Bouck would willingly sacrifice Van Buren, but not if it meant the governor's defeat. Each party has a strong motive to keep the peace." Seward had reached a comparable conclusion several months earlier: "The factions among our opponents will combine on Van Buren and increase his strength. I indulge no hope of their division . . . as things now stand."[5]

Another mistake came in response to the clamor for land reform on the Manor of Rensselaerwyck. The legislature's Democratic majority was anxious to cast responsibility for the seemingly hopeless tenant agitation on the Whigs, but the opposition outfoxed them. Progressive Whigs in the legislature and the press condemned manorial tenures and blamed the landlords, not the tenants, for the Anti-Rent movement. Beginning in September, the party's Seward-Weed wing approached the question of "voluntary slavery" in precisely the same way it approached the increasingly salient issue of African American slavery. The result was paradoxical. Every signal from the legal environment in 1844 indicated that the Anti-Rent legislative program was patently unconstitutional. Yet encouraging signals from the political environment suggested that the tenants had cause to persevere. By early September, when the state's Whig and Democratic parties nominated candidates for governor, tenant leaders in the counties of Rensselaer, Albany, and Schoharie had transformed the Anti-Rent associations into political action groups and had carried their case against "feudal servitude interminable" into a half-dozen other counties. Party leaders acknowledged that the growing Anti-Rent movement, like the burgeoning drive to annex the Republic of Texas, not only posed a threat to the public peace but would be a factor in the autumn election.

Petitions and Partisanship

Early in January 1844, Smith Boughton arrived in Albany carrying a sheaf of identical petitions signed by the 4,000 members of the Anti-Rent Association of Rensselaer County. The statement of grievances proclaimed that the "unjust and oppressive" leases on Rensselaerwyck "are opposed to the spirit of our republican institutions" and declared that "the claim of those who assume to be lords of the manor, is unfounded and fictitious." Unlike previous tenant petitions, which merely prayed for redress of grievances, this one specified a course of action designed to extinguish the lease in fee. Annexed to the complaint was the proposed Act Concerning Tenures by Lease. It contained two sections. The first provided for the suspension of rent collections until landlords holding under grants from the British government had established the validity of their titles in a court of law. The second authorized the extinguishment of all landlord interests in tenant farms upon payment of compensation fixed by "three disinterested persons."[6]

Jonathan Whipple of Rensselaer laid the Anti-Rent petition before the assembly on January 19. He proposed that it be referred to a select committee composed of "the first legal talent of the house." Jesse Palmer, a Democrat from Delaware County, countered by moving that the petition be sent to a select committee composed of the members from Albany and Rensselaer counties. Palmer's motive was clear enough. All six assemblymen from Albany and Rensselaer were Whigs; he wanted them to tell the tenants that the Anti-Rent bill was unconstitutional. Whipple objected to Palmer's motion. So did his Rensselaer colleague George B. Warren and Levi Shaw of Albany. Each emphasized that the vast majority of their tenant constituents were in a state of high excitement. "It would be better," Whipple remarked, "to refer the matter to a select committee who are wholly uninterested." The reluctance of the Rensselaer and Albany representatives merely stiffened the Democrats' resolve to give them the Anti-Rent petition. Clark Cochrane, the last Democrat to speak, disclaimed "any political considerations" in supporting Palmer's motion. "If the matter is referred to these two delegations, who are presumed to be favorably disposed to the subject, and if they are to report that there is no relief here," he declared, "it will quiet the excitement and set the matter to rest—and the state will be put to no more expense to carry on wars against the tenants." Palmer's motion passed a few moments later with all but two of the Whig votes cast against it.[7]

The assembly took up the matter again on Tuesday, January 22. Samuel Stevens of Albany had been absent the previous week; he now asked to be excused from the Select Committee which the house had charged with reporting on the petition from the Anti-Rent Association of Rensselaer County. Stevens explained that he was counsel for the estate of Stephen Van Rensselaer III. "Should an adverse report be made," he asserted, "the tenants might say their cause has not had a fair hearing, inasmuch as one of their judges was interested as counsel for the landlords." Nobody was disposed to deny Stevens's request. But a Democrat from Queens suggested that all the members from Albany and Rensselaer be excused. This proposition evoked a lengthy speech by Michael Hoffman. "I was not in my seat the other day when the unfortunate reference of this subject was made by the house," he said. "We should not only excuse the gentleman who now asks it, but every member of the Select Committee and send the subject [to the Judiciary Committee] where it should have been in the first instance." Hoffman brandished *Bronson v. Kinzie* as a bar to the first section of the bill proposed by the petitioners; he held up *Taylor v. Porter* as a bar to the second section. "No law can be passed to set aside the objectionable features of these leases," he declared. "We can only provide against like evils for the future—and for the future only. We can say that hereafter, no lease shall contain such clauses as are in these complained of. That is all we can do. We can speak for the future—we must be dumb for the past."[8]

Hoffman's speech might have stampeded the assembly if it had been delivered three days earlier. But it came too late. Whipple stood up as soon as Hoffman sat down; he asked the house "if it is customary to discharge a committee before they ask it themselves." William F. Allen, chairman of the Judiciary Committee, replied that it was not and Whipple remarked that he "would have nothing to say." Warren, his more loquacious Rensselaer colleague, explained why the members of the Select Committee had no intention of relinquishing their charge. "On Saturday I opposed the motion to refer to the joint delegation from Albany and Rensselaer with all my might," he said. "But the house in its wisdom . . . sent the subject to this committee, thus by its act alleging that interest was no objection, and I consider that vote as a virtual instruction to the committee to make out as good a case for the tenants as possible." Warren's remarks must have stunned Palmer, Cochrane, and the other Democrats who had cheerfully surrendered their party's control of the matter on January 19. Instead of acting responsibly and telling the anti-renters that the legislature could not pass their unconstitutional proposal, the Select Committee seemed determined to increase the Whig Party's political capital among the tenants. Stevens's request to be excused was carried by a voice vote; when the house adjourned shortly afterward, the Democrats went away muttering about how they had outsmarted themselves.[9]

The assembly's Democratic majority had an opportunity to mitigate the damage a few days later. Assemblyman Cole presented a petition signed by 2,000 members of the Anti-Rent Association of Albany County on January 26, and Horatio Seymour immediately moved that it be referred to the Judiciary Committee. Allen, who chaired that body, professed to be puzzled by the motion. "Is it the design," he asked, "to have two reports, adverse perhaps to

each other?" Seymour ducked the question, but he claimed that such a reference was "proper and parliamentary" all the same. Hoffman, though inclined to
disagree with Seymour, stated that he would "be governed . . . not so much by
my own view of propriety, as by other considerations." Warren of Rensselaer
had promised to put the anti-renters' proposed legislation in the best possible
light, and Hoffman wanted to make sure that the Judiciary Committee would
have time to kill the bill with a report of its own. "If at this time they are still in
doubt—if they have taken no decisive action," he said, "it will make some
difference in my vote." Warren's answer satisfied Hoffman; the house rejected
Seymour's motion on a voice vote and referred the petition to the Select
Committee. But a plot line for the remainder of the legislature's 1844 session
had been established. The Whigs from Albany and Rensselaer were going to
report out the Anti-Rent bill, and the Democrats on the Judiciary Committee
were going to reject it on constitutional grounds. Hoffman's call for prospective
legislation prohibiting leases in perpetuity, which would have done nothing
to alter conditions on Rensselaerwyck in any event, got lost in the ensuing
shuffle.[10]

The report of the Select Committee contained no surprises. Whipple declared that the Van Rensselaer family's perpetual leases tended "to convert their
tenants into abject serfs or slaves, and make them mere appendages of the soil,
and to be kept forever in a condition of hopeless vassalage, without a prospect
of relief." In theory, at least, they could sell their farms and walk away. But
nobody wanted to buy property encumbered in perpetuity with an "intolerable" legal relation to "the lords of the manor." The value of the tenants'
houses, barns, and other improvements—fruits of backbreaking labor—was
thus artificially low. Heads of households determined to bite the bullet and sell
out at "great sacrifice" were nonetheless bound by contract to forfeit one-
quarter of the purchase price as well. Although "the American people are
emphatically an emigrating people," it was not surprising that relatively few
inhabitants of Rensselaerwyck had joined the vast stream of "farmers and
mechanics [who] have emigrated to new settlements in the West."[11]

Whipple emphasized that manorial tenures not only blighted New York
society but also oppressed the tenants. The lease in fee included covenants that
"obstruct trade, by fettering the transfer of property." It tended "in a very
material degree to discourage that spirit of improvement so indispensable to the
growth of every community." And it deprived the tenants of "that spirit of
independence which is not humbled by the payment of an annual tribute,
acknowledges no superior, and which raises the American farmer of more
favored districts to a rank in the social scale never attained by the working man
of any country but our own." Withal, the conditions in rural Albany and
Rensselaer constituted "a reproach to the intelligence and civilization of a free

republic." Something had to be done. The petitioners' grievances were very real, and there was "abundant evidence that a deep and enduring feeling of discontent pervades the whole agricultural population of the Manor of Rensselaerwyck." If the legislature hesitated before doing something decisive, Whipple reported, "it may reasonably be presumed that this feeling will increase, and that the public peace will again be disturbed, and the welfare of society be endangered thereby. The good of the community seems, therefore, to require immediate legislative action, if any is practicable."[12]

Practicability was the rub, but the members from Albany and Rensselaer had a convenient excuse for ignoring it. "Your committee not being any of them members of the legal profession," Whipple explained, "do not deem themselves qualified to suggest any specific plan of relieving the tenants of Rensselaerwyck from the oppressions of which they complain." Nor were they competent to evaluate the Act Concerning Tenures by Lease, which the committee submitted to the house "in compliance with the wish of the petitioners." Whipple dutifully summarized the main points of the argument against the Van Rensselaer family's title. He also reported that the second section, authorizing tenants to extinguish their landlord's interest in the land upon payment of just compensation, was attractive because it would "put an end to the system . . . in case the proper law tribunals shall decide the title of the proprietors of the Manor of Rensselaerwyck to be valid." But the committee said nothing about the legislature's competence to enact the eminent domain scheme.[13]

Summarizing the report of the Select Committee is easier than characterizing it. Two interpretations of Whipple's handiwork spring to mind; they are not mutually exclusive. The first would take the members from Albany and Rensselaer at their word. They saw a wrong and wanted to make things right. "The power to remedy the grievances complained of by the petitioners must reside somewhere," Whipple remarked. "If so, where else can it reside but in the representatives of the people of the state?"[14] Yet the arguments of the lawyers who appeared before the committee, replete with subtle variations on "the rule" of *Bronson v. Kinzie* or *Taylor v. Porter*, confused and eventually disabled them. Viewed from this perspective, the report was directed at the Judiciary Committee; its message could not have been more clear. Whipple and his colleagues told the assembly's lawyers that the leases in force on Rensselaerwyck were sores on the body politic and the proposed Act Concerning Tenures by Lease would provide an effective remedy. If the legislature could not enact the bill, the considerations of justice and policy underlying any constitutional impediments should be more persuasive than the case against manorial tenures.

The second interpretation would dismiss the Select Committee's report as partisan propaganda. The Whig members from Albany and Rensselaer, having championed the tenant cause and declared that only "immediate legislative action" could forestall violence in the manor counties, neither evaluated nor endorsed the Anti-Rent bill. They merely shifted the entire burden of political responsibility to the Democratic Party. They did so, moreover, knowing full well that the Democrats on the Judiciary Committee were prepared to kill the measure on constitutional grounds. Viewed from this perspective, the report was directed at the New York electorate; its message could not have been more clear. If the "Indians" returned to Rensselaerwyck and the manor became a blood-stained battleground, the people should blame the Democrats and not the Whigs.

William F. Allen, chairman of the Judiciary Committee, instinctively grasped this second interpretation. He was angry about the Select Committee's performance, too, especially after Thurlow Weed, quick as always to disseminate an effective piece of partisan literature, printed Whipple's report in the *Evening Journal* on April 4. Allen understood that his principal duty was to explain why the bill framed by the Anti-Rent associations, as he put it, "would be declared unconstitutional" and thus "would but subject [the tenants] to an expensive litigation, without being of the least service."[15] The legal analysis had to be so convincing, moreover, that the Anti-Rent agitation would subside before the presidential election. But the report of the Select Committee complicated the task in ways that he understood only dimly. Allen regarded the Democratic Party as his principal client in the cause; he felt compelled to respond to the transparently partisan salvos Whipple and his colleagues had fired at the Democracy. Doing so, however, required him to address New York voters as well as the tenants of Rensselaerwyck. Allen never did get a clear fix on his audience; consequently his report blended equal measures of thoughtful legal analysis, partisan invective, and impolitic exaggerations. The resulting mixture was highly explosive. It enraged the tenants, and it gave the landlords a false sense of security. The only beneficiary was the Whig Party.

Land Reform and Democratic Constitutionalism

Assemblyman Allen, a stodgy conservative from Oswego, dissected the proposed Act Concerning Tenures by Lease with the same plodding precision that later characterized his opinions for the New York Supreme Court. He began by describing the purpose and effect of the bill's first section, which provided that all "persons who claim to derive title from the British government" had to establish the validity of their title before the conditions of any long-term lease might be enforced by law. Counsel for the Anti-Rent associations, Allen reported, conceived this provision as a mere relaxation of the common law rule, in force "from time immemorial," prohibiting the tenant from questioning the title of his landlord. Yet that conception was not strictly accurate. In point of fact, "the proposed law not only provides that the tenant may dispute the title of his landlord, but goes farther, and puts the landlord upon proof of title before he can enforce the conditions of the lease, or even put the tenant on his defense." The burden of proof thus imposed upon Hudson Valley landlords would not be easy to meet. Parties and witnesses to the British land grants had long since died; parts of the documentary record for some titles had no doubt been lost or destroyed by fire. The purpose of the bill's first section, then, was to compel Hudson Valley landlords to prove something that in a great many instances might be unprovable.[16]

In New York, as in all other common law jurisdictions, the statute of limitations ordinarily spared landowners from such an ordeal. *Humbert v. Trinity Church*, decided by the New York Supreme Court in 1840, was a leading case in point. There the court, speaking through Justice Esek Cowen, rebuffed an attempt to impeach the title of New York City's largest landlord. "Statutes limiting real actions . . . have with great propriety been termed statutes of repose," Cowen explained. "They fix a term broadly marked and easily proved [twenty years, with some qualifications, in New York], at which litigation is arrested; beyond which every man is enabled to pronounce that his possessions are no longer open to disturbance." In Allen's judgment, Justice Cowen's remarks on the gravity of the problem posed by *Humbert* were also instructive. The petitioner had asked the court to withdraw Trinity Church from protection of the statute on the ground that a fraud had been committed in the seventeenth century. "We are asked to throw both parties back upon the litigation of a documental title, which looks for its origin to the Dutch Dynasty before 1663," Cowen replied. "This it is conceded must be done, if at all, not merely through evidence obscured by the ordinary mists of tradition in a settled government, and under a well regulated system of conveyancing; but evidence which comes to us through the mutations of empires, the fury of revolutions, repeated changes in the law of descents . . . and great defects at all times in the method of perpetuating the evidence of their existence." Enacting the first section of the Act Concerning Tenures by Lease would impose those very insuperable difficulties on the parties and on the courts.[17]

Allen was equally troubled by the anticipated effect of the bill's first section. "The tenants insist," he wrote, "that they should be permitted to remain in possession, rent free, unless the lessor shall prove by *legal evidence* his title, leaving them to take advantage of any apparent defect in the title, whether growing out of the loss of documentary evidence or any other cause." This result seemed just to anti-renters steeped in the labor theory of value. Allen, working from the quite different maxim that "he who asks equity must do equity," disagreed. "The petitioners, or those under whom they claim, have come into the occupation of the land by the consent of him whose title they now seek to dispute and ask to have established, under a contract which is mutual, imposing conditions upon each of the parties," he wrote. "They now ask that they may be allowed to remain in possession of the lands, and that the landlord shall abide by his contract by which he has engaged to suffer them to remain in possession, and to guarantee to them the quiet enjoyment of the premises, but that they shall be released from the performance of their part of the same contract." Allen believed that the "bare statement of this proposition" undercut the high moral ground claimed by anti-renters. It also supplied ammunition for his own claim that the first section of the proposed Act Concerning Tenures by Lease would violate the Constitution's prohibition of laws impairing the obligation of contracts.[18]

Counsel for the tenants strenuously argued that the bill's first section did not disturb rights secured by the Contract Clause. But the Supreme Court's "recent decision" in *Bronson v. Kinzie* compelled a different conclusion. The stay laws of Illinois had been struck down, Allen pointed out, because the Court declined to "sanction a distinction between the right and the remedy which would render the [Contract Clause] illusive and nugatory." Yet stay laws were puny instruments of oppression and injustice compared with the first section of the proposed Act Concerning Tenures by Lease. The purpose of the bill was to "absolutely destroy many contracts of lease, not from any actual want of title, but from the want of the necessary evidences of that title, . . . [by] imposing conditions upon the landlord to which he never would have assented in making the contract." And the effect of the bill was to secure the tenants' possession of their farms while nullifying the contracts that enabled them to enter the land in the first place. If the Anti-Rent measure did not impair a right through the remedy, it was hard to imagine one that would.[19]

Allen was just as adamant about the legislature's want of power to enact section two of the bill. It provided that "any person holding lands by lease in perpetuity" might petition for an appraisal of his contractual obligations and, upon payment of such a sum, extinguish the landlord's interest in his farm. "We suppose," Allen said, "that this section was framed in pursuance of the suggestions contained in the report of 1840." William A. Duer Jr., his Whig rival at the Oswego bar, had "read the words 'public use' as synonymous with 'public purposes,' or 'public good,'" and had "contend[ed] that it is as much for the public use or public good that the tenures by which land is held, should be so regulated as to promote agricultural improvement and enterprise, as that highways and canals should be constructed." In Allen's view, this conception of the eminent domain power, though "ingenious," was unsound. Acting on it "would, by implication, enlarge the power of . . . [state government] beyond the strict letter of the constitution." Allen's most arresting claim, however, was that "no precedent can be found to sanction" the general theory of eminent domain embedded in the bill's second section. Duer had claimed otherwise in his 1840 report. He put special emphasis on *Beekman v. Saratoga & Schenectady Railroad Co.* (1831) and *Harding v. Goodlett* (1832), a Tennessee decision upholding an act that authorized private property to be taken, upon payment of just compensation, for "a mill site." Allen reported that every member of the Judiciary Committee had read both cases. All of them agreed that Duer's first authority was weak and the second weaker still.[20]

The language in *Beekman* was merely obiter dictum in Allen's eyes. At issue there, he explained, was the devolution of the state's eminent domain power in a charter granted to a railroad corporation. Comparable legislation had been enacted throughout the Union, and appellate courts had found such laws to be constitutional everywhere the issue arose. "But they have been so held," Allen wrote, "because, although the corporation was a private corporation, yet the use of the land appropriated was public." Every statute incorporating a railroad company invested the firm with public duties, including a duty to transport all freight and passengers on reasonable terms. It followed that a railroad corporation qualified, under the "public use" requirement, to expropriate landowners for a right-of-way. An excellent test for distinguishing public uses from private ones, Allen observed, had been formulated by Justice Henry Baldwin in *Bonaparte v. Camden & Amboy Railroad* (1830): "The true criterion is, whether the objects, uses and purposes of the incorporation are for public convenience or private emolument, and whether the public can participate in them by right or only by permission." Acts chartering railroad corporations met this test; the second section of the proposed Act Concerning Tenures by Lease did not.[21]

Allen understood Duer's reliance on the *Beekman* case. Focusing on the language of a prior decision, while ignoring both the facts and alternative grounds for reaching the same result, was a time-honored technique for capitalizing a welcome precedent. But Allen was perplexed by Duer's decision to invoke *Harding v. Goodlett*. There the Tennessee Supreme Court had indeed upheld the taking of private property for gristmills, but its opinion exploded the Whig theory of eminent domain. "By the laws of that state," Allen reported, "grist mills are public—the public have a right to use them." In return for the privilege conferred, the Tennessee statute required mill keepers to grind everyone's grain "according to turn," regulated their measures, and fixed their rates. It also exempted them from serving in the militia and from working on the public highways. As the Tennessee court flatly stated, "it is emphatically a public use for which the property is required and to which it is appropriated. The grist mill is a public mill—the miller is a public servant." In the same case, moreover, the court held that the plaintiff's land could not be flooded under the statute because the petitioner also planned to build a sawmill and a papermill on the site. Those mills, explained the Tennessee court, "have no public character." The identical principle could be found in *Taylor v. Porter*. Legislatures were competent to authorize compensated takings for public roads, railways, and gristmills because the public used those things as a matter of right. But legislatures had no power to authorize compensated takings for private roads, sawmills, and ironworks because the public used those facilities only with the owner's permission. Because the farms of Albany and Rensselaer fell into the latter category, section two of the Anti-Rent bill was clearly unconstitutional.[22]

Allen packaged his legal analysis in an explosive wrapper. His report began with scathing attacks on Governor William Seward's message to the legislature in 1840, on the act establishing the Manor Commission passed later the same year, and on Whipple's report for the Select Committee. In each instance, he asserted, "vague promises and assurances of relief have been held out to the tenantry, [but] no definite action has been proposed or had. . . . Hopes have been excited and kept alive, only to be blasted and disappointed." As they awaited the day of deliverance dangled before them, moreover, anti-renters had periodically assaulted law enforcement officials. Allen argued that Seward was as responsible as anyone for the "pernicious and dangerous" situation that now loomed so large before the New York body politic. Although the Whig governor had denounced manorial tenures as " 'oppressive, antirepublican and degrading' " in 1840, he never explained "how, by acting upon the remedies only, and without impairing the obligation of contracts, the legislature could evisc[er]ate the covenants in the leases complained of, and assimilate them to the more modern leases." Duer had shown that any hope of relief through the right-remedy distinction was "illusory and deceptive" and held up the eminent domain power as a plausible alternative. Yet the Whigs had not acted on Duer's "dangerous doctrine." They "merely recommended the appointment of a commission to negotiate between the landlord and the tenants, and the commission was appointed and of course effected nothing."[23]

Thus the Select Committee organized in 1844 merely followed the Whig Party's established routine. Having once again informed the tenants "that their condition is degrading and serf-like in the extreme," the Select Committee had reported out a bill but "nowhere recommended its passage." In Allen's view, the only possible explanation for such a consistent pattern of behavior was the Whig quest for partisan advantage in the manor counties. He deplored the consequences. "To say that there are great and grievous wrongs resting upon a large and respectable class of citizens, and that we have the power to redress those wrongs, and yet do it not," Allen wrote, "is to inflict an injury greater than the injury sought to be redressed." In contrast to the Whigs, whose unscrupulous manipulation of the manor question "only tends to add fuel to the flame already kindled," Allen promised "to meet the questions presented by the [tenant] memorialists fully, and to express an opinion with candor and justice, but with fearlessness." He vowed, in other words, to extinguish the Anti-Rent "flame" forever.[24]

Allen returned to this objective after he had condemned the proposed Act Concerning Tenures by Lease on constitutional grounds. He made two moves. First, he grasped an old adage—"If it ain't broke, don't fix it"—and turned it topsy-turvy. "It is idle to talk of the degradation and hardships of the tenants when it is well known that no relief can be extended," he declared. "But your committee are firmly convinced that the degradation and hardships exist but in the imagination." Second, he took up the title to the Manor of Rensselaerwyck. He described the contents of the "numerous papers connected with the title" and attempted to answer, by the evidence and logical inferences drawn from it, every allegation of fraud and chicanery that Anti-Rent witnesses had raised during the Select Committee's hearings. Allen should have known better. His constitutional objection to the first section of the proposed Act Concerning Tenures by Lease was predicated on the difficulty, not to say impossibility, of proving the validity of "ancient titles." But the impulse to resolve the manor question for all time distorted his judgment. "In conclusion," he reported, "your committee are compelled to say, that if possession under color of title for 207 years, and actual title under the legitimate government of the land, for 140 years . . . is not a perfect title, it would be extremely difficult to find one; there can certainly be none in this state."[25]

The attempt to square the circle did not succeed. Allen's condescending claim that tenants in perpetuity had no legitimate complaints bordered on the outrageous. And his analysis of the Van Rensselaer title contained several errors of fact and a great many interpretive leaps of faith, all of which the anti-renters on Rensselaerwyck immediately identified and rebutted. Under the circumstances, they had cause for refusing to believe a word of the Judiciary Committee's demonstration that the Anti-Rent bill was unconstitutional. The *Freeholder*, an Albany newspaper established in 1845, called the Allen Report "a gross insult to the tenants, an unpardonable neglect of duty, a gratuitous fraud upon the public." Anti-Rent publicists elaborated the claim for audiences all over the state. "The tenants deem themselves to have a just cause of complaint," Troy attorney Henry Z. Hayner explained to the readers of Horace Greeley's *Tribune*. "They think it might about as well have been left to Van Rensselaer to draw the report. They do not mean to be crowded out of the legislature in this contemptuous and contemptible manner." Burton A. Thomas, secretary of the Anti-Rent Association of Rensselaer County, even retailed the motive for Allen's handiwork. "The Committee of the Judiciary, you may be assured," he declared in May 1844, "has made a handsome sum of money out of the Van Rensselaers."[26]

The gravity of the charges against the Judiciary Committee underscored the tenants' desperation. If Allen was right about the constitutional limitations that fettered the legislature, the Anti-Rent movement had no future. The leadership's first task, then, was to sustain the morale of association members; Thomas concocted the bribery story to rally the tenant membership rather than to persuade the general public. But the movement could not survive without influential allies in government and the press. How to get them, how to transform the structure of political opportunity at Albany, became the question of the hour following the legislature's adjournment on May 10. While the Anti-Rent associations fretted about their precarious situation, however, help came from an unanticipated source. The emergence of an urgent new issue in national politics disrupted the calculations of New York Democrats, altered the configuration of party dialogue, and enhanced the tenants' chances of getting another hearing in Albany.

Texas and the Reorientation of Parties

On April 27, 1844, one day after the New York assembly received the Allen Report and tabled the proposed Act Concerning Tenures by Lease, the *Evening Post* published a secret treaty of annexation that had been concluded between the United States and the Republic of Texas. President John Tyler had submitted the treaty, still under a ban of secrecy, to the Senate for its "advice and consent" on April 22. Senator Benjamin Tappan, an Ohio Democrat, leaked the agreement and the accompanying State Department correspondence, and William Cullen Bryant printed the documents with alacrity.

The treaty itself, though inherently controversial, had been rumored for weeks and contained few surprises. Texas agreed to become a territory of the United States and to cede its public domain for a consideration of $350,000 in cash and the assumption of its public debt (up to $10 million) by the United States. The instrument also guaranteed "all titles and claims to real estate," which included some 65 million acres and a few land claims that rivaled Rensselaerwyck in size. But the big scoop in the pile of documents Bryant acquired from Senator Tappan was a diplomatic dispatch, dated April 18, from newly appointed Secretary of State John C. Calhoun to Sir Richard Pakenham, the British minister to the United States. Calhoun's letter claimed that African Americans had achieved the highest elevation of intelligence and civilization in the slaveholding South, implied that the free states had been wrong to abolish property rights in people, and declared that the determination of the United States to annex Texas arose from its duty to protect and perpetuate slavery, "in reality a political institution essential to the peace, safety, and prosperity" of the American republic. "After reading this paper," Bryant told a Senate investigating committee a week later, "the people of the United States will not hesitate in making up their minds in respect to the infamy of the project."[27]

The Washington press printed two documents of equal national interest on the same day Bryant broke the treaty story. The *National Intelligencer*, a Whig print, carried Henry Clay's "Raleigh Letter" on the Texas question; the *Globe* printed Martin Van Buren's letter on the same topic to William H. Hammet of Mississippi. Neither presidential hopeful had seen Calhoun's dispatch to Pakenham, and neither addressed the relationship between annexation and slavery. Instead, they underscored the fact that Mexico had never acknowledged Texan independence. Clay described the proposed treaty as "a measure compromising the national character, involving us certainly in war with Mexico." His vision of North America comprehended three republics—the United States, Texas, and Canada—with common interests but separate governments. "True wisdom," wrote Clay, "points to the duty of rendering [the Union's] present members happy, prosperous, and satisfied with each other, rather than an attempt to introduce alien members, against common consent, and with the certainty of deep dissatisfaction." Van Buren's letter was much longer. He recounted the history of American relations with Mexico since the declaration of Texan independence in 1836, emphasizing that "the contest between Texas and Mexico, for the sovereignty of the former," had been the crux of his opposition to immediate annexation during his term in the White House. "It has hitherto been our pride and our boast," Van Buren remarked, "that while the lust of power, with fraud and violence in its train, has led other and differently constituted nations of the earth to aggressive action and conquest, our movements in these respects have always been regulated by reason and justice."[28]

Clay's position was standard Whig doctrine even in the South, and the party unanimously nominated him for president five days later. But "Texas fever" permeated the southern Democracy; the Hammet letter put Van Buren's quest for a third consecutive nomination into instant jeopardy. Silas Wright, New York's senior member of the United States Senate, reported from Washington on May 6 that "the state of things here is as bad as it can be." Thomas Ritchie, editor of the *Richmond Enquirer* and a close friend of Van Buren's for twenty years, felt "compelled" to inform him that the Hammet letter "has produced a condition of political affairs which I did not believe to be possible. . . . We cannot carry Virginia for you." Even Andrew Jackson deserted him. "The die was cast" with the publication of the Hammet letter, he wrote from the Hermitage. Electing Van Buren now would be like trying "to turn the current of the Mississippi."[29]

The New York Democracy, anticipating the erosion of support for their man in the South, tried to do what Jackson said could not be done. On April 24 a huge throng attended a "Great Anti-Annexation Meeting" at the Broadway Tabernacle, where Theodore Sedgwick Jr. insisted that "the government seems to be acting under a perfect hallucination as to the subject of slavery," and David Dudley Field, his former law partner, urged Democrats everywhere to think hard about the treaty's consequences. "The annexation of Texas is war with Mexico!" Field proclaimed. "Your troops must occupy the fortresses of Texas. Your troops instead of Texan troops must defend them against Mexico. Are you prepared for war?" In the hectic days that followed, Bryant appealed to the principles that had cemented the Democratic coalition for a generation. "If we understand the doctrine of states rights," the *Evening Post* asserted on May 6, "it is that the different states are only members of a general partnership, and not the elements of a consolidated government. According to this theory, it is manifest, certainly, that no new partner should be admitted into the firm, until the older members have been regularly consulted."[30]

Bryant spoke "with great frankness" about the party's future on the eve of the Democratic National Convention. "Make it a test of competency to be for the annexation of Texas, and you disband the Democratic Party," he observed. "With Mr. Van Buren for a candidate, we shall carry New York triumphantly. Set him aside because he does not entertain the opinion concerning the occupation of Texas which is most in fashion at the South, and the vote of New York is inevitably lost." Silas Wright posited the same ominous result. Stand firm against annexation, he wrote Van Buren, and "leave to the convention the responsibility of disbanding the Democratic Party of the nation, if that must be done."[31]

When the Democratic Convention assembled in Baltimore on May 27, between 148 and 154 delegates were pledged to vote for Van Buren. One of them, Henry D. Gilpin, immediately reported his disgust with the "most reckless and desperate system of political intrigue that I have ever witnessed." Much of the "intrigue" focused on the question of whether two-thirds or a simple majority should be necessary for nomination. On the convention's first day, Benjamin F. Butler, Van Buren's floor manager, delivered an impassioned speech in favor of "the good old doctrine of democracy that the majority should rule," but the unanimous vote of the South plus Michigan, Indiana, and Illinois and a few scattered votes from other states passed the two-thirds rule 148-116. After eight ineffectual ballots, Butler withdrew Van Buren from the race and cast New York's vote for James K. Polk of Tennessee. The ensuing stampede to "Young Hickory" culminated in his unanimous nomination. To appease the Van Buren forces, the convention offered Silas Wright the party's nomination for vice-president. Wright declined. George M. Dallas of Pennsylvania accepted the second spot on the ticket, and the convention adjourned on May 30. Ten days later, the Senate rejected President Tyler's annexation treaty. But the New York Democracy had already suffered a crushing blow. The national party's decision at Baltimore required the New Yorkers to parade before the voters saddled with a presidential candidate expressly committed to annexation "at the earliest practical moment" and implicitly devoted to the luxuriation of slavery within the United States.[32]

Van Buren and his New York friends found some consolation in the fact that Polk was a Democrat of the Jackson school. "Young Hickory" favored tariff reduction and a revival of the Independent Treasury; he opposed all forms of government spending for internal improvements, including the distribution of public-land receipts among the several states. In early June, the stalwarts of the New York Democracy lauded Polk's public philosophy and the "uprightness of his course" at the convention. "If we could not have Mr. Van Buren," John A. Dix wrote Comptroller Azariah Flagg on June 14, "certainly they could not do so well as to give us Colonel Polk." Wright felt the same way. "Our Democracy will support faithfully the Baltimore ticket," he informed Joel R. Poinsett, the staunch Jacksonian from South Carolina, "if there be no more southern bad faith, no [more] sectional issues raised, to produce further suspicions." Bryant, Sedgwick, Field, and four other Barnburners believed that Wright's terms were too generous. Early in July they circulated a letter that endorsed Polk but called on Democrats to repudiate the annexation plank in the Baltimore platform as having "no relation to the principles of the party" and urged the defeat of pro-Texas candidates for Congress. The "secret circular" did not remain a secret for very long; none of the targeted party leaders endorsed the course of action proposed by the *Evening Post* crowd. Yet the circular underscored the radicals' discontent and reinforced their principal demand on the state organization. If the New York Democracy intended to rally around Polk and battle the Whigs on questions of economic policy, the Barnburners wanted Wright, not Bouck, on the ticket for governor.[33]

Nominating Wright for governor made sense. He had been in Washington for more than a decade and had tactfully remained aloof during the fierce intraparty struggles in Albany over internal improvements and constitutional reform. Conservatives liked him and respected him as much as the radicals. Even Marcy, who favored Bouck's renomination, called Wright "the most perfect specimen of a Democrat in the nation, and one of its ablest statesmen." Nobody doubted that the addition of Wright would strengthen the Democratic ticket, reduce the saliency of Texas annexation in the New York campaign, and enhance Polk's chances of capturing the state's crucial electoral votes. But Wright did not want to be governor. His wife loved Washington and hated the state capital; he could hardly bear the thought of officiating the "miserable Albany feuds" among Democrats. Besides, he confided to Albert H. Tracy, "local interests and desire for office have become so predominant in our state, that I see no opportunity for any man to gain strength by administering our government." On August 1, after several county conventions already had declared for him, Wright wrote a public letter unequivocally stating that "I cannot, under any circumstances, consent to become a competitor for the nomination." His "policy of declination," as Van Buren termed it, was genuine. Yet it also helped the party. For several weeks prior to the state convention, which assembled in Syracuse on September 4, Democratic journalists focused on Wright's availability rather than on disputes with the opposing faction in the state organization and the Texas enthusiasts in the party's southern wing. His very name helped to keep the peace.[34]

The Whigs bubbled with confidence all summer. Every issue before the voters of New York seemed to portend victory in November. A spurt in manufacturing output spearheaded a growing national economy in 1844; Horace Greeley and Thurlow Weed gleefully attributed the recovery to the Tariff of 1842, and they retailed the gospel of protection almost daily in the *New York Tribune* and the *Albany Evening Journal*. Whig organs promised that the recovery would surge forward with the election of Henry Clay. The resumption of distribution, which President Tyler's vetoes had suspended, would not only assist Pennsylvania, Michigan, Indiana, and Illinois "in meeting their engagements and redeeming their faith" but also enable New York to repeal the contractionist Stop and Tax Act. Whigs believed that a majority of New York voters approved all these measures; the Democrats opposed them. "Their policy, so far at least as the business and industry and general prosperity of the country are concerned, or may be affected, is a negative one," Daniel Dewey Barnard wrote in an early August letter to his constituents. "Their doctrine is that the people should not expect too much from the government. In this respect, they seem to me to think very much of the offices of government, and very little of the obligations of government." For Barnard, as for Greeley, Clay's vaunted American System was "the paramount issue of the campaign." But the "nefarious" scheme to annex Texas supplied an impelling means for securing that long-deferred mix of public policies.[35]

The Texas question did not merely hurt the New York Democracy. It also had a synergistic effect on the principles Whigs always had espoused. Day after day, Greeley and Weed claimed that the "slave power" held the Democratic Party in thralldom. "Locofocos" from the South demanded a pro-Texas candidate at Baltimore, and they got one. "Locofocos" from the South also favored free trade; if Polk were elected, they would get that as well. Yet the "slave power" had no principles. When "the embarrassed states in our confederacy" asked the national government for assistance in refinancing their crushing debts, Weed pointed out in late June, "Locofocoism had no friendship or sympathy for sister states. They were left to struggle with debts which involved us all in pecuniary dishonor." But the Democratic Party walked a different walk in order to bring Texas into the Union. If they succeeded, "we assume and pay the national debt of Texas for the inglorious privilege of allowing the American eagle to soar, and the American flag to float, over millions of acres of newly acquired slave territory!" Weed claimed that the Whig Party, in contrast, was the party of peace, prosperity, and free labor. Clay opposed the annexation of Texas; when the Senate rejected President Tyler's treaty, all but one of the Senate's twenty-six Whigs voted against it. Now that the Texas question had unmasked the "Locofocos" of the North, revealing them to be "doughfaced" minions of the slaveocracy, the result would surely be defeat for the New York Democracy in November. "We believe there are five thousand voters in the state, who have hitherto voted the Van Buren ticket," Greeley declared, "who have immovably resolved not to vote for Polk and Dallas. Some of them have gone over to Abolition; others will not vote at all. . . . Such is our undoubting conviction."[36]

New York Whigs stood shoulder to shoulder on the interlocking issues of protection, distribution, and Texas annexation. On one tactic involving the "slave power" theme, however, the party's progressives and conservatives divided just as they had on land reform in 1840–41. Barnard, for example, vigorously attacked the Democratic Party's commitment to the extension of slavery within the Union. "Increasing the political power of the slave interest," he said in August, would perpetuate the "great evil" of African American bondage. Barnard was quick to add, however, that "the compromises of the Constitution," not to mention the doctrine of vested rights, barred any attempt to meddle with slavery where it already existed. The progressives advocated a stronger stand against slavery—one designed, as Seward later represented it to Clay, to recapture the 13,000 New York abolitionists, drawn "chiefly from the Whig Party," who had voted the Liberty ticket in 1843.[37]

The *Evening Journal* held out an olive branch to "Whig abolitionists" all summer. Weed exulted on the first day of July, when he reprinted a two-column letter from a Liberty Party member who explained why he planned "to discharge my duty . . . toward God and man" by voting for Clay. Seward pursued the abolitionists more aggressively. "Friends of Emancipation! Advocates of the Rights of Man!" he proclaimed in a speech at Syracuse on July 13. "I am one of you. I have always believed and trusted that the Whigs of America would come up to the ground you have so nobly assumed." Seward meant what he said. The "nomination of Polk," he wrote Weed three weeks earlier, "seems to me to convert Clay into the Abolition candidate of the North."[38]

Seward chose his words with care in the Syracuse speech. He identified himself as a friend of emancipation and of the rights of man. He did not identify himself as a friend of the Liberty Party. By 1844 the Liberty creed had two basic articles, and Seward opposed both of them. Liberty voters advocated "the absolute and unconditional divorce" of the national government from slavery, a program that entailed constitutional amendments to repeal the Three-Fifths Clause and the Fugitive Slave Clause as well as statutes to prohibit slavery in the District of Columbia and on the high seas. Liberty voters also refused to cast ballots for slaveholders under any circumstances. In Seward's judgment, the Liberty Party's "cornerstone principles" forestalled the flexible statecraft that effective political action against slavery required. He thought the first principle was too legalistic, the second too self-righteous. Underlying the Liberty creed, however, lay four assumptions with which Seward fully concurred. He agreed that human bondage was a moral wrong that victimized slave and slaveholder alike. He agreed that the people had "the duty of resisting it by the right of suffrage." He agreed that political agitation of moral questions shaped public opinion. And he agreed that in a republican polity, animated by the doctrine of popular sovereignty and destined to achieve progress through time, freedom possessed the inherent power to triumph over slavery. On those grounds, Seward felt justified in saying "I am one of you" to the abolitionists at Syracuse.[39]

The attachment to the goal of universal emancipation Seward proclaimed in 1844 was romantic, not programmatic. But he took it seriously enough to describe how political agitation, public opinion, and flexible statecraft might succeed:

> The work of manumission begun in the Revolutionary age as a natural work, prosecuted until it reached Mason and Dixon's line and suspended there long ago by force of political combinations, is to be resumed, to be arrested no more. How is it to be prosecuted? I think by firm decisive urgent advocacy in the North, tempered nevertheless by . . . conciliation. Let the world have assurance that we neither risk nor sympathize with convulsive, revolutionary or sanguinary measures. Caution and compensation should always be proclaimed, and they will ultimately commend our great enterprise to the wise and good men of the South of whom there are enough to join us when the character of our designs shall be truly understood.

Seward had been down this road before. Following the Helderberg War of 1839, he had expressed comparable sentiments and pursued a comparable course of action with respect to "voluntary slavery" on the Manor of Rensselaerwyck. Seward's fuzzy commitment to the abolition of slavery, like his fuzzy call for the abolition of manorial tenures four years earlier, infuriated Democrats and conservative Whigs who regarded all talk of emancipation as "demagoguery." In their view, agitation to effect what the Constitution rendered impossible would only sunder the body politic and return its constituent members to a Hobbesian state of war.[40]

Anti-Rent organizers saw something very different in Seward's speech at Syracuse. His politics of hope and moral purpose, progress and goodwill, had always attracted a large following. Those very people—people who were impatient with legalism and sensitive to cries of injustice—were logical targets of opportunity for Anti-Rent political action. But movement leaders had learned something from the disappointments of 1840–41. Cultivating the support of progressive Whigs did not require tenants to rely exclusively on vague promises of future legislation. An independent political party, rooted in the Anti-Rent associations and designed to function like the early Liberty Party, could "call out" the views of Whig and Democratic candidates on the proposed Act Concerning Tenures by Lease and bestow the Anti-Rent nomination on anyone who endorsed the measure. Installing a handful of Anti-Rent loyalists in the state legislature was only part of the new strategy. Tenant leaders aimed to show Weed and his ilk that Anti-Rent voters, not the abolitionists whom the Whigs were wooing so assiduously, would determine which major party carried New York State in the presidential election.

The Luxuriation of Anti-Rent

On May 25, 1844, four days before the Democracy dumped Van Buren and nominated Polk, "friends of the cause" from Albany, Rensselaer, and Schoharie counties assembled for a Saturday morning strategy session at the home of John J. Gallup in East Berne. The participants included Lawrence Van Deusen and Hugh Scott (tenants of Stephen Van Rensselaer IV), Smith Boughton and Burton A. Thomas (residents of William P. Van Rensselaer's domain across the Hudson), John Mayham of Blenheim (a tenant of John A. King), and David L. Sternberg of Livingstonville (a tenant on the Scott Patent). All of them thought that the Allen Report was likely to precipitate landlord attempts to break the rent strikes, and Thomas reported that agents of William P. Van Rensselaer already had "served a notice upon Geo. Clipperley, Esq., the treasurer of the [Rensselaer] Anti-Rent Association, for him to remove the dam of his factory out of the creek within thirty days, and now they are up."[41]

Thomas avowed that any deputy sheriff who attempted to execute a writ of ejectment "will get a wet jacket." Law officers bearing distress warrants for the collection of rent could expect the same treatment. "Our all was at stake," Boughton explained in a reminiscence of the meeting on Gallup's farm.

> The law was on their side and we were at their mercy. We resolved to adopt the same kind of protection resorted to by the people of Boston when the tea was thrown into the water of the bay. We raised in the counties a large force of men to . . . be on hand to protect the tenants from legal hounds. No one knew who they were, except the individuals. This force was to be used only until we could get judicial or legislative redress.

Settling on a resumption of "Indian" activity came easily. Van Deusen, Scott, and Gallup were veterans of the campaign in Albany County during 1841. They described how their defensive tactics not only had staved off Deputy Sheriff Bill Snyder but also had rallied public opinion favorable to the tenants' cause.[42]

The tenant leaders wrestled longer with the problem of devising a new political strategy. Two "lessons" from the state legislature's 1844 session generated their conclusion. First, the members from Albany and Rensselaer had embraced the Anti-Rent critique of manorial tenures yet had not endorsed the bill framed for the Anti-Rent associations. It seemed easy enough to keep people like Whipple, as well as landlord attorneys like Samuel Stevens, out of the legislature in the future. The creation of an Anti-Rent party, capable of delivering thousands of votes in each county, would enable the tenants to secure pledges of support from major-party candidates and result in the election of a few legislators already committed to enactment of the proposed Act Concerning Tenures by Lease. But Van Deusen, Boughton, and their associates recognized that political action could not bear much fruit if Anti-Rent operations were confined to the counties of Albany, Rensselaer, and Schoharie. In their judgment, Assemblyman Allen and his Judiciary Committee had pilloried the Anti-Rent measure because the tenant vote was not large enough to threaten Democratic hegemony. The "friends of the cause" therefore decided, as Gallup put it in an open letter written two days after the meeting adjourned, "to send an agent to every manor in the state."[43]

Smith Boughton volunteered to organize the tenants on Livingston Manor and Claverack in Columbia County, but events kept him in Rensselaer until November. John Mayham of Schoharie, who agreed to spread the Anti-Rent gospel among tenants on the west side of the Hudson River, got started immediately. Early in June he orchestrated the creation of the Blenheim Anti-Rent Association. On the motion of Dr. John Cornell, like Boughton a country physician, the Schoharie rank and file put up "the tallest and straightest pole that could be found" and raised a flag bearing the words, "Down with the Rent." Three tribes of "Indians" were soon organized. Christopher Decker, called "Black Hawk," led the band on Blenheim Hill. Henry A. Cleveland, "Red Jacket," became chief of the Middleburgh tribe; John McEntyre, "Tecumseh," directed the braves from Gilboa. All three tribes were composed, it is said, "of the younger and more reckless men" on the Blenheim Patent. While the Schoharie tenants drilled, Mayham and Cornell visited community leaders on the Hardenbergh Patent, a domain of more than 1 million acres granted by Viscount Cornbury in 1708. It covered nearly half of Delaware, Greene, Sullivan, and Ulster counties; the vast majority of the inhabitants held their land under durable leases, most of them in perpetuity and the balance for two or three lives. When Mayham and Cornell returned in late June, the chiefs of the three Schoharie tribes had their "Indians" ready to march into Delaware County.[44]

The trek was great fun for the participants. Enthusiastic crowds summoned

MAP 3. West Side Organizing Drive of 1844

by colorful handbills watched the "Indians" maneuver in Roxbury, Bovina, and Andes. Delaware farmers learned how to conduct a rent strike, how to finance the struggle, how to resist deputy sheriffs bearing distress warrants, and how to sing "The End of Bill Snyder." Anti-Rent organizations sprang up overnight along the headwaters of the Delaware River. When the Schoharie "Indians" returned home, Mayham led the newly established Delaware bands into the Catskills for a mammoth rally at Pine Hill, Ulster County; some 5,000 people attended the Pine Hill conclave, 300 of them in disguise. "The association is said to extend over all the leasehold lands in the counties of Delaware, Schoharie, Greene, Ulster, and Sullivan," the *Evening Post* reported on July 26. "A set of regulations has been drawn up, disguises have been procured and are kept ready by the tenants, and wherever a horn is sounded in the region, it is a token that the officers of the law are engaged in the collection of rents, and the conspirators assemble in their disguises to prevent by any means of annoyance, or of force, if necessary, the execution of legal process."[45]

Anti-Rent was suddenly a big regional movement, and the Van Rensselaers had company in their misery. Samuel A. Law, land agent for the proprietors of the Franklin Patent in western Delaware County, wrote indignantly on July 30 about the "racket, all around us, of tenants refusing to pay rent." The level of concern was undoubtedly higher among the proprietors of the Hardenbergh Patent: John Hunter and Henry Overing (at least 100,000 acres under perpetual lease in Delaware, Greene, and Sullivan), James Desbrosses (75,000 acres under perpetual lease in Greene and Sullivan), Gulian C. Verplanck and his aunt Charlotte Verplanck (20,000 acres under perpetual lease in Delaware), the descendants of Morgan Lewis (15,000 acres under perpetual lease in Delaware), and the heirs of Robert R. Livingston (32,000 acres under lease in perpetuity or for three lives in Delaware, Sullivan, and Ulster).[46]

One piece of encouraging news reached the landlord class early that summer. In *Quackenbush v. Danks*, decided in May 1844, the New York Supreme Court held that the Exemption Act of 1842, which enabled debtors to protect "necessary household furniture and working tools" valued up to $150 against distress for rent or levy and sale under execution, could not be interpreted so as to affect contracts made prior to its passage. The matter at issue was whether a creditor, seeking to recover on an 1837 agreement, could reach a horse and harness, valued by the jury at $65, belonging to the judgment debtor. The debtor owned nothing else on which the creditor might levy in satisfaction of the contract. Justice Greene Bronson, author of the landmark disquisition on the eminent domain power in *Taylor v. Porter*, spoke for the court. He began by considering the policy of such legislation. "Whatever may be thought of the expediency of passing exemption laws, if they are wholly prospective in their operation, no wrong is done to the creditor," Bronson said. "He has the law before him when he parts with his money or his property; and it will not be the fault of the government if the debt is lost." When exemption laws were applied to "past transactions," however, "they take the property which in honesty and fair dealing belongs to the creditor, and, without his consent, transfer it to the debtor."[47]

Bronson pointed out that the Exemption Act did not expressly mandate a retrospective operation. On the other hand, he admitted, "the general words in which the law is framed are broad enough to include contracts already in existence, as well as those which should afterwards be made." It followed that the controversy called for application of a "well established rule" of statutory construction: "A statute shall not be so construed as to give it a retrospect beyond the time of its commencement." In point of fact, the legislature had intended to give the Exemption Act a retrospective operation. On March 31,

1842, the senate defeated an amendment designed to accomplish precisely what the court ruled in the *Quackenbush* case. Bronson had a fallback position, however. "Granting that this statute is broad enough to cover the plaintiff's case," he wrote, "the question then arises whether it is not a 'law impairing the obligation of contracts.' " In the court's judgment, the Exemption Act was such a law.[48]

Justice Bronson's analysis of the right-remedy distinction echoed Assemblyman Allen's treatment of the proposed Act Concerning Tenures by Lease earlier in the year. "If the legislature can deprive [the creditor] of the right to reach the [debtor's] property—a right which existed at the time the contract was made," Bronson explained, "it is evident that nothing will then remain of the obligation of the contract beyond an empty name. . . . For all honest and practical purposes, the legislature might just as well say that the debt shall be blotted out, as to deny the creditor all means of enforcing payment." He conceded that Chief Justice Roger Taney, speaking for the Supreme Court of the United States in *Bronson v. Kinzie*, had included exemption laws on a list of measures "properly belonging to the remedy" and therefore immune to attack under the Contract Clause. But that was only "a *dictum*." "If the question turns on what is 'necessary' for the debtor and his family," Bronson remarked, "the learned chief justice will find it impossible to stop with the articles he has mentioned. The husbandman stands in as much need of a *farm*, as he does of the 'implements of agriculture,' and 'household furniture' is not more essential to the head of a family than a *house* to live in." The judicial department had to draw a line somewhere; in Bronson's view, the prospectivity norm answered the requirement with precision and justice.[49]

The *Quackenbush* decision effectively restored the Hudson Valley landlords' right to collect rent by distress, and the result was a new offensive against the several thousand tenants on strike. William P. Van Rensselaer moved first. On July 16, 1844, his lawyers handed Gideon Reynolds, the Whig sheriff of Rensselaer County, a batch of distress warrants to be served on tenants near Alps. The sheriff and two deputies tried to do their duty that afternoon, but a small band of "Indians" intercepted them at Stephentown and the officers turned back. Reynolds returned a week later with a posse of thirty-five men. This time more than 100 "Indians" armed with pistols and tomahawks surrounded the sheriff's party, released their horses into the woods, and compelled them to march a mile and a half into Alps. There the lawmen were searched. The chief—probably Smith Boughton disguised as "Big Thunder"—told the sheriff that anyone found with a distress warrant in his possession would be tarred and feathered. The unlucky victim was George B. Allen, one of Reynolds's deputies. Another deputy, Jacob Lewis, endured still greater torment a few days later. When anti-renters learned that his home contained a bundle of distress warrants, the Rensselaer "Indians" descended at midnight, ransacked the house, and burned his papers "at a powwow in the center of the village." The next morning Lewis bragged that he would get even. Instead, the "Indians" pulled him out of bed at midnight once again; according to a report reprinted in *Niles' Register*, Lewis was "covered with a thick coat of tar and feathers, and was then compelled to run around the town pump, and up and down the streets for the amusement of his persecutors."[50]

Sheriff Reynolds asked Governor William C. Bouck for state assistance in late July. The request put Bouck in a quandary. He still entertained hopes of being renominated at the Democratic Party's state convention, scheduled for September 4, despite the groundswell of support for the reluctant Silas Wright. Bouck assumed that decisive action against the rebellious Rensselaer tenants would kill his chances. Thus he took refuge in the New York statute that spelled out the governor's duties during times of civil disorder: "In case it shall appear to the governor, that the power of any county will not be sufficient to enable the sheriff thereof to execute process delivered to him, he shall, on the application of such sheriff, order such a military force from any other county or counties of this state, as shall be necessary." Bouck recited the applicable law to Reynolds in a letter of August 1. He acknowledged that the Anti-Rent resistance posed a serious problem for law enforcement in Rensselaer. In his view, however, the resources at Sheriff Reynolds's command had not been exhausted.[51]

Eight days later, Bouck journeyed to West Sandlake for a meeting with Anti-Rent representatives of Rensselaer County's eight townships. While more than 1,000 people looked on, a great many of them in "Indian" disguise, he offered to mediate the tenants' dispute with their landlord. Anti-Rent negotiators proposed, instead, that the governors of any three New England states except Connecticut be empowered to adjudicate the validity of William P. Van Rensselaer's title. Bouck rejected that impertinent suggestion, and the *Argus* reported that the conference broke up after three or four hours of discussion. Whether or not anything else got resolved at West Sandlake, two things became clear in the weeks that followed. Sheriff Reynolds had no intention of attempting to collect rents without state assistance, and Bouck had no intention of calling up the militia until the sheriff tried harder to crush the "Indian" force. The stalemate infuriated William P. Van Rensselaer. Early in December the *Evening Post* reported that he was "about to remove to Pennsylvania, in order to be enabled to commence suits in the United States courts, as a non-resident against his tenants in this state." The rumor spoke volumes about landlord frustration with the politics of law in New York State.[52]

Stephen Van Rensselaer IV fared no better that summer. Christopher Batterman, the sheriff of Albany County, attempted to serve distress warrants near Rensselaerville beginning in mid-August. Anti-renters foiled Batterman's first

foray into the Helderbergs by shooting his horse. When he returned with three
deputies on August 30, sixty "Indians" ambushed the lawmen and bound them
with a rope. The chief sought to persuade Batterman to renounce his rent-
collecting duties while the other "Indians" destroyed his papers. But "the
sheriff replied that he was there to do his duty, and that he would not be
frightened or coaxed back." As a result, he returned to Albany in the back of a
wagon, "his legs and feet plentifully supplied with a coat" of tar and feathers.
Timothy Corbin, a deputy sheriff in Roxbury, Delaware County, got a "wet
jacket" from another band of "Indians" early in September. In Delaware, as in
Albany and Rensselaer, all attempts to serve process on tenants ceased for
several months. On December 24, the Argus reported that neither Batterman
nor his deputies had ventured to collect rents in the Helderberg towns since
September.[53]

The autumn truce that brought an uneasy peace to the manors and great
patents of eastern New York differed substantially from the lull of 1841–43. This
time neither secret deals nor legal impediments stayed the hand of landlords.
And this time the "Indians" did not demobilize. The savage disguise had
become a source of identity as well as a means of resistance. Young men wore it
with pride. When a Rensselaer shoemaker got thrown from his horse and died
during Anti-Rent drills in August, an honor guard of ninety-six "Indians"
escorted the casket to the funeral. "They were on horseback, riding two and
two, in costume and masked; and at a little distance, made a strange and
somewhat formidable appearance . . . [to the] two thousand five hundred
people on the ground," reported a newspaper correspondent. "The band rode
up to the green where the services were to be performed. The war chief . . .
directed the spectators to keep silent, and requested the ministers to begin."
After the clergymen had performed their duties, the "Indians" led a procession
to the burying ground. "They formed a circle around the grave," the reporter
continued.

> And the deceased warrior being deposited, one of the chiefs designated as
> the "the prophet of the tribe," addressed the people. He entered into an
> explanation of the object of the association. They were contending for the
> freedom of which a usurper had deprived them. They were not contend-
> ing against the usurper himself, but against the wrong, and resistance to
> that wrong had grown into a principle, and as long as that principle
> existed, they would never lay down the steel and the gun.

At the conclusion of his remarks, the "prophet of the tribe"—almost certainly
Boughton—announced that he would receive contributions for the cause in
memory of the deceased.[54]

This unusually vivid display of community solidarity awed the reporter.

"Nearly the whole of that county approves of the resistance which is offered to the service of Mr. Van Rensselaer's papers," he wrote, "and a feeling of confidence has been infused into the ranks of the insurgents by the fact that Governor Bouck has met to negotiate with them on their own ground." One suspects that Anti-Rent leaders actually put very little stock in Bouck's apparent sympathy with their cause. Short-run political calculations shaped the governor's policy of appeasement, and the tenants knew it. If the state government declared war on them after the election, however, the "Indians" were prepared to fight. Tenant "chiefs" believed that state intervention would at least give them another opportunity to tell the Anti-Rent story. Progressives in their own way, Boughton and his associates never ceased to rely on public opinion for a just resolution of tenant grievances. But resistance was not the only move open to them in the fall of 1844. The Democratic state convention assembled at Syracuse on September 4; the Whigs met in the same hall a week later. Tenant delegates convened shortly afterward to make the Anti-Rent Party's first nominations to public office.

7

Resistance and Reform

Despair gripped Thurlow Weed as New York Whigs descended on Syracuse to nominate his handpicked gubernatorial candidate, Millard Fillmore, on September 11, 1844. A letter from Henry Clay to a voter in Alabama produced Weed's woe. *Niles' Register*, the nation's premier weekly newspaper, published the "Alabama letter" on August 31; once again, the Whig candidate for president addressed the propriety of annexing the Republic of Texas. After reviewing the threat of war with Mexico and various other impediments to the project, Clay flatly stated that slavery "ought not to affect the question one way or another." Seward was campaigning in western New York at the time. "[I] met *that letter* at Geneva," he wrote Weed from Auburn on September 2, "and there, here, and until now everybody droops, despairs. . . . It jeopards, perhaps loses this state." Congressman Washington Hunt had the same reaction. "We had the Abolitionists in a good way, but Mr. Clay seems determined that they shall not be allowed to vote for him," he wrote Weed from his home in Lockport. "I believe his letter will lose us more than two hundred votes in this county." Offsetting the anticipated defection of Whigs to the Liberty standard became an obsession with Weed, and it led him willy-nilly to the anti-renters.[1]

For the first time in anyone's memory, Weed stayed home when the New York Whigs convened to nominate a candidate for governor and frame an address to the voters. But he did not remain in Albany to lick his wounds. His lead editorial on September 11 addressed the Anti-Rent agitation, a subject on which he had been silent for years. Weed wove several inconsistent themes into a powerful, remarkably coherent endorsement of the tenant cause. He began by decrying the "Indian" attacks. "Resistance to laws, *per se*, is always wrong," he said. "The outrages perpetrated upon the sheriff of this county and the deputy sheriff of Rensselaer, demand prompt and exemplary punishment." Setting an example was especially important because, as Weed put it, "there is contagion" in the Anti-Rent violence. "The spirit of resistance is spreading. Tenants in neighboring counties, where, but for this tree of bitterness [called Rensselaerwyck] no such roots would have sprung up, are forming Anti-Rent associations. The mischief is becoming every day more formidable." Yet the situation called for something more than "the efficient execution of the laws." Some legal rights, Weed averred, were so "obnoxious" that attempts to exercise them "will be the cause of perpetual strife and contentions." The indentures in force on Rensselaerwyck, "relic[s] of feudalism . . . at war with our general laws and against our public policy," were a case in point.[2]

Weed conceded that "the answer to all this is, that the state is bound to protect the Messrs. Van Rensselaer in their legal rights." What, then, was to be done? His approach was a variation on Seward's prescription for political action against slavery. "Those who are called upon to take ground in favor of these proprietors against their tenants," Weed said, "are likely to find an onerous duty cast upon them." The body politic was certain to balk at a policy of armed suppression; the vast majority of New Yorkers wanted to put down manorial tenures, not the farmers who protested them. "And the community is not unreasonable," he wrote, "in asking the Messrs. Van Rensselaer, instead of reposing upon their legal rights, to make an earnest effort to change these offensive and impolitic tenures."

Weed expected "these proprietors to put their shoulders to the wheels of their own car" just as Seward expected slaveholders to accommodate the laws of progress by extinguishing property rights in people. Weed offered his prescription "with no unkind feelings to the proprietors" just as Seward recommended that the abolitionist approach to slaveholders be "tempered by conciliation." Weed denounced anti-renters for permitting "flagrant outrages" against deputy sheriffs that "weakened their claim for consideration" just as Seward condemned "convulsive, revolutionary or sanguinary measures" against slavery. And Weed announced that land reform was a live political issue in New York just as Seward announced that "slavery is now henceforth and forever among the elements of political action" in the United States. For Weed, as for Seward, solutions to wrongs like slavery and manorial tenures could not come from the law. Rights vested by law created the problems that had to be overcome. In a republican polity, however, progress could be achieved by urgent advocacy and by resistance at the polls, both of which enhanced the wrongdoer's incentive to capitulate voluntarily. The solutions, in other words, had to come from politics.[3]

Weed's editorial heralded the first conventions of the Anti-Rent Party that gathered at New Scotland, Albany County, and Sandlake, Rensselaer County, ten days later. It also justified them. Ambitious young Whigs were quick to capitalize on the resulting opportunity. Two lawyers, Ira Harris of Albany and William H. Van Schoonhoven of Troy, managed to be nominated for the assembly by the Anti-Rent associations as well as by the Whigs. Securing the Anti-Rent nomination, however, compelled them to take a more programmatic stance than Weed's. The county associations demanded replies to three inter-rogatories. One asked potential candidates whether they had any objection to running on the Anti-Rent ticket. Another asked them whether, if elected, they would "use all honorable means efficiently and promptly to redress the griev-ances of the tenants." The third asked whether they endorsed the proposed Act Concerning Tenures by Lease, which William F. Allen's report for the Judiciary Committee had strangled in April.

Van Schoonhoven gave the right answers to all three questions. Harry Betts and Roger Heermance, two Whigs from rural Rensselaer, apparently did so as well. Harris, the only major party candidate in Albany County to accept the nomination of the Anti-Rent Party, was more circumspect. "I gratefully appreci-ate the confidence of those you represent," he wrote the nominating committee, "and should I be elected to the assembly, my best exertions shall be given, not only to secure prompt and favorable action upon the petitions of the tenants, but to obtain *all the relief* consistent with fair and constitutional legislation." Harris also remarked that he could "see no objection" to the bill's first section but was "inclined to think" that the second section, grounded on the eminent domain power, "would, if brought in question before a judicial tribunal be declared unconstitutional." Nevertheless, Harris kept "the flame" of Anti-Rent hope, as Allen had derisively called it, burning brightly. "If, however, the object contemplated by such an act can be constitutionally attained, I should not hesitate to give the measure my cordial support."[4]

The questions posed to Harris, Van Schoonhoven, and the others were cleverly framed. Whig "modernizers" could endorse the Anti-Rent commit-ment to the abolition of manorial tenures. They could not endorse the tenants' rent strikes—a form of repudiation—or the "Indian" resistance to actions at law for the enforcement of contracts. Anti-Rent leaders understood the distinction in Whig thought and tried to separate resistance at the polls from resistance on the land. Yet the separation was incongruous. The tenant movement began with a rent strike on Rensselaerwyck, and its leaders carried the cause elsewhere in "Indian" garb. Strikes provided direct benefits for the rank and file and funds for political action. Resistance songs sustained the promise of victory. The processes of commitment, recruitment, education, and organization—the very "movement culture" that pulsed within the Anti-Rent associations—hinged on the rent strike.[5] Thus the architects of the Whig/Anti-Rent alliance built on quicksand. Whig leaders could not sponsor land reform while the "Indian" resistance continued; anti-renters could not renounce resistance without im-pairing the vitality of their county associations. The incongruity crippled the Anti-Rent agitation for many months. Still, the allied Whigs and anti-renters knew what they were doing. Whig candidates needed votes, and the tenant associations needed spokesmen at the state capital. Anti-renters got something more out of the deal. The fusion movement generated a jolt to the New York Democracy, and it persuaded some Democratic leaders that the party should at least rethink the manor question. Martin Van Buren went further. He identified a new method of abolishing "feudal" tenures without impairing vested rights of property or contract.

The Election of 1844

Democrats started down the campaign's homestretch with Silas Wright on their ticket for governor. At the state convention William C. Bouck got only 30 of the 125 votes cast on the first ballot; the incumbent's manager, Horatio Seymour, immediately moved that the party's decision be made unanimous. "My nomination," Wright told a delegation from Syracuse on September 4, "is a decision by the convention that my personal wishes in relation to the office should yield to my obligations to the Democratic Party of the state . . . and the unanimity of expression leaves me no alternative but to yield to the call made upon me." Next day the Democracy adopted a lengthy address to the voters that said nothing at all about Texas. Putting Wright's name on the ticket just below James K. Polk's said enough. It justified the New York Democracy's claim that the election could not be considered a referendum on annexation or the extension of slavery. It also provided what the *Albany Atlas*, a radical print, called "a point of union to the whole Democratic Party under which they can march, like brethren, shoulder to shoulder, in solid, unbroken array, to the victory that ever awaits their united efforts."[6]

Only the Whig Party's dalliance with the anti-renters disturbed the composure of Democrats. *Argus* editor Edwin Croswell was especially alarmed. In Rensselaer, he informed Wright shortly after the Anti-Rent nominating conventions adjourned, Sheriff Gideon Reynolds had been acting in "perfect understanding" with the rebellious tenants for two months, his object being to collect votes rather than rents. Furthermore, Whig operatives already had effected a coalition with the Anti-Rent Party in Rensselaer and, to a lesser degree, in Albany; "Weed and Co." was likely to engineer comparable alliances in Delaware, Greene, Schoharie, Sullivan, and Ulster. Croswell warned Wright that the anti-renters might even ask the gubernatorial candidates to make "a declaration of principles for the public eye." Consequently he had better be prepared to answer. "Mr. Fillmore will be perfectly in the hands of Weed," Croswell added, "and will try anything and write anything which Thurlow should dictate."[7]

Wright had no idea what to say if "called out" by the anti-renters. He immediately solicited the advice of Azariah Flagg, the state's comptroller and an old friend. "I have long heard of the Helderberg War," Wright wrote on September 25, but "nothing which I recollect to have seen gives a statement of the facts about which the troubles arise, or . . . what the tenants demand, or desire, or expect to obtain, either from the landlords or from the legislature. All I have been able to discover is a determined and organized resistance against the collection of rent." Surely, he said, the tenants did not expect the legislature to nullify their contractual obligations or endorse their riotous conduct. "These people cannot place themselves upon a ground so hard, and which appears to me to be so wholly indefensible constitutionally, legally, and morally." Wright assumed that there must be more to the dispute than met the eye, and he asked for "all the information which our friends can give" about what the anti-renters "suppose the legislature can do for them."[8]

Very little of Wright's incoming correspondence has survived. Circumstantial evidence indicates that Flagg supplied him with the terms of the proposed Act Concerning Tenures by Lease as well as a copy of Assemblyman Allen's report to the legislature during the previous session. Others rendered advice. Michael Hoffman, for example, told him to just say no. "The renters will work mischief," he wrote; "but don't let our people whore with them." Governor Bouck already had done "enough in that line." As for the Whigs, Hoffman counseled, their penchant for unscrupulous manipulation knew no bounds yet posed no genuine risk. "Whatever Weed can do by bargains with Nativism, Anti-Rentism, Abolitionism will be done—but *payment*, cash payment will be scarce." Hoffman urged Wright to "make no compromise with any *isms*. Democracy or nothing. Hold to this and we are safe."[9]

Martin Van Buren suggested a very different response. He recommended a new departure in New York property law. Leases in perpetuity, Van Buren wrote Wright in early October, posed the same problem as entails and might be extinguished in much the same way. Although the rights of the existing proprietors had vested and could not be disturbed, the interests of their heirs stood on a different footing. As Blackstone said, "wills and testaments, rights of inheritance and succession, are all of them creatures of the civil or municipal laws, and accordingly are in all respects regulated by them." It followed that the legislature might enact a statute authorizing tenants for lives or in perpetuity, upon the death of their landlord, to convert the value of all rents, services, and reservations on their land, as ascertained by the New York Court of Chancery, into a mortgage that could be paid off in five or ten years. Van Buren recognized that a statute of this sort would merely phase out manorial tenures. But legislation mandating a gradual emancipation of the tenants would give landlords an incentive to begin the process voluntarily, thus reducing the threat of both additional "Indian" violence and Whig gains in the Anti-Rent counties. Van Buren was certain about one thing. No principle of constitutional law barred the enactment of such a statute. Like the eighteenth-century act abolishing entails, it would impair no contractual obligations and disturb no vested rights.[10]

"Upon the first reading . . . your letter appeared to me to be pretty radical," Wright replied on October 8.

Upon the second its aspect was somewhat ameliorated, and I do not know but it may come to look quite rational, if I can get to look at it without having the very bad conduct of the ["Indian"] disturbers in my mind. Yet my present inclinations are that it will not be best for me to broach the idea predicated upon the abolition of the entails. . . . I cannot help but like the principle, but to suggest it now I think would give a ground to the disturbers stronger and more plausible than any they have attempted to occupy, and put an end to all hope of reasonable compromises with them.

Pursuit of Van Buren's idea also involved political risks at a time when government spending for internal improvements and constitutional reform already threatened to divide the Democratic Party. The legislature might "expressly repudiate it," Wright wrote, "in which case I should be left with the anti-renters, with the Whigs and our own folks upon my back." As a result, Wright preferred to shelve Van Buren's scheme for the time being.[11]

Wright's cautious response to Van Buren's ingenious suggestion came at a critical moment. If he had placed it before the public immediately, the announcement might have averted the loss of three lives and large expenditures of tax dollars on military action against the "Indian" insurgents. But Wright was a politician, not a seer. Even his predisposition to "urge the landlords the duty of reasonable compromises" remained a secret in the fall of 1844. The Anti-Rent Party neither called upon Wright and Fillmore to state their views nor framed tickets in counties other than Albany, Rensselaer, and Schoharie. Its aspirations exceeded the resources at hand to organize all the state's tenants before the election. And the Democracy prevailed. Polk carried New York by about 5,000 ballots; Wright defeated Fillmore by twice that number, 241,096 to 231,057. "We have done our duty, as a private, in the campaign that has just closed," Weed wailed on November 8, but "the electors of the State of New York have rendered their verdict in favor of Polk, Texas, foreign free trade, and slavery!"[12]

Contemporary observers agreed that Polk's victory in New York was vital to his election, and many of them pointed to the 15,000 votes for James G. Birney as the principal source of Whig defeat. "The cause of human freedom has been sacrificed by its professed advocates," Weed declared. "The Slave Party owes its triumph to the 'Liberty Party.'" Other analysts argued that the abolitionist vote, though important, had not been decisive. Horace Greeley attributed Whig defeat to the party's misguided pursuit of nativists in New York City. The American Republican Party, established in 1843 to strengthen the naturalization laws and thereby reduce the political power of Irish Catholic immigrants, had persuaded the city's Whig leadership to endorse "Native American" candidates for the state legislature in return for nativist support of Clay and Fillmore. "This new element in our politics," Greeley complained, triggered an "immense naturalized vote against us."[13]

Democratic commentators focused on the sources and significance of their victory, not the causes of Whig defeat. William Cullen Bryant and his fellow Barnburners at the *Evening Post* were especially anxious to controvert the "erroneous" presumption that, as David Dudley Field put it, Polk's election constituted "a final decision of the people" on the desirability of annexing Texas. A great many other issues were before the people in 1844, Field wrote in a widely noticed article. "Unless an election turns upon a single question, in which personal preferences and party attachments have no part, it cannot be a test of opinion, in respect to it." Democrats opposed to annexation were equally anxious to explode the impression that they had been unfaithful to the national ticket. "I refer," Wright wrote Polk on December 20, "to the difference between the vote given to yourself, and that which I received in this state." The impulse to "impute the disaffection to the more peculiar friends of Mr. Van Buren," Wright explained, "is wholly without foundation." The governor-elect attributed the differential to nominally Whig "capitalists and heavy merchants" who supported the Stop and Tax Act, "desire that the policy of 1842 should continue to govern the financial affairs of our state, and consequently do not wish a reascendancy of their own party here, for the present."[14]

As party managers and publicists studied the returns in search of evidence for their self-serving arguments, two other results must have caught their eye. First, the Whigs and American Republicans had cut deeply into the Democracy's muscle in the New York assembly. Democrats had enjoyed a 92-36 majority in 1844. The newly elected members of the lower house included 67 Democrats, 46 Whigs, and 15 American Republicans. Second, the anti-renters had come to the polls in droves. Each of the three Whig/Anti-Rent candidates for the assembly in Rensselaer had run well ahead of Clay and carried the county by very large majorities. Ira Harris had become the first Whig in Albany County history to defeat his Democratic opponent by more than 2,000 votes. Seymour Boughton, a Democrat, and Elisha Tibbets, a Whig, had accepted the Anti-Rent nomination in Schoharie; both had been elected. These two developments, taken together, augured a promising future for the Anti-Rent experiment with independent politics. In 1845 the Democratic assembly would lack the two-thirds majority required to adopt the five constitutional amendments approved the previous session. And the alternative, a constitutional convention, would provide an effective focal point for the Anti-Rent agitation. In a convention of the people, anti-renters could outflank the troublesome doctrine of vested rights and put an eminent domain measure into the New York Constitution. Before the newly elected legislators departed for Albany in

January, however, Smith Boughton and his Rensselaer "Indians" changed the terms of public debate on the Anti-Rent movement.[15]

Bloodshed

Shortly after the election of 1844, Smith Boughton journeyed into Columbia County to lay the foundation for a rent strike and an Anti-Rent Party on Livingston Manor. Community leaders in the villages of Taghkanic, Copake, Hillsdale, and Ancram greeted him enthusiastically and agreed to arrange mass meetings at which "Big Thunder" could address the people early in December. Yet talk of the risks involved in organizing Columbia County dogged Boughton everywhere. Livingston Manor, unlike Rensselaerwyck and the Hardenbergh Patent, contained a great many enclaves in which former tenants already had purchased the proprietor's interest in their farms. The 140,000-acre manor had been subdivided repeatedly since Robert Livingston Jr. died in 1790; of the thirty-odd Livingstons who subsequently inherited shares of the estate, about a quarter had sold their interests to the tenants in possession. More than 800 families on Livingston Manor still held their farms for two lives, paid wheat rents substantially higher than those stipulated on Rensselaerwyck, and owed their proprietors "four fat fowl" and two days of "riding" each year. But the 300 families who had acquired allodial titles within the old manor, most of them during the 1830s, were not Anti-Rent material. At least some of the independent farmers could be expected to cooperate with Sheriff Henry C. Miller in the suppression of "Indian" disorders. And the sheriff of Columbia County, warned Boughton's contacts, was a tough and resourceful man.[16]

Boughton promised to be careful. Nevertheless, he was more impressed by the Anti-Rent potential in the hundreds of families still oppressed by "the last relics of feudalism" than by the supposed dangers arising from a minority who had escaped "voluntary slavery." Suspicions about the validity of the Livingston family's title were as old as the estate itself, and spectacular tenant uprisings had engulfed the manor in 1755, 1766, and 1777. Boughton intended to rekindle the discontent which the tenants' forebears had acted upon in the eighteenth century. He believed that the recipe for success in Rensselaer—organize, strike, resist, and vote the Anti-Rent ticket—would work anywhere the majority labored under "feudal servitude interminable." And he had an answer for the Livingston tenants who feared Sheriff Miller. The "Natives will come out from their glens and caves in the rocky mountains, and drive off the sheriffs," one Columbia inhabitant later quoted Boughton as saying. "They will come at night and return at night, and no one will know whence they came or where they went." In other words, Boughton was not prepared to be careful enough.[17]

The first stop on Boughton's tour, at Taghkanic on Saturday, December 7,

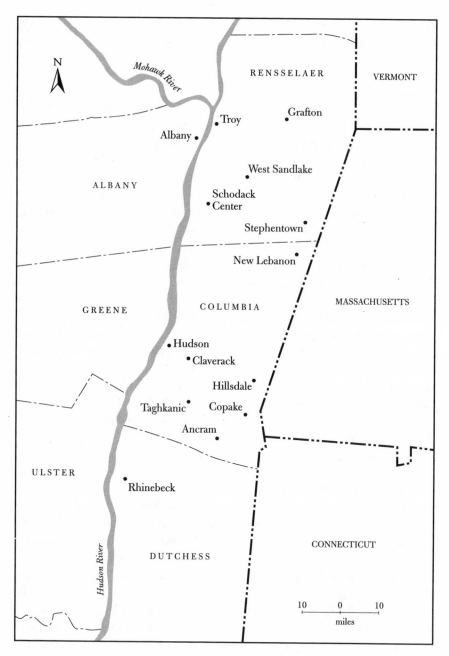

MAP 4. East Side Organizing Drive of 1844

was a great success. His upriver braves delighted a large crowd with intricate "Indian" drills and a lusty performance of the Anti-Rent anthem, "The End of Bill Snyder." A rousing speech by "Big Thunder" followed. "Down with the rent!" shouted the disguised Boughton. "The aristocrats have taken from us and our fathers in rent many times what the land is worth. They will take no more. We have ten thousand Indians ready at the first blast of the horn to drive their paid agents from our farms. . . . They are sworn to protect you in your homes!" After he had finished speaking, a Copake tenant named Stephen Decker requested the very aid "Big Thunder" promised to supply. Sheriff Miller had appeared at his farm with a distress warrant just the day before, Decker explained. His stock, equipment, and grain had been inventoried and advertised for sale on Wednesday. Would the "Indians" be there to drive the sheriff away?[18]

An estimated 200 "Indians" and 1,500 "citizen spectators" awaited the sheriff at the Decker place as he came up the road from Hudson, the county seat, on December 11. Miller later testified that he heard the din of the crowd and ducked into a nearby tavern. But the sheriff had been seen. "Big Thunder" and several other chiefs soon cornered him; with a show of drawn swords and leveled pistols, the "Indians" persuaded him to hand over his papers. "The *whole assembly* gave three cheers" when the braves ceremoniously tossed the distress warrant and the inventory into a bonfire ready for the occasion. Sheriff Miller was allowed to go unharmed, and he returned to Hudson determined to learn the identity of the masked men who had robbed him. By the weekend he had succeeded. An anonymous tip, corroborated by bits of information discreetly collected by deputies in Taghkanic and Copake, gave Miller sufficient evidence to arrest Boughton though not yet enough to secure an indictment. The sheriff's opportunity came, tragically, at the Rensselaer leader's next Anti-Rent rally.[19]

On December 18 a huge crowd gathered at Smoky Hollow to watch the "Indians" maneuver, sing the down-rent songs, join the newly established Anti-Rent Association of Columbia County, and pay the membership dues of two cents per acre. Handbills announcing the rally said that "Big Thunder" would expose the flaws in the Livingston family's title. But he never got a chance to speak. The "Indian" demonstration had scarcely begun when a stray bullet killed William Rifenburgh, a teenage spectator from Hillsdale. While the stunned crowd slowly dispersed, Sheriff Miller's men raced to Hudson to report the incident; Boughton and Mortimer Belden ("Little Thunder") were in custody before nightfall. Sheriff Miller and his hastily assembled posse found them, no longer clad as "Indians," in a roadside tavern near the shooting scene. Both were collared after a brief scuffle. In a search incident to the arrest, Miller discovered in the suspects' baggage "two complete disguises, two brace of pistols, loaded with balls, a powder flask, [and] a sword." Hours later at the Hudson jail, Boughton and Belden found themselves charged with manslaughter in the death of young Rifenburgh as well as robbery and assault with a deadly weapon in resisting the execution of legal process at Copake.[20]

The first news out of Hudson was pure fiction. On December 20 the *Albany Argus* reported that Rifenburgh had been shot dead by a Columbia "Indian" for refusing to cry "down with the rent." The *Evening Journal* repeated the story. In a grotesque way, however, the misinformation proved prophetic. That very day, a band of fifty "Indians" killed Elijah Smith in Grafton, Rensselaer County. Smith and his uncle, Plumb Martin, were lumbermen; their traitorous conduct, as triggerman Norman Goyer and his fellow braves saw things, consisted in their willingness to validate William P. Van Rensselaer's title by purchasing a woodlot from the patroon. The "Indians" did not tell the lumbermen to shout "down with the rent." Instead, they surrounded Martin's loaded wagon and ordered him to dump the logs beside the road. Smith rushed from the woods to assist his embattled uncle, "his axe swinging carelessly in his hands." Goyer cocked his pistol and said, " 'If you advance any farther I will blow you through.' " Moments later, Goyer carried out the threat. The "Indians" scattered in all directions; Martin carried his fallen nephew into a neighboring house. Smith died shortly afterward.[21]

News of this second death at the hands of "Indian outlaws" electrified the Empire State just as the significance of what had occurred in Columbia became clear. On December 20 a Hudson coroner's jury determined that the Rifenburgh shooting had been accidental, concluding Boughton and Belden's jeopardy on the manslaughter charge. But the sheriff's determination to hold them on the robbery and assault charges outraged the county's anti-renters. Crossroads orators denounced the arrest as "the crowning injustice of a century of tyranny" and talked boldly about an attack on the jail to liberate their champions. Panic gripped the little city of Hudson. The threats and rumors prompted the mayor to station a local militia company at the jail; Sheriff Miller dispatched a messenger to Albany, asking Governor Bouck to call up troops "from abroad." This time Bouck did not hesitate. More than 300 citizen-soldiers from Albany and New York City had arrived in Hudson by New Year's Day. Detachments of militia smashed the "Indian" resistance in the countryside, and scores of men were arrested. A grand jury later indicted fifty of them for riot or conspiracy to riot. On January 2, 1845, twenty-four hours after the inauguration of Silas Wright, the mayor of Hudson reported that "the happiest results" had attended the state government's intervention. "We hear of the public burning of many of the masks and dresses," he wrote. "Another encouraging fact is that many of the wheat rents were yesterday paid promptly, and by several of the most noisy anti-renters. I hope it is all over, except a few more arrests." The disorders arising from Boughton's ill-fated foray into Columbia were over. But their reverberations in New York public life had only begun.[22]

Mixed Reactions

The bloodshed on Livingston Manor and Rensselaerwyck evoked a flurry of public discourse on the Anti-Rent agitation. Whig and Democratic organs used their distinctive idioms to say much the same thing. Horace Greeley's *Tribune* insisted that "the reign of violence and homicide in the manor counties must be put down, and so decidedly that the 'Indian' operations will stay down." James Watson Webb's *Courier and Enquirer* asserted that government officials had a duty "to teach Jacobinism that it can never maintain its footing in this land of law." William Cullen Bryant's *Evening Post* declared that "nothing but the same vigorous determination with which nullification was put down by President Jackson will answer any purpose." The people of New York stood atop a steep and very dangerous slope, Bryant observed. "Large amounts of capital are invested in agricultural securities, and these securities are blank paper if the present state of things is allowed to remain unchecked. Anti-Rent is next door to anti-interest, and mortgages will follow the same way as leases." Still, Bryant remarked that he did not speak "in the interest of the capitalist." Tenant lawlessness, he emphasized, was not consonant with the republican form of government. "In the most anarchical countries on the face of the globe the great rich man protects himself—fraud, cabal, bribery, secure his position in troubled times," Bryant explained. "It is for the industrious classes . . . that a system of law and order is indispensable. A free people cannot subsist in a state of violence and anarchy."[23]

Only the expected bickering about political responsibility disturbed this consensus. Rufus King, in charge of the *Evening Journal* while Weed and his family vacationed in the Caribbean, blamed the deaths of Rifenburgh and Smith on Governor Bouck. If the Democratic governor had fulfilled "his oath of office to see that the laws were faithfully executed" back in August, King wrote on December 21, "Big Thunder" and the "ascendancy of anarchy" would have been nipped in the bud. Croswell replied for the Democracy. "Attempting to stem the torrent of facts which connect the *Evening Journal* and its party with the Anti-Rent combinations in the late campaign, it [now] . . . attempts to shift the responsibility of action from its own local officers to the shoulders of the executive." But the Whig ploy would not succeed. "We have no doubt," Croswell asserted, "that the organ of Governor Seward, who may be said to have originated these difficulties in their more serious aspect, and the organ also of the combined Whig and Anti-Rent tickets, is sufficiently understood, and will be rightly appreciated by all fair-minded and considerate men." Bryant thought of himself as a "fair-minded" man; he contended that "crafty demagogues and timid leaders" from both parties had "trifled" with the anti-renters. "A Whig governor was found with little enough knowledge of constitutional law, and a Whig legislature with little enough knowledge of common right to organize a commission to inquire at the 'just and fair value' of contracts guaranteed by the law of the land," he wrote, "while on the other hand a Democratic governor was found with so little regard to his own dignity to negotiate with a band of outlaws armed in hostility to the laws of the state." In Bryant's judgment, however, the "time for crimination or recrimination" had passed: "The question is what should be done to suppress a growing evil."[24]

The big-city journalists identified the "Indians," not manorial tenures, as the "growing evil" that had to be suppressed. Yet most of them showed signs of ambivalence toward the Anti-Rent movement. Bryant acknowledged "that the system of landholding out of which these agitations have arisen, is a bad one." "It is better, there can be no question," he said, "that the population of any district should be the owners in fee of the soil they cultivate: it is the true way to avoid discontents, and it fills the region with a better population." Greeley went further. He declared that "there is *another* right in these manors beside the right of the Van Rensselaers—a right surely recognized in the chancery of heaven though not in that of New York." And that right arose from the tenants' labor. Surely, Greeley argued, the labor theory of value vested "*some* right in those whose hard toil has made the lands what they are." Yet neither Greeley nor Bryant had a clue about how to extinguish manorial tenures. Attacking the validity of landlord patents seemed fruitless. "We don't believe it will do you a particle of good," Greeley counseled Anti-Rent leaders. "Prescription and long usage are against you; wealth is against you; and we believe the law is against you." Even that will-o'-the-wisp had been extinguished by the "Indian" outrages of December. "Now that the lives of two worthy and unoffending citizens have been sacrificed," Greeley wrote on December 26, "we apprehend that [the Anti-Rent] cause is . . . irrevocably ruined by the crimes of a portion of its advocates, and that neither from the legislature nor [from] the landlords can any measure of relief be expected."[25]

Greeley's presumption was correct, at least in the short run. Silas Wright's plans for the 1845 legislature had never included land reform, and the bloodshed on Livingston Manor and Rensselaerwyck seemed to make his task easier. On December 4, as a draft of his message to the legislature began to take shape, he told Azariah Flagg that "I will make but one remark" on the Anti-Rent agitation: "Without the slightest sympathy of feeling for the landlords, I am so utterly disgusted with this mob law course, and mock Indian mummery, on the part of the tenants, that . . . [I intend] to give them to understand that men who dare not show their own faces as a sanction of their acts should hope little from honest administration of the law." Wright's revulsion with the "Indians" ran deep. In early December, however, he worried about the political consequences of a policy that distinguished the Anti-Rent movement's tactics from its goals and refused to consider the latter until the former had been suppressed. The killings east of the Hudson, then, came at precisely the right moment for the Democratic Party. "It is fortunate for those who have to deal officially with this ugly question, that blood has been first drawn by the Indians," Flagg wrote Van Buren on December 23. "This bloody argument prepares the public mind to look favorably on the adoption of energetic measures for the cure of these disorders, where without it the same measures might be regarded as unnecessarily harsh and uncalled for." Van Buren, who had previously argued that a gradual emancipation act would disband the "Indians," fell into step. "We are apparently on the eve of a bloody insurrection by the tenants against their landlords," he wrote Joel Poinsett four days later, "although I have strong hopes that the matter will be suppressed without much bloodshed."[26]

Most of the Hudson Valley landlords cared less about the possibility of more bloodshed than about the protection of their legal rights. On December 19 "about twenty" absentee proprietors assembled at the City Hotel in Manhattan to consider their situation, and none of them advocated compromise with the rebellious tenants. Gulian C. Verplanck chaired the meeting. The other participants included John J. Hunter and his son, "most of the Livingstons," Campbell P. White, "the Armstrongs," James McBride and his son-in-law Aaron Vanderpoel, "the Ludlows," J. Watts De Peyster, William S. Johnson, and John A. King. Together they owned close to a million acres under lease for lives or forever, mostly west of the Hudson in the counties of Delaware, Greene, Schoharie, Sullivan, and Ulster. Their agenda contained two items. The first was a memorial to be delivered to Wright upon his arrival at Albany on December 26. The memorial, as King summarized it for Stephen Van Rensselaer IV shortly afterward, stated "the utter helplessness" of the landlords "to collect dues, or to enforce their legal remedies," and called upon the governor-elect to "sustain the office of the law, in the discharge of his duties, with the whole power of the state." The memorial also implored Wright to recommend that a statute be enacted "making the assembly of armed and disguised men highly penal."[27]

King regarded the second item on the agenda as the more important one. It authorized the creation of an executive committee "whose duty, among other things, is to collect contributions from those interested, for the purpose of defraying all necessary and proper expenses, to pay two agents to attend at Albany, during the winter [session of the legislature] and generally, to take care of the general interest confided to them, in such manner as they should think best." King did not specify what the hired agents might do besides work the legislature's lobby. By retaining the services of James Powers and Charles Hathaway, however, the executive committee signaled that the landlords' plans included close collaboration with local officials in attempts to collect rents. Powers, a Catskill attorney, was the resident agent for the Hunter and Debrosses families in Ulster County. Hathaway, a Delaware County lawyer, managed the Hardenbergh Patent lands owned by Campbell P. White and the Livingstons. His cousin, Osman N. Steele, was the undersheriff of Delaware County.[28]

The executive committee's principal duty was to raise money, and King wrote the Van Rensselaers on Christmas Eve hoping to collect necessary funds. The proprietors of Rensselaerwyck disappointed him. Although the executive committee raised (and spent) $1,060 during 1845, the Van Rensselaers did not contribute a dime. William P. Van Rensselaer responded to an assessment of $250 with a scathing letter to Verplanck and Johnson, denouncing the New York City group's lack of support in the years when his family battled the anti-renters alone. But the division in the landlord ranks transcended matters of dollars and cents. It involved strategy. Late in 1844 the Van Rensselaers revived their offer, laid before the Manor Commission in 1841, to sell their interest in tenant farms for four dollars per acre. By their calculations, that sum, invested at 5 percent interest, would produce an annual revenue equal to the annual rent plus the value of their other interests in each farm—quarter sales, mineral- and water-right reservations, the one day's "riding," and the "four fat fowl." Negotiators for the Anti-Rent associations refused to pay more than two dollars per acre. As the Van Rensselaers waited patiently for their tenants to increase the counteroffer, the "Indians" disappeared from Rensselaerwyck. The aggressive policy pursued by the New York City group, in contrast, evoked massive resistance and eventually resulted in a third fatality.[29]

The sensational events of December 1844 spawned comparable divisions among the Anti-Rent faithful. Henry Z. Hayner, a Whig lawyer from Troy and cocounsel for Smith Boughton in the legal proceedings at Hudson, emerged as the principal Anti-Rent spokesman in Rensselaer following the arrest of "Big Thunder." Hayner's message was simple and direct. "The death of Rifenburgh and the murder of Smith will certainly have one good effect," he wrote in a Christmas day letter to the *Tribune*. "We shall see no more 'Indians.'" But their "folly and madness" Hayner insisted, "will not end the discussion of the iniquity and antirepublicanism of perpetual leases." The work of the Anti-Rent Party, which already had coalesced with the Whigs in Rensselaer, would continue until the state legislature had devised "some mode of rooting out the perpetual curse of perpetual leases." In a second letter, dated January 6, 1845, Hayner took up the problem of government action at some length. He denounced the "contemptuous and contemptible" Allen Report and called for a thorough reconsideration of the proposed Act Concerning Tenures by Lease drafted for the Anti-Rent associations. "Our state has been plastered over with patents obtained . . . by bribery, fraud and favoritism, to which Texas furnishes the only parallel," Hayner declared; because the measure laid before the legislature in 1844 would destroy the "landed aristocracy," it merited a "full and impartial" hearing. So did other measures designed to break the landlords' will to fight. "Perhaps the legislature may lay an income tax which shall reach ground-rents and make the owners of them more favorably disposed to a sale of them to the tenants," he suggested. "There is no good reason why bank, insurance, railroad and other stocks should be taxed, and ground-rents should escape."[30]

Hayner's call for a new Anti-Rent strategy resounded through Rensselaer in early January. At West Sandlake on January 4, "a large and respectable" mass meeting adopted resolutions framed by Burton A. Thomas, secretary of the Anti-Rent Association of Rensselaer County:

> Resolved, That this Association disapprove[s] of using any other means of redress, except those which the existing laws and the legislative power can furnish us, against the vassalage, created by the feudal leases of the Manor of Rensselaerwyck.

> Resolved, That in the opinion of this meeting, all ground-rents ought to be specifically taxed, as high as bank stock, or bonds and mortgages; and the present exemption of ground-rents from taxation, is antirepublican and unjust.

An "address to the people," issued a week later by the local Anti-Rent association at Schodack, sounded many of the same themes. "That any considerable portion of the landholders of this manor are 'Indians' or have opposed the execution of legal process," the Schodack tenants averred, "we believe to be false."[31]

In the Schodack address, however, the tenants advocated legislation grounded on the eminent domain power rather than the power to tax. "The Boston Railroad passes through this town, and so far as they occupy the lands, the landlord's covenants have been extinguished without his consent, and that under a power granted by our legislature," the address pointed out. "This would be justified on the ground, not that it is strictly for public use, but the prosperity and welfare of the country require it. Then if the prosperity of the welfare of the country would be promoted by removing the evils we complain of, why should not the same rule be applied and a similar course adopted?" The author of the Schodack address acknowledged that a "different reading" of the eminent domain power had been set forth in the Allen Report of 1844. Allen and the Democrats had approached the question, however, in the wrong spirit. "This state," proclaimed the tenants at Schodack, "must no longer remain the only civilized government on earth which leaves so important matters in the social polity [as land tenure] to the unrestrained direction of individual contracts."[32]

The unmistakably Whiggish tone of these documents was no accident. Boughton had been jailed and the "Indians" discredited; but the coalition that had elected Van Schoonhoven, Betts, and Heermance to the legislature in November remained intact. Even the new Anti-Rent rallying cry in Rensselaer, adopted by the Sandlake local on January 11, echoed the doctrines of Seward and Weed: "Let our motto be AGITATE, AGITATE, AGITATE, peaceably and lawfully, and victory will yet be ours." A studied disclaimer issued by Henry Z. Hayner did as well. On Christmas day, he flatly stated that "I am no agrarian, who would rob the rich of his lands to divide them among the poor." Such a disclaimer meant something in 1844. Earlier that year the National Reform Association, a social movement orchestrated by George Henry Evans's *Working Man's Advocate*, the voice of New York City's radical artisans, had taken an active interest in the tenant cause. Evans and most of his associates were nominal Democrats, and they charted an altogether different course for the Anti-Rent movement after the arrest of "Big Thunder" in December.[33]

Natural law was the wellspring of National Reform. Evans subscribed to the idea that property rights derived their legitimacy from the right of every human being to himself and the fruits of his labor. But land was the gift of God, not the product of toil. It followed that "the land should not be a matter of traffic, gift, or will" and government's duty to preserve natural rights entailed a duty to regulate land tenure for the common good. "If any man has a right on earth, he has a right to land enough to raise a habitation on," Evans wrote in 1841. "If he has a right to live, he has a right to land enough for his subsistence. Deprive anyone of these rights, and you place him at the mercy of those who possess them." National Reformers claimed that the doctrine of natural rights provided both a diagnosis and a cure for the crisis of republican government in America—a crisis manifested by "the haggard, care-worn countenance of the daily laborer, the wasting form of the overtasked seamstress . . . [and] the squalid children trained to beggary and deceit." The surplus of "white slaves" caused by the mechanization of labor meant that working people were rapidly losing the autonomy necessary for responsible citizenship. "By restoring his natural right to the soil," Evans insisted, "the laborer would not be dependent on the employer, and would consequently rise to his proper rank in society." All the people's representatives had to do was fix a limit on the amount of land any individual might own.[34]

Evans acknowledged that implementing this policy would be easier on the public domain of the United States than in states where land titles already had been allotted to individuals. But the concept of vested rights, though central to

American constitutional law, posed no barrier to the National Reformers. In their view, established wrongs created no prescriptive rights. "I am of Jefferson's opinion," Evans asserted. Neither natural rights nor the sovereignty of the people could be bargained away. "The people are beginning to 'repudiate' the idea that one generation may be bound, during the whole course of their existence, to the payment of interest on a debt, which they had no voice in contracting," declared the *Working Man's Advocate* in 1844. The same principle applied to land titles and justified tenant resistance in "the Anti-Rent districts" of eastern New York. "The statutes may be against the farmers," Evans wrote on September 14. "But these statutes may not be law, for law (see Blackstone) must be founded on natural right: although the ancestors of the farmers may have agreed that their descendants to all eternity should pay rent to the descendants of some Dutch king's favorite, these [tenant] descendants, not having been consulted in the matter, may reasonably conclude that they have a right to live on the land of their birth without paying tribute to any scion of monarchy."[35]

Evans did not despair on December 28, 1844, when the *Working Man's Advocate* announced that two deaths had resulted from the Anti-Rent disturbances. "Has landlordism never caused death?" he asked. "And if not guilty of deliberate murder, is it not at this moment the unquestionable cause of thousands upon thousands of cases of pinching want, if not many of actual starvation?" Evans blasted the Whig press for advocating the "employment of force by the state against the anti-renters," and he chided Bryant's *Evening Post* for subordinating "its love of justice" to its veneration of the law. "If the spirit shown in Columbia County is a 'disease,'" he asked, "then was that spirit a 'disease' that threw the tea chests overboard at Boston, and that threw monarchy overboard at Bunker Hill?" Evans strenuously urged members of the militia to ignore Governor Bouck's order to make war on their fellow citizens. "No power on earth," he declared, "should coerce me to support laws violating natural rights." His "hints to the anti-renters" were equally direct: "Carry on a *guerilla warfare*. The landless will be with you." Only unrelenting resistance, Evans argued, could keep the tenants' grievances before the public and allow "a right plainly asserted in the Declaration of Independence" to prevail. Evans urged all "anti-renters, all holders of small farms, and all mechanics and laboring men, throughout the state," to join in the National Reform Association's drive "to restrain anyone *hereafter* from obtaining possession, by gift, will, or purchase of more land than will be sufficient for a reasonable sized farm (say 160 acres)."[36]

Whig anti-renters, especially in Rensselaer, paid no attention to Evans's counsel. On the west side of the Hudson, however, the National Reformers got a hearing. Tenants in the hills of Albany and Schoharie counties were already familiar with the land-limitation scheme. Thomas A. Devyr, editor of the *Na-*

tional Reformer, a Long Island monthly, had corresponded with Anti-Rent leaders in the Helderberg towns since 1842 and had delivered a series of lectures there in October 1844. But the reception anti-renters gave to National Reform did not depend on men and measures. It depended on the status of rent strikes. In February 1845, when the proprietors unleashed deputy sheriffs in Delaware, Schoharie, and Ulster, the affected tenants listened more closely to the National Reformers than ever before. "They seek with avidity, and devour with eagerness, all that emanates from the press friendly to their view and opposed to feudalism," a Delaware anti-renter wrote Evans in mid-February. "This is proved to my satisfaction by the rapid increase to the subscription list of your *Advocate*, from this county, when, but a few days ago, it was unknown." Tenant tactics and agendas tended to correlate with landlord tactics and agendas. As the new year began, however, everyone with a stake in the land question recognized that his immediate fate hinged on Governor Wright. He set the agenda for the state legislature.[37]

Stalemate

Silas Wright had very little sympathy for the landlords and less for the likes of Henry Z. Hayner and Ira Harris, George Henry Evans and Thomas A. Devyr. He just wanted the "Indians" suppressed. Wright apparently did not consider how the pursuit of such a single-minded policy might affect the balance of power between landlords and tenants, Whig anti-renters and National Reformers. Perhaps he would have given the matter more thought if the perilous condition of his party had not distracted him. The movement to annex Texas, which resumed in earnest when Congress reassembled on December 3, 1844, threatened to exacerbate Democratic divisions on state policy and impair the party's ability to govern in Albany. Thus the bulk of the governor's message to the legislature, delivered on January 7, 1845, amounted to a high-wire balancing act on canal policy and constitutional reform. Wright asked for no new measures; he implored radicals and conservatives alike to put aside their pet projects while Congress deliberated on Texas and President-elect Polk deliberated on cabinet appointments. Because the Democracy's prospects in New York depended on developments in Washington, Wright urged the state legislature to act with caution until the national situation stabilized.[38]

The governor called for decisive action only on the tenant disorders in eastern New York. He condemned the "Indian" resistance, lamented the loss of life in Columbia and Rensselaer, and delivered a long homily on the obligations of citizenship in a republican polity. Wright acknowledged that the tenants' grievances had some merit. Under different circumstances, he told the lawmakers, "I might have invited your careful attention" to a determination of "in what way contracts, onerous in their exactions, and tenures in their nature and character uncongenial with the habits and opinions of our people could be peaceably and justly and constitutionally modified to meet the changed circumstances of the times." The governor felt "precluded from discussions of this character," however, "so long as the present position of the controversy on the part of the tenants is maintained." He did ask the legislature to enact two statutes, one making it a crime to go on the public highway "under the protection of masks and other disguises" and another authorizing the state government to provide county sheriffs with "the arms and munitions of war" required to suppress civil disorders. This was the only legislation, on any matter of public interest, Wright requested in 1845.[39]

The legislature tackled the "Indian" measures with extraordinary dispatch. "An Act to prevent persons appearing disguised and armed," introduced in the senate by Erastus Corning on January 8, breezed through both houses, and Wright signed it into law on January 28. The statute not only authorized every local peace officer to pursue and arrest masked people "of his own authority, and without process" but also empowered him "to command any male inhabitant of his county, or as many as he shall think proper, to assist him." Two years of imprisonment was prescribed for persons convicted of riot, or conspiracy to riot, while disguised and armed. A second statute authorized a special session of the Court of Oyer and Terminer in February to try Smith Boughton and the other prisoners already in custody at Hudson. Even the Whigs elected with Anti-Rent support in Albany, Rensselaer, and Schoharie voted for the two measures.[40]

Tenant leaders reacted to Wright's message as fast as the legislature did. A call went out for the Anti-Rent Party's first state convention on January 8; one week later, nearly 200 delegates from eleven counties gathered in the Lutheran church at Berne, Albany County. Devyr and five other National Reformers were seated but could not vote for want of affiliation with a county Anti-Rent association. The turnout astonished all who participated. Veteran anti-renters expected large delegations from counties on both sides of the Hudson and from Delaware. But the Mohawk country sent representatives as well. Fourteen delegates arrived from Schenectady and Montgomery counties, where rent strikes had just begun on the 30,000-acre Duanesburg estate and the 13,000-acre Corry Patent owned by George Clarke Jr. Every long-term tenant in the state, it seemed, wanted to protest Governor Wright's stance on the Anti-Rent agitation.[41]

Two resolutions adopted on January 15 reflected the Anti-Rent Party's immediate concerns. "Public functionaries, and also the press, both powerful organs," the preamble proclaimed, "have widely spread charges of combinations of tenants for the secret purpose of hiring persons disguised as Indians, to set law at defiance, . . . [but] we publicly declare—before God and man—that no such combinations have been made within our knowledge or belief, and can exist only in imagination." The resolutions followed:

> *Resolved*, That we deeply regret that the governor of this state should "feel himself precluded from inviting the careful attention of the legislature to the consideration" of the acknowledged grievances of the tenants, by reason of the lawless and indefensible acts of a misguided few, with whose acts . . . [they] are in no wise connected, and which they totally discountenance—and we cannot but deprecate this act of injustice, in making the sins of others the ground of witholding all relief from the acknowledged burden of oppression resting upon us.

> *Resolved*, That we cannot conceive of any sufficient cause for the continuance of "contracts" which are acknowledged to be "onerous in their exactions, and tenures which in their nature and character are uncongenial with the habits and opinions of a free people," and the principles of a free government.

The committee on petitions, which reported on the adoption of the resolutions, proposed a way to trump Governor Wright's policy. It framed a uniform petition for "a general and prompt circulation" in all eleven counties. The petition called upon the legislature to abolish the remedy of distress for rent, subject personal property in the form of ground rents to state taxation, and pass the Act Concerning Tenures by Lease. The convention resolved that "none but legal voters" should sign the document; one delegate predicted that 15,000 signatures could be obtained before March 1. Anti-renters collected more than 25,000.[42]

John Mayham, founder of the Anti-Rent Association on Blenheim Hill, Schoharie County, delivered a rousing speech that evening. He denounced the rent system as "a relic of barbarous times," called the land titles of the great proprietors "the barest frauds," and referred to the remedy of distress for rent and the exemption of ground rents from taxation as "special and antidemocratic privileges" that violated "immutable principles of equal rights." Mayham's speech concluded, as it began, with an indictment of Governor Wright. "It has been truly remarked," he said, "that 'prejudice closes the eyes as well as the ears to reason,' and thus bars every avenue to the heart against the conviction of truths presented."[43]

Charles Hathaway, the agent retained by the absentee New York City proprietors in December, immediately responded for the landlords in a series of articles for the *Evening Journal*. Writing under the pseudonym "Justus," Hathaway termed each of the Anti-Rent Party's proposed measures "absurd, unjust, and unconstitutional." The "cool impudence" in Mayham's speech evoked more extended comment. "There is scarcely in the whole of it a plain statement of facts; there is scarcely a line of even pretended argument," Hathaway wrote. "But woven, and thickly woven, in and out, through the whole length and breadth, are such phrases as these—'subservient vassal'—'liege lord'—'oppressed tenantry'—'noble landlord'—'humble tiller of the soil'— 'haughty and purse proud aristocrat.' " Hathaway complained that the impression conveyed by such talk "is, in fact, untrue." The landlord-tenant relation arose from contract only. As for equal rights, which Mayham invoked so "indiscriminately," it "does not mean that the debtor is inferior to the creditor, and that he shall be made equal by abolishing the debt, but this is what they ask." Instead, the equal-rights principle "mean[s] that he who makes a contract shall fulfill it, but this they repudiate. They ask for special legislation." Hathaway concentrated most of his fire, however, on the Anti-Rent claim that their associations had nothing to do with the tenant resistance. "It may be that the Anti-Rent associations have not, as such, employed these bands of 'Indians,' " he wrote. "It may be that not a red man has ever been seen at any of their meetings, but has not this been because some of the members had just washed their faces?" Although he could not prove that the "Indians" and the tenant associations "are composed of the same persons," Hathaway could reinforce Governor Wright's policy by provoking additional "Indian" activity.[44]

Hathaway's cousin, Osman N. Steele, rekindled the excitement in Delaware County. Beginning on February 11, Undersheriff Steele and his deputies advanced against the anti-renters on two fronts. They arrested Daniel Squires, a Roxbury tenant, for directing the tar-and-feather assault on deputy sheriff Timothy Corbin the previous September; they began serving distress warrants in Roxbury, Bovina, and Andes. On February 15, one day before the first scheduled sale, nine "Indians" threatened a deputy named J. A. Berson with tar and feathers if he ever returned to serve papers on striking tenants. Berson claimed that he recognized five of the disguised men; early the following morning, Steele raised a posse in Delhi, the county seat, and raided the farms of Anson K. Burrill, Ezekiel C. Kelley, Lewis Knapp, John Osterhout, and Silas Tompkins. All five were arrested on charges of violating the newly enacted Armed and Disguised Act. (Kelley subsequently pleaded guilty and was fined $250; the others were tried, convicted, and sentenced to two years imprisonment.) But the distress sale scheduled for that afternoon had to be postponed. "Not less than 400 persons, disguised as Indians, armed with muskets, rifles, and pistols, were seen on the mountain today to attend a sale of property to collect a rent of sixteen dollars," a Delhi resident wrote "a gentleman in Albany"— probably Hathaway—on February 16. "The sheriff immediately adjourned the sale. . . . It may be safely affirmed that the anti-renters are insincere in their professions of submission to the laws, and that they are determined to persist in their defiance of law and order to the utmost extremity."[45]

Steele went after the "Indians," not their rents, in the weeks that followed. The resistance leaders focused on the prisoners in custody. Steele and a deputy, each commanding parties of between 30 and 40 volunteers, succeeded in capturing Warren W. Scudder ("Bluebeard") and 5 others near Roxbury. But a foray into Andes on March 11 was less successful. An estimated 100 "Indians" trapped the undersheriff in Hunting's tavern, apparently hoping to trade their prisoner for the 12 anti-renters already in jail awaiting trial. The siege lasted all night. Just before dawn, however, Steele managed to get a messenger through the "Indian" lines. His note to Sheriff Green More, as recorded and perhaps edited by a Delhi newspaper correspondent, was certainly evocative: "They intend, as near as I can ascertain, to take my papers, tar and feather me, and pass me over to the Middleburgh tribe. I shall never be able to reach home, unless you come over with all the force you can raise. Let every man come armed and determined to do his duty or die on the spot. Lose no time, but get here as soon as possible." Sheriff More came and the "Indians" melted away as the posse marched up the road.[46]

Delhi remained an armed camp for the next ten weeks. The sheriff persuaded Colonel James Marvin, commander of the local militia unit, to fortify the jail with his Delhi men; Hathaway arranged for the shipment of 100 sabres, 100 pairs of pistols, and 600 cartridges from the state arsenal. But the Delaware authorities controlled only the county seat and its overcrowded jail. No distress sales were conducted, and "the anti-renters kept the countryside in a state of constant alarm by blowing their horns and firing their guns." Sheriff More "will not meet in council with us," a Delaware anti-renter complained in a letter to Greeley's *Tribune* on April 5. "Perhaps it may not be amiss here to say that if the sheriff's advisors expect to break down 'Anti-Rent' by any course they may pursue, they greatly overrate themselves and underrate us, as a more determined spirit never actuated a community of men. . . . The landlords who direct the sheriff's movements have thus far only bound [us] more strongly together as a band of brothers who are determined to free the land of this curse that it labors under."[47]

Similar standoffs, punctuated by discriminating "Indian outrages" and a few arrests under the Armed and Masked Act, materialized in Ulster and Schoharie counties. Henry P. Shultis, resident agent for the heirs of Robert L. Livingston in Woodstock, Ulster County, had an especially trying time. Three of his men got a coat of tar and feathers from "a gang of 15 or 16 armed men, disguised as Indians" early in March. One of the victims pulled off two masks during the affray; arrest warrants for both people were issued on March 7. "The proprietors of the land are determined not only to arrest the offenders, but to collect every cent of rent now due, by legal proceedings," the commander of the Ulster militia wrote his superior in Albany that afternoon. Next day the Ulster "Indians," led by Asa Briggs ("Blackhawk"), ambushed a deputy sheriff and burned his papers. A posse of fifty men largely recruited in Kingston, the county seat, pursued Briggs and his braves "in a pelting snow" for four days and made seventeen arrests. But most of the "Indians," including Briggs, escaped into adjacent Delaware County. "From the nature of this country," a Kingston correspondent for the *Argus* explained on March 14, "those accustomed to it can defy pursuit and can only be arrested by strategem." In a letter to the proprietors on April 2, Shultis underscored the arrests that had been made and boasted that he had begun to receive "some [rent] money daily in small sums." The most graphic commentary on the situation in Ulster, however, was made by Briggs and his men as they temporarily fled the county. The "Indians" poured tar and feathers on a roadside stone that marked the boundary of Shultis's farm in the hills above Woodstock. "For many years," the local historian reports, "the 'Tory stone' was given an annual coat of tar and feathers as an expression of lasting Anti-Rent feeling."[48]

The sheriff of Schoharie County, John S. Brown, collected no rents and made no arrests that spring. On March 24, he and a deputy tried to serve distress warrants on the Blenheim Patent, owned by John A. King. They stopped first at the home of Stephen Mayham, treasurer of the county Anti-Rent association. "On our way and while we were at Mayham's," the sheriff wrote in a statement published five days later, "we several times heard the blowing of horns." Nevertheless, Brown and his aide proceeded to home of Orra Ferguson, "against whom we had an execution, not for rent." Ferguson was not at home, but the lawmen encountered him on the road a few minutes later; Ferguson said that he would meet them at Fink's tavern that evening and pay the execution. Shortly after Ferguson showed up at the tavern, as promised, "Mrs. Fink came into the barroom and informed us that the house was surrounded by *Indians*." The sheriff subsequently claimed that "at this juncture the countenance of Mr. Ferguson brightened into a smile, and he immediately disappeared." The "Indians" did not.

Sheriff Brown reported that at least 150 men, "disguised and armed with deadly weapons," marched the lawmen through the woods for several hours, amusing themselves with "ribald language" and intermittent talk of tar and feathers while "forcing us through the muddiest places they could find . . . and poking us with their guns." The Blenheim tribe released them unharmed but issued a warning. "They demanded that I should resign my office or swear that I would not again come in that region on like business," Brown said. "And if I did come with a posse, they would select me, and put a ball through my horse, and would not be particular if it took effect in the rider." Schoharie officials did not return for several months.[49]

A different sort of standoff occurred in the Columbia County trial of Smith

Boughton for robbery and conspiracy to obstruct justice. On March 30, after hearing two weeks of testimony and the defense lawyers' insistent claim that "the Big Thunder at Copake was not Dr. Boughton," members of the jury returned and announced that they would be unable to reach a verdict "if they were kept together for a year." Judge Amasa J. Parker polled the jurors and reluctantly discharged them. "Eight were for acquittal," reported the *Tribune* correspondent in Hudson. "Two [others] were willing to agree either to acquittal or conviction." Boughton was remanded to jail where he remained until July, when the authorities quietly released him on bail and ordered him to return for a second trial during the court's September term. George Henry Evans predicted the outcome of the first trial and lambasted the government's course. "In one half of the time, and for one half the expense, that these trials will occupy," he wrote on March 29, "the legislature might pass a law to prevent any further land monopoly in this state, and give some relief to those who are now suffering from this monarchical curse; but they seem to prefer a resort to prison, sword, and bayonet arguments. We shall see the effect."[50]

One immediate effect was another triumph for the Whig/Anti-Rent coalition in the Albany and Rensselaer local elections on April 1. Henry Z. Hayner, fresh from his victory in the Boughton trial, exulted at the returns. "Every town upon the Manor of Rensselaerwyck elects an anti-renter," he wrote Greeley two days later.

> How absurd and ridiculous to suppose that a majority of all the voters in nine large and populous towns are Indians, or countenance the disguised opposition to the laws! . . . Do you think they can be outwitted by such poor trickery as that of Governor Wright in his message, who could not hearken to their complaints, or inquire into their grievances, or propose any measures for their relief, because, forsooth, some persons without warrant or authority, without countenance or assistance from them, had assumed to take up arms in their behalf, and had violated the laws? This was too stale a trick of tyranny to succeed in this land of intelligence and freedom.

Evans also rejoiced that "the entire Anti-Rent ticket was put through" in Albany and Rensselaer. But he cautioned the faithful to discount Hayner's rhetorical disdain for the "Indian" bands. "Some of the anti-renters are denouncing any violent resistance of injustice," Evans declared shortly after the April elections. "Where inalienable rights are concerned, those who are robbed of them are daily losing part of their existence, and should never voluntarily resign the quickest mode of recovering their rights."[51]

The next move belonged to Governor Wright and the Democratic majority in the state legislature. Twenty-five thousand tenant petitioners from eleven counties could not be ignored. Yet anti-renters had little cause to expect a favorable response. The proposed Act Concerning Tenures by Lease remained at the top of their wish list; no reputable lawyer, Whig or Democrat, had contested the imposing constitutional arguments against it. *Bronson v. Kinzie*, decided by the Supreme Court of the United States in 1843, still stood as a barrier to the measure's first section, authorizing tenants to set up want of title in their landlord as a defense against actions for rent. *Taylor v. Porter*, decided under the state constitution's due process clause that same year, still stood as a barrier to the measure's second section, authorizing tenants to purchase their landlords' interest in the land upon payment of just compensation. The taxation of ground rents, a new Anti-Rent proposal, stood on a different footing. It posed no constitutional difficulties. But the governor had linked the consideration of land reform with the cessation of "Indian" hostilities, and the tenant resistance had not ceased. By the adjournment of the legislature on May 13, 1845, however, the Wright administration had endorsed the taxation of ground rents. A bill authorizing a constitutional convention, which suddenly made an eminent domain measure feasible, had been enacted as well. Sanctimonious denunciations of the "Indians" by Whig anti-renters had nothing to do with the changing environment for land reform. The impetus came from Washington.

Political Crossroads

Horatio Seymour, the speaker of the New York assembly in 1845, once re-marked that Silas Wright "was a great man, an honest man: if he committed errors, they were induced by devotion to his party. He was not selfish: to him his party was everything—himself nothing." Examples of Wright's selflessness were legendary. In 1844 alone, he declined both an appointment to the Supreme Court of the United States and the Democratic Party's nomination for vice-president. Yet he agreed to run for governor, an office that repulsed him and his wife more than any other, because his party beckoned at a critical stage of the campaign. "The only safe hope and dependence for the republican principle in this country, from this time forth," he wrote George Bancroft in September 1844, "rests upon the Democracy of the North; and th[at] deep conviction . . . has forced me to submit myself to almost anything." In the immediate aftermath of his election, however, Wright did not tell Bancroft or anyone else what the New York Democracy might do to secure "the republican principle" against the unnamed forces that imperiled it. He spoke, instead, in metaphors that con-veyed his sense of bewilderment about what had happened to his party, as well as to his wife and himself, during the previous six months. "I think the case may be likened to a family burned out and left houseless and homeless, with the reflection that the insurance was good and ample," he confided to Azariah Flagg on November 12. "We feel that we are broken up, and do not know exactly how we shall fare in another establishment."[1]

Wright had reason to be uncomfortable with the prospect of moving into the statehouse. Few incoming governors in American history faced a more paradox-ical political situation. For his entire career, the party that meant "everything" to him had been dedicated to frugal government and the containment of sectional struggles over slavery. But internal-improvement enthusiasts in the state party's conservative wing had breached the one principle at Albany in 1843–44, and Texas enthusiasts in the national party had violated the other at the Baltimore convention that dumped Martin Van Buren and nominated James K. Polk for president. Wright thought both developments, especially in combination, jeopardized the future of the Democracy; he longed to guide the party back toward the safe path that Van Buren had blazed, with his assistance, in the 1820s and 1830s. Taking a firm stand against both the New York conservatives' plans for canal construction and Polk's plans for Texas, however, was almost certain to hasten the demise of the old Democracy he wanted to restore. The incoming Polk administration had a great many federal offices to distribute. And the conservatives—William C. Bouck, Edwin Croswell, Daniel S. Dickinson, William L. Marcy, and their followers—not only "hunkered" for the spoils but avowed their support for Texas annexation from the outset. Wright's first objective as leader of the New York Democracy, then, was to prevent Polk and the conservatives from uniting. This could be accomplished by neutralizing the Texas question in state politics and delaying it on the national scene until new terms of annexation, conformable to "the republican principle," had been established. Neither move would be easy to execute, but Wright was an adroit and influential politician.

Wright excelled at mending political fences, and he worked hard at it between his nomination and inauguration. "If I was ever your friend," he wrote Polk on December 20, "I was never more sincerely so than at this moment." Equally reassuring letters went out to Dickinson, Marcy, and conservative state senator Erastus Corning. Wright's best friends, however, called themselves radicals. Michael Hoffman, William Cullen Bryant, Theodore Sedgwick Jr., Samuel Young, and others shared his fears about the party's trajectory and engineered his nomination for governor because they regarded him as one of their own. The radicals advocated a constitutional convention to check the luxuriation of conservative power in Albany and condemned the Texas project from the beginning. Wright's heart was with them. If he expected to shape Polk's decisions, however, he had to keep the radicals at arm's length.[2]

Silas Wright was not the first governor of New York who hitched his state party's future to national decisions that he could influence but not control. William Henry Seward had done much the same thing in 1840–41. Seward looked to Washington for money; Wright looked to Washington for a solution to the Texas question that all New York Democrats could live with. Neither of them succeeded. But Wright's position in 1845 was stronger than Seward's in 1841. Seward pegged everything on new sources of revenue and had nowhere to turn when the anticipated funds did not materialize. Wright had a well-marked line of retreat. He could take up the radicals' call for a constitutional convention, hold out an olive branch to the anti-renters, and mesh the Democracy's new commitments with some old reliable ones to maintain a working majority in the state legislature. Adverse circumstances prompted Wright to take each of those steps during the spring of 1845. As he gradually changed course, the tenants were invited to change theirs as well. When the New York legislature's 1845 session came to an end in May, the Anti-Rent movement stood at a political crossroads.

The Washington-Albany Connection

Governor Wright's first official duty, delivering a message to the state legislature that convened in January, provided him with a customary occasion for exercising party leadership. Yet he dreaded the assignment. He could not define the Democracy's mission in coherent terms without alienating either the conservatives or the radicals, and he remained uncertain about how to split the difference until the last minute. The fatal gunshots in Columbia and Rensselaer exploded his doubts about what to say about the Anti-Rent agitation. But other December developments in Washington and in New York only increased his anxiety.[3]

The final session of the Twenty-eighth Congress began on December 3, 1844, and President Tyler urged the lawmakers to reconsider the annexation of Texas. Success was possible, Tyler declared in his message to Congress, if annexation were understood as a problem in state making (which required a simple majority in both houses) rather than as a problem of treaty making (which required a supermajority in the Senate). Annexationists favored the joint-resolution scheme because it made immediate action feasible. Yet offering the Republic of Texas admission as a state, rather than a territory, posed other difficulties. The treaty, which Texas officials already had approved, resolved the problems of slavery, land titles, and the public debt. Consideration of a joint resolution meant reopening those matters. Tyler's recommendation evoked an abundant response all the same. Beginning on December 10, seven annexation resolutions were introduced in the Senate and ten in the House of Representatives. Each of them stipulated different terms for admitting Texas to the Union; some stipulated no terms whatsoever. Adopting a resolution of the latter sort would permit the president to make a new deal with Texas, subject to approval by the Twenty-ninth Congress, which assembled in December 1845. Polk did not commit himself to any particular formula for a joint resolution. The president-elect let it be known, however, that he wanted Congress to pass one of them before it adjourned on March 4, the day of his inauguration.[4]

Just before the debate on Texas began in Congress, Governor Bouck made two interim appointments to the United States Senate. Wright's uncommon sense of rectitude had prompted him to resign his seat upon accepting the Democracy's nomination for governor; Nathaniel P. Tallmadge, a Whig whose term expired on March 4, had resigned a few weeks later to accept an appointment as governor of Wisconsin Territory. Bouck named two conservatives,

Daniel S. Dickinson and Henry A. Foster, both of whom immediately began to collaborate with the Senate annexationists. The appointments outraged the radicals associated with the *Evening Post*. Bryant, assisted by Sedgwick and David Dudley Field, conducted a fierce anti-Texas campaign throughout December and January, elaborating a plausible case against the constitutionality of annexation by joint resolution and decrying any measure that "irrevocably fastens on us the infinite curse and disgrace of slavery." When the state legislature convened in January, they argued, both of Bouck's men should be canned. Congressman Lemuel Stetson of New York City, Wright's former messmate, concurred. Foster had gone "hook and line for Calhoun," he wrote Flagg from Washington on December 31. "Send such men back here and you . . . will have a member of the cabinet from the State of New York hostile to [Wright]; all the patronage of the administration will flow into similar channels."[5]

Wright saw things differently, in part because he knew things the radicals did not. Polk wrote him on January 4, saying that he intended to select a New Yorker as head of either the State Department or the Treasury. The president-elect sent a similar letter to Van Buren on the same day. Polk asked both of them for names and strongly implied that he would appoint one of the people they recommended. Wright and Van Buren agreed that Benjamin Butler was right for State, Azariah Flagg for Treasury; but the prospect of Butler's appointment thrilled them. If Congress passed an annexation resolution that gave Polk a free hand, a stalwart of the New York Democracy would conduct the negotiations with the Republic of Texas and perhaps with Mexico. War might be averted. Flagg's appointment, though less desirable, would at least give the Van Buren men a voice in the new administration and ensure an acceptable distribution of the federal offices in New York State. All they had to do was straddle the senatorial question. Jettisoning both Dickinson and Foster, if such a thing were possible, could not be accomplished without signaling Polk that the state party had fallen into the hands of the radicals. Wright and his advisors concluded that John A. Dix should replace Foster but Dickinson should be retained in Washington for a full term. The decision to mollify both factions on national affairs inclined Wright to approach divisive questions of state policy in much the same way.[6]

Governor Wright's first message to the state legislature, delivered on January 7, 1845, elaborated one main theme. He was neither a conservative Hunker nor a radical Barnburner, and he expected all members of his party to work together as Democrats. Edwin Croswell called the message a "great state paper." Horace Greeley characterized it more accurately as "shreds of party patchwork." Despite his preoccupation with national affairs during the preceding month, Wright said very little about "the interests of our state as a member of the Union." He did proclaim that the "solemn decision of the people" had settled the bank, tariff, and distribution issues. In New York, "the most commercial state of the Union," he remarked, "we have felt, with great severity, the uncertainty, the change and the prospect of change, which, for many years past, have almost constantly surrounded all these questions." But the principal threat to national repose evoked only passing mention. "I firmly believe," Wright declared, "that a calm and statesmanlike course in the management of our relations with other powers . . . will continue us in peace, or if it lead to a war, it will be such a war as every patriotic heart in the country will sustain and approve." Democrats understood the meaning implied in these brief remarks. The governor did not want the state legislature to consider any resolutions on the Texas question pending in Congress. A substantial majority of the New York electorate disagreed with Polk's views on the matter; if a resolution that denounced annexation came to a vote, the legislature's Democrats would have to disappoint the voters or the president-elect. Hoping for an acceptable outcome in Washington, as Wright did, was the more prudent course.[7]

The bulk of the governor's message addressed the state debt, the constitutional amendments passed by the legislature in 1844, and the tenant disorders in eastern New York. His observations on the debt amounted to a veto threat. The surplus money available for new construction under the Stop and Tax Act, he declared, "is entirely too inconsiderable to make any useful progress with the works, and especially so, if it must be divided among them." It was "not likely," moreover, that "the large and worthy portions of our fellow citizens" interested in either the Erie Canal enlargement, the Genesee Valley Canal, or the Black River Canal "will consent that the money shall be diverted from the debt and also from their favorite improvement." Using the surplus to begin paying off the principal, then, was the only thing that made sense.[8]

Wright coupled his vow to restrain government spending, a blow to conservatives, with a request designed to muzzle the radicals on their favorite project, a constitutional convention. Five constitutional amendments had been passed by the legislature in 1844; the New York Constitution provided that both houses had to approve them again in 1845, this time by a two-thirds majority, before they could be submitted to the voters for ratification. The pending amendments would constitutionalize the Stop and Tax Act, mandate a referendum on construction projects requiring substantial new debt, and effect modest reforms in the judicial system. But the 1844 legislature had refused to address four other items on the radical agenda for constitutional reform. Radicals wanted to prevent stockholders in business corporations from evading their debts under the principle of limited liability, to separate the legislative and judicial departments, to curtail the executive's enormous patronage powers, and to facilitate constitutional reform in the future by requiring a convention of the people every twenty years. Conservatives strenuously opposed change on all these matters.[9]

Wright asked the legislature to adopt the pending amendments and quash the movement for a constitutional convention. The amendments passed in 1844 "have taken hold of the public mind, and have been received with strong favor," he said. "It is not given to you to incorporate the provisions in, and make them a part of, our constitution. This is wisely left for the people themselves." If the amendments failed for want of the requisite action by the legislature, however, "discontents will be experienced, and other forms of amendment will be proposed and perhaps successfully urged." These remarks, ostensibly aimed at the conservatives who had opposed the People's Resolution in 1842 and 1843, imposed a more significant obligation on the radicals who had suspended their quest for a convention in 1844. Wright expected them to maintain their silence until the fate of the constitutional amendments had been determined.[10]

Everything went the Wright way in January and early February. The legislature's Democratic caucus seethed with dissension, but its members followed the course the governor had set. Dickinson and Dix got the two Senate seats; the party's two wings split the state offices (radicals Azariah Flagg and John Van Buren for comptroller and attorney general, conservatives Nathaniel S. Benton and Benjamin Enos for secretary of state and treasurer). Martin Van Buren and William C. Bouck were named to the state university's board of regents. Resolutions on the Texas question, introduced day after day by Whigs in both houses, got rebuffed by the Democratic majority. Meanwhile, welcome news reached New York from Tennessee. Polk wrote Van Buren on January 30 to thank him for the recommendation of Butler for the State Department and Flagg for the Treasury. "I think it probable that I may want one of the gentlemen mentioned for a place in my cabinet," he said; "but which one of them I think it prudent to leave open until I reach Washington."[11]

Trouble loomed only for the five constitutional amendments. In the senate, where the Democracy occupied twenty-seven of the thirty-two seats, the amendments passed by the requisite two-thirds majority on February 4. But the chamber's four Whigs, led by Gideon Hard of Albion, Orleans County, voted against the amendments. "The objection which Mr. Hard and other [Whig] members in the legislature . . . take to this tinkering with the constitution," remarked the *Evening Journal*, "is that the remedy does not reach the disease." The judiciary amendments "simply create five additional offices," three vice-chancellors and two justices of the New York Supreme Court. "This is well pleasant enough for Governor Wright, who is to dispense, and for 'the faithful,' who are to receive, these crumbs of patronage." But the people wanted to curtail, not enhance, the executive's appointive powers. "A convention alone," proclaimed the organ of progressive Whiggery, "can carry out the desired reform."[12]

The *Evening Journal* did not mention one thing Hard hoped to secure from a convention of the people. When the senate considered constitutional reform in 1844, he had introduced an unsuccessful amendment to repeal the property qualification for black voters. The first sentence of the Declaration of Independence, Hard said on that occasion, laid down "the grand political thesis" of the American republic. "The universality of that proposition embraces *all men*, and includes as well the African race as the Asiatic, European, or American races. And no where in that instrument can any distinction be found between men on account of color; hence in most of the states of this Union all free men of color are admitted to the right of suffrage." For Hard, as for most Whigs in western New York, the struggle for equal voting rights also provided a means of luring Whig abolitionists away from the Liberty Party. "In this state," Seward wrote Liberty leader Gerrit Smith on January 21, 1845, "the obvious interests of the Whig party (to do no violence to their sympathies) lead to efforts for a convention to extend the right of suffrage. I doubt not we shall have your aid."[13]

Democratic managers recognized that Whig talk of a convention put the constitutional amendments in jeopardy. Democrats held 67 of the 128 seats in the assembly, 19 fewer than the two-thirds majority required to amend the state's fundamental law. The New York City nativists, who had been elected with Whig support, had 15 votes and the Whigs 46. As the session got under way, Croswell grew increasingly alarmed. Greeley came out for a constitutional convention on January 30; John Young, the minority whip in the assembly, followed suit in a speech delivered on February 11. "There is no doubt a good reason for the sudden effervescence of the Whigs for a convention," Croswell declared in a derisive editorial three days later. "No doubt the honest Whigs, thoroughly beaten before the people and the Democratic ascendancy restored, are extremely anxious to try their hand over again, under new issues and other questions of difference. No one will doubt, that their votes against any amendment of the constitution, by which reforms may be made in the constitutional mode, spring from this patriotic desire [in John Young's words] to 'upturn the whole machinery of state government.'" What really concerned Croswell was the prospect of a Barnburner-Whig alliance on the convention question. For three months, however, the radicals acquiesced to Wright's plea for party discipline.[14]

The new politics of constitutional reform could not have been more ironic. The conservative Democrats, who had grudgingly accepted the pending amendments in 1844, became their greatest defenders. The Whigs, who had never shown much interest in the matter, became champions of a convention. And the radical Democrats, who had launched the controversy and established the reform agenda, became mere spectators as Whigs and Hunkers hurled brickbats at one another in the press and in the legislature. The assembly took up the question on January 31 and debated it almost daily for two months before a breakthrough occurred. None of the state's party leaders and publicists considered the possibility that the distinct movements for land reform and constitutional reform might converge. Nobody in the Anti-Rent ranks did either. Anti-renters were still in the throes of confusion arising from their commitment to both rent strikes and political action.

Dilemmas for the Democracy

James K. Polk changed the course Governor Wright had set in January. The president-elect wrote Martin Van Buren on February 22 and reported that he had decided to offer Benjamin Butler the War Department. Van Buren received the letter at Lindenwald, his Columbia County estate, four days later. The more he thought about its contents, the more furious he became. Polk had spoken of "a place in my cabinet" for either Butler or Flagg on January 30; Van Buren had persuaded himself that Butler was likely to get the State Department, an appointment that might "save us," he wrote Francis Preston Blair on February 11, "from a war for the acknowledged or known purpose of extending or perpetuating slavery." The president-elect's February 22 letter dashed that dream and conjured up a nightmare. Butler had made it clear in January that he would not accept anything less than the State Department. He had been attorney general under Andrew Jackson and would not give up his lucrative Manhattan law practice for a lesser post. Van Buren feared that Polk might use Butler's rejection as an excuse to appoint William Marcy, a conservative whose suitability for Treasury or War had been openly pressed by William C. Bouck and Senator Daniel S. Dickinson.[15]

Van Buren hurried to Albany for a consultation with Wright on February 27. Next day they dispatched Smith Van Buren to New York and on to Washington with one message for Butler, urging him to swallow his pride for the good of the party, and another for Polk, "answering for Mr. Butler that he will accept" and warning the president-elect that it would be "a fatal mistake in this state" to appoint Marcy. Should Butler decline, Van Buren wrote, "by all means . . . take Mr. [Churchill] Cambreleng," another New York City radical, for the War Department. Smith Van Buren arrived too late at both destinations. In New York he learned that Butler already had sent Samuel J. Tilden to Washington with a letter declining the appointment. A railroad accident in Baltimore prevented young Van Buren from getting to Washington before Polk offered the War Department to Marcy. "New York is, I fear, betrayed," Senator John A. Dix wrote Flagg from Washington on March 3. "I only desire to say that the president-elect acts with full knowledge of the probable consequences, and with a view of the whole ground." Maybe not. Dix's voice carried no more weight than Dickinson's, and Polk had not heard either Van Buren's or Wright's at the critical moment. But the feeling of betrayal remained. "The nomination of

Mr. Marcy," remarked the *Albany Atlas* on March 12, "[has] caused a wider and deeper feeling of disappointment than the accredited rumor that no place had been assigned to New York."[16]

The resolution of the Texas question upset Wright and his Barnburner friends as much as the Marcy appointment. On January 25, the House of Representatives passed a joint resolution proposed by Milton Brown, a Tennessee Whig, by a vote of 120-98. It purported to admit the Republic of Texas as a state and left jurisdiction over its debt and public lands to Texans themselves. The resolution also provided that up to four additional states might be carved out of Texas at a later date, with slavery permitted in any new states located south of the 36°30′ Missouri Compromise line and prohibited in any new states established north of the line. This provision, designed to mollify southern Whigs, repulsed most representatives from the free states. Every northern Whig voted against Brown's resolution; the Democratic delegation from New York stood nearly two to one against it. "I do not believe the Democracy of the state would sustain us in the annexation without some fair compromise of the slave question," Wright wrote Dix on February 15. "Hence I do not believe you would be sustained in voting for the proposition which passed the House. I look upon that proposition as more unfortunate than if it had proposed no line, because all our people know that the line it marks does not touch one inch of the territory which Texas owns, or over which Texas has ever practically exercised jurisdiction and government. It is therefore no compromise in fact, while it is one in form, and almost every man you meet calls it a cheat and a fraud." Preston King, a Barnburner from upstate New York, predicted that the Democrats would "fall in every free state except Illinois" if the party were "made responsible for legalizing slavery in the whole of Texas."[17]

Wright and the New York radicals preferred a measure that Thomas Hart Benton of Missouri introduced in the Senate on February 5. Benton's bill simply appropriated $100,000 to defray the expenses necessary to establish new terms for the admission of Texas, either by treaty or by articles submitted to Congress as the president might direct. Annexationists opposed this approach for the same reason their adversaries favored it. Starting from scratch entailed delay and possible defeat for the project. The result was compromise. On February 27, following three weeks of delicate negotiations in which Polk took an active part, the Senate adopted a bill that vested the president with discretion to implement either the Benton plan or the joint resolution that had passed in the House. Three southern Whigs joined the unified Democrats to see the bill through the Senate; the House accepted it by a larger majority than Milton Brown's resolution had received in January. President Tyler signed the measure into law on March 1.[18]

In a letter to Wright, Dix explained why the Democratic delegation from New York embraced the compromise measure.

I had a conversation with the president-elect, whose solicitude on the subject is very great, and he assured me if he had any discretion placed in his hands, he would exercise it in such a manner as to satisfy us. That same evening I saw Haywood [of North Carolina] . . . [and] told him I would, with the consent and approbation of Benton, vote for a union of the two propositions with a proviso that the president in his discretion might, without submitting the conditions of the joint resolution to Texas, open negotiations immediately under Benton's bill.

Dix's understanding contained a blind spot. Tyler did not have to leave the choice to his successor. With the connivance of Secretary of State John C. Calhoun, Tyler immediately dispatched a messenger offering statehood to Texas under the House resolution. Polk might have nullified those instructions following his inauguration. On March 10, however, his cabinet agreed that the action of the previous administration should be confirmed in order to avoid confusion and delay in effecting annexation. Van Buren's quest to put Butler, not Marcy, inside Polk's inner circle had been propelled by this very sort of contingency. But nothing had worked according to plan. "Your course was right and will be sustained by your friends," Wright assured Dix on March 11, "even if *the two presidents* should defraud you of the understanding."[19]

New York Whigs reveled in the misery of Governor Wright and his friends. Weed's *Evening Journal* interrupted a steady stream of editorials advocating a constitutional convention to pillory the "slave power" and its benighted creature, the Democratic Party. "The issue of the Texas question serves to establish, beyond all future cavil, the utter hollowness and hypocrisy of the claims and pretensions, so constantly and ostentaciously put forward by the Locofoco party to the name and principles of DEMOCRACY," he wrote on March 5.

As Democrats, they profess to be in favor of equal rights; yet what grosser outrage upon equal rights can be imagined than a measure which imparts new strength and sanction to the doctrine that one human being can hold another, created, like himself, in the image of his Maker, in hopeless and perpetual bondage. As Democrats, they claim to read the Constitution strictly; yet when was a more latitudinarian construction ever given to the Constitution than that under which Congress is invested with power to acquire, by mere joint resolution, a foreign republic?

Whether the New York Democracy liked it or not, opposition to slavery and a war with Mexico—issues they had finessed in 1844—now belonged to the Whigs and their nemeses in the Liberty Party.[20]

Hunkers welcomed the emergence of clear party distinctions on territorial expansion and a constitutional convention. Edwin Croswell's *Argus* hailed the impending annexation of Texas and lauded Polk's continental vision. "The anti-American course of the Whig press," Croswell remarked on March 6, "will not be sustained by the people." The radicals had other ideas. In their judgment, the time had come for the New York Democracy to reclaim its traditional role as the tribune of popular sovereignty and natural rights. Nothing could be done to reassert the Barnburner position on the extension of slavery until the new Congress assembled in December. But constitutional reform was another matter. The reasons for postponing the agitation for a convention had dissipated, and the Whig minority in the assembly had all but killed the pending constitutional amendments. On March 4, Michael Hoffman and Arphaxed Loomis summoned Assemblyman William Crain of Herkimer home for a conference. He returned to Albany four days later with a bill authorizing a plebiscite in November on the question of "convention" or "no convention."[21]

Crain took the case for a constitutional convention to Governor Wright on March 9. They discussed the matter again two, perhaps three, days later at a meeting that Hoffman and Loomis came down from Herkimer to attend. Although no record of the conversations has survived, the gist of what transpired seems clear enough. Wright acknowledged that a convention had become necessary to constitutionalize the Stop and Tax Act, secure some form of the People's Resolution, and put the state debt question to rest. But he thought the Whigs should be required to defeat the existing constitutional amendments before Crain introduced his bill. Only then could a modicum of Democratic discipline be maintained in the legislature. Hoffman and Loomis worried about the consequences of delay. Whig assemblymen and Whig editors had been pounding the drums for a convention since January; Democrats needed to engage them, emphasizing party differences on public spending and limited liability for business corporations, before the people forgot that the very idea of a convention had originated in the Democracy.[22]

The course of events suggests that they made a deal. Crain introduced "An act recommending a Convention of the People of this State in 1846" on March 13, but he said nothing about his bill until after the pending constitutional amendments had been defeated. Meanwhile, the organs of radical Democracy resumed the agitation. "We shall never have a reform of the constitution from the hands of the legislature," wrote William Cullen Bryant on March 20. "Our only reliance is upon the old fashioned method of a convention." Arphaxed Loomis, writing under the pseudonym "Citizen," supplied the *Evening Post* with five articles that week on the "radical reforms . . . essential to our prosperity and security, and . . . why these reforms should be sought only through the agency of a convention." In 1845, as in 1843, the abolition of manorial tenures was not on the reform agenda.[23]

Yet the Whigs, not the radical Democrats, forced the convention issue in the state legislature. Assemblyman John Young, a handsome Geneseo trial lawyer and former congressman, devised the Whig plan of attack on the divided Democrats. Jabez Hammond called him "one of the ablest party leaders and most skillfull managers in a popular body that ever entered the assembly chamber; [he was] quick to perceive how an advantage might be gained over an adverse party . . . but no man could wait more quietly for the arrival of the proper time for action than he." Young's opportunity came on April 2, when seventeen Democrats took the day off. Calvert Comstock, chairman of the Select Committee on Constitutional Amendments to which Crain's bill had been referred on March 13, introduced a seemingly innocuous resolution scheduling the final vote on the pending amendments for April 9. Alvah Worden, the lone Whig on the Select Committee, offered a substitute for Comstock's resolution. It moved the final vote on the constitutional amendments to April 10 and instructed the committee to report Crain's bill without amendment on April 4.[24]

Bedlam ensued. Thomas R. Lee, a Hunker from Westchester, insisted that the house had a "constitutional duty to act first upon the amendments passed upon by the preceding legislature." "The question of a convention cannot legitimately be brought up," he screamed, "before these amendments are disposed of." In Young's view, the objection was immaterial. "All I want is to ascertain if there are *any* of the majority upon this floor who are really in favor of a convention," he remarked. "We were charged at an early period of the session with not being in favor of a convention, but of being only desirous to make political capital. I would not retort this charge upon others, but I desire by this test, to know how many of the political majority here are ready to introduce a bill for examination and discussion." John L. Russell, Governor Wright's protégé and his acknowledged mouthpiece in the assembly, protested Young's attempt "to get up party tests for the majority" but said that he was "now willing to suffer the vote to be taken." Moments later, Worden's resolution carried by a vote of 55-47. Whigs and New York City nativists, plus Crain and two other radical Democrats, constituted the majority. The minority consisted entirely of Democrats. For years afterward, Whigs pointed to this roll call as evidence that they had given the people of New York a constitutional convention. John Young instantly became a household name and the likely Whig choice to run for governor against Wright in 1846.[25]

The constitutional amendments failed to secure the requisite two-thirds majority on April 10. Earnest debate on Crain's convention bill began the next day. Hunkers guided the discussion toward methods of hamstringing the constitutional convention, and Wright supported them in a vain quest for party unity. One proposed amendment to the bill prohibited the convention from tampering with the existing qualifications for suffrage. Another compelled the convention to produce a provision constitutionalizing the Stop and Tax Act. A third required the convention to submit any constitutional changes to the people as distinct propositions, so that each might be separately accepted or rejected in the ratification election. All of them were defeated "for the plain reason," Theodore Sedgwick Jr. explained in the *Evening Post*, that no true Democrat could permit the legislature to circumscribe a convention of the people. "A legislature acts in subservience to rules that the people have prescribed," he declared. "A convention is the people itself. A legislature can control its own action and can limit that of a subsequent legislature, but how can it lay down the law for a convention?" Nevertheless, Russell and a handful of other Wright loyalists voted with the irreconcilable conservatives. Only the strange combination of Whig discipline and radical principle staved off the drive for a limited convention.[26]

On the final roll call, taken on April 22, Russell joined thirty other Democrats and all but four of the Whigs to pass Crain's bill by a vote of 83-33. Thirty-one conservative Democrats voted against it and hoped for a different result in the upper house.[27] But the fireworks in the assembly had by no means concluded. Governor Wright modified his position on more than the quest for a constitutional convention in the midst of the legislature's 1845 session. Early in April, he endorsed the taxation of rent charges requested by the 25,000 tenant petitioners from eastern New York. Political logic dictated his reluctant embrace of the tax scheme. An opportunistic Whig Party not only had seized the slavery issue and laid claim to the call for a constitutional convention but also had taken up the tenant cause in the Anti-Rent counties. Wright could not allow the Whigs to monopolize the popular side of every issue in the New York elections of 1845.

Land Reform and Constitutional Reform

Answering the tenant petitions was the responsibility of Assemblyman J. Anthony Constant, a conservative Democrat from Westchester County and chairman of the Select Committee appointed by Speaker Horatio Seymour to report on the "numerous petitions from manor tenants." The committee reported on April 8, just as the nine-week debate on constitutional reform reached a climax. Constant did not regard his task as a difficult one. Governor Wright had coupled the consideration of government action with the cessation of "Indian" resistance, and the resistance had not ceased. But Constant did not dwell on Wright's controversial policy. Nor did he dismiss the tenant complaints out of hand. "It cannot be denied," he remarked, "that many of the covenants, reservations and restrictions contained in these leases, are unusual, and in some respects repugnant to the spirit of the age and of our institutions." He emphasized, instead, "that no constitutional power exists in the legislature to alter, modify, or in any way interfere with existing covenants in leases."[28]

Constant disposed of the proposed Act Concerning Tenures by Lease, the centerpiece of the Anti-Rent agitation for two years, with a few sentences and a citation to the Allen Report of 1844. The first section of the bill, authorizing tenants to allege "want of a good and sufficient title to the premises in the landlord" as a defense against actions for rent, he said, would violate the Contract Clause of the Constitution. The eminent domain scheme envisioned in the second section was equally objectionable. "A law compelling every man to sell his property at an appraisement to any person who shall happen to covet it," he asserted, "would, in the opinion of your committee, be an outrage upon the rights of the citizens of this state."[29]

Constant lingered over the Anti-Rent convention's tax proposal a bit longer than the others. As early as 1835, he pointed out, a senate committee had reported on the subject and concluded that ground rents might lawfully be included in the annual assessment of taxable personal property. But no action had been taken on the committee report. In 1844, however, William F. Allen and his associates on the Judiciary Committee had recommended "that the comptroller be requested to report to the next legislature whether any, and what, alteration in the law is required, to subject the ground rents, extra rents, incomes from quarter sales and interest in unlocated and undefined water right reservations, to taxation; and whether if not now taxable, they ought to be." Comptroller Flagg had not yet reported, but Constant was certain that the proposed tax would fall on the tenant petitioners rather than their landlords. "The leases on the Manor of Rensselaerwyck," Constant observed, "contain a covenant, on the part of each lessee," to pay all taxes imposed on the proprietors' interest in their farms. If rent charges were taxed, then, "the tax imposed, when collected from the landlord, would be by him collectable of the tenant under that covenant." It followed that "the only mode . . . which remains to those petitioners who feel aggrieved in the conditions under which they hold their lands, is to seek relief by negotiation and compromise with their landlords." Constant appended a letter from Stephen Van Rensselaer IV. "It will be seen," the committee reported, "that so far as the county of Albany is concerned, the tenants can be released of all the covenants and reservations complained of, on terms most easy and accommodating." In point of fact, however, the terms Van Rensselaer offered in 1845 were almost identical to the deal manor tenants had rejected in 1839 and 1841.[30]

The report caused a stir in the assembly on April 8. Ira Harris and Seymour Boughton complained that they had no idea Constant intended to report so soon. Both were members of the committee on tenant petitions, both had been elected with Anti-Rent support, and both had expected to present a "counter report" on the same day Constant reported for the majority. Harris was especially upset. He had been working on one bill to tax rent charges, another "to modify the right of distress, perhaps to abolish it in certain cases," and a third designed to test the validity of landlord titles. "I should have introduced them now," he remarked, "had I had notice that this report was coming in today." John L. Russell, the governor's spokesman in the assembly, had a different and more arresting complaint. He claimed that the committee had misunderstood the Anti-Rent case for the taxation of rent charges. "I have no doubt," he said, "that the legislature has power to enforce a greater equality of taxation, by compelling the holders of these rent charges to pay their due proportion, which they never have done." Constant pointed out that the report did not say rents should escape taxation, only that the tax would fall on the tenants. Russell insisted that the committee erred. "The effect," he asserted, "will be to relieve the tenants." Russell had no time to elaborate. The clock struck the noon hour as he spoke; the assembly, by prior agreement, went into committee of the whole to discuss constitutional reform.[31]

Russell's remarks suggested that Governor Wright wanted to recoup his party's political capital in eastern New York. Of the eleven counties that sent delegations to the Anti-Rent Party's state convention in January, Wright had carried all but Albany, Rensselaer, and Schenectady in the election of 1844. Fourteen of the Democracy's sixty-seven assemblymen, more than one-fifth of the party's strength in the lower house, hailed from Columbia, Delaware, Greene, Montgomery, Otsego, Schoharie, Sullivan, and Ulster. In each of those new Anti-Rent strongholds, Wright's policy of suppressing the "Indians" before considering legislative action against manorial tenures had proved extremely unpopular. Invoking the tax power provided a means of retreat. The doctrine of equal rights, a Democratic rallying cry for more than a decade, readily accommodated the Anti-Rent claim that the state should tax ground rents for the same reason it taxed mortgages and bank stocks. Best of all, however, Comptroller Flagg's duty to report on the subject gave Wright an opportunity to put the administration's imprimatur on an Anti-Rent proposal. The governor's prodding no doubt accounted for the unexpected appearance of Constant's report. On April 15, precisely one week after the proposed Act Concerning Tenures by Lease had been slain, the comptroller laid before the assembly his observations on the taxation of income from ground rents.[32]

Flagg produced a masterpiece of legal and political argument. When Benjamin Butler, John Duer, and John C. Spencer revised the New York statutes in 1828, Flagg reported, they expressed surprise that rent charges had escaped taxation in the state's first levy on intangible property. The architect of that measure, enacted in 1823, had also been surprised. Comptroller John Savage had recommended new levies on rent charges as well as mortgages, bank stocks, and other credits in the hands of investors. "The plain inference," Flagg wrote, "is that the legislature of 1823 did not intend that rents, or leases, should be taken into the estimate of the assessors in making up the value of the taxable estate of the landlord." The reason for the omission was equally plain. A powerful landlord interest in the legislature had overwhelmed the reasoned arguments of distinguished public servants devoted to the public good. In Flagg's judgment, the time had come "to equalize the burdens of taxation among all its citizens, by assessing specifically every species of property according to the ability which that property gives to its possessor to pay taxes."[33]

Framing an appropriate statute posed some problems. "A tax on short leases," Flagg said, "would tend to increase the burden on the lessee." Owners of apartment buildings, for example, could be expected to raise rents in the face of new taxes. Consequently "it would be necessary to designate the character of the leases which should be included in the assessment roll." Flagg recommended that the legislature tax only "rents reserved in any leases in fee," ranging from one or more lives (the standard Livingston family lease) to forever (the standard Van Rensselaer family lease). Landlords with interests in durable leases could not respond with rent hikes because their contracts fixed rents for one life, two lives, or in perpetuity. The sleight of hand incident to this move was visible only to the most acute observer. Flagg invoked the equal-rights principle to justify the taxation of ground rents, then qualified the principle to achieve his main objective. He favored the taxation of rent charges, not to raise revenue or to "equalize the burden" of taxation among all citizens, but to give the landlords of eastern New York an added incentive to extinguish manorial tenures voluntarily and on terms favorable to their tenants.[34]

Flagg tackled the tax covenants with comparable verve. Some simple observations resolved the difficulty that Assemblyman Constant regarded as an insurmountable one. Unlike taxes on real estate, which county officials collected from the person in possession, a tax on rent charges would be collected directly from the landlord. If the landlord failed to pay the levy, Flagg pointed out, existing state law authorized the comptroller "to sell the interest which the landlord reserves out of the granted premises including the streams and the soil under them." In the first instance, then, landlords would have to pay the new levies or, better yet, escape liability by selling their reserved interests in the land. Few if any landlords, Flagg reported, would be inclined to go after their tenants under the tax covenants included in every lease. Apportioning the levy among hundreds, sometimes thousands, of families would be an accountant's nightmare; the attorney's fees and court costs required to collect each tenant's proportional share would exceed the amount collected. Flagg did not deign to mention another factor likely to shape the landlord response to the proposed tax law. As long as the tenant resistance continued, attempts to enforce court orders for the collection of money owed under tax covenants would be as fruitless as attempts to collect rents.[35]

Flagg did more than call for the enactment of appropriate legislation. He drafted a bill. Assemblyman Russell, chairman of the Ways and Means Committee, was no doubt anxious to introduce it. But the administration settled on a different procedure. On April 8, Ira Harris had announced that he planned to introduce a batch of measures in conformity with the proposals made at the Anti-Rent Party's state convention. Flagg apparently offered him the tax bill in return for Harris's promise to delay both his minority report and any bills grounded on the right-remedy distinction or the eminent domain power. Harris introduced the Act to Equalize Taxation on April 22. He did not produce his minority report or his other promised bills until May 10. The legislature adjourned three days later.[36]

Russell reported the tax bill out of his Ways and Means Committee on April 28. The nativists from Manhattan, primed with arguments supplied by Hathaway and Powers, lobbyists for the city's absentee proprietors, led the opposition. Roderick Morrison spoke twice, Thomas Oakley three times. Both denounced the bill because it contemplated "double taxation," once on the land in the tenant's possession and again on the rents reserved to the landlord. Daniel Lee, a progressive Whig, replied that the bill purported to treat landlords no differently than mortgagees; he described the measure as "in all respects right and proper." Harris of Albany and Van Schoonhoven of Rensselaer defended the bill on the same grounds. Horatio Seymour raised a more pertinent objection. He pointed out that the "bill proposes to tax the landlord on his rent charge, and to give him no right as the mortgagee has to set off his debts against the assessment on his rent interest." Seymour claimed that the vaunted principle of equal rights, as applied to the bill at hand, was a sham and a delusion.[37]

The bill was ready for a third reading and a vote on May 10. This time the New York City nativists let Democrats carry the burden of opposition. Thomas R. Lee and Thornton Niven, conservatives, reiterated Seymour's claim that taxing the owners of rent charges, without permitting any deduction for their debts, was to countenance unequal and oppressive legislation. Benjamin Bailey, a radical, urged "the injustice of taxing these rent charges which are not collectable without a military force, and not even then." Nobody answered these arguments before the roll call began. Yet the bill passed by a vote of 49-46. The five Whig/Anti-Rent members from Albany, Rensselaer, and Schoharie said aye. So did twelve Democrats from Columbia, Delaware, Greene, Otsego, Montgomery, Schoharie, Sullivan, and Ulster. The nativists from New York City stood 10-1 against the bill. But the rest of the members divided rather evenly. The remaining Democrats voted 19-24; the remaining Whigs 12-12. John Young, the Whig Party's ambitious legislative leader, did not vote. Every member from an Anti-Rent county except C. D. Fellows of Otsego and Irwin Pardee of Ulster, who also preferred not to be counted, could return home and report that a means of extinguishing manorial tenures not only had been identified but also had passed the house. Because the senate had no time to consider the Act to Equalize Taxation before adjournment, the year of decision would be 1846.[38]

Something else marked 1846 as a year of decision for the people of New York State. Two days after the house passed the tax bill, the senate enacted the convention bill. Governor Wright signed it into law on May 13. The act provided that if a majority of those voting in November declared in favor of a constitutional convention, a special election would be held on the last Tuesday of April 1846, and the delegates so chosen would assemble in convention at the state capital on the first Monday in June. Contemporary commentators took it for granted that the people would approve the proposal. "The convention will be called, by a fifty thousand majority," Horace Greeley predicted on May 21. And he underestimated. New York voters approved the call by a vote of 214,700 to 33,032. The legislature's 1845 session thus ended on a decidedly different note than it began. In his January message, Governor Wright had slammed the door on land reform and discouraged agitation for a constitutional convention. Yet the house had passed a tax bill framed by his closest advisor, and a convention bill had become law with the support of his best friends in the legislature. Nobody had better cause for rejoicing than the state's tenant farmers. Anti-Rent leaders had urged them to "AGITATE, AGITATE, AGITATE" in January, but great uncertainty remained about what they could get from government and how they could get it. Nevertheless, two different but compatible routes to land reform had been thrown open in May.[39]

One route led through the next session of the legislature. Flagg's tax measure provided a way to induce serious settlement talks. Everyone who spoke on the Act to Equalize Taxation, whether for it or against it, assumed that landlords would be inclined to offer acceptable terms in the face of increased tax liability. The other route led through the impending convention of the sovereign people. It provided an opportunity to abolish the rent system without any bargaining at all. If the convention adopted the eminent domain scheme William A. Duer Jr. had recommended in 1840, the tenants could buy out their landlords at prices fixed by government appraisers. The decision of the New York Supreme Court in *Taylor v. Porter* (1843), which obstructed this route during the legislature's 1844 session, could not fetter a constitutional convention. No principle of federal law prevented the states from authorizing compensated takings of private property, whether to establish private roads or extinguish manorial tenures. But other well-trodden paths, including the provision for contesting landlord titles in the proposed Act Concerning Tenures by Lease, were still blocked by the Contract Clause doctrine expounded by the Supreme Court of the United States in *Bronson v. Kinzie* (1843). The national Constitution was "the supreme law of the land." It could not be transgressed by state constitutional conventions any more than by state legislatures.

Anti-renters stood at a crossroads, then, in mid-1845. American legal theory designated some routes as passable, others as almost certain dead ends. Party battles between Whigs and Democrats, Barnburners and Hunkers, deposited the tenants at this juncture without much warning. But the Anti-Rent associations had to decide which route to take. Although major party managers coveted the Anti-Rent vote, neither Whigs nor Democrats were likely to make good choices if tenant spokesmen made bad ones. Unfortunately, the Anti-Rent associations were not prepared to select an appropriate legal strategy. The rank and file, especially in Delaware and Schoharie, confronted implacable landlords bent on breaking rent strikes. Resistance, not reform, was the first priority of people on the ground. "Indians" already in custody wrote letters urging the faithful to continue, in Smith Boughton's words, "the glorious work of emancipating a wronged and insulted people from a state of slavery and land-ridden tyranny, which would be a disgrace to modern *Russia*."[40] Getting out of jail remained their top priority all the same. The most disturbing sign of inertia, however, came from members of the Whig/Anti-Rent contingent in the state legislature. Their performance during the session's waning days suggested that the new opportunities suddenly at hand might not be seized.

Partisan Mediators of Anti-Rent Decisions

Among the more durable traditions in historical writing about the Anti-Rent movement is the impulse to give considerable credit for the enactment of the convention bill to Ira Harris (W.-Albany), William H. Van Schoonhoven (W.-Rensselaer), Harry Betts (W.-Rensselaer), Roger Heermance (W.-Rensselaer), Elisha Tibbets (W.-Schoharie), and Seymour Boughton (D.-Schoharie). Each of them had agreed to run on an Anti-Rent ticket in 1844 after having already accepted a nomination from one of the major parties. "Of all the members who supported the bill for calling a convention, vested with unrestricted powers, the Anti-Renters were probably the most sincere," Jabez Hammond wrote in 1852. "They could not anticipate any effectual relief from the evils of which they complained, without some radical alteration of the fundamental law, and they therefore approached the convention question with great and no doubt honest zeal." Hammond's observation makes so much sense on its face that seven generations of historians have repeated his claim. Edward P. Cheyney, a student of Frederick Jackson Turner, even abandoned Hammond's circumspection. "It was the Anti-Rent agitation," he wrote in 1934, "that gave the final push to the pressure for the calling of a constitutional convention and the adoption of the constitution of 1846." Yet there is very little evidence to support Hammond's weak version, let alone Cheyney's stronger one, and much to suggest that potential connections between land reform and constitutional reform eluded "the Anti-Renters" in the legislature.[41]

The standard interpretation contains two distinct elements. Hammond asserted that "the Anti-Renters" voted for the convention bill; he declared that they did so because "some radical alteration of the fundamental law" provided the only hope of "effectual relief from the evils of which they complained." The first claim is at once accurate and misleading. Every legislator named on an Anti-Rent ticket in 1844 voted for the convention bill, but their votes were consistent with their major-party allegiances. Clarkson Crosby (W.-Albany) and Elisha Litchfield (W.-Albany) denounced the Anti-Rent agitation at every opportunity and voted against the Act to Equalize Taxation. Nevertheless, they stood shoulder to shoulder with Ira Harris on the convention question. The behavior of the Albany delegation suggests that the partisan commitment of each assemblyman, not his stance on the Anti-Rent movement, governed his vote on the convention bill. The votes cast by the fourteen Democrats from eastern New York suggest the same thing. Eight, including Boughton of Schoharie, supported both the tax bill and the convention bill. But six Democrats from Greene, Montgomery, Otsego, and Ulster opposed the call for a constitutional convention. Because the Democrats who voted on the convention bill divided 31-31, the 8-6 split in eastern New York suggests the tenacity of factional identities among the region's assemblymen. Apprehensions about Anti-Rent demands on the proposed convention had absolutely no effect on the roll call. The New York City nativists endorsed the convention bill 14-0; they voted 10-1 against the taxation of rent charges.

Hammond's second claim, then, is the more important one. The voting behavior of "the Anti-Renters," though consistent with their major-party allegiances, might have been shaped by the perception that land reform could be achieved only in a convention of the people. But the evidence for that claim is weaker still. Nobody breathed a word about constitutional reform at the Anti-Rent Party's state convention on January 15. Six weeks later, well after the Whig drive for a constitutional convention had gathered momentum in the legislature, Harris told the house that "the great evil of which [the tenants] complain . . . is susceptible of legislative redress." Betts of Rensselaer, one of the Anti-Rent Party's half-dozen state committeemen, echoed Harris in a long speech delivered on March 6. The *Freeholder*, co-owned by Harris and edited by Thomas A. Devyr, published its first number on April 9. Although Devyr lambasted the Constant Report and tirelessly promoted both Harris's title-test bill and the proposed Act to Equalize Taxation, he said nothing about the constitutional convention as a forum for land reform until long after the legislature had adjourned on May 13.[42]

Horace Greeley read the *Freeholder*, and he reached a conclusion that ran counter to the subsequent presumptions of Jabez Hammond and the historians who followed him. "We have seen no evidence," the discerning Whig editor remarked on May 20, "that the Anti-Renters, as such, have taken ground in favor of a convention." Greeley did not speculate on why this was so, but the reason is plain. An eminent domain measure, the one item on the Anti-Rent wish list that could be constitutionalized with finality in a convention of the people, did not figure in the immediate plans of the assemblymen from Albany, Rensselaer, and Schoharie. All of them preferred to push for the enactment of a statute authorizing the tenants to allege want of title in their landlords as a defense against actions for rent. In some ways, their preference made sense.[43]

Testing landlord titles had three advantages relative to the compensated emancipation plan Duer devised in 1840 and the Anti-Rent associations wove into their proposed Act Concerning Tenures by Lease in 1843. The first advantage was manifest. If the projected title litigation were successful, landlord interests in tenant farms would be instantly extinguished. In theory, at least, the tenants in possession could acquire unqualified titles by adverse possession or by purchase on nominal terms from the state government. Tenant families might get something for nothing, or next to nothing, under a title-test measure. But the eminent domain scheme would require them to compensate their landlords for everything divested, including the value of the "four fat fowl" and the quarter-sale reservations. Once the landlord titles had been shown to be tainted with "fraud and illegality," the *Freeholder* later explained, "the whole manor system and all its feudal incidents and disabilities will fall at once to the ground."[44]

The second relative advantage, though less apparent, appealed at least as strongly to the legislature's Whig/Anti-Rent members as to their tenant constituents. If a title-test statute were enacted, its immediate effect would be a moratorium on both distress sales and actions for ejectment. The "Indian" disorders, which had been defensive from the outset, would cease until the validity of landlord titles had been established. So would the need for the Whig/Anti-Rent leadership to engage in pharisaical censure of the tenant resistance while promoting the tenant cause. An eminent domain measure, on the other hand, would not stay the hand of landlords. Each tenant would be empowered to purchase his landlord's interest at a price fixed by government appraisers. Until the tenant secured a loan and set the condemnation machinery into motion, however, his obligation to pay rent would continue. Only the title-test scheme, in other words, could dissolve immediately and everywhere the tension between resistance and reform that had vexed the Anti-Rent movement since the fall of 1844.

Harris and Van Schoonhoven, the two lawyers in the legislature's Whig/Anti-Rent contingent, saw a third relative advantage in the title-test strategy.

Both hoped to commit the Whig Party to land reform and drive Silas Wright out of office with Anti-Rent assistance in the election of 1846. Yet their plans might be derailed if the legislature enacted the tax bill in the spring of 1846 and a constitutional convention embraced the eminent domain scheme in the summer. The people of New York would not elect a new governor until November. Only the title-test measure, which the Democrats had repudiated in 1844 and again in 1845, could keep the Anti-Rent agitation alive long enough to help the Whig Party. Harris, Van Schoonhoven, and others repeatedly denied conjectures about their political motives, and they did so with a clean conscience. Leaders of the Anti-Rent associations in Albany and Rensselaer counties had been fanatically devoted to the title-test measure since 1843. It was no accident that the proposed Act Concerning Tenures by Lease put the title-test provision in section one and the eminent domain safety net in section two. By making the title-test scheme the sine qua non of land reform, Harris and his Whig/Anti-Rent colleagues carried out the wishes of their tenant constituents.[45]

The title-test measure had one imposing disadvantage. It was almost certainly unconstitutional. Three days before the legislature adjourned in May 1845, Harris introduced a new title-test bill, "An Act Concerning Tenures." His bill differed slightly from the Anti-Rent bill that Assemblyman William F. Allen had condemned during the 1844 session. Harris remodeled the first section so that it provided a more accurate legal description of manorial tenures; he jettisoned the second section grounded on the eminent domain power, the constitutionality of which he had questioned in October 1844.[46] But the heart of the measure—a bar on rent collections until New York courts sustained landlord titles—still remained subject to Allen's objections. He had claimed that one effect of such legislation would be to "destroy many contracts of lease, not from any want of title, but from the want of the necessary evidences of that title." Another effect would be to secure the tenants' possession of their farms while nullifying the contracts that enabled them to enter the land in the first place. According to Allen, the title-test bill impaired the obligation of contracts more severely than did the Illinois statutes that the Supreme Court struck down in *Bronson v. Kinzie*.

Harris did not contest Allen's analysis in his report on the 1845 bill. Instead, he emphasized that a title-test law would fulfill compelling state interests Allen had overlooked. "The opinion has become general throughout the whole territory covered with this system of tenures," he observed, "that the original title of those who have assumed to dispose of their lands, claiming to hold under grants from the British government, is invalid." Harris acknowledged that this opinion might not be "well founded." In his view, however, "nothing short of a full and fair investigation of these titles before a competent and impartial judicial tribunal, untrammelled by the existing rules of evidence, will ever allay this alarming and perilous excitement." Even the landlords should favor the "thorough legal investigation" contemplated by the bill. "It cannot be doubted," Harris declared, "that if after a fair and unrestricted trial, the tenants should become satisfied that they have been laboring under misapprehensions," the Anti-Rent resistance would cease and the tenants "would cheerfully yield that obedience to the law which is due from every good citizen." Harris claimed that a bill with such wholesome effects could not possibly violate the Contract Clause of the Constitution. The proposed Act Concerning Tenures had nothing in common with the "stay laws" at issue in *Bronson v. Kinzie*, a precedent he did not mention and undoubtedly endorsed on its facts. The measure he had framed, Harris insisted, could "not be distinguished in principle" from statutes of limitation and other remedial legislation that courts had sustained against Contract Clause challenges since 1789.[47]

Harris merely feinted at the imposing constitutional arguments arrayed before him. Nothing in the case law justified his presumption that a statute's wholesome effect on the body politic might counteract its pernicious effect on the vested rights of parties to executory contracts. The general effect of statutes, however beneficial or benign, had never been the focus of Contract Clause adjudication. Chief Justice Roger Taney, speaking for the Court in *Bronson v. Kinzie*, had refrained from taking judicial notice of the fact that "stay laws" were enacted to facilitate the resumption of specie payments, something he personally endorsed. The Court struck down the Illinois legislation because it did "not act merely on the remedy, but directly upon the contract itself, and . . . engraft[ed] upon it new conditions injurious and unjust to the mortgagee." Taney even addressed Harris's supposed analogies. "Whatever belongs merely to the remedy may be altered according to the will of the state, provided the alteration does not impair the obligation of contract," he proclaimed. "But if that *effect* is produced, it is immaterial whether it is done by acting on the remedy or directly on the contract itself. In either case it is prohibited by the Constitution."[48]

Assemblyman Harris averted his eyes from the legal doctrines that impeded his way and blithely started the Anti-Rent movement down the one impassable route to land reform. He controlled the *Freeholder*; consequently his voice was a powerful one. Before the state legislature reassembled in January, however, other formidable voices contested Harris's program and offered rival solutions to the Anti-Rent difficulties. All of them got a full hearing from the people of New York State. The most shocking event of the Anti-Rent era occurred in August 1845, and the manor controversy finally became the central preoccupation in New York public life.

9

A Cacophony of Voices

The sixth anniversary of the Anti-Rent movement passed quietly on May 22, 1845. It was a bittersweet occasion for Lawrence Van Deusen, president of the Anti-Rent Association of Albany County. Van Deusen took pride in the unity and staying power of his fellow tenants since 1839, when Stephen Van Rensselaer IV rejected the demands he wrote up for them at Dunbar's tavern. Yet the strike had merely nullified the contractual obligations that bound anti-renters to the patroon, and Van Rensselaer still refused to sell his interest in the land on acceptable terms. How the struggle would end remained as uncertain as on the day it began. Van Deusen felt confident of victory all the same. The cry of "down with the rent" had spread from Albany to Rensselaer and Schoharie counties in 1842–43, to Columbia and the four Hardenbergh Patent counties in 1844, to Otsego and Montgomery and Schenectady early in 1845. Anti-Rent voters had demonstrated their power at the polls, and it seemed logical to assume that increasing the pressure on the state was to increase it on the landlords. As the Anti-Rent agitation grew in magnitude, however, so did its vulnerability to schism. And a schism came.

Disagreement about means, not ends, generated the rift in the Anti-Rent ranks. Van Deusen and his Delaware County counterpart, Martin Kelley, shared a commitment to the abolition of manorial tenures. But tenants on the various manors and great patents faced very different situations in the summer of 1845. When members of the Albany County association got together in Berne or New Scotland, discussion focused on supposed flaws in the Van Rensselaer title and ways to put it on trial. Their homes and chattels seemed safe for the time being. Sheriff Christopher Batterman and his deputies had not ventured into the Helderberg towns since September 1844; Albany anti-renters had renounced the "Indian" resistance without compromising the common cause. On the Hardenbergh Patent, where an imminent landlord offensive loomed, desperation prevailed. Anti-Rent investigators in Delaware County had discovered an apparent discrepancy between the boundaries specified in the Hardenbergh grant and the location of the land actually patented, but they had not come up with a plausible argument to contest its validity.[1] When tenants got together in the Delaware hamlets of Andes or Bovina, then, discussion focused on the immediate threat of distress sales rather than the promise of political action. "Indian" chiefs, not lawyers and politicians, spoke for the Anti-Rent Association of Delaware County.

The legislature's authorization of a constitutional convention acted as the catalyst that transformed Anti-Rent differences into a bitter schism. Beginning in June 1845, George Henry Evans wrote long essays on "the new constitution" for three successive issues of his new land reform weekly, *Young America*. Evans did more than propose an agenda for the constitutional convention. He belittled the idea of taxing rent charges and scorned the idea of contesting the validity of landlord titles in the New York courts. Ira Harris tried to read Evans and his disciples out of the movement; factions loyal to each Anti-Rent spokesman battled for control of the county associations beginning in July. Harris partisans predominated in Albany and Rensselaer, Evans men in Delaware. But the rancorous local quarrels among anti-renters proved less significant than the general response to their rival programs for political action. Not a single politician or pundit outside the Anti-Rent counties endorsed either "the new constitution" proposed by Evans or the title-test scheme promoted by Harris.

The schism climaxed at a moment when public interest in the Anti-Rent question mushroomed. On August 7, 1845, a band of "Indians" shot and killed a deputy sheriff in Delaware County. Expressions of shock and fury reverberated from Manhattan to Buffalo; Whigs and Democrats alike demanded that the killers be apprehended, tried, and punished. As the government war against the "Indians" proceeded, commentaries of a different sort rolled off the presses. Two eminent Whigs, Horace Greeley and Daniel Dewey Barnard, tried to explain what the rent strike was really about, why it had lasted so long, and how the deplorable state of affairs on the manors and great patents of eastern New York might be resolved. They agreed on very little besides the gravity of the situation. Yet the Greeley-Barnard exchange, which the entire New York press followed very closely, clarified three things about the future of the tenant agitation. The controversy could not be resolved on the terms set by putative Anti-Rent leaders. Neither Greeley nor any other progressive Whig had the imagination to devise an alternative means of extinguishing manorial tenures. And the taxation of rent charges, the course of government action favored by Democrats, might induce the proprietors of the Hardenbergh Patent to sell out but it would have no effect on Rensselaerwyck. At the close of 1845, the incentives for forging a political solution had never been greater. The range of options at the command of lawmakers, however, seemed as small as ever.

The "New Constitution"

The explosive articles George Henry Evans published in June 1845 appeared in a logical sequence. His first number emphasized the "glorious" opportunity that "the young men of the present generation" now had to establish "a perfect constitution" and exert a "stupendous effect on . . . the destiny of the republic." "An object no less than that of securing to all men in the State of New York all their inalienable rights will be urged upon the convention," Evans declared. This objective, "if attained, will present a model constitution to the other states." Michael Hoffman, Theodore Sedgwick Jr., John Bigelow, and Elisha P. Hurlbut—the radical Democrats who started the agitation for a constitutional convention—had been saying the same thing since 1843.[2]

Evans parted company with the radical Democrats in the second article. Hoffman and the *Evening Post* crowd used the language of natural rights against government's powers to tax and spend, to confer special privileges on favored forms of enterprise, and to impair contractual obligations. But they treated interests in land as the very sort of rights that constitutional compacts among the people had been designed to protect. In Evans's view, this was "a fundamental error, adopted from the monarchical system" and reinforced by the blind devotion of American lawyers to Magna Carta, the common law, and other inherited institutions still encrusted with feudal forms. The seminal writers on natural rights and republican government had seen things more clearly. John Locke and James Harrington understood that, as Evans put it, "every man has an indisputable right and title to land enough to live upon; and no one has a just title to a foot more than is necessary for the subsistence of his family while another is without land. Land is an inalienable right." Because the radical Democrats misconceived the doctrine of natural rights, moreover, they had not come to grips with the source "of the evils which have rapidly grown upon us in this infant republican state, until the only difference between us and the rotten-ripe English tyranny is, that there one in *ten* are paupers, while here it is only one in twenty-six!" Property rights in rented and wild lands, not unjust exercises of the state government's inherent powers, generated "the monstrous anomaly of poverty among the producing classes in proportion to the increase of national wealth." It followed that the principal duty of the constitutional convention was to "restore the land of New York State to the people."[3]

Abolishing property rights in land did not occur to Evans. The republican tradition grounded the personal independence required for citizenship in the ownership of real estate; he aimed to "perfect" the republican form of government, not replace it with something new. His agenda for the New York convention had three main components:

That no one *hereafter*, shall, under any circumstances, become possessed of more than 160 acres of land in this state.

There shall be a special court or commission, composed of landholders and (poor) lacklanders proportioned to the numbers of their respective classes in this state, who shall, in all cases where land is held by a twenty years' or more, or a life, or a perpetual lease, determine, on principles of *equity*, what (or whether any) compensation shall be paid to the claimant in full extinguishment of his claim.

The homestead . . . shall be inalienable, except at the will of the occupant, and then only transferable to a landless person.

Evans described his agenda as a "just and reasonable compromise on the part of the landless." Natural law mandated a less gradual program. "But there is no example in history in which the mass of the people, on a reformation of government, have asserted more than half the rights they were entitled to," he declared. "Therefore it is not wisdom in a reformer to propose measures that there is no reasonable hope of accomplishing."[4]

The notion that such an agenda had a "reasonable hope" of adoption might have been a delusion. Yet all three propositions did accommodate the doctrine of vested rights. A qualifier, "*hereafter*," was the key word in his first recommendation. Evans did not propose to disturb existing titles to New York real estate. "At the death of the possessor," moreover, "his landless heirs, no matter how numerous, could each inherit the possession of a lot or a farm." Only "the remainder" would have to be sold to landless purchasers and the proceeds divided among the heirs of the deceased. Evans had studied Blackstone's *Commentaries*. Even Blackstone, a thoroughgoing "Tory," recognized that the right to inherit "was no natural, but merely a civil right" and might be regulated in the public interest. American state governments had relied on the distinction to justify the abolition of entails in the eighteenth century; although Evans did not know it, Martin Van Buren had invoked the distinction to justify the gradual abolition of manorial tenures in an 1844 letter to Silas Wright. Van Buren targeted a particular form of land tenure for gradual extinction. Evans called for the eventual elimination of all estates that exceeded 160 acres in size. But both proposals were based on the same legal theory.[5]

Land limitation was the heart of Evans's program for reconstructing the republican order in New York State. If the people put it into the state constitution, he said, "freeholds would gradually cheapen, as they came into the market from the death of the monopolists, until, as none could purchase but landless men or women, everyone in the state would become a freeholder." But he regarded the third item on his agenda, providing for prospective limitations on the alienability of land, as a necessary component in any new system of tenure. Owners of 160-acre farms might put their independence in jeopardy by mortgaging their freeholds. "How long would it be," Evans asked, "before [land] would again be monopolized under the operation of existing laws?" Only by limiting freedom of testation and freedom of contract on the part of "monopolists" and "homesteaders" alike, then, could the poverty and privilege that imperiled the republic be gradually abated.[6]

Anti-Rent support was indispensable to Evans. Thus his second proposition, "a special court or commission" empowered to extinguish landlord interests in tenant farms upon payment of just compensation, offered the victims of "patroonery" an immediate remedy for their grievances. He took the eminent domain idea from William A. Duer Jr. But he resisted the assumption, posited in the Whig lawmaker's 1840 report, that the tenants had a duty to pay for the market value of every right reserved to their landlords in the indentures. "The [national] Constitution guarantees the validity of contracts, it is true, but not of contracts which the parties had no right to make," Evans wrote. "Vested *rights* cannot be infringed upon, I willingly admit; but vested *wrongs* can and ought to be infringed upon in the speediest manner." He believed that a couple of analogies clinched the point. "No parent," Evans remarked "could rightfully contract his children into slavery." Nor could a parent rightfully agree to sell his children's limbs "to the surgeons for dissection, and thereby place burdens on the public." Because the right to land, like the right to life and limb, was an inalienable one, members of one generation had no authority to fetter the rights of the next with contracts that ran forever. Viewed from this perspective, the agreements in force throughout eastern New York vested very little in the landlords. "On principles of equity," the valuation basis Evans trumpeted, "feudal" proprietors had a rightful claim only to the value of the land at the moment settlers first entered it, less the value of all rents and services their heirs and assignees had been wrongfully compelled to pay over the years.[7]

Evans did not insist on the implementation of any one formula for the valuation of landlord interests in tenant farms. He proposed to leave that decision to an adjudicatory body, authorized by the new state constitution and "composed of landholders and (poor) lacklanders proportioned to the numbers of their respective classes in the state." But he did claim that his recommendation had ample precedent in New York law and practice. Since 1817 the Board of Canal Appraisers, consisting of three officers appointed by the governor for two-year terms, had been empowered "to make a just and equitable estimate and appraisement of the loss and damage, if any, over and above the benefit and advantage to the . . . proprietors" whose land or water rights were taken for the public works. If the canal appraisers could offset the value of benefits arising from improved access to transportation against the value of property taken, Evans thought it would be equally "just and equitable" for the proposed land reform commission to offset rents the tenants already had paid against the value of property rights taken from their landlords. He also insisted that only his eminent domain proposal would completely extinguish every vestige of "feudalism" in New York State. "Taxing rents is only treading on the corns of patroonery," he asserted. "The plan is to knock his gouty old legs from under him." Evans's objection to the idea of contesting landlord titles in the courts ran much deeper.[8]

Impediments to the title-test scheme arising from the Supreme Court's decision in *Bronson v. Kinzie* did not concern Evans so much as the scheme's effects on the "noble cause" of the tenants. Focusing on the validity of landlord titles, he pointed out, effectively transformed a general social problem—an anti-republican system of land tenure—into a number of very particular problems that affected relatively few individuals. Of the dozens of huge manors and patents in eastern New York, each had a different history, a different source and chain of title. Thus arguments about supposed flaws in the title to Rensselaerwyck could not be used by tenants on the Hardenbergh Patent, the Blenheim Patent, or the Livingston Manor. "Suppose," Evans wrote, "that the Van Rensselaers have no parchment title, and that in consequence the tenants become freeholders under the present system. In what a position does this place the tenants under all other monopoly leases throughout the state?" Putting the Van Rensselaer title on trial, moreover, was not to extinguish it. A judicial decision that upheld the "monarchical sheepskin" was at least as likely as a decision that voided the British grant. Yet Assemblyman Harris had solemnly informed the state legislature that the tenants "would cheerfully submit" to their landlords "after a fair and unrestricted" investigation of the region's land titles. If Harris meant what he said, a great many Anti-Rent families—perhaps all of them—were destined to remain mired in perpetual tenancy with no hope of escape for themselves and their posterity.[9]

Evans refused to believe that the tenants would harness their movement to such a "narrow-souled" course of action. Enactment of the title-test scheme would compel them to rely on "a lawyer's argument" tailored to account for the distinctive history of each British land grant and addressed to judges steeped in "the hoary iniquities of the Norman land pirates" that made up the common law of real property. It would incline anti-renters to think of themselves as tenants of the Van Rensselaers, of the Livingstons, of the Verplancks, or of some other family with a paper claim to the soil they farmed. It would divide and almost certainly defeat them. Evans insisted that his plan, in contrast, would enable the tenants "to place themselves upon the broad platform of their equal rights *as men*" and to argue their case before delegates of the sovereign people gathered in convention. "To secure a redress of your own grievances, you must show a disposition to aid in redressing the grievances of others," he admonished the anti-renters. "There should be a union, and the way to effect such a union is to contend for such general measures in the constitutional convention as will effectually put an end to land monopoly . . . and enable every citizen to obtain an inalienable freehold."[10]

Evans's critique of the title-test proposal had some merit. So did the "special court or commission" he advocated in its stead. By packaging the eminent domain remedy between two more far-reaching proposals, however, Evans ensured that it would get very little attention. Beginning in August, his call for a 160-acre limit on landholding and for restrictions on alienability served as a lightning rod for political debate on land reform and popular sovereignty. Horace Greeley, a Whig, and Theodore Sedgwick Jr., a Democrat, assailed the idea of linking land reform with the drive for a constitutional convention. Both rejected Evans's main premise, and they did so for the same reason. Positing an irrepressible conflict between republican government and a liberal political economy, as Evans did, amounted to a denial of American exceptionalism—of the hopeful Jeffersonian presumption that the United States, with its free markets, its vast expanse of "vacant" land in the West, and its boundless opportunities for capitalist accumulation by independent producers, could escape republican decline for ages to come. "Great landed property and the descent of enormous and unbroken fortunes are, on any large scale, wholly incompatible with our institutions," Sedgwick wrote on September 23. "All our legislation tends to secure equality of condition, and this is at once our glory and our safeguard. But on the other hand, the right of property, the right to enjoy undisturbed the fruits of legitimate acquisition, whether of one's own or of ancestral labor, is the first badge of a civilized society, and to it every other principle gives way." Arguments like those expounded by Evans might make some sense, claimed Sedgwick, if "the evil" of inequality had "reached a pass, as once in France, perhaps now in England, it could only be solved by revolution." But the free people of New York understood that America was different. Here the certain rewards of labor sustained republican citizenship and moral progress. The "new constitution" Evans advocated, Sedgwick declared, "will not be tolerated by the people of this state." Greeley concurred. "We have not a particle of apprehension," he wrote on September 23, "that any anarchical or destructive proposition will prevail in the constitutional convention. We have faith in the people."[11]

Conservative Whigs were not so certain about the people of New York. James Watson Webb, in particular, linked the Anti-Rent agitation with Evans's program of "spoilation" and the menace of agrarianism with the legislature's authorization of a constitutional convention. His *Courier and Enquirer* called on Whigs to disavow the former by voting against the latter. "Does any one suppose," he remarked in August "that the caveat against touching vested rights would weigh very much in the [convention's] scale against the irritated feeling, excited prejudices, long cherished resentment—and strong personal interests [of anti-renters] in the other?" The events of 1845 called to Webb's mind James Madison's sharp response to Thomas Jefferson's argument that every generation had a right to refashion its institutions in a convention of the people. Implementing such a notion, Madison wrote in 1790, would produce "the most violent struggles . . . between the parties interested in reviving and those interested in reforming the antecedent state of property." And so it had.[12]

Schism

Ira Harris condemned Evans's "agrarianism" six weeks before Webb sounded the alarm. When the legislature adjourned in May 1845, however, the Whig/ Anti-Rent leader regarded Silas Wright and the New York Democracy as the principal threat to his own agenda for the tenant movement. Henry Z. Hayner and William Van Schoonhoven, Harris's closest associates in Rensselaer County, no doubt felt the same way. The tenants on Rensselaerwyck had swelled Whig majorities in the election of 1844, and they were unlikely to settle for anything less than a statute authorizing them to allege want of title as a defense against actions for rent. The situation was different, however, in the other Anti-Rent counties of eastern New York. Arguments contesting landlord titles had neither been fully developed nor widely disseminated. Equally distressing to Whigs like Harris was the fact that tenant voters in Columbia, Delaware, Greene, Montgomery, Schoharie, Sullivan, and Ulster had been overwhelmingly Democratic for a generation. Harris and his compatriots assumed that Governor Wright would make a concerted effort to keep all those counties in the Democratic column.

It required little effort, then, for Harris to imagine a scenario in which his hopes for the tenants of Rensselaerwyck and for the Whig Party were smashed in 1846. Governor Wright might sell the legislature on the taxation of rent charges as the final solution to the problem of manorial tenures. Democrats might persuade the Anti-Rent associations, excepting only those in Albany and Rensselaer, that government could do nothing more for the tenant cause. The absentee proprietors of Livingston Manor and the great patents west of the Hudson might give up the fight, liquidate their interests in tenant farms on favorable terms, and leave the people of Rensselaerwyck as isolated as they had been before the organizing drive of 1844. If all those things happened, the Whig Party would make no headway in the Anti-Rent counties and Governor Wright would be reelected in 1846.

For politicians, as for military commanders and litigators, imagining the opposition's strategy is the first step in the formulation of means to counteract it. Harris's key move was to persuade his law partner's roommate, Robert D. Watson, to join him on the Anti-Rent ticket for the assembly in 1845. Watson was not only a Democrat but a Hunker already inclined to oppose Wright's leadership and to challenge the governor's control of the party. The conservative Democrat launched his campaign in Harris's *Freeholder*; his first four-column article, "The Anti-Rent Question," appeared on May 28. A longer piece followed on June 4. Watson described the leases in force throughout eastern New York and emphasized "the incompatibility of these feudal tenures with the genius of our institutions." But the vast bulk of his remarks focused on landlord titles, not the terms on which tenants held the land. Only the enactment of Harris's title-test bill, he asserted, would put an end to centuries of "tyranny, and despotism, and fraud" and ensure domestic tranquillity in eleven counties seething with resistance to the law—resistance "for which we can find no language sufficiently strong to express our condemnation." He did not mention the Contract Clause of the Constitution, the eminent domain power, or the impending constitutional convention.[13]

Thomas A. Devyr, editor of the *Freeholder*, fit less snugly into Harris's plans. In March, when Harris and Charles F. Bouton put up the money to establish an Anti-Rent organ, the Albany assemblyman wanted no part of an Evans disciple as editor. But Bouton insisted on Devyr. So did Lawrence Van Deusen, president of the Anti-Rent Association of Albany County. Harris balked, then stalled, and finally gave in. Bouton and Van Deusen had cause to hold out for Devyr. A man with an unusual combination of great empathy and boundless energy, Devyr spent several days each week on the road attending meetings of Anti-Rent locals in Albany, Rensselaer, and Schoharie counties. He respected the farmers, listened to their hopes and fears, and summarized their concerns in his weekly editorials. He neither talked down to them nor claimed to speak for them. The tenants loved him. Until the end of June, moreover, Devyr gave Harris no cause to complain. The *Freeholder* praised the title-test bill and disavowed resistance "save in the last, the very last, resort—when all peaceful means have failed to vindicate our undoubted rights." Aside from his advocacy of free homesteads on the nation's public lands, nothing Devyr wrote evinced his commitment to the principles of National Reform.[14]

The publication of Evans's articles on "the new constitution" changed everything. Devyr's first impulse was to claim that the National Reform barrage on the Harris-Watson combination did not really matter. Tenants in eleven counties were bound to entertain "diverse views in the relation to the means of redress, and even the nature of the evil," he observed in the *Freeholder* on June 25. "Some, for example, may hold that if the title of the patroons is legitimately derived from legitimate kings and queens, and regularly endorsed by our state authorities—why, then, there is an end of the dispute." But others might "hold that men have certain rights conferred upon them by the Deity, and that no deliberative body of mere men have any power to *take away* those natural rights." Devyr acknowledged that the two perspectives yielded different prescriptions for relief, both as to measures and as to forum. But the authority to establish the Anti-Rent agenda did not belong to him, to Evans, or to Harris. It belonged to the farmers themselves. "Every town in all the patriotic counties," Devyr asserted, should send delegates to a "MONTHLY CONVENTION" of the Anti-Rent Party. Only then could the views of "each township—its wishes—its resources—its public opinion—be spread out before the collected wisdom of the whole." Only then could the course of events, which "may take unexpected turns," be closely monitored and shaped in conformity to the will of the tenant community.[15]

Nine days later, tenant farmers and their families did assemble in force for Independence Day rallies throughout the region. Thousands of wagons decorated with Anti-Rent banners and flags streamed into New Scotland, Albany County, and Sandlake, Rensselaer County. Thousands more journeyed to Durant's Grove near Blenheim, Schoharie County, and Peter's Grove near Roxbury, Delaware County. Smaller but no less festive conclaves of anti-renters gathered at designated sites in Columbia, Montgomery, Schenectady, Otsego, and Sullivan counties. The crowds of Anti-Rent faithful were larger, the feelings of solidarity and expectations of victory greater, than ever before. At the New Scotland rally, William Holmes read the Declaration of Independence under a banner that read "Resistance to tyrants is obedience to God!" A Rensselaerville band played patriotic marches and its director conducted 5,000 voices through verse after verse of "The End of Bill Snyder." Resolutions were passed by acclamation, one of which praised Devyr's manifold contributions to the cause.[16]

Robert D. Watson, the principal orator at New Scotland on July 4, 1845, spoke for two hours. He did not mention Devyr's call for open discussion of strategy and tactics by the rank and file. In Watson's judgment, those matters already had been decided. "Will the descendants of the Revolution, the countrymen of George Washington," he asked in his opening paragraph, "allow feudal barons to hold large tracts of land without title to them, and stifle all enquiry and investigation into them, and not allow the tenants to have a law passed by which landlords shall be compelled to prove their title?" Public opinion, which was "omnipotent" in America, would not permit such a state of affairs to continue. But the quest for support from the people of New York, Watson insisted, had to be managed with circumspection. "No agrarian or levelling doctrines should be presented, for . . . they will destroy the cause. This position cannot be too fully presented to the people of the state, that the tenants are not destructives, not levellers, not agrarians; that they are opposed to all violations of the law: that they want no man's property, and no man shall hold theirs by fraud." Hold fast to these guidelines of "prudent" agitation, Watson declared, and "public opinion in our free government will carry your cause triumphantly through."[17]

Devyr returned to Albany in a rage. It was regrettable, he wrote in the *Freeholder* on July 16, that Watson should give countenance to the "absurd impression that there is an agrarian movement going on." National Reformers believed, first, in free homesteads for settlers on the public lands; their "secondary object" was "the breaking down of all feudal tenures in the state." Only prospective measures had been advocated. Equating those measures with agrarianism, Devyr declared, was "a miserable, contemptible device of the enemy which should be scouted with dignity by every man engaged in the glorious work" of emancipating New York's tenant farmers.[18]

Evans responded to Watson's fire at greater length. "Mr. Watson makes, by implication, a lying charge against the National Reformers," he wrote a few days after Devyr's editorial appeared. "There is no 'agrarian movement' in this country but theirs and that of the anti-renters; and his language implies that the National Reformers wish to divide or destroy men's property, a charge for which there is not the shadow of a foundation." All the National Reformers proposed, Evans explained, "is to prevent *further* monopoly." But the "slander" in Watson's oration was merely a symptom of the cancer within the Anti-Rent movement—the increasing authority of "self-aggrandiz[ing]" party politicians. The "dishonest" title-test scheme neither addressed the real grievances of the tenants nor guaranteed the extinguishment of "feudal" tenures. "It will be well," Evans concluded, "if there be not more Mr. Watsons in the Anti-Rent ranks." Harris and Bouton fired Devyr forty-eight hours later. Alexander G. Johnson of Troy, Hayner's young law partner, replaced him as editor of the *Freeholder*.[19]

The firing of Devyr caused an uproar in eastern New York. Acrimony and backbiting disrupted the meetings of Anti-Rent locals in late July; Devyr published the first number of his own Albany paper, the *Anti-Renter*, on August 16. Alvan Bovay, an eloquent National Reformer from New York City, spoke to "large and enthusiastic crowds" in thirteen Albany County locales during early August and carried Evans's gospel into a dozen other towns in Rensselaer and Columbia before the month ended. But he had to cancel his plans to lecture in Delaware County. On August 8, the Delhi correspondent for the *Albany Argus* dispatched a story that electrified the people of New York State. "We have at length the climax of outrage and murder in this county," he wrote. "The 'Indians,' as they are called—disguised whites, who appropriately assume the name of 'Indians'—yesterday not only resisted the lawful authorities, but wantonly shot down deputy sheriff Osman Steele, a valuable and highly esteemed citizen and officer; and here all is excitement and the highest feeling." The excitement became general, not merely local, as news of Steele's murder spread. So did concern about the implausible programs for state action urged by the Anti-Rent movement's two warring wings.[20]

The Rout of the "Indians"

Undersheriff Steele died in the line of duty on the south one-half of Great Lot No. 39, Hardenbergh Patent, a 160-acre farm near Andes that Moses Earle held in perpetuity at an annual rent of twenty cents per acre. The rent had been payable to Charlotte D. Verplanck of New York City for as long as anyone could remember. Earle was one of the more prosperous farmers in Delaware County, and a pasture full of livestock plainly showed his ability to fulfill his contractual obligations. Landlord lawyers bent on breaking the rent strike picked his place as a logical spot to launch another offensive. On June 4, 1845, Verplanck's resident agent issued a distress warrant for $64, two years rent in arrear. Sheriff Green More distrained six cows and eight hogs belonging to Earle on July 23, scheduled a sale to satisfy the warrant for July 29, and published the five-day notice required by New York law in the *Delaware Gazette*. Although fifty "Indians" showed up before dawn on July 29, they hid in the woods behind Earle's barn. The sheriff never saw them. A contingent of undisguised anti-renters in Earle's pasture kept up the bidding until sunset, and More finally adjourned the sale until August 7 at one o'clock in the afternoon.[21]

The postponement produced a tragedy of errors. Warren Scudder and Edward O'Conner, the "Indian" chiefs in Andes and Bovina, respectively, assumed that a landlord hireling would come to bid at the second auction. Consequently they decided to scuttle the scheme that had worked on July 29 in favor of armed intimidation. Delaware "Indians" had repeatedly violated the Armed and Disguised Act since its enactment in January; the chiefs had no reason to suspect that the risks incident to willful lawbreaking on August 7 might be greater than ever before. They miscalculated. Sheriff More miscalculated as well. Because the tenant resistance had been peaceable on July 29, he did not summon a posse to overawe the anti-renters ten days later. More did order Steele to show up at the Earle place shortly after noon on August 7. When the sheriff started up Dingle Hill that morning, however, his only companion was Peter P. Wright, law partner of landlord lobbyist Charles Hathaway. Wright had been retained by Verplanck's agent to outbid the anti-renters on the ground. Neither the sheriff nor the Delhi lawyer seems to have understood that their mission constituted a violation of New York law. In 1841 a state court had held that "a sale under a distress warrant cannot be postponed beyond the five days limited by the statute."[22]

Everyone concerned had a last clear chance to avoid the bloodshed nobody wanted. A crowd of spectators already had assembled at the Earle farm when More and Wright arrived about ten on the morning of August 7. Shortly afterward, a small body of "Indians" came up the road and marched through the pasture to a rendezvous in the woods. Additional warriors, amounting in all to more than 200, paraded past Sheriff More and the hired bidder before noon. Yet the sheriff did not back off once it became clear that this attempt to sell Earle's cattle would be more dangerous than the last one. Instead, he and Wright tried to persuade Earle to pay his rent. "You will have to go on and make it out of the property," the farmer declared. "I shall fight it out to the hardest." At one o'clock the "Indians" marched single file across the pasture and lined up along the rail fence that kept Earle's livestock out of the road. Sheriff More warned them that they were violating the law. "Damn the law," one of the "Indians" in the line replied; "we mean to break it." Other warriors threatened Wright. "I told them," the Delhi attorney later testified, "if the property was offered for sale, I should bid on it. They then said that if I bid on the property, I should go home feet foremost in a wagon." More decided to wait for Steele's arrival before proceeding any further; the "Indians," sweltering in their disguises under the midday heat, refreshed themselves from a pail of whiskey carried down from Earle's house.[23]

Undersheriff Steele and Erastus Edgerton, the Andes constable, rode up about two o'clock. "I talked with Steele and Edgerton about adjourning the sale," Peter Wright testified at the coroner's inquest. "We thought it best to offer one article." Steele suggested that Wright take a position between his horse and Edgerton's so that the lawmen could escort him through the "Indian" line and into the pasture. As they walked toward the gate, the horses six to eight feet apart and Wright in the middle, one of the chiefs shouted "Shoot the horses!" A volley of shots rang out, followed about fifteen seconds later by another. Edgerton's wounded horse reared up and plunged into the road; the constable jumped clear of the animal as it fell. Steele was not so fortunate. Bullets ripped into his chest, bowels, and right arm as well as into his horse. He died in Moses Earle's bed early that evening. The undersheriff's uncle, Dr. Ebenezer Steele, was there at the end. "I pointed to the body and said it was a very hard case," the physician later reported. "Earle said he did not know; he had been created for the very course he had taken, and [the lawman] was ordained to die in that way. I told him then he must be a fatalist. Earle replied that the Almighty made no mistakes."[24]

Osman Steele's funeral had to be held outdoors so great was the crowd. Two thousand people listened to sermons on justice and vengeance delivered by three Delhi clergymen, and Sheriff More found that townsmen who had declined to help him execute distress warrants were now eager to help him catch "Indians." The arrests began the following day. Frederick Steele, brother of the decedent and a graduate of West Point, led one posse of volunteers. James B. Howe, a brother-in-law, took charge of another. Timothy Corbin, a deputy sheriff whom the Roxbury tribe had tarred and feathered in the fall of 1844, headed a third. Charles Hathaway's law office served as the campaign's command and control center. The "reign of terror," as George Henry Evans characterized it, lasted three weeks. Day after day posses went out from Delhi while construction crews built log jails near the courthouse to hold the prisoners. About 300 men were arrested and confined in the "Delhi Bastille." Warren Scudder, the chief of the Andes "Indians," was not among them. He got away.[25]

Rumors that Scudder had been seen in Schoharie County reached Delhi on August 20, and a 150-man Delaware posse joined up with another at Gilboa headed by Sheriff John S. Brown. The ensuing raids netted fourteen more arrests, mainly on charges of violating the Armed and Disguised Act in February or March. But the foray into Schoharie embarrassed the authorities. Neither Scudder nor any other Delaware fugitive was apprehended; the posse's excessive zeal evoked a chorus of complaints about warrantless searches, careless gunfire, trampled crops, and forcible seizures of private property to feed the volunteers and their horses. Every "atrocity" got broadcast across the state by the big-city reporters who had hustled to "the seat of war" following the Steele shooting.[26]

On August 27, Governor Silas Wright issued a proclamation declaring Delaware County to be "in a state of insurrection." Calling the disorders an insurrection stretched the truth. Nobody in Delaware had seen an "Indian" in twenty days, and the anti-renters responsible for the death of Osman Steele either had been jailed or had burned their disguises and gone into hiding. There was method in the proclamation all the same. It enabled Wright to put his own man, Adjutant General Thomas Farrington, in charge of destroying the "Indian" organizations and restoring peace to the countryside. Delaware officials welcomed Farrington and his troops to Delhi. The "act to enforce the laws and preserve order," enacted on April 15, 1845, authorized the state government to pay for the suppression of civil uprisings that localities could not put down. Farrington spent at least $129,000 before Governor Wright revoked the insurrection proclamation on December 18; the people of New York State, not just the taxpayers of Delaware County, picked up the tab.[27]

The proclamation also strengthened Wright's hand in the disposition of prosecutions under the Armed and Disguised Act. A grand jury in Kingston, Ulster County, already had indicted twenty-six men implicated in the March uprising near Woodstock; trial had been set for October. Fourteen more suspects had been jailed in Gilboa, Schoharie County, where they awaited the summoning of a grand jury. But those numbers were dwarfed by the 346 indictments that a Delhi grand jury handed down beginning on August 22.

Approximately half of them charged the person named with the murder of Undersheriff Steele. The county prosecutor's hair-raising legal theory, which Judge Amasa J. Parker had endorsed in his charge to the grand jury, held that the "Indians" who assembled at Moses Earle's farm on August 7 had committed murder whether they fired their guns or not. New York law provided that every fatality arising from the commission of a felony (assembling armed and disguised) constituted murder in the first degree. Proof of intent to kill was not required. Nelson K. Wheeler, a Democratic wheelhorse in Delhi, believed that the prosecutions would wipe out the Democratic Party in Delaware County. "I am clearly of opinion that the we have made too many arrests," he wrote Azariah Flagg. "We cannot send a fourth of our citizens to the state prison and hang another fourth of them!" Only timely intervention by Governor Wright, Wheeler counseled, could forestall such a calamity.[28]

Wright's proclamation served a third function as well. It gave him an opportunity to address the people of New York State, and his message sent clear signals to anti-renters and landlords alike. The era of the "Indian," of "mak[ing] might the measure of right between citizen and citizen," he said, had come to a tragic yet foreseeable end. "The present presents a peculiarly appropriate occasion," Wright declared, for "tenants who disapprove of this disguised and armed force . . . to mark more distinctly their separation from proceedings which cannot fail to be fatal to a good cause, and to prejudice good men." Again the governor insisted, as he had in January, that land reform could not be effected until the "Indian" tribes disbanded. Only then could the "natural sympathies of the great body of our freeholders" be rallied behind a drive to extinguish a form of land tenure "not in accordance with the genius of our institutions, or the spirit of our people." Wright added that "the present crisis should not be without its lessons" to the great proprietors of eastern New York. "While the power of the state must and will be exerted to enforce the law," he said, the landlords had a corresponding duty to "put an end forever to this perpetual relation of landlord and tenant . . . by tendering generous terms to the tenants."[29]

Adjutant General Farrington began to implement Wright's peace policy on August 27. His first stop en route to Delhi was Gilboa, Schoharie County, where he conferred with Sheriff Brown and John Mayham, leader of the county Anti-Rent association. Together they negotiated "the treaty of Gilboa." Mayham and other "men of influence among the anti-renters, named in writing," agreed to collect and deliver to the authorities all masks and disguises in the possession of association members. They also promised "to use their influence throughout the county to restore peace, good order and a proper respect for the laws." In return Sheriff Brown released the fourteen "Indian" suspects in custody, disbanded his posse, and agreed to "refrain from arresting any more [anti-renters] on suspicion of appearing in disguise." The era of the "Indian wars" on the Blenheim and Scott patents thus ended with no prosecutions and therefore no "political prisoners" for Schoharie tenants to rally around. A comparable denouement occurred in Ulster County. Asa Briggs ("Blackhawk"), the Wood-stock tenant leader who had escaped into Delaware in March, surrendered early in September. But no trials followed. The circuit judge released the men under indictment, some on bail and others on their own recognizance, and continued all twenty-six Armed and Disguised Act prosecutions until the court's spring term. Eventually the charges were dismissed.[30]

The politically explosive situation in Delaware County could not be defused so easily. Farrington marched into Delhi at the head of 300 militiamen on August 28; the "reign of terror," orchestrated by landlord lobbyist Charles Hathaway, soon ceased. But a general clearing of the "Delhi Bastille" was out of the question. The prisoners included Edward O'Conner, chief of the Bovina "Indians," and John Van Steenburgh, an illiterate youth who was said to have boasted after Steele's murder, pointing between his legs, "[I] put a ball into him here." Scores of other prisoners had been artfully examined by local magis-trates, and many had confessed to being armed and disguised at the shooting scene. Delhi residents had been quoted as saying that Moses Earle, also under indictment for murder, "is sure of the rope" and would get it sooner rather than later "but for respect to law and order." Anti-renters had given the people of Delhi a martyr, and Steele's friends seemed determined to have a New York trial court give the anti-renters martyrs of their own.[31]

Farrington won some small victories for the Wright administration in Delhi. When the trials began on September 22, only O'Conner and Van Steenburgh stood accused of capital murder. The county prosecutor had accepted pleas of guilty to manslaughter by Earle and eight others. Murder charges against an-other sixty-eight prisoners had been dropped in exchange for pleas of guilty to assembling at Earle's farm armed and disguised. All of the latter ultimately avoided prison sentences. Thirty convicted "Indians" were fined sums varying between $500 and $25; the other thirty-eight had their sentences suspended. But trying even one Delaware anti-renter for a capital offense meant risking a political backlash from tenant voters. Jury selection in *The People v. Van Steen-burgh*, the first case on the docket, began on September 23. Three days later, Nelson K. Wheeler wrote Flagg from Delhi that "of the first 50 talesmen summoned . . . only five jurymen [were] sworn."[32]

Impaneling a jury took an equally long time in the second trial of Smith Boughton—"Big Thunder"—for taking distress warrants at gunpoint from the sheriff of Columbia County back in December. Boughton's ordeal in Hudson resumed on September 3. Seventy talesmen were questioned during the first ten days, and the court accepted only four of them. An astute reporter for the *Argus* explained the difficulty on September 17. In the landmark case of *The People v. Bodine* (1845), decided two months earlier, the New York Supreme Court had set aside a murder conviction on the ground that Judge Parker, who also presided in the first Boughton trial, had refused to reject prospective jurors unless they expressed "a fixed and absolute opinion" about the guilt or innocence of the accused. The proper standard in a challenge to a juror "for favor," Justice Samuel Beardsley declared for the high court, was "any fact or circumstance from which bias or prejudice may justly be inferred, although weak in degree." The rule expounded in the *Bodine* case, remarked the reporter in Hudson, "allows counsel on either side an almost unlimited range of enquiry in examining a [potential] juror." It also reduced the possibility of jury nullification, the deed that had vexed prosecutors in the first Boughton trial.[33]

Prosecutors had to be patient to get convictions at Hudson and Delhi, but the convictions came. Boughton's trial started first and concluded first. On September 28 the Hudson jury, having been purged of everyone with even a hint of Anti-Rent sympathy, found him guilty of highway robbery; two days later, Judge John Worth Edmonds, a Wright appointee, sentenced Boughton to a life term in the state prison. For Boughton and his many friends in the Anti-Rent movement, the harsh sentence had only one plausible rationale. "The affair in Delaware County," he wrote in a memoir, "caused Governor Wright to declare that I being the principal [tenant] leader must be made an example of." Van Steenburgh and O'Conner, who stood sobbing before Judge Parker on October 11, had no explanation for the death sentences imposed upon them. A poem O'Conner wrote for his sweetheart just before the sentencing indicated his state of mind:

> Oh Janet, dear, I little thought that this would be my lot—
> I fear I'll die a shameful death and be by man forgot.
> But should I meet so hard a fate, my foes I do forgive them,
> We'll rise triumphant from the grave—we'll meet again in Heaven!

O'Conner was not forgotten. Neither were Van Steenburgh, Boughton, Earle (sentenced to life imprisonment), and the twelve other Delaware anti-renters convicted of manslaughter and put behind bars for long terms. On October 4, George Henry Evans put a new line of bold-faced type on the masthead of *Young America*: "Liberation of Dr. Boughton." Two weeks later, he added the names of the Delaware anti-renters condemned to death or sent to the state prison at Clinton to serve their allotted time. "There is nothing to equal it in this country," Evans wrote of the trials on October 18, "since the hanging of witches in New England." Anti-renters throughout New York tended to agree.[34]

Very few people expected O'Conner and Van Steenburgh to hang. "Great exertions will made to induce the governor to commute their sentences," Farrington wrote Flagg from Delhi on October 17. "It is not proven that either of them shot Steele; therefore the murder so far as the people here are concerned is a constructive murder, a legal murder and not an actual murder." Every member of the Van Steenburgh jury and all but one member of the O'Conner jury recited these arguments in petitions to Governor Wright. With the exception of James Watson Webb, reactionary editor of the *Courier and Enquirer*, even the state's Whig journalists urged the governor to commute the sentences. Hanging Van Steenburgh and O'Conner, Greeley contended, would "counteract the influence of the Andes tragedy" and "render difficult and distant that pacification and adjustment of the landlord and tenant differences which all good men must earnestly desire."[35]

Nobody yearned for "pacification and adjustment" more than Silas Wright. Anti-Rent agitation had been a bone in his throat since he accepted the Democratic nomination for governor in 1844. The power of the "Indians" had been broken, but the bone had not been dislodged. Wright waited until after the November 1845 election to commute the death sentences; his message on the subject was generally well received. The election returns gave him less satisfaction. Democrats captured 73 of the 128 seats in the assembly, a gain of six over the previous year, and retained a substantial 25-7 majority in the senate. In the Anti-Rent counties, however, Wright's party took a beating. An independent Equal Rights Party drubbed the Democrats in Delaware and sent two anti-renters, Reuben Lewis and Orrin Foote, to the assembly. Ira Harris and Robert D. Watson won easily in Albany. So did Henry Z. Hayner, Samuel Mc-Clellan, Justus Nolton, and Thomas Smith, the Whig/Anti-Rent candidates in Rensselaer and Schoharie counties. But the most significant Democratic setback occurred in the third senate district. William Van Schoonhoven, the nominee of both the Whig and Anti-Rent parties in a district comprising Albany, Rensselaer, Columbia, Greene, Delaware, Schoharie, and Schenectady counties, defeated his Democratic opponent by nearly 7,000 votes. Wright had carried the same district in 1844 with a majority of 2,220. Party managers immediately grasped the implications of Van Schoonhoven's strong showing. If the Whig candidate for governor ran as well among anti-renters in 1846, Wright could not be reelected.[36]

Wright believed that the tenant voters who had deserted the Democracy could be coaxed back. Early in December he quietly contrived a new package of land reform measures. Its key item was the gradual emancipation plan Martin Van Buren had suggested the previous fall and Wright had then dismissed as too "radical." If the legislature enacted the entire package in 1846, the extinction of manorial tenures would be assured and the appeal of Anti-Rent politics greatly reduced. The schism in the Anti-Rent movement gave Wright one reason to hope for success. Bitter strife within the Whig Party gave him another.

Whig Recriminations

The death of Osman Steele on August 7, 1845, generated an insatiable public appetite for Anti-Rent news and analysis. New York journalists stoked the public interest with sensational accounts of the manhunts, the militia movements, and the trials. Landlord agents and tenant spokesmen sustained it with press releases designed to sway public opinion. Each side blamed the other, of course, for the deplorable state of affairs in the Anti-Rent counties.[37] An anxious public, troubled by the violence and by the rhetoric of conflict, wanted to know why the controversy still raged and how it might be resolved. Democrats responded cautiously. The party press dutifully supported Governor Wright's pacification policy and waited for him to initiate new proposals for government action. Whigs did not have that luxury; they also lacked a common point of view. As progressives, conservatives, and Anti-Rent fusionists proceeded to offer different diagnoses of the difficulties or to advocate different cures, moreover, they lambasted one another unmercifully. Two mighty Whig commentators, Horace Greeley and Daniel Dewey Barnard, stood at the center of the resulting storm.

Greeley filled the *Tribune* with a steady stream of editorials on the Anti-Rent agitation beginning on August 11. His first piece, " 'Indian' Outrages," reported the Steele shooting and condemned the tenant resistance. He took it for granted that "the authors of this outrage" would be captured and punished, "no matter whether they fired or not." But he was more concerned about what would happen after "the wild hurrah against the murderers at Andes" had run its course. "Will the imprisonment of some 'Indians' allay the excitement now pervading the leasehold counties?" Greeley asked. "Will it adjust the controversy? Will it collect the withheld rents? Will it ensure future quiet, harmony and order? . . . Is it not well to consider these points? Is it not high time they *were* considered?" A "few facts" followed.[38]

The leading "fact," as Greeley saw it, was that the tenant movement could not be put down with force. Time and again since 1839, he said, "the military have marched up their hills and then marched down again; yet here is Anti-Rent." Tenant voters had elected six members to the state legislature in 1844; the Anti-Rent Party, he correctly predicted, "will hardly elect fewer this year." Some of the new assemblymen, moreover, were almost certain to be exponents of the "ultra" land reform program trumpeted by George Henry Evans. The movement's growth, staying power, and increasing radicalism alarmed Greeley. But "distress warrants and the wholesale ejectment of families from the[ir] humble homesteads," he asserted, "will only enlarge the sphere and increase the power of Anti-Rentism."[39]

In his most provocative article, "The Pro and Con of Anti-Rent," Greeley provided an imaginative account of how the lease in fee generated the tenant movement. "Consider a poor farmer (not merely a poor man)," he wrote in the September 6 piece, "living in the house built by his father and on the farm which he inherited from his father—such farm having been first taken on a perpetual lease when entirely wild by some ancestor of the family." Suppose the farm to consist of 160 acres at an annual rent of twenty cents an acre or thirty-two dollars. "(Cheap enough, will be the general exclamation.)" Because the rent system stifles his incentive to improve the farm, however, "the tenant . . . sneers at 'book-farming' and tills just as his grandfather did, except where the grandfather's system of tillage has worn out the soil, and even white beans and buckwheat have refused longer to grow." As a result, the farm yields "less than $300" of produce a year, "of which two-thirds is directly consumed in the family; the rest is pretty much mortgaged to the neighboring 'storekeepers' before it is harvested." Still, the tenant "calls the farm his own, as did his father before him, looking on the rent merely as a disagreeable incumbrance or formality, like one of the whimsicalities by which land is held in England under feudal tenures."

"But the rent is no abstraction," Greeley insisted as he developed the implications of his story. "Every year must see it paid, though frosts kill, crops fail or cattle die." Only the proprietor's paternalism could be counted on for a stay. "Sickness, death, or any mischance becomes the pretext for a petition of forbearance," thus the tenant habitually "makes a journey to the landlord, states his case, and is generally excused." As "the evil day" of reckoning is postponed year after year, however, the tenant's restive feelings of dependence "wake new thoughts" in his mind:

At home, he is the equal of the best around him; when he approaches the landlord or agent to supplicate forbearance, he feels himself an inferior being. He is a slave addressing a master, who has power to work him deadly injury. . . . He ponders on his difficulties and perplexities, calculates the gross amount of rent which his ancestors and he have paid, and the question will force itself upon him—"*For what* should I pay this rent? To what end are some men landlords and other tenants? Was it right in the government to give this landlord's ancestors all the earth hereabouts and mine none? Had they any rightful power to fence up the God-created elements against the use of those who should need them? Why the earth more than the air? And if the grant was wrong at first, how can it have been made right since? No! The rent is a venerable fraud—an impudent juggle of rulers to enrich their pampered favorites at the expense of the toiling masses. . . . This farm is no more than the fair share of my family—our labor has made it what it is, paid the taxes, made the roads. The rent is the great curse of our community—*down with the rent!*"

And so it began.[40]

Greeley claimed that "the political theorizing of our day" kept the Anti-Rent movement going. "The reference to the glorious deeds of our ancestors in resisting law and order in defense of human rights—the pregnant language of the Declaration of Independence," he explained, "are listened to and commented on by the unknown Gracchi of a rural neighborhood, who argue, 'If life and the pursuit of happiness are inborn, inalienable rights, they include space to labor and live on, without which life could not be preserved nor happiness obtained; wherefore, the laws which give some men a thousand times as much land as they can use and thus deprive millions of any at all, are invalid, being contrary to the fundamental principles of our government.'" In Greeley's judgment, arguments of this sort were no more persuasive than those expounded by radical abolitionists, "pioneers in this school of logic." "The fact is," he said, "abstract notions of natural right and justice cannot override and nullify sovereign grants and title-deeds." But another "fact" seemed equally plain. As long as eastern New York remained in the grip of perpetual tenancy, "the fallacies and misrepresentations of the Anti-Rent orators" would continue to gain ground among the inhabitants and "might lead to events perilous to some established rights of property." Already a great many tenants had embraced "the new constitution" proposed by George Henry Evans.[41]

Accounting for the luxuriation of the Anti-Rent movement was a didactic exercise for Greeley. In his hands, the story revealed truths that progressive Whigs had long regarded as self-evident. For years they had taught that individual effort, the engine of progress in a republic, could thrive only in an environment of equal opportunity, secure possession of the fruits of labor, and harmonious social relations. The rent system violated all those principles, and New York was reaping the whirlwind. The improvident land grants of the colonial era had been "a flagrant and pernicious error." "Were it to do over again," Greeley wrote, "we should sternly resist any alienation of the ownership originally, and necessarily vested in the state or sovereignty, except in small lots to actual settlers." Manorial tenures aggravated the initial mistake. The landlord's property interest in tenant improvements "robbed the farmers of rights founded in labor," encouraging "bad husbandry" and the construction of "poor shacks." As for landlord paternalism, it merely put a temporary lid on volatile class resentments that eventually burst forth with great fury.[42]

Greeley might have invoked another cardinal Whig principle—the public sector's responsibility to shape an environment conducive to progress—as a guide to resolution and reform. But this he declined to do. "Looking over the whole ground," Greeley told his anxious readers on September 6, "we do not see how the anti-renters can succeed in obtaining titles to their lands otherwise than by paying the landlords for them." Landlords had a social obligation to sell their reserved interests on equitable terms; tenants had a social obligation to accept such offers. Greeley repeated the admonition day after day beginning on August 11. "This can be done at once," he said entreatingly, "without troubling legislatures, lawyers, agents, sheriffs, posses, or anybody else but the parties actually interested." Having defined the rent system as a public problem of great magnitude, Greeley entrusted its resolution to private bargaining in the shadow of public opinion.[43]

Two forces pushed Greeley in this direction. The first sprang from the rural landlords who resided in New York City. On August 18, seventeen proprietors of estates in the counties of Columbia, Delaware, Greene, Schoharie, Sullivan, and Ulster published a circular in which they offered, as the circular put it, "to sell our rents, and make grants in fee, on fair terms." The signatories included Frederick De Peyster, John Hunter, Campbell S. White, the Verplancks, the Armstrongs, the Ludlows, and the Livingstons. All of them were founding members of the landlords' executive committee, established in Manhattan on December 19, 1844, to break the "Indian" resistance and restore the steady flow of rent payments. The circular did not state their buyout terms, but the New York City group had clearly decided to give up the fight and change their investment portfolios. Only John A. King, the chairman of the executive committee, released his terms to the press. Following "the treaty of Gilboa," he announced his willingness to commute the perpetual rents payable on Blenheim Patent into a principal sum, which, invested at 6 percent, would produce an annual income equivalent to the rent. He also promised to forgive the rents in arrear. Greeley had reason to hope that all the New York City absentees would follow King's lead. Even the proprietors of Rensselaerwyck might be persuaded to sell out on comparable terms. "The Van Rensselaer estate might have been settled up in this way several years ago, to the advantage of all parties," Greeley remarked on September 23. "We hope it may yet be."[44]

The split in the Anti-Rent ranks was a second factor that impelled Greeley to link the abolition of manorial tenures with voluntary action, not state intervention. He had studied the arguments for and against both Evans's "new constitution" and the title-test scheme favored by Ira Harris. Neither proposal, Greeley informed his readers, had any merit. But Evans's critique of the Harris bill impressed him, as did Harris's critique of the "destructive" restrictions on freedom of testation and alienation advocated by Evans. In effect, Greeley summarized those critiques for *Tribune* subscribers who knew nothing about the weekly war of words between the *Freeholder* and the *Anti-Renter*. The title-test proposal, he reported, was underinclusive; the "new constitution," overinclusive. Harris's bill targeted supposed irregularities in landlord titles, not the manorial tenures that produced the indomitable spirit of Anti-Rent. Enacting the measure would only escalate the mutual enmity of the parties, provide employment for pettifogging lawyers, and prolong the agony of the New York body politic. The "new constitution," on the other hand, targeted the conventional rights of all New York landowners, not merely those implicated in the "sore mischief" of manorial tenure. Implementing the land-limitation scheme would depress the market for real estate, check the improvement of land, and diminish the incentives to exertion in every branch of industry. It would supplant the "blight" incident to the rent system with another, more general blight arising from "agrarianism."[45]

Greeley had no intention of arguing natural law with the Evans crowd or the validity of landlord titles with the Harris people. He was shrewd enough to understand that neither contest could be won. Instead, he tried to convince anti-renters of all persuasions that they should not pin their hopes on new statutes or constitutional reforms any more than landlords should pin theirs on state enforcement of existing contractual obligations. His was the logic of prudence, not the logic of rights. Yet the most striking thing about Greeley's repeated entreaties for a negotiated settlement was his quiet, perhaps unconscious suppression of an eminent domain alternative. Time and again he insisted that the state "cannot resume or reappropriate private property without making full compensation for it." In the summer of 1845, however, only George Henry Evans pointed out that the constitutional convention could revive the eminent domain option recommended by the Duer Committee in 1840. Once the eminent domain idea had been contaminated with "agrarianism," Greeley and his progressive Whig associates put it out of mind. Compensated emancipation became unthinkable.[46]

Nobody noticed Greeley's reluctance to embrace an eminent domain solution. People reacted to what he said rather than to what he did not say. And indignant reactions came from all manner of Whigs. Henry Z. Hayner, leader of the Whig/Anti-Rent fusionists in Rensselaer County, objected to Greeley's conclusion that tenants had no choice but to throw themselves upon the mercy of their landlords. "You are wrong in admitting that the legislature has no power to abolish perpetual leases," he wrote the *Tribune* from Troy on September 27. "I can prove that it has ample power in two ways," presumably via Harris's title-test bill and the taxation of rent charges. "It can be done according to law, and without impairing the obligation of contracts. It does not need the aid of a [new] constitution." Besides, Hayner admonished Greeley, to confess collective powerlessness in the face of "a heavy curse, an abominable tenure, overspreading a very large portion of this state," was to impugn the principle of free government: "Are we the citizens of a republic, yet cannot lift the burden of serfdom from our shoulders? We may as well be without laws and constitutions, if we are to be hampered and enslaved by them. Freemen want the unrestrained use of their limbs."[47]

James Watson Webb bashed Greeley's diagnosis of the problem harder than

Hayner assailed his prescription. " 'The Pro and Con of Anti-Rent,' " he wrote on September 11, "is the most reprehensible article we have ever seen in a press calling itself Whig." According to Webb, the "inflammable material at the bottom of the Anti-Rent excitement" was not, as Greeley supposed, the contractual relation between landlord and tenant. It was the "disorganizing" batch of ideas the *Tribune* "put in the mouths of anti-renters." Yet Greeley strained to make such ideas seem sensible. He supplied a "specious defense" of the Anti-Rent argument, a "covert apology" for the "banditti" who had repudiated their debts and assaulted sheriffs for six years and more. Greeley's work, charged the *Courier and Enquirer*, had "no other tendency than to encourage and keep alive the spirit of insubordination," which government had a duty to crush. Because the anti-renters had "taken up arms against the sovereignty of the state and set at defiance the power and the reason of the commonwealth of which they are members and to which they owe allegiance," Webb thundered, "it would be better, far better, that a thousand of th[em] . . . should be shot down without mercy, than that the majesty of the law should remain unvindicated for a single hour."[48]

Daniel Dewey Barnard supplied a philosophical foundation for Webb's wild talk in "The 'Anti-Rent' Movement and Outbreak in New York," published in the December number of the *Whig Review*. It, too, caused a sensation. For Barnard, as for Greeley, recounting the Anti-Rent story provided an opportunity to preach on the woeful consequences of transgressing Whig principles. But the two men had always expounded a different version of the party creed; their narratives contained few common threads. Barnard described the landlord-tenant relation in different terms, attributed the Anti-Rent movement to different causes, and distilled altogether different lessons from the events of 1839–45. He also subverted the solution Greeley advocated so strenuously. Barnard, the longtime spokesman for the Van Rensselaer family, made it clear that the proprietors of Rensselaerwyck had no intention of negotiating a compromise with the anti-renters. Webb claimed that his reasoning was unanswerable. "In a little over twenty pages," he gushed on December 12, "the whole subject is so clearly, so fairly and so forcibly treated as to leave no room for cavil or complaint."[49]

The No-Compromise Persuasion

Barnard's account of the Anti-Rent controversy pivoted on a concept he called "public licentiousness." Throughout history, he explained, republics had been subject to "popular commotions" that contested private rights and disturbed the public peace. In the United States, then, "the existence of such evil opinions and practices, here and there, now and then, must be expected, and need not excite serious fears in any mind, provided they do not invade and infect the healthier portion of the community." Mere "popular licentiousness," Barnard insisted, "easily subsides, if left to itself, under the influence of a sound public sentiment—gentle yet firm, charitable yet uncompromising." Under optimal conditions, such would have been the fate of the "proposed plunder of Mexican territory," as well as the Anti-Rent movement. But in each instance "a local and temporary ebullition of popular heat and impatience" had been "patronized and advocated, or at the least encouraged because not condemned, by those who, by their position in society, their calling and their associations, command public attention, possess, in some degree, the public confidence, and exercise, therefore, a strong influence over public opinion." Agitation with a "vulgar or ignoble origin" thus became respectable and formidable. The complicity of elites, in other words, transformed harmless "popular licentiousness" into dangerous "public licentiousness."[50]

Readers of the *Whig Review* did not have to be told that Democratic statesmen and publicists had converted the "disreputable and scandalous" agitation for Texas annexation into a vital public question. What made the Anti-Rent story so poignant was the role of Whigs in the movement's efflorescence. The villains in Barnard's piece were William Henry Seward, Thurlow Weed, and Horace Greeley. The rent strike that began on Rensselaerwyck in 1839, he observed, amounted to "a general repudiation of debts, existing in the form of rent charged on lands." Explaining how "the design of repudiation" had been conceived and implemented posed no problems for Barnard. It was sufficient, he thought, to point out that every farmer in Albany County had the same landlord and that "purposes which solitary individuals dare not avow or entertain, on account of their profligacy or injustice, communities of men, composed of just such individuals, will oftentimes boldly embrace." Indeed, he added, "there seems to be nothing so intrinsically base or wicked, that respectable and apparently well-meaning persons may not be found to encourage and support it, provided only it have the sanction of numbers in its favor." But the logic of numbers that generated the Helderberg War had a still more pernicious effect. It inclined Seward, Weed, and Greeley to take up the tenant cause, to give it a "public character and consequence," and to sustain it even as the murderous "Indian" commotion spread to other counties. They had "nothing else in view but the success of party," Barnard argued, "and will not submit to let any portion of the people who have votes to bestow on election days, slip away from them."[51]

Barnard wrote as a private citizen, not as a Whig member of Congress. Fearing defeat and at odds with Weed over party strategy, he had refused to run for reelection in 1844. Polk's triumph disturbed him. "I grieve and lament," he told Hamilton Fish, "as if [the United States] were conquered by a horde of barbarians." Nevertheless, the election of Ira Harris and his Whig/Anti-Rent brethren in Albany and Rensselaer disturbed him more. The success of fusion politics prolonged the rent strike, emboldened the "Indians," and compelled Barnard to wait still longer for the $35,000 Stephen Van Rensselaer IV had owed him since 1839. Yet he understood that stating the "public licentiousness" thesis was not to prove it. Barnard had to show that no foundation existed for the "customary clamor" against the rent system that Seward, Weed, and Greeley had amplified. He relished the task.[52]

As a matter of law, Barnard insisted, there was nothing "feudal" about the relationship. When Stephen Van Rensselaer III conveyed his lands to settlers between 1785 and 1815, "such conveyances were contracts, which meant just what was expressed on the face of them, and nothing more." The agreements, moreover, were mutual. "Both parties . . . stood before the law of the land upon a footing of perfect civil equality," and every purchaser of land on Rensselaerwyck became the owner of "a freehold estate of inheritance." All the patroon acquired in return was a debt due from the purchasers, "secured by a pledge, first, of the personal effects of the debtor on his premises [recoverable by distress warrant] and next of his land [recoverable by writ of ejectment]." The debt took the form of a rent charge, in effect "a very moderate annual interest upon the value of the lands, as a capital or principal sum, at the time of the sale." Because the contracts barred the Van Rensselaer family from demanding the principal sum, the debtors' obligation to pay "interest" ran with the land in perpetuity. And so it would remain until debtor and creditor, by mutual consent, made new contracts that provided for payment of the principal. "If there is anything 'feudal' about this," Barnard exclaimed, "then every pledge of personal property, and every mortgage of real estate, as security for debt, is feudal. . . . We know of nothing in the payment of interest, or in the payment of rent, which makes a man a vassal. If it be so, the state is crammed with vassals."[53]

It took some doing to characterize as "interest" rents payable in grain ready for milling, in labor with team and wagon, and in fat fowl. So did the formulation of a liberal, as opposed to a feudal, justification for the quarter-sale provisions in every agreement. But Barnard was good at that sort of thing. "The rent was exceedingly moderate—not two per cent, taking the average, on the value of the farms—when the rent first became payable," he explained. Nevertheless, Stephen Van Rensselaer III had bargained away any right to raise the rent as the value of the land increased. Only the quarter-sale conditions permitted him to share in the prosperity that "his policy in bringing the lands generally into speedy cultivation" made possible. "There was no reason," Barnard asserted, why the initial purchasers "should be allowed to put the whole profit in their own pockets" as they sold out in a rising market; "a portion of it, in all fairness, might be claimed by Mr. Van Rensselaer." Barnard acknowledged that "when time had elapsed and the value of the farms had been fixed . . . any rigorous exaction of a claim to quarter-sales might have been unjust and oppressive." In 1832, however, Van Rensselaer had promulgated a general offer to sell his quarter-sale rights forever for $30 per farm. The offer still stood.[54]

Barnard proceeded in this manner for page after page. He took up every Anti-Rent complaint and "put [it] to silence, so far as truth can," by analogizing the covenant in question to conventional commercial practices. He did not expect to persuade Weed and Greeley, let alone the Anti-Rent agitators and politicians. Barnard wrote primarily for the monied men of New York State, for its bankers and mortgagees and rentiers. His message was plain. The contracts in force on Rensselaerwyck, like mortgages and other legal forms used to finance land development, were nothing more than instruments of credit. And an attack on vested rights in one form of credit was an attack on all. The Van Rensselaers had a duty to ensure that the Anti-Rent movement did not succeed, and the Whig party's men of means had a corresponding duty to support them.[55]

Only one conclusion to the Anti-Rent agitation could be acceptable to Barnard. The farmers had to "abandon their unlawful combinations" and "give up their political organizations." Such associations "are out of place," he said, "where mere private contracts are in question." Above all, anti-renters had to renounce the "absurd notion" that collective action might effect "a compromise" of some sort "at the expense of creditors." No principled landlord could possibly capitulate to such "wicked" pressure. "It is just as base an act of turpitude . . . to compel a creditor . . . to give up a part of what is honestly and fairly due to him on a legal contract, as it would be rob him of the whole," Barnard exclaimed. "The highwayman who divides with his victim on the road, after he gets him in his power, may be called a generous fellow, but he is a robber nevertheless."[56]

This did not mean that the existing legal relations on Rensselaerwyck must endure without change forever. "The time has now come," Barnard remarked, "when the farmers should think of buying off the rents against them, and so ridding themselves of perpetual debt." But it did mean that Stephen Van Rensselaer IV, at least, had no intention of giving quarter to "public licentiousness" by bargaining over terms. Neither the threats of Anti-Rent associations nor the entreaties of misguided journalists like Greeley would improve the "reasonable and moderate terms" Van Rensselaer had laid before the Manor Commission in 1841, before legislative committees in 1844 and 1845, and before the general public in a letter to the Albany newspapers on September 18, 1845. When the people of Rensselaerwyck accepted the offer already on the table, the Anti-Rent era would come to an appropriate end. In the meantime, Barnard concluded, "the honest fulfillment of just contracts is what is required of them, and without which all sympathy with them is only an insult and a curse."[57]

The happy ending Barnard postulated was not very realistic. For one thing, the buyout terms offered by Stephen Van Rensselaer IV were less "liberal" than Barnard let on in the *Whig Review*. Back rents had to be paid and the quarter-sale covenants extinguished at $30 per farm before Van Rensselaer would agree to sell his other interests in the land. What is more, the general offer to convert the perpetual rent into a mortgage for $2.60 an acre (a principal sum that, invested at 6 percent, would produce an interest equivalent to the annual rent) applied only to "the farms in the four hill-towns of Albany county." Tenants in townships closer to the Hudson River, including the Anti-Rent stronghold of New Scotland, had to pay more. And the patroon's agents drove hard bargains. John A. King, in contrast, offered identical terms to all the farmers on his Blenheim Patent. The absentee proprietors of Livingston Manor and the Hardenbergh Patent offered comparable deals to their tenants before the year ended. In December 1845, one could imagine tenants lining up to buy out their landlords in the counties of Columbia, Delaware, Greene, Schoharie, Sullivan, and Ulster. It was harder to imagine such a thing happening on Rensselaerwyck.[58]

Anti-Rent had a stronger foundation on Rensselaerwyck than in neighboring counties, and Barnard knew it. The "Indian" organizations had collapsed everywhere following the murder of Osman Steele, and some rents had even been collected in Delaware County. But the tenant resistance had not been subdued on Rensselaerwyck. Christopher Batterman, the sheriff of Albany County, had tried to resume distress sales following the Steele shooting in August. Time and again Anti-Rent activists frustrated him by arranging for the disappearance of livestock or other chattels advertised for sale. Attempts to serve writs of *fieri facias* (attaching chattels for sale under a court order) had been no more successful. Whenever a law enforcement official "suspected to be serving process is discovered to be on the road," Batterman testified some months later, "an alarm is generally given by blowing horns, or sending messengers in some other way, and usually a company is gathered who surround and accompany him, which makes his progress a matter of very general notoriety." Once the process server arrived at farms named in the writs, "the dwellings are generally found either locked, or apparently in the keeping of females, . . . and the persons upon whom service is desired are either concealed or absent from their residences." Batterman had "abandoned such attempts as useless" in November 1845, the very month Barnard sent his article to the *Whig Review*.[59]

Yet the intransigent position Barnard staked out for Stephen Van Rensselaer IV did have a certain logic. Anti-Rent could not be proclaimed a success even if all the other proprietors sold out on easy terms. The movement had begun on the Manor of Rensselaerwyck, and it had to end there whatever happened elsewhere. Barnard believed that the farmers of Albany County would be compelled to accept defeat in a year or two. His own account of the movement's origin and progress suggested why. Although "public licentiousness" had sustained Anti-Rent, he observed, "the most rational of the measures of pretended relief that have been proposed . . . have had, and are calculated to have, little other effect than to flatter and deceive." Only one of them, the taxation of rent charges, stood a chance of being enacted. An eminent domain law had been proposed, discussed, and buried. Nobody talked about it any more. Meanwhile the "'subterranean' Democracy" had proposed a "new constitution," and the Anti-Rent associations of Albany and Rensselaer had devised a title-test measure. But those schemes had so little merit that even Greeley condemned them. In Barnard's judgment, the taxation of rent charges was an equally bad idea. It "look[s] more like vengeance towards one party than relief of the other," he complained. Tax assessors might make the proprietors' resolve costly, but Van Rensselaer would pay the levy under protest before he would give in to the anti-renters. Indeed, nothing government might plausibly do could prevent him from standing up for his rights. Property, not "the spirit of the age" retailed by the likes of Greeley, was indomitable. And so it had to be if the American republic were to survive.[60]

The course of events disappointed Barnard. He underestimated the farmers' tenacity and the ingenuity of their lawyers and elected representatives. But he and the Van Rensselaers were not the only people whose expectations got dashed. Lawrence Van Deusen, president of the Anti-Rent Association of Albany County and one of the architects of the rent strike, eventually lost his farm. So did many of his friends. The radical visions of George Henry Evans and Thomas A. Devyr came to nothing. Ira Harris, Henry Z. Hayner, William H. Van Schoonhoven, and Robert D. Watson won some political skirmishes but never vanquished the contracts in force on Rensselaerwyck. For all of them, things began to fall apart in 1846. The travail of Governor Silas Wright ended sooner than theirs. Despite a substantial effort to resolve the Anti-Rent controversy, Wright's world lay in ruins when that year of decision concluded.

10

Democratic Futility

Elementary arithmetic told Silas Wright that his political future hinged on decisive action against manorial tenures during the state legislature's 1846 session. In the election of 1844, he ran up a 2,200 majority in the third (Albany) senate district and defeated Millard Fillmore, the Whig candidate for governor, by a 10,000 majority. The tenant vote wiped out both margins of victory in 1845. William H. Van Schoonhoven, the senate nominee of the Anti-Rent Party as well as of the third-district Whigs, beat his opponent by 7,000 votes. Unless thousands of tenant voters were brought back into the Democratic fold, then, the Whig Party was almost certain to win the statewide election in November 1846. Yet the taxation of rent charges, which had seemed so promising to Governor Wright in the spring of 1845, would no longer help the Democrats. Daniel Dewey Barnard had made it clear that new taxes would not change the buyout terms offered by the Van Rensselaers. Besides, Ira Harris and Van Schoonhoven backed the tax scheme too; so did Horace Greeley and Thurlow Weed. Democrats could roll back the Whig/Anti-Rent tide in eastern New York only by sponsoring land reform legislation altogether different from anything yet proposed. They needed a measure that would enable them to reach over the heads of Anti-Rent politicians and give the tenants something they could never get from the Whig Party.[1]

Wright had known for some time what that measure must be, and he put Attorney General John Van Buren to work on it in December 1845. The result was the most radical land reform bill considered by the New York legislature during the Anti-Rent era. Entitled "An Act to amend the Statute of Devises and Descents, and to extinguish certain Tenures," it set new regulations for the transmission of landlord interests from one generation to another. The bill provided that upon the death of any landlord whose tenants held "in fee, for life or lives, or for any period exceeding twenty-one years," the tenants might petition the Court of Chancery "to ascertain the value of [all] rents, services, and privileges reserved to the lessor or grantor, and to convert the same into a mortgage on the lands." In effect, the bill required the New York judiciary to do precisely what the Rensselaerwyck anti-renters asked Stephen Van Rensselaer IV to do voluntarily in 1839. Rents and services payable forever were to be transformed into a principal sum which, invested at the legal rate of interest, would yield the same annual return in perpetuity. The lease in fee would disappear as the five-year mortgages for the principal sum were paid off.[2]

The devise-and-descent plan had many virtues. Its enactment would ensure that the dead hand of oppressive contracts would be lifted and every tenant's aspiration to own the family farm would ultimately be fulfilled. Even its gradual implementation could be seen as a strength. If the bill became law, only tenants who avoided ejectment by performing their contractual obligations would be able to take advantage of it upon the death of their landlord. The devise-and-descent plan thus provided mutually reinforcing guarantees of law and order on the one hand, land reform on the other. The constitutionality of the bill, moreover, was beyond reproach. Unlike the compensated emancipation scheme William A. Duer Jr. proposed in 1840, the new Democratic measure was not grounded on the eminent domain power. It was grounded, instead, on the power to regulate rights of inheritance. And unlike the title-test bill Ira Harris sponsored in 1845, the new Democratic measure would neither subvert vested rights of property nor impair the obligation of contracts. At common law the right to inherit arose from law rather than from property or contract. "Nothing, therefore, can be clearer," Joseph Story wrote in his *Commentaries on the Constitution* (1833), "than that the rules of descent are subject to be changed by legislative authority."[3]

The political implications of the devise-and-descent plan impressed Wright more than anything else. He believed that the Whig Party had benefited from the Anti-Rent agitation for years without doing anything to earn tenant votes. Harris and Van Schoonhoven had grown powerful by condemning the "Indian" violence while currying the favor of its perpetrators; Weed and Greeley had helped the Whig/Anti-Rent leaders seize control of the third senate district while withholding support for their title-test scheme. Whigs had gotten away with such shenanigans because Democrats lacked a solution of their own. But the devise-and-descent bill would change everything. During the legislature's 1846 session, Democrats could expose Whig perfidy and exploit Whig divisions with new confidence. Democrats could even pose as the true champions of the tenant cause. They held 73 of the 128 seats in the assembly, 25 of the 32 seats in the senate. Enactment of the devise-and-descent bill would make the gradual abolition of manorial tenures a Democratic achievement.

Governor Wright understood that many tenants would remain loyal to Harris and Van Schoonhoven whatever the Democrats did in 1846. On the Manor of Rensselaerwyck, in particular, Anti-Rent leaders had persuaded the rank and file that their "pretended proprietors" never had a valid title to the land. Tenants who expected to get something for nothing had little use for legislation that would compel them to pay for Van Rensselaer interests in their farms. But the governor did not need the support of every New York tenant in the November election, and he had reason to think that the devise-and-descent bill would be acclaimed in Anti-Rent counties where the title-test mania had not taken hold of the tenant associations. Wright had still another reason, however, to believe that a partisan debate on Anti-Rent measures would help his party. Staging a fight with the Whigs was a time-honored technique for unifying the Democracy.

Wright came into office distressed by "the miserable Albany feuds" among Democrats, and the Barnburner-Hunker rift had widened during the legislature's 1845 session. Yet restoring a semblance of party harmony seemed possible in 1846. The annexation of Texas, which had divided Democrats for two years, agitated the body politic no more. Congress admitted Texas to the Union on December 29, 1845, and Mexico agreed several weeks earlier to receive John Slidell as a special United States envoy. "The reasonable presumption," Wright told the people of New York, "is that all differences will be amicably adjusted, and the peace of the two nations continue unbroken." Meanwhile, the economic issues that divided Democrats had been committed to another forum. "The success of the [constitutional] convention question before the people" in November 1845, the *Evening Post* remarked on the eve of Wright's second annual message, "has left the legislature little to do." Deliberation on Anti-Rent measures, then, figured to be "the great feature" of the 1846 session. A united Democracy rallying behind the devise-and-descent bill and pummeling the Whig alternatives was a prospect that gave Wright immense satisfaction.[4]

The toughest decision Wright faced as he awaited the lawmakers' arrival in January was whether to promote the devise-and-descent idea in his annual message. Grappling with that matter compelled him to rank and balance his goals for the session. He wanted the bill to become law. He also wanted his Democratic brethren arrayed against the Whigs rather than against one another as in 1845. The best way to achieve his first objective was to feature the bill in his message, explain how the measure would work, and urge the legislature to enact it for the common good. Every daily newspaper printed the governor's message; editors wrote about his recommendations and voters talked about them from one end of New York to the other. There was no better way of mobilizing public support for an act of state. Showing his hand at the outset of the legislative session, however, threatened to undermine the achievement of Wright's partisan objectives. Harris and company might immediately endorse the devise-and-descent plan while continuing to clamor for a title-test measure. In that instance, the Democratic Party would gain no advantage in the Anti-Rent counties.

Wright instinctively subordinated his policy goals to his partisan goals. He wanted voters to think of the devise-and-descent bill as a Democratic measure, not merely as a good idea that merited the support of all well-meaning people. Wright said nothing about the plan in his annual message; he put the bill in the hands of Assemblyman Bishop Perkins of St. Lawrence, an old friend who agreed to spring it on the unsuspecting Whigs when the governor gave the word. Meanwhile, Wright instructed other Democratic lieutenants—Benjamin Bailey of Putnam, Levi Chatfield of Steuben, and Samuel J. Tilden of New York City—on how to bait the Whigs so that Perkins's introduction of the devise-and-descent bill would have maximum effect on both the dialogue of parties and public opinion.[5] Hitching the devise-and-descent bill to partisan objectives was a perilous business. Wright knew it too. He might fail to keep intraparty warfare between Hunkers and Barnburners at bay and, in the process, lose his chance of extinguishing manorial tenures. For Wright, however, "party was everything," and he assumed the risk willfully. He paid the price in November. The people of New York State paid in a different way for decades afterward.

Land Reform at the Shrine of Party

Anti-Rent history and policy dominated the message Governor Wright delivered to the state legislature on January 6, 1846. He introduced the subject with a brief recitation of the Democratic creed. "Attempts to confer favors by law upon classes or localities," he declared, "produce a competition destructive to profitable industry—a strife, not to earn, but to gain the earnings of others." He urged New York lawmakers to disavow "this false system" because it tended to "produce the singular result that he who labors least may accumulate most, and he who works the hardest may know the most want." The legal relation between landlord and tenant in eastern New York illustrated the point. Leases for lives or forever, Wright explained, "are not in accordance with the genius of our institutions or with the feelings of our people," and they could not have survived in a regime of law that "equalizes the benefits and burdens of government, extends the same encouragement to the enterprise and industry of all in every situation and employment, and attempts to secure no special privileges to any." But the rent system had been nourished by a legal order that immunized property in the form of rent charges from taxation and vested landlords with extraordinary remedies for the collection of debts. The time had come to rectify the inequities of the past.[6]

Wright was the first governor in New York history to request specific action against the lease in fee. He asked the legislature to tax rent charges in a bill that assimilated the suggestions, "sound in principle and practical in detail," which Comptroller Azariah Flagg had laid before the assembly in April 1845. He also recommended the enactment of a bill abolishing the remedy of distress for rent.

The legislature had an obligation to do everything it could, consistent with the protection of "existing contracts" required by the Constitution, he said, to mitigate "the odious character, and evil influences, of the leasehold tenures" that government had sustained for so long. Wright kept the devise-and-descent scheme under wraps. But he emphasized that tenant aspirations and his own objectives were precisely the same. "The change of the tenures from leasehold to fee simple estates," he asserted, "I have ever understood, and supposed to be, the great object of desire on the part of the tenants."[7]

The governor did not ignore the cause of his current unpopularity in the Anti-Rent counties. In January 1845, he confessed, "I considered myself precluded from discussing the real merits of the differences existing between the landlords and tenants, by the violent and criminal conduct of those who assumed to act for the latter, and in their name, and apparently by their approbation." Yet he insisted that his "peace first" policy had been justified. Wright pointed out that the shooting of young Rifenburgh at Smoky Hollow, Columbia County, in December 1844 had outraged the body politic and served notice on the Anti-Rent associations that the tenant resistance had "changed the issue" from wrongs arising from manorial tenures to wrongs arising from "wanton disturbances of the peace." Still, two more lives had been lost before the violence ceased. The subsequent murder trials, moreover, had provided conclusive proof of the links between the "Indians" and the Anti-Rent Association of Delaware County, exploding the protestations to the contrary by their "pretended friends." Wright hoped that every tenant who had donned an "Indian" disguise now regretted his participation in "aggravated trespasses on the rights and lives" of others. He trusted that every tenant who had supported the "disturbers" now repudiated "the designing and selfish counselors" who led his kinsmen and neighbors astray. And he asked the tenant community to believe that their institutions of self-government would now do whatever could be done to extinguish the lease in fee.[8]

Wright's remarks on the Anti-Rent question were so sensible that even the Whig press found no fault with them. "The governor discusses, frankly and fairly, the evils of which the tenants complain, and the remedies which have been suggested," Thurlow Weed reported. "His views upon these points are coincident with those presented by Governor Seward, for which *he* was denounced in the . . . Locofoco papers, in all of which we shall find these views now warmly commended." Horace Greeley put a slightly different spin on the land reform recommendations set forth in Wright's message. "His suggestions on this hand strike us favorably," he wrote. "With the governor's process of reasoning designed to show that it is *now* proper to consider carefully the complaints of the anti-renters, though it would have been *im*proper a year ago, we willingly let pass without objection." Weed and Greeley, writing with their eyes fixed on the November election, discerned the same implications in the governor's message. Wright remained vulnerable on the "peace first" point; the Whigs could claim credit for the measures he recommended even if the Democrats went ahead and enacted them. Their party's hold on tenant voters seemed secure.[9]

Assemblyman Ira Harris, leader of the Whig/Anti-Rent contingent in the legislature, interpreted the message as an invitation to go forward with the battery of bills he had sponsored in 1845. On January 7 he gave notice of his intention to introduce one bill to "equalize taxation," a second to abolish distress for rent, and a third to suspend rent collections until the landlords had proved their titles. Harris also moved that the tenant petitions submitted in previous years be pulled from the assembly's files and referred to a select committee. A subject "so varied and extensive," he said, "could not belong to any one of the standing committees of the house." But one Democrat after another objected that the motion was premature. Governor Wright's message had not yet been referred, and the Democratic members claimed that the committee having jurisdiction of the tenant petitions should also be charged with consideration of the governor's call for action against manorial tenures. Harris's resolution was therefore laid on the table. "The vote to postpone," Greeley's *Tribune* reported, "means simply that the majority want to keep the whole business in their own hands." Actually it meant a great deal more.[10]

Harris called up his Select Committee resolution on January 9, and Benjamin Bailey moved to refer it to the committee of the whole on the governor's message. The two motions, taken together, provided a parliamentary justification for the partisan forays both sides were prepared to make. Harris spoke first. "I supposed," he remarked, "after we had heard what the governor had to say on the subject of these difficulties—after even he has so far got over the scruples which he entertained last year that he felt himself at liberty . . . now to discuss, and actually to recommend action on this subject—that there would be no disposition here to delay action." Yet it was "manifest" that the course Bailey advocated "must necessarily tend to delay." According to Harris, "all experience proved that several weeks must elapse" before the sundry resolutions distributing the governor's message among appropriate committees were passed. Bailey's reply deftly undercut Harris's main point. He accepted the idea of a select committee, suggested that the committee be clothed with jurisdiction over Governor Wright's recommendations as well as the tenant petitions, and urged that the committee be appointed immediately to ensure "early action" on land reform.[11]

A portentous exchange followed between Samuel J. Tilden and John Young, the likely Whig candidate for governor in the fall. "No man came to the house more determined than I am," Tilden asserted, "to give to this important question an early, a careful, and a candid consideration." He also contended that "it would be unwise and unparliamentary to refer the [tenant] petitions to one committee, and a portion of the message on the same subject to another." When Tilden sat down, Young asked him if he shared Bailey's inclination to organize such a committee without delay. Tilden replied that he did; Young protested that the course contemplated by the Democratic majority would be unfair to the Whig minority. The governor's message was now before the house "for discussion and review," he declared, "and yet, before a word has been spoken," Democratic leaders wanted to bury it in a select committee. "Why not appoint a committee as the gentleman from Albany proposes?" Young pleaded. "Why not let us say one word on about half this message, when it comes up properly for discussion?" Meanwhile, the committee advocated by Harris could "go forward in their examination of the [tenant] petitions."[12]

John Young's remarks thrilled the Democratic leadership. Bailey leaped to his feet and claimed that the Whig Party was more interested in posturing for the anti-renters than in enacting land reform legislation. Indeed, he said, Whigs had always been so inclined. Bailey charged that Seward had used the manor question in 1840 "to manufacture for himself a little party capital, regardless of the consequences," and John Young had the same intention now. As for Harris, he fretted about delay but actually feared decisive government action. If the legislature mitigated the conditions that generated the Anti-Rent agitation, his political organization would collapse. Only the Democrats, Bailey insisted, were ready "to do speedily all that can be done."[13]

Bailey held the floor all afternoon and much of the following day. He berated the chamber's Whig/Anti-Rent members for their "demagoguery" at one moment and for their "ridiculous" title-test scheme the next. Bishop Perkins, the custodian of Wright's devise-and-descent bill, assumed a more statesmanlike posture as he closed for the Democrats on Saturday, January 10. The Anti-Rent counties, he declared, "are now at peace . . . and it has now become our duty to legislate in such manner as to bring these leases and feudal tenures to an end." Democratic lawmakers, Perkins avowed, "will go to the very verge of what we can do, consistently with a proper respect for vested rights, and long respected principles of law, in granting relief to these tenants." The "responsible majority," he said, "want no delay." Democrats were ready to proceed as soon as the fractious minority finished discussing the governor's message. "It is to us, if nothing is done," he reminded the Whigs, "that will be attributed the odium of doing nothing." Shortly after Perkins sat down, the house adjourned until Monday.[14]

The Whig press jumped into the fray, as expected, over the weekend. Greeley and Weed produced long editorials that defended Seward against the "unfounded aspersions" of the "Locofoco legislature." What the Democrats "rail at as 'demagoguism,'" Greeley wrote, "will yet appear to have been prompted by far-seeing statesmanship and *genuine* democracy." Weed elaborated the same points with a graphic that juxtaposed excerpts from Seward's message of 1840 and Wright's message of 1846. The similarities between their sentiments and language were indeed striking. Both governors described the lease in fee as an odious legal form utterly inconsistent with the spirit and genius of the age. Both governors called for its abolition. Weed believed that the evidence admitted of only one conclusion. "The real difference, therefore, between Governor Seward and his assailants," he wrote, "is that in wisdom and foresight, he was six years in advance of th[em]."[15]

Weed overlooked three things in the haste of composition. First, by focusing on manorial tenures, not manorial titles, he added strength to the Democratic case against Harris's title-test bill. Second, by quoting Seward's words while saying nothing about what the Whig legislature had done about them, he begged questions about the resulting eminent domain scheme that even Greeley had since abandoned. Third, by stressing the identical aspirations of Seward and Wright, he forgot one crucial difference between them. The Whig governor had failed; the Democratic governor still had a chance to succeed. When he read the Saturday edition of the *Evening Journal*, Wright knew that the time to unlimber the devise-and-descent bill had arrived.

On Monday morning, January 12, Assemblyman Perkins moved that a series of resolutions, which together summarized the gist of Wright's devise-and-descent bill, be "referred to the committee of the whole on the message of the governor." He read the resolutions; Harris, stunned, "called for the reading of the resolutions again." While Harris regained his composure, Perkins explained that he was not prepared to introduce a bill. All he wanted was "to call out discussion, and elicit the view of members on the points involved" before the resolutions went to a select committee on the tenant petitions and the governor's land reform recommendations. Harris spoke next. He professed to be "gratified at the tenor of the resolutions" but thought the motion was "not now in order, as the house has not yet ordered a committee on the subject." Harris was right about one thing. Although the floor leaders of both parties had agreed on a select committee, custom barred the Democratic majority from organizing such a committee until the Whigs had said everything they wanted to say about the governor's message. Harris was wrong, however, on the point of order. Governor Wright had done his homework; Perkins moved to refer the resolutions to the committee of the whole, not the proposed select committee, and Speaker William Crain ruled the reference "perfectly in order." The Whigs had nothing else to say. Bailey moved that the resolutions be printed, "which was agreed to," and the sundry elements of the devise-and-descent plan were suddenly thrust before the house and the people of New York State.[16]

Neither the Whig press nor the *Freeholder* breathed a word about the Perkins Resolutions. Governor Wright's principal organ featured them on the editorial page. "Mr. Perkins of St. Lawrence," crowed William Cassidy of the *Albany Atlas*, "has indicated a channel of inquiry which seems to have escaped not only the attention of the tenants, during the prolonged agitation of this subject, but of the many jurists and statesmen who have made its consideration their study." Cassidy claimed that regulating the devise and descent of manorial tenures was an ingenious idea as well as a new one. For six years, he wrote, "no subject . . . has so deeply occupied the public mind as how to reconcile the requirements of the public necessity, which seems to demand a modification of the tenures in the rent district, with the positive constitutional enactment which forbids state interference with contracts." But the constitutional difficulty that "exercised many minds" had been resolved in the Perkins Resolutions. "The action of the proposed law will be prospective," Cassidy observed, yet will provide "remedies for present evils and many safeguards against their further recurrence."[17]

Wright's people in the lower house pressed their advantage in the days that followed. Bailey contrasted the Democratic Party's devise-and-descent approach, which could be "rightfully and constitutionally" enacted, with Assemblyman Harris's "impossibly unsound and unconstitutional" title-test bill. Yet the Harris bill, he pointed out on January 13, was not the only Whig response to the Anti-Rent agitation. Brandishing a copy of the *Whig Review*, Bailey asked "the great leaders on that side of the house . . . [to] come out and show their hands, and tell us plainly whether they take sides with Mr. Barnard" or with Assemblyman Harris. Thomas Smith, a Whig/Anti-Rent member from Schoharie, responded with alacrity. "Barnard has been too long pent up in the city, and under the influence, if not the pay of patroons and landlords," Smith declared, "to know much of the interests, feelings or wants of the tenants." The main-line Whig members, however, maintained what Bailey derisively termed "a studied silence on this momentous question."[18]

Levi Chatfield, a lawyer of some repute, taunted the Whigs and reinforced his party's position in a different way. For two days beginning on January 14, he recounted a Democratic interpretation of the Anti-Rent question during the Whig ascendancy. Seward's purpose in 1840, Chatfield argued, was not to emancipate the people of Rensselaerwyck but "to assimilate their politics, to induce the tenants to attorn the Whig party." The Duer Committee reinforced the "delusive hopes" held out by Governor Seward. Its eminent domain theory, grounded in the "India rubber rule or manner of construing constitutions," suggested that state legislatures might "take from one man his property give it to another without his consent." Not even the murder of Undersheriff Steele, Chatfield insisted, had stopped the Whig Party from "tampering with this question." John Young still wanted "to agitate, and keep up agitation" in the

Anti-Rent counties; as a result, he supported Harris's "unparliamentary" motion "to have the [tenant] petitions singled out and made to take a different direction from the [governor's] message." But the tenant community, Chatfield declared, could be "deluded" no longer. Its leaders had read the Perkins Resolutions, and now they appreciated the "active determination" of the Democracy "to do what may be done justifiably . . . in the spirit of sympathy mingled with justice."[19]

Only the members from Albany, Rensselaer, and Schoharie tried to fight off the Democratic onslaught. Harris, Hayner, Smith, and Watson made some good points too. They emphasized that Governor Wright's party had controlled the legislature since 1842 yet had done nothing for the tenant cause. They talked endlessly about the Allen Report of 1844, mocking its claim that "the degradation and hardships" protested by anti-renters "exist but in the imagination" and reviling its conclusion that the Van Rensselaers had a "perfect" title to the Manor of Rensselaerwyck. Each of them returned time and again to one dominant theme: Democrats, not Whigs, sought to make "political capital" out of the Anti-Rent question. Smith put it best on January 13. "It is the 7,000 majority rolled up in this senate district which I imagine has wrought this sudden change in his excellency's views," he remarked. "The governor is shrewd enough to see when he gets upon the wrong track. He never likes to be found on the wrong side of a popular question." Wright had taken up "the cause of justice and the oppressed" in eastern New York for the same reason Democrats "stole the Texas thunder from John Tyler." What galled the Whig/Anti-Rent contingent, however, was not so much Democratic intentions as the success the Democrats were enjoying. Orrin Foote and Reuben Lewis, the Anti-Rent assemblymen from Delaware County, preferred the course of action outlined by the Perkins Resolutions to a title-test measure that had never enthused their constituents. So did the members from Greene, Sullivan, and Ulster counties.[20]

Signs of Democratic success in the struggle for tenant votes evoked Whig countermeasures. Weed orchestrated them as usual. First, he persuaded Harris that a new title-test bill, one that Whig progressives could support with the same fervor as tenants on the Manor of Rensselaerwyck, had to be laid before the legislature. Harris introduced the resulting bill on January 15. Entitled "An Act to provide for the Investigation of Titles to Manorial Lands and the Extinguishment of the Same," the bill authorized Eliphalet Nott, president of Union College, and former governors Seward and Bouck "to investigate and report upon the validity of the titles to lands held upon manorial tenures, and to hear and determine all disputes and controversies between the landlords and tenants." It vested the commissioners with the power to summon witnesses and subpoena documents; it required them to inform the legislature "in case it shall appear that the people of this state, or any other party, other than the claimants, are the real owners of the land." Nott, Seward, and Bouck were to complete the assignment no later than January 1848. "The bill introduced yesterday by Mr. Harris," Weed exclaimed in the *Evening Journal* on January 16, "suggests the proper and perhaps the only mode of settling this 'vexed question.'" It was certainly the only title-test scheme that he and Greeley, who promoted it the following day, could approve. Because the tenants' contractual obligations would remain in force while the commissioners deliberated, the doctrine laid down by the Supreme Court in *Bronson v. Kinzie* (1843) would not come into play.[21]

Meeting the challenge posed by the Perkins Resolutions in the Hardenbergh Patent counties was trickier than consolidating the Whig Party's hold on the Manor of Rensselaerwyck. It required a revival of the eminent domain alternative. William A. Duer Jr. happened to be in Albany during the legislature's "great debate" on manorial tenures, and Weed persuaded him to write a defense of the Whig record in 1840 that not only answered the Democratic calumnies but also provided a restatement of the eminent domain scheme's rationale and relative merits. One advantage was apparent to Weed already. The eminent domain law Duer once proposed, like the Democratic Party's new devise-and-descent idea, would compel tenants to compensate their landlords. Yet an eminent domain act would authorize tenants to condemn landlord interests in their farms right away while the Democratic plan would keep them in "voluntary slavery" until their landlords died. If the Democrats enacted a devise-and-descent law, Weed believed that the Whigs should be ready to compete for tenant votes with an eminent domain measure. The 5,000-word document Duer produced, framed as letter to the editor of the *Evening Journal*, supplied the wily Whig tactician with more ammunition than he expected. Weed published the letter on January 17, touting it as a "triumphant" piece of work.

Duer aimed to vindicate both "my character as an honest man" and the legal theory embedded in his 1840 report. Economy of effort served him well in the first task. Duer rebuffed the "false and wanton" claim that his report had inspired the Anti-Rent violence with a single penetrating question about the mainspring of tenant motivation. "What man is there of common sense that does not know, or of common candor who will not acknowledge," he asked, "that it is the hope or the 'delusion,' not of getting their lands by *paying*, but *without* paying, that has led to 'bloodshed and other unhappiness?'" Duer relied on facts rather than logic to explode Democratic talk about his "demagogic" motives in 1840. At the heart of such allegations, he wrote, lay a presumption that his report "expressed the views and complied with the desires of those known as anti-renters." In point of fact, however, "the reverse" was true. His committee killed the bill introduced by Assemblyman Wheaton, counsel for the tenants on Rensselaerwyck, and did so on constitutional grounds. In proposing, instead, "a modification of the tenures for public purposes and on full and adequate compensation to the landlords," Duer insisted, "I sought to please neither tenants nor landlords."[22]

The bulk of the document elaborated the reasons Duer remained "satisfied" with his eminent domain theory. He began by pointing out that in 1846, as in 1840, the drive to extinguish manorial tenures had to get over the Contract Clause hurdle prohibiting state laws that dispensed with the performance of executory contracts. What is more, the hurdle constrained more than land reform legislation. "Now there is nothing lawful at the time," Duer observed, "that may not become the subject of an executory contract, and that may not too, upon this principle, by being made the condition on which land is held in a perpetual lease, be made perpetual itself." Among the reforms that engaged "philanthropists at the present day," Duer pointed out, was the prohibition of traffic in alcoholic beverages. "But suppose A. (it being lawful at the time) should lease to B. and his heirs, for 999 years, a lot of land, on the condition and with a covenant on the part of B. that he and his assignees should during the term of the lease sell to the lessee and his descendants spirituous liquors at so much by the glass." Existing standards of Contract Clause interpretation would bar state governments from interfering with such liquor sales. But "might the legislature prohibit this traffic," Duer asked, "and direct that something else should be paid as a substitute by the lessee?" He thought so in 1840, and he still thought so in 1846. "In the progress of civilization," Duer wrote, "it constantly becomes a matter of state policy to prohibit something once permitted or perhaps commanded."[23]

Duer conceded that his theory of the eminent domain power differed from that "popularly entertained within as well as without the legal profession." He also acknowledged that his view had been rejected by the New York Supreme Court in *Taylor v. Porter*. But this "opposite doctrine," Duer argued, had a fatal vice. It effectively transformed every private contract into "*a law* that can never be repealed," thus "limit[ing] the power of the states to legislate for the public good." Duer's conclusion impressed Harris as much as Weed. "I am inclined to believe, after perusing the very able argument of Mr. Duer," the Whig/Anti-Rent leader told the house on February 4, "that his proposition is constitutional. But I have no desire to enforce such a remedy, or to take questionable ground at this time." For Harris and Weed in 1846, as for Duer in 1840, the eminent domain option was available as a last resort. If Governor Wright signed a devise-and-descent bill into law in May, Whig delegates to the constitutional convention would push for an eminent domain amendment in June.[24]

The party competition for Anti-Rent votes amazed George Henry Evans. "A marvelous change of opinion in favor of Anti-Rentism has taken place in the legislature," he wrote in *Young America* on January 24. "The question will soon be who are the best anti-renters!" The tenant community had reason to be encouraged, but nobody had greater cause to be satisfied with the new state of affairs than Silas Wright. In two weeks his party had turned a weakness into a possible strength; the very existence of Whig countermeasures implied that the Democratic offensive was working. Just as he began to feel good about what already had been achieved in the assembly, however, the senate's Whig minority stirred up the old enmities between conservative and radical Democrats. The state printing contract generated this latest spat between Barnburners and Hunkers, and it took Wright by surprise. A constituent of Samuel J. Tilden crisply stated its significance on January 26. "The match appears to have been touched," he wrote, "that will blow up and tear in fragments the Democratic party of the state."[25]

Political Fratricide

Martin Van Buren once called the New York Democracy "a political brotherhood" because its members were loyal to an organization rather than to a single leader or idea. The image of party as a kind of family impelled Democrats to take seriously their mutual obligations. For the original Albany Regency group, in particular, majority decisions reached in caucus or convention were subject to neither remonstrance nor appeal; this fundamental precept disciplined the Democracy's often fractious members for more than two decades. Party lore celebrated one example after another of forbearance and self-sacrifice that carried the organization through intense disagreements over nominations, policy positions, and the division of spoils. Governor Marcy swallowed the Independent Treasury in 1838 and accepted defeat with equanimity. Silas Wright gave up his seat in the Senate to run for an office he did not want to hold, and Michael Hoffman stopped agitating for his pet project, a constitutional convention, during 1844 and part of 1845. Edwin Croswell balked, however, when his turn to sacrifice for the good of the Democratic family came around in January 1846. Croswell did not violate the letter of party rules. But he killed the spirit of fraternity that animated them and dealt the New York Democracy a blow from which it never fully recovered.[26]

The state printing contract, which the *Argus* had held for all but three of the previous twenty-two years, expired on January 24, 1846, and Croswell knew that the Democratic caucus would not recommend its renewal. In the county conventions of 1845 Democrats repudiated virtually all the lawmakers who had fought shoulder-to-shoulder with him against the constitutional convention bill. Only a fourth of the Democrats in the 1846 legislature, most of them holdover senators, called themselves conservatives. Radical domination of the Democratic caucus meant that William Cassidy's *Atlas* would get the three-year contract that had made *Argus* one of the half-dozen most important newspapers in the country. Croswell did the logical thing in December 1845. He proposed a merger of the two Albany papers, telling John Van Buren and several other party leaders that he was prepared to retire from public life as long as his nephew and partner, Sherman Croswell, could have a share in both the ownership and editorial responsibilities of the consolidated enterprise. Cassidy accepted the proposal in principle, and Governor Wright presumed that it was a done deal. But a mid-January roll call in the senate persuaded Croswell to change his mind.[27]

The ongoing merger negotiations remained a tightly held secret when the legislature's 1846 session began. As a result, two senators launched projects for reforming the state printing while the assembly debated the Anti-Rent question. John Porter, a radical, introduced a bill on January 12 that provided for competitive bids on the legislature's journals and documents. John C. Wright proposed a conservative "counter plan" on January 15. His measure required all government printing to be awarded to the lowest bidder and abolished the office of state printer altogether. Wright pointed out that his bill, unlike Porter's, covered "printing for the executive departments—no small item in printing expenses" and more perfectly accommodated the radicals' professed goal of "reforming abuses in the public printing." The radicals, sensing a plot to subvert the Democratic caucus scheduled for January 22, tried to refer the "much entangled" matter of printing reform to a select committee. And they failed. All seven Whigs voted with the conservative Democrats to keep the matter before the senate.[28]

Croswell was struck by the delicious irony of the situation. During the legislature's 1845 session, the Democracy's radical minority had voted with the Whigs to thrust a constitutional convention down the throats of conservatives. Retrenchment and reform had been the radical watchwords. Suddenly the shoe was on the other foot, and Croswell saw a way to keep the state printing contract without being absorbed into the *Atlas*. Senator Orville Clark put the plan into effect. At the Democratic caucus on January 22, Clark read a letter from Croswell asking that his name not be placed in nomination for state printer. He also implored the caucus to refrain from nominating anyone else until the legislature had decided whether to abolish the office. "In the great family to which we all belong," Clark declared, "some little differences occur, which should, in no way, affect the unity, the honor, the harmony or the permanence of the party." He insisted that the state printing question was one of them.[29]

Samuel Young scoffed at Clark's plea for party unity. "Mr. Clark asks the republican family to harmonize, when he and those with whom he especially acts have been harmonizing for the last three or four days with the Whigs of the senate," Young exclaimed. "Now if that is the kind of harmony to be inculcated upon us here, I for one do not want such harmony." A very large majority of the

Democratic caucus shared Young's view, and Cassidy was nominated by a vote of 73-15. But the Democratic Party had to deal with Clark's "kind of harmony" anyway. Twelve hours after the caucus adjourned, the Whig-Hunker phalanx in the senate passed the bill abolishing the office of state printer. Moments later, the senate received an assembly resolution scheduling a joint session of the legislature to elect the state printer. Senator Clark immediately moved that the joint session be postponed from Monday, January 26, the date fixed in the assembly resolution, until the first Monday in June—the date already fixed for the constitutional convention to begin. The effect of Clark's motion, which prevailed 17-11, was to defy what the *Argus* termed the "so called" Democratic caucus. Croswell would remain the state printer unless the assembly enacted the reform bill produced by the Whig-Hunker alliance in the senate.[30]

The Democratic "family" went through a sort of divorce proceeding in the weeks that followed. The charges were the same on both sides. Radicals and conservatives alike claimed to be victims of habitual desertion, extreme cruelty, and adultery with the Whigs. They reopened old wounds and vented resentments that had been repressed for years. "Eccentric memories" and "fertile imaginations" figured prominently as one Democrat after another recounted stories, some going back as far as 1824, that always were saturated in the "acrimony of personal hate." The *Atlas* complained about the conservative penchant for "duplicity, venom, and recklessness of imputation." Croswell, not to be outdone, denounced the "coarseness of invective" and "the storm of obloquy" that flowed from the radicals. The "running fire of savage personalities," as Greeley described it, began in the upper house on January 23. It continued for three weeks, "without much regard to the question before the senate," and engulfed the assembly when the Committee on Printing reported out a substitute for the senate bill on February 18. By then even the Whigs had heard enough. "The fact that all the parties are Locofoco of some sort and able to tell much truth of each other," Greeley remarked in mid-February, "gave the discussion some piquancy at first, but it has been continued till everybody but the wranglers themselves is heartily tired of it." Still, the impassioned "reminiscences of the past" did not come to an end until March 4. On that afternoon, thirteen Democrats combined with the Whigs to kill the assembly substitute and pass the senate bill by a vote of 65-52. In the state legislature, at least, the Democratic Party already had ceased to exist.[31]

Whig votes contributed to the distress of the New York Democracy, but Weed disclaimed all responsibility for the opposition's agony. "We have preserved a 'masterly inactivity' in regard to the pending conflict," he insisted in the *Evening Journal* on February 13. "Nor do our friends in the legislature interfere, further than to vote with the section of the 'happy family' that presents the fairest proposition." Weed derived a moral from the Democratic Party's woes all the same. Three days later, he submitted that the warfare between Hunkers and

Barnburners was "the legitimate fruit of Van Burenism." The builder of the New York Democracy "made devotion to party the only test of merit . . . [and] made office-seeking a regular business—a trade," Weed wrote. "He founded the school in which all these vile tactics were taught, and in which these *lazaroni* [homeless beggars] graduated." It was altogether fitting, then, that "the Van Buren family, hav[ing] been billeted upon the treasury for more more than thirty years," should fall apart on a question of spoils.[32]

Yet the causes of the Democratic breakup impressed Weed and his Whig associates less than its consequences. A divided Democracy seemed beatable, first in the April 28 election of constitutional convention delegates and then in November. Seward was especially optimistic. "It is universally conceded," he blustered in a letter to John McLean, "that the Whig Party will regain political control over the state immediately." The two journalists in the progressive Whig troika were not so sure. "Isn't Seward too sanguine?" Greeley wrote Weed on March 13. "He talks as though we had carried the convention, the state next fall, and everything else. I don't feel all this in my bones." Weed and Greeley grasped a fact that apparently eluded Seward. The spontaneous collaboration of Whigs and Hunkers that carried the day in the state printer contest could not be easily duplicated in an electoral campaign. "If the Old Hunkers mean to help us," Greeley asked, "why should they not come out for free [black] suffrage . . . and everything else tending to break up the old machinery?" While the Whigs waited in vain for Hunker assistance during March and April, Greeley and Weed concentrated on another crucial bloc of voters. They still believed that the primary road to Whig recovery ran through the Anti-Rent counties of eastern New York.[33]

The political imponderables that vexed Weed and Greeley gave Governor Wright a reason to hope. In a March 10 letter to John L. Russell, his right-hand man during the legislature's 1845 session, Wright acknowledged that "the false lights" of the *Argus* had put the Democratic ship on the rocks. It was much too soon, however, to presume that the "sound Democracy" would go down. "There is abundant cause for grief and deep concern," he wrote another St. Lawrence friend, "but after we have done all we can do, we must trust to Providence and the people, and [a]wait patiently the developments of time." The one thing Wright and "the sound Democracy" could do right away was try to finish the task they set for themselves in January. They had to reclaim a healthy portion of the tenant vote from the Whigs.[34]

The Anti-Rent Measures

The forty-day debate on land reform in the assembly ended on February 16, two days before the lower house took up the state printing bill that had temporarily supplanted Governor Wright's devise-and-descent plan as "the great measure of the session of 1846." Samuel J. Tilden, who chaired the resulting Select Committee, fused autobiography and partisanship in a powerful closing argument. Shortly before his birth in 1814, Tilden told the house, his father and mother joined the Yankee migration out of Connecticut and bought a farm in New Lebanon, Columbia County. "Until near manhood," he said, "I lived . . . where the cultivators are also proprietors, but between the manors of the Van Rensselaers on the north and of the Livingstons on the south; I had some opportunity of observing and comparing the condition of agriculture and society under the different tenures so nearly contiguous." Tilden explained that he had been "inclined to the study of such questions" from an early age, and his own investigation confirmed his father's intuitive judgment. The conditions on Rensselaerwyck and Livingston Manor "repress[ed] the disposition, the habit, and the opportunities of enterprise." On the farms of New Lebanon, in contrast, "the mere idea of proprietorship" had the effect of "inculcating habitual self-respect and self-reliance; elevating the moral and mental dispositions, and enlarging the capacities for action; cultivating at once a manly sense of individual independence, and a generous subordination to the collective will."[35]

Tilden claimed that he brought "such prepossessions" to Albany in January and had been ready for weeks to begin "doing everything consistent with the Constitution, with the rights of individuals and the public welfare," to extinguish manorial tenures. Assemblyman Harris and his friends, however, preferred talk to constructive action. And the talk was not in the public interest. "In a speech which occupies eight columns of the *Evening Journal*," Tilden pointed out, Harris said nothing about the merits of the devise-and-descent plan but dwelled instead on the impeachment of landlord titles, "which we know finally will be disappointed." Nor did Harris "deal frankly" with his subject. "Why does he throw vague doubts upon the Van Rensselaer title," Tilden asked, "and still shrink from the responsibility of saying, on his character as a lawyer and a citizen, that it is bad; or, on the other hand, of telling the tenants that it is good?" Tilden insisted that "the policy of sympathetic inaction . . . and empty generalities—the fatal fruits of which we are now reaping—however it may subserve the interests of ambitious politicians, or conciliate the votes of those whom it deceives, is unworthy of enlightened legislators. It is a detestable fraud upon these tenants. It is treason to the peace, the order, the prosperity of the state."[36]

Moments after Tilden sat down, the assembly finally established a committee with jurisdiction over Governor Wright's recommendations, the tenant petitions, and the Perkins Resolutions. A comparable senate committee, though organized more than a month earlier, had been "sleep[ing]" ever since with bills in their hands providing for the taxation of rent charges and the abolition of distress sales. It consisted of Whig/Anti-Rent leader Van Schoonhoven, two

Hunkers, one Barnburner, and a conservative Whig. William Crain, the speaker of the assembly, named a committee more favorable to Governor Wright. It included five radicals—Tilden, Perkins, Bailey, Chatfield, and Clark Grinnell; three other spots went to Reuben Lewis of Delaware, Ira Harris, and John Young. The strategy of the "sound Democracy" was clear. Wright's people in the lower house hoped to drive a wedge between Lewis and Harris, compel Whig gubernatorial candidate Young to choose between them, and report out a battery of Anti-Rent measures by the end of March. Tilden announced that committee members from both houses would sit together for hearings on March 4–6.[37]

Five days before the hearings began, the Anti-Rent Party held its second state convention in downtown Albany. The turnout startled Anti-Rent leaders. Nearly 200 delegates from eleven counties attended the first convention in 1845, but only 57 delegates from seven counties showed up on February 27, 1846. Nobody came from Delaware, Otsego, Sullivan, or Ulster. Eighty percent of the tenant delegates lived on the Manor of Rensselaerwyck. Everywhere else the demise of the "Indian" auxiliaries had enfeebled the tenant associations, though farmers throughout the region were still passionately attached to the Anti-Rent cause. The convention did attract a great many politicians and sympathetic outsiders. Thomas A. Devyr, Robert D. Watson, and Calvin Pepper Jr. of Albany were admitted as voting delegates. So were *Freeholder* editor Alexander G. Johnson of Troy and Jacob W. Ryckman, a National Reformer from New York City. Thurlow Weed, Senator Van Schoonhoven, and Assemblyman Hayner attended as "honorary members of the convention."[38]

The animus between Johnson and Devyr, who had been sniping at one another for months, dissolved under these straitened circumstances. The two Anti-Rent editors cochaired the committee on resolutions, and they produced a platform that satisfied everyone. The convention endorsed both Harris's title-test bill and George Henry Evans's land-limitation scheme. It also called for the enactment of every Anti-Rent measure then before the state legislature, including the devise-and-descent idea embedded in the Perkins Resolutions. One plank soon attracted more attention than all the others combined:

Resolved, That in the opinion of this convention the legislature ought to pass a law setting at liberty the men who have been sentenced to state prison under the statute of 1845, against appearing disguised and armed. If we have read the testimony right in the case of Mr. Boughton and the men convicted at Delhi, they are all only technically guilty of the offenses for which they are suffering punishment, and we believe that the sentences are greatly disproportioned to their offense, excessively and vindictively severe.

The troublesome nexus between Anti-Rent resistance and Anti-Rent politics took a new turn with the adoption of this resolution. In 1845 the party's delegates sought to influence public opinion outside the leasehold counties; as a result, the convention "totally discountenance[d]" any connection with the "Indians" and condemned their "lawless and indefensible acts." Different political circumstances dictated a different strategy in 1846.[39]

Since the summer schism, debate on land reform measures had divided members of the Anti-Rent Party just as it divided members of the Whig and Democratic parties. But anti-renters everywhere had been "Indians" themselves or knew someone—a father, son, brother, uncle, or cousin—who had worn the disguise with pride. The "Indian" bands had been organized to protect communities against rapacious landlords, not to prey on their neighbors; no tenant thought of his family and friends as criminals. Devyr's pardon resolution focused these feelings on the twenty-two men in the state prison at Clinton and gave tenants in all eleven counties one standard they could rally around together. Weed and the Whig/Anti-Rent politicians at the convention saw something else in the drive to free the "political prisoners." Returning the convicted anti-renters to their families was an idea they could promote but Governor Wright could not. When he commuted the two death sentences in November 1845, Wright promised the sheriff of Delaware County that no pardons would follow. "If I could, in my classification, call this insurrection, commenced and prosecuted to resist the collection of admitted debts, a rebellion," Wright wrote in a letter released to the press, "I should find, I fear, more room to add the crime of treason to the catalogue already made up, than to discover a ground for indulgence in its political character."[40]

The fate of the Anti-Rent convicts was not on the Joint Legislative Committee's agenda for the hearings, and nobody mentioned it. A new man on the scene, Albany attorney Calvin Pepper Jr., turned out to be the star witness. Pepper practiced law on High Street with his father, a self-styled "attorney for the damned" who specialized in criminal defense work. Most any cause involving "the bone and sinew of the country" engaged young Pepper. He presented a plan for an "industrial exchange," a kind of cooperative for the producing classes, at a June 1845 meeting of the National Reform Association in Manhattan, and the "feudal abominations" at the root of the Anti-Rent agitation induced him to conduct a legal and historical study of manorial tenures in New York State. Pepper's work generated a loosely reasoned yet electrifying pamphlet, *Manor of Rensselaerwyck*, that became available on the newsstands of Albany and Troy in January 1846.[41]

Pepper added two new wrinkles to the Anti-Rent case against the Van Rensselaer title. First, he showed that the statute Quia Emptores, enacted by Parliament in 1290, barred the creation of new manors in England. According to

Pepper, it followed that "a feudal system could not be imposed upon a free, intelligent, and patriotic people under British rule." Yet the patents of 1685 and 1704 under which the Van Rensselaer family claimed title purported to do that very thing. "The Manor of Rensselaerwyck," Pepper declared, "is not a *relic* of feudalism, but an infamous and presumptuous attempt at *revival*, and it is an insult to the age and generation in which we live, for any person to pretend that this preposterous claim was ever founded in reason, justice or law." Because the British patents authorized the grantees to hold a court leet and a court baron, to have the waifs and estrays, deodands, and other feudal privileges—that is, to enjoy a characteristic manorial estate—they violated the statute Quia Emptores. The grant vested nothing in the Van Rensselaers because it was void from its inception. Second, Pepper argued that "should their paper title fail," the Van Rensselaers could not derive title to manor lands by possession. Acquiring title by possession, he pointed out, required "actual occupancy, positive, notorious, uninterrupted, and continued for twenty years." By his lights, "the possession of a grantee, or lessee, is no part of this possession." But the rights of Van Rensselaer tenants had vested. "*They* having been in actual possession for more than twenty years," Pepper insisted, "could maintain that possession . . . as against the the whole world" once the Van Rensselaer family "was out of the way."[42]

Pepper's testimony before the Joint Legislative Committee caused a sensation. The *Freeholder* reported that Senator Joshua A. Spencer, a fifty-six-year-old conservative Whig and former United States attorney, "plied Mr. Pepper with many law questions and cross-examined him rigidly." One would expect as much. Pepper's argument assumed that all acts of Parliament had been in force in colonial New York. It assumed that the lawyers who drafted the Van Rensselaer patents and framed their indentures did not know the first thing about the law of real property. It assumed that nothing was saved by the saving clause of New York's version of Quia Emptores, the Act Concerning Tenures passed in 1787, which expressly protected "any rents certain or other services . . . due or to grow due to any mesne lord, or other private person." And it assumed that the Van Rensselaers did not acquire anything from the British patents yet their own grantees could claim fee-simple titles by possession. Accepting all these propositions required an unusual legal imagination. Nevertheless, Assemblyman Harris swallowed Pepper's argument whole. Senator Spencer, on the other hand, refused to take it seriously; ten days later, he flatly stated that the validity of the Van Rensselaer title had been established beyond peradventure in the Allen Report of 1844.[43]

Tilden had a different response to Pepper's testimony. He bought a copy of *Manor of Rensselaerwyck* and spent some time in the library trying to make sense of the state's complicated land law. The result was a new theory of the statute Quia Emptores in New York law. A thoughtful reading of *Jackson* ex dem. *Lewis and Wife v. Schutz* (1820) exploded Pepper's argument. James Emmot, counsel for the plaintiffs in *Schutz*, claimed that Quia Emptores had not been in force in colonial New York; Chief Justice Ambrose Spencer declared that the court "never supposed" it had. Tilden believed that Emmot and Spencer had reached the correct conclusion too. There was no other plausible explanation for the creation of the Manor of Rensselaerwyck and the ensuing luxuriation of the lease in fee. The *Schutz* court's construction of the Act Concerning Tenures, however, seemed wrong. "Our statute of 1787," Tilden explained in his committee report, "substantially reenacted" Quia Emptores and thereby prohibited fines on alienation. Yet Justice Platt, speaking for the court in *Schutz*, had upheld the tenth-sale condition in the indenture at issue. "He construed the statute," Tilden pointed out, "as merely reversing the feudal rule . . . and making the right of alienation incident to a grant in fee, unless that right was qualified by express stipulation, which, he said, the parties might lawfully do." Tilden disagreed. "The Act Concerning Tenures," he wrote, constituted "an authoritative declaration of public policy, the principle of which no private contract could be allowed to contravene." New York's version of Quia Emptores saved rents and services "due or to grow due" to landlords, and the Contract Clause forbade state legislation impairing the right to collect them. But covenants reserving tenth sales, quarter sales, and the like stood on a different footing. The act of 1787 abolished those conditions, retrospectively and generally, two years before the Constitution of the United States was ordained and established.[44]

Tilden's theory of New York land law enabled the Select Committee to sweeten the devise-and-descent bill for tenant voters. The measure he reported out on March 28 still provided for the conversion of reserved rents and services into mortgages upon the death of existing proprietors. But it also provided that the value of quarter sales, tenth sales, "and charges or penalties of every kind and description, payable . . . on the alienation of any lease or grant, shall not be estimated." Those reservations, the Select Committee explained, "are not believed to be valid by the existing laws of this state." Tilden told the house that every member of his committee advocated the enactment of the devise-and-descent bill, as well as the bills reported out the same day for the taxation of rent charges and the abolition of distress sales. "The adoption of the[se] measures," he said, "will . . . produce a gradual and rapid extinction of leasehold tenures without injustice to any person."[45]

The committee divided, as expected, on the legislature's competence to enact Harris's title-test bill. Tilden spoke of the wisdom and policy of the "statutes of repose" that figured so prominently in the Allen Report of 1844. He reported that the proposed legislation was "very analogous to the law of Illinois" struck down in *Bronson v. Kinzie* (1843), "except that it is more extreme and indefensible." And he argued that Harris and Pepper were wrong to suppose that the adverse-possession principle aided their cause. "The very idea of an adverse possession is of a possession claimed to be in the occupant's own right, and adverse to every other right," Tilden wrote. "A submission to another title," whether by entering the land under a grantor's indenture or paying any rent at all, "destroys its character and effect." For Tilden, however, the most objectionable thing about Harris's bill was that its enactment would not extinguish manorial tenures. The primary effect of the title-test agitation, he contended, was to "divert attention from other and more practical remedies and from all effectual measures, by legislation or by compromise, of terminating a relation which has been so fruitful of mischief." Lewis of Delaware concurred. So did John Young. In his brief dissent, Harris spoke only for himself.[46]

Harris knew how to mitigate any political advantage the "sound Democracy" might gain from the Tilden Report. On March 31, just three days after the Select Committee finished its work, the Whig/Anti-Rent leader introduced a resolution that Greeley's *Tribune* featured on the front page:

> Resolved, (if the senate concur), As the sense of this legislature, that it be recommended to his excellency the governor to take immediate measures for the release of the several persons above mentioned, and for that purpose to issue pardons in their behalf, respectively.

The people "above mentioned" were, of course, the twenty-two anti-renters confined in the state prison at Clinton for murder, manslaughter, robbery, or appearing on the public highway disguised and armed. "It is not perhaps to be expected that the pardoning power vested in the executive will be exercised in relation to so many persons," Harris declared in his sponsor speech, "unless he first has the countenance of the legislature." An *Evening Journal* editorial that defended Harris's motion a few days later was almost as disingenuous. "For the most part," Weed wrote, "they were men into whose hearts the thought of crime had not entered—men who would not rob, or steal, nor bear false witness—men, moreover, of good moral character. Such, and other considerations which Mr. Harris presented very effectively to the house, induces the effort on behalf of these prisoners." The "Indians" no longer threatened the peace, but they still had a role to play in the savage warfare of the Second Party System.[47]

A Sinking Ship

Tilden's three bills sailed through the lower house. The "sound Democracy," the Whig/Anti-Rent members, and the Whig progressives all backed them. Hunker votes were not necessary to see the measures through. The devise-and-

descent bill, the newest and most important land reform proposal, got such a
good press that opponents hesitated to speak against it. Robert H. Ludlow, a
Manhattan Hunker whose family owned a piece of the Hardenbergh Patent,
was the only person who did. He complained about the "arbitrary exclusion"
from the valuation process of the quarter-sale reservations, "which are as much
a part of the contract as the rent." He also remonstrated against the stipulated
mortgage terms, arguing that "no prudent man ever takes a mortgage for the
whole amount of a sale" as the bill required. Not even Ludlow, however,
conjured up the specter of "agrarianism." Tilden quashed that kind of talk with
thoughtful analogies to earlier New York legislation affecting future interests in
land, including the abolition of entails in 1782 and the regulation of trusts in the
Revised Statutes of 1828.[48]

The bill to abolish distress for rent passed by a vote of 94-7, and the Act to
Equalize Taxation passed 84-9. But the 63-18 vote on the devise-and-descent
bill concerned Governor Wright. The nays included one-fourth of the Whigs
and five of the thirteen Hunkers who had joined the opposition in the state
printer contest. If Whigs and Hunkers massed against the bill in the senate, the
centerpiece of his land reform program would fail. The senate's response to the
arrival of the assembly bills intensified Wright's fears. The tax and distress
measures went on the calendar right away. But the devise-and-descent bill was
referred to the Judiciary Committee because the upper house had not yet
considered anything like it. Wright's decision in January to keep the scheme
under wraps, rather than promoting it in his message, now came back to haunt
him. The Judiciary Committee consisted of a Whig lawyer from Attica named
Harvey Putnam and two outspoken Hunkers, John A. Lott of Brooklyn and
John C. Wright of Schoharie. Prying the bill out of their hands would be
difficult. Only the public demeanor of the *Argus* encouraged the struggling
governor. "The Anti-Rent bills, as they are called, passed the house yesterday
by large majorities," Croswell reported on May 5. "The bill to amend the law of
devises and descents is *the* important measure of the three."[49]

The final results of the constitutional convention balloting, announced on
the same day the assembly passed the Anti-Rent measures, contained a comparable mixture of good news and bad news for Governor Wright. Democrats
won 76 seats, the Whigs 52. Conservatives in both parties took a beating. Only a
handful of successful candidates were votaries of old-guard Whiggery; although
the Hunkers ran separate tickets in two dozen upstate counties, few of their
nominees won. Almost half of the twenty-one Hunker delegates would come
from Manhattan, where the Democracy trounced the Whigs with a Tammany
Hall slate that named an equal number of conservatives and radicals. Wright's
people would have to accommodate the views of progressive Whigs on some
issues and the Hunkers on others, but the "sound Democracy" had elected

enough delegates to organize the convention and staff the key standing committees with a Barnburner majority. The returns from the Anti-Rent counties, on
the other hand, were discouraging. Harris and Van Schoonhoven won by huge
majorities; Ambrose Jordan, chief counsel for "Big Thunder" the previous
year, led the combined Whig/Anti-Rent ticket to its first victory in Columbia
County. Thirteen delegates in all had been elected with Anti-Rent support, and
eleven of them were Whigs. It was clear that the Democratic Party's fate in
eastern New York depended on passage of the devise-and-descent bill.[50]

Wright recruited Senator George D. Beers, an upstate Hunker, to force the
bill out of committee. Beers was a logical choice for the job. The administration
could not succeed without some help from the conservatives, and Beers had
shown a keen interest in the Anti-Rent measures since the Tilden Committee
reported in March. The process of counting heads, cajoling, and guessing what
the Whigs would do began on May 6. It continued for three days. Wright
presumed at the outset that he could rely on each of the senate's twelve radicals;
but two headstrong Barnburners, John Porter and Samuel Young, soon disappointed him. Both stood fast on the libertarian principle that government had
no business interfering with contracts at all, and they refused to vote for any of
the Anti-Rent measures. Thomas Barlow and Richard H. Williams, a freshman
who ordinarily took his cues from Porter, refused to commit themselves one
way or the other. Beers and the agreeable radicals thus constituted only nine of
the necessary fifteen or sixteen votes. Still, the cause was not hopeless. John C.
Wright was from Schoharie, an Anti-Rent constituency, and Beers assured the
governor that other Hunkers would go along. Van Schoonhoven, the Whig/
Anti-Rent leader, dared not oppose the devise-and-descent bill; Gideon Hard,
the senate's outstanding progressive Whig, seemed unlikely to kill a measure
that, as Greeley's *Tribune* remarked, "will, if passed, rid the state of its present
curse of feudal tenures within twenty years."[51]

Decision day was May 9. Beers got the floor and moved that "the Judiciary
Committee be discharged from the further consideration of the assembly bill
entitled 'An act to amend the Statute of Devises and Descents, and to extinguish
certain Tenures,' and that the same be ordered to a third reading, and the final
vote be taken thereon on the 12th of May, at twelve o'clock noon, without
debate." The motion lost 14-10. Van Schoonhoven and Hard did not vote. Nor
did Barlow and Williams. All but one of the Hunkers deserted Beers at the
critical moment. Fifteen or twenty minutes later, Van Schoonhoven moved that
the distress and tax bills be referred to a select committee to "report complete"
and ready for a vote. His motion passed 19-11. Three main-line Whigs joined
Van Schoonhoven, Beers, John C. Wright, and the eight radical Democrats in
the majority. So did Barlow, Williams, and three Hunkers who had voted
against Beers's motion. The distress bill passed 23-3 on May 12, and the tax bill

passed 15-11 shortly before the session ended the next day. Governor Wright signed both into law on May 13. The devise-and-descent bill never reached the senate floor.[52]

The death of the devise-and-descent bill was a strange one. Only a handful of people opposed the measure on its merits, nobody claimed credit for killing it, and none of the party editors who had been chattering about it for months conducted an autopsy. Political prudence dictated silence. Although the Whigs and Hunkers could never admit as much, they were glad the bill had not become law. Weed, Greeley, and *Freeholder* editor Johnson regarded it from the outset as an administration measure designed to strengthen Governor Wright in the Anti-Rent counties. Its failure meant that the third senate district was theirs. Croswell welcomed the result for a comparable reason. After the state printer fight began, his principal aim was to prevent Wright's renomination in the fall. "He has not consulted the interests or the wishes of the entire party," Croswell wrote a Hunker colleague on March 2. "He has failed, with all the elements on his hands, to unite the Democratic Party—and he cannot command its united vote."[53] The death of the devise-and-descent bill meant that Wright had no chance of winning in November. If the radicals succeeded in renominating him anyway, rule-or-ruin Hunkers could stay home on election day and blame the party's defeat on the anti-renters.

Wright and his Barnburner friends took it for granted that Weed and Croswell had worked quietly behind the scenes to defeat the measure. Months of toil and trouble had proved to be an exercise in futility, but there was nothing for the "sound Democracy" to say in Cassidy's *Atlas* or Bryant's *Evening Post*. The devise-and-descent bill had been conceived in partisanship, and the strategy Wright concocted in January relied on party discipline to get it through the legislature. He was as responsible for the outcome as the Whigs and Hunkers who combined to kill the bill. Still, it was ironic that Wright's land reform project died in a senate composed of three parties, two of which professed to be Democratic. When Martin Van Buren suggested the devise-and-descent scheme in October 1844, Wright invoked party harmony as an excuse for resisting the idea. The pursuit of land reform, he replied, might divide the Democracy, "in which case I should be left with the anti-renters, with the Whigs and our own folks upon my back."[54] Things played out in the opposite way when Wright took the plunge in January 1846. First his "own folks" went through a nasty divorce, then the Hunkers helped the Whigs bury the devise-and-descent bill and lock up the Anti-Rent vote.

The experience chastened Wright. He washed his hands of the Anti-Rent agitation and began to focus on the constitutional convention that would begin on June 1. Yet there was no repose for the weary and disheartened governor. On May 9, the very day his devise-and-descent bill died in the senate, reports of skirmishes along the disputed Texas boundary reached New York and Washington. Wright still hoped that war with Mexico might be averted, but President Polk had other plans. For a year or more, Polk had been prepared to accept war as a means of acquiring California and fulfilling the republic's "manifest destiny." The fighting enabled him to persuade a reluctant Congress that a state of war already existed. Wright despaired. All of his political objectives had been exploded, and he longed for retirement. If his friends in the "sound Democracy" insisted on running him again, however, Wright could not and would not refuse their nomination. "I am not, in any event," he wrote Van Buren on May 17, "to flee a sinking ship."[55]

The state's tenant farmers did not yet know it, but their ship was sinking too. Major party competition for the Anti-Rent vote during the 1846 session produced both the Democratic devise-and-descent bill and the Whig revival of Duer's eminent domain scheme. Once the "sound Democracy" conceded the tenant vote to their opponents, however, the hothouse atmosphere for compensated land reform suddenly cooled. Harris, Van Schoonhoven, and their Whig/Anti-Rent brethren still had ambitious plans for the tenant movement. They also contrived an ingenious way to attract main-line Whig support for their pursuit of legislation to test the validity of landlord titles. But they did not anticipate the corrosive effect of the republic's "manifest destiny" on the structure of New York politics. Manor tenants ended up settling for a Whig resolution that brought them nothing but grief.

Whig Resolution

Thurlow Weed made an uncharacteristic prediction when the devise-and-descent bill died in the senate on May 9, 1846. He insisted that the constitutional convention would resolve the Anti-Rent controversy. "Things at war with the general welfare will be reformed," he wrote in that evening's lead editorial. "The constitution will be purged of whatever of feudalism remains in our form of government, and the elements of discord will pass away." At the root of Weed's forecast lay convictions which delegates articulated time and again during the 110-day constitutional convention that began on June 1. George Simmons, a prominent Whig, declared that if the rent system were "general all over the state," rather than being confined to eleven counties, "there would be a revolution as quick as that which took place under [King] Charles" in 1640. Levi Chatfield, an influential Democrat, exclaimed that rents payable in perpetuity were "as much at war with the spirit of our institutions as the government against which our fathers rebelled." Delegates on both sides of the aisle announced their willingness to pass any measure, "short of the abrogation of the great principles upon which the government was founded," to abolish the evil. "The interests of the state would be advanced, and the character of humanity elevated," said a Whig from Utica, "by the adoption of some principle which should induce the landlords to part with their lands to those who occupy and till them." Yet no such principle was incorporated into the constitution of 1846. Manorial tenures survived despite Weed's confident prediction to the contrary.[1]

The convention of the people did address the rent system in New York's very Bill of Rights:[2]

Section 11. All feudal tenures of every description, with all their incidents, are declared to be abolished, saving, however, all rents and services certain which at any time heretofore have been lawfully created or reserved.

Section 12. All lands within this State are declared to be allodial, so that, subject only to the liability to escheat, the entire and absolute property is vested in the owners, according to the nature of their respective estates.

Section 13. No lease or grant of agricultural land for a longer period than twelve years, hereafter made, in which shall be reserved any rent or service, of any kind, shall be valid.

Section 14. All fines, quarter sales, or other like restraints upon alienation, reserved in any grant of land hereafter to be made shall be void.

As statements of the body politic's revulsion with "voluntary slavery," these provisions spoke volumes. As instruments of land reform, however, they had negligible utility. Each of the prohibitions spoke to the future and not to the past. For the holder of a lease for two or three lives, the constitution of 1846 merely created a different transaction setting when the existing agreement expired and his family's house, barn, and other improvements reverted to the landlord. For the holder of an existing lease in fee, it changed nothing at all. The tenant and his heirs would remain in "feudal servitude interminable" unless the state government subsequently intervened or a new agreement could be worked out with the landlord.

Ira Harris framed the pathetic constitutional amendments that the Committee on the Creation and Division of Estates in Land reported out on September 16. Of the convention's eighteen standing committees, Harris's was one of only two with a majority of Whig members. Democrats had learned a lesson during the state legislature's 1846 session. Manor tenants regarded Harris as their "good and faithful servant," and no political solution to the Anti-Rent controversy could succeed without his active support. Allowing him to establish the convention's land reform agenda, instead of encouraging him to oppose Democratic recommendations, made partisan sense. The proposals Harris reported out annoyed the Democrats all the same. When debate began, Charles Ruggles of Dutchess County asked the Whig/Anti-Rent leader to explain "what possible use these provisions could be to those who complained of the present state of things." Ruggles, an eminent lawyer who later sat on the New York Court of Appeals, pointed out that all but one of the proposed measures (the prospective bar on leases or grants in fee, reserving rents, longer than twelve years) simply constitutionalized existing New York law. The first two proposed amendments came right out of the *Revised Statutes* of 1828; the fourth restated in different terms a rule established by the Act Concerning Tenures passed in 1787. "[I] have no more fears of a restoration of feudal tenures in this state," Ruggles declared, "than of an attempt on the part of the legislature to establish a monarchy here."[3]

Harris acknowledged the validity of Ruggles's legal analysis but contested his conclusion. "[My] only object," he explained, "was to obtain for this body and the people a formal . . . declaration that the feudal system is not congenial with our institutions, and ought to be utterly eradicated from among us." Harris claimed that the aim was a worthy one because the state constitution had a "moral influence" on New York public life. Ambrose Jordan, a Whig/Anti-Rent member from Columbia County, agreed. "So far as these tenures can be brought into disrepute and yet preserve the faith of the state, and individual and private rights," he said, "it should be done." William H. Van Schoonhoven went further. He reminded the convention that written constitutions did more than guarantee the people rights enforceable in courts of law. Bills of rights also ordained standards of liberty and justice around which the people could rally in future struggles against oppression. It followed that the irrepressible conflict between manorial tenures and the republican form of government was "a principle which should be as distinctly asserted in our fundamental law as any other which has been placed there."[4]

Harris and Van Schoonhoven might have asked the convention for something more if the devise-and-descent bill had become law during the legislature's 1846 session. From January to March, the two Whig/Anti-Rent leaders and *Freeholder* editor Alexander G. Johnson had joined Weed and William A. Duer Jr. in reviving the eminent domain plan as an alternative to the Democratic land reform measure. The constitutional convention was certainly an appropriate forum for securing an immediate, compensated emancipation of manor tenants. In *Taylor v. Porter* the New York Supreme Court had held that the due process principle forbade legislation that took private property for private use. On the very day the delegates voted to append Harris's land law measures to the Bill of Rights, however, they overruled the landmark 1843 decision on its facts and expressly authorized compensated takings for private roads. A large majority also rejected an amendment, offered by Arphaxed Loomis, mandating that "in such roads, when opened, the public shall have the right of way." Taken together, the two votes on private roads resolved any doubts about the convention's power to enable manor tenants to extinguish landlord interests in their farms upon payment of compensation fixed by government commissioners or a jury of the vicinage. But abolishing manorial tenures with the eminent domain power required more than formal authority. It required political will.[5]

Forgoing the eminent domain option was an easy decision for Harris and Van Schoonhoven to make. Their constituents on the Manor of Rensselaerwyck expected to acquire full title to their farms without paying anything to their landlords; beginning in 1843, Anti-Rent doctrine held that a title-test measure coupled with a rent moratorium should precede the implementation of compensated emancipation. "All they have ever asked," Johnson explained in the *Freeholder* upon the adjournment of the constitutional convention, "is that the manor lords shall be required to prove that they have a good and valid title, and then they are willing to buy it out at a fair value." The eminent domain power still remained a fixture in Whig/Anti-Rent contingency plans. "Whenever the public good seems to require it," Johnson observed in the same editorial, "governments have always exercised the power of taking private property for public uses, even against the will, and against the interests of the individual landowner." For Harris and Van Schoonhoven, as for Johnson, it was inconceivable that the jurisprudence of *Taylor v. Porter* might ultimately prevail over the claims of social progress, the demands of an enlightened public opinion, and the "moral influence" of the new state constitution's antifeudalism provisions. They took it for granted that "patroonery" would be destroyed with an eminent domain law if the title-test campaign came to naught.[6]

Weed saw things differently. He did not criticize what Harris had done in the constitutional convention. Nor did he upbraid Harris for passing up a golden opportunity to constitutionalize the eminent domain scheme. Weed had groomed the young Albany lawyer as a Whig/Anti-Rent politician in 1844 and had been promoting his work in the manor counties ever since. (Asked many years later if he knew Harris personally, Weed replied that "I should rather think I do. I invented him!") He had no intention of disturbing their relationship just as it was about to bear fruit in the election of 1846. In a roundabout fashion, however, Weed suggested that Harris would come to regret his decision to put the eminent domain idea on a back burner rather than striking when the iron was hot. He did so by lamenting the Duer Committee's hesitation and the Whig Party's default in 1840. "If the state, in virtue of its right of eminent domain, had taken, appraised, and sold these lands, itself paying to Mr. Van Rensselaer their value," he confessed on October 5, "its peace and honor would have been preserved for less money than has been drawn from the treasury for the payment of troops." Weed feared that history was about to repeat itself in a new political context, and this time his forecast proved to be accurate.[7]

Anti-Rent and the Balance of Power

Preparation for the campaign of 1846 began long before the constitutional convention adjourned, and the political objectives pursued by Weed and Harris shaped their opposing responses to the eminent domain option. Both men realized that the Anti-Rent vote would be decisive in the fall election and both thought land reform fit logically into the Whig Party's progressive mission. The difference between them, as Harris viewed it, was small. Weed preferred a compensation approach to a title-test measure because he believed that mainline Whigs would swallow the former more easily than the latter. Unlike the state's Democratic spokesmen, however, the wily Whig boss had neither denounced Harris's title-test measure nor pronounced it unconstitutional. Weed had kept his options open, and the Whig/Anti-Rent leader aimed to force "the dictator" to come out for the bill. Harris's plan was simple, audacious, and so explosive that he kept it under wraps until the Anti-Rent Party's state convention on October 6. In the election of 1846, tenant voters would be directed to defeat the Whig nominee for lieutenant governor as well as Silas Wright. Once the Anti-Rent Party had shown that it held the balance of power in New York politics, Harris assumed that Weed would move heaven and earth to convert Anti-Rent voters into steadfast Whigs. And the title-test bill would become law. The *Freeholder* described the plan's premise, though not its mechanics, in a September editorial. "No party can be long sustained in this country with but one idea for its basis and but one measure for its object," Johnson wrote. "But a body of men, comparatively few in numbers, may engraft a favorite measure upon one, or the other, of the two parties into which the people are inevitably divided . . . and thus secure success for their cause."[8]

Whig progressives courted Harris with the promise of high office rather than support for his title-test bill. Weed spoke of him in May as an appropriate candidate for lieutenant governor; Greeley thought he "deserved better" and suggested that the Whigs run him for Congress. Anti-renters set their sights higher. At the traditional Independence Day rally in New Scotland, Albany County, the tenants cheered heartily when John Slingerland offered a resolution nominating Harris for governor. And in Kortwright, Delaware County, where Harris spoke on July 4, the crowd toasted "*The next governor*—With Ira Harris for governor, we look for just and equal laws, the suppression of aristocracy, a free soil and a happy people." The third-district Whigs paid attention. In the Whig Party's county conventions, assembled to select delegates for the state nominating convention at Utica on September 23, all but four of the twenty-five delegates from the Anti-Rent region promised to support him for governor. Harris had no illusions about winning the top spot, and he wanted no part of a lieutenant governor nomination. His choice for governor was John Young. But he liked the idea of posting the Anti-Rent flag at Utica. Henry Z. Hayner, a delegate from Rensselaer and a member of the Whig central committee, was charged with the management of Harris's forces.[9]

Millard Fillmore, the favorite of Whig conservatives, approached the state convention in much the same spirit as Harris. On August 27, Fillmore told Greeley that he had settled on Young as his candidate and did "not feel at liberty" to enter the race himself. When the Harris bandwagon began to roll in the Anti-Rent counties, however, Fillmore decided that a summary withdrawal of his name would be unwise. His friends demanded an opportunity to muster their own show of strength, one that would upstage the rumblings on the left and emphasize their resistance to everything associated with the Anti-Rent movement. Fillmore let them have their way. But he also pledged the Erie County delegation to vote for Young on the second ballot and asked George Babcock to announce that "the name of Mr. Fillmore has been used against his expressed wishes" before the third. The upshot at Utica was a kind of factional

TABLE 1. Ballots at Whig State Convention, September 1846

	First	Second	Third
Fillmore	55	61	45
Young	36	44	76
Harris	21	10	0
Scattered	16	13	7

melodrama. It climaxed with a resolution Weed had scripted weeks in advance (see Table 1). The forty-five votes for Fillmore on the final ballot provided a good index of conservative dissatisfaction with the party's direction; Christopher Morgan, Seward's law partner, mollified them by proposing that Hamilton Fish of New York City be nominated for lieutenant governor by acclamation. When the ensuing huzzahs subsided, the convention adjourned without adopting a platform. Whig divisions on the Anti-Rent question ran so deep that no statement of principles could evoke unanimous assent.[10]

Young maintained the Whig policy of silence for the duration of the campaign. William Cullen Bryant, frustrated by the Whig nominee's refusal to answer inquiries about his views on the vested rights of landlords, called him "the pig in a poke." Young did make one campaign promise. In a letter to Harris on September 29, the candidate vowed to pardon the eighteen Anti-Rent convicts still being punished "for offenses quasi-political." Harris did not release the document to the press, but it caused a sensation anyway. Prominent antirenters claimed to have read Young's letter, Whig spokesmen disputed its existence, and journalists in both parties reported so many conflicting rumors that most voters outside the Anti-Rent district did not know what to think.[11]

Weed grasped the situation right away. During the spring he had helped Harris lay the foundation for using the "Indian" convicts as a Whig issue in the Anti-Rent counties, and Young's eagerness to play the pardon card made sense. James Watson Webb would howl in the *Courier and Enquirer* just as he had when the *Evening Journal* supported Harris's "political prisoner" resolution in April. But the damage could be controlled unless the tenants compounded it by naming Young for governor on their own ticket. What gave Weed pause was the possibility that Harris might use Young's pardon pledge to stampede the Anti-Rent convention. Greeley presumed that "the dictator" had everything under control. "It will not be best to have Young nominated for governor by the Anti-Rent convention, even if practicable," he wrote Weed from Manhattan on September 28. "It would gain him few votes, and enable his enemies to excite great odium against him." In point of fact, Weed had no more wires to pull.

Whig conventions already had nominated Harris for the state senate and his friend Slingerland for Congress. The initiative belonged to the man Weed had "invented."[12]

The Anti-Rent Party's convention was held on October 6 at Beardsley's hotel in Albany. Thirty-four delegates attended, nearly half of them from the counties spanned by the Manor of Rensselaerwyck. With the exception of Albany attorney Edward S. Willett, an Anti-Rent candidate for the assembly, the fourteen members from Albany and Rensselaer were manor tenants. William B. Wright, a Whig/Anti-Rent lawyer in town for the constitutional convention, represented Sullivan County. Other delegates from the Hardenbergh Patent counties and from Columbia, Montgomery, and Schoharie had been elected by grass-roots assemblies. One organizational detail, established at the convention's outset, was new. Friendly journalists and politicians had been invited inside the hall as "honorary members of the convention" at the party's March conclave. This time the delegates resolved to meet behind locked doors. Harris paced outside with Weed, Johnson, and Thomas A. Devyr; some of the talk in the lobby was paradoxical. Weed told everyone who would listen that the convention should not make any nominations. Devyr blustered about a Whig conspiracy to saddle the tenants with Young.[13]

The convention deliberated for four hours. Harris's people, armed with the pardon-pledge letter from Young, won every battle. They defeated one resolution providing that no candidates be named for statewide office and another making any nomination contingent on the nominee's written endorsement of particular Anti-Rent measures. The arguments for both resolutions packed some punch. Russell G. Dorr of Columbia, who offered the first one, declared that the nomination of either Young or Governor Wright would "have a direct tendency to separate and to destroy the Anti-Rent organization, and divide its members into their former political and party associations." Proponents of the second resolution emphasized Anti-Rent tradition. But most of the delegates concluded that the opposing arguments, recited in "an elaborate speech" by William B. Wright, were more persuasive. Silas Wright would never pardon Smith Boughton and his Anti-Rent companions in prison, Young would not endorse specific tenant demands before election day, and nominating one of their own people "would be a useless piece of formality, for there could not be the remotest possibility of his election." Seven delegates walked out when Young won the nomination on the first ballot. The big bombshell for Weed and the Whig Party was still to come. After the bolters departed, the convention unanimously nominated Addison Gardiner, the Democratic incumbent, for lieutenant governor.[14]

Weed did what he could to stem the imminent conservative revolt. "The action of the Anti-Rent convention was independent of and adverse to the views and wishes of the *Evening Journal*," he wrote on October 8. "We stand un-flinchingly by the whole Whig ticket." Greeley said much the same thing a few days later in a widely noticed speech in Columbia County; meanwhile, he sang the virtues of Hamilton Fish in the *Tribune*. Webb tried to drown them out. "John Young stands before the state as fully committed to Anti-Rentism as Ira Harris," the *Courier and Enquirer* roared when news of the Anti-Rent nomi-nations reached Manhattan. A vote for Young was a vote for "repudiation of the most solemn contracts," for "cold-blooded murder perpetrated in resisting the laws," and for the "fiendish plot" hatched by Weed and Greeley. "Their game with the Anti-Renters was all arranged in advance," Webb charged. First they engineered Young's nomination at Utica and put Fish in the second spot. Then they encouraged their Anti-Rent friends to neutralize Fish and strengthen Young. If "true Whig" voters allowed "the *Evening Journal* and *Tribune* clique" to get away with its juggle, he wrote, "our party may never recover from this descent into darkness."[15]

Jacob Livingston, one of the proprietors of the Scott Patent in Schoharie County, did not need Webb's guidance to reach the same conclusion. "I do not intend to support any but a Whig but cannot support and will not support Young," he told a friend on October 8. "Young, Seward, and Weed are deter-mined to drive all those whom they cannot manage from the party and then . . . to set the poor against the rich and thus control the state by destroying the minority who ought to have as much protection as the majority." Greeley wrote Weed the same day and grimly predicted that the Anti-Rent nominations would cost the Whigs 5,000 votes in the governor's race. Yet the good news ultimately overshadowed the bad. Fish refused to subscribe to Webb's conspiracy theory; he absolved Weed and even Harris of responsibility for the Anti-Rent nomina-tions. A letter from Henry Clay, which the *Tribune* published on October 29, rallied most of the disaffected conservatives. "If there be a desire to ensure, two years hence, the election of a Whig president for the United States," he wrote, "you may be sure that it is of the first importance to secure the election of a Whig governor at your approaching election." Clay's missive broke Webb's back. Two weeks later, the Whig central committee of New York City passed a resolution declaring that "the opposition of the *Courier and Enquirer* not to the nomination but the election after nomination of John Young as governor has made it the duty of this Committee to say that the *Courier and Enquirer* has no longer the confidence of the Whig Party of this city."[16]

The ostracism of Webb thrilled Harris. So did the equally self-defeating opposition by his nemesis on the left. Devyr and a small band of discontented anti-renters assembled on October 22 to compose a Free Soil ticket. They named Lewis Masquerier, a National Reformer, for governor and abolitionist William Chaplin for lieutenant governor. But their most conspicuous nominee was Thomas L. Shafer, the Democratic candidate for the very third-district senate seat Harris sought. Devyr staked everything on the outcome. The embattled editor of the *Anti-Renter* vowed that he would quit the movement and go back to New York City if "humbuggery [and] conservatism" prevailed. Should tenant voters shun the Free Soil ticket and choose, instead, to "chime in with the corruption that seeks only to strengthen the Whig party," Devyr warned on October 31, "in sackcloth and ashes they will repent it." This forlorn admonition was his last one. New Yorkers went the polls early the next week, and the *Anti-Renter* did not appear on the first Saturday in November. Nobody tried to resurrect it upon Devyr's departure from Albany.[17]

The electorate's verdict fulfilled Harris's every dream. In the three races he targeted, the returns told an unmistakable story (see Table 2). The unprecedented 9,000-vote majority Harris rolled up in the senate contest not only had been delivered to Young and Gardiner, the Anti-Rent Party nominees, but also had provided their margin of victory. Tenant voters in counties outside the third district—Montgomery, Sullivan, and Ulster—accounted for the difference between Young's majority and Harris's. "We hold the balance of power in the state," the *Freeholder* crowed on November 4. "We can put in our friends and put out our enemies." Many leaders of the Whig Party admitted as much. "Our noble friend Hamilton Fish," Greeley wrote Clay on November 15, "has got exactly the vote Mr. Fillmore would have received had he been put up and commended as the enemy of the Anti-Renters." Fish was even more forthright. "Mr. Young received the support of the Anti-Renters and they have a right to claim the victory," he lamented in a letter to Daniel Dewey Barnard. "Theirs is a complete victory, while the two permanent parties can claim each but half the battle, and neither can say that its own merits or its own strength gave it the little of victory which it has obtained."[18]

The "ominous" implications of Young's victory concerned Fish more than his own defeat. For him, as for conservative Whigs throughout New York State, the big question was what "*our* governor" would do to accommodate his Anti-Rent constituency. "Will he speak and act only as a Whig executive should speak and act," Fish asked, "or shall we have an effort to coax the new party into the Whig ranks?" He assumed that Barnard would accept such a union, as he had once accepted fusion with the Antimasons, "if the Anti-Renters are satisfied with their efforts and require no further legislation, and if the tenants are buying out the landlords' rights and thus creating within the disaffected corps a body whose interest will call for order." Another scenario, however, seemed far more likely. "Emboldened by success," Anti-Rent leaders might "require concessions of principle" in the form of title-test legislation that impaired vested rights of property and contract. "If this be yielded," Fish submitted, "we shall have but one more effort as 'Whigs' under our present organization. I think

TABLE 2. Election Returns, November 1846

Governor	Lieutenant Governor	Senate, Third District
Young (W) 198,878	Gardiner (D) 200,970	Harris (W) 31,738
Wright (D) 187,306	Fish (W) 187,613	Shafer (D) 22,744

there is too much love of law and order, too much conservatism in the Whig ranks, to consent to part with all principle and retain only the name of Whig."[19]

Weed understood the anxiety that pervaded his party. Instead of articulating the Whig predicament, however, he denied the Anti-Rent Party its putative victory. Day after day beginning on November 4, the *Evening Journal* attributed Fish's defeat "wholly to the wanton and persevering assaults of the *Courier and Enquirer* upon the electors of this senate district." According to Weed, "it was the indignation these aspersions created that extorted from Anti-Rent Whigs, a reluctant acquiescence in the nomination of Lieutenant Governor Gardiner." The reasons for Young's victory were different. "Silas Wright," the *Evening Journal* explained, "was identified in the public mind with the national administration" that "heedless[ly]" plunged the nation into war in May, slashed the protective tariff in July, and reinstituted the credit-killing Independent Treasury in August. Democrats registered their discontent by staying home; Wright's total vote declined more than 22 percent between 1844 and 1846. Whigs, on the other hand, turned out in force to protest "the ill-judged conduct" of President Polk and Congress. "For the first and only time," Weed pointed out, the Whigs had captured a majority of New York's thirty-four seats in the House of Representatives. All "those Locofoco editors who attribute the election of Young to the Anti-Rent vote," he remarked on November 13, "find themselves befogged the moment they attempt to explain the election of twenty-two members of Congress!" Weed's analysis yielded a conclusion that was implausible but not impolitic: "John Young would have been elected *without* the Anti-Rent vote."[20]

Few of Weed's subscribers concurred with his interpretation of the election returns. Hunker opposition to Barnburner control of the state government, not opposition to Polk's policies at the national level, induced many Democrats to stay home. The low turnout accounted for Whig gains in the state's congressional delegation. In the statewide races, however, the Anti-Rent vote was decisive. Yet people did not look to the *Evening Journal* for objective journalism. They read it to get the Whig party line, and nobody appreciated Weed's performance more than governor-elect Young. Weed emphasized the issues that united the party, downplayed those that threatened to sunder it, and assured everyone in the winning coalition—"Anti-Rent Whigs" included—that they belonged. Above all, he signaled that the message Harris and his friends worked so hard to send had not been received. Weed prepared the Whig mind for the release of the Anti-Rent convicts, but the *Evening Journal* did not breathe a word about Harris's title-test measure. If the Whig/Anti-Rent crowd expected Whig regulars to take up the struggle for legislation to test the validity of landlord titles, the Anti-Rent Party would have to exert the "balance of power" in the election of 1847 without any help from the Whig machinery.[21]

A Troublesome Constituency

John Young became the second Whig governor of New York on January 1, 1847. Tactical partisanship was his forte. He emerged as a rising Whig star in 1845 by deftly exploiting Democratic divisions on the idea of a constitutional convention, and he duplicated the feat a year later in the state printing fight. In the one instance, Young threw his Whig forces on the Barnburner side to defeat the Hunkers; in the other, Whig votes helped the Hunkers rout the radicals. Constant application of Whig pressure in the state legislature caused the New York Democracy to crumble. Young's greatest fear as he took the helm of state government, then, was that the Democratic opposition would employ the same disorganizing tactics to polarize his Whig and Anti-Rent constituencies. William H. Seward, the state's first Whig governor, treated the manor question as an opportunity for constructive statecraft. Young regarded it as problem to be fixed.

Young's legislative experience did enable him to see every facet of the problem at a glance. There was nothing he could do to prevent the introduction of Harris's Act Concerning Tenures, with its controversial link between title-testing and a rent moratorium. But the governor could preclude debate early in the session by ignoring the Anti-Rent question in his annual message. Debate on the bill could be stifled by referring it to a hostile committee or declining to permit a second reading after a favorable committee reported it to the floor. Each maneuver would soothe apprehensive Whigs and disarm Democrats poised to stir up hostilities between his Whig friends and Anti-Rent friends. Without the cooperation of Harris and his Whig/Anti-Rent people, however, neither ploy could succeed. If the *Freeholder* blasted the message or clamored incessantly for action on the bill, the Whig press was certain to reply and the factional quarrel Young wanted to suppress would merely rage in the newspapers instead of the legislature.

Harris and Young reached an understanding shortly before inauguration day. They agreed, first, that two gubernatorial messages should be delivered in January. One of them, addressed to the legislature as the state constitution required, would not discuss the Anti-Rent agitation. The other one, drafted by *Freeholder* editor Alexander G. Johnson in return for his silence on the annual message, would announce the pardon of the Anti-Rent convicts, retail a sympathetic history of the tenant movement, and affirm the governor's commitment to the abolition of manorial tenures.[22] The pardon proclamation, unlike the message delivered to the legislature, would not be a legitimate subject of debate in either house. As the senate's Judiciary Committee observed during the 1846 session, the power to pardon belonged exclusively to the executive. Young also persuaded Harris that they shared a common interest in choking off debate on the proposed Act Concerning Tenures. With the senate still in Democratic hands and main-line Whigs still opposed to the bill, it had no chance of passing in 1847. A floor fight would not only divide the Whig and Anti-Rent members but also harden attitudes. Thus the chances of success in 1848, when the tenant vote figured to be crucial in a presidential campaign, would be greater if the bill were allowed to slumber for the time being.

Careful preparation resulted in a long honeymoon for Governor Young. His annual message, delivered on January 5, focused entirely on the duties thrust upon the legislature by the newly ratified constitution of 1846. Until the requisite enabling acts had been passed, Young pointed out, corporations could not be organized under the mandated general incorporation laws and judges could not be elected to the enlarged New York Supreme Court or the new Court of Appeals. Nor could canal construction be resumed with the receipts remaining after the state debt had been serviced under the constitutionalized Stop and Tax Act. Even the Democrats found much to praise and nothing to criticize in the governor's remarks. Still, the response to his pardon proclamation pleased him more. It evoked joyous celebrations in the Anti-Rent counties, laudatory editorials in the *Freeholder* and *Evening Journal*, and circumspect defenses in the rest of the Whig press. Only the radical Democratic editors cried foul. The attacks helped Young more than they hurt him, for they reinforced Anti-Rent identification with the Whig Party.[23]

Things went just as well in the state legislature. Assemblyman Edward Carpentier, a Democrat from New York City, greeted Young's annual message with a resolution "asking whether the governor has any information to communicate in regard to the subject of landlord and tenant." But the well-drilled Whig and Anti-Rent members refused to discuss the matter and eventually tabled the resolution by a vote of 53-42. The only debate occurred on January 13. Jonathan C. Allaben of Delaware County moved that a select committee be appointed to consider land reform legislation; Bishop Perkins, after expressing surprise that the governor's message had not considered the subject, claimed that "nothing more could be done" for the tenants. Perkins pointed out that the new constitution had abolished the New York Court of Chancery and its army of chancery masters. As a result, the machinery for administering the devise-and-descent bill "of last winter" no longer existed. What, then, did the proposed committee expect to accomplish? Thomas Smith, a Whig/Anti-Rent member from Schoharie, taunted Perkins instead of answering his question. It was "regrettable," he remarked, "to see the gentleman from St. Lawrence manifesting a disposition to turn his back on these tenants" now that his friend Silas Wright had been defeated. The house adopted Allaben's resolution moments later, and the Act Concerning Tenures did not reach the assembly floor before the session ended in May.[24]

Seward marveled at Young's achievement. "Today I have been at St. Peters," he wrote his wife from Albany on January 17.

> There was such a jumble of wrecks of party in the church that I forgot the sermon and fell to moralizing on the vanity of political life. You know my seat. Well, half-way down the west aisle sat Silas Wright, wrapped in a coat tightly buttoned to the chin, looking philosophy, which it is hard to affect and harder to attain. On the east side sat Daniel D. Barnard, upon whom "Anti-Rent" has piled Ossa, while Pelion only has been rolled upon Wright. In the middle of the church was Croswell, who seemed to say to Wright, "You are welcome to the gallows you erected for me." On the opposite side sat John Young, the *saved* among the lost politicians. He seemed complacent and satisfied.

Seward knew from experience that Young's serenity had an unstable foundation. Resisting new legislation to resolve the Anti-Rent question meant relying on the willingness of landlords and tenants to settle their differences through private bargaining. Negotiation had not worked for him in 1840–41. Yet Seward understood Young's inclination to hope for a different outcome in 1847. There was no better way to harmonize the discordant elements of the Whig coalition, and there was no greater "vanity of political life" than the presumption that an effective party leader satisfied everyone who counted.[25]

One stalwart Whig proprietor was happy to oblige Governor Young. John A. King and his tenants on the 17,000-acre Blenheim Patent came to terms on January 6, 1847. King promised to sell his entire interest in hundreds of Schoharie County farms, payable over three years and secured by mortgages carrying 10 percent interest, at prices ranging from $1.87 per acre (for land carrying an annual rent of 20¢ per acre) to $1.50 per acre (for land carrying an annual rent of 12¢ per acre). The articles of agreement provided that all existing "liabilities or charges," including back rents, would be waived upon the receipt of a 5 percent down payment on November 15. King insisted on something else in return. The Anti-Rent association not only had to guarantee that a majority of the patent's tenants would subscribe to the deal but also had to collect the down payments, service the mortgages, and remit the money to King at the appointed times. It was a shrewd bargain. The tenants got the allodial titles they always wanted; King took $25,000 out of the vexatious land business and put it into the rising market for railroad securities in a costless transaction.[26]

King's ingenious method was hard to replicate in other Anti-Rent counties. More than two dozen proprietors owned bits of Livingston Manor and the Hardenbergh Patent, and no landlord in Columbia, Delaware, Greene, Sullivan, or Ulster proposed a uniform deal administered by the Anti-Rent associations. Yet all of them offered to sell their interests for an amount that, invested at 5 percent interest, would yield the annual rent in perpetuity. Spurred by the taxation of rent charges that began in 1847, the conversion business grew large enough to be called "a land rush." Half the remaining tenants on Livingston Manor bought out their landlords between 1846 and 1848, and voluntary sales of reserved rents proceeded at much the same rate across the Hudson on the Hardenbergh Patent. By 1850 agents for the Livingstons, Ludlows, and Verplancks were collecting mortgage payments from almost as many families as they collected rents.[27]

The sales encouraged Governor Young, but they neither proceeded fast enough nor affected enough great estates to unify his Whig and Anti-Rent constituents. George Clarke Jr., the proprietor of several Mohawk country patents, refused to sell out to his tenants on any terms. Stephen Van Rensselaer IV complained loudly about the tax liability imposed by the 1846 act, stood firm on his prior offers, and found very few willing buyers. His half brother went further. William P. Van Rensselaer challenged the right of Rensselaer County assessors to put rent-charge income on the tax rolls; he continued the fight until the New York Supreme Court upheld the assessments in February 1850. Uncompromising landlords strengthened the hand of uncompromising tenants. During the late 1840s, the title-test mania gripped the Anti-Rent associations in Montgomery and Otsego counties as well as the parent organizations in Albany and Rensselaer. It also animated a small pocket of Anti-Rent resistance in Taghkanic, Columbia County, where a band of twenty-five to thirty armed "Indians" led by Calvin and Peter Finkle committed a stunning new outrage just six weeks after Young issued his pardon proclamation.[28]

The chain of events that generated the "Indian" revival on Livingston Manor began at the Tilden Committee hearings in March 1846. George I. Finkle of Taghkanic heard the testimony of Calvin Pepper Jr. and was floored by the Albany lawyer's Quia Emptores argument against the Van Rensselaer title. Finkle instantly recognized its applicability to Livingston Manor; several weeks later, his nephews launched a plan to test the title of Charles J. Livingston. Agents for the twenty-five-year-old absentee landlord had ejected a tenant named Peter Houghtaling from a Taghkanic farm in April 1846. Peter Sheldon bought it shortly afterward. Calvin and Peter Finkle entered the farm before Sheldon took possession, and they dared Livingston's people to try running them off the land. Because the Finkles were squatters rather than tenants, the common law rule barring them from contesting the Livingston title would not apply.[29]

Pepper agreed to defend the Finkles as soon as the resulting ejectment action had been filed. At first, however, the Anti-Rent lawyer believed that they had no case. "Supposing that Mr. Livingston would rely for recovery solely upon the ground of prior actual possession on his part," Pepper later explained in the *Freeholder*, "[I assumed] that the legality of the manor grant to the Livingstons would not be made an issue upon the trial." But early in June, E. P. Cowles, counsel for Charles Livingston, assured Pepper that he intended "to make an exhibit of the entire Manor of Livingston." Pepper urged every Columbia tenant to contribute "at least fifty cents" for legal expenses. "You have not a moment to lose," he wrote in a broadside for the *Freeholder*, "in preparing for the most important trial that has ever taken place in your county."[30]

Nothing went right for the Columbia anti-renters in the trial before Circuit Judge Bowen Whiting. Counsel for Livingston entered into evidence the 1686 manor patent, a confirmatory 1715 patent, and sundry other documents bearing on the authenticity of the title. But Cowles also offered proof of Charles Livingston's prior possession of the farm at issue. Seward represented the Anti-Rent association; although he elaborated the Quia Emptores argument for the jury "in a speech of unsurpassed power and beauty," it did not help the Finkles. Judge Whiting charged the jury that they were to bring in a verdict for Livingston if the evidence showed that, upon the ejectment of Houghtaling, the landlord owned the premises on the basis of either title or possession. The jury held for Livingston, and the quest to isolate the burning Anti-Rent question of the day—whether the enactment of Quia Emptores in 1290 barred the creation of manors in colonial New York—thus came to naught.[31]

Calvin and Peter Finkle compounded the costs of defeat in the months that followed. First they attempted to hold the farm in defiance of the court's process. Cowles, the attorney who had bested them at trial, was attacked with "fists and clubs" in the ensuing affray; he spent the night in the hospital while Columbia deputies put Peter Sheldon, the purchaser of the farm, into possession of the land. The Finkle brothers went into hiding. On March 24, 1847, they returned to the farm in "Indian" garb and, in Governor Young's words, "with force and violence broke and entered the said dwelling house and forcibly removed therefrom the person and property of the said Sheldon and his family, in violation of the laws of this state, especially the act entitled, 'An act to prevent persons appearing disguised and armed.'" Sheldon got a coat of tar and feathers; Peter and Calvin Finkle received sentences of three years and four months in state prison. As the Finkle brothers left the Hudson courthouse following the trial in June, they threatened "to raise forces from abroad to rescue them" and even "to fire the city." Twenty-five special deputies guarded the Columbia County jail for weeks afterward. Meanwhile, the progressive Whigs wrestled with the problem of how to pacify the tenants without losing the Anti-Rent vote that had been so decisive in the election of 1846.[32]

Horace Greeley developed the line of argument Governor Young ultimately embraced. The proximate cause of the "troubles" in Columbia County, he wrote in a series of spring 1847 editorials, was landlord intransigence. Lawyers for Charles J. Livingston had promised the Columbia anti-renters "a comprehensive litigation, arbitration, and adjustment of *all* the questions in controversy between the assumed landlords and those they claim as tenants." After the Anti-Rent association had raised the funds to retain counsel and put the matter to rest, however, landlord attorneys kept the title question "covered up under legal cobwebs." Greeley made it clear that neither deceitful lawyers nor the "miserable cobhouse of fiction" called the common law justified resistance to legal process. But "deep-seated" tenant convictions about defective landlord titles, whether "unfounded" or not, could be ignored no longer. Anti-renters demanded to know "the *truth*," and the demand was a reasonable one.[33]

Greeley took this position without his usual enthusiasm. He had remonstrated against the title-test scheme for years because of its seeming futility, and the newly minted Quia Emptores argument had not changed his mind. "*Have* the Van Rensselaers a good title?" Greeley asked on March 17. "In our opinion they have; and this is what puzzles us when we see so much higgling and coddling to screen them from any obligation to prove their title."[34] But the logic of politics finally drove Greeley to advocate some kind of title-test measure. Enacting one would channel the troublesome Anti-Rent agitation into the courts yet enable the Whigs to retain the loyalty of tenant voters. If the title-test litigation failed, as Greeley anticipated, angry tenants would have no reason to blame the Whig Party. Partisan imperatives thus transformed an imprudent land reform policy into a necessity.

Young was more fussy than Greeley about the details of title-test legislation. The governor doubted the constitutionality of any measure that would compel landlords to prove their titles as a prerequisite for collecting rent; besides, he could not recommend the enactment of Harris's Act Concerning Tenures without provoking a revolt of Whig conservatives. It followed that law officers of New York State, rather than Pepper, Seward, and other private attorneys general, should file the necessary challenges. Young recognized that legislation authorizing government suits against the proprietors of British grants also confronted formidable legal obstacles. The biggest one was the Quiet-Title Act of 1788. As codified in the *Revised Statutes*, it promised the landlords repose from the very sort of legal action he contemplated:

The people of this State will not sue or implead any person for or in respect to any lands, tenements, or hereditaments . . . by reason of any right or title of the said people to the same, unless,

1. Such right or title shall have accrued within twenty years before any suit, or other proceeding, for the same shall be commenced; or unless,

2. The people, or those from whom they claim, shall have received the rents and profits of such real estate, or of some part thereof, within the said space of twenty years.

Neither condition obtained in 1847.[35] By the adjournment of the legislature in May, however, Young had reason to believe that the Anti-Rent associations would embrace his approach to litigating landlord titles and give up their long struggle for the proposed Act Concerning Tenures. Ira Harris's vaunted "balance of power" strategy had been wrecked by new developments on the national stage.

Antislavery and Anti-Rent

One of the most fateful controversies in American history began on August 8, 1846. President Polk asked the House of Representatives for an appropriation of $2 million to be used in communicating peace terms to Mexico through diplomatic channels. David Wilmot, a Democrat from Pennsylvania, proposed that the bill be amended to conform with the antislavery sensibilities of northern voters. His amendment, modeled on the Northwest Ordinance of 1787, prohibited slavery and involuntary servitude "as an express and fundamental condition to the acquisition of any territory from the Republic of Mexico by the United States by virtue of any treaty which may be negotiated between them." The bill passed the House with the Wilmot Proviso attached, but it did not come to a vote in the Senate before the session ended forty-eight hours afterward. Polk complained about the "demagogues and ambitious politicians" who promoted the antislavery provision in 1846, and he condemned the "mischievous and wicked . . . agitation of the slavery question" when Preston King, a Barnburner from Silas Wright's congressional district, revived the measure in January 1847. John C. Calhoun's answer to the Wilmot Proviso, introduced in the form of resolutions for consideration by the Senate, constitutionalized the sectional feeling Polk reviled. Calhoun insisted that Congress, as the "joint agent" of the sovereign states, had no power to forbid citizens who owned slaves under state law from "emigrating, with their property, into any of the territories of the United States."[36]

The Wilmot Proviso thrust the slavery question to the center of New York public life. William Cullen Bryant's *Evening Post* defined opposition to the extension of slavery as a moral and political necessity in September 1846, and the entire radical Democracy fell into step after the Whig victory in November. Bryant pointed out that Mexican law forbade slavery in California and New Mexico. "If we, who boast of being the freest people in the world," he wrote, "should, upon coming into possession of any one of these provinces, so change its institutions as to create a new class of men to be held in perpetual bondage, our confederacy would stand disgraced in the eyes of all mankind." Wright saw things in precisely the same way. "The principle asserted [in the proviso] is clearly right," he insisted in a January letter to Senator John A. Dix, "and its assertion now is, in my judgment, not merely expedient, but positively necessary." Wright presumed that "no part and no party of the free states will consent that territory be purchased or conquered to extend this institution to countries where it does not and cannot now constitutionally and lawfully exist."[37]

Samuel Young, the redoubtable Barnburner state senator, carried the radical Democracy's case for the Wilmot Proviso into the New York legislature on January 16, 1847. Fifteen days later, New York became the first state to go on record in favor of prohibiting slavery from any territory acquired from Mexico. The debate on Colonel Young's antislavery resolutions, first in the legislature and then in the press, arrayed the Democrats in predictable formations. Hunkers curried Polk's favor by decrying the agitation. "We would prohibit slavery in the new territory—and we would moot the question whenever the territory shall have been acquired, and upon its admission into the Union, either as a state or territory," the *Argus* observed on January 22. "We would not attempt to do it *now*. While it would scarcely fail to embarrass the administration, it could serve no immediate good purpose." Barnburners dismissed such arguments as the rantings of "southern mercenaries." The time had come, the *Atlas* remarked on February 3, for "Northern Democrats" to take a stand: "The degradation of labor, which results from a system of compulsory servitude, has a contagion that affects with dishonor all who are associated with it."[38]

New York Whigs were quick to endorse the Barnburner resolutions in the state legislature. Weed, Seward, and Greeley had long portrayed their organization as the antislavery party of the North, and they had no intention of allowing Democratic rivals to monopolize "the great issue" of the day. But nobody expressed the progressive Whig position more fully or faithfully than Ira Harris. "Let the North, *now*, with a united front . . . say to the South openly and boldly, and yet kindly and affectionately, that they intend to fix *unalterably* the bounds of slavery," he declared in the senate on January 19, "and a glorious victory will yet be won in behalf of human freedom." Harris, unlike most Barnburners, identified the containment of slavery by force of law as only the first step in its abolition. "Public opinion is omnipotent in a country like ours," he proclaimed. "It is yet destined to break the chain of the slave, and lift him up from his present degradation to the level of intelligent manhood." Seward himself could not have summarized the creed of antislavery Whigs more elegantly. Weed published Harris's speech in the *Evening Journal*, and Greeley praised it in the *Tribune*. James Watson Webb declared a pox on all their houses. The clamor for the "hydra-headed monster" Wilmot Proviso, he told *Courier and Enquirer* readers, was of a piece with the Anti-Rent agitation. "Demagoguery" sustained both movements. The emerging combination of antislavery and Anti-Rent, Webb argued, threatened to bring "all the horrors of the French Revolution" upon the American republic.[39]

Webb buried a good point in his fulminations. It was true that the same politicians and pundits who remonstrated against the extension of slavery also decried the lease in fee. Whig progressives and Democratic radicals even projected images of the South that bore a striking resemblance to their descriptions of manorial society. They claimed that the "pestilence" of slavery, like the "blight" caused by manorial tenures, was recognizable in "worn out soil, dilapidated fences and tenements, and an air of general desolation." They asserted that slavery, like the form of land tenure in the Anti-Rent counties, was "a curse," an "enormous evil" that degraded labor, stunted the incentive to improvement, forestalled the influx of a useful population, and acted as a brake on economic development. If California remained free, the *Evening Post* observed with a flourish that echoed countless commentaries on Rensselaerwyck, "in a few years the country will teem with an active and energetic population, and its resources will be developed in every possible manner that human ingenuity or enterprise can invent." Nobody doubted that the oppression suffered by manor tenants paled in comparison with the condition of the slaves. But the free-soil argument focused primarily on the incompatibility of perpetual bondage and free labor. So did the argument against manorial tenures. For progressive Whigs and radical Democrats alike, neither slavery nor the lease in fee fulfilled what Willard Hurst termed "the proper property function of generating a constantly expanding reach of human creative power."[40]

Yet the ideological affinity between antislavery and Anti-Rent, though strong in the abstract, weakened significantly on exposure to the legal and political environment of New York State in 1847. One countervailing force was the doctrine of vested rights. Manor tenants had no use for legislation prohibiting the luxuriation of "voluntary slavery" where it did not yet exist. They rallied behind Harris's Act Concerning Tenures because it would release them from contractual obligations until their landlords had established legal title to the land. Few progressive Whigs and still fewer Barnburners believed that the proposed statute's immediate effect was constitutional or its objective—the destruction of "patroonery" by judicial invalidation of land titles—realistic. Anti-Rent was grounded on a "constitutional utopianism" comparable with the radical abolitionism of Gerrit Smith and Lysander Spooner. Political antislavery, on the other hand, accommodated the prospectivity norm in legislation. Its much broader appeal flowed in part from the Wilmot Proviso's conformity to conventional maxims of American constitutional law.[41]

Vested rights constitutionalism merely inhibited the fusion of antislavery with Anti-Rent. The bastard pragmatism of New York politicians sapped the Anti-Rent Party's very foundation. Short-run calculations shaped both the Barnburner agitation for the Wilmot Proviso and the responses of Hunkers and Whigs. In 1847, at least, the radical Democracy did not ask for the aid of land reformers, Liberty men, or Whigs; the formation of a new, broad-gauged antislavery party never occurred to Barnburner leaders. They fought for the soul of the Democratic Party, not for the soul of the nation. After the defeat of the Wilmot Proviso in the United States Senate on March 1, moreover, it became increasingly apparent that the Barnburners were going to lose. President Polk opposed them. Senator Daniel S. Dickinson denounced them. And the Hunkers, sustained by the national party machinery as well as the *Argus*, persuaded one Democratic county organization after another to pass resolutions declaring that "he is an enemy to his party and his country who encourages these dissensions."[42] The deepening Democratic schism gratified the Whig leadership. Weed and Greeley embossed their party's antislavery pedigree in the *Evening Journal* and the *Tribune* all through the spring. They also anticipated a smashing victory over the divided Democrats in the November general election. For Ira Harris, however, the impending dissolution of the New York Democracy meant trouble. The Anti-Rent Party's "balance of power" strategy hinged on keen competition for voters between two major parties having roughly equal strength. No leverage could be exerted on the Whigs if the Hunkers and Barnburners insisted on running separate tickets.

Harris bailed out in May 1847. He accepted the Whig nomination for a seat on the New York Supreme Court and sold his interest in the *Freeholder* to longtime partner Charles F. Bouton. Harris and William B. Wright, his Whig/Anti-Rent colleague from Sullivan County, won handily in the new third judicial district. So did Malbone Watson of Greene and Amasa J. Parker of Albany, the two Democrats named by the Anti-Rent convention. The June 8 special election turned out to be the last time Anti-Rent Party nominations affected the outcome. Not coincidentally, it was the last election for two years in which New York Democrats worked together. Hunkers and Barnburners coalesced without much effort to keep the state judiciary in Democratic hands. "The higher judiciary is invested in this country with power unknown to the English courts," the *Evening Post* explained on May 20. "It is of extreme importance, therefore, . . . that a majority of the judges should be Democrats, or at least should entertain those views in regard to constitutional questions which are held by the Democratic Party." The warring factions split the judicial nominations; Democrats captured twenty-two of the thirty-two seats on the Supreme Court. Greene

Bronson, Addison Gardiner, Freeborn Jewett, and Charles Ruggles were elected to the Court of Appeals.[43]

But the powerful New York Democracy disintegrated at its state convention in Syracuse on September 29. Following an acrimonious fight over contested seats, a slim Hunker majority put staunch conservatives in every slot on the party's ticket and named a Hunker-dominated committee to frame resolutions. David Dudley Field proposed a Wilmot Proviso plank from the floor; when the chair ruled his motion out of order, the Barnburner delegates walked out amid "a scene of indescribable tumult." Four days after the Democrats went home, the Whigs convened in the same Syracuse building and adopted a verbatim copy of the Field Resolution rejected by the Hunkers. Hamilton Fish was nominated for lieutenant governor, Millard Fillmore for comptroller, Christopher Morgan for secretary of state, and Anti-Rent champion Ambrose Jordan for attorney general. "Weed came last evening and gave me a full account of the convention at Syracuse, which seems to have proceeded exactly as he wished," Seward wrote home from Albany on October 9. "The 'Barnburners' are bent on defeating the Democratic ticket; and John Van Buren had a meeting at the capital last night, in which the position of the 'Barnburners' was eloquently set forth. The Whigs may expect to carry their ticket by some 30,000 majority."[44]

The Democratic schism that elated Whigs threw the Anti-Rent Party into complete disarray. Tenant voters had no chance of influencing the outcome of an election purposefully boycotted by half of the New York Democracy. Making nominations at the Anti-Rent state convention, scheduled for October 13, thus became an empty gesture. Nor was that the only problem looming before the tenant delegates. In 1846 their nominations for governor and lieutenant governor had been all that mattered. The longer ballot mandated by the new state constitution put twelve statewide offices up for grabs in 1847, and the Anti-Rent Party had established no working principle for distributing its nominees among the Whigs and Hunkers. The result was chaos. Anti-Rent leaders with roots in the Whig Party, led by *Freeholder* editor Alexander G. Johnson, supported the entire Whig slate; delegates with Democratic connections backed either the Hunker nominees or the Liberty Party candidates. Only the nomination of Jordan for attorney general was unanimous. The rest of the ticket made no sense at all. Morgan, a Whig progressive, failed to get the Anti-Rent nomination but Fillmore won it. "At the conclusion," the *Freeholder* reported a week later, "we were surprised to see Doctor Boughton rise and declare that he was dissatisfied with the nominations, and threaten to get up mass meetings and denounce them." But the surprise was feigned. At the outset, Boughton had joined Jonathan C. Allaben of Delaware in protesting the convention's exclusion of thirty-three National Reform delegates from New York City. They believed that the Anti-Rent Party's future lay in fusion with the Barnburners rather than the exploded "balance of power" strategy.[45]

Subsequent developments at the local level destroyed the Anti-Rent organization. The major parties nominated candidates for the legislature during the second week in October, and their conventions operated under a new set of rules. The constitution adopted in 1846 created single-member districts. Thus the old third senate district, which Van Schoonhoven and Harris once carried on the Whig and Anti-Rent tickets, had been broken up and its component counties scattered among six smaller units. Valentine Treadwell, a friend of Harris's, secured the Whig nomination in the new Albany-Schenectady senate district and won easily in November. Elsewhere, however, the major party conventions snubbed Anti-Rent activists. Allaben got clobbered by his Hunker opponent in the Delaware-Schoharie senate district because the Barnburners sat out the election and the Whigs put up their own man. Anti-Rent took a beating even in Rensselaer. The Whig convention discarded Van Schoonhoven in favor of a party regular; Johnson declined the Anti-Rent nomination. "I stand no possible chance of election," he announced in the *Freeholder*. "There are in Rensselaer County about 12,000 voters, of whom not more than 2,500 are Anti-Renters. Either the Whig or Democratic candidate would receive, upon a full poll, nearly or quite twice as many votes as I should. I am not able to spend the time, or incur the expense, of carrying on a hopeless contest." Johnson soon gave up on the cause entirely. At year's end he quietly resigned as editor of the *Freeholder* and accepted an appointment as Christopher Morgan's chief deputy in New York's State Department.[46]

Weed declared that a "gratifying truth" had been demonstrated in the election of 1847. "The vote of the State of New York can never, at any future period, be secured for a known advocate of slavery extension," he wrote on November 8. " 'Free Labor upon Free Soil' is the settled doctrine of at least three fourths of the electors of this state." The result of the Barnburner boycott gratified Weed more. Whigs won 94 of the 128 seats in the assembly, 24 of the 32 seats in the senate, and all of the state offices. Only one set of numbers troubled the Whig leadership. Fillmore ran nearly 5,000 votes ahead of Fish in the eleven Anti-Rent counties. Daniel Dewey Barnard congratulated Fish for having won without "the compliment of a place on the Anti-Rent ticket," but even Fish conceded that something had to be done to consolidate Whig strength in eastern New York. As it turned out, Governor Young's solution for the manor question helped Fish's political career more than anything Barnard had ever done for him.[47]

Dead Ends

On January 4, 1848, John Young told the New York legislature that the time had come to put the Anti-Rent agitation to rest. "The principle which has been so often asserted, that these tenures are not in harmony with our institutions, exists no longer in mere speculation," he said. "It has received the sanction of the constitution of the state, and is now a part of its fundamental law." Having identified the form of tenure as the crux of the problem and reminded the legislators of their "high duty . . . to seek out and remove any causes of discontent that may exist among the people," Young effortlessly shifted gears. He took up the quite different question of landlord titles. "It is believed," he remarked, "that one of the fruitful sources of disquietude among these tenants is the apprehension that after paying rents and making improvements for a long series of years," they might lose their farms to landlords claiming title under defective British grants. At common law the tenants had no right to contest the patents of their proprietors, and the Constitution forbade legislation that would authorize them to do so. Yet "the object to be attained by the tenants" might be achieved in suits brought by government lawyers. "If an action or actions of ejectment shall be brought by the state, in such case or cases as you may in your wisdom prescribe," Young concluded, "the state will have discharged a duty which, in my judgment, it owes to the importance of the subject."[48]

Young's recommendation evoked a favorable response from Whig and Anti-Rent commentators alike. "We have no doubt, if the titles to the manor lands can be reached in the way laid down in the message," Charles Bouton announced in the *Freeholder*, "that the tenants will be as fully, if not better satisfied than they would be if they were allowed to test the title themselves." Greeley focused on public opinion generally; the *Tribune* declared that "three-fourths of the whole people, upon a fair statement of the case, will concur in Governor Young's views." Greeley trusted that the legislature would give the new title-test scheme "a very earnest consideration," and it promptly did. On January 13, without a word of debate, the Whig speaker of the assembly named a select committee to consider the matter. Its chairman was Edward S. Willett of Albany, the one remaining Whig/Anti-Rent member of the house.[49]

Willett's report was a quintessential exercise in political sophistry. The committee simply ignored the difficulty posed by the bar on government challenges to land titles in the Quiet-Title Act of 1788. Rather than proposing a statute, Willett introduced a resolution that passed the buck to newly elected Attorney General Ambrose Jordan:

> *Resolved*, (if the senate concur), That the attorney general be instructed carefully to inquire and ascertain whether, in any of the lands in this state now claimed to be held under any of the manorial titles, . . . the claim of the present landlords be open to just doubt and question, and whether in his judgment this state may justly and legally lay claim to the title of the same or to any part thereof, by escheat or otherwise; and if in his opinion the title of the present claimants may be justly questioned . . . that he take

such measures, either by suit at law or other proper proceedings, as will test the validity of such titles or claims.

Charles G. Myers of St. Lawrence, the lone Barnburner on the committee, filed a minority report. Neither the governor nor his Whig colleagues, he declared, had shown how the state could "justly and legally lay claim" to land held under quiet titles. In his view, the proposed title-test resolution was "calculated" to direct the Anti-Rent movement down a cul-de-sac. Its passage, he said, would merely "excite hopes and expectations, which can end only in disappointment, 'to keep the word of promise to the ear and break it to the hope.' "[50]

The *Freeholder* pilloried Myers in an editorial published on March 29, two days before the assembly passed the title-test resolution by a vote of 65-29. Bouton did not answer the claim that the Quiet-Title Act forbade the projected government suits. Instead, he put Myers's motives into question. "This loud-mouthed Democrat of ultra professions despises the two hundred thousand citizens cursed by land monopoly," Bouton wrote, "and is the obsequious worshipper of some twenty landlords." Valentine Treadwell, who shepherded the resolution through the upper house, employed a similar tactic in an exchange with Senator William S. Johnson, a conservative Whig from New York City, on April 7. Johnson contended that the contemplated government suits would inflict trouble and expense on the landlord defendants yet do the tenants no good; Treadwell replied that nothing said by "the premier of the landlords" deserved any weight. "Now the senator from New York says that the resolution is entirely useless," Treadwell remarked. "If it is so utterly useless, it certainly can do no harm, and what objection can there be to its passage? The anti-renters desire it, and it is the recommendation of Governor Young. I ask the senate if it is not best for the good order of the country to satisfy these men." The resolution passed by a vote of 18-7 two days later. "Great benefits will result from it," the *Freeholder* proclaimed on April 12. The title-test resolution "will go much farther towards relieving the tenants from their present embarrassed condition than any act done by any former legislature."[51]

Bouton and Treadwell were right about the enthusiasm for Young's title-test scheme at the grass roots. Mass meetings in Delaware and Rensselaer counties endorsed it several weeks before the legislature did. But the resolutions produced by the Anti-Rent associations sounded another theme as well. The tenants presumed that the eminent domain safety net was still available. Harry Betts, author of the document adopted at West Sandlake on March 2, put it this way:

Resolved, That we ask for the investigation of the claims of title in the landlord as recommended in the governor's annual message; and if, in the event, our landlord's title is confirmed, we ask for the abolition of this odious rent-paying system—giving us the privilege of buying the soil at a fair and reasonable rate.

The renewed call for compensated-emancipation legislation fell on stony ground. Whig leaders assumed that the drive for land reform had come to an end upon passage of the title-test resolution; the New York Court of Appeals accentuated the point during its January 1848 term. In *Gilbert v. Foote* the court reaffirmed the due process limitations on takings for private use laid down in *Taylor v. Porter* (1843).[52]

The 1816 statute challenged in *Gilbert*, entitled "An Act for Draining Swamps and Other Low Lands," was cut from the same mold as the Private Road Act of 1772. It authorized farmers who wanted to reclaim wetlands with a ditch "through lands belonging to other persons, in case the owners of such lands shall refuse to permit the opening of such ditches," to petition the local justice of the peace for permission to proceed. The act directed the magistrate to notify the affected landowners, "summon twelve reputable freeholders," and guide the jury's deliberations on both the suitability of the project and (if found "necessary and proper") the compensation that the petitioner had to pay his neighbors for the right-of-way. New York's high court held that the legislature could not authorize such an unconstitutional proceeding.[53]

The court reached the result in *Gilbert* without difficulty. Five years earlier in *Taylor v. Porter*, Justice Greene Bronson had said that the legislature had no power "to compel any man to sell his land or goods, or any interest in them, to his neighbor, when the property is not to be applied to public use." And the Wetlands Act, though consonant with the public good, made no pretense of devoting the resulting drainage ditches to public use. It not only bestowed all use rights on the petitioner and "his heirs and assign[ee]s forever" but also clothed them with a cause of action against "any person who shall dam up, obstruct, or in any way injure" the ditches so opened. The court insisted that the New York Constitution of 1846, which overruled *Taylor v. Porter* on its facts, had actually strengthened the due process principle at hand. The sovereign people's deputies "must have appreciated the full force of the [1843] decision," Justice Charles Mason explained, "as they have provided . . . that so far as private roads are concerned they may be opened in the manner to be prescribed by law, but they have not extended the right to take private property for private use, beyond the case of opening private roads; and from the very fact that they have not, I think the inference is irresistible that they did not intend it should be." The "moral influence" Ira Harris had ascribed to the new constitution's antifeudalism provisions was thus subverted. If the eminent domain power could not be exercised to reclaim wetlands, it could not be invoked to extinguish manorial tenures.[54]

The *Freeholder* acknowledged the unhappy implications of the *Gilbert* decision in a plaintive editorial on May 10, 1848. Bouton was at once angry, incredulous, and contrite. A legislature having no power to suppress "a public evil," he wrote, "is a worthless political machine." The eminent domain idea proposed by Assemblyman Duer in 1840, Bouton pointed out, "only compels, for the welfare of the whole people, a few of the people to change the form of their property; to take an equivalent gross sum of money in full satisfaction and discharge of a perpetual rent. There is in this no robbery, no wrong, no hardship." Landlord and tenant alike would reap "a positive benefit" from the abolition of manorial tenures on a compensated basis, "for it would make the capital of each more disposable and profitable." Yet the Court of Appeals had spoken; the constitutional moment for an eminent domain measure had passed. Bouton in 1848, like Weed in 1846, looked backward with regret. "It is a solemn truth," he lamented, "that if the constitutional convention had permitted a commutation of rents, the great mass of them would have been extinguished by this time, and the land well nigh freed from feudal exactions and restraints."[55]

Bouton's gloom flowed from a gathering sense of doom. As the year wore on, he grew increasingly apprehensive about the Anti-Rent Party's dependence on Governor Young's title-test scheme. "It may be that the passage of the resolution was only throwing a rat to the whale," the *Freeholder* declared on August 30. "The attorney general is pursuing his investigation under the resolution, but he has not yet commenced any suit, and it may be that he will not think it his duty to commence any, for in his opinion all the manorial titles may be valid and indefeasible." Bouton's main concern, however, was the state of his party. Anti-Rent leaders had permitted the Whigs to commandeer their legislative program; meanwhile, the "exciting" question of slavery in the Mexican cession had tempted a great many tenants to stray from the Anti-Rent standard. By August 16, when Martin Van Buren accepted the Free Soil nomination for president, three other parties were competing for voters in the rural villages of eastern New York. Bouton pleaded for Anti-Rent unity. "The moment we break up our political organization," he insisted, "that moment our influence is lost." But the only rallying cry at his command was the promise of uncertain future rewards once the Second Party System had been restored. "Whenever the two great parties into which the state is almost equally divided come fairly into the field again," Bouton contended, "the Anti-Renters will still hold the balance of power."[56]

Three candidates for governor already had been nominated when the Anti-Rent Party held its state convention on October 4. John A. Dix had been named by the Barnburner-dominated Free Soilers and Reuben Walworth, the former chancellor, by the Hunkers in control of the regular Democratic organization. Governor Young's usefulness as the nominal head of the New York Whigs had ceased with the passage of the title-test resolution. Weed, anxious to appease the conservatives, backed Hamilton Fish for governor and his man won the nomination without a struggle. All three candidates attracted some support in the Anti-Rent convention. Congressman John Slingerland, whom the Whigs already had dumped in favor of Albany banker John L. Schoolcraft, endorsed Fish because he was "the only candidate we can elect." Bouton, the Hunker nominee for Congress in the Albany district, preferred Walworth. Nevertheless, Dix won the Anti-Rent nomination on the third ballot. It scarcely mattered. Only 3,500 tenants voted the Anti-Rent ticket in 1848, and the Whigs trounced the divided Democrats. Attorney General Jordan helped the Whig cause in Albany County. Early in October he filed a title-test suit against Stephen Van Rensselaer IV; Schoolcraft ran ahead of Bouton even in Berne, the birthplace of the Anti-Rent movement.[57]

On November 29, 1848, the *Freeholder* announced that the tenant organ had been sold to Philander S. Grant, the weekly newspaper's shop foreman since its founding in 1845. Bouton had finally conceded that the Anti-Rent Party was dead. The new state of affairs suited Hamilton Fish. He became the first New York governor in a decade to serve an entire term without having to address the Anti-Rent controversy in his annual messages. Weed was ecstatic for another reason. On February 6, 1849, the New York legislature elected Seward to the United States Senate. John Young, the odd Whig out, died of "pulmonary consumption" on April 22, 1852. Obituary writers who portrayed him as the victim of Weed's dictatorship did not mention the title-test resolution Young's own political legerdemain set into motion in 1848. The litigation had not yet run its course. When the New York Court of Appeals finally quashed the government assault on landlord titles in December 1853, the Whig Party itself stood at death's door.[58]

12

Enmeshed in Law

The collapse of the Anti-Rent Party compelled tenant leaders to reassess the movement's prospects. Minor Frink, the new editor of the *Freeholder* in January 1849, found the situation exasperating. "There is but one sentiment everywhere expressed by the people of this state, not even the landlords themselves excepted," he wrote, "and that is that the manorial tenures ought to come speedily to an end." Yet it was not happening. Tenant purchases of landlord interests, in theory the easiest way to extinguish the rent system, required agreement on the terms of sale; several proprietors, led by the Van Rensselaers, still refused to negotiate with the Anti-Rent associations. Only the impending title-test suits kept the movement going. Three outcomes were imaginable, two of which buoyed tenant hopes. Government lawyers might win the cases and thus nullify the property rights of the several great proprietors. Alternatively, the landlords might decide to sell on Anti-Rent terms rather than endure the cost and uncertainty of lengthy litigation. But defeat in the courts, the third possible result, would be disastrous. It would put anti-renters wholly in the power of their landlords. "A morbid anxiety," Frink reported that winter, "prevails very generally among the tenants."[1]

Anti-Rent leaders had not given up on a political solution to the long impasse. "It must at no moment be forgotten that we live under a republican government, a government the chief glory and excellence of which is that it admits of change," Frink reminded *Freeholder* readers. "Under the salutary operation of this principle, an astonishing progress never before known in the history of the world has been made . . . in protecting the rights and property of the masses." Still, the Anti-Rent associations had no legislation to recommend in 1849. The climate for land reform had not been so unfavorable for ten years.[2]

Compensated emancipation was no longer an option. *Gilbert v. Foote* (1848) turned out to be only the first in a flurry of new rulings that converted the state constitution's due process clause into a makeweight for the negative state. Justice Augustus Hand, writing later the same year, emphatically denied the legislature's competence to permit takings by water-powered manufacturing firms for the construction of raceways. "That would be giving the property of A. to B. for private purposes, which cannot be done," he said. "Sites for steam engines, hotels, churches, and other public conveniences might as well be taken by the exercise of this extraordinary power." In 1850 the Court of Appeals announced that previous decisions prohibiting compensated takings, except for facilities that the people generally might use as a matter of right and not merely as a favor, "should be regarded as having settled the point."[3]

Other developments reinforced the growing sense of limits on public institutions. New York's constitution of 1846, with its new restrictions on the state legislature's power to borrow money and bestow privileges on favored corporations, geared the political process more tightly to a market calculus. The election of 1848 tilted national economic policy in the same direction. Two years earlier, when Congress enacted the Walker Tariff and reinstituted the Independent Treasury, Whigs expected deflation and depression to ensue; they gleefully predicted that voters would rally around the American System and sweep Henry Clay into the White House. Events proved them wrong on all counts. Massive exports of grain, stimulated by Parliament's repeal of the Corn Laws and crop failures on the continent, fueled an economic boom. State governments long in default resumed payment of their debts, the volume of bank loans swelled, foreign investment revived, and an era of frenzied railroad construction began. Democrats crowed that they had been right all along. The invisible hand of the market, not the fostering hand of government, generated prosperity. At the Whig convention in June 1848, the party's leadership admitted as much by discarding Clay in favor of Mexican War hero Zachary Taylor. In public policy, as in constitutional law, the Democratic faith in private ordering had trumped the Whig idea of progress nourished by a beneficent state.[4]

Yet the urge to resolve the Anti-Rent controversy was so great that a "new project" blossomed during the New York legislature's 1850 session. This scheme, cosponsored by a Whig and a Democrat, sought to achieve the same ends as an eminent domain law by different means. Its foundation was simple. Landlords hated the idea of defending their British patents in the New York courts. The tenants professed their willingness to buy their farms at a fair price. And the title-test suits, six of which were filed against great proprietors during 1849, gave the legislature a unique opportunity to broker a settlement. The pending lawsuits could be dismissed and the challenged titles confirmed (something the landlords wanted) on condition that every tenant be guaranteed a right to buy out his landlord on terms established by law (something the Anti-Rent associations wanted). While the compromise bill was being framed in committee, however, the New York Supreme Court unwittingly changed the odds of its enactment.[5]

The court's decision in *Overbaugh v. Patrie* (1850), an ejectment case for breach of a quarter-sale condition in an Albany County lease in fee, subdued the anxiety on Rensselaerwyck. The court not only ruled that the quarter-sale requirements were void and unenforceable but grounded its holding on a legal theory that, to Anti-Rent minds, exploded the legality of the rent system. Tenant leaders became convinced that all the "feudal" conditions and covenants in manor contracts were as invalid as the Van Rensselaer land title. Victory seemed once again to be the movement's destiny. The *Freeholder* came out against the compromise bill. So did the state senators from Albany and Rensselaer counties. In 1850, as in 1840 and 1846, a fleeting chance to extinguish manorial tenures by force of law slipped away.[6]

Staking everything on a strategy of litigation proved to be a mistake. When the litigation campaign began, nobody knew for certain how the lease in fee had taken root in New York. Nor did anyone know precisely how to conceptualize the unusual legal form. People had simply presumed its validity for generations. After the initial Anti-Rent triumph in *Overbaugh*, however, the landlords paid for a thorough investigation. Landlord lawyers rediscovered long forgotten statutes and built new defenses on principles of equity jurisprudence that their opponents had overlooked. The battle in the courts transformed New York land law. But the Anti-Rent lawyers, like the founders of the Anti-Rent Party before them, eventually got clobbered from their blind side. When the litigation campaign concluded in April 1859, the remaining Anti-Rent faithful found themselves trapped in a legal labyrinth from which even sympathetic judges and legislators could not help them escape.

Lawyers in Charge

Attorney General Ambrose Jordan and Azor Taber, counsel for the Anti-Rent Association of Albany County, directed the tenant cause in 1849. Both lawyers were Whigs, and both learned their trade in the shadow of manorial tenures. Jordan was born in 1789 at Hillsdale, Columbia County, studied for the bar under Jacob R. Van Rensselaer of Claverack, and practiced in Otsego County for eight years before returning to his native ground in 1820. He headed the team that defended Smith Boughton in the sensational "Big Thunder" prosecutions of 1845. Jordan's ringing critiques of the rent system in the courts and in the constitutional convention of 1846 made him an Anti-Rent favorite. Taber, a native of rural Albany County, had closer ties to tenant leaders at the grass roots. Along with Henry G. Wheaton, his law partner for a time, Taber negotiated the Helderberg War truce during Governor Seward's first term. Defending anti-renters against ejectment became his specialty, then his passion, from 1847 until his death in 1853. *Overbaugh v. Patrie* was his most important case.[7]

Jordan and Taber attacked "patroonery" in different ways. The attorney general challenged the validity of landlord property rights; Taber contested the validity of the conditions and covenants in manor contracts. At one significant point, however, their litigation strategies overlapped. Both claimed that the statute Quia Emptores, enacted by Parliament in 1290, had entered New York law upon the English conquest of New Netherland in the mid-seventeenth century. Taber argued that the quarter-sale conditions in Van Rensselaer indentures were invalid because in colonial New York, as in England, Quia Emptores prohibited fines on alienation whenever the landlord conveyed the land itself (as in a lease in fee) and not merely a right to possess the land for a term of years or lives (as in a conventional lease). Jordan took a similar approach in *People v. Van Rensselaer*. He proceeded on the theory that the original British patent creating the Manor of Rensselaerwyck was void because, as Blackstone had said, "it is essential to a manor, that there be tenants who hold of the lord . . . and no tenant of a common lord since the statute Quia Emptores could create any new tenants to hold of himself."[8] The attorney general was prepared to argue that New York's royal government had violated English law by authorizing the heirs of Kiliaen Van Rensselaer to establish a manor and subinfeudate the land.

The two lawyers neither collaborated nor pursued their tasks with the same enthusiasm. Jordan harbored grave doubts about the title-test campaign from the beginning. He worried, first, about the uncertain foundation of the Quia Emptores argument. The state judiciary had not yet decided when the English statute had entered New York law, let alone considered its effects, and two other theories packed as much punch as the instant-reception doctrine he had to argue. Samuel J. Tilden claimed in 1846 that Quia Emptores had not come into force until the state legislature expressly adopted it following the American Revolution. Joshua A. Spencer, writing the same year, insisted that even if British grants of manor privileges had been illegal in colonial New York, the accompanying grants of land stood on a different footing. In his view, it was immaterial whether Rensselaerwyck had ever been a lawful manor because the Van Rensselaer family's title to the land had vested anyway. Yet the uncertainty surrounding the Quia Emptores question did not concern Jordan as much as the Quiet-Title Act of 1788. It jeopardized all the projected title contests. The act not only compelled the state to prove that the proprietors' British patents were invalid but also that the people of New York had "accrued" title to the land or "received the rents and profits of such real estate" within the previous forty years. Jordan had no idea how such doubtful propositions might be established.[9]

Jordan yearned for a political solution. He took up the tenant cause in 1845 because the rent system had no place in a republican regime dedicated to individual liberty and collective pursuit of the public good. "We are not like

England, wedded to her errors because they are ancient," he remarked during the constitutional convention. "In England, all is stable; here all is changing. There a man reveres as sacred the ancient stone walls of the family mansion occupied by his ancestors a thousand years ago, however uncouth or inconvenient; here we would demolish them and build better." In the fall of 1848, however, Jordan could no longer imagine a substitute for testing landlord titles that was both workable and constitutional. Besides, he understood the partisan character of his job. Over, under, and between the lines of the title-test resolution, the Whig legislature had indicated that the New York judiciary, not the attorney general, should decide whether the people of New York might "lay claim" to the great estates held under "manorial titles."[10]

Preparing the suits vexed Jordan all the same. Tenant leaders crowded his office to press for action, offer advice, and present him with documents. Writers for the *Freeholder* clamored for progress reports. The law gave him trouble too. At the outset, Jordan assumed that the state could attempt to recover any land claimed under the British manor and patent grants. "I want you by some means to procure and send to me a [legal] description of some farm on the Rensselaer tract," he wrote a subordinate in September 1848. "I thought some of commencing the suit on the farm upon which Mr. Van Rensselaer has erected the large house on the east side of the river, but I have no particular choice that I know of: any other farm, one held under a Rensselaer lease will do as well." Jordan still did not comprehend the lease in fee. In March 1849 a circuit judge dismissed the initial complaints Jordan filed against the Van Rensselaers. The people of New York could proceed, explained the judge, only in an action for possession of land held by the landlord. Real estate leased in fee belonged to the tenant, not to the proprietor whose remaining interest arose from conditions and covenants annexed to the land rather than the land itself.[11]

Jordan filed against wild land claimed by the proprietors in the spring of 1849, and this time the complaints survived preliminary motions to dismiss. Hurrahs and hosannas greeted Jordan's announcement of suits against Henry Overing and John Gemmel (Delaware), Stephen Van Rensselaer IV (Albany), William P. Van Rensselaer (Rensselaer), Herman Livingston (Columbia), and George Clarke Jr. (Montgomery and Otsego). But the anti-renters who cheered him were not entirely satisfied. In June the tenant associations revived their call for a law that would suspend rent collections until the validity of landlord titles had been ascertained. The resulting excitement was not surprising. Farmers in all six counties would benefit from a moratorium on rent collections; tenant leaders believed that the struggle for new legislation would enable them to reestablish the Anti-Rent Party. For Jordan, however, the rent-suspension clamor amounted to a last straw. One distinguished lawyer after another had insisted that the proposed legislation was unconstitutional since the decision in

Bronson v. Kinzie (1843), and he agreed with them. Two weeks before the Whig convention on September 26, 1849, Jordan told John L. Schoolcraft, the party's state chairman, that he could not accept a renomination. Another attorney general would have to try the title cases and fight off the rent-suspension bill.[12]

Azor Taber, in contrast, relished his work for the Anti-Rent Association of Albany County. He believed in what he was doing. The gist of his defense in *Overbaugh v. Patrie,* an action of ejectment for breach of a quarter-sale covenant in a lease in fee, was simple yet far-reaching. Taber conceded that the plaintiff would have a right to recover if the legal relation between the parties could be defined as one of landlord and tenant. But he denied the presumption that the plaintiff was a landlord and the defendant a tenant. The so-called tenants of rural Albany County actually owned their farms in fee simple, he argued, and restraints on alienation in fee-simple conveyances had been unlawful since the enactment of Quia Emptores in 1290. Samuel Stevens, the dean of the Albany bar and Taber's opponent in *Overbaugh,* replied that the New York Supreme Court already had considered—and rejected—this very argument in *Jackson* ex. dem *Lewis & Wife v. Schutz* (1820). Nor was *Schutz* the only case on point. Stevens directed the court's attention to the string citation in *Livingston v. Stickles* (1843), where Justice Samuel Nelson had observed that "these covenants, though in restraint of alienation, have been repeatedly held lawful and binding upon landlord and tenant." The trial judge stood on the New York precedents in October 1847. Taber appealed.[13]

Stevens had two things right. Counsel for the defendant in *Schutz* had in fact made the same argument Taber now advanced. Thomas J. Oakley had pointed out that the indentures in force on the Rhinebeck Patent, like those on Rensselaerwyck, were grants "to a man and his heirs and assign[ee]s forever, without any reservation of any part of the interest, to create a reversion." Because the relation of landlord and tenant was, by definition, a relation between one person having the reversion and another having possession, the indenture could not be defined as a lease. It was a grant in fee. And the estate vested in the grantee, Oakley had argued, "must be deemed a fee simple." Stevens was also right about the *Schutz* court's response. It had indeed said that Oakley's claim was "without foundation." Justice Jonas Platt had used the term "lease in fee" to describe the relation between the parties; the term itself implied that the proprietor stood as both grantor and landlord to his tenants in fee. But Stevens overlooked something in *Schutz* that Taber noticed. At no point in Platt's opinion had he indicated the nature and source of the proprietor's reversion. Calling the relation a lease in fee was not to explain how, let alone why, the indenture could be understood as a lease as well as a grant in fee.[14]

Taber was the first person to notice something else in the case law. Of all the reported New York decisions involving the validity of quarter sales, sixth sales, and tenth sales, every one but *Schutz* concerned leases for years or for lives.

Most were Livingston Manor leases or Livingston family leases on the west side of the Hudson. Nevertheless, judges and legislators had cited *Schutz* and the other cases indiscriminately for a generation. Taber insisted that the habit was wrong. At the expiration of every Livingston lease, he pointed out, the land reverted back to the landlord. Restraints on alienation were valid even in long leases because the landlord had a reversion to protect; it followed that the Livingston cases had been decided correctly. In *Schutz*, however, a grievous error had been committed and the court had a duty to overrule it. Ownership of the reversion had provided the only justification for restraints on alienation since the enactment of the statute Quia Emptores. The grantors on Rhinebeck and Rensselaerwyck had reserved a right of reentry for breach of the stipulated conditions and covenants, but they had conveyed the land itself. How, then, could the quarter-sale condition at issue in *Overbaugh* be lawful?[15]

Taber's penetrating question had a sensible answer in 1820. James Emmot supplied it in his *Schutz* argument. He claimed that grants of land in perpetuity, with a reservation of rent and with covenants and conditions annexed, established the feudal tenure Blackstone termed rent service. Landlords who used the lease in fee retained a reversionary interest called an escheat; the "fat fowl" and personal service covenants in every indenture signified a privity of estate between each tenant in fee and his feudal lord. Rent service, though long dead in England, thrived in colonial New York because the act of Parliament that prohibited subinfeudation at home did not apply to the crown's dominion on the Hudson. Quia Emptores entered New York law only upon the legislature's enactment of the Act Concerning Tenures in 1787, Emmot maintained, but even then it did not affect land belonging to British grantees. The New York statute, as Emmot interpreted it, applied only to land conveyed "under the great seal of the State."[16]

When the *Overbaugh* case reached the New York Supreme Court in December 1849, Stevens might have answered Taber's question the same way Emmot had three decades earlier. But the archaic tenure known as rent service provided the legal foundation for a regime that was too hierarchical, too "antirepublican," for the New York mind of 1850. It connoted a monarch who took care of the aristocracy, a landed gentry who took care of the poor, and bonds of reciprocal service that held everything together and everyone in his place. Even conservative Whigs like Stevens and Barnard could not imagine their New York in feudal terms. They understood the lease in fee as a contract between people who, as Barnard said in 1845, "stood before the law of the land upon a footing of perfect civil equality." For Stevens, as for the *Schutz* judges, neither the moment Quia Emptores became part of New York law nor its effect on British grantees had any bearing on the question at hand. "The parties" to manor contracts, Platt had declared, "have a right to bargain as they please."[17]

But the freedom-of-contract principle, vigorous and supple though it was in nineteenth-century America, did not supply a persuasive answer to Taber's argument in *Overbaugh*. Tilden had exposed the *Schutz* court's fallacy in 1846. Platt's opinion "made no distinction between leases in fee and other grants in fee; and applied his construction to both equally," Tilden wrote. "If his dictum that the consent of the grantee can make . . . a condition [restraining alienation] valid is right, then the whole current of English and American adjudications on the point, for five centuries, is wrong." Tilden's withering critique of the *Schutz* decision did not undercut Emmot's theory. The mighty "current" of reported cases turned on the legal consequences of Quia Emptores. And Emmot not only denied that the ancient statute had been in force in colonial New York but also insisted that its adoption in the Act Concerning Tenures did not affect land belonging to British grantees, their heirs, and their assignees. Yet one thing was clear three years before *Overbaugh* reached the New York Supreme Court. The quarter-sale question could not be resolved without considering the timing and scope of New York's reception of Quia Emptores. The court would have to adopt Emmot's rent-service theory, Taber's instant-reception theory, or a third theory that Tilden offered in his committee report of 1846. He claimed that fines on alienation, whether lawful or not in colonial New York, had been abolished generally and retrospectively by the Act Concerning Tenures in 1787.[18]

Stevens lost the *Overbaugh* case by default. The rent-service theory provided the only plausible reply to Taber's argument, and Stevens did not make it. He stood on the authority of *Schutz*; for a conservative Whig that seemed enough. It did not satisfy Justices Amasa J. Parker, Malbone Watson, and William B. Wright. During its February 1850 general term, the New York Supreme Court overruled *Schutz* and distinguished all the precedents involving leases for lives. Parker spoke for the court; he "d[id] not think it necessary" to determine the precise moment when Quia Emptores had become incorporated into New York law. It was sufficient, he thought, to say that ever since the Act Concerning Tenures, if not before, "the common law exist[ed] here under the same statutory modification as in England." The rest of the opinion paraphrased Taber's brief. "To impose a restraint upon alienation," Parker wrote for the court, the grantor "must have a right to the reversion of the estate." The right of reentry reserved in the typical Albany County indenture had never been regarded as a reversion, or a possibility of reverter, at common law. It was a mere right of action. "I think, therefore," Parker concluded, "that the whole estate having been granted in fee, the restraint imposed upon alienation was repugnant to the grant, and is void, and the void condition being a condition subsequent, the estate stands divested of the condition."[19]

Justice Parker's words, strictly construed, meant nothing more than the demise of quarter-sale conditions, which the Van Rensselaers had offered to waive for $30 a farm since 1832. But tenant leaders on the Manor of Rensselaerwyck, in particular, were inclined to read the opinion more broadly. Taber argued that Quia Emptores had entered New York law before the British patents to the manor were issued. And he won. It seemed increasingly likely that Attorney General Jordan's title-test suit, grounded on the theory that the ancient act of Parliament prohibited the manor's very creation, would be a winner too. Nor was that all. Anti-Rent spokesmen had often claimed that manor contracts contained provisions "contrary to the law at the time they were given." *Overbaugh* "divested" one condition in the standard Van Rensselaer indenture; tenant leaders imagined subsequent decisions that would sunder the rent covenants as well. So did a pair of creative Anti-Rent lawyers. In the spring of 1850, Anson Bingham and Andrew J. Colvin began the process of transforming Taber's argument against restraints on alienation into a formidable assault on the enforceability of covenants for rent in a lease in fee. Hot pursuit of their project, however, awaited the response to *Overbaugh* in the New York Court of Appeals. Stevens appealed Parker's decision in March. He and Taber did not square off before the state's highest court until October 1852.[20]

Minor Frink, the editor of the *Freeholder* in 1850, had less patience than the Anti-Rent lawyers. By his lights the collapse of the rent system was at hand. "In view of the redress already obtained in the courts, and of able opinions strongly indicating that much greater advantages are in reserve," Frink declared on April 24, any "landlord who opposes this movement contends against 'manifest destiny,' against an irresistible tide of public opinion and course of human events, and like one climbing against sliding banks of sand, will be overborne and crushed by the superintending weight which overhangs and surrounds him." Frustration, not just overweening confidence, produced Frink's bluster. A showdown between tenants and landlords had occurred during the legislature's 1850 session. Tenant spokesmen demanded a rent moratorium until the long delayed title-test suits had been decided; landlord lawyers strenuously opposed the Anti-Rent measure. Meanwhile, a bipartisan coalition of radical Democrats and conservative Whigs proposed a compromise that would have extinguished manorial tenures in return for the government's dismissal of the title-test suits. Neither bill passed. Frink's editorial, entitled "A Plain Talk with Landlords," grudgingly accepted the stalemate and the resulting all-or-nothing struggle. He assumed that the proprietors had no chance of winning. "Revolutions—especially when they are based on the moral convictions of mankind, and appeal to the innate sense of justice implanted in man," he told them, "never go backward."[21]

The Failed Compromise of 1850

The 1849 election marked the beginning of the end of Whig rule in New York State. During the spring and summer, the Democratic Party's warring factions gradually negotiated a truce. The federal patronage that had sustained the

Hunkers since 1845 now belonged to the Whigs, and the radicals pressed their advantage. John Van Buren and William Cassidy, editor of the *Atlas*, laid down the Barnburner terms for reunion. The main one was toleration of "the free exercise of individual opinions" on the slavery question; William L. Marcy and Horatio Seymour persuaded most conservatives to accommodate the radicals at the party's state convention on September 14. "The day of compromises is past," Van Buren announced shortly before the reunion convention. "But, in regard to candidates for state offices, we are still a commercial people. We will unite with our late antagonists." All but a few "hard-shell" Hunkers ratified the deal in November. Democrats won exactly half of the assembly races, trimmed the Whig majority in the senate to 17-15, and elected Levi Chatfield attorney general.[22]

Tenant voters enabled Chatfield to roll up a larger majority than anyone else on the Democratic ticket. Yet anti-renters did not rally behind him so much as they cast their ballots against the Whig candidate. At the Whig convention on September 26, Samuel Stevens was nominated "peremptorily and without a vote" moments after Schoolcraft read Ambrose Jordan's letter of declination. "This will be news to most of our readers," Frink remarked dryly in the *Freeholder*. Frink's call for an Anti-Rent state convention did not evoke the response he expected. Only a handful of delegates showed up on October 17; they declined to make any nominations for the state offices and thus confirmed the death of the Anti-Rent Party. Twenty-four hours later, however, Albany County anti-renters convened a mass meeting that urged tenant voters everywhere to spurn "the landlord lawyer" at the polls. Cassidy's *Atlas* helped spread the word by featuring the Anti-Rent resolution in its columns and recounting details of Stevens's long association with the Van Rensselaer family. Approximately 4,000 "Anti-Rent Whigs" voted for Chatfield.[23]

Attorney General Chatfield paid his debt to manor tenants on January 14, 1850. Prodded by a senate resolution asking for information on the pending title-test litigation, he described the suits already filed and reported that he intended to prosecute them to a conclusion. "Suggestions have been made to me, that while these manorial titles are undergoing judicial investigation under the joint resolution of the two houses of the legislature, collection of rents on leases, and principal and interest on contracts of sale, should cease, and should be restrained by legislative enactment," Chatfield wrote. "This measure seems to me to be just; for if the claims of the state shall be finally established, and the pretended title of the landlords be declared void for any reason, the tenants will have paid money to which the landlord is not justly entitled; and being voluntarily paid on the claim of right, can never be recovered by the tenant." Hamilton Fish, the Whig governor, had ignored the clamor for a rent moratorium in his annual message. Chatfield, the Democratic attorney general, forthrightly recommended that such an act be passed.[24]

Legislation of the sort Chatfield endorsed already had been introduced in the assembly by his friend Edward Pratt, a Democrat from Otsego, and in the senate by an Albany Whig named S. H. Johnson. Both bills were reported out of committee on February 13. Assemblyman Pratt filed a written report. Until the title-test litigation had run its course, he contended, tenants on the affected estates had no duty to pay rent. "The state having set up an original and exclusive claim to these lands, it remains good until somebody establishes a better one," Pratt explained. "In the meantime the tenants of the same are the tenants of the state, and must be considered as occupying the property of the state." Reuben Walworth, counsel for George Clarke Jr., disagreed. The former chancellor argued that John Marshall's "strong and conclusive reasoning" in *Fletcher v. Peck* (1810) exploded Pratt's main premise. Whatever the merits of the pending title suits, Walworth insisted, the government's mere assertion of a superior claim to land could not justify legislation disturbing contracts among persons with vested rights in the same land. In his judgment, it was absurd to think that calling the lessees of New York's great proprietors "tenants of the state" might dissolve their legal obligations. Because the proposed rent moratorium amounted to a stay law, Walworth observed, it would surely be struck down for the same reason analogous Illinois legislation had been declared unconstitutional in *Bronson v. Kinzie* (1843). The stage was set for another floor fight in the New York legislature. Its unhappy conclusion persuaded Whigs and Democrats alike to give up the search for a political solution to the Anti-Rent controversy.[25]

The debate began in the senate with a sponsor speech by S. H. Johnson on February 18 and ended in the lower house at two o'clock in the morning on April 11, the final day of the legislature's 1850 session. Two things became clear right away. First, the rent system had no defenders. Henry B. Stanton, a renowned radical Democrat, spoke for all his colleagues in the senate when he decried "the curse of the feudal system on our republican soil." "While I will maintain to the letter all the constitutional rights of these landlords," he declared, "yet, so abhorrent is their unnatural and antirepublican system to every feeling of my heart . . . that I will go to the very verge of the Constitution to . . . bring this system to a perpetual end." Second, Johnson and his Rensselaer colleague Thomas B. Carroll—a Democrat—were the only senators who believed that the moratorium bill could pass constitutional muster. Even the members from other Anti-Rent counties remained unpersuaded. Yet the naysayers offered two different ways of approaching the seemingly insuperable Contract Clause obstacles to the bill demanded by "some five thousand tenant petitioners."[26]

Each alternative method attracted bipartisan support. One group of senators favored a substitute that, like the title-test resolution that engendered it, was designed to throw the matter into the courts. The substitute, proposed on February 21 by Marinus Schoonmaker (W.-Ulster) and John Snyder (D.-Columbia), provided "that if any landlord or proprietor, during the pendency of any suit against him by the attorney general to test his title, shall commence any suits or proceedings to collect rents . . . the Supreme Court, upon special motion, may on such terms and upon payment of the rent or money into court, or filing of such security as the court shall direct in view of the particular equities and circumstances of the case, stay all proceedings until the further order of the court." Other senators opposed the substitute for the same reason they opposed Johnson's bill. Charles A. Mann, a radical Democrat from Utica, and George Babcock, a conservative Whig from Buffalo, believed that both measures evaded the real issue at hand. Each was predicated on the assumption that the title-test litigation should go forward. Mann and Babcock insisted that the legislature should focus, instead, on the abolition of manorial tenures. On February 20, Johnson challenged them "to concoct some plan for the settlement of these manorial difficulties in a constitutional manner." Mann not only "accepted the invitation" but soon produced a bill that Babcock compared with the "omnibus resolutions" Senator Henry Clay had just proposed as a solution to the sectional crisis over slavery. Both relied on the spirit of compromise to harmonize dangerously estranged social interests.[27]

Floor discussion ceased temporarily on March 12, when the senators referred both the original rent-moratorium bill and the proposed substitute to a select committee. Johnson and Carroll lost the ensuing fight in committee; nine days later, the milk-and-water substitute was reported out and ordered to a third reading. The senate agreed to resume debate on March 23. Meanwhile, the Judiciary Committee reported out the promised Mann-Babcock bill. Introduced on March 20, it provided for a conditional yet "full and complete confirmation, on the part of the people of this state," of all "titles, estates and interests now held and claimed by the landlords or grantors" in the several Anti-Rent counties. The bill's "express condition" incorporated the very demand set forth in the "Anti-Renters' Declaration of Independence" (1839). Proprietors could not obtain the proffered confirmation of title, thus triggering the dismissal of title-test suits, until the attorney general had received a promise to sell all reserved interests in tenant farms for "a sum of money which, invested at the rate of seven percent interest, will yield the annual income equal to the rent reserved in such grant or lease." Where the existing indenture stipulated payment in wheat, its value was to be estimated at one dollar per bushel; where the rents reserved were payable "in articles other than money or wheat, or in services," the bill provided for their extinguishment at a value determined by three persons chosen by the affected proprietors and tenant associations.[28]

Mann consulted with Minor Frink before taking the bill to the senate floor. Their conversation did not result in a meeting of minds. On March 20, the very day Mann introduced the measure, Frink denounced it in the *Freeholder*. "That this scheme originated with the landlords," he reported, "there cannot be a doubt." Mann and Babcock claimed otherwise in their committee report, but the charge contained a kernel of truth. Their inclination to seek Frink's advance assent suggests that they had discussed the measure with spokesmen for the great proprietors. Rents in arrear posed one problem as the advocates of compromise tried to accommodate everyone concerned. The Van Rensselaers refused to forgive the back rents and thus ratify the legitimacy of the eleven-year rent strike; because the bill hinged on voluntary action on the part of landlords, it provided that rents in arrear had to be "satisfactorily secured" by a mortgage as part of the final settlement. Yet the back-rent provision, though necessary to obtain Van Rensselaer cooperation, made the Mann-Babcock bill unacceptable to Anti-Rent leaders. They, too, demanded the right to declare victory after such a long and bloody struggle. Like their landlords, manor tenants were inclined to take their chances in the title-test suits rather than submit to a dishonorable compromise.[29]

The *Overbaugh* decision shaped the Anti-Rent response to the Mann-Babcock bill. Frink interpreted the quest for compromise as a sign that the Van Rensselaers were attempting to pull victory from the jaws of certain defeat. He jumped to the conclusion that the statute Quia Emptores, which had beaten the patroons in the quarter-sale case, would beat them again in the title-test suit. "The very fact of the state's relinquishing its claims to these lands, the title of which is in dispute," Frink told *Freeholder* readers, "implies that those claims are good—that the lands are vested in the people." Senators Carroll of Rensselaer and Johnson of Albany saw things the same way. After opposing the Schoonmaker-Snyder substitute to the bitter end, they became its most vocal supporters when debate resumed. Enacting the court-supervised suspension measure figured to perform two functions. It would definitely kill the "landlord inspired" Mann-Babcock bill, and it might induce the Van Rensselaers to offer better terms in subsequent settlement talks.[30]

When the senate took up the Schoonmaker-Snyder bill on March 23, Babcock pleaded with his colleagues to recommit it so that the Judiciary Committee's compromise measure could be discussed instead. The adoption of the title-test resolution in 1848, he said, marked "an evil hour for the honor of the state, and the peace and welfare of the tenants." The suits were bound to drag on for years and result in landlord victories, for the Quiet-Title Act of 1788 meant "the state is estopped at every point of attack." Enabling the courts to prolong the agony by acting as receivers of rent, then, was exactly the wrong thing to do. Babcock's motion to recommit lost all the same; the senate proceeded to pass the emasculated moratorium bill by a vote of 18-10. Anti-Rent leaders hailed the senate's action less for its practical significance than its symbolic import. They won because the landlord agents had been beaten. "If the assembly will pass the constitutional, just, and politic bill which has passed the senate and is now before them," the *Freeholder* declared on April 3, "by another session of the legislature the landlords will be willing to settle this vexed question on reasonable terms, and the tenantry and people will be relieved from an odious system and a disgraceful controversy."[31]

The senate bill failed in the assembly. Attorney General Chatfield urged the Democratic members to pass it and thus reestablish the party's strength in the Anti-Rent counties. The vast majority complied. Of the 56 assemblymen who voted for the bill, 45 were Democrats. Only 5 Democrats and 31 Whigs said nay. But the constitution of 1846 provided that "no bill shall be passed unless by the assent of a majority of all the members elected to each branch of the legislature," and one-fourth of the house—22 Whigs and 14 Democrats—refused to vote at all. Henry J. Raymond, a progressive Whig, had the last word in the legislature's fruitless 1850 session. "I should be very glad," Raymond said as he cast his vote against the measure, "to aid in the passage of some law which would convert, more or less rapidly, by a just, fair and satisfactory process, these leasehold estates into estates in fee." But the bill before the house, he insisted, would merely "create new occasions of controversy and dissension." Raymond contended that the oppressive landlord-tenant relation in eastern New York required government intervention of an altogether different kind, "involving appropriations to be made and borne by the people of the whole state." This cry for compensated emancipation was the last one heard from a public official during the Anti-Rent era.[32]

Raymond spoke in protest, not to offer a prescription for government action. He knew that his Whig colleague, Joel B. Nott of Guilderland, Albany County, had introduced a resolution early in the session that instructed the Judiciary Committee to report out an eminent domain measure. In a long February 12 speech, Nott supported his resolution with an analogy the Anti-Rent associations had often drawn since 1840: "I say if you can pass such an act for the purpose of a railroad, *a fortiori*, you may pass an act for the benefit of these tenants who have . . . been ground to dust by the operation of this system, derived from one of the darkest ages the world ever knew." But the call for an eminent domain law went nowhere. All the lawyers in both parties flogged the railroad analogy, invoked the lengthening list of judicial decisions holding that "reasons and motives of public policy do not constitute a 'public use,'" and asked Nott why he had not proposed, "as consistency would require him," the appointment of government commissioners "to regulate the price at which all lands should be sold . . . as well as the price of bank stock, canal boats, horses, cattle and, in fine, of every description of merchantable property."[33]

Neither Raymond nor anyone else defended Nott's resolution in February.

But its demise in the assembly, coupled with the death of the Mann-Babcock bill in the senate, created a situation that was as "antirepublican" as the manorial tenures supposedly at issue in the house vote on April 11, 1850. Lawmakers supported the landlord position, the Anti-Rent position, or fled the chamber to avoid being counted on one side or the other. In effect, Raymond deplored the conditions of law and politics that had converted the New York legislature from the deliberative, public-regarding body Whigs had celebrated since the party's founding into a powerless forum for the expression of class conflict. His melancholy remarks amounted to a requiem for the Anti-Rent era in New York politics.

Division and Decline

In the early summer of 1845, when the Anti-Rent associations stood at a crossroads and considered various routes to land reform, George Henry Evans issued a warning. Pursuit of the title-test scheme, he said, would divide the tenantry. Each manor and great patent derived from a different British grant; thus arguments about the validity of "monarchical parchments" would incline the Anti-Rent region's farmers to think of themselves as tenants of particular landlords rather than as a body of "*men*" united to destroy an "antirepublican" land system.[34] Evans's forecast proved prophetic. Litigating landlord titles highlighted differences among the tenants and sapped their shared aspirations. As the government suits went forward, it became increasingly clear that Assemblyman Raymond's disillusionment with the legislative process would be nothing compared to Anti-Rent disillusionment with the judicial process.

The first effect of the title-test suits was to crush the movement in five counties. Attorney General Jordan disappointed tenants in Schoharie and Schenectady by determining that the state had no case against the proprietors of either the 50,000-acre Scott Patent or the 30,000-acre Duanesburg estate. Anti-Rent arguments against both patents focused on the conditions annexed to the British grants that required settlement of a specified number of families within a prescribed number of years. And the conditions had not been fulfilled in the allotted time. According to Jordan, however, the settlement requirements had been conditions subsequent to the acquisition of title. Because both grants had been valid in British law before the American Revolution, the validity of both had been guaranteed by the Treaty of Paris that confirmed American independence. Levi Chatfield agreed with his predecessor's view, and the Anti-Rent era ended overnight in two movement strongholds.[35]

The state's case against Henry Overing and John Gemmel had a comparable effect on the tenant movement in Greene, Ulster, and Sullivan counties. *People v. Overing*, which went to trial in October 1850, turned on the "true" western boundary of the Hardenbergh Patent. The state tried to prove that the British grant extended only to the East Branch of the Delaware River; the proprietors claimed that it ran to the West Branch. But even if the government's argument prevailed, one result would be to confirm all landlord titles on the patent between the Hudson River and the East Branch of the Delaware. Tenant families on the half-million uncontested acres had no choice but to surrender on whatever terms their landlords demanded.[36]

Azor Taber's litigation strategy divided anti-renters along still other lines. His attack on the lease in fee as a violation of the statute Quia Emptores provided a backstop for tenants on Rensselaerwyck. If the title litigation failed and the Court of Appeals accepted his position in *Overbaugh*, a new and possibly passable route to victory over "patroonery" would burst open. At the heart of Taber's argument, however, lay a distinction between grants in fee having conditions and covenants that ran forever (the standard indenture in force on Van Rensselaer lands) and leases for lives (the legal form employed on Livingston Manor, much of Delaware County, and the George Clarke Jr. tracts in Montgomery and Otsego). Taber conceded the lawfulness of the latter legal relation. In the spring of 1850, then, only one frayed thread connected the remaining Anti-Rent faithful as brothers in a common cause. The tenants of Clarke, Overing, the Livingstons, and the Van Rensselaers all hoped that the Quiet-Title Act of 1788 would not serve as a bar to the state's assault on landlord titles. The great proprietors, on the other hand, felt confident of victory. Their attorneys could not see how the state could possibly win.

Landlord lawyers assumed at the outset that the government suits might be answered with demurrers grounded on the Quiet-Title Act. In other words, they could simply deny that the people's supposed title had "accrued" since 1809 and deny that the people had received any rents or profits from the land at issue during the previous forty years. If the demurrers were upheld, the attorney general would have to begin each case by establishing one of those extremely doubtful propositions. In *People v. Van Rensselaer*, decided in May 1850, Justice Augustus Hand dealt the landlords a temporary setback. The court held that title must be presumed to be in the people whenever an action of ejectment had been brought in their name. For Hand, it followed that the defendant proprietors had to answer the state's case against their British patents yet could assert their Quiet-Title Act defenses in the same trial.[37]

Justice Hand's ruling merely prolonged the agony of Anti-Rent defeat. John C. Spencer for William P. Van Rensselaer immediately amended his pleadings to conform with the court's decision. But the resulting trial, the only one to feature the Quia Emptores argument, did not occur until September 1852. Counsel for Henry Overing and Herman Livingston followed Spencer's lead and got earlier dates on court calendars. The *Overing* case, tried at Delhi in

October 1850, lasted two weeks and resulted in a hung jury; the *Livingston* case went to trial in Hudson a month later. Justice William B. Wright, who had been elected on the Whig and Anti-Rent tickets in 1847, surprised his tenant friends by holding that the British patents for Livingston Manor were valid. Yet nothing was settled. Attorney General Chatfield vowed to retry *Overing*, and he filed an appeal in *Livingston*.[38]

People v. Clarke, decided in March 1851, had the same procedural history as the others but yielded a more ominous result. Chatfield and his hired special counsel, John Van Buren, argued that the 12,700-acre Corry Patent in Montgomery County had been obtained by fraudulent means. George Clarke, the ancestor of the defendant, had been lieutenant governor of New York when the grant was made in 1737; British law authorized him to grant land and issue letters patent to anyone except himself. Chatfield and Van Buren tried to prove an allegation that has been sustained by modern scholarship. William Corry, the formal grantee, was nothing more than a dummy entryman who conveyed every acre to Clarke for no consideration the following year. Nevertheless, Justice Daniel Cady ruled that the Quiet-Title Act compelled a judgment for the defendant. Because the Clarke family had held the land adversely to the people for the forty years prescribed by the statute, Cady declared, the defendant's title was as good as anyone's in New York State. Attorney General Chatfield appealed, and Minor Frink remonstrated in the *Freeholder*. "How an admitted and palpable fraud can ever become a right," Frink fumed, "is what puzzles those unused to legal abstractions. If it is a right, it must be the same sense in which catching Negroes in the free states is a legal right (or rather wrong)." He and Chatfield both reported that the government's appeal in the *Clarke* case would determine the fate of the Anti-Rent movement.[39]

Chatfield should have known better. *People v. Arnold*, one of two suits filed under the title-test resolution of 1848 that did not involve the Anti-Rent agitation, had a distinctive procedural history and reached the Court of Appeals well ahead of the others. William Arnold, the defendant, was the resident agent for a group of British and Dutch capitalists who claimed title to the Pultney estate in western New York. Sir William Pultney had apparently died intestate in 1805. At trial Attorney General Jordan told Justice Thomas A. Johnson that the people of New York intended to recover possession on an escheat theory; the demurrer entered for Arnold merely recited the provisions of the Quiet-Title Act. Justice Johnson, unlike his colleague Hand in *People v. Van Rensselaer*, sustained the demurrer and gave judgment for the defendant in October 1849. If the Court of Appeals affirmed the decision, the title-test enterprise would conclude before the showcase prosecution against the Van Rensselaers even went to trial.[40]

The *Arnold* case was argued in the Court of Appeals during its January 1851 term. Chatfield insisted that the defendant could not merely invoke the Quiet-Title Act, deny the people's title, and thrust the entire burden of proof upon the state. The challenged proprietor had to establish some right in himself. "To succeed with such a defense," he contended, "the defendant must show an adverse possession of forty years or a grant from the people." The attorney general claimed that when the legislature enacted the 1788 law, its "intention . . . was [only] to protect a party who had been in possession for forty years." Chatfield made the only argument that would permit the government suits to go forward. Yet the assault on landlord titles became a meaningless exercise when Chief Justice Greene Bronson, speaking for the court, accepted his main point. Even if the government eventually won every suit against the proprietors, it would not help their tenants. All of them—whether they lived on estates claimed by the Van Rensselaers, the Livingstons, Clarke, or Overing—had held their farms, adversely to the supposed title of New York State, for more than forty years.[41]

An appropriate messenger delivered the bad news to manor tenants. When *People v. Van Rensselaer* finally went to trial in September 1852, Justice Ira Harris ruefully explained that the very rationale of the government's challenge had been annihilated by the *Arnold* decision. "To the owners of the 3,000 farms which for more than forty years have been occupied by persons who entered under, and have held in subordination to the manor title," Harris said, "it is quite immaterial whether that title was, in its origin, legal or illegal." The Quiet-Title Act, "as construed by the Court of Appeals," barred government action against "the occupants of such lands, and those under whom they occupy." He pointed out that the adverse possession principle, though unwelcome in this context, had a reasonable basis. "As twenty years continued adverse possession of land will bar the right of an individual, however good his title, or however defective the title under which the occupant entered," Harris declared, "so a continued holding in hostility to the people for forty years is held to bar the right of the people, however valid that right might otherwise have been." Tilden told Harris as much in 1846, but the Whig/Anti-Rent leader had been so intoxicated by the Quia Emptores argument that he had refused to listen.[42]

Harris sought a measure of vindication all the same. His opinion for the court authorized the people of New York to seize possession of the Van Rensselaer wild lands at issue in the suit. He negated the Quiet-Title defense by ruling that neither regular payment of taxes nor periodic action against trespassers amounted to possession of the premises in hostility to the state's title. And he held that the British patents for the Manor of Rensselaerwyck were void because they conferred "manorial privileges and franchises . . . upon the lord of the manor" in "express violation of the established law" laid down by Parliament. The decision failed to stick. In December 1853, the Court of Appeals unanimously rejected both strands of Harris's opinion. Even if Quia Emptores had been in force in colonial New York, Justice Hiram Denio explained, the court below erred in supposing that the grant of manor privileges was inseparable from the British government's conveyance of the land. Denio pointed out that "there is no legal difficulty in declaring," first, that the Van Rensselaers were "entitled to retain the lands" and, second, that their tenants held of the British crown until 1776 and the people of New York thereafter "instead of the patentee and his heirs." Harris's defeat was complete.[43]

The title-test fiasco destroyed the last remnants of the Anti-Rent movement in Columbia, Montgomery, Otsego, and Delaware counties. Chatfield dismissed the pending appeals in *Livingston* and *Clarke* as he left office on December 31, 1853; the *Overing* case was never retried. Governor Horatio Seymour, a long-standing opponent of testing landlord titles, insisted that the result benefited everyone. "The principal obstacles to negotiation between the parties have been removed," he told the state legislature in January 1854. "In numerous instances the tenants have availed themselves of the abundance of money and the high prices commanded by the productions of the soil, to secure full ownership of their lands upon favorable terms." Voluntary transactions were indeed wiping out the rent system in much of eastern New York. But Seymour's commitment to private ordering blinded him to its principal weakness. Landlords had no legal obligation to sell out at all, let alone "upon favorable terms." George Clarke Jr. defiantly turned down every tenant offer to buy the family farm; he converted leases for lives into leases for years, as required by the constitution of 1846, when the existing tenants died or moved away. There were reports as late as 1878 of Montgomery County farmers who burned down their houses and threw down their fences rather than allow the fruits of their labor to vest in Clarke when their leases expired. The spirit of Anti-Rent died hard.[44]

Only on the Manor of Rensselaerwyck did the tenants still have a chance of defeating their landlord foes after 1853. Azor Taber's second line of defense against the Van Rensselaers had been strengthened by the New York Court of Appeals during its October 1852 term. In *De Peyster v. Michael*, a quarter-sale suit arising on Claverack that was argued with *Overbaugh v. Patrie* and decided the same day, the court not only held that fines on alienation were unlawful in a lease in fee but also laid the foundation for a subsequent attack on the enforceability of Van Rensselaer rent covenants. The decision evoked celebrations from the eastern villages of Rensselaer County to the Helderberg towns in western Albany. It offset the humiliating defeat in the title contest and saved the tenants from having to visit the manor offices, hat in hand, to accept the Van Rensselaer terms of sale. Anti-Rent lawyers hailed the decision for another reason. The statute Quia Emptores finally cut as large a figure in New York law as it had in Anti-Rent politics.

The Lease in Fee Besieged

Chief Justice Charles Ruggles, one of the New York Democracy's most capable jurists, spoke for the Court of Appeals in the *De Peyster* case. He had good reason to keep the opinion for himself. Taber's brief, read with Tilden's previous argument against the validity of quarter-sale conditions, made it clear that a major landmark in the law of real property was about to be laid down. Ruggles wanted to produce an opinion as great as the occasion. His first few paragraphs tracked Judge Parker's reasoning in the court below. He distinguished leases from grants in fee, mustered a spate of authorities to show that a grantor in fee lacked the reversion necessary to fetter the grantee's right of alienation, and overruled the *Schutz* decision of 1820. But he did not stop there. Ruggles, being a good Democrat, located the ultimate source of the bar against restraints on alienation in natural law. "The reason why such a condition cannot be made good, by agreement or consent of the parties," he wrote, "is that a fee-simple estate and a restraint upon its alienation cannot in their nature co-exist." Aristotle understood that " 'it is the definition of property to have in one's self the power of alienation.' "[45]

Saying that one incident of the lease in fee violated natural law ineluctably begged several linked questions. How did such an unnatural legal form take root in New York? What extinguished it in law, if not in practice, such that the court's decision in *De Peyster* became predestined? And how could the resulting legal relation between the Van Rensselaers and their fee-simple grantees be defined with precision? Ruggles answered the first question the same way James Emmot did in 1820. He concluded that Quia Emptores had not been incorporated into New York law during the long period of British rule. "This assumption," he said, "is in conformity with the action and understanding of the colonial government." After all, New York's royal governors not only created manors but also permitted their grantees to subinfeudate the land. What emerged on the Manor of Rensselaerwyck and the Claverack proprietorship carved from it in 1704, then, was the archaic feudal tenure known as rent service. The patroon in each Van Rensselaer household was both grantor and landlord to his tenants in fee, and the resulting privity of estate sanctioned the quarter-sale conditions throughout the colonial era.[46]

Ruggles followed Tilden rather than Emmot on the second question. He declared that the Act Concerning Tenures, passed in 1787, "took effect retrospectively, and operated upon all lands and tenures held under colonial grants." Ruggles conceded that his interpretation of the Revolutionary era statute, unlike his assessment of the situation in colonial New York, was at odds with the behavior of the very people most responsible for its passage. Still, he stuck to his guns. The "indirect and consequential" effect of the 1787 act, Ruggles asserted, "may not have been observed by the landholders, or the scriveners who drew their leases. The legality of these restraints on alienation in leases in fee, before the Revolution, and their legality in leases for lives and years, before and after that period, may have led, and most probably, did lead, to their continuance in the leases in fee." Whatever the Revolutionary era's lawyers and landholding politicians thought, however, the fact remained that the Act Concerning Tenures strangled fines on alienation in all the fee-simple conveyances of New York State just as Quia Emptores had in England.[47]

Chief Justice Ruggles's answer to the third question evoked another round of acrimonious litigation. The act of 1787, he said, "converted all rents upon leases in fee, from rent-service, into rent charges . . . and by taking away the grantor's reversion or escheat, removed the entire foundation on which the power of a grantor to restrain alienation by his grantee formerly rested." This transformation established a legal regime on Rensselaerwyck that was not feudal at all. "It is what was anciently called a fee-farm estate," Ruggles explained. "A fee-farm rent is a rent charge, issuing out of an estate in fee; a grant of lands in fee, reserving rent, is only letting lands to farm *in fee-simple*, instead of the usual methods for life or years." In other words, the Van Rensselaers were not really landlords. Manor farmers did not hold of the patroons or have privity of estate with them. Two distinct estates were created by conveyances reserving a rent charge. "The grantor owns the rent," Ruggles said, "and the grantee owns the land." The problem with this analysis—if a problem it was—lay in its ahistorical foundation. The eighteenth-century proprietors worked from the premise that they stood as both landlord and grantor to their tenants in fee. By cutting down the Van Rensselaers's right to act as landlords, Ruggles set forces into motion that also threatened their right to collect the rents reserved forever in the manor grants to settlers.[48]

Two thoughtful lawyers, Anson Bingham of Troy and Andrew J. Colvin of Albany, were quick to see the possibilities implicit in *De Peyster*. In 1853 they announced a new and electrifying Anti-Rent argument: Stephen Van Rensselaer III once "own[ed] the rent," as Chief Justice Ruggles said, but his sons no longer did. Prodigious research in law books ancient and modern enabled Bingham and Colvin to show that covenants for rent could run with the land at common law only in the landlord-tenant relation. The landlord's reversion legitimated such covenants in leases for lives or years; the tenurial connection between grantor and grantee performed the same function where grants in fee established a rent service. Grantors and grantees with a rent-charge relation, in contrast, lacked the privity of estate necessary to make the obligation to pay rent a real one (attached to the land) rather than a personal one (between the contracting parties). Bingham and Colvin found English cases indicating that rent charges were not legally binding on the grantee's devisees or assignees, and they found still others holding that grantors could not devise rent charges by will or assign them to strangers. For the young Anti-Rent lawyers, the implications were clear and incontrovertible. Upon the death of Stephen Van Rensselaer III in 1839, both the right to collect rent and the right of reentry for failure to pay it had been cut off by operation of law. Any intention to the contrary by the original parties to Rensselaerwyck contracts was immaterial. Just as the Act Concerning Tenures had the "indirect and consequential" effect of extinguishing fines on alienation, so it nullified the Van Rensselaer attempt to fasten liability for rent to the land in perpetuity.[49]

Bingham and Colvin provided a powerful summary of their case against the most important reservation in the Van Rensselaer indentures. "A covenant for the payment of rent, when made by a grantee in fee, has never been held to run with the land in England since the statute of Quia Emptores was enacted, nor in any state of our own country where a similar act prevails," they declared. "If there be a covenant to pay, it is only personal and collateral, and can never, by possibility, become a burden upon the land." The farmers on Rensselaerwyck grasped the gist of the argument. In the *De Peyster* decision, New York's highest court had said that the Van Rensselaers were not their landlords and they were not tenants. Why, then, should they pay rent? And so the rent strike continued with a new justification.[50]

The anti-renters of Albany and Rensselaer counties stood alone in 1853 just as they had in 1839. But the politicians and journalists who took up their cause at the outset had stopped paying attention. The quest for a political solution to the Anti-Rent agitation had ended in exhaustion after a decade of effort; even the *Freeholder* had ceased to exist. Daniel Dewey Barnard said it would end like this shortly after Evans implored the Anti-Rent faithful to swear off the title-test chimera. They bet on the same horse too. Barnard insisted that "there are too many men of property in this country . . . to allow debts, in any form, finally to be repudiated," and Evans contended that reliance on "a lawyer's argument" would mean certain defeat. In the Anti-Rent controversy, as in the sectional conflict over slavery, people on the far right and the far left saw the future more clearly than their peers.[51]

Perpetual Rent

A new order emerged on Rensselaerwyck as the next phase of Anti-Rent litigation began. In 1853 Stephen Van Rensselaer IV, besieged by creditors and tired of paying taxes on rent charges he could not collect, sold his interests in the Albany County farms to a speculator named Walter S. Church. The asking price was lower than anything he had ever offered manor families; Stephen accepted a bid of sixty cents on the dollar. But he did not surrender. Unlike

John A. King, who had struck a mutually beneficial bargain with the Blenheim Anti-Rent Association in 1847, Stephen preferred to make his refractory tenants suffer as much as he did. The contract with Church required the speculator to collect and remit the back rents on each farm before taking title to the indentures. Stephen got $210,000 in cash, paid off Barnard and his other creditors, and lived on the income generated by the 150,000 acres that had never been leased in fee and the Court of Appeals had said belonged to him. William P. Van Rensselaer held out for another four years. He offered anti-renters in Rensselaer the same terms his half brother accepted from Church, and about half of them took the deal. In 1857 he conveyed all his interests in the other farms, including the back rents, to Church for forty cents on the dollar. William already had sold his "magnificent mansion" and 650 acres of ground at Bath, just across the Hudson from the state capital, to Paul C. Forbes of Boston. He got $62,500 for the house, accepted $42,000 for the last of the manor contracts in Rensselaer, and lived out his final days peacefully in Westchester County.[52]

Most of the writs that beset anti-renters and kept their lawyers bustling still carried the Van Rensselaer name. Yet everyone knew that Church was the real party in interest. Beginning in 1854, he offered to sell out for $2.60 an acre and carry a mortgage that secured the principal sum, plus the back rents and accrued interest, at a rate of 7 percent. And he made it clear that anyone who declined the offer would lose his farm. Church's lawyers, Charles M. Jenkins of Albany and William A. Beach of Troy, ran two of the nation's busiest law offices during the late 1850s. Some 2,000 writs of ejectment were drafted and filed in the court of record; the Act to Abolish Distress for Rent, passed in 1846, required every such writ to be preceded by a fifteen-day notice of the grantor's intention to reenter. Church often traveled along with the process server and restated his settlement terms to farmers who would listen. "We hated him like pisen," an Albany County native recalled many years later. "It finally got so he was too scared to come up here 'cause they shot through his plug hat once and another time just under his buggy seat."[53]

Bingham and Colvin kept the county sheriffs at bay for years with demurrers, lengthy trials, and motions to stay execution as they worked to get a test case before the Court of Appeals. The opposition they encountered from the judiciary, however, matched the resistance Church met in the countryside. Anti-renters expected a more sympathetic response from the New York Supreme Court of the third district. A three-judge panel heard oral argument in the batch of key cases reported together as *Van Rensselaer v. Smith* (1858), and two of the judges had strong records of devotion to the cause. Ira Harris was once the most prominent figure in the Anti-Rent movement. His public persona rested on the proposition that, as he put it in 1846, "manorial tenures have many of the badges of slavery, that devouring cancer upon the very intestines of our republic." William B. Wright, the presiding justice in *Smith*, had been a steadfast Whig/Anti-Rent politician before going on the bench with Harris in 1847. And his complaints about manorial tenures had not abated. "The enlightened of all classes admit," Wright declared in 1850, that the rent system "retards the accumulation of property by those immediately engaged in cultivating the soil," "paralyzes their energies," "weakens [their] innate sense of independence," and "fosters invidious distinctions amongst our citizens." Bingham and Colvin presented these men with an opportunity to make a bold, perhaps decisive, emancipation proclamation for the people on Rensselaerwyck. Yet neither Harris nor Wright could bring himself to write the requisite judicial opinion.[54]

The burden of New York's manorial past crushed the land reform impulses of the two Anti-Rent judges. In one respect, the argument of Bingham and Colvin in *Smith* mirrored the argument Taber advanced so successfully in the cases involving restraints on alienation. The young Anti-Rent lawyers distinguished a lease from a grant in fee and stressed the legal consequences of the lessor's reversion and the grantor's failure to retain one in the land conveyed. In another respect, however, the two arguments diverged. The quarter-sale conditions Taber attacked had not been sanctioned by the New York legislature; he merely had to persuade the courts to declare them inoperative. But the rent covenants Bingham and Colvin attacked did not have their foundation in contract alone. New York lawmakers had presumed for seventy years that "feudal" tenures survived the American Revolution in the eastern counties. As a result, the *Revised Statutes* included provisions investing Church with the legal capacity to do what Bingham and Colvin contended could not be done at common law.

Three statutes, in particular, undermined the ingenious Anti-Rent argument framed by the movement's second generation of lawyers. One was the very Act Concerning Tenures that Chief Justice Ruggles had invoked in the *De Peyster* case to wipe out fines on alienation. It not only incorporated Quia Emptores into New York law but also stated that "this act . . . shall not take away, nor be construed to take away or discharge any rents certain or other services . . . due or to grow due to any mesne lord, or other private person." A more significant statute, enacted in 1805, had been forgotten by the New York bar until Church's counsel rediscovered it. Passed in response to an obscure New York Supreme Court decision holding that rent charges were not assignable in law, though the grantor's executors could enforce them in equity, the act clothed persons claiming through grantors in fee with what Justice Wright termed a *"pro hac vice* equivalent to a reversion." It made rights stipulated in a lease in fee transferable in law and provided that the grantor's assignees might take advantage of any remedy for the collection of rent available to lessors for lives or years. An Anti-Rent measure, the Act to Abolish Distress for Rent, played an equally important role in the *Smith* decision. The lawmakers of 1846 worked from the premise that legislation divesting landlords of all remedies for nonpayment of rent would violate the Contract Clause of the Constitution. As a result, the act confirmed the preexisting right of both grantors and lessors to reenter by ejectment. It reduced the thirty-day notice required by the *Revised Statutes* to fifteen days and provided that "the said notice may be served personally on such grantee or lessee, or by leaving it at his dwelling house on the premises."[55]

Bingham and Colvin implored the *Smith* court to spurn the conventional plain-meaning and legislative-intent standards in interpreting the statutes. All three public laws, they pointed out, had been passed at a time when government officials—former Assemblymen Harris and Wright included—labored under the "assumed theory" that the lease in fee was an unfortunate yet lawful remnant of feudalism. In *De Peyster*, however, the "manor pretensions" of the Van Rensselaer family had been exploded. Chief Justice Ruggles announced that rent service had been abolished generally and retrospectively in 1787, and the tenants on Rensselaerwyck had become landowners holding in fee simple. Fundamental principles of both the land law and the law of the land, insisted the Anti-Rent lawyers, forbade any construction of the statutes that would effectively convert fee-simple tenures into mere leases.[56]

Their revisionism did have an attractive logic. According to Bingham and Colvin, the saving clause in the Act Concerning Tenures was designed to protect only those rent obligations secured by leases for lives or years. Grants in fee with an annexed rent-charge reservation stood on a different footing because "the inevitable consequence" of adopting Quia Emptores in the same statute was to divest the grantor's reversion and hence the capacity of the rent covenants to run with the land. Insofar as the acts of 1805 and 1846 clothed the Van Rensselaers with an "equivalent to a reversion," they argued, the legislation was unconstitutional. "It is not possible," Colvin remarked, "to pass the right of property from one person to another without his consent or without due process of law." Yet both statutes purported to invest the grantor's assignees with new legal rights that, in practical application, took away everything that made the grantee's fee-simple tenure valuable. Bingham urged the court to invoke the well-established maxim that no law could be given a retrospective operation if the result would impair vested rights. It followed that the acts of 1805 and 1846, like the Act Concerning Tenures passed in 1787, should apply "only where the conventional relation of landlord and tenant exists." Because the Van Rensselaer indentures "created no such relation as landlord and tenant," neither the patroons nor Church had a legal right to reenter the land.[57]

Justices Harris and Wright refused to swallow these anachronistic claims. Bingham and Colvin not only asked them to make history in *Smith* but to remake it as well. Accepting their gloss on the statutes meant holding that the saving clause in the 1787 act protected the Livingstons and the Clarkes but not the Van Rensselaers. It meant holding that the 1805 act, though designed to preserve the lease in fee, applied only to conventional leases that did not require additional statutory support. And it meant holding that the 1846 act, which Harris had helped push through the legislature, did not confirm the Van Rensselaer right of reentry as a quid pro quo, mandated by the Constitution, for the abolition of their right to collect rent by distress. The new Anti-Rent argument seemed so perverse that Harris and Wright simply ignored counsel's canny reliance on the vested rights doctrine. For the aging Anti-Rent judges, logic and experience reinforced one another; each led to the same conclusion. The lease in fee was rooted so deeply in the New York legal order that it could not be abolished by judicial decision. In effect, they used the statutory materials at hand to reconstruct the anomalous legal form without disturbing the authority of *De Peyster*. "Under our laws," Wright wrote, "the relation of landlord and tenant *is* made to exist as between grantor and grantee in a conveyance in fee, of manor lands, reserving rents." Harris concurred.[58]

Two of the cases decided with *Smith* reached the Court of Appeals in 1859. The result was no different. In *Van Rensselaer v. Hays*, an action for sixteen years of back rent, the court confirmed plaintiff's right to enforce the rent-charge covenant under the statute of 1805. In *Van Rensselaer v. Ball*, an eject-ment suit, the court grounded plaintiff's right to reenter on the legislature's "manifest" intention to preserve that remedy in the act of 1846. Unlike the judges below, however, Justice Hiram Denio gave serious consideration to counsel's claim that the statutes, thus construed, took property from the defen-dants without due process of law. His mind had been receptive to such argu-ments for years. Speaking for the Court of Appeals in *Westerfeldt v. Gregg* (1854), Denio held that the Married Women's Property Act violated the due process principle when applied to property interests vested in the husband before the statute's enactment in 1848. "No power in the state," he said on that occasion, "can legally confer upon one person or class of persons the property of another person or class, without their consent, whatever motives of policy may exist in favor of such transfer." For Denio, then, the constitutional question posed by the Anti-Rent lawyers was both legitimate and imposing. If the Van Rensselaer conveyances had vested the fee in the grantees and the Act Concern-ing Tenures had cut off the Van Rensselaer reversions, as the court ruled in *De Peyster*, how could subsequent statutes qualify the one and confer the other without running afoul of the due process clause?[59]

Justice Denio's answer exploited a blind spot in the Anti-Rent argument. Bingham and Colvin had mastered the common law authorities on covenants for rent, but they had ignored the pertinent principles of equity jurisprudence. Speaking for the court in *Hays*, Denio conceded that rent charges were not assignable at common law. Nevertheless, he insisted that rent charges, like all property rights arising from executory contracts, were assignable in equity. It followed that "if the statute [of 1805] had not passed, the assignee could have prosecuted in the name of the grantor or his heirs for the benefit of the [rent's] equitable owner." Thus the act did not clothe Stephen Van Rensselaer III or his sons with property rights they lacked before. Nor did the act divest Van Rensselaer grantees of rights previously vested in them. Because the statute merely transformed an equitable cause of action into a legal one, Denio declared, "the legislature acted only on the remedy, which all the [vested rights] cases agree it was competent for it to do."[60]

The high court rejected Bingham and Colvin's due process challenge to the 1846 act for a similar reason. At common law, Denio pointed out in *Ball*, grantors in fee could reenter the land for unpaid rent if their indentures expressly reserved that remedy. And every contract in force on Rensselaerwyck contained such a reservation. Just as rent charges were assignable in equity, so was the capacity to enforce them by reentering the land for nonpayment of rent. By abolishing the remedy of distress and authorizing the devisees of Stephen Van Rensselaer III to renter by ejectment, then, the legislature did not take property from anyone. "The estate of the grantee was subject to be destroyed by a reentry for nonpayment of rent before the statute," Denio explained, "and no new or further liability is attached to it now."[61]

Justice Denio's opinions for the Court of Appeals did more than reconstruct the lease in fee. He made it invulnerable. Two distinct strands of interpretation emerged as he responded to the various arguments of counsel. The first one repulsed the Anti-Rent argument at common law. Denio read the acts of 1805 and 1846 in the same way Justices Harris and Wright had read them; he affirmed their conclusion in *Smith*. The judiciary could not extinguish the lease in fee because the legislature had placed grants in fee, reserving rents, on the same legal footing as conventional leases. Bingham and Colvin disdained this view yet knew how to subvert it. In theory, at least, the legislature might take away remedies previously conferred in derogation of common law. But the second strand of Denio's opinion signaled that any attempt to modify the statutes would be futile. This strand, woven to repulse the Anti-Rent lawyers' due process challenge to the acts of 1805 and 1846, actually made the legislation immaterial. Denio identified preexisting grantor remedies in equity and held that the legislature had merely converted them into remedies at law. Rights enforceable in equity, having vested under contracts that ran forever, could not be impaired by retrospective legislation. And the preexisting equitable remedies would remain even if the legislature repealed the statutes that neutralized the Bingham-Colvin argument at common law. After twenty years of agitation and litigation, *Hays* and *Ball* enmeshed the dwindling Anti-Rent movement in a web of law from which there was no escape.

It was not the same web Stephen Van Rensselaer III and "the scriveners who drew [his] leases" thought they had spun in the eighteenth century. They no doubt understood the legal relation established by the indentures as a rent service. Van Rensselaer wanted to develop the Manor of Rensselaerwyck with the form of land tenure that had long prevailed on the family estate, and his Federalist lawyers were delighted to frame a legal instrument that would counteract "the contagion of liberty" in a republican regime. The resulting manor contracts mandated rituals of fealty that not only signified a rent service but also ensured the tenant's dependence on his superiors. Van Rensselaer and his lawyers failed as social engineers. Manorial society collapsed in the Panic of 1819; the patroon's paternalism merely postponed the day of reckoning until his death twenty years later. But the "scriveners" built better than they knew. Although the Court of Appeals ruled in 1852 that the legal relation was really a rent charge, the lease in fee survived in its new legal wrapper. Manor contracts expressly provided that the grantor's reserved interests were to be assignable in perpetuity and expressly reserved a right of reentry. No conveyancer in Anglo-American history had ever drafted a grant in fee, understood as reserving a rent charge, having both of these extraordinary terms. Because the Van Rensselaer indentures contained them, however, the Court of Appeals felt compelled to uphold the lease in fee as a distinctive yet valid form of the rent-charge relation. New York State became the world's only common law jurisdiction in which rent-charge covenants ran with the land forever, and a primary objective of Van Rensselaer's eighteenth-century lawyers remained intact. The obligation to pay perpetual rent could not be sundered by democratic means. It could be extinguished only with the great proprietor's consent and on the great proprietor's terms.[62]

When the rent strike started on Rensselaerwyck in 1839, Governor William H. Seward refused to accept the proposition that a republican remedy might not exist for an "antirepublican" legal relation. He insisted that the pursuit of "social perfection" was a collective obligation imposed on the New York body politic by its devotion to "the democratic principle." And the quest for land reform began. When the Court of Appeals finally ruled that nothing could be done, however, its decision evoked expressions of relief rather than cries of woe. "All the judges concur in the opinion that the rents and arrears must be paid," Thurlow Weed announced in the *Evening Journal* on April 15, 1859. "This action of the court of last resort is necessarily final. It has been looked for with deep interest by the parties concerned and the public, and terminates a long and exciting controversy." William Cassidy of the rival *Atlas and Argus* said much the same thing. Both editors told anti-renters that they must look to Church, not to the legislature, for relief.[63]

Many already had. In Rensselaer County, approximately 250 farmers still held their land as tenants in fee. The others had bought out the interests of William P. Van Rensselaer before he conveyed the indentures to Church. Although the terms offered to Albany County tenants were less generous, the *Smith* decision persuaded most families to give up the struggle. Of the 1,397 manor contracts that bound Albany County farmers to "feudal servitude interminable" in 1839, only 580 still existed in 1859. Poverty prevented some manor families from dealing with Church. But many of the holdouts could afford the required mortgage payments; they remained in "voluntary slavery" as a matter of principle. Peter Ball of Berne, the losing party in the landmark Court of Appeals case, was among them. He still believed that the sovereign people had an obligation to resolve the irrepressible conflict between manorial tenures and the republican form of government.[64]

Bingham and Colvin encouraged such sentiments. Neither lawyer grasped the implications of Justice Denio's answer to their due process argument in *Hays* and *Ball*. Consequently they launched a campaign in the fall of 1859 to modify the statutes that the New York judiciary had used to reconstruct the lease in fee. Bingham ran for the assembly on the Republican ticket in Rensselaer. Colvin, a Democrat, pursued the Albany-Schenectady senate seat. Two tenant allies, former Whig/Anti-Rent congressman John Slingerland of Bethlehem and Stephen Merselis of Knox, were nominated for the assembly by Republican conventions in the largely rural districts of Albany County. All of them won. So did another candidate whom the four Anti-Rent activists boosted on the stump. He was a Democrat named Rufus Peckham, Ira Harris's opponent in the Supreme Court race. Weed and Cassidy did not comment on either the revival of Anti-Rent political action or its decisive impact on the local election.[65] The partisan editors, one now a Republican and the other still a Democrat, wanted no part of a hopeless cause that could end only in violence. Church appreciated their cooperation. Armed with the *Hays* and *Ball* decisions, he stood poised to break the twenty-year rent strike by throwing intransigent Anti-Rent families out of their homes.

13

The End of an Era

For more than a century, two defining moments of Anti-Rent history have been recounted time and again by the people of rural Albany County. One was the ejectment of Peter Ball by the county sheriff on February 18, 1860. Shortly after the sheriff finished his work, the Anti-Rent leader's neighbors restored Ball to possession. Local "Indians" sustained his claim to the family farm for several years afterward, underscoring the power of community. The other defining moment was the second and final ejectment of Ball by the state militia on May 29, 1865. It demonstrated the power of contract, backed by the state's legitimate monopoly of force, to overwhelm communities, tear apart lives, and suppress land reform aspirations that had once pervaded the New York body politic.[1]

The central event of United States history occurred between the two ejectment proceedings. Ball lost a son in the Civil War; scores of other young men from rural Albany County fought in the Union army. In April 1865, while the decisive battles in Virginia were being waged, the New York legislature ratified a thirteenth amendment to the Constitution that confirmed the abolition of slavery and involuntary servitude "within the United States, or any place subject to their jurisdiction."[2] The ordeals and achievements of the Civil War shaped reactions to the fate of Anti-Rent following the Confederate surrender. For anti-renters it seemed perverse that the same New York soldiers who helped to destroy chattel slavery in the southern states would invade the Manor of Rensselaerwyck, throw some victims of "voluntary slavery" out of their homes, and compel others to fulfill the obligations of "feudal servitude interminable." For the New York authorities, on the other hand, it seemed natural to crush Anti-Rent rebels who defied state law just as the Union army had crushed Confederate rebels who defied federal law. Yet nobody celebrated the outcome. The citizen-soldiers of the Albany County Artillery did not march in grand review after smashing the last of the "Indians." Public officials declined to claim credit for putting down the quarter-century rent strike on Rensselaerwyck. And none of the state's renowned journalists identified a theme worthy of elaboration on their editorial pages. In their judgment, the violent end of the Anti-Rent era was at once necessary and embarrassing.

Tension between the spirit of Anti-Rent and the political establishment was as old as the movement itself. Beginning in the Helderberg War of 1839, journalists and politicians repeatedly said that community resistance to law could never be justified in a republic. But the tension had a creative dimension until the very end of the Anti-Rent era, for the molders of public opinion also insisted that manorial tenures had no place in nineteenth-century New York. Tenant resistance on the ground and the quest for land reform at the state capital reinforced one another through the explorations of the eminent domain option, the taxation of rent-charge income, the struggle for the devise-and-descent bill, and the ill-advised attack on proprietor titles. Tenant intransigence and widespread hatred of "patroonery" coalesced again to produce the Anti-Rent Act of 1860. When the state judiciary nullified the legislature's last-ditch effort to extinguish the lease in fee, however, the drive for land reform concluded. The politicians and the press accepted the survival of manorial tenures with quiet resignation and moved on; the last beleaguered remnant of the Anti-Rent movement refused to surrender. In May 1865 there was nothing to celebrate, indeed nothing to say, because everyone suffered from the denouement. Ball lost his farm, and a generation of people lost their faith in the capacity of republican self-government to right admitted wrongs.

The Anti-Rent Act of 1860

On February 17, 1860, Sheriff Thomas W. Van Alstyne journeyed to Berne, Albany County, with Walter S. Church and a posse of eight officers to carry out the Court of Appeals decision authorizing the ejectment of Peter Ball. Church's original demand for back rents totaling $150, served fifteen days before filing suit in 1855, had grown to more than $800 with the costs of litigation. Ball could have raised the money all the same. The "city news" editor of Thurlow Weed's *Evening Journal* estimated the value of the 125-acre farm, graced by a two-story frame house and three barns, at $8,000. It was said that Church wanted Ball to pay because of the "influence it might exert at the same time upon other anti-renters to come forward and settle exacted claims." Ball, an Anti-Rent militant for twenty years, refused to make a deal for that very reason. Sheriff Van Alstyne begged the tenant in fee "to arrange the matter, and save him the unpleasant duty of dispossessing him." He even offered $50 from his own pocket. Ball politely declined to take the sheriff's money, and the operation began.[3]

Almost every inhabitant of Berne was present when the sheriff's men went to work that Friday afternoon in a pelting snowstorm. The crowd, fortified by "lookers on" from Knox and Rensselaerville, grew much larger the next day in spite of freezing temperatures and the eight inches of new snow on the ground. But there was no resistance. The assembled multitude sang the Anti-Rent songs while the posse, with "gentlemanly deportment," emptied the house and out-buildings. Provisions and dishes, tables and chairs, beds and bedding, stoves and fuel were placed in neat piles on the icy public road. The officers tethered horses and cattle outside the front fence. Stacks of hay filled the highway nearby. At nightfall on February 18, Sheriff Van Alstyne put Church into posses-sion; the entire party, including the farm's new owner and the newspapermen who tagged along, returned to Albany the next morning. "It is a sad spectacle," an *Atlas and Argus* writer remarked in the "local affairs" column of the Monday edition, "to see the home and property of so comfortable and thrifty a farmer as Mr. Ball once was, thus lost by ruinous litigation." Twenty miles away at the state capital, people did not know that everything had been moved back into the house and barns as soon as Church departed.[4]

There was method in the Anti-Rent restraint during the ejectment. Ball and his neighbors counted on an aroused public opinion to help them triumph in a last, desperate campaign to extinguish the lease in fee by force of law. Assembly-man Anson Bingham, a member of the Judiciary Committee, already had framed three measures designed to stay Church's hand. The first one, which Bingham introduced on January 20, would modify the Act to Abolish Distress for Rent. It provided that the landlord's right of reentry, preserved by the 1846 act, could be exercised only by "the grantee or owner of the reversion, but not otherwise." The second one, introduced by John Slingerland the same day, would pull the teeth that the New York judiciary had found in the statute of 1805. It aimed to take from grantors in fee any "equivalent to a reversion" supplied by the act. "No person can recover in ejectment by means of any condition of reentry," the Slingerland bill provided, "unless the reversion of such estate shall have remained in the person to whom, and in whose favor, such condition shall have been made, at the time of the making thereof; and unless the person bringing the action shall, at the time of its commencement, have been the owner of such reversion." The third one, introduced by Stephen Merselis, would amend the saving clause in the Act Concerning Tenures of 1787. It provided that "no covenants or conditions, made by or on the part of the grantee of any conveyance of real estate, by which conveyance such grantee shall have acquired the whole legal estate of the grantor in the premises, shall attach to, or run with the land, as a burden upon subsequent grantees." Bing-ham described the theory of the proposed legislation in a committee report issued on February 24, five days after the "sad spectacle" at the Ball farm concluded. Each of the bills, he said, "is only declaratory of the common law."[5]

When the bills came up for a second reading and debate on March 13,

Assemblyman Slingerland translated Bingham's recondite measures into terms fellow lawmakers could understand and appreciate. "Listen while I tell a 'plain, unvarnished tale,' which any gentleman on this floor can verify by traveling a few miles west of this city," he began. "There lives (or *did* live, for God only knows where he finds a shelter now), in the town of Berne, in this county, an honest, industrious, respectable, and very much respected farmer by the name of Peter Ball." Once he had described the ejectment in graphic detail, Slingerland fused old Anti-Rent arguments and new Anti-Rent arguments into a powerful plea for government action. The result was the longest, most effective Anti-Rent speech ever made in the New York legislature. It proved to be the last one as well.[6]

The labor theory of value provided the foundation for the first of Slingerland's four main themes. Between the initial settlement of William Ball under a Van Rensselaer indenture in 1792 and the formation of the Anti-Rent Association of Albany County in 1839, he pointed out, the Ball family had paid rents amounting to three or four times the value of the land in its original state. Meanwhile, members of the Ball household "spent the dew of youth and the energy of manhood" transforming wild land into a productive farm. The hard work of "improving and beautifying" continued after William died and his son Peter joined the Anti-Rent movement. Yet "the fruits of many a lifetime of toil" had been seized by another person with no interest in the land except a legal right to collect both the rents in arrear and future rents in perpetuity. This "enormous wrong," moreover, was about to be duplicated again and again. "Ball's situation is the situation of thousands of respectable farmers," Slingerland told his colleagues in the assembly. "Nor can they avert the threatened destruction by paying, for many of them are entirely unable to pay because of the extent to which these liabilities have accumulated." Unless the legislature acted with dispatch, then, "the unfortunate victims of feudal wrong must be precipitated at one blow from happy homes to a state of homelessness. And for what?"

Slingerland's answer to the rhetorical question got him going on a second theme. He insisted that the impending ejectments could not be justified by any sound principle of law or morality. "A favorite argument with the friends of patroonery," he remarked, "has been that the land having been taken possession of, with a full knowledge of all the rents, covenants and conditions that are said to belong to it, and these having been voluntarily accepted, the occupants have now no right to complain, and cannot with even a shadow of consistency, or even of honesty, ask for relief." In Slingerland's view, however, it was more accurate to level the charge of hypocrisy at those who reviled Anti-Rent on freedom-of-contract grounds. Turning the tables on his adversaries required two steps. First, he invoked Thomas Jefferson's maxim that the dead had no right to fetter the living. "Suppose our forefathers, the first grantees under manorial titles, did enter these agreements voluntarily and with open eyes," Slingerland said. "Was it right, or even possible, for them to bind their heirs?" Second, he showed that even the most rabid opponent of Anti-Rent could not deny the applicability of Jefferson's precept in the context at hand. The personal service requirement in every Van Rensselaer indenture enabled him to drive home the point.

"Gentlemen," he asserted, "it is a serious fact that there is *slavery* in this relic of feudalism—a compulsory obligation on the part of the so-called tenants to perform manual labor" one day a year in perpetuity for every heir or assignee of Stephen Van Rensselaer III. The contracts in force on Rensselaerwyck prescribed neither the type of work required nor the time of its performance:

> We may be directed to clean his pig pen or black his boots. If . . . all the landholders under these titles should come to perform their services on one day, the city of Albany, said to be the capital of a free state, will behold a man with a larger retinue of slaves than ever called any one hundred cotton planters "master." This is not a picture of the imagination. It is in plain black and white in my deed. . . . And how did it get there? How did I and every other descendant of the original grantees become thus enslaved? I answer (and I want every man who says we have no moral right to complain to hear me), it never got there by our act or with our consent. We never agreed for *any* consideration to perform menial labor for the lord of any manor. No! We became enslaved by our own birth and the death of our ancestors, two circumstances over which we had not the slightest control.

Slingerland claimed that the very existence of the covenant for compulsory labor exploded the favorite argument of Anti-Rent foes. If a deal was a deal, not only between the contracting parties but across generations until the end of time, then honest consistency required "the friends of patroonery" to insist on enforcement of the servile labor with the same ardor they insisted on enforcement of the rents payable in fowl and wheat. Yet nobody could in 1860. "It involves something," Slingerland proclaimed, "which, to an American citizen of the Empire State, is of vastly greater importance . . . than mere dollars and cents." In a free society, the individual's "exemption from service except at his own free will" was his most precious personal liberty.

The legislation framed by his Anti-Rent colleague served as the frame of reference for Slingerland's third theme. The general rule that tenants had an obligation to pay their rent, he emphasized, was a salutary one. "I am a landlord myself, and I will not vote away the right of collecting my rents." But the bills Bingham had reported out of the Judiciary Committee would have no effect on the property rights of legitimate landlords. Enacting the three measures would merely prevent persons having no reversionary interest in the property—persons who, rightly understood, were not landlords at all—from reentering land previously conveyed in fee simple. "The principle which these bills assert," he said, "is simply that a man cannot sell a piece of land 'out and out,' and at the same time reserve rents upon it forever. They simply assert that these farmers have bought their land, paid for it and paid all it is worth, received a good deed for it, and are therefore under no further obligation to their grantors." The legislation before the house responded to "the anomalous spectacle of landless landlords—a contradiction in terms which was never reconciled till our solemnly sapient Court of Appeals undertook the job" in *Van Rensselaer v. Hays* and *Van Rensselaer v. Ball.* Both 1859 decisions, Slingerland explained, were grounded on the "old and gray" statutes that the Anti-Rent bills proposed to modify. "And now I ask, is it right, in the middle of the nineteenth century, to leave on our statute books laws that are so contrary to freedom, to the spirit of our republican institutions, and to the best interests of the state?"

For Slingerland, the question admitted of one answer only. "Incalculable benefit" would result from legislation that drove "from our presence" the "serpent" that Stephen Van Rensselaer III had thrown into Albany and Rensselaer counties. It would "encourage and stimulate agricultural industry." It would "beget confidence in the title to an immense amount of real estate, which at present no one with open eyes can be induced to buy." Above all, it would "secure independent homes to a multitude of innocent women and children, who at present possess no assurance that at the expiration of the next fifteen days they will not be driven from hearths which they themselves have laid and . . . into the street, with no shelter but the blue canopy of heaven." Slingerland urged lawmakers on both sides of the aisle to do the right thing. "We are sent here to make laws for the *people*," he reminded them, "and it is our duty to endeavor to do the greatest good to the greatest number."

Slingerland's speech persuaded a great many uncommitted lawmakers and disarmed others predisposed to vote against the Anti-Rent measures. Only four assemblymen, three Republicans and one Democrat, spoke against the proposed legislation. All of them were lawyers; none of them defended "patroonery." Nor did they contest Slingerland's claim that bedrock principles of property, contract, and public responsibility supplied ample support for Bingham's bills. Instead, they identified blind spots in the Anti-Rent argument and explained that equally weighty principles of law and prudence inclined them to oppose the bills. Theophilus Callicott (D.-Brooklyn), David R. Jacques (R.-Manhattan), W. T. B. Milliken (R.-Westchester), and Lucius Robinson (R.-Chemung) made the same three points in different ways. First, they pointed out that the proposed legislation could not pass constitutional muster. Its very purpose was to deprive persons claiming through Stephen Van Rensselaer III of every remedy for the breach of rent covenants. "The legislature may modify and take away, to a certain degree, the remedies provided by the law or the contract," Callicott asserted. "But it cannot take away all remedies" without violating the Constitution's prohibition of state laws impairing the obligation of contracts.[7]

Second, the four lawyers claimed that the Anti-Rent argument overlooked a countervailing legal and moral principle. The proposed legislation would take property from one person and vest it in another. Slingerland erred, Robinson told his fellow lawmakers, when he claimed that the farmers of Albany and Rensselaer counties "have bought their land, paid for it and paid all it is worth." In point of fact, the tenants in fee on Rensselaerwyck had entered the land for nothing and rent had not been required for the first seven years. It was immaterial, then, whether the farmers had subsequently paid "all it is worth" under an abstraction like the labor theory of value. Church still had legal rights in the rents reserved. Establish a beachhead in New York law for the proposition that property might be taken from A. and given to B., Callicott warned, and "no person will regard any property of value."[8]

Finally, the opponents of government action insisted that the tragic ejectments, which Slingerland claimed were imminent, could and should be avoided. Church had offered to sell his interest in every farm for $2.60 an acre, just a dime per acre more than the figure proposed in 1839 by the Anti-Rent Association of Albany County. Furthermore, he had agreed to carry a mortgage for the back rents as well as the principal sum. Peter Ball might have saved his farm by accepting Church's terms; the enactment of new legislation would only encourage other tenants to fight on toward a bitter end. What kept the Anti-Rent agitation going, Callicott declared, was "the hope that they may, by legislative action or continued litigation, be enabled to maintain their own rights under the Van Rensselaer contracts, and either destroy or evade the rights of the other parties." But the hope was a delusion because Bingham's bills were unconstitutional. The remaining tenants in fee could deal with Church now, or they could deal with him after another disappointing yet inevitable defeat in the courts. Robinson insisted that the wise policy was to hasten the process of settlement by voting down all three Anti-Rent measures.[9]

The roll call, taken on March 29 without a recorded debate, was very close. Bingham put up the bill to repeal the 1805 act first; it lost by a vote of 54-58. Milliken of Westchester, who opposed all the Anti-Rent bills from the outset, kept the measure alive by asking the house "to reconsider said vote" and then lay the matter on the table. This parliamentary maneuver allowed the original legislation, or a substitute for it, to be revived by a simple majority of the house.

And the motion passed. The rationale for Milliken's action soon became clear. Along with Martin Finch, another Republican member of the Judiciary Committee who voted nay on March 29, Milliken had worked up a substitute that accommodated the principal Anti-Rent objective yet had a chance of withstanding judicial review. It read as follows:

> Chapter 98 of the Laws of 1805, passed April 9, 1805, entitled "An act to amend an act entitled 'An act to enable grantees of reversions to take advantage of conditions to be performed by lessees,' " . . . shall not apply to deeds of conveyance in fee made before the ninth day of April, 1805, nor to such deeds hereafter to be made.

Finch laid the substitute before the house with Bingham's support on April 5. Slingerland and Callicott endorsed the new measure; Robinson was the only member who denounced it. The substitute passed that afternoon by a vote of 74-34. Andrew J. Colvin shepherded it through the senate, and Governor Edwin D. Morgan signed the bill into law on April 14. By its own terms, the act was to "take effect immediately."[10]

The making of the Anti-Rent Act of 1860 provides an exemplary illustration of how lawyers and legal doctrine influenced the legislative process in the nineteenth century. Very few members of the assembly had a firm grasp on the theory of either Bingham's bills or the Finch substitute, and the political parties did not take a stand on the proposed legislation. In the March 29 roll call, lawmakers took their cue from Slingerland or from the lawyers who remonstrated against Bingham's measures. And the bill failed. When two of the four nay-saying lawyers joined the Anti-Rent members in endorsing the Finch substitute on April 5, however, about half of the people who voted no in the first roll call decided to say yes. The influential lawyers were driven in turn by a solicitude for vested rights. The bill that passed, unlike the bill that lost, was designed to accommodate the prospectivity norm in legislation. Finch, Milliken, and Callicott believed that it neither impaired the obligation of contracts nor redistributed property rights for the benefit of some people at the expense of others. They also persuaded Bingham to let his other two measures die. As the architects of the substitute read their handiwork, it gave the Anti-Rent lawyers everything they needed to prevail in the next round of litigation.

Seeing what the sponsors of the Anti-Rent Act saw in its brief, opaque provisions requires some patience. Consider first the Act Concerning Tenures passed in 1787. As interpreted by the Court of Appeals in *De Peyster v. Michael* (1852), the act "t[ook] away the grantor's reversion or escheat" and therefore "converted all rents upon leases in fee from rent service into rent charges." It did not disturb the right of Stephen Van Rensselaer III, stipulated in every manor indenture, to reenter the land for nonpayment of rent. Because the patroon always conveyed the fee, however, Bingham had argued for years that the act of 1787 effectively cut off his legal right to sell or devise the rents. Finch and Milliken agreed. Rent-charge covenants did not run with the land at common law, and the patroon's assignees could not reenter under a 1788 statute authorizing the grantees of reversions to collect rents. Whatever reversions Stephen Van Rensselaer III previously owned had been divested by the Act Concerning Tenures. Finch and Milliken concluded that the New York legislature had attempted to rectify the situation in 1805. The resulting statute, which the Anti-Rent Act of 1860 purported to amend, provided that the 1788 act "shall be construed to extend as well to grants or leases in fee reserving rents, as to leases for life and years, any law, usage or custom to the contrary thereof notwithstanding."[11]

The theory of the Anti-Rent Act was based on the sequence of legislation enacted between 1787 and 1805. Finch and Milliken worked from the premise that the right of reentry claimed by Stephen Van Rensselaer IV, William P. Van Rensselaer, and Walter S. Church—the direct and indirect assignees of Stephen Van Rensselaer III—might be made contingent on the date of the original conveyance. The act acknowledged that state action could not prevent Church from reentering any farm held under a lease in fee contracted after April 1805 and before April 1860. Once the legislature had enacted a prospective statute making the right of reentry assignable, as it clearly did in 1805, rights arising from subsequent indentures became vested. The federal Constitution forbade state laws impairing the obligation of contracts that were lawful at the time of the transaction.

But the framers of the 1860 law believed that leases in fee established before April 1805 stood on a different footing. The assignment covenant in every indenture that went into force before 1787 had been nullified by the Act Concerning Tenures; the assignment covenant in indentures made between 1787 and 1805 had not been lawful at the time of the transaction. With respect to those leases in fee, then, no right of reentry had vested in the patroon's assignees. Nor had the act of 1805 created vested rights where none existed previously. In the *Hays* and *Ball* decisions, the Court of Appeals held that the act applied to leases in fee executed before 1805 as well as afterward. It applied, however, in a different way. Justice Hiram Denio, speaking for the court, justified the retrospective operation of the 1805 law as a benign modification of the remedies available to the grantor's assignees.[12] The Anti-Rent Act of 1860 was grounded on the sensible proposition that no person could acquire a vested right in any remedy that the law supplied after the original deal had been struck. What the legislature conferred retrospectively in 1805 could be divested retrospectively in 1860.

Bingham, Colvin, and Slingerland embraced the Finch-Milliken theory with alacrity. Virtually all of the Van Rensselaer indentures still in force in Albany and Rensselaer counties had been contracted before April 1805. What is more, the act of 1860 undermined Church's right of reentry not only under the act of 1805 but also under the Act to Abolish Distress for Rent passed in 1846. Once the legislature had taken away the "equivalent to a reversion," which the courts had found in the retrospective operation of the 1805 law, no legal foundation existed for the presumption that the 1846 statute merely confirmed a preexisting right in the assignees of Stephen Van Rensselaer III. Still, the theory of the Anti-Rent Act rested on a misconception. Bingham, Colvin, and Slingerland assumed that the "old and gray" statutes had beaten them in *Van Rensselaer v. Hays* and *Van Rensselaer v. Ball*. Finch and Milliken assumed the same thing. Yet none of the lawmakers read the court's opinions with sufficient care. Justice Denio had sent a clear signal that modifying the statutes would be an exercise in futility. And so it was.

Defeat

The Anti-Rent Act of 1860 had two immediate effects. It stayed the impending ejectments until the statute's implications had been determined by the courts, and it put Walter S. Church into financial difficulty. Mortgage payments from the manor farmers who bought out his interest in the rents between 1854 and 1859, though sufficient to cover his debt to the Van Rensselaers, did not generate enough cash to pay his lawyers. Church had filed suit against each of the intransigent anti-renters beginning in 1855. But he had obtained a final judgment authorizing him to reenter by ejectment only in the Peter Ball case. The remaining tenants in fee—about 800 of them—now had a new defense grounded in the Anti-Rent Act, and Church could not use those indentures as collateral for additional loans unless the New York Supreme Court upheld his right of reentry. For him, *Main v. Green* and *Van Rensselaer v. Secor*, argued on September 3, 1860, meant the difference between solvency and bankruptcy. Anson Bingham, counsel for both defendants, liked his chances of destroying Church. The theory of the act seemed right and so did the judges. Rufus Peckham, who succeeded Ira Harris in January 1860, owed his election to the Anti-Rent vote; Henry Hogeboom, the presiding justice, had argued *De Peyster v. Michael* with Azor Taber in 1852. Better than anyone else on the New York bench, Hogeboom figured to understand the "inevitable consequence" of the decision that changed the legal relation on Rensselaerwyck from a rent service into a rent charge.[13]

At issue in *Green* and *Secor* was the right of reentry under a Rensselaer County lease in fee contracted in 1793 and an Albany County lease in fee made the previous year. Justice Hogeboom remarked at the threshold that the two cases were "in all material respects, except a single particular," identical to *Van Rensselaer v. Ball.* "The only distinguishing feature that I am able to discover," he said, "is as to the effect of the law of 1860 repealing or limiting the former statutes extending certain remedies to the grantees or assignees of reversions." Hogeboom, speaking for himself and Peckham, saved Church by holding that the Anti-Rent Act did not have the effect Bingham supposed. In the court's judgment, the state legislature had misinterpreted *De Peyster*, misunderstood *Ball*, and misconstrued the law passed in 1805. If the Anti-Rent Act of 1860 meant what Bingham said it meant, however, the statute would be unconstitutional.[14]

Justice Hogeboom unraveled Bingham's tissue of errors with an impatient air. It was true, he said, that the Act Concerning Tenures passed in 1787 had divested the reversions previously owned by Stephen Van Rensselaer III. The *De Peyster* case established the point with clarity and force. It was also true that at common law "a mere right of reentry is not assignable so as to authorize an action by the assignee in his own name." But there was no foundation in *De Peyster* for the assumption that covenants for rent could run with the land only when the landlord retained a reversion. If the indenture provided that the rents reserved to the grantor were assignable, the right of reentry for nonpayment of rent had always been enforceable in equity. As the Court of Appeals explained in *Ball*, "the assignee could have prosecuted in the name of the grantor or his heirs for the benefit of the equitable owner" in the absence of legislation conferring a right to proceed at law. Hogeboom crisply stated the only logical conclusion. The ejectment actions at issue in *Green* and *Secor*, he declared, could be maintained "independent, therefore, of any of these statutes."[15]

The court's holding begged a fair question. If the legislature of 1805 did not intend to restore landlord rights that had been cut off with their reversions in 1787, why had the measure been enacted? Hogeboom answered with aplomb. He began by insisting that it "was professedly only a declaratory act." The very language of the 1805 statute, he said, "implies a legislative opinion" that the act of 1788 authorizing grantees of reversions to enforce rent covenants "was broad enough, when construed according to its spirit and intent, to reach grants and leases in fee, and that the later act of 1805 was enacted for more abundant caution." The legislature framed both statutes, however, to address procedural irregularities rather than substantive ones. Justice Denio's opinion for the Court of Appeals in *Ball*, Hogeboom pointed out, made it clear that even in 1787 the assignees of rent charges could have reentered for nonpayment of rent in the name of the grantor. Construing the 1805 law as a declaratory act meant that assignees of rent charges could reenter in their own name beginning in 1788; interpreting it otherwise meant that they could not reenter in their own name until 1805. But the right of reentry vested in Van Rensselaer assignees flowed from the indentures, not from the statutes. The legislation of 1788 and 1805 merely transformed preexisting rights enforceable in equity into rights enforceable at law.[16]

Hogeboom's construction of the "old and gray" statutes was grounded firmly in *Ball*. It also collapsed the distinction at the heart of the Anti-Rent Act. Vested rights enforceable in equity could not be extinguished by retrospective legislation any more than rights vested under the standing law. It followed that leases in fee contracted before 1805 stood on the same footing as leases in fee made after that year. The only remaining problem for the court in *Green* and *Secor*, then, was what to say about the statute enacted in 1860. As interpreted by Bingham, the Anti-Rent Act impaired the obligation of contracts and was therefore unconstitutional. Viewed through the lens of *Ball*, on the other hand, it had no bearing on the rights of Van Rensselaer assignees. They could reenter for unpaid rent in spite of the Anti-Rent Act; as a result, it would be supererogatory for the court to strike down the law.

Justice Hogeboom resolved the difficulty by salvaging a role for the statute. He relied on a canon of statutory interpretation James Kent had articulated in 1805, Greene Bronson had invoked in 1844, Ira Harris had trumpeted in 1848, and Theodore Sedgwick Jr. had endorsed with enthusiasm in his *Treatise on the Rules which Govern the Interpretation and Application of Statutory and Constitutional Law* (1857). Bingham himself deployed it unsuccessfully before the Court of Appeals in 1859. The canon, in Hogeboom's words, required that "no enactment, however positive in its terms, is to be so construed as to interfere with existing contracts, rights of action or suits, unless it expressly declares that intention." The upshot was just as devastating to the hopes of anti-renters as an outright judicial veto. "I doubt if the legislature by this act of 1860 intended to take away rights already vested," Hogeboom wrote. "There will scope and verge enough for the operation of the act of 1860, if it is limited to rights acquired by means of assignments or transfers of leases in fee made or executed since the passage of the act."[17]

Giving the Anti-Rent Act a wholly prospective operation transformed it into a vain and idle enactment that accomplished nothing. The constitution of 1846 prohibited new leases in fee designed to last longer than twelve years, and it was very unlikely that conveyancers would use the anomalous legal form after April 1860. Justices Hogeboom and Peckham understood this as well as anyone. They also knew that old Anti-Rent friends were going to call them turncoats. Yet it did not matter. Precedent and principle tied their hands just as it had constrained the lawmakers who passed the 1860 law. Hogeboom was justified in expressing "doubt" that the legislature "intended to take away rights already vested." Bingham's bills had failed in part because Assemblymen Callicott and Milliken argued that they were unconstitutional; the Finch substitute passed when both lawyers, one a Democrat and the other a Republican, assured their colleagues that it accommodated the prospectivity norm in legislation.

Hogeboom's opinions in *Green* and *Secor* showed why the framers of the Anti-Rent Act had been mistaken. The court's holding also underscored the common commitment of Federalists, Democrats, Whigs, and Republicans to the vested rights doctrine. From the early republic it had been a fixed star in a changing political universe.[18] The "basic doctrine of American constitutional law" fettered the drive for land reform at the beginning of the Anti-Rent era and foreclosed the possibility of relief for manor tenants at the end. Whatever compunction Hogeboom and Peckham felt while performing their thankless task was overshadowed by an unshakeable conviction in its necessity. Property rights legitimately vested through contract could be extinguished only through contract. The judges who handed down *Green* and *Secor* in September 1860 believed that it would ever be so.

A "landholders convention" gathered in downtown Albany on October 2 to protest the New York Supreme Court decisions that preserved "the system of feudal tenures." All the Anti-Rent arguments were restated in forceful resolutions, but the assembled tenants had run out of ideas for constructive government action. Besides, the movement's political capital had been spent. The convention did not even ask John Slingerland to run again for the state legislature. He was nominated instead for Congress. At the county's Republican convention ten days later, Slingerland received only seventeen votes; the other eighty-seven delegates massed behind Thurlow Weed's man, Albany businessman Thomas W. Olcott. The stay on ejectments, however, remained in force. Bingham filed appeals in *Green, Secor*, and every other case Hogeboom's court disposed on the same grounds. One of them was *Van Rensselaer v. Slingerland*. Until the Court of Appeals construed the Anti-Rent Act of 1860, Church could not attempt to reenter farms owned by the remaining tenants in fee. And all of them had an incentive to stay in possession for as long as possible.[19]

The cloture of public debate on the Anti-Rent question encouraged Church to lay plans for a triumphant return to Berne. He did not anticipate the coming of the Civil War. On May 1, 1861, two weeks after the guns of Fort Sumter boomed, Church had to sell all of the Rensselaer County leases in fee to pay his creditors. It was not until June 1863, when every available New York soldier was either fighting at Gettysburg or putting down the draft riot in Manhattan, that the Court of Appeals unanimously sustained the right of reentry vested in Van Rensselaer assignees. Church had to wait two more years before an armed force could be raised to enforce the court orders in western Albany County. On May 23, 1865, the very day Generals Grant and Sherman marched their victorious armies through the streets of Washington, the sheriff of Albany County ejected Hiram Secor from his farm in Berne. Church put two men into possession before departing. The expected headline—"Anti-Rent Outbreak"—appeared in the Albany press three days later. "Twenty or thirty persons, disguised as Indians," reported the *Argus*, "entered upon the premises, turned [Church's people] out of doors, and replaced the goods and furniture of Secor." At dawn on Monday, May 29, the Albany County Artillery headed toward the Helderbergs with Church and the sheriff. The soldiers carried rifles and sidearms, a "thousand round of cartridges, one barrel of pork and one of beef, with other provisions." They camped that night on the farm of Peter Ball. The end of the Anti-Rent era was at hand.[20]

Aftermath

The invasion of the Helderbergs in 1865 had a very different character than the first one. In 1839 Governor Seward insisted that the situation required government action against manorial tenures as well as against the riotous tenants. The politicians and the chattering class saw only "Indians" in 1865. Civil War imagery abounded in local press coverage of the campaign. "The loyal do not question that in the end the government will triumph and the rebellion will be quelled," the *Evening Journal* proclaimed after the Albany County Artillery marched out of town on May 29. "And they rejoice that Colonel Church is at last a believer in 'coercion.'" George Dawson, the longtime associate editor who bought the newspaper from Weed in 1863, complimented Church two days later for "courageously" taking on "the rebels" and "determinedly proceeding with the work of confiscation." William Cassidy of the *Argus* defended military action against the tenants more readily than he accepted coercion of the South in 1861. "The law must be enforced," he declared, "and at this day military force is an accustomed resort."[21]

Peter Ball, in the eyes of the law a mere trespasser since his first ejectment, was the first anti-renter to be driven from his home. The same operation, conducted with "gentlemanly deportment," took two days in February 1860. Church and the militia, unrestrained by public opinion sympathetic to the tenants, finished the job in two hours; Ball's farm became "Camp Church," headquarters of the ensuing campaign. Robert Hays and Hiram Secor were ejected the next day. Beginning on May 31, the troops marched up every road in the county's western townships and called at every remaining Anti-Rent home. Many were already vacant. Scores of families avoided the indignity of ejectment by packing up their things and leaving the county before the militia arrived. The majority who stayed heard Church make his standard pitch while the soldiers milled around in the road. Tenants in fee could avoid the fate of Ball, Hays, and Secor by immediately remitting the back rents (in which case they would remain liable for annual rents in perpetuity) or buying out his interest in their farms for $2.60 an acre (in which case he would carry a mortgage for the principal sum plus the back rents). Some of them signed mortgage agreements and made the requisite down payment, but a much larger number of tenant families stayed in possession by paying only the back rents and accrued interest. Robert Hays did so on June 1 and moved back into the house that the militia had emptied two days earlier. As late as 1884, more than 300 leases in fee still existed in Albany County.[22]

When the militia went home in June, Anti-Rent militants responded in the traditional way. At four o'clock in the morning on July 14, the barn and wagon shed on the Secor place burned to the ground while Church's armed guards slept in the house. The "Indians" made their last forlorn appearance three weeks later. About thirty of them sneaked into "Camp Church" at dawn on August 12 to harvest Peter Ball's crop. But this attempt to prevent landlord expropriation of the fruits of tenant labor did not succeed. "Colonel Church, with five or six men, was in possession of the premises," the *Evening Journal* reported. "The colonel ordered the anti-renters to leave, which they did, but afterward returned, and were again driven off." Next day a gang of Church hirelings harvested the fields and shipped the crop to market, thus denying the people of Berne even a symbolic victory. The rent strike had been broken and so had the tenant pledge "each unto the other," announced a quarter-century before in the "Anti-Renters' Declaration of Independence," to protect "our rights and property from being wantonly and unjustly forced from us."[23]

The spirit of Anti-Rent did not die after the struggle ceased. It lived on in the movement's songs and in the stories that the defeated farmers told their children and grandchildren. Not surprisingly, the dominant theme of songs and stories alike was community resistance to tyrannical outsiders—to the landlords, to the courts whose writs sustained "patroonery," and to the public officials who ejected Ball and others in the name of the people of New York State.[24] Anti-renters understood a truth that judges, journalists, and politicians refused to acknowledge in 1865. Government enforcement of property and contract rights involves something more than faithful execution of the laws. It puts the whole power of the state at the command of private parties accountable to nobody but themselves. The resort to "coercion" enabled Church to dictate the settlement terms or, if he so chose, to reenter the land without giving tenant families any opportunity to pay the back rents or buy out his interest in their farms. Authorities constituted by the people dispossessed the tenants in fee who could not or would not accept Church's offer, but the vested rights doctrine barred the people's deputies in the state legislature from having any say in the matter. Anti-renters regarded the denouement as a reproach to the idea of republican self-government.

Yet rights of property and contract have always been ultimately grounded on the state's willingness to defend them with force. The invasion of the Helderbergs in 1865 loomed so large in the Anti-Rent mind that the people who experienced it either forgot how long "patroonery" had been held at bay or attributed the previous success of nullification to the "Indian" resistance. Both perspectives were short-sighted. Manor tenants sustained the rent strike for twenty-six years because Anti-Rent voters outnumbered their landlord foes and party leaders despised the lease in fee almost as much as they despised the "Indians." The Anti-Rent era began when Governor Seward condemned manorial tenures as "oppressive, antirepublican and degrading" and urged the state legislature to intervene "not only upon considerations of justice and equality, but by sound and enlightened policy." As long as "voluntary slavery" remained a public problem that seemed to require a public solution, the state government tried to preserve law and order yet declined to pursue a policy of "coercion." Even Governor Wright, a fixture in Anti-Rent demonology from his first day in office, vowed to propose a land reform measure as soon as the "Indian outrages" stopped. The struggle for the devise-and-descent bill showed that he meant it.

For two decades, legislators and litigators explored solutions under the power to divest landlord remedies, the eminent domain power, the tax power, the power to regulate inheritance, the power to contest the validity of land titles, and the legality of the lease in fee in a real property regime bottomed on the statute Quia Emptores. Some proposals failed in the legislature. Others failed to achieve the intended objective or failed to pass judicial muster. The Anti-Rent era did not come to an end, however, until every possible means of extinguishing manorial tenures by force of law had been exhausted. William Cassidy, an indefatigable advocate of the devise-and-descent bill in 1846, defended "coercion" in May 1865 on the ground that no other option existed. "Litigation, protracted through twenty years, has brought no relief to the tenants," he reported, "and political agitation has been even more futile."[25] This last *Argus* editorial on the subject provided a sad yet accurate epitaph for the Anti-Rent movement.

Conclusion

Thurlow Weed, writing in 1844, aptly termed the Manor of Rensselaerwyck a "tree of bitterness." Its fruit brought sorrow to all who sought a share of the contested harvest. Stephen Van Rensselaer IV and his half brother William eventually sold their reserved interests in tenant farms for less than their tenants had been willing to pay in 1839. Yet none of the tenants got a better deal than the initial Van Rensselaer offer. In every instance, the accumulated back rents increased the price of extinguishing the lease in fee. Walter S. Church, the third party who tried to capitalize on the long rent strike, fared badly too. Years of litigation and the costs of borrowed money gradually ate up his anticipated windfall; he was ultimately compelled to declare bankruptcy. Everyone with a stake in the old manor felt wronged, even betrayed, in the end. Church, the Van Rensselaers, and the tenants all blamed their bitter fate on the connections between law and politics in mid-nineteenth-century New York. Their inter- pretations of what had happened to them were neither entirely wrong nor altogether right.[26]

Church and the Van Rensselaers attributed the destructive Anti-Rent contro- versy to the excesses of democracy. Like hard-line conservatives before and since, they believed that government never had any business contesting their property rights or considering ways to sunder the contractual obligations of their tenants. The decisions of the Court of Appeals upholding great proprietor land titles, repulsing attacks on manor rent covenants, and emasculating the Anti-Rent Act of 1860 simply confirmed what should have been true all along. As Daniel Dewey Barnard put it in 1845, appeals to the public interest were "out of place where mere private contracts are in question." But the politicians could not leave well enough alone. The logic of democracy impelled party managers to curry the favor of any big bloc of voters with real or imagined grievances. Whigs and Democrats alike denounced the rent system, talked up impossible relief schemes that the legislature never enacted, and reinforced the tenant inclination to reject the buyout terms offered by their landlords. Law enforcement officials behaved just as badly. County sheriffs either shirked their duty to serve legal process or passed responsibility for the "Indian" resistance to equally reluctant governors. Demagoguery thus subverted the rule of law until the number of Anti-Rent votes had become insignificant. And everyone suffered from the consequences. One commentator saw things precisely as Church and the Van Rensselaers did. "Anti-Rent put itself above the law," the *Troy News* remarked after the rent strike collapsed. "It elected governors, judges, congressmen, senators, legislators, town and county officers, ruined the Van Rensselaers, and worried them out of their handsome estate, was petted and patronized as long as it had votes to give, and now after long years of struggle the law finally put its broad hand upon Anti-Rentism and hopelessly squelche[d] it."[27]

The conservative view, though attractive to some people even now, always rested on two false premises. First, it overestimated the sanctity of property and contract rights in the American constitutional order. Henry George captured the gist of the Church–Van Rensselaer legal understanding in *Progress and Poverty* (1880). "We of the English-speaking nations," he wrote, "still wear the collar of the Saxon thrall, and have been educated to look upon the 'vested rights' of land owners with all the superstitious reverence that ancient Egyptians looked upon the crocodile." But the Van Rensselaers, in particular, should have known better. During the 1840s their lawyers claimed that manor indentures, buttressed by the Contract Clause, barred the taxation of rent-charge income and forbade legal challenges to the quarter-sale conditions annexed to every lease in fee. New York courts proved them wrong on both counts. Nor was that all. Compensated emancipation schemes, unlike the all-or-nothing Anti-Rent Act of 1860, had solid constitutional foundations when lawmakers proposed them. The devise-and-descent bill, which a large majority of the lower house passed in 1846, did not evoke a single objection on constitutional grounds; Stephen Van Rensselaer IV took the eminent domain plan so seriously in 1841 that he ordered his own valuation of the water rights reserved in manor contracts. *Taylor v. Porter* (1843) shut down the eminent domain route for a time, but the drive for a constitutional convention quickly reopened it. Even the absurd attack on landlord titles provided the legislature with substantial leverage to broker a compromise in 1850. Political constraints, not constitutional barriers, checked the responsible exercise of public power at key junctures of the Anti-Rent era.[28]

The second false premise was closely related to the first. In retrospect, at least, conservatives underestimated the possibility of land reform; consequently they underestimated the commitment of party leaders to achieving it. New York politicians tried to suppress manorial tenures because the lease in fee fostered dependence in social relations, retarded the spirit of improvement, and threatened the public peace. Just as African American slavery became a logical target for political action on the national stage, so "voluntary slavery" became a logical target for political action at the state capital. The "demagoguery" theme in conservative commentary said more about their ideology than it did about the situation at hand. Emphasizing the baneful effects of "king numbers" in New York politics made more sense. Party managers courted Anti-Rent voters with vigor, and they did so for the same reason bankers attempted to increase their loans. Votes are the currency of democratic politics. But party competition for the Anti-Rent vote shaped the legislative process in one significant way that conservatives overlooked. As the Anti-Rent Party grew larger, political credit for extinguishing manorial tenures became a kind of public good that neither major party wanted the other to appropriate. Democrats scorned the eminent domain option put forward by Whig lawmakers; the Whigs helped Governor Wright's intraparty enemies bury the devise-and-descent bill. Party competition for tenant voters not only sustained the Anti-Rent agitation, as conservatives charged throughout the era, but also frustrated the enactment of statesmanlike solutions.

One conservative argument cannot be contradicted. Manor tenants did put themselves above the law. In the Anti-Rent view, however, the law of property

and contract gave them no other choice. The rent strike signaled tenant repudiation of both the archaic lease in fee and the unreasonable buyout terms
their landlords offered. It promoted tenant unity, provided funds for Anti-Rent
politics, and dramatized the tenant plight for the general public. Year after year,
moreover, Anti-Rent appeals to public opinion evoked favorable responses
from the state. From the Manor Commission of 1840 through the Anti-Rent Act
of 1860, landlord attempts to break the rent strike were followed by intervention
on the tenants' behalf. None of the government forays proved decisive. But
tenant leaders on Rensselaerwyck always assumed that a final solution lay just
around the corner. They did not understand the synergy between law and
politics any better than their landlords did.

Anti-Rent activists took it for granted that excessive claims grounded in
rights of property and contract might be checked by democratic action. Talk of
constitutional limitations evoked their scorn. "The influence of the landed
aristocrat is felt" even in the state legislature, "the lawmaking power of the
people," John Mayham exclaimed at the first Anti-Rent state convention in
1845. "Entwining himself with his golden chords around those ever ready to
raise false constitutional objections to every measure designed for the common
good," the landlord "shelters himself from all legislative change in his relations
with his tenant, under that clause of the United States Constitution which
provides that no state shall pass any law impairing the obligation of contracts—a
position totally foreign to the intent of that Constitution." Anti-renters never
ceased to believe that the "golden chords" would be snapped, for public
opinion was "omnipotent" in America. Alexis de Tocqueville had said so in
1835. "The people reign in the American political world as the Deity does in the
universe," he wrote in *Democracy in America*. "They are the cause and aim of
all things; everything comes from them, and everything is absorbed in them."
The *Freeholder* merely echoed him and countless others. "In this country
public opinion controls our laws and institutions," Charles F. Bouton declared
in 1848. "All that has to be done is to convince the public mind that a cause has
merits, and the people will in the end work out strict justice." Minor Frink,
Bouton's successor at the *Freeholder*, told anti-renters that "revolutions never
go backward." When theirs did in 1865, manor tenants instinctively branded
the outcome as a failure of democracy.[29]

The Anti-Rent view, though attractive to some people even now, overestimated the promise of democracy in the nineteenth-century "polity of courts
and parties."[30] At no point could the people of New York State speak directly or
with one voice capable of trumping all other voices. Every forum of republican
self-government clothed agents of the people, not the people themselves, with
the authority to find an appropriate means of extinguishing the lease in fee.
Most of the agents whom party machines selected and the voters elected—

governors, legislators, judges, and members of the 1846 constitutional convention—were lawyers. Training and experience inclined them to take seriously the
constitutional constraints that Anti-Rent leaders assailed as mere landlord talis-
mans. Political principle and partisan interest, on the other hand, made them
responsive to the tenant cry for action against manorial tenures. But the people's agents never spoke in unison. Whigs resisted appeals to class feeling;
Democrats encouraged such appeals when oppressive social relations in the
present stemmed from grants of "privilege" or government "corruption" in the
past. Rival constitutional understandings compounded the difficulty of political
choice in a culture of partisanship. Whigs celebrated a positive liberalism
grounded in broad constructions of legislative power; Democrats trumpeted a
negative liberalism critical of the Whig penchant for "India rubber" standards
of constitutional interpretation. Party loyalty, shaped by distinctive constella-
tions of political and constitutional ideas, thus transformed the very concept of
a body politic into a legal fiction.

Bipartisan support for a single, decisive land reform measure never materialized. Factionalism within the major parties, often aggravated by unanticipated events in Washington, disrupted the quest for constructive solutions even
when one party controlled both houses of the New York legislature. Opportunities for resolute action passed, subsequent developments in constitutional
law foreclosed the political possibilities of previous years, and the lease in fee
survived. William H. Seward and Silas Wright, the era's most popular and
powerful governors, took up the cause of land reform only to learn the same
humbling lesson. Abraham Lincoln described it forthrightly in 1864. "I claim
not to have controlled events," Lincoln said, "but confess plainly that events
have controlled me."[31]

Anti-Rent reliance on public opinion, like the Church–Van Rensselaer reliance on the rule of law, gradually stoked a sense of bewildered disillusionment
with the performance of major party leaders. What the conservatives derided as
"demagoguery," however, was regarded by manor militants as perversity. Whigs
and Democrats insisted time and again that manorial tenures could be extinguished only upon payment of compensation, but neither the eminent domain scheme nor the devise-and-descent bill became law. Meanwhile, the Anti-
Rent movement's own lawyers persuaded the rank and file on Rensselaerwyck
that the well-meaning people affiliated with the major parties had been wrong
on the compensation question. Ira Harris argued that the legislature could pass
a rent moratorium law designed to test the validity of proprietor land titles.
Calvin Pepper Jr. contended that the Van Rensselaer family's British patents
violated the statute Quia Emptores. Azor Taber, followed by Anson Bingham
and Andrew J. Colvin, claimed that the common law barred landlords having
no reversions from ejecting tenants in fee who refused to pay fines on alienation

or even the rent itself. Anti-Rent pursuit of these all-or-nothing arguments estranged the movement from the major parties, hardened the Van Rensselaer commitment to their no-compromise persuasion, and ultimately brought grief to everyone with a stake in the old manor. At the end of the era, the lease in fee no longer presented a problem to be solved. It served, instead, as a symbol of the self-defeating posturing by landlords and tenants alike. Both spurned compromise, both posed as noble victims deprived of their rights, and both blamed their unhappy fate on the corrosive interaction between law and politics. In 1865 nobody else cared.

Monuments to the blood, treasure, and emotion expended during the Anti-Rent era still exist in the eastern counties of New York State. Roadside historical markers designate places where deputy sheriffs were coated with tar and feathers. A placard outside the Berne Historical Society informs visitors that the village was once "the capital of the Anti-Rent movement." Across the Hudson River in Rensselaer County, rural people gather in Hoags Corners every July to celebrate "Big Thunder Day."[32] But the most appropriate monuments to the Anti-Rent era are buried in county land records. Astonished home buyers sometimes learn that they are required every year to pay a nominal rent charge to some remote assignee of Stephen Van Rensselaer III. Their title deeds stand as reminders of how law, politics, and ideology frustrated the achievement of a reform everyone wanted to achieve during a supposed "golden age" of American democracy. We forget them at our peril.

Notes

ABBREVIATIONS AND FREQUENTLY CITED SHORT TITLES

AEJ	*Albany Evening Journal* (daily)
AHR	*American Historical Review*
AIHA	Albany Institute of History and Art
Allen Report	*Report of the committee on the judiciary on the petition of sundry residents of the Manor of Rensselaerwyck, praying for certain modifications of the law respecting the rights of landlord and tenant, &c.*, NYAD 183, 67 sess. (1844)
Anti-Renter	(Albany) *Anti-Renter* (weekly)
Argus	*Albany Argus* (daily)
Atlas	*Albany Atlas* (daily)
Blackstone, *Commentaries*	William Blackstone, *Commentaries on the Laws of England*, ed. Joseph Chitty, 4 vols. (New York: W. E. Dean, 1832)
Courier and Enquirer	*New York Courier and Enquirer* (daily)
Democratic Review	*United States Magazine and Democratic Review*
Dickinson, *Speeches*	John R. Dickinson, ed., *Speeches, Correspondence, Etc. of the Late Daniel S. Dickinson of New York*, 2 vols. (New York: G. P. Putnam, 1867)
DLC	Library of Congress, Washington, D.C.
Duer Report	*Report of the Committee on so much of the Governor's Message as relates to the difficulties between the landlord and tenants of the Manor of Rensselaerwyck*, NYAD 271, 63 sess. (1840)
Freeholder	(Albany) *Freeholder* (weekly)
Gillet, *Wright*	Ransom H. Gillet, *The Life and Times of Silas Wright* (Albany: Argus, 1874)
Hammond, *Political History*	Jabez D. Hammond, *Political History of the State of New York, From January 1, 1841 to January 1, 1847* (Syracuse: L. W. Hall, 1852)
Herald	*New York Herald* (daily)
JAH	*Journal of American History*
JEH	*Journal of Economic History*
Kent, *Commentaries*	James Kent, *Commentaries on American Law*, 4th ed., 4 vols. (New York: E. B. Clayton, 1840)
Lincoln, *Governor Messages*	Charles Z. Lincoln, ed., *Messages from the Governors of the State of New York*, 11 vols. (Albany: J. B. Lyon, 1909)
"LNY"	"Legislature of New York" (daily proceedings)

(m)	microfilm
McAdam, *Bench and Bar*	David McAdam et al., *History of the Bench and Bar of New York*, 2 vols. (New York: N.Y. History, 1897)
NYAD	New York Assembly Document
NYAJ	*New York Assembly Journal*
NYEP	*New York Evening Post* (daily)
NYH	*New York History*
NYHS	New-York Historical Society
NYHSQ	*New-York Historical Society Quarterly*
NYPL	New York Public Library
NYRS	*New York Revised Statutes*
NYSD	New York Senate Document
NYSJ	*New York Senate Journal*
NYSL	New York State Library
Proctor, "Albany Bar"	L. B. Proctor, "The Bench and Bar, or Legal History of Albany," in *History of Albany County*, ed. George R. Howell and Jonathan Tenney (New York: W. W. Munsell, 1886)
PSQ	*Political Science Quarterly*
Richardson, *President Messages*	James D. Richardson, ed., *A Compilation of the Messages and Papers of the Presidents, 1789–1908*, 11 vols. (Washington, D.C.: Bureau of National Literature and Art, 1909)
Seward, *Autobiography*	Frederick A. Seward, ed., *Autobiography of William H. Seward, from 1801 to 1834. With a Memoir of His Life, and Selections from His Letters from 1831 to 1846* (New York: D. Appleton, 1877)
Seward, *Works*	George E. Baker, ed., *The Works of William H. Seward*, 3 vols. (New York: J. S. Redfield, 1853)
Thorpe, *Constitutions*	Francis N. Thorpe, ed., *The Federal and State Constitutions*, House Doc. 357, 59th Cong., 2d sess. (1909)
Tribune	*New York Tribune* (daily)
UR	Rush Rhees Library, University of Rochester
WA	*Working Man's Advocate* (weekly)
Weed, *Memoir*	Thurlow Weed Barnes, ed., *Memoir of Thurlow Weed* (Boston: Houghton, Mifflin, 1884)
Whig Review	*American Whig Review*
Whipple Report	*Report of the select committee, to whom was referred the petitions from numerous tenants of the manor of Rensselaerwyck*, NYAD 189, 67 sess. (1844)
YA	*Young America* (weekly)

CHAPTER ONE

1. "Anti-Renters' Declaration of Independence, July 4, 1839," in *We the Other People: Alternative Declarations of Independence by Labor Groups, Farmers, Woman's Rights Advocates, Socialists, and Blacks, 1829–1976*, ed. Philip S. Foner (Urbana: University of Illinois

Press, 1976), 60–62. The size of the manor and the number of tenant families in 1839 are drawn from *People v. Van Rensselaer*, 9 N.Y. 291, 292 (1853) (statement of facts stipulated by the parties); Edward P. Cheyney, *Anti-Rent Agitation in the State of New York, 1839–1846* (Philadelphia: University of Pennsylvania Press, 1887), 14.

2. A. J. F. Van Laer, "The Patroon System and the Colony of Rensselaerswyck," *Proceedings of the New York State Historical Association* 8 (1909): 222–33; Clarence W. Rife, "Land Tenure in New Netherland," in *Essays in Colonial History Presented to Charles McLean Andrews by His Students* (New Haven: Yale University Press, 1931), 41–73; Donna Merwick, *Possessing Albany, 1630–1710: The Dutch and English Experiences* (New York: Cambridge University Press, 1990), 6–67.

3. Richard Hofstadter, *America at 1750: A Social Portrait* (New York: Alfred A. Knopf, 1971), 151; Julius Goebel Jr., *Some Legal and Political Aspects of the Manors of New York* (Baltimore: Order of Colonial Lords of Manors in America, 1928); Sung Bok Kim, *Landlord and Tenant in Colonial New York: Manorial Society, 1664–1775* (Chapel Hill: University of North Carolina Press, 1978), 3–128, 162–234.

4. Irving Mark, *Agrarian Conflicts in Colonial New York, 1711–1775* (New York: Columbia University Press, 1940), 14, 73–75, 107–63; Kim, *Landlord and Tenant in Colonial New York*, vii, 281–415; Patricia U. Bonomi, *A Factious People: Politics and Society in Colonial New York* (New York: Columbia University Press, 1971), 179–228; Staughton Lynd, "The Tenant Rising on Livingston Manor, May 1777," in *Class Conflict, Slavery, and the United States Constitution* (Indianapolis: Bobbs-Merrill, 1967), 63–78. Mark and Lynd interpret the uprisings as episodes of class conflict; Bonomi and Kim emphasize the fact that the insurrections flared up near the disputed eastern boundary with Connecticut and Massachusetts and interpret the uprisings in terms of tenant opportunism. For a thoughtful attempt to establish a *via media* through this historiographical dispute, see Cynthia Kierner, *Traders and Gentlefolk: The Livingstons of New York, 1675–1790* (Ithaca: Cornell University Press, 1992), 86–87, 110–25. The outstanding treatments of the boundary controversy and the relatively neglected disorders on Claverack at the turn of the century, respectively, are Julius Goebel Jr. and Joseph M. Smith, *The Law Practice of Alexander Hamilton: Documents and Commentary*, 5 vols. (New York: Columbia University Press, 1964–81), 1:531–84, 3:315–66. But see also Alfred F. Young, *The Democratic Republicans of New York: The Origins, 1763–1797* (Chapel Hill: University of North Carolina Press, 1967), 204–7, 533–35.

5. *Message from the Governor, in relation to the difficulties in the Manor of Rensselaerwyck* (hereinafter cited as *Seward Report*), NYSD 70, 63 sess. (1840), 15–16.

6. *AEJ*, Nov. 13, 16, 1838. For the numbers, see Elliott Robert Barkan, *Portrait of a Party: The Origins and Development of the Whig Persuasion in New York State* (New York: Garland, 1988), 267–68; for the record turnout and a perceptive assessment of its causes and consequences, see Joel H. Silbey, *The American Political Nation, 1838–1893* (Stanford: Stanford University Press, 1991), 26–32.

7. [John A. Dix], "Address of the Republican State Convention to the Democracy of the State of New York," *Argus*, Sept. 15, 1838; *AEJ*, Nov. 9–10, 1838; Dixon Ryan Fox, *The Decline of Aristocracy in the Politics of New York, 1801–1840* (New York: Columbia University Press, 1919), 398–401. See also Arthur M. Schlesinger Jr., *The Age of Jackson* (Boston: Little, Brown, 1945), 47–50, 88–259.

8. Marcy to Prosper M. Wetmore, Dec. 11, 1838, quoted in James C. Curtis, *The Fox at Bay: Martin Van Buren and the Presidency, 1837–1841* (Lexington: University Press of Kentucky, 1970), 137; *Argus*, Nov. 16, 1838; Fillmore to George W. Patterson, Feb. 6, 1839, quoted in Robert J. Rayback, *Millard Fillmore: Biography of a President* (Buffalo: Buffalo

Historical Society, 1959), 106–7. For the resumption of specie payments and the recovery of 1838, see Bray Hammond, *Banks and Politics in America: From the Revolution to the Civil War* (Princeton: Princeton University Press, 1957), 477–81. See also VETO [Theodore Sedgwick Jr.], "Position of the Democratic Party: Causes of Our Recent Defeat," *NYEP*, Dec. 3, 1838.

9. W. H. Seward to Francis Miller Seward, Nov. 23, 1833; Weed to W. H. Seward, Nov. 9, 1838, Seward, *Autobiography*, 231, 379. Outstanding accounts of the Seward-Weed path to power and the political ideas, cultural attitudes, and social forces that sustained them include Lee Benson, *The Concept of Jacksonian Democracy: New York as a Test Case* (Princeton: Princeton University Press, 1961), 4–109; Daniel Walker Howe, *The Political Culture of the American Whigs* (Chicago: University of Chicago Press, 1979), 1–122, 181–84, 197–200; Thomas Brown, *Politics and Statesmanship: Essays on the American Whig Party* (New York: Columbia University Press, 1985), 1–48, 93–104; Harry L. Watson, *Liberty and Power: The Politics of Jacksonian America* (New York: Hill and Wang, 1990), 177–87.

10. Seward, *Works*, 2:197, 205.

11. Ibid., 190, 197–98.

12. John A. Garraty, *Silas Wright* (New York: Columbia University Press, 1949), 150; Marvin Meyers, *The Jacksonian Persuasion: Politics and Belief*, 2d ed. (Stanford: Stanford University Press, 1960), 31.

13. Seward, *Works*, 2:183, 199–205. For a brief but shrewd discussion of just how new the departure Seward proposed was, see Nathan Miller, *The Enterprise of a Free People: Aspects of Economic Development in New York State during the Canal Period, 1792–1838* (Ithaca: Cornell University Press, 1962), 252–53.

14. *Argus*, Jan. 24, Feb. 20, Mar. 9, 1839; *NYEP*, May 7, 1839; Ronald E. Shaw, *Erie Water West: A History of the Erie Canal, 1792–1854* (Lexington: University of Kentucky Press, 1966), 319–23.

15. *AEJ*, May 10, 1839.

16. Seward, *Works*, 2:343; *Argus*, Jan. 28, Feb. 1–2, 1839; John C. Fitzpatrick, ed., "The Autobiography of Martin Van Buren," in *Annual Report of the American Historical Association for the Year 1918*, vol. 2 (Washington, D.C.: Government Printing Office, 1920), 514; Bayard Tuckerman, ed., *The Diary of Philip Hone, 1828–1851*, 2 vols. (New York: Dodd, Mead, 1889), 1:349; Daniel D. Barnard, *A Discourse on the Life, Services and Character of Stephen Van Rensselaer Delivered Before the Albany Institute, April 5, 1839* (Albany: Hoffman and White, 1839), 91–92.

17. Robert R. Palmer, *The Age of Democratic Revolution*, 2 vols. (Princeton: Princeton University Press, 1959–64), 1:235; Martha J. Lamb, "The Van Rensselaer Manor," *Magazine of American History* 11 (1884): 1. See also William B. Fink, "Stephen Van Rensselaer: The Last Patroon" (Ph.D. diss., Columbia University, 1950), 1–22.

18. Kim, *Landlord and Tenant in Colonial New York*, 144–45, 157 (quotation), 161, 167–68, 235; Thomas Eliot Norton, *The Fur Trade in Colonial New York* (Madison: University of Wisconsin Press, 1974), 3–8, 43–59, 83–100. A "groat" was the old English four-penny coin.

19. Edward Countryman, *A People in Revolution: The American Revolution and Political Society in New York, 1760–1790*, 2d ed. (New York: W. W. Norton, 1989); New York, *Laws*, 10 sess. (1787), 415–16. For land redistribution during the Revolution, with copious citations to the manor-by-manor case studies, see Young, *Democratic Republicans of New York*, 62–66. The opening of western New York following the Treaty of Fort Stanwix (1784) is treated from different perspectives in Barbara Graymont, "New York State Indian Policy after the

Revolution," *NYH* 57 (1976): 438–74; William Chazanof, *Joseph Ellicott and the Holland Land Company* (Syracuse: Syracuse University Press, 1970); Robert W. Silsby, "Mortgage Credit in the Phelps-Gorham Purchase," *NYH* 41 (1960): 3–34.

20. Barnard, *Life, Services and Character of Stephen Van Rensselaer*, 11–13; Fink, "Stephen Van Rensselaer," 23; Kim, *Landlord and Tenant in Colonial New York*, 176.

21. For the number of tenants and the yearly price of wheat at Watervliet beginning in 1793, see the deposition of Andrew D. Lansing, a clerk in the manor office since 1812, in *Report of the select committee on so much of the Governor's message as relates to the difficulties existing between the proprietors of certain leasehold estates and their tenants*, NYAD 156, 69 sess. (1846), 49–50. For the Yankee migration, see David Maldwyn Ellis, "Rise of the Empire State, 1790–1820," *NYH* 56 (1975): 5–27; David Paul Davenport, "The Yankee Settlement of New York, 1783–1820," *Genealogical Journal* 17 (1988–89): 63–88.

22. Fink, "Stephen Van Rensselaer," 36. The wheat rent on Rensselaerwyck had been the lowest in the Hudson Valley since 1767 when Stephen II, as a direct sequel to the tenant uprising of the previous year, called in all the old indentures (fixing the annual rent at 10 percent of produce) and issued new ones (setting the rent at ten bushels of wheat for every 100 acres). See Kim, *Landlord and Tenant in Colonial New York*, 194; William P. McDermott, "The Livingstons' Colonial Land Policy: Personal Gain over Public Need," in *The Livingston Legacy: Three Centuries of American History*, ed. Richard T. Wiles (Annandale-on-Hudson, N.Y.: Bard College Office of Publications, 1987), 10–37. For tabular data and scholarly estimates on acres of land cleared per man per year, wheat yields per acre, and the relationship between wheat prices and transport costs in the 1789–1819 period, see David Maldwyn Ellis, *Landlords and Farmers in the Hudson-Mohawk Region, 1790–1860* (Ithaca: Cornell University Press, 1946), 74, 105, 123; Paul W. Gates, *The Farmer's Age: Agriculture, 1815–1860* (New York: Holt, Rinehart and Winston, 1960), 35; William N. Parker, "Sources of Agricultural Productivity in the Nineteenth Century," *Journal of Farm Economics* 49 (1967): 1455–68; Charles Sellers, *The Market Revolution: Jacksonian America, 1815–1846* (New York: Oxford University Press, 1991), 14–16.

23. Cheyney, *Anti-Rent Agitation*, 15; Fox, *Decline of Aristocracy*, 32; John M. Duncan, *Travels through Part of the United States and Canada in 1818 and 1819*, 2 vols. (London: Hurst, Robinson, 1823), 2:326.

24. Ellis, *Landlords and Farmers*, 124 (quotation), 126, 136, 185, 223–24, 233; Gates, *Farmer's Age*, 160; "List of Rent due in East Manor, 1811–1823," William Paterson Van Rensselaer Collection, box 4, folder 1, AIHA. Before the Panic of 1819, Van Rensselaer routinely took legal action against tenants in default of their contractual obligations. See Fink, "Stephen Van Rensselaer," 41–42. For the difficulties of agricultural readjustment, even for farmers having conventional fee-simple tenures, see Clarence H. Danhof, *Change in Agriculture: The Northern United States, 1820–1870* (Cambridge: Harvard University Press, 1969).

25. Palmer C. Ricketts, *The Centennial Celebration of Rensselaer Polytechnic Institute* (Troy: RPI Board of Trustees, 1925), 64; Miller, *Enterprise of a Free People*, 46–47; Donald B. Marti, "Early Agricultural Societies in New York: The Foundations of Improvement," *NYH* 48 (1967): 313–31; *Report of the commissioners appointed to effect a settlement of the disputes existing between the landlord and tenants of the Manor of Rensselaerwyck*, NYAD 261, 64 sess. (1841), 5.

26. Fink, "Stephen Van Rensselaer," 251–53.

27. "Schedule of the ascertained debts on Bonds and Notes owed by Stephen Van Rensselaer deceased . . . having been divided into nearly two equal parts" [May 1839], William Paterson Van Rensselaer Collection, box 2, folder 2, AIHA.

28. "Agreement between Stephen Van Rensselaer and William P. Van Rensselaer, May 28, 1839," ibid.

29. For details on William P. Van Rensselaer's debt-collection policy in Rensselaer County, see Casparus F. Pruyn to W. P. Van Rensselaer, Dec. 15, 1839, Jan. 16, 24, Mar. 24, 1840, ibid., box 1, folder 8. Pruyn, a manor employee since 1805, remained reluctant to press the Rensselaer County tenants for payment until his retirement in 1844; there is no evidence suggesting that Pruyn's boss urged him to do otherwise. See Charles Elliott Fitch, *Memorial Encyclopedia of the State of New York* (New York: NYHS, 1916), 3:276-77. For the $35,580 debt to Barnard, see "Schedule of the ascertained debts," William Paterson Van Rensselaer Collection, box 2, folder 2, AIHA.

30. Daniel Dewey Barnard, "The Anti-Rent Movement and Outbreak in New York," *Whig Review* 2 (1845): 581.

31. Lawrence Van Deusen et al. to Stephen Van Rensselaer IV, May 22, 1839, *Argus*, Dec. 6, 1839.

32. Van Rensselaer to Van Deusen et al., May 29, 1839, ibid., Dec. 6, 1839.

33. "Anti-Renters' Declaration of Independence," ibid. The quest for solidarity already had met some success. Delegates from five townships remonstrated with Van Rensselaer on May 22; Anti-Rent committeemen from a sixth township, Guilderland, signed the July 4 manifesto.

34. *Seward Report*, 21-22.

35. Ibid., 25-26.

36. Ibid., 22-24.

37. Artcher to Seward, Dec. 4, 1839, ibid., 18-19.

38. Ibid., 19-20.

39. *AEJ*, Nov. 8, 1839; Thurlow Weed, *Autobiography*, ed. Harriet A. Weed (Boston: Houghton Mifflin, 1884), 476-79.

40. Pruyn to Van Rensselaer, Dec. [7], 1839, William Paterson Van Rensselaer Collection, box 1, folder 8, AIHA; *NYEP*, Dec. 11, 1839. See also the comparable editorials reprinted in *Argus*, Dec. 19, 21, 1839.

41. In 1840 Wheaton's colleague, Fred A. Tallmadge (W.-Manhattan), referred to him as "the counsel of the tenants" on the senate floor. See "LNY," *Argus*, May 13, 1840.

42. *AEJ*, Dec. 10, 1839; Wheaton and Taber to Seward, Dec. 11, 1839, *Seward Report*, 34-35; *Argus*, Dec. 11-13, 1839. See also *Report of the Comptroller, in answer to a resolution of the Senate, relative to paying the militia called out to assist the Sheriff of Albany*, NYSD 67, 63 sess. (1840).

43. *AEJ*, Dec. 12, 1839; *Argus*, Dec. 13, 1839.

44. Robert T. Swaine, *The Cravath Firm and Its Predecessors*, 2 vols. (New York: Ad Press, 1946), 2:52-73 (quotation at 56). For a representative indenture, see *Report of the Committee on so much of the Governor's Message as relates to the difficulties between the landlord and tenants of the Manor of Rensselaerwyck*, NYAD 271, 63 sess. (1840), 23-27. For the form of real-estate development Seward knew best, see William Wyckoff, *The Developer's Frontier: The Making of the Western New York Landscape* (New Haven: Yale University Press, 1988).

45. See, generally, John N. Taylor, *A Treatise on the American Law of Landlord and Tenant*, 2d ed. (New York: J. S. Voorhies, 1844). The quotation in the text is from *Spencer's Case*, 77 Eng. Rep. 72 (K.B. 1583). Whether leasehold covenants ran with the land at common law remained uncertain until Henry VIII plundered the monasteries in 1540. Because much of the church land was under lease and the king wanted to sell the reversions, he asked Parliament to enact a statute expressly authorizing grantees of reversions to enforce

covenants in leases and making the tenants' assignees liable for the rent. The New York legislature adopted a version of the statute in 1788. See A. W. B. Simpson, *A History of the Land Law*, 2d ed. (Oxford: Clarendon Press, 1986), 255–56; New York, *Laws*, 11 sess. (1788), 604.

46. Kent, *Commentaries*, 3:460–61. See also Emory Washburn, *A Treatise on the American Law of Real Property*, 2d ed., 2 vols. (Boston: Little, Brown, 1864), 2:9–11.

47. Kent, *Commentaries*, 4:127; William Rawle, *A Practical Treatise on the Law of Covenants for Title*, 2d ed. (Philadelphia: T. and J. W. Johnson, 1854), 341–42; Thomas Platt, *A Practical Treatise on the Law of Covenants* (London: Saunders and Benning, 1829), 65; John William Smith, *A Selection of Leading Cases on Various Branches of the Law, with Notes*, 2 vols. (Philadelphia: J. S. Littell, 1838–40), 2:37–38. See also Edward Sugden, *A Practical Treatise on the Law of Vendors and Purchasers of Estates*, 7th ed. (Springfield, Mass.: George and Charles Merriam, 1851), 728–31, 736–42.

48. Kent, *Commentaries*, 4:131; *Newkirk v. Newkirk*, 2 Caines 345, 352–53 (N.Y. Sup. Ct. 1805).

49. *Jackson* ex dem. *Lewis & Wife v. Schutz*, 18 Johns. 174 (N.Y. Sup. Ct. 1820) (hereinafter cited as *Schutz*); Philip L. White, *The Beekmans of New York in Politics and Commerce, 1647–1877* (New York: NYHS, 1956), 92–94, 118, 161–63, 206–7; Staughton Lynd, *Anti-Federalism in Dutchess County, New York* (Chicago: Loyola University Press, 1962), 23–25.

50. *Schutz* (arg.), 176, 179, 182. Emmot and Oakley were natives of Dutchess County; both were prominent members of the Federalist Party. For biographical sketches, see David Hackett Fischer, *The Revolution of American Conservatism: The Federalist Party in the Era of Jeffersonian Democracy* (New York: Harper and Row, 1965), 313, 316.

51. Blackstone, *Commentaries*, 2:42–92. In modern legal scholarship, the Quia Emptores story has been told with greater sensitivity to social context. See, in particular, Alan Harding, *A Social History of English Law* (London: Penguin Books, 1966), 30–35, 88–96; A. W. B. Simpson, "Land Ownership and Economic Freedom," in *The State and Freedom of Contract*, ed. Harry N. Scheiber (Stanford: Stanford University Press, 1998), 13–24.

52. Blackstone, *Commentaries*, 2:42, 91–92. See also Simpson, *History of the Land Law*, 54–55, 77–78; C. F. Kolbert and N. A. M. Mackay, *History of Scots and English Land Law* (London: Geographical Publications, 1977), 70–73, 100–103. The rights of distress and reentry, which had to be expressly annexed to a grant reserving a rent charge, were "inseparably incident" to rent service because of the tenure existing between grantor and tenant in fee. See Kent, *Commentaries*, 3:461.

53. *Schutz* (arg.), 179 (Emmot's emphasis). See also Goebel, *Legal and Political Aspects of the Manors*, 9–11; William R. Vance, "The Quest for Tenure in the United States," *Yale Law Journal* 33 (1924): 248–71. For a stunning reinterpretation of *Calvin's Case*, 77 Eng. Rep. 377 (K.B. 1608) (distinguishing the jurisdiction of Parliament in crown lands acquired by descent from crown lands acquired by conquest), see Barbara A. Black, "The Constitution of Empire: The Case for the Colonists," *University of Pennsylvania Law Review* 124 (1976): 1157–1211.

54. *Schutz* (arg.), 180. For the statute, see New York, *Laws*, 10 sess. (1787), 415–16.

55. *Schutz* (arg.), 180; New York, *Laws*, 10 sess. (1787), 415–16. In the feudal law, a "mesne lord" was an intermediate lord who stood between the king and the tenants in fee.

56. *Schutz*, 184. For biographical sketches of the justices, two Federalists and two Jeffersonians (Ambrose Spencer, principal manager and advisor of De Witt Clinton, moved back and forth between the parties), see Fischer, *Revolution of American Conservatism*, 309–10, 318–19; McAdam, *Bench and Bar*, 1:484, 522.

57. *Schutz*, 186–87.

58. Kent, *Commentaries*, 4:131(a).

59. *Seward Report*, 16; *NYAJ*, 35 sess. (1812), 110. The 1812 report, which responded to tenant petitioners on the George Clarke estate in Otsego County, was quoted by Seward in his message to the legislature on January 7, 1840. See Seward, *Works*, 2:221.

60. *Argus*, Dec. 19, 1839 (quoting from *New York Gazette*); *Cochran v. Van Surlay*, 20 Wend. 365, 384 (N.Y. Ct. Errors 1838). See also Thomas L. Haskell, "Capitalism and the Origins of the Humanitarian Sensibility, Part 2," *AHR* 90 (1985): 547–66.

61. Howe, *Political Culture of the American Whigs*, 87–92; Brown, *Politics and Statesmanship*, 11, 30–31. For an excellent discussion of the ideas about the separation of powers that Whigs revived, see Gordon S. Wood, *The Creation of the American Republic, 1776–1787* (Chapel Hill: University of North Carolina Press, 1969), 150–59.

CHAPTER TWO

1. Thorpe, *Constitutions*, 2643.

2. *Argus*, Jan. 8, 1840; Seward, *Works*, 2:216, 219, 221, 250, 253. For an account of the Harrisburg convention, see Robert Gray Gunderson, *The Log-Cabin Campaign* (Lexington: University of Kentucky Press, 1957), 41–66.

3. Seward, *Works*, 2:190, 213, 242, 249–50.

4. Ibid., 221.

5. *Beers v. Haughton*, 9 Pet. 329, 359 (U.S. 1835); Seward, *Works*, 2:221. See also *Holmes v. Lansing*, 3 Johns. Cas. 73 (N.Y. Sup. Ct. 1802); *Sturgis v. Crowinshield*, 4 Wheat. 122, 200 (U.S. 1819); *Mason v. Haile*, 12 Wheat. 370, 378 (U.S. 1827).

6. Seward, *Works*, 2:183, 224; Reginald McGrane, *The Panic of 1837: Some Financial Problems of the Jacksonian Era* (Chicago: University of Chicago Press, 1924), 70–81, 85–90, 204–7; Peter Temin, *The Jacksonian Economy* (New York: W. W. Norton, 1969), 148–55.

7. Carter Goodrich, *Government Promotion of American Canals and Railroads, 1800–1890* (New York: Columbia University Press, 1960), 275. See also B. U. Ratchford, *American State Debts* (Durham: Duke University Press, 1941), 88; Harry N. Scheiber, *Ohio Canal Era: A Case Study of Government and the Economy, 1820–1861* (Athens: Ohio University Press, 1969), 156–57.

8. Seward, *Works*, 2:224, 227, 254. For the political controversies summarized here through Seward's eyes, see Arthur M. Schlesinger Jr., *The Age of Jackson* (Boston: Little, Brown, 1945); Thomas Payne Govan, *Nicholas Biddle: Nationalist and Public Banker, 1786–1844* (Chicago: University of Chicago Press, 1959); John M. McFaul, *The Politics of Jacksonian Finance* (Ithaca: Cornell University Press, 1972); Daniel Feller, *The Public Lands in Jacksonian Politics* (Madison: University of Wisconsin Press, 1984); Merrill D. Peterson, *The Great Triumvirate: Webster, Clay, and Calhoun* (New York: Oxford University Press, 1987).

9. *Argus*, Oct. 31, 1839; Daniel S. Dickinson, "Speech upon the Governor's Message in the Senate of New York, January 11th, 1840," Dickinson, *Speeches*, 2:103.

10. Seward, *Works*, 2:212, 232–33, 236–37.

11. *NYEP*, Jan. 14, Apr. 29, 1840; *Argus*, Jan. 14, May 13, 1840.

12. "LNY," *Argus*, Jan. 11, 1840; *NYSJ*, 63 sess. (1840), 77.

13. "LNY," *Argus*, Jan. 11, 1840 (Young's emphasis).

14. "The Manor Difficulties: Conclusion of the debate . . . on the motion of Mr. Edwards," *Argus*, Jan. 13, 1840 (Dickinson's emphasis).

15. "LNY," *Argus*, Jan. 11, 1840; "The Manor Difficulties," ibid., Jan. 13, 1840; *NYSJ*, 63 sess. (1840), 78.

16. *AEJ*, Feb. 18, 1848; *NYAJ*, 63 sess. (1840), 107; [Benjamin F. Butler, John Duer, and John C. Spencer], "Revisers' Reports and Notes," *NYRS*, 2d ed., 3:571; Lawrence M. Friedman, *A History of American Law*, 2d ed. (New York: Simon and Schuster, 1985), 240. See also Seward, *Autobiography*, 47-48; Katherine A. Jacob and Bruce A. Ragsdale, eds., *Biographical Directory of the United States Congress, 1774-1989*, Senate Doc. 34, 100th Cong., 2d sess. (1989), 933. The outstanding account of the pioneering *NYRS* is Gregory S. Alexander, *Commodity and Propriety: Competing Visions of Property in American Legal Thought, 1776-1970* (Chicago: University of Chicago Press, 1997), 97-126.

17. Proctor, "Albany Bar," 144. For the introduction of the bill, see *NYAJ*, 63 sess. (1840), 146. The provisions of Wheaton's bill are printed in *Duer Report*, 6.

18. Kent, *Commentaries*, 3:473, 485. The thirty-day-notice prerequisite for actions of ejectment was codified in *NYRS*, 2d ed. (1836), 1:745.

19. Kent, *Commentaries*, 3:472-73 (digesting statutes and "contrary to public policy" decisions in other jurisdictions). See also Elizabeth Blackmar, *Manhattan for Rent, 1785-1850* (Ithaca: Cornell University Press, 1989), 219-27.

20. "LNY," *Argus*, Feb. 8, 1840.

21. *NYAJ*, 63 sess. (1840), 312.

22. *Duer Report*, 3-4. The quoted words are Duer's, summarizing tenant complaints; the actual petitions were destroyed, along with all other legislative-branch manuscripts, in the New York State Library fire of 1911.

23. Ibid., 4.

24. James Willard Hurst, *The Growth of American Law: The Lawmakers* (Boston: Little, Brown, 1950), 70-71, 78-79. For an excellent account of comparable developments in England, see P. S. Atiyah, *The Rise and Fall of Freedom of Contract* (Oxford: Clarendon Press, 1979), 91-102, 250-55. Although the New York legislature retained jurisdiction over petitions for divorce throughout the nineteenth century, it rarely dissolved marriages. See Nelson Manfred Blake, *The Road to Reno: A History of Divorce in the United States* (New York: Macmillan, 1962), 64-79.

25. *Seymour v. Delancey*, 3 Cowen 445, 525 (N.Y. Ct. Errors 1824); Kent, *Commentaries*, 2:485; Francis Bohlen, "Voluntary Assumption of Risk," *Harvard Law Review* 20 (1906): 22. For an elaborate compilation of cases on "inadequacy pure and simple" and "inadequacy coupled with other inequitable incidents," see John Norton Pomeroy, *A Treatise on Equity Jurisprudence*, 3 vols. (San Francisco: A. L. Bancroft, 1882), 2:428-33. See also Morton J. Horwitz, *The Transformation of American Law, 1780-1860* (Cambridge: Harvard University Press, 1977), 160-80; James Gordley, *The Philosophical Origins of Modern Contract Doctrine* (Oxford: Clarendon Press, 1991), 202-8.

26. Kent, *Commentaries*, 1:455; Edward S. Corwin, "The Basic Doctrine of American Constitutional Law," *Michigan Law Review* 12 (1914): 247-76. The cases referred to in the text are *Holden v. James*, 11 Mass. 396 (1814); *Allen's Administrator v. Peden*, 4 N.C. 442 (1816), explained in *Hoke v. Henderson*, 15 N.C. 1, 17 (1831); *Bank of the State v. Cooper*, 2 Yerg. 599 (Tenn. 1831). See also *Dash v. Van Kleeck*, 7 Johns. 477, 508-9 (N.Y. Sup. Ct. 1811). For a splendid account of the emergence of the "basic doctrine" in one jurisdiction, see Timothy A. Lawrie, "Interpretation and Authority: Separation of Powers and the Judiciary's Battle for Independence in New Hampshire, 1786-1819," *American Journal of Legal History* 39 (1995): 310-36.

27. *Duer Report*, 4-5.

28. Blackstone, *Commentaries*, 2:288; Adam Smith, *An Inquiry into the Nature and Causes of the Wealth of Nations*, ed. Edwin Cannan (New York: Modern Library, 1937), 363. For an excellent discussion of Jefferson's views, see Stanley N. Katz, "Thomas Jefferson and the Right to Property in Revolutionary America," *Journal of Law and Economics* 19 (1976): 467–88. Entails were abolished in New York, *Laws*, 6 sess. (1782), 501–2.

29. *Duer Report*, 5–6.

30. Ibid., 7–8. Duer's assumptions about original intent were on the mark. See Benjamin F. Wright, *The Contract Clause of the Constitution* (Cambridge: Harvard University Press, 1938), 3–12; Jennifer Nedelsky, *Private Property and the Limits of American Constitutionalism: The Madisonian Framework and Its Legacy* (Chicago: University of Chicago Press, 1990).

31. *Duer Report*, 8–9. Duer's argument tracked Joseph Story, *Commentaries on the Constitution of the United States*, 3 vols. (Boston: Hilliard, Gray, 1833), 3:236–37. For Duer, as for Story, the mischief arising from the right-remedy distinction stemmed from the Court's rejection of Chief Justice Marshall's position in *Ogden v. Saunders*, 12 Wheat. 213 (U.S. 1827). His father provided an elaborate indictment of the *Ogden* holding and its repercussions in *A Course of Lectures on the Constitutional Jurisprudence of the United States*, 2d ed. (Boston: Little, Brown, 1856), 355–81. Even Duer's "secondary contract" principle, invoked against the first section of the Wheaton bill, seems to have been derived from Marshall's claim, dissenting in *Ogden* (353), "that obligation and remedy are distinguishable from each other . . . [in] that the first is created by the act of the parties, the last is afforded by government." See also G. Edward White, *The Marshall Court and Cultural Change, 1815–1835* (New York: Macmillan, 1988), ch. 9.

32. *Duer Report*, 9–11; Theodore Sedgwick Jr., ed., *A Collection of the Political Writings of William Leggett*, 2 vols. (New York: Taylor and Dodd, 1840), 1:166. See also Richard Hofstadter, "William Leggett, Spokesman of Jacksonian Democracy," *PSQ* 58 (1943): 581–94. Duer's invocation of Adam Smith on corn rents came right out of Kent, *Commentaries*, 3:462–63.

33. *Duer Report*, 11.

34. Ibid., 12–13.

35. Ibid., 14.

36. Ibid., 19.

37. *Beekman v. Saratoga & Schenectady Railroad Co.*, 3 Paige 45, 73 (N.Y. Ch. 1831); *Bloodgood v. Mohawk & Hudson R. R. Co.*, 18 Wend. 9 (N.Y. Ct. Errors 1837).

38. *Duer Report*, 19–20. Duer cited only two cases from another jurisdiction. *Willson v. Blackbird Creek Marsh Co.*, 2 Pet. 245, 251 (U.S. 1831), justified the construction of a dam across a tidal creek because "the value of the property on its banks must be enhanced" by draining the swamp; *Harding v. Goodlett*, 3 Yerg. 40 (Tenn. 1832), construed a mill act so as to permit condemnation of private property for a gristmill but not for a sawmill or papermill. Neither citation provided much support for Duer's claim; the latter provided fodder for a powerful Democratic counterblast in 1844. Yet there were Massachusetts and New Jersey mill-act decisions directly on point. See *Boston & Roxbury Dam Co. v. Newman*, 12 Pick. 467, 480 (Mass. 1832); *Scudder v. Trenton Del. Falls Co.*, 1 N.J. Eq. 694, 727 (1832); Harry N. Scheiber, "Property Law, Expropriation, and Resource Allocation by Government, 1789–1910," *JEH* 33 (1973): 232–51. Duer was apparently the victim of the sources closest at hand. Walworth's only citations in *Beekman* were to Kent's *Commentaries*, 2:340, and John Marshall's opinion for the Court in *Willson*. Kent cited *Harding*, an opinion that Duer seems never to have read, beginning in the 4th edition (1840); but he never cited *Newman* or *Scudder*, decisions he probably disapproved.

39. Don C. Sowers, *The Financial History of New York State from 1789 to 1912* (New York: Columbia University Press, 1914), 336; Harry Pierce, *The Railroads of New York: A Study of Government Aid* (Cambridge: Harvard University Press, 1953), 16.

40. *Duer Report*, 21. The bill is printed in "LNY," *Argus*, Mar. 24, 1840.

41. "LNY," *AEJ*, May 12, 1840.

42. Casparus F. Pruyn to William P. Van Rensselaer, Mar. 24, 1840, William Paterson Van Rensselaer Collection, box 1, folder 8, AIHA; "LNY," *Argus*, May 12–13, 1840. The Locofocos were a radical faction of the Manhattan Democracy that ran an independent ticket, dedicated to the equal-rights principle, during the the mid-1830s. Beginning in 1837, Whigs referred to all Democrats as Locofocos and did so with derision.

43. The act "to provide for the settlement of disputes existing between the landlords and tenants of the Manor of Rensselaerwyck" is in New York, *Laws*, 63 sess. (1840), 223. The railroad-aid laws are in ibid., 129, 141, 144, 147, 152, 241, 244, 291. For a legislative history of the canal appropriations in 1840, see Ronald E. Shaw, *Erie Water West: A History of the Erie Canal, 1792–1854* (Lexington: University of Kentucky Press, 1966), 323–24. For the roll calls on the Duer bill, see *NYAJ*, 63 sess. (1840), 1390–91; *NYSJ*, 63 sess. (1840), 556–57, 562.

44. *AEJ*, May 16, Aug. 5, 1840; Gideon Lee to Seward, May 21, 1840 (declining appointment); Gary V. Sacket to Seward, June 10, 1840 (accepting appointment on condition that he could stay at home until after the harvest), Seward Papers, UR (m).

45. Weed to Francis Granger, Nov. 10, 1840, Weed, *Memoir*, 87; *AEJ*, Nov. 5, 1840.

46. The numbers and the analysis are from Michael F. Holt, "The Election of 1840, Voter Mobilization, and the Emergence of the Second Party System: A Reappraisal of Jacksonian Voting Behavior," in *A Master's Due: Essays in Honor of David Herbert Donald*, ed. William J. Cooper Jr. et al. (Baton Rouge: Louisiana State University Press, 1985), 16–58. The quotations are from Gunderson, *The Log-Cabin Campaign*, 118, 125; William Nisbet Chambers, "The Election of 1840," in *History of American Presidential Elections, 1789–1968*, ed. Arthur M. Schlesinger Jr. and Fred L. Israel, 4 vols. (New York: Chelsea House, 1971), 1:677 (emphasis in original); Norma Lois Peterson, *The Presidencies of William Henry Harrison and John Tyler* (Lawrence: University Press of Kansas, 1989), 29.

CHAPTER THREE

1. *NYEP*, Jan. 7, 1841; Seward, *Works*, 2:287; *Washington National Intelligencer*, Feb. 15, 1841 (letters from New York business correspondent); Robert Sobel, *The Big Board: A History of the New York Stock Market* (New York: Free Press, 1965), 50; William Bard to G. C. Verplanck, Feb. 24, 1841, Verplanck Papers, box 1, NYHS; Samuel B. Ruggles to Verplanck, Feb. 11, 1841, ibid., box 6. See also Walter Buckingham Smith, *Economic Aspects of the Second Bank of the United States* (Cambridge: Harvard University Press, 1953), 223–30.

2. Seward, *Works*, 2:287–94.

3. Ibid.

4. Ibid., 290–91. I have made one important change in Seward's text. His estimate of New York's first-year share in the *Works* was "nearly three hundred thousand dollars," half the figure that all the newspapers reported in January 1841. I have used the 1841 number.

5. The term "inexpedient" was Duer's. See William A. Duer Jr. to Thurlow Weed, *AEJ*, Jan. 17, 1846.

6. Leland H. Jenks, *The Migration of British Capital to 1875* (New York: Alfred A. Knopf, 1927), 73–103; B. U. Ratchford, *American State Debts* (Durham: Duke University Press, 1941), 89–98; Ralph W. Hidy, *The House of Baring in American Trade and Finance: English Merchant Bankers at Work, 1763–1861* (Cambridge: Harvard University Press, 1949), 288–

94; Thomas Payne Govan, *Nicholas Biddle: Nationalist and Public Banker, 1786-1844* (Chicago: University of Chicago Press, 1959), 373-75, 383-84, 392-97; James Roger Sharp, *The Jacksonians versus the Banks: Politics in the States after the Panic of 1837* (New York: Columbia University Press, 1970), 274-75, 292-96. For the quotation, see Harry N. Scheiber, *Ohio Canal Era: A Case Study of Government and the Economy, 1820-1861* (Athens: Ohio University Press, 1968), 149.

7. Calvin Colton, ed., *The Works of Henry Clay*, 10 vols. (New York: G. P. Putnam and Sons, 1904), 8:198, 207, 232, 263; Clay to John M. Clayton, Mar. 3, 1841, Robert Seager II, ed., *The Papers of Henry Clay*, vol. 9, *The Whig Leader* (Lexington: University Press of Kentucky, 1988), 509-10.

8. *Washington National Intelligencer*, Feb. 5, 1841; *Washington Globe*, Feb. 8, 1841; "Notes for Newspaper Editorial," Feb. 4, 1841, Seager, *Papers of Henry Clay*, 495-96. See also Richard Lowitt, *George W. Norris: The Persistence of a Progressive, 1913-1933* (Urbana: University of Illinois Press, 1971), 155-57, 515-18.

9. *AEJ*, Jan. 19, Mar. 22, 1841; Richardson, *President Messages*, 4:21; George Rawlings Poage, *Henry Clay and the Whig Party* (Chapel Hill: University of North Carolina Press, 1936), 28-32; Sydney Nathans, *Daniel Webster and Jacksonian Democracy* (Baltimore: Johns Hopkins University Press, 1973), 154-60.

10. Hammond, *Political History*, 290-91, 380-81; Proctor, "Albany Bar," 140-41; Sherry Penney, *Patrician in Politics: Daniel Dewey Barnard of New York* (Port Washington, N.Y.: Kennikat Press, 1974).

11. Seward, *Works*, 3:374; Louis Hartz, *The Liberal Tradition in America* (New York: Harcourt Brace and World, 1955), 111. See also Lee Benson, *The Concept of Jacksonian Democracy: New York as a Test Case* (Princeton: Princeton University Press, 1961), 11-46, 104-9; Elliott R. Barkan, "The Emergence of a Whig Persuasion: Conservatism, Democratism, and the New York State Whigs," *NYH* 52 (1971): 367-95.

12. Arthur M. Schlesinger Jr., *The Age of Jackson* (Boston: Little, Brown, 1945), 299-304, 313 (quoting Brownson's "Address to the Workingmen" [1841] and describing Whig attacks on him during the 1840 campaign). For the agrarian tradition Barnard feared, see Thomas P. Govan, "Agrarian and Agrarianism: A Study in the Use and Abuse of Words," *Journal of Southern History* 30 (1964): 35-47; Paul K. Conkin, *Prophets of Prosperity: America's First Political Economists* (Bloomington: Indiana University Press, 1980), 222-45.

13. Barnard waited until 1845 before taking his case against Seward before the public. For details on King's estate, see *Report of the select committee on so much of the Governor's message as relates to the difficulties existing between the proprietors of certain leasehold estates and their tenants*, NYAD 156, 69 sess. (1846), 4. King's vote on the Duer bill is recorded in *NYAJ*, 63 sess. (1840), 1390-91. See also McAdam, *Bench and Bar*, 1:388.

14. *AEJ*, Dec. 24, 1840, quoted in Isabel Thompson Kelsay, "Down with the Rent! A Story of Social War in Rural New York" (Ph.D. diss., Columbia University, 1950), 80.

15. *Report of the commissioners appointed to effect a settlement of the disputes existing between the landlord and tenants of the Manor of Rensselaerwyck* (hereinafter cited as *Manor Commission Report*), NYAD 261, 64 sess. (1841), 1. For the statute, see New York, *Laws*, 63 sess. (1840), 223.

16. *Manor Commission Report*, 7-9.

17. Ibid., 9-10.

18. Ibid., 2; Jon Jenkins to Andrew Lansing, Feb. 5, 1841, William Paterson Van Rensselaer Collection, box 6, file 11, AIHA.

19. *Manor Commission Report*, 10; Sacket to Seward, Feb. 8, 1841; Maxwell to Seward,

Apr. 14, 1841, Seward Papers, UR (m). For the reception of the report, see *NYAJ*, 64 sess. (1841), 955.

20. *NYEP*, Mar. 23, 1841.

21. *Report of the Committee on the Judiciary, on several petitions for a law to extend the exemption of personal property from sale on execution or distress for rent* (hereinafter cited as *Sibley Report*), NYSD 81, 64 sess. (1841), 1–4; *NYSJ*, 64 sess. (1841), 343. The "ancient" statutes were codified in *NYRS*, 2d ed. (1836), 2:290.

22. *Sibley Report*, 2–4.

23. *Argus*, May 12, 1841; *AEJ*, Apr. 26, 28, May 4, 7, 8, 11, 17, 20, 1841.

24. "LNY," *AEJ*, May 6, 1841. For the roll call, see *NYSJ*, 64 sess. (1841), 490–92.

25. "LNY," *AEJ*, May 6, 7, 13, 21, 1841.

26. *AEJ*, May 26, 1841.

27. Ibid., Apr. 26, 1841.

28. Seward, *Autobiography*, 547.

29. *Argus*, May 6, 1841.

30. *Courier and Enquirer*, May 12, 1841; Orestes Brownson, "The Laboring Classes," *Boston Quarterly Review* 3 (1840): 358–95, 420–510 (quotation at 389). Thorough treatments of Skidmore's world, thought, and influence include Edward Pessen, *Most Uncommon Jacksonians: The Radical Leaders of the Early Labor Movement* (Albany: State University of New York Press, 1967); Sean Wilentz, *Chants Democratic: New York City and the Rise of the American Working Class, 1788–1850* (New York: Oxford University Press, 1984).

31. Clinton Rossiter, ed., *The Federalist Papers* (New York: New American Library, 1961), 275–76 (Madison's emphasis); William M. Wiecek, *The Guarantee Clause of the U.S. Constitution* (Ithaca: Cornell University Press, 1972), 40–42, 66, 72, 150–51, 157–58.

32. Daniel T. Rodgers, *Contested Truths: Keywords in American Politics Since Independence* (New York: Basic Books, 1987), 78. The link between "constitutional utopianism" and theories of legal obligation was first suggested by Robert M. Cover, *Justice Accused: Antislavery and the Judicial Process* (New Haven: Yale University Press, 1975), 154–58. See also Daniel R. Ernst, "Legal Positivism, Radical Litigation, and the New Jersey Slave Case of 1845," *Law and History Review* 4 (1986): 337–66.

33. *NYRS*, 2d ed. (1836), 2:415; *Herald*, Apr. 2, 1841. See also Kelsay, "Down with the Rent," 82–85. Resistance by white "Indians," though new to New York in 1841, had occurred in other rural conflicts following the American Revolution. For a compendium of episodes and a speculative interpretation of the cultural meanings participants attached to the disguise, see Alan Taylor, *Liberty Men and Great Proprietors: The Revolutionary Settlement on the Maine Frontier, 1760–1820* (Chapel Hill: University of North Carolina Press, 1990), ch. 7.

34. *Argus*, Sept. 9, 1841.

35. Seward, *Autobiography*, 358; *Argus*, Sept. 10, 1841, Apr. 27, 1842; *Herald*, Sept. 11, 16, 1841; *AEJ*, Sept. 10, 1841, Apr. 21, 1842. The removal of distrained chattels from the premises was, of course, unlawful. New York law authorized "the person aggrieved" to recover treble damages in a "special action on the case . . . against the owner of the goods distrained, in case the same be afterwards found to have come to his use or possession." *NYRS*, 2d ed. (1836), 2:414.

36. *AEJ*, Sept. 22, 1841; *Argus*, Sept. 21–22, 1841; Henry Christman, *Tin Horns and Calico* (New York: Henry Holt, 1945), 42–45, 326–27.

37. *Argus*, Sept. 9, 1841; "Man O' the Hills" to James Gordon Bennett, *Herald*, Sept. 11, 1841.

38. The quotations are from Penney, *Patrician in Politics*, 79. For a brilliant analysis of the dynamics and legacies of the special session, see William R. Brock, *Parties and Political Conscience: American Dilemmas, 1840–1850* (Millwood, N.Y.: KTO Press, 1979), ch. 3.

39. Arthur H. Cole, "Cyclical and Sectional Variations in the Sale of Public Lands, 1816–1860," in *The Public Lands: Studies in the History of the Public Domain*, ed. Vernon Carstensen (Madison: University of Wisconsin Press, 1968), 233; Thomas C. Donaldson, *The Public Domain: Its History with Statistics* [1884], House Misc. Doc. 45, 47th Cong., 2d sess. (serial 2158), 753.

40. John Bach McMaster, *A History of the People of the United States from the Revolution to the Civil War*, 8 vols. (New York: Appleton, 1915), 6:623–28; Ratchford, *American State Debts*, 98, 105–7; Reginald C. McGrane, *Foreign Bondholders and American State Debts* (New York: Macmillan, 1935), 133–34, 200–203. Arkansas and Mississippi, the first states to default, were also the first to begin shutting down banks that had suspended specie payments in violation of their charters. See Sharp, *The Jacksonians versus the Banks*, 66–80, 117–19.

41. Don C. Sowers, *The Financial History of New York State* (New York: Columbia University Press, 1914), 69–70, 83–84.

42. The evidence for "the deal," though entirely circumstantial, is very strong. Unlike many agreements that historians have reconstructed from such evidence, moreover, every element of this one was fulfilled. Compare, for example, C. Vann Woodward, *Reunion and Reaction: The Compromise of 1877 and the End of Reconstruction* (Boston: Little, Brown, 1951); Allan Peskin, "Was There a Compromise of 1877?," *JAH* 60 (1973): 63–75; Woodward, "Yes, There Was a Compromise of 1877," ibid., 215–23.

43. *AEJ*, Oct. 8–9, 1841; Seward to John Quincy Adams, Nov. 6, 1841, Seward, *Autobiography*, 570; Glyndon G. Van Deusen, *Thurlow Weed: Wizard of the Lobby* (Boston: Little, Brown, 1947), 124. For the election returns, see *Argus*, Nov. 4–9, 1841.

44. McMaster, *History*, 7:2–3; Michael F. Holt, "The Election of 1840, Voter Mobilization, and the Emergence of the Second American Party System: A Reappraisal of Jacksonian Voting Behavior," in *A Master's Due*, ed. William J. Cooper Jr. et al. (Baton Rouge: Louisiana State University Press, 1985), 38–39; Ratchford, *American State Debts*, 98; McGrane, *Foreign Bondholders*, 204; Jenks, *The Migration of British Capital*, 104–5.

45. John V. Orth, *The Judicial Power of the United States: The Eleventh Amendment in American History* (New York: Oxford University Press, 1987), 42–46.

CHAPTER FOUR

1. Hammond, *Political History*, 247; *Argus*, Nov. 4, 9, 1841 (Croswell's emphasis); *NYEP*, Mar. 19, Nov. 8, 1841; Arthur M. Schlesinger Jr., *The Age of Jackson* (Boston: Little, Brown, 1945), 392.

2. *NYEP*, Oct. 1 (quotation), Dec. 4, 1841, Jan. 12–13, 1843. For a useful account of Bryant's thought and that of his closest associates in the *Evening Post* circle, see Edward K. Spann, *Ideals and Politics: New York Intellectuals and Liberal Democracy, 1820–1880* (Albany: State University of New York Press, 1972).

3. *New State Ice Co. v. Leibmann*, 285 U.S. 262, 280 (1932); *NYEP*, Dec. 12, 1839; "The Manor Difficulties: Conclusion of the debate . . . on the motion of Mr. Edwards," *Argus*, Jan. 13, 1840.

4. Daniel S. Dickinson, "Address Delivered at the Fair of the Queens County Agricultural Society, October 17, 1843," Dickinson, *Speeches*, 1:116.

5. Seward, *Works*, 2:301, 312.

6. Ibid., 321–25, 608–9; Richardson, *President Messages*, 4:82.

7. *NYEP*, May 3, 1841, Mar. 21, 1842, Sept. 28, 1848; *Argus*, Jan. 24, 1842; Hoffman to Azariah Flagg, [1842?], quoted in Schlesinger, *Age of Jackson*, 286. For a discussion of Seward's personal debt, see Glyndon Van Deusen, *William Henry Seward* (New York: Oxford University Press, 1967), 87–88.

8. Michael Hoffman, "Remarks . . . on the Message of the Governor," *Argus*, Jan. 21, 24, 1842.

9. Ibid.

10. New York, *Laws*, 65 sess. (1842), 79, 418; *Report of the committee on public lands, in relation to so much of the Governor's Message as relates to the share of the State of New-York in the proceeds thereof*, NYAD 122, 65 sess. (1842); Thomas C. Donaldson, *The Public Domain: Its History with Statistics* [1884], House Misc. Doc. 45, 47th Cong., 2d sess. (serial 2158), 753. See also Raynor G. Wellington, *The Political and Sectional Influence of the Public Lands, 1828–1848* (Cambridge, Mass.: Riverside Press, 1914), 105–13.

11. George W. Smith, "Arphaxed Loomis—His Career and Public Services," *Papers Read before the Herkimer County Historical Society* 2 (1899–1902): 109–27.

12. Arphaxed Loomis, "Remarks . . . on the Resolutions to Amend the Constitution," *Argus*, May 9, 1842.

13. *AEJ*, Apr. 22, 1842. The intra-Democratic debate on the People's Resolution is expertly treated from a different perspective in L. Ray Gunn, *The Decline of Authority: Public Economic Policy and Political Development in New York State, 1800–1860* (Ithaca: Cornell University Press, 1988), ch. 5.

14. John W. Tamblin, "Speech . . . on Mr. Loomis's Resolution," *AEJ*, Apr. 22, 1842.

15. John A. Dix, "Remarks . . . on the Resolution for an Amendment to the Constitution in Relation to the Borrowing of Money or the Issuing of State Stocks," *Argus*, Mar. 31, 1842.

16. Samuel Young, *Lecture on Civilization, delivered before the Young Men's Association of Saratoga Springs, March 8th, 1841* (Saratoga Springs: G. M. Davison, 1841), excerpted in the *Argus*, Nov. 30, 1841. Orestes Brownson reported that Young's pamphlet "may be obtained at the principal bookstores in New York, Albany, Troy, and Schenectady." See "Literary Notices," *Boston Quarterly Review* 5 (1842): 126. For an especially thoughtful account of the famous principle, see Herbert Sloan, "The Earth Belongs in Usufruct to the Living," in *Jeffersonian Legacies*, ed. Peter S. Onuf (Charlottesville: University Press of Virginia, 1993), 281–315.

17. Dix, "Remarks."

18. The quotation is from the *Argus*, Apr. 12, 1842. See also *NYEP*, Apr. 13, 1842. For the roll call on the People's Resolution, see *NYAJ*, 65 sess. (1842), 837–38. Article VIII of the New York Constitution spelled out the rigorous requirements for amending the instrument. A majority of all members in each house had to assent during one session, followed by two-thirds of all members in the next session, before the proposed amendment could be submitted to the voters for ratification. See Thorpe, *Constitutions*, 2650.

19. Theodore Sedgwick, *Public and Private Economy in Three Parts, 1836–1839*, ed. Joseph Dorfman (Clifton, N.J.: Augustus M. Kelley, 1974), 2:121; Richardson, *President Messages*, 3:330, 344.

20. *NYSJ*, 65 sess. (1842), 245; "LNY," *AEJ*, Jan. 5, Mar. 16, 1842.

21. *Report of the committee on the judiciary in relation to the exemption of property from levy or sale, on execution, or distress for rent* (hereinafter cited as *Strong Report No. 1*), NYSD 76, 65 sess. (1842), 2–3, 15.

22. Ibid.; *Report of the Committee on the Judiciary in relation to the exemption law* (hereinafter cited as *Strong Report No. 2*), NYSD 43, 66 sess. (1843), 3–4 (Strong's emphasis).

23. *Strong Report No. 1*, 3–4; *Argus*, Mar. 28, 1842 (Croswell's emphasis). For the text of Strong's bill as it came out of committee, see "LNY," *AEJ*, Mar. 16, 1842.

24. *NYSJ*, 65 sess. (1842), 364–67; *NYAJ*, 65 sess. (1842), 902–3; New York, *Laws*, 65 sess. (1842), 193–94.

25. "LNY," *Argus*, Feb. 1, 5, 7, 8, 9, 1842; David Maldwyn Ellis, *Landlords and Farmers in the Hudson-Mohawk Region, 1790–1850* (Ithaca: Cornell University Press, 1946), 242–43.

26. "LNY," *Argus*, Mar. 4, 1842; Charles Warren, "*Volenti Non Fit Injuria* in Actions of Negligence," *Harvard Law Review* 8 (1895): 457–71. For a reinterpretation of the maxim's social foundations, see Christopher L. Tomlins, "'A Mysterious Power': Industrial Accidents and the Legal Construction of Employment Relations in Massachusetts, 1800–1850," *Law and History Review* 6 (1988): 375–438.

27. *Report of the majority of the committee on the judiciary, in relation to sundry petitions . . . in relation to the tenure by which they hold their lands* (hereinafter cited as *Loomis Report*), printed in "The Helderberg Difficulties," *Argus*, May 5, 1842. Thurlow Weed, the state printer, did not publish Loomis's majority report in the New York Assembly Documents. The cause of the omission remains unclear. See also "LNY," *Argus*, Apr. 11, 1842 (reporting that on April 9 the Loomis Report "was ordered to be printed . . . and laid on the table").

28. See *Report of the minority of the committee on the judiciary, in relation to titles of certain land* (hereinafter cited as *Simmons Report*), NYAD 177, 65 sess. (1842). In 1840 Simmons had been a member of the Judiciary Committee that reported out the Wheaton bill. See "LNY," *Argus*, Jan. 14, 17, 1840.

29. *Loomis Report*, 3; Alexis de Tocqueville, *Democracy in America*, ed. Phillips Bradley, 2 vols. (New York: Alfred A. Knopf, 1945), 1:48–49. See also James L. Huston, "The American Revolutionaries, the Political Economy of Aristocracy, and the American Concept of the Distribution of Wealth, 1765–1900," *AHR* 98 (1993): 1079–1105.

30. Stanley N. Katz, "Republicanism and the Law of Inheritance in the American Revolutionary Era," *Michigan Law Review* 76 (1977): 1–29 (quotation at 26n). See also John V. Orth, "After the Revolution: 'Reform' of the Law of Inheritance," *Law and History Review* 10 (1992): 33–44.

31. *Simmons Report*, 1–2.

32. The anonymous anti-renter is quoted in Henry Christman, *Tin Horns and Calico* (New York: Henry Holt, 1945), 46. See also *Report of James Seymour, relative to a railroad between Albany and Goshen*, NYAD 108, 65 sess. (1842); New York, *Laws*, 65 sess. (1842), 293.

33. *AEJ*, Apr. 27, 1842; *Herald*, Apr. 30, 1842; *Argus*, May 5, 1842; Michael Hoffman to Azariah Flagg, June 30, 1842, Flagg Papers, box 3, NYPL.

34. The quotation is from Ellis, *Landlords and Farmers*, 243. For the rent strike on King's estate, see Albert Champlin Mayham, *The Anti-Rent War on Blenheim Hill: An Episode of the 40's* (Jefferson, N.Y.: Frederick L. Frazee, 1906), 31.

35. "LNY," *AEJ*, Aug. 17, 22 (quotation), 24–27, 29–31, Sept. 1–3, 5–7; Lincoln, *Governor Messages*, 4:40; *Strong Report No. 2*, 6.

36. Daniel Dewey Barnard, "The 'Anti-Rent' Movement and Outbreak in New York," *Whig Review* 2 (1845): 581. For the ejectment regulations, see *NYRS*, 2d ed. (1836), 1:745.

37. "LNY," *Argus*, Jan. 20, 1844; *Herald*, July 29, 1844; Ellis, *Landlords and Farmers*, 243, 248.

38. For printed versions of the Dongan (1685) and Cornbury (1704) patents, respectively,

see S. G. Nissenson, *The Patroon's Domain* (New York: Columbia University Press, 1937), 381-85; *Allen Report*, 47-55. The argument against the Van Rensselaer title summarized in this paragraph and the two that follow has been pieced together from the account of counsel's brief in *People v. Levi Culver* (Rensselaer Co. General Sessions, 1844), *Argus*, Mar. 11, 1844, and the description of counsel's main points for the petitioners in *Whipple Report*, 6-7. See also the long letter from Rufus S. Waite to Burton A. Thomas, Jan. 14, 1844, *Freeholder*, Mar. 3, 1847. Anti-renters had been suspicious about the validity of the Van Rensselaer title since at least 1830. See Isabel Thompson Kelsay, "Down with the Rent! A Story of Social War in Rural New York" (Ph.D. diss., Columbia University, 1950), 45.

39. The quoted remark on the William and Mary seal is from "D. B." to George Henry Evans, *YA*, Dec. 20, 1845. For an excellent discussion of the bar on landownership by aliens and its consequences in colonial America, see James H. Kettner, *The Development of American Citizenship, 1608-1870* (Chapel Hill: University of North Carolina Press, 1978), chs. 4-5.

40. *Allen Report*, 31-32; Richard B. Morris, *Studies in the History of American Law* (New York: Columbia University Press, 1930), 79. See also Nissenson, *The Patroon's Domain*, 329-45, 386-87. An explanation for the allegedly fraudulent seal on the 1704 patent, which vexed the Judiciary Committee in 1844 (*Allen Report*, 37-38), did not materialize for some time. At trial in *Van Vechten v. Clute* (Albany Co. Circuit Court, 1847) (ejectment by plaintiff claiming title through Van Rensselaer patents of 1685 and 1704), counsel introduced into evidence authenticated copies of an order from Queen Anne in 1705, establishing and accompanying a new seal for the colony of New York, and a letter from Governor Cornbury in 1706, acknowledging the receipt of the new seal. Formalizing the monarchical succession took time in the early eighteenth century, especially in the crown's dominions across the Atlantic. See "Title of Van Rensselaer Estate," *AEJ*, Feb. 10, 1847.

41. Reports and rumors about Sill, Schuyler, and other Van Rensselaer descendants claiming to have been unlawfully divested of an interest in Rensselaerwyck abounded in the mid-1840s. The earliest one that I have seen is in an undated letter from "Justice" to the editor, *Tribune*, Oct. 31, 1844. See also Nissenson, *The Patroon's Domain*, 345-48 (suggesting that this version of the Anti-Rent argument was not implausible).

42. Christman, *Tin Horns and Calico*, 49-50.

43. *Argus*, Mar. 11, 1844.

44. The bill was printed in the *Whipple Report*, 11.

45. Chief Justice James Kent announced the "settled rule" forbidding a tenant from questioning his landlord's title in *Jackson* ex dem. *Bleecker v. Whitford*, 2 Caines Rep. 215 (N.Y. Sup. Ct. 1804); but the classic statement of the principle came in John Marshall's opinion for the Supreme Court in *Blight's Lessee v. Rochester*, 7 Wheat. 535, 547 (U.S. 1822).

46. For a digest of Mill Acts in force throughout the Union, see Justice Horace Gray's elaborate note in *Head v. Amoskeag Mfg. Co.*, 113 U.S. 9, 17 (1883). Excellent discussions of their operation and policy include Morton J. Horwitz, *The Transformation of American Law, 1780-1860* (Cambridge: Harvard University Press, 1977), 47-53; Louis C. Hunter, *Waterpower: A History of Industrial Power in the United States, 1780-1930* (Charlottesville: University Press of Virginia, 1979), 139-58. Neither Horwitz nor Hunter noticed that the New York legislature did not enact a mill act during the nineteenth century, although it did authorize mills to appropriate heads of water generated by the state-owned canal system. See *NYRS*, 2d ed. (1836), 1:217-21; *Varick v. Smith*, 5 Paige 137, 158-60 (N.Y. Ch. 1835). The Private Road Act of 1772, codified in *NYRS*, 2d ed. (1836), 1:510-14, supplied an alternative source of analogy for Anti-Rent lawyers.

47. For the petition of the Schoharie tenants (quoting from the Scott Patent), dated Feb. 14, 1844, see *Whipple Report*, 13–15.

CHAPTER FIVE

1. Arthur H. Cole, "Statistical Background of the Crisis Period, 1837–1842," *Review of Economic Statistics* 10 (1928): 186; Bessie L. Pierce, *A History of Chicago*, 3 vols. (New York: Alfred A. Knopf, 1937–57), 1:69; George Rogers Taylor, *The Transportation Revolution, 1815–1860* (New York: Holt, Rinehart and Winston, 1951), 345–46; James Roger Sharp, *The Jacksonians versus the Banks: Politics in the States after the Panic of 1837* (New York: Columbia University Press, 1970), 79. See also Samuel Rezneck, "The Social History of an American Depression, 1837–1843," *AHR* 40 (1935): 662–87.

2. Orestes Brownson, "The Policy to be pursued hereafter by the Friends of the Constitution, and of Equal Rights," *Boston Quarterly Review* 4 (1841): 108–9.

3. *NYEP*, Mar. 4, 1841; *Washington Globe*, Oct. 14, 1841.

4. *NYEP*, Mar. 25, 1841.

5. Berrien's remarks appeared in *Report of the Committee on the Judiciary, to whom were referred a bill from the Senate entitled "An act to repeal the bankruptcy law*," Senate Doc. 121, 27th Cong., 3d sess. (1843) (serial 415), 23. For the resumption and stay laws, see Mississippi, *Laws* (1840), 13, 30; *Woods v. Buie*, 5 How. 285 (Miss. Sup. Ct. 1840) (sustaining the Valuation Act on the ground that it impaired only the creditor's remedy, not the debtor's obligation); Arkansas, *Laws*, 3 sess. (1840–41), 51, 58; Illinois, *Laws*, 12 sess. (1841), 168, 172; Indiana, *Laws*, 26 sess. (1841), 130; Indiana, *Laws*, 27 sess. (1842), 82; Virginia, *Acts of the General Assembly* (1842), 54, 61; Pennsylvania, *Laws* (1842), 68, 407; Ohio, *Laws*, 40 sess. (1842), 13; Ohio, *Laws*, 41 sess. (1843), 10 (referring to Valuation Act enacted on March 4, 1842, which the state printer neglected to publish in the session laws); Michigan, *Laws* (1842), 5, 135; Alabama, *Acts Passed at the Annual Session of the General Assembly* (1841–42), 8–9. My data on the impact of the resumption acts draw on the *Washington Globe*, June 17, 1842; Sharp, *The Jacksonians versus the Banks*, 203, 246.

6. *Hunt's Merchants' Magazine* 8 (1843): 273, quoted in Reginald Charles McGrane, *The Panic of 1837: Some Financial Problems of the Jacksonian Era* (Chicago: University of Chicago Press, 1924), 139–40.

7. *Sturgis v. Crowinshield*, 4 Wheat. 122, 200 (U.S. 1819); John Marshall, *The Life of George Washington*, 2d ed., 2 vols. (Philadelphia: J. Crissy, 1836), 2:103, 192. In modern legal scholarship the right-remedy distinction is conventionally treated as an incoherent one. See Laurence Tribe, *American Constitutional Law* (Mineola, N.Y.: Foundation Press, 1978), 467; Richard Epstein, "Toward a Revitalization of the Contract Clause," *University of Chicago Law Review* 51 (1984): 746. Marshall's claims about the impact of the Contract Clause on public policy and commercial morality in the early republic were overly sanguine. See Steven R. Boyd, "The Contract Clause and the Evolution of American Federalism, 1789–1815," *William and Mary Quarterly* 44 (1987): 529–48; Murray N. Rothbard, *The Panic of 1819: Reactions and Policies* (New York: Columbia University Press, 1962), ch. 2.

8. *Ogden v. Saunders*, 12 Wheat. 213, 302 (U.S. 1827). Justice Joseph Story did not participate in the *Bronson* case, but he endorsed the Court's holding all the same. "I read the opinion with the highest satisfaction, and entirely concur in it," he wrote Taney a few days later. "There are times in which the Court is called upon to support every sound constitutional doctrine in support of the rights of property and of creditors." Story to Taney, Mar. 25, 1843, quoted in Charles Warren, *The Supreme Court in United States History*, 2 vols. (Boston: Little, Brown, 1926), 2:103–4.

9. John Denis Haeger, *The Investment Frontier: New York Businessmen and the Economic Development of the Old Northwest* (Albany: State University Press of New York, 1981), 88–94, 99–102, 169, 181–82, 196–98.

10. *Bronson v. Kinzie*, 1 How. 311, 315–16, 319–20 (U.S. 1843) (hereinafter cited as *Bronson*).

11. Ibid., 326, 330.

12. Ibid., 317–18.

13. *Tribune*, Mar. 22, 1843; *NYEP*, Mar. 3, 1843; *Argus*, Mar. 3, 1843. For sketchy details on the response in the West, see John Bach McMaster, *A History of the People of the United States from the Revolution to the Civil War*, 8 vols. (New York: D. Appleton, 1915), 7:47; Carl B. Swisher, *The Taney Period, 1836–1864* (New York: Macmillan, 1974), 150–51.

14. For a discussion of the "secondary contract" principle Duer favored, see chapter 2 above at notes 30–31. In *McCracken v. Hayward*, 2 How. 608, 614 (U.S. 1844), a second case involving the Illinois stay laws in which Taney's *Bronson* opinion was reaffirmed, the Court expressly disapproved Duer's argument. "No agreement or contract can create more binding obligations than those fastened by the law, which the law creates and attaches to contracts," Justice Henry Baldwin insisted. "The express power which a mortgagor confers on the mortgagee to sell as his agent is not more potent than that which the law delegates to the marshal, to sell and convey the property levied on, under an execution." The principle expounded in *McCracken* saved a great many subsequent statutes, including the New York legislature's abolition of distress for rent in 1846, from being declared unconstitutional. For a convenient summary of the leading cases, see Thomas M. Cooley, *A Treatise on the Constitutional Limitations Which Rest upon the Legislative Power of the States of the American Union* (Boston: Little, Brown, 1868), 288–89.

15. *NYRS*, 2d ed. (1836), 1:510–14; *Taylor v. Porter*, 4 Hill 140 (N.Y. Sup. Ct. 1843) (hereinafter cited as *Taylor*).

16. *Beekman v. Saratoga & Schenectady Railroad Co.*, 3 Paige Ch. 45, 73 (N.Y. Ch. 1831).

17. *Taylor*, 147, 153; *Stone v. Green*, 3 Hill 469–70 (N.Y. Sup. Ct. 1842).

18. *Taylor*, 142–43 (emphasis in original).

19. Ibid., 143–44.

20. Ibid., 144–45; John Locke, *The Second Treatise of Government*, ed. Thomas P. Peardon (Indianapolis: Bobbs-Merrill, 1952), 79.

21. *Taylor*, 144–45. The literature on implied limitations in the cases and commentaries of the early republic is simply immense. For a good bibliography, see Leslie Friedman Goldstein, "Popular Sovereignty, the Origins of Judicial Review, and the Revival of Unwritten Law," *Journal of Politics* 48 (1986): 51–71. For recent accounts that reach different conclusions, see Thomas C. Grey, "The Original Understanding and the Unwritten Constitution," in *Toward a More Perfect Union: Six Essays on the Constitution*, ed. Neil L. York (Albany: State University of New York Press, 1988), 145–73; Helen K. Michael, "The Role of Natural Law in Early American Constitutionalism: Did the Founders Contemplate Judicial Enforcement of 'Unwritten' Individual Rights?," *North Carolina Law Review* 69 (1991): 421–90.

22. *Butler v. Palmer*, 1 Hill 324, 329 (N.Y. Sup. Ct. 1841); *Cochran v. Van Surlay*, 20 Wend. 365, 381 (N.Y. Ct. Errors 1838).

23. *Taylor*, 143. Here, in particular, Bronson built on Cowen's opinion in *The Matter of John & Cherry Streets*, 19 Wend. 659, 676–77 (N.Y. Sup. Ct. 1839) (striking down the condemnation of property in excess of that actually required for a public street). For the concepts of "law of the land" and due process in eighteenth-century American thought, see Robert E. Riggs, "Substantive Due Process in 1791," *Wisconsin Law Review* (1990): 941–1005.

24. *Taylor*, 145–47. The important North Carolina decision was *Hoke v. Henderson*, 15 N.C. 1 (1833), which is elaborately treated in Walter F. Pratt Jr., "The Struggle for Judicial Independence in Antebellum North Carolina: The Story of Two Judges," *Law and History Review* 4 (1986): 129–59.

25. *Taylor*, 147.

26. Edward S. Corwin, "The Doctrine of Due Process of Law before the Civil War," *Harvard Law Review* 24 (1911): 374.

27. *Taylor*, 151; *Bronson*, 326. For an excellent profile of Gibson and his jurisprudence, see Stanley I. Kutler, "John Bannister Gibson: Judicial Restraint and the 'Positive State,'" *Journal of Public Law* 14 (1965): 181–97.

28. *Chadwick v. Moore*, 8 Watts & Serg. 49, 50, 52 (Penn. Sup. Ct. 1844).

29. *Harvey v. Thomas*, 10 Watts 63, 66–67 (Penn. Sup. Ct. 1840).

30. The first quotation is the title of Carter Goodrich's classic article, "The Revulsion against Internal Improvements," *JEH* 10 (1950): 145–69; the second is from an editorial in an Ohio newspaper, quoted in Rezneck, "The Social History of an American Depression, 1837–1843," 678. The stay law decisions referred to in the text are *Willard v. Longstreet*, 2 Doug. 172 (Mich. Sup. Ct. 1845); *Hunt v. Gregg*, 8 Blackf. 105 (Ind. Sup. Ct. 1846); *Moore v. Fowler*, 17 Fed. Cas. 679 (C.C.D. Arkansas 1847); *Shaffer v. Bolander*, 4 Greene 201 (Iowa Sup. Ct. 1854). See also Louis Hartz, *Economic Policy and Democratic Thought: Pennsylvania, 1776–1860* (Cambridge: Harvard University Press, 1948), 232–33. For a different interpretation of the luxuriation of judicial review, predicated on the assumption that until the 1840s judges conceived of the people as "a single, cohesive and indivisible body politic" rather than an aggregation of interest groups, see William E. Nelson, "Changing Conceptions of Judicial Review: The Evolution of Constitutional Theory in the States, 1790–1860," *University of Pennsylvania Law Review* 120 (1972): 1166–85.

31. [Peter S. DuPonceau], "The Security of Private Property," *American Law Magazine* 1 (1843): 318–47 (quotations at 333, 335, 337, 347); Howard J. Graham, "Procedure to Substance: Extra-Judicial Rise of Due Process, 1830–1860," *California Law Review* 40 (1952): 483–500.

32. Theodore Sedgwick [Jr.], *A Treatise on the Rules which Govern the Interpretation and Application of Statutory and Constitutional Law* (New York: John S. Voorhies, 1857), 155n, 160, 164, 166–67. See also Wallace Mendelson, "A Missing Link in the Evolution of Due Process," *Vanderbilt Law Review* 10 (1956): 125–37.

33. Sedgwick, *Statutory and Constitutional Law*, 144, 178, 505–6, 676, 678.

34. VETO, "Copyrights—To Foreigners," *Plaindealer*, Jan. 21, 1837; Theodore Sedgwick Jr., "Speech . . . at the Broadway Tabernacle," *NYEP*, Aug. 17, 1843.

35. [John Bigelow], "Constitutional Reform," *Democratic Review* 13 (1843): 563–76 (quotation at 570); E[lisha] P. H[urlbut], "Constitutional Reform," *NYEP*, July 26, Sept. 26, 1843. Bryant published thirteen other articles on constitutional reform by Hurlbut that summer. For evidence on the Sedgwick-Bigelow and Bigelow-Hurlbut connections, see John Bigelow, *Retrospections of an Active Life*, 5 vols. (New York: Baker and Taylor, 1909–13), 1:40, 53, 70; Margaret Clapp, *Forgotten First Citizen: John Bigelow* (Boston: Little, Brown, 1947), 33–35.

36. E. P. Hurlbut, *Essays on Human Rights and Their Political Guaranties* (New York: Greeley and McElrath, 1845), 63; Bigelow, "Constitutional Reform," 564–65, 567. See also *NYEP*, Mar. 22, 1844 (calling Bigelow's piece "profound and brilliant"); *Courier and Enquirer*, Dec. 5, 1843 (describing Bigelow's argument as "sheer humbug"). For the connection between Jefferson's views on the intergenerational obligation of public debts and consti-

tutional forms, see Merrill D. Peterson, *Thomas Jefferson, the Founders, and Constitutional Change* (Claremont, Calif.: Claremont Institute for the Study of Statesmanship and Political Philosophy, 1984).

37. Hammond, *Political History*, 283-86; Herbert D. A. Donovan, *The Barnburners* (New York: New York University Press, 1925), 32-35; Ronald Shaw, *Erie Water West: A History of the Erie Canal* (Lexington: University of Kentucky Press, 1962), 334-41.

38. Lincoln, *Governor Messages*, 4:9, 17-18.

39. Van Buren to Marcy, Jan. 13, 1843, quoted in Shaw, *Erie Water West*, 342; Marcy to Prosper M. Wetmore, Sept. 20, 1843, quoted in John A. Garraty, *Silas Wright* (New York: Columbia University Press, 1949), 293; Hoffman to Azariah Flagg, June 30, 1842, Mar. 16, 1843, Flagg Papers, box 3, NYPL.

40. Hoffman to Flagg, Aug. 3, 1842, quoted in Donovan, *The Barnburners*, 44. For Hoffman's stop-Bouck campaign prior to the Democratic state convention in 1842, see Hammond, *Political History*, 307-14.

41. *Report of the majority of the select committee on the Herkimer Memorial*, NYAD 152, 66 sess. (1843), 6-7; *NYEP*, May 22, 1843; Shaw, *Erie Water West*, 342; Harry H. Pierce, *Railroads of New York: A Study of Government Aid, 1826-1875* (Cambridge: Harvard University Press, 1953), 14-15; L. Ray Gunn, *The Decline of Authority: Public Economic Policy and Political Development in New York State, 1800-1860* (Ithaca: Cornell University Press, 1988), 173-74.

42. Hoffman to F. Byrdsall, Corresponding Secretary of the State Constitutional Reform Association, *Argus*, Aug. 22, 1843. See also *NYEP*, June 1, 14, 29, July 20, 29, 1843; John L. O'Sullivan to H. O'Reilly, Secretary of the State Constitutional Reform Association, ibid., Sept. 19, 1843.

43. Sedgwick, "Speech . . . at the Broadway Tabernacle," *NYEP*, Aug. 17, 1843.

44. Hoffman to F. Byrdsall, *Argus*, Aug. 22, 1843; Sedgwick, "Speech . . . at the Broadway Tabernacle"; "Address of the Executive Committee of the State Association for Constitutional Reform," *NYEP*, Oct. 23, 1843. New York's radical Democrats supported Thomas W. Dorr's suffragists and retailed their arguments all the same. See ibid., Apr. 27-28, May 11, 21-23, June 1-2, 1842; David Dudley Field to Dorr, Mar. 16, 1844, Dorr Papers, John Hay Library, Brown University, Providence, R.I.

45. *Barron v. Baltimore*, 7 Peters 243, 247 (U.S. 1833).

CHAPTER SIX

1. *NYEP*, Dec. 9, 1843; [John Bigelow], "History of Constitutional Reform in the United States—New York," *Democratic Review* 18 (1846): 405-6. For the Whig presumption, see Washington Hunt to Thurlow Weed, Dec. 19, 1844, Weed, *Memoir*, 112. See also John Niven, *Martin Van Buren: The Romantic Age of American Politics* (New York: Oxford University Press, 1983), 489-94, 505-15.

2. Hammond, *Political History*, 385; Lincoln, *Governor Messages*, 4:50-57.

3. Lincoln, *Governor Messages*, 4:57-60.

4. Herbert D. A. Donovan, *The Barnburners* (New York: New York University Press, 1925), 50; Stewart Mitchell, *Horatio Seymour of New York* (Cambridge: Harvard University Press, 1938), 71-76; Ronald E. Shaw, *Erie Water West: A History of the Erie Canal, 1792-1854* (Lexington: University of Kentucky Press, 1966), 343-45; New York, *Laws*, 67 sess. (1844), 411-13, 538-44.

5. Hammond, *Political History*, 433-34; Hand to Van Buren, May 11, 1844, Van Buren

Papers, DLC (m); Niven, *Van Buren*, 515; Seward to Christopher Morgan, Jan. 31, 1843, Seward Papers, UR (m). See also Richard P. McCormick, *The Presidential Game: The Origins of American Presidential Politics* (New York: Oxford University Press, 1982).

6. *Whipple Report*, 11, 16. Henry Christman, *Tin Horns and Calico* (New York: Henry Holt, 1945), 62–63, claimed that Boughton already had secured one favorable assessment of the bill from Ira Harris and another from Daniel Webster. But the claim is not credible. Speaking on the floor of the legislature in 1846, Harris declared that he had no connection with the Anti-Rent movement until the fall of 1844. Webster, arguing a case before the Supreme Court in 1848, decried the eminent domain theory embedded in the Anti-Rent bill. If "the legislature or their agents, are to be the sole judges of what is to be taken, and to what public use it is to be appropriated," he said, "the most levelling ultraisms of Anti-rentism or Agrarianism or Abolitionism may be successfully advanced." See "LNY," *Argus*, Jan. 12, 1846; *West River Bridge v. Dix* (arg.), 6 How. 507, 520 (U.S. 1848).

7. "LNY," *Argus*, Jan. 20, 1844; *NYAJ*, 67 sess. (1844), 105–6. The vote was 71 in favor of Palmer's motion, 49 against.

8. "LNY," *AEJ*, Jan. 22, 26, 1844; "LNY," *Argus*, Jan. 23, 1844.

9. "LNY," *AEJ*, Jan. 22, 1844.

10. "LNY," *Argus*, Jan. 27, 1844. The petition from Schoharie did not come in until late February; the Select Committee devoted only one paragraph of its report to the Anti-Rent agitation on Blenheim Hill and the Scott Patent. See *NYAJ*, 66 sess. (1844), 381.

11. *Whipple Report*, 3.

12. Ibid., 3–6.

13. Ibid., 8.

14. Ibid., 5.

15. *Allen Report*, 11.

16. Ibid., 9, 15. Allen's conservatism, though certainly apparent in the land reform report, is more striking in his *Report of the committee on the judiciary, on petitions asking passage of a law for the protection of married women*, NYAD 96, 67 sess. (1844). He was elected to a seat on the New York Supreme Court in 1848 and served until 1863. For a brief biographical sketch, see McAdam, *Bench and Bar*, 1:247.

17. *Humbert v. Trinity Church*, 24 Wend. 587, 609 (N.Y. Sup. Ct. 1840). For the origins and development of Trinity Church's holdings in New York City, see Elizabeth Blackmar, *Manhattan for Rent, 1785–1860* (Ithaca: Cornell University Press, 1989), 30–33.

18. *Allen Report*, 9, 24–25 (Allen's emphasis).

19. Ibid., 8, 10, 13, 19.

20. Ibid., 16–17. For the Allen-Duer rivalry at home, see Charles M. Snyder, *Oswego: From Buckskins to Bustles* (Port Washington, N.Y.: Ira J. Friedman, 1968), 248–49. Allen was wrong, of course, about the want of precedent to support Duer's argument; but the latter's hasty research in 1840 opened the door for such a charge. See the discussion in chapter 2 at note 38.

21. *Allen Report*, 18–19 (in part quoting from *Bonaparte v. Camden & Amboy Railroad*, 1 Baldwin 205, 220 [C.C.D.N.J. 1830]).

22. Ibid. (in part quoting from *Harding v. Goodlett*, 3 Yerg. 40, 52–54 [Tenn. 1832]).

23. Ibid., 4–7.

24. Ibid., 2–4.

25. Ibid., 22, 27, 43.

26. B. A. Thomas to Thomas A. Devyr, *WA*, June 1, 1844; "Anti-Rent" [Henry Z. Hayner] to Horace Greeley, *Tribune*, Jan. 11, 1845; *Freeholder*, Mar. 4, 1846.

27. *NYEP*, Apr. 27, 1844; Charles H. Brown, *William Cullen Bryant: A Biography* (New York: Charles Scribner's Sons, 1971), 290; *Senate Journal*, 28th Cong., 1st sess. (1844) (serial 430), 426–43. The literature on the Texas-annexation movement is immense. For a narrative and a valuable compilation of sources, see Frederick Merk, *Slavery and the Annexation of Texas* (New York: Alfred A. Knopf, 1972). But see also Elgin Williams, *The Animating Pursuits of Speculation: Land Traffic in the Annexation of Texas* (New York: Columbia University Press, 1949); William W. Freehling, *The Road to Disunion: Secessionists at Bay, 1776–1854* (New York: Oxford University Press, 1990), 353–425. For a shrewd assessment of Calhoun's motives in framing the Pakenham letter, see William J. Cooper, *The South and the Politics of Slavery, 1828–1856* (Baton Rouge: Louisiana State University Press, 1978), 375–76.

28. *Washington National Intelligencer*, Apr. 27, 1844; *Washington Globe*, Apr. 28, 1844.

29. Wright to Van Buren, May 6, 1844; Ritchie to Van Buren, May 5, 1844, Van Buren Papers, DLC (m); Jackson to Van Buren, [May 1844], quoted in Robert V. Remini, *Andrew Jackson and the Course of American Democracy, 1833–1845* (New York: Harper and Row, 1984), 498. For the mood and proceedings of the Whig convention, see Merrill D. Peterson, *The Great Triumvirate: Webster, Clay, and Calhoun* (New York: Oxford University Press, 1987), 360–61.

30. *NYEP*, Apr. 25, May 6, 1844; Henry M. Field, *The Life of David Dudley Field* (New York: Charles Scribner's Sons, 1898), 111–13. See also Theodore Sedgwick Jr., *Thoughts on the Proposed Annexation of Texas to the United States* (New York: S. W. Benedict, 1844).

31. *NYEP*, May 24, 1844; Wright to Van Buren, May 6, 1844, Van Buren Papers, DLC (m).

32. Butler to Van Buren, May 23, 1844; Gilpin to Van Buren, May 26, 1844, Van Buren Papers, DLC (m). For the Senate vote that killed the treaty, see Merk, *Slavery and the Annexation of Texas*, 78–82. The proceedings of the Democratic convention are thoroughly recounted in John A. Garraty, *Silas Wright* (New York: Columbia University Press, 1949), ch. 12; Charles Sellers, *James K. Polk, Continentalist, 1843–1846* (Princeton: Princeton University Press, 1966), ch. 3.

33. Dix to Flagg, June 14, 1844, Flagg Papers, box 2, NYPL; Wright to Joel R. Poinsett, June 26, 1844, quoted in Sellers, *Polk, Continentalist*, 115; Hammond, *Political History*, 499–500. See also *NYEP*, May 31, July 3–4, 6, 23–29, 1844.

34. Marcy to P. M. Wetmore, May 9, 1844, quoted in Ivor Spencer, *The Victor and the Spoils: A Life of William L. Marcy* (Providence: Brown University Press, 1959), 128; Wright to Tracy, Aug. 5, 1844, Tracy Papers, NYSL; Wright to Mssrs. Hitchcock and Smith, Aug. 1, 1844, Hammond, *Political History*, 486–87. See also Garraty, *Wright*, 291–304.

35. *AEJ*, June 26, 1844; "Letter of Daniel D. Barnard to His Constituents, No. 5," ibid., Aug. 5, 1844; Glyndon G. Van Deusen, *Horace Greeley: Nineteenth-Century Crusader* (Philadelphia: University of Pennsylvania Press, 1953), 90; *Tribune*, July 25, 1844.

36. *AEJ*, June 26, 1844; *Tribune*, June 10, July 29, 1844. See also James L. Crouthamel, *James Watson Webb: A Biography* (Middletown: Wesleyan University Press, 1969), 97.

37. "Letter of Daniel D. Barnard to His Constituents, No. 5," *AEJ*, Aug. 5, 1844; Seward to Clay, Nov. 7, 1844 (copy), Seward Papers, UR (m).

38. Charles Burchard to "Abolitionists of Hamilton County," *AEJ*, July 1, 1844; "Governor Seward's Speech at the Great Syracuse Convention," ibid., July 20, 1844; Seward to Weed, June 20, 1844, quoted in Jane H. Pease, "The Road to the Higher Law," *NYH* 40 (1959): 124.

39. For detailed discussions of the tactical differences that divided antislavery Whigs and Liberty leaders, see Seward to Gerrit Smith, *AEJ*, Dec. 14, 1844; Richard H. Sewell, *Ballots*

for Freedom: Antislavery Politics in the United States, 1837–1860 (New York: Oxford University Press, 1976), 3–110; William M. Wiecek, *The Sources of Antislavery Constitutionalism in America, 1760–1848* (Ithaca: Cornell University Press, 1977), 202–18.

40. Seward to Edward A. Stansbury, Sept. 2, 1844, quoted in Glyndon G. Van Deusen, *William Henry Seward* (New York: Oxford University Press, 1967), 103. For the conservative resistance to Seward-Weed "demagoguery" in 1844, see Lee H. Warner, "The Silver Grays: New York State Conservative Whigs, 1846–1856" (Ph.D. diss., University of Wisconsin, 1971), 15–17.

41. John J. Gallup to Thomas A. Devyr, May 27, 1844; B. A. Thomas to Devyr, May 24, 1844, *WA,* June 1, 1844.

42. Christman, *Tin Horns and Calico,* 74.

43. *WA,* June 1, 1844.

44. Albert Champlin Mayham, *The Anti-Rent War on Blenheim Hill: An Episode of the 40's* (Jefferson, N.Y.: Frederick L. Frazee, 1906), 31–33, 39. For the origin and development of landlord-tenant relations on the Hardenbergh Patent, see David Maldwyn Ellis, *Landlords and Farmers in the Hudson-Mohawk Region, 1790–1860* (Ithaca: Cornell University Press, 1946), 9, 59–62. One student of the Anti-Rent movement used the manuscript census to assemble a profile of the "Indians" in Delaware, Columbia, and Rensselaer counties. His findings comported with the impressions of Mayham quoted in the text. See Eldridge Honaker Pendleton, "The New York Anti-Rent Controversy, 1830–1860" (Ph.D. diss., University of Virginia, 1974), 171–285, 293.

45. *NYEP,* July 26, 1844; Alf Evers, *The Catskills: From Wilderness to Woodstock* (New York: Doubleday, 1972), 410–11, 756n.

46. Samuel A. Law to Francis Wharton, July 30, 1844, quoted in Ellis, *Landlords and Farmers,* 246. For the data on the Hardenbergh Patent proprietors, see *Report of the select committee on so much of the Governor's message as relates to the difficulties existing between the proprietors of certain leasehold estates and their tenants,* NYAD 156, 69 sess. (1846), 5–6.

47. *Quackenbush v. Danks,* 1 Denio 128, 130–31 (N.Y. Sup. Ct. 1844) (hereinafter cited as *Quackenbush*).

48. Ibid. See also chapter 4 at note 24 (describing legislative history of the 1842 Exemption Act). Counsel did not examine the legislative history of the statute; at the time, accepted principles of statutory construction discouraged the practice. See J. Willard Hurst, *Dealing with Statutes* (New York: Columbia University Press, 1982), ch. 2.

49. *Quackenbush,* 131–33 (Bronson's emphasis).

50. "New York, Anti-Rent Rebellion," *Niles' Register* 57 (Sept. 17, 1844): 2; Christman, *Tin Horns and Calico,* 86–87; *Argus,* July 26, 1844. See also *Herald,* July 31, 1844. As he launched the offensive, William P. Van Rensselaer snubbed overtures from Daniel Gardner, a Troy attorney authorized to negotiate a settlement for the Anti-Rent Association of Rensselaer County. See Gardner to Van Rensselaer, July 3, July 27, Aug. 1, 1844, William Paterson Van Rensselaer Collection, box 3, folder 4, AIHA.

51. *NYRS,* 2d ed. (1836), 2:359; Bouck to Reynolds, Aug. 1, 1844, Pendleton, "The New York Anti-Rent Controversy," 126; Bouck to Azariah Flagg, Sept. 3, 1844, Flagg Papers, box 2, NYPL.

52. *Argus,* Aug. 12, 1844; *NYEP,* Dec. 2, 1844.

53. *Argus,* Aug. 16, Sept. 2, 12, Dec. 24, 1844; "New York, Anti-Rent Rebellion," *Niles' Register* 67 (Sept. 7, 1844): 2; John D. Monroe, *The Anti-Rent War in Delaware County, New York: The Revolt against the Rent System* (Jefferson, N.Y.: privately printed, 1940), 18–19.

54. *Herald,* Aug. 17, 1844.

CHAPTER SEVEN

1. *Niles' Register* 66 (Aug. 31, 1844): 439; Seward to Weed, Sept. 2, 1844, Seward, *Autobiography*, 724 (Seward's emphasis); Hunt to Weed, [Sept. 1844], Weed, *Memoir*, 123. See also Robert J. Rayback, *Millard Fillmore: Biography of a President* (Buffalo: Buffalo Historical Society, 1959), 152–55. For especially lively Democratic commentary on Clay's letter and its presumed impact on the campaign, see *NYEP*, Sept. 10, Oct. 2, 16, 1844. Whig slaveholders put enormous pressure on Clay. See William J. Cooper, *The South and the Politics of Slavery, 1828–1856* (Baton Rouge: Louisiana State University Press, 1978), 210–16.

2. *AEJ*, Sept. 11, 1844; Glyndon G. Van Deusen, *Thurlow Weed: Wizard of the Lobby* (Boston: Little, Brown, 1947), 135.

3. *AEJ*, Sept. 11, 1844 (Weed's emphasis). All the Seward quotations are from his letter of Sept. 2, 1844, cited and discussed in chapter 6 at note 40.

4. *Argus*, Nov. 1, 1844 (Harris's emphasis). See also ibid., Sept. 27, 1844. The best biographical sketch of Harris is Proctor, "Albany Bar," 147–48. Although he claimed to be a commercial lawyer, Harris did at least some personal injury work. See his letter to William P. Van Rensselaer, Mar. 29, 1842, William Paterson Van Rensselaer Collection, box 2, folder 7, AIHA, threatening to file suit on behalf of a client injured by the patroon's watchdogs and reciting terms for a settlement. Van Schoonhoven is listed as a lawyer in Troy (New York), *City Directory, for the Year 1844–1845, Containing the Names of Residents, with their Trades and Occupations* (Troy: N. Tuttle, 1844), 127. Betts resided in Brunswick, Heermance in Nassau; both were tenants of William P. Van Rensselaer. See "Veritas" to Horace Greeley, *Tribune*, Jan. 10, 1845.

5. The concept of "movement culture" is defined and elaborated in Lawrence Goodwyn, *Democratic Promise: The Populist Moment in America* (New York: Oxford University Press, 1976).

6. John A. Garraty, *Silas Wright* (New York: Columbia University Press, 1949), 305–8; Gillet, *Wright*, 1571. See also "Mr. Wright and Texas," *NYEP*, Sept. 19, 1844. For a description and analysis of the Democracy's address to the voters, see Benson, *The Concept of Jacksonian Democracy: New York as a Test Case* (Princeton: Princeton University Press, 1961), 227–37. Azariah Flagg apparently wrote it. See Jabez Hammond to Flagg, Sept. 15, 1844, Flagg Papers, box 2, NYPL.

7. Wright to Flagg, Sept. 25, 1844, Flagg Papers, box 2, NYPL (summarizing contents of Croswell's letter).

8. Ibid.

9. Hoffman to Flagg, Oct. 21, 1844, Flagg Papers, box 3, NYPL (Hoffman's emphasis).

10. I have inferred Van Buren's suggestion from Wright's reply; Van Buren's letter no longer exists. Fourteen months later, Wright asked Attorney General John Van Buren to draft legislation along these very lines. The quotation is from Blackstone, *Commentaries*, 2:12. For the New York act abolishing entails, see New York, *Laws*, 6 sess. (1782), 501–2.

11. Wright to Van Buren, Oct. 8, 1844, Van Buren Papers, DLC (m).

12. *AEJ*, Nov. 8–9, 1844.

13. *Tribune*, Nov. 6, 1844; *AEJ*, Nov. 9, 1844; Ira M. Leonard, "The Rise and Fall of the American Republican Party in New York City, 1843–1845," *NYHSQ* 50 (1966): 151–92. For useful discussions of the New York results, see Garraty, *Wright*, 326–28; Rayback, *Fillmore*, 155–59. A shrewd assessment of the national returns is Lex Renda, "Retrospective Voting and the Presidential Election of 1844: The Texas Issue Revisited," *Presidential Studies Quarterly* 24 (1994): 837–54.

14. *NYEP*, Nov. 26, 1844; D. D. F., "The Election—What Does it Signify as to Texas?," ibid., Nov. 28, 1844; Wright to Polk, Dec. 20, 1844, Gillet, *Wright*, 1632-39.

15. For the "official" returns in Rensselaer and Albany, respectively, see *Argus*, Nov. 15, 18, 1844. Leonard Litchfield and Clarkson F. Crosby, the two Whig assembly candidates in Albany who wanted no part of the Anti-Rent agitation, also won. Litchfield won by 619 votes and Crosby by 536 votes; Harris, in contrast, won by 2,476. For a roster of the newly elected legislators, see *AEJ*, Nov. 19, 1844.

16. Isabel Thompson Kelsay, "Down with the Rent! A Story of Social War in Rural New York" (Ph.D. diss., Columbia University, 1950), 108-9; James D. Livingston and Sherry H. Penney, "The Breakup of Livingston Manor," in *The Livingston Legacy: Three Centuries of American History*, ed. Richard T. Wiles (Annandale-on-Hudson, N.Y.: Bard College Office of Publications, 1987), 406-26.

17. "The Anti-Rent Trial at Hudson," *NYEP*, Sept. 22, 1845.

18. Henry Christman, *Tin Horns and Calico* (New York: Henry Holt, 1945), 99.

19. *Tribune*, Dec. 18, 1844 (Greeley's emphasis); Kelsay, "Down with the Rent," 109-10; *People v. Smith Boughton*, 1 Edmonds 140, 142 (N.Y. Oyer & Terminer, Columbia Co., 1845) (hereinafter cited as *Boughton*).

20. "The Anti-Rent Trial at Hudson" (summarizing testimony); "New York, Anti-Rent Disturbance," *Niles' Register* 67 (Jan. 11, 1845): 291-92.

21. *Tribune*, Dec. 25, 1844 (reprinting "probably correct account" of the Smith murder from the *Troy Budget*). See also the corroborative accounts in ibid., Jan. 1, 1845 (letter from Troy attorney Henry Z. Hayner); ibid., Jan. 10, 1845 (letter from "Veritas" naming Goyer as the triggerman and listing "Indian" accessories in custody).

22. David Maldwyn Ellis, *Landlords and Farmers in the Hudson-Mohawk Region, 1790-1850* (Ithaca: Cornell University Press, 1946), 261; "New York, Anti-Rent Disturbance," *Niles' Register* 67 (Jan. 11, 1845): 291-92; *Boughton*, 142. See also Kelsay, "Down with the Rent," 112-20. Bouck did not act unilaterally. See A. C. Niven to Flagg, Dec. 27, 1844, Flagg Papers, box 2, NYPL (inviting Flagg to attend a meeting with Bouck and Wright "in reference to an application from Columbia County to detail a military force to assist the sheriff").

23. *Tribune*, Dec. 26, 1844; *Courier and Enquirer*, Jan. 6, 1845; *NYEP*, Dec. 18, 23, 1844.

24. *AEJ*, Dec. 21, 1844; *Argus*, Dec. 24, 1844 (quoting at length from Weed's Sept. 11 editorial, discussed at notes 2-3); *NYEP*, Dec. 23, 1844. See also Van Deusen, *Weed*, 137. King's uncle, John A. King, owned the Blenheim Patent.

25. *NYEP*, Dec. 18, 1844; *Tribune*, Aug. 27, Dec. 26, 1844 (Greeley's emphasis).

26. Wright to Flagg, Dec. 4, 1844, Flagg Papers, box 3, NYPL; Flagg to Van Buren, Dec. 23, 1844, Van Buren Papers, DLC (m); Van Buren to Poinsett, Dec. 27, 1844, Gilpin Collection, Pennsylvania Historical Society, Philadelphia.

27. John A. King to Stephen Van Rensselaer, Dec. 24, 1844, William P. Van Rensselaer Collection, box 3, folder 4, AIHA.

28. Ibid. See also Alf Evers, *The Catskills: From Wilderness to Woodstock* (Garden City: Doubleday, 1972), 429; Charles Hathaway to Greeley, *Tribune*, Aug. 15, 1845 (describing estate-management duties of Powers and Hathaway, respectively). For the kinship ties between Hathaway and Steele, see John D. Monroe, *The Anti-Rent War in Delaware County, New York* (Jefferson, N.Y.: privately printed, 1940), 17.

29. Ellis, *Landlords and Farmers*, 293-94. Cortlandt Van Rensselaer, the third son of Stephen Van Rensselaer III and a Presbyterian minister in New York City, laid down the new sale terms in a 20,000-word circular published in *AEJ*, Dec. 19, 1844.

30. "Anti-Rent" [Henry Z. Hayner] to Greeley, *Tribune*, Jan. 1, 11, 1845. See also Smith A. Boughton to Thomas A. Devyr, *WA*, Mar. 1, 1845. Hayner was admitted to the bar in 1830 and ran for the state senate (third district) on the Whig ticket in the election of 1844. John P. Beekman, an Albany physician and president of the New York Agricultural Society, defeated him. See *AEJ*, Nov. 9, 1844.

31. *AEJ*, Jan. 8, 17, 1845.

32. Ibid., Jan. 17, 1845.

33. *Argus*, Jan. 14, 1845; *Tribune*, Jan. 1, 1845. National Reform has attracted considerable attention from scholars. Especially useful titles include Helene Sara Zahler, *Eastern Workingmen and National Land Policy, 1829–1862* (New York: Columbia University Press, 1941); Sean Wilentz, *Chants Democratic: New York City and the Rise of the American Working Class, 1788–1850* (New York: Oxford University Press, 1984), 335–43, 356–58, 369, 383; Michael A. Bernstein, "Northern Labor Finds a Southern Champion: A Note on the Radical Democracy, 1833–1849," in *New York and the Rise of American Capitalism: Economic Development and the Social and Political History of an American State, 1780–1870*, ed. William Pencak and Conrad Edick Wright (New York: NYHS, 1989), 147–67.

34. Wilentz, *Chants Democratic*, 336–37 (quoting Evans's editorials in the *Radical*); *WA*, May 18, 1844.

35. Bernstein, "Northern Labor Finds a Southern Champion," 151 (quoting *Radical* piece of 1841); *WA*, Aug. 17, Sept. 14, 1844.

36. *WA*, Dec. 28, 1844, Jan. 25, 1845 (Evans's emphasis).

37. "Junius" to George Henry Evans, *WA*, Feb. 22, 1845; Thomas Ainge Devyr, *The Odd Book of the Nineteenth Century, or "Chivalry" in Modern Days, A Personal Record of Reform—Chiefly Land Reform, for the Last Fifty Years* (Greenpoint, N.Y.: author, 1882), pt. 2, 42–43. For Devyr's lecture tour, see *WA*, Oct. 5, 1844.

38. The nature and sources and Wright's balancing act, the events that upset it, and the implications for land reform are the subjects of chapter 8.

39. Lincoln, *Governor Messages*, 4:139, 141, 148, 150.

40. *Argus*, Jan. 9, 1845; New York, *Laws*, 68 sess. (1845), 3, 5; "LNY," *AEJ*, Jan. 15, 17, 24–25, 1845.

41. "Anti-Rent State Convention," *Argus*, Feb. 10, 1845; Ellis, *Landlords and Farmers*, 42–45, 252.

42. "Anti-Rent State Convention" (quoting in part from Wright's message); *Report of the minority of the select committee on landlord and tenant*, NYAD 247, 68 sess. (1845), 1.

43. "Anti-Rent State Convention."

44. "Justus" to Rufus King, *AEJ*, Feb. 12, 14, 18, 1845. See also the rejoinders by "Franklin," ibid., Feb. 19, 25, 1845.

45. "Extract from a letter dated at Delhi on the 16th . . . to a gentleman in this city," ibid., Feb. 19, 1845; David Murray, "The Antirent Episode in New York," in *Annual Report of the American Historical Association for the Year 1896*, 2 vols. (Washington, D.C.: Government Printing Office, 1897), 1:157; Ellis, *Landlords and Farmers*, 265; "Anti-Rent Trials," *AEJ*, May 2, 1845.

46. *NYEP*, Mar. 14, 18, 1845; Murray, "The Antirent Episode in New York," 157–58.

47. "An Anti-Renter of Delaware" to Greeley, *Tribune*, Apr. 11, 1845; Ellis, *Landlords and Farmers*, 265, 293. See also Charles Hathaway to James Dexter, Mar. 22, 1845, Anti-Rent Papers, NYSL; *NYEP*, Apr. 1, 4, 1845; Christman, *Tin Horns and Calico*, 140–45. The legislature did not enact the armament-sharing law Governor Wright had requested until April 15, three weeks after Delaware authorities procured supplies from the state arsenal. For

the statute, entitled "An Act to enforce the laws and preserve order," see New York, *Laws*, 68 sess. (1845), 53.

48. Joseph S. Smith to Adjutant General Thomas Farrington, *Argus*, Mar. 10, 1845; ibid., Mar. 13, 17, 1845 (printing letters from Kingston correspondent); Alf Evers, *Woodstock: History of an American Town* (Woodstock, N.Y.: Overlook Press, 1987), 197–98. See also *WA*, Mar. 22, 1845.

49. *Argus*, Mar. 29, 1845 (Brown's emphasis). Stephen Mayham is identified as treasurer of the Anti-Rent association in *Freeholder*, Apr. 9, 1845.

50. *Tribune*, Apr. 1, 1845; *AEJ*, Apr. 1, 1845 (reporting an 11-1 deadlock); *YA*, Mar. 29, 1845. In this very issue of the National Reform Association weekly, Evans parted with the title *Working Man's Advocate* "with some reluctance." The new one underscored his belief that "the movement of the entire civilized world is toward republicanism" and the American people had an obligation both to guarantee the nation's youth and to show others the way by reforming the land law.

51. "Anti-Rent" to Greeley, *Tribune*, Apr. 5, 1845; *YA*, Apr. 12, 19, 1845.

CHAPTER EIGHT

1. Hammond, *Political History*, 53; Wright to Bancroft, Sept. 11, 1844, quoted in John A. Garraty, *Silas Wright* (New York: Columbia University Press, 1949), 308; Wright to Flagg, Nov. 12, 1844, Flagg Papers, box 3, NYPL. The nature and sources of Wright's commitment to his party are set forth brilliantly in Michael Wallace, "Changing Concepts of Party in the United States, 1815–1828," *AHR* 74 (1969): 453–91.

2. Wright to Polk, Dec. 20, 1844, Gillet, *Wright*, 1632–39. See also Wright to Corning, Sept. 11, 1844, ibid., 1587–89; Wright to Marcy, Sept. 13, 1844, Marcy Papers, DLC; Wright to Dickinson, Oct. 9, 1844, Dickinson, *Speeches*, 2:371.

3. Jabez Hammond reported that Wright invited Marcy, Croswell, and Justice Greene Bronson (conservatives) to meet with Flagg, Samuel Young, and George P. Barker (radicals) to read and discuss his message before he delivered it to the state legislature. See Hammond, *Political History*, 536n. It seems to me that Wright's inclination to secure advance assent to the message suggests his uncertainty about how to straddle the Democracy's two factions. For a different interpretation of Wright's situation and his response to it in January 1845, emphasizing his penchant for putting principle before the exigencies of party management, see Garraty, *Wright*, 333–39.

4. Frederick Merk, *Slavery and the Annexation of Texas* (New York: Alfred A. Knopf, 1972), 101–51; Charles Sellers, *James K. Polk, Continentalist, 1843–1846* (Princeton: Princeton University Press, 1966), 173.

5. VETO, "Mr. Tyler's Message," *NYEP*, Dec. 5, 1844; D. D. F., "Is Mr. McDuffie's Resolution for Annexation Constitutional?," ibid., Dec. 16, 1844; L. Stetson to Flagg, Dec. 31, 1844, quoted in Garraty, *Wright*, 343. See also Michael Hoffman to Flagg, Nov. 22, 1844, Flagg Papers, box 3, NYPL; Preston King to Flagg, Dec. 21, 1844, ibid., box 2; "Our Senators in Congress," *NYEP*, Jan. 20, 1845. Stetson's patronage fears stemmed from the custom of senatorial courtesy—presidential selection of officials from names supplied by senators of the state in which the job would be performed.

6. Sellers, *Polk, Continentalist*, 174–80, 184.

7. *Argus*, Jan. 14, 1845; *Tribune*, Jan. 9, 1845; Lincoln, *Governor Messages*, 4:151–53.

8. Lincoln, *Governor Messages*, 4:95, 101–3.

9. See the discussion in chapter 5 at notes 40–44. For the conservative objections to a convention in 1843, see L. Ray Gunn, *The Decline of Authority: Public Economic Policy and*

Political Development in New York State, 1800-1860 (Ithaca: Cornell University Press, 1988), 177-78.

10. Lincoln, *Governor Messages*, 4:108-9.

11. Polk to Van Buren, Jan. 30, 1845, Van Buren Papers, DLC (m); Hammond, *Political History*, 524-31; *Argus*, Jan. 29, 1845; Wright to Dix, Feb. 15, 1845, Gillet, *Wright*, 1623-27; "Address of the Whig Members of the Legislature," *AEJ*, May 24, 1845. Van Buren declined the appointment to the board of regents; Jabez Hammond, one radical who did refuse to vote for Polk in 1844, served in his stead. See *Tribune*, May 12, 1845; Hammond to John Van Buren, Dec. 1, 1844, Van Buren Papers, DLC (m).

12. *AEJ*, Feb. 5, 1845 (King's emphasis). See also "The Project of a Convention," ibid., Feb. 6, 1845; "The Regency against a Convention," ibid., Feb. 13, 1845.

13. Gideon Hard, "Remarks . . . in Support of the Amendment to Extend the Right of Suffrage," ibid., Apr. 1, 1844 (Hard's emphasis); Seward to Gerrit Smith, Jan. 21, 1845, Seward Papers, UR (m). Hard did not have an opportunity to renew his call for equal suffrage in 1845 because, as the *Evening Journal* explained on February 4, "the amendments to the constitution, adopted last session, were hurried through the senate to-day under 'whip and spur,' and almost without debate. The evident object of this 'hot haste' is, if possible, to 'nip in the bud' the project of a Convention." Hard was wrong about the suffrage laws of the several states. Free blacks voted on the same terms as whites only in northern New England. See Paul Finkelman, "Prelude to the Fourteenth Amendment: Black Legal Rights in the Antebellum North," *Rutgers Law Journal* 17 (1986): 415-82. See also Phyllis F. Field, *The Politics of Race in New York: The Struggle for Black Suffrage in the Civil War Era* (Ithaca: Cornell University Press, 1982), 19-47.

14. *Tribune*, Jan. 30, 1845; "LNY," *AEJ*, Feb. 11, 1845; *Argus*, Feb. 14, 1845. See also *NYEP*, Jan. 8, 1845.

15. Sellers, *Polk, Continentalist*, 184-99 (quotation at 186). See also Ivor Spencer, *The Victor and the Spoils: A Life of William L. Marcy* (Providence: Brown University Press, 1959), 129-36; John Niven, *Martin Van Buren: The Romantic Age of American Politics* (New York: Oxford University Press, 1983), 550-65.

16. Van Buren to Polk, Feb. 27, 1845, Polk Papers, DLC (m); Dix to Flagg, Mar. 3, 1845, Flagg Papers, box 2, NYPL; *Atlas*, Mar. 12, 1845, quoted in Garraty, *Wright*, 347-48; Sellers, *Polk, Continentalist*, 200-204.

17. Wright to Dix, Feb. 15, 1845, Gillet, *Wright*, 1623-27; Preston King to Van Buren, Feb. 14, 1845, Van Buren Papers, DLC (m); Sellers, *Polk, Continentalist*, 170-73.

18. For favorable commentary on the Benton plan, see *NYEP*, Feb. 8, Mar. 1, 1845; Preston King to Flagg, Feb. 8, 1845, Flagg Papers, box 2, NYPL; Wright to Dix, Feb. 15, 1845, Gillet, *Wright*, 1623-27. For the compromise and its enactment, see William Nisbet Chambers, *Old Bullion Benton: Senator from the New West* (Boston: Little, Brown, 1956), 288-91.

19. Dix to Wright, Feb. 27, 1845, quoted in Sellers, *Polk, Continentalist*, 207n; Wright to Dix, Mar. 11, 1845, Gillet, *Wright*, 1627-28 (Wright's emphasis).

20. *AEJ*, Mar. 5, 8, 1845. See also *Tribune*, Mar. 3-4, 1845.

21. *Argus*, Mar. 3-4, 6, 1845; "LNY," *AEJ*, Mar. 4, 1845; Hammond, *Political History*, 540-41, 754.

22. Hammond, *Political History*, 541-42; Wright to Polk, July 21, 1845, Gillet, *Wright*, 1648-53.

23. *NYEP*, Mar. 20, 1845; *NYAJ*, 68 sess. (1845), 500. For the "Citizen" essays, see *NYEP*, Mar. 20, 21, 24, 25, 27, 1845.

24. Hammond, *Political History*, 537; *NYAJ*, 68 sess. (1845), 677-81.

25. "LNY," *AEJ*, Apr. 2-3, 1845 (Young's emphasis). For the roll call, see *NYAJ*, 68 sess. (1845), 681-83. For the Wright-Russell relationship, see Garraty, *Wright*, 146n, 263, 288, 305, 324, 334-35, 404.

26. VETO, "A Convention," *NYEP*, Apr. 29, 1845. For the votes on the unsuccessful amendments to Crain's bill in the assembly, see *Argus*, Apr. 24, 1845. See also "A Limited Convention," *AEJ*, May 5, 1845 (echoing Sedgwick on incoherence of the limited-convention argument).

27. *NYAJ*, 68 sess. (1845), 904. For the conservative case against a convention, see *Report of Mssrs. Comstock, McKey, Sage and Pierce, from the select committee . . . to which was referred Mr. Crain's bill relative to a Convention*, NYAD 231, 68 sess. (1845).

28. *Report of the majority of the select committee on numerous petitions from the manor tenants in several counties of this State for relief*, NYAD 222, 68 sess. (1845), 7.

29. Ibid., 2, 4.

30. Ibid., 6-7 (quoting in part from the *Allen Report*). See also *Report of the committee on finance, in obedience to a resolution of the Senate of 9th February last*, NYSD 83, 58 sess. (1835). The revival of the taxation scheme in 1844 did not come directly from Assemblyman Allen, as Constant supposed. In his report for a select committee earlier that session, Jonathan Whipple (W.-Rensselaer) suggested that if the Judiciary Committee determined that the legislature was incompetent to enact the proposed Act Concerning Tenures by Lease, then it should "recommend that a law be passed taxing the income and ground rents of the owners of such property, provided that such a law can be framed in a manner to prevent the proprietors from compelling the tenants to reimburse to them the amount of such tax." *Whipple Report*, 8. The impulse to treat the taxing power as an inferior, though marginally useful, alternative to the police and eminent domain powers also figured in the work of Henry G. Wheaton, the Albany assemblyman who served as counsel for the tenants of Stephen Van Rensselaer IV in the 1839-41 period. Three days after the Manor Commission reported, he introduced a bill "authorizing the taxing of landlords in the towns where the lease lands lie." It never got out of committee. See "LNY," *AEJ*, Apr. 26, 1841.

31. "LNY," *Argus*, Apr. 9, 1845.

32. Wright beat Fillmore by a 442 majority in Columbia, a 475 majority in Delaware, a 594 majority in Greene, a 456 majority in Montgomery, a 1,418 majority in Otsego, a 559 majority in Schoharie, a 238 majority in Sullivan, and a 52 majority in Ulster. For the numbers, see *The Whig Almanac and United States Register for 1845* (New York: Greeley and McElrath, 1845), 43-44.

33. *Report of the Comptroller, in answer to a resolution of the Assembly of 1844, in relation to taxing rents, quarter sales, interests in water right reservations, etc.* (hereinafter cited as *Flagg Report*), NYAD 228, 68 sess. (1845), 3-4, 7. For the 1823 statute and the revisers' notes, see *NYRS*, 2d ed. (1836), 3:496.

34. *Flagg Report*, 7.

35. Ibid., 6-7.

36. *NYAJ*, 68 sess. (1845), 889, 1169, 1219-20.

37. "LNY," *Argus*, Apr. 29, 1845.

38. "LNY," ibid., May 12, 1845. For the roll call, see *NYAJ*, 68 sess. (1845), 1208-10.

39. *Tribune*, May 21, 1845. In the senate, the enabling act passed by a vote of 18-14, all the nays being Democrats. See "LNY," *Argus*, May 13, 1845. For the statute, see New York, *Laws*, 68 sess. (1845), 270; for the popular vote approving the call, with county-by-county totals, see *Argus*, Nov. 24, 1845.

40. Smith A. Boughton to Thomas A. Devyr, *YA*, July 19, 1845 (Boughton's emphasis).

41. Hammond, *Political History*, 537; Edward P. Cheyney, "The Antirent Movement and

the Constitution of 1846," in *History of the State of New York*, vol. 6, *The Age of Reform*, ed. Alexander C. Flick (New York: Columbia University Press, 1934), 308. See also Christman, *Tin Horns and Calico*, 147–48; Ellis, *Landlords and Farmers*, 277–78; Gunn, *The Decline of Authority*, 180–81; David Montgomery, *Citizen Worker* (New York: Cambridge University Press, 1993), 105–6.

42. Ira Harris, "Remarks . . . on the Bill to Pay the Troops Called into the service of the State at Hudson," *AEJ*, Mar. 1, 1845; Harry Betts, "Remarks . . . on so much of the Governor's Message as relates to the Manor Question," ibid., Mar. 11, 1845. The first mention of the constitutional convention in the *Freeholder* did not occur until July 16. For editorials on the tax bill and the proposed measure to test the validity of landlord titles, see Apr. 9, 23, May 14, 21, June 4, 11, 1845. See also C. F. Bouton, "To the Public," ibid., Aug. 6, 1845 (stating that he and Harris owned the newspaper).

43. *Tribune*, May 20, 1845.

44. "Anti-Rentism," *Freeholder*, May 10, 1848.

45. In the fall of 1845, Harris and Van Schoonhoven openly acknowledged that they were Whigs first and Anti-Renters only secondarily. See *Freeholder*, Oct. 1, 1845; *Tribune*, Oct. 29, 1845.

46. For Harris's bill, see *Report of the minority of the select committee on landlord and tenant*, NYAD 247, 68 sess. (1845), 16. The 1844 bill spoke exclusively of leases; Harris's measure recognized that indentures stipulating the payment of rent in perpetuity were actually grants in fee and were distinguishable from leases for lives or for years. The 1845 bill, now called an Act Concerning Tenures, authorized tenants subject to both legal forms to contest their landlords' title.

47. Ibid., 7–9.

48. *Bronson v. Kinzie*, 1 How. 311, 316, 319 (1843) (my emphasis).

CHAPTER NINE

1. *Freeholder*, June 11, 1845; *Tribune*, Aug. 28, 1845.

2. *YA*, June 14, 1845.

3. Ibid., June 21, 28, 1845 (Evans's emphasis).

4. Ibid., June 28, 1845 (Evans's emphasis). Three other propositions rounded out the plan. One provided that no person, "*hereafter*, shall, under any circumstances, become possessed of more than one lot in a city or village (the size of which may be regulated by the city or town authorities)." Another required corporations "now holding land" to sell it to "landless persons, under the above restrictions, excepting the lots and buildings occupied for their business." The third authorized "associations of persons," such as Fourierist phalanxes, to hold land in common. For a brief discussion of the connection between National Reform and associationism, see Helene S. Zahler, *Eastern Workingmen and National Land Policy, 1829–1862* (New York: Columbia University Press, 1941), 52–55. See also Carl Guarneri, *The Utopian Alternative: Fourierism in Nineteenth-Century America* (Ithaca: Cornell University Press, 1991).

5. *YA*, June 28, 1845; Blackstone, *Commentaries*, 2:12.

6. *YA*, June 28, July 26, 1845. Evans's proposal must not be confused with homestead-exemption acts that permitted landowners to waive the exemption in contracts with financial intermediaries. See Paul Goodman, "The Emergence of the Homestead Exemption in the United States: Accommodation and Resistance to the Market Revolution, 1840–1880," *JAH* 80 (1993): 470–93.

7. *YA*, June 28, Sept. 27, 1845 (Evans's emphasis).

8. Ibid., June 28, July 26, Aug. 16, 1845; New York, *Laws*, 59 sess. (1836), 406, amending the parent statute in *Laws*, 40 sess. (1817), 301. For a useful history of the offset principle in American eminent domain law, see Charles M. Haar and Barbara Hering, "The Determination of Benefits in Land Acquisition," *California Law Review* 51 (1963): 833–81.

9. *YA*, July 26, 1845; *Report of the minority of the select committee on landlord and tenant*, NYAD 247, 68 sess. (1845), 8.

10. *YA*, July 26, 1845 (Evans's emphasis). The phrase "hoary iniquities of the Norman land pirates" is from Evans's famous pamphlet, "Vote Yourself a Farm," first published on March 15, 1845. It is reprinted in Zahler, *Eastern Workingmen and National Land Policy*, 207–8.

11. VETO, "The Convention," *NYEP*, Sept. 23, 1845; *Tribune*, Sept. 17, 23, 1845. Especially perceptive treatments of American exceptionalism in the era's thought include Drew R. McCoy, *The Elusive Republic: Political Economy in Jeffersonian America* (Chapel Hill: University of North Carolina Press, 1980); Dorothy Ross, "Liberalism," in *Encyclopedia of American Political History: Studies of the Principal Movements and Ideas*, ed. Jack P. Greene (New York: Charles Scribner's Sons, 1984), 2:750–63. See also Merrill D. Peterson, *The Jefferson Image in the American Mind* (New York: Oxford University Press, 1960), 67–111.

12. J. W. W[ebb], "Convention or No Convention," *Courier and Enquirer*, Aug. 1, 5 (quotation), 14, 1845. Madison's rejoinder to the idea that "the earth belongs to the living" is in *The Papers of James Madison*, ed. Charles Hobson and Robert Rutland (Charlottesville: University Press of Virginia, 1981), 13:23. For an analysis of the Jefferson-Madison exchange, see Stephen Holmes, "Precommitment and the Paradox of Democracy," in *Constitutionalism and Democracy*, ed. Jon Elster and Rune Slagstad (New York: Cambridge University Press, 1988), 195–240.

13. *Freeholder*, May 28, June 4, 1845. Watson and Harris's law partner, S. O. Shepard, roomed together at the American Hotel. See L. G. Hoffman, *Albany Directory and City Register for the Years 1845-46* (Albany: L. G. Hoffman, 1845), 31–32, 196, 310, 351.

14. *Freeholder*, June 11, 1845; Henry Christman, *Tin Horns and Calico* (New York: Henry Holt, 1945), 152–55. See also Devyr, "To the Farmers of Albany and Schoharie Counties," *WA*, Feb. 1, 1845; Devyr, "What is to Be Done?," *YA*, May 10, 1845.

15. *Freeholder*, June 25, 1845 (Devyr's emphasis).

16. Christman, *Tin Horns and Calico*, 159–62.

17. Robert D. Watson, "Oration . . . delivered at the Great Anti-Rent Celebration, held at New S[cotland] on the Anniversary of our Independence," *Freeholder*, July 9, 1845.

18. Christman, *Tin Horns and Calico*, 163–64.

19. *YA*, July 26, 1845; C. F. Bouton, "To the Public," *Freeholder*, Aug. 6, 1845. Bouton edited the paper until Johnson, who had been admitted to the New York bar in 1843, came aboard. See ibid., Oct. 1, 1845; Nathaniel Bartlett Sylvester, *History of Rensselaer County, New York* (Philadelphia: Everts and Peck, 1880), 135.

20. *YA*, Aug. 9, 16 (quotation), 23, 30, Sept. 6, 1845; *Argus*, Aug. 11, 1845.

21. *People v. Van Steenburgh*, 1 Parker Crim. Cas. 39 (N.Y. Oyer & Terminer, Delaware Co., 1845) (hereinafter cited as *Van Steenburgh*); Christman, *Tin Horns and Calico*, 176; Eldridge Pendleton, "The New York Anti-Rent Controversy, 1830–1860" (Ph.D. diss., University of Virginia, 1974), 3.

22. John D. Monroe, *The Anti-Rent War in Delaware County, New York* (Jefferson, N.Y.: privately printed, 1940), 22–24, 31–34; *Morrill v. Jenkins*, 2 N.Y. Legal Observer 214 (1841). See also *NYRS*, 2d ed. (1836), 2:411–15.

23. *Van Steenburgh*, 40–41 (summarizing Wright's testimony). See also David Murray,

"The Antirent Episode in New York," in *Annual Report of the American Historical Association for the Year 1896*, 2 vols. (Washington, D.C.: Government Printing Office, 1897), 2:159.

24. *Van Steenburgh*, 42–44; Monroe, *Anti-Rent War in Delaware County*, 29–30. For a different account, see S. D. C., "Law and Order," *Freeholder*, Aug. 20, 1845. See also Christman, *Tin Horns and Calico*, 176–82.

25. *Tribune*, Aug. 23, 1845; Monroe, *Anti-Rent War in Delaware County*, 35–38; Christman, *Tin Horns and Calico*, 182–93, 197–201. The phrase "Delhi Bastille" was coined by J. C. Allaben, treasurer of the Anti-Rent Association of Delaware County and one of the inmates. See Allaben's letter to Evans in *YA*, Aug. 30, 1845.

26. *YA*, Aug. 23, 30, 1845 (reprinting excerpts from newspapers throughout the state); "New York Anti-Rent Disturbances," *Niles' Register* 68 (Aug. 23, 1845): 393–95; ibid., 69 (Sept. 6, 1845): 7–8 (summarizing press reports).

27. Lincoln, *Governor Messages*, 4:297–308; New York, *Laws*, 68 sess. (1845), 53; Roger Sherman, "Anti-Rent War—Flagg's False Returns," *Tribune*, Mar. 15, 1847.

28. N. K. Wheeler to Azariah Flagg, Sept. 13, 1845, Flagg Papers, box 2, NYPL; Alf Evers, *Woodstock: History of an American Town* (Woodstock, N.Y.: Overlook Press, 1987), 199; Monroe, *Anti-Rent War in Delaware County*, 42–45; Pendleton, "The New York Anti-Rent Controversy," 150–51; *Van Steenburgh*, 39–40.

29. Lincoln, *Governor Messages*, 4:306–7.

30. *Argus*, Aug. 29, Sept. 19, 1845; Evers, *Woodstock*, 199.

31. *Herald*, Aug. 21, 23, 1845.

32. N. K. Wheeler to Flagg, Sept. 26, 1845, Flagg Papers, box 2, NYPL; Murray, "Antirent Episode," 162.

33. *People v. Bodine*, 1 Denio 281 (N.Y. Sup. Ct. 1845); *Argus*, Sept. 17, 1845. Governor Bouck had appointed Beardsley to the court upon the death of Esek Cowen in the fall of 1844. Silas Wright, who hated Beardsley, called him "the master-spirit" of the Hunker Democracy. Wright to Cave Johnson, Oct. 12, 1846, Gillet, *Wright*, 1703. For a biographical sketch, see McAdam, *Bench and Bar*, 1:258–59.

34. Christman, *Tin Horns and Calico*, 204; *Herald*, Oct. 27, 1845; *YA*, Oct. 4, 18, 1845. See also [Thurlow Weed], "Anti-Rent Trials," *AEJ*, Oct. 1, 1845 (defending the trial judges); [A. G. Johnson], "Trial by Jury," *Freeholder*, Oct. 1, 1845 (castigating the trial judges). In the spring of 1846, Polly Bodine was acquitted of murder by a second, more carefully selected jury, thus illustrating the other face of dismissing jurors for favor in the American system of criminal justice. See *AEJ*, Apr. 20, 1846.

35. Thomas Farrington to Flagg, Oct. 17, 1845, Flagg Papers, box 2, NYPL; Lincoln, *Governor Messages*, 4:316, 318–19; *Tribune*, Oct. 17, Nov. 11, 1845; *AEJ*, Nov. 12, 1845. For Webb's bloodthirsty editorials, see *Courier and Enquirer*, Oct. 24, Nov. 12–13, 1845.

36. For the response to Wright's death sentence message, see *Argus*, Nov. 28–29, 1845. But see also *YA*, Nov. 29, 1845. For assessments of the election returns, see *Argus*, Nov. 5–7, 1845; *Tribune*, Nov. 5, 10, 12, 1845; *Freeholder*, Nov. 12, 1845. The allotment of counties to senate districts is in *NYRS*, 2d ed. (1836), 3:364–65; to calculate Wright's 1844 majority in the third district, I relied on the numbers in *The Whig Almanac and United States Register for 1847* (New York: Greeley and McElrath, 1847), 44. For a roster of the members elect, see *Argus*, Nov. 13, 1845. Democratic gains in the lower house were generated by the collapse of the American Republican Party in New York City. Democrats won all fifteen seats occupied by nativists in 1845.

37. "Coeymans" to Horace Greeley, *Tribune*, Aug. 18, 26, 1845; "A Landholder" to Edwin Croswell, *Argus*, Sept. 4, 1845.

38. *Tribune*, Aug. 11, 13, 18, 22, 23, 28, 30; Sept. 2, 6, 12, 17, 20, 23, 26, 29, 1845 (quotations from issues of Aug. 11, 18) (Greeley's emphasis).

39. Ibid., Aug. 11, Sept. 6, 20, 1845.

40. Ibid., Sept. 6, 1845 (Greeley's emphasis).

41. Ibid., Sept. 6, 12, 17, 1845.

42. Ibid., Aug. 30, Sept. 15, 1845.

43. Ibid., Aug. 11, Sept. 6, 29, 1845.

44. *Argus*, Aug. 18, 1845; *Tribune*, Sept. 23, 1845.

45. *Tribune*, Sept. 15, 17, 23, 26, 29, 1845.

46. Ibid., Sept. 6, 12, 23, 1845. Evans wrote two articles pillorying Greeley's positivism and challenging him to an exchange on natural rights in the American political tradition. He got no response. See "What Is Law?," *YA*, Aug. 30, 1845; "The City Press," ibid., Sept. 13, 1845.

47. "Anti-Rent" to Greeley, *Tribune*, Sept. 19, 29, 1845.

48. *Courier and Enquirer*, Sept. 11, 13, 16, 18, 28, Dec. 1, 1845.

49. Ibid., Dec. 12, 1845.

50. D. D. Barnard, "The 'Anti-Rent' Movement and Outbreak in New York," *Whig Review* 2 (1845): 577-78.

51. Ibid., 577-78, 580.

52. Ibid., 578, 596; Sharon Hood Penney, "Daniel Dewey Barnard: Patrician in Politics" (Ph.D. diss., SUNY-Albany, 1972), 107-8, 118. Barnard announced his retirement from Congress on September 23, 1844, twelve days after Weed's endorsement of fusion with the Albany and Rensselaer anti-renters. See *AEJ*, Sept. 11, 23, 1844, and the discussion in chapter 7 at notes 2-4. The district's Whig convention nominated Henry G. Wheaton; he lost in November.

53. Barnard, "The Anti-Rent Movement," 579, 583, 585-86, 588.

54. Ibid., 593-94.

55. Ibid., 587, 595. For Whig and Anti-Rent critiques of Barnard's argument, see *AEJ*, Dec. 9, 1845; *Tribune*, Dec. 13, 1845; *Freeholder*, Dec. 17, 24, 31, 1845.

56. Barnard, "The Anti-Rent Movement," 582, 587, 597.

57. Ibid., 593-94, 597-98.

58. Ibid., 594. See also [C. F. Bouton], "The Patroon's Offer," *Freeholder*, Sept. 24, 1845; John I. Slingerland to Weed, *AEJ*, Oct. 29, 1845; [A. G. Johnson], "The Anti-Rent Movement," *Freeholder*, Dec. 17, 1845. For a summary statement of the terms proposed in late 1845 by the proprietors of the Hardenbergh Patent and Livingston Manor, respectively, see Alf Evers, *The Catskills: From Wilderness to Woodstock* (Garden City, N.Y.: Doubleday, 1972), 429-30; James D. Livingston and Sherry H. Penney, "The Breakup of Livingston Manor," in *The Livingston Legacy: Three Centuries of American History*, ed. Richard T. Wiles (Annandale-on-Hudson, N.Y.: Bard College Office of Publications, 1987), 415.

59. "Affidavit of Christopher Batterman," *Memorial of Stephen Van Rensselaer*, NYSD 47, 70 sess. (1847), 9-10. See also Alvan Bovay's account of a futile New Scotland distress sale in *YA*, Aug. 30, 1845.

60. Barnard, "The Anti-Rent Movement," 578, 597.

CHAPTER TEN

1. For the progressive Whig support of rent-charge taxation, see *Tribune*, Dec. 2, 1845; *AEJ* Dec. 9, 1845. For the numbers that imperiled Wright, see chapter 9 at note 36.

2. The bill is printed in *Report of the select committee on so much of the Governor's message*

as relates to the difficulties existing between the proprietors of certain leasehold estates and their tenants (hereinafter cited as *Tilden Report*), NYAD 156, 69 sess. (1846), 31–34. The bill did not disturb the right of existing proprietors to sell their interests to persons other than the tenants in possession. But it did contain a safeguard so that the death sentence for manorial tenures could not be evaded by proprietor sales or gifts. Section 11 of the bill, as reported out of committee on March 28, provided that if the specified rents, services, and other reservations were "hereafter conveyed," they would become subject to the provisions of the act "at the time at which they would, if not so conveyed, have become so subject in passing by devise or descent."

3. Joseph Story, *Commentaries on the Constitution of the United States*, 3 vols. (Boston: Hilliard, Gray, 1833), 3:670.

4. Wright to Albert H. Tracy, Aug. 5, 1844, Tracy Papers, NYSL; Lincoln, *Governor Messages*, 4:249–50, 285; *NYEP*, Jan. 5, 1846; *Courier and Enquirer*, Jan. 1, 13, 23, 1846 ("Sentinel" letters from Albany). For the abortive Slidell mission, see David M. Pletcher, *The Diplomacy of Annexation: Texas, Oregon, and the Mexican War* (Columbia: University of Missouri Press, 1973), 286–91, 352–72.

5. For Wright's relationship with Perkins, see Wright to Azariah Flagg, Sept. 25, 1844, Flagg Papers, box 3, NYPL. In one of the strategy sessions, Wright and Tilden whispered through cupped hands for two hours while a third Democrat sat restlessly across the room. See John Bigelow, *Retrospections of an Active Life*, 5 vols. (New York: Baker and Taylor, 1909–13), 1:66. John L. Russell, Wright's right-hand man during the legislature's 1845 session, had lost a coin toss with Asa Hazelton, the other assemblyman from St. Lawrence County in 1845, and withdrew his candidacy for renomination in conformity to the Democracy's rotation-in-office principle. The principle held that each county must elect at least one new assemblyman every year; the new member was Bishop Perkins. See Russell's letter, "To the Democratic Electors of St. Lawrence," *Argus*, Oct. 8, 1845.

6. Lincoln, *Governor Messages*, 4:232, 244.

7. Ibid., 240–43.

8. Ibid., 233–40 (all quotations at 239).

9. *AEJ*, Jan. 6, 1846 (Weed's emphasis); *Tribune*, Jan. 7, 1846 (Greeley's emphasis). See also Greeley to Schuyler Colfax, Jan. 12, 1846, Greeley-Colfax Letters, NYPL.

10. *NYAJ*, 69 sess. (1846), 66; "LNY," *AEJ*, Jan. 7, 1846; "The Anti-Rent Troubles," *Tribune*, Jan. 9, 1846.

11. "LNY," *Argus*, Jan. 10, 1846.

12. Ibid.

13. Ibid.

14. "LNY," *Argus*, Jan. 12, 1846; *NYAJ*, 69 sess. (1846), 85.

15. *Tribune*, Jan. 10, 1846; *AEJ*, Jan. 10, 1846.

16. "LNY," *Argus*, Jan. 13, 1846.

17. "Legislation on Land-Tenures," *Atlas*, Jan. 13, 1846.

18. "LNY," *Argus*, Jan. 13, 1846; Thomas Smith, "The Manor Difficulties: Remarks . . . on the motion of Mr. Harris," ibid., Jan. 20, 1846. See also Henry Z. Hayner, "The Anti-Rent Question: Remarks on . . . the Governor's Message," *AEJ*, Feb. 25, 1846; Ira Harris, "The Anti-Rent Question: Remarks . . . in Committee of the Whole," ibid., Feb. 10, 1846.

19. Levi Chatfield, "The Anti-Rent Question: Remarks . . . in Committee of the Whole," *Atlas*, Jan. 20, 1846. Chatfield served as the state's attorney general from 1850 through 1853; he later taught in the law department of the City University of New York. See McAdam, *Bench and Bar*, 2:278–79.

20. Smith, "The Manor Difficulties"; Robert D. Watson, "Remarks in Committee of the Whole on . . . the Governor's Message," *Argus*, Feb. 4, 1846.

21. *NYAJ*, 69 sess. (1846), 129–30; "LNY," *AEJ*, Jan. 15, 1846; "Anti-Rent Difficulties," ibid., Jan. 16, 1846. See also *Tribune*, Jan. 17, 1846; *Freeholder*, Jan. 21, 1846.

22. *AEJ*, Jan. 17, 1846 (Duer's emphasis).

23. Ibid. Historians of American constitutional law will recognize that Duer's analogy foreshadowed the famous case of *Wynehamer v. People*, 13 N.Y. 378 (N.Y. Ct. Appeals 1856).

24. *AEJ*, Jan. 17, 1846 (Duer's emphasis); Harris, "The Anti-Rent Question." See also Van Schoonhoven's speech in the senate, "LNY," *Argus*, Feb. 20, 1846; Harry Betts's testimony before the Tilden Committee, summarized in "The Legislative Committees on the Subject of Landlord and Tenant," *Freeholder*, Mar. 11, 1846; Alexander G. Johnson's editorial, "Eminent Domain—Senator Spencer," ibid., Mar. 18, 1846.

25. *YA*, Jan. 24, 1846; J. Kellog to Tilden, Jan. 26, 1846, Tilden Papers, box 4, NYPL.

26. Jean H. Baker, *Affairs of Party: The Political Culture of Northern Democrats in the Mid-Nineteenth Century* (Ithaca: Cornell University Press, 1983), 125–32 (quotation at 127). See also Joel Silbey, *The American Political Nation, 1838–1893* (Stanford: Stanford University Press, 1991), 115–18.

27. For conflicting accounts of the merger proposal's rise and fall, see *Atlas*, Feb. 25, 1846; *Argus*, May 13, 1846. See also Cassidy's rebuttal, supported by lengthy statements by Senator John Beekman and Attorney General Van Buren, *Atlas*, May 14, 1846. A statute enacted in 1843 fixed the state printer's tenure at three years. See New York, *Laws*, 66 sess. (1843), 5–6.

28. "LNY," *Argus*, Jan. 14, 16 (quotation), 17, 1846. See also *NYSJ*, 69 sess. (1846), 66, 94–95. The Democrats who joined the Whigs in the upper house included all ten holdover senators who voted against the constitutional convention bill in 1845.

29. "Democratic Legislative Caucus," *Atlas*, Jan. 23, 1846.

30. Ibid.; *NYSJ*, 69 sess. (1846), 131–37; "Democratic Legislative Caucus," *Argus*, Jan. 31, 1846. See also Croswell's editorial, "Retrenchment and Reform," ibid., Jan. 26, 1846, and Cassidy's counterblast, *Atlas*, Jan. 26, 1846.

31. For highlights of the divorce proceeding, see "The Public Printing: Sketch of the Debate," *Argus*, Jan. 27, 1846; D. R. F. Jones, "Remarks . . . on his resolutions in relation to the Annexation of Texas," ibid., Jan. 31, 1846; Orville Clark, "Speech in Reply to Col. Young," ibid., Feb. 24, 1846; W. S. Sherwood, "Printing Bill: Remarks . . . in the Assembly," ibid., Feb. 27, 1846; Bishop Perkins, "Speech . . . on the bills to provide for the Public printing," *Atlas*, Mar. 6, 1846. For the quotations, see *Atlas*, Feb. 14, 23, 1846; *Argus*, Jan. 31, 1846; *Tribune*, Jan. 26, Feb. 13, 1846. For the votes on printing reform in the assembly, see "LNY," *Argus*, Mar. 5, 1846. The statute is in New York, *Laws*, 69 sess. (1846), 20–22.

32. *AEJ*, Feb. 13, 16, 1846.

33. Seward to McLean, Mar. 20, 1846, Seward Papers, DLC; Greeley to Weed, Mar. 13, 1846, Weed Papers, UR. See also Michael F. Holt, "Winding Roads to Recovery: The Whig Party from 1844 to 1848," in *Essays on American Antebellum Politics*, ed. Stephen F. Maizlish and John J. Kushma (College Station: Texas A&M University Press, 1982), 147–48. Greeley already knew the answer to his rhetorical question about the Hunkers and black suffrage. Croswell and his conservative associates, like most of their Democratic brethren in the Barnburner ranks, had always opposed it. So did most Whig voters. Greeley even anticipated the final outcome. "We shall have [equal suffrage] inserted into the new constitution, but shall be compelled to submit it separately to the people," he wrote a friend that spring,

"and there all the white niggers of both parties will unite to kill it." See Greeley to Schuyler Colfax, Apr. 22, 1846, Greeley-Colfax Letters, NYPL. See also John L. Stanley, "Majority Tyranny in Tocqueville's America: The Failure of Negro Suffrage in 1846," *PSQ* 84 (1969): 412-35.

34. Wright to Russell, Mar. 10, 1846, Gillet, *Wright*, 1731-32; Wright to John Fine, Mar. 30, 1846, Hammond, *Political History*, 756.

35. Samuel J. Tilden, "Remarks . . . in relation . . . to the Manor difficulties," *Atlas*, Feb. 23, 1846; *Tilden Report*, 7-8. For a splendid account of Tilden's life and thought, see Robert Kelley, *The Transatlantic Persuasion: The Liberal-Democratic Mind in the Age of Gladstone* (New York: Alfred A. Knopf, 1969), 238-92. The intentionally ironic "great measure" remark was Weed's. See his editorial, "The State Printing," *AEJ*, Mar. 3, 1846.

36. Tilden, "Remarks."

37. *NYAJ*, 69 sess. (1846), 383, 428; *NYSJ*, 69 sess. (1846), 63, 69, 76. For the quotation, see "LNY," *Argus*, Apr. 6, 1846.

38. "Anti-Rent State Convention," *Tribune*, Mar. 4, 1846.

39. Ibid. The title-test bill endorsed at the Anti-Rent Party's convention was Harris's first one, "allowing a tenant in all suits upon leases in perpetuity, for life, or for a term exceeding twenty years, to show want of title in the grantor, and thereby defeat a recovery," and not the later one, introduced at Weed's behest on January 15, that would authorize Nott, Bouck, and Seward to conduct an investigation. For the rancor between Johnson and Devyr, see the former's two editorials, both entitled "Agrarianism," *Freeholder*, Jan. 21, Feb. 4, 1846; Devyr's piece, "The Right of Man to the Earth," *Anti-Renter*, Feb. 14, 1846. See also Henry Christman, *Tin Horns and Calico* (New York: Henry Holt, 1945), 252-53.

40. Wright to Green More, Nov. 22, 1845, Hammond, *Governor Messages*, 4:325. For the resulting flood of petitions to free the Anti-Rent prisoners, see *NYAJ*, 69 sess. (1846), 406, 461, 466, 467, 625, 658, 686-87, 715, 735, 863, 973; *NYSJ*, 69 sess. (1846), 198, 202, 215, 233, 236, 246, 258, 262, 270, 174, 280, 284, 296, 302, 310, 315, 322, 334, 351, 353, 371, 458, 551, 600. In the senate, a resolution comparable with Harris's was killed on the ground that the power to pardon belonged exclusively to the governor. See *Report of the committee on the judiciary, on petitions for pardon of persons convicted for offenses growing out of the difficulties between landlord and tenant*, NYSD 142, 69 sess. (1846).

41. *YA*, June 14, 1845; *Annals of Albany*, 10 vols. (Albany: J. Munsell, 1850-59), 2:36, 9:268; L. W. Hall, *Albany Directory and City Register for the Years 1845-6* (Albany: L. W. Hall, 1845), 282. For the availability of Pepper's pamphlet, see *Freeholder*, Jan. 28, 1846.

42. Calvin Pepper Jr., *Manor of Rensselaerwyck* (Albany: J. Munsell, 1846), 23-24, 28, 29 (Pepper's emphasis).

43. For Harris's infatuation with Pepper's Quia Emptores argument, see his unreported opinion for the New York Supreme Court, published as "Manor of Rensselaerwyck: Opinion of Judge Harris, The People v. William P. Van Rensselaer," *AEJ*, Sept. 11, 1852. For the quotations, see "The Legislative Committees on the Subject of Landlord and Tenant," *Freeholder*, Mar. 11, 1846; *Report of the minority of the select committee on so much of the Governor's message as relates to leasehold tenures*, NYSD 92, 69 sess. (1846), 16. For a biographical sketch of Spencer, see McAdam, *Bench and Bar*, 1:486.

44. *Tilden Report*, 26-28; *Jackson ex dem. Lewis & Wife v. Schutz*, 18 Johns. 174, 180 (N.Y. Sup. Ct. 1820).

45. *Tilden Report*, 25, 29, 31-32.

46. Ibid., 15-16, 19, 21-22, 29; *Courier and Enquirer*, Apr. 6, 1846 (report of "Sentinel" from Albany); *Tribune*, Apr. 6, 1846 (report of Albany correspondent).

47. Ira Harris, "Discharge of Anti-Rent Prisoners: In Assembly, March 31," *Tribune*, Apr. 4, 1846; *AEJ*, Apr. 7, 1846; *NYAJ*, 69 sess. (1846), 739-40. See also James Watson Webb's hysterical reaction, "The Murder of a Sheriff," *Courier and Enquirer*, Apr. 10, 1846.

48. *Tilden Report*, 24-25; Robert H. Ludlow, "Remarks . . . in opposition to the bill to amend the statutes of Devises and Descents," *Argus*, Apr. 21, 1846. For comparable complaints about the bill, see Gulian C. Verplanck to Tilden, Apr. 2, 1846, Tilden Papers, box 4, NYPL. The laudatory press reports include *Atlas*, Mar. 28, 1846; *NYEP*, Mar. 30, 1846; *AEJ*, Mar. 31, 1846; *Freeholder*, Apr. 1, 1846. But see also Webb's editorial, written months afterward, denouncing the devise-and-descent bill as "the most barefaced attempt at legislative ROBBERY—the most manifest outrage against vested rights, that has ever been brought forward in a civilized community." *Courier and Enquirer*, Oct. 14, 1846.

49. *NYAJ*, 69 sess. (1846), 1109-12; *Argus*, May 5, 1846 (Croswell's emphasis); *NYSJ*, 69 sess. (1846), 67, 611. For sketches of the Judiciary Committee members, see Hammond, *Political History*, 370, 372-73.

50. *Atlas*, May 5, 1846; *Tribune*, May 5, 1846; *Freeholder*, May 6, 1846; Hammond, *Political History*, 605-10. For the party and factional loyalties of the delegates, I have relied on Philip L. Merkel, "Party and Constitution Making: An Examination of Selected Roll Calls from the New York Constitutional Convention of 1846" (University of Virginia seminar paper, 1983), supplemented and sometimes corrected by data on county nominations in the *Herald*, Apr. 18-20, 1846.

51. *Tribune*, May 6, 1846. Beers voted against the constitutional convention enabling act in 1845 and for the state printing bill the following January. For his interest in the land reform measures, see *NYSJ*, 69 sess. (1846), 530.

52. *NYSJ*, 69 sess. (1846), 663, 672, 695, 710, 745, 774; New York, *Laws*, 69 sess. (1846), 369, 466-68.

53. Croswell to "Colonel" Seaver, Mar. 2, 1846, quoted in Garraty, *Wright*, 366.

54. Wright to Van Buren, Oct. 8, 1844, Van Buren Papers, DLC (m).

55. Sellers, *Polk, Continentalist*, 416-21; Wright to Van Buren, May 17, 1846, Van Buren Papers, DLC (m).

CHAPTER ELEVEN

1. "Feudal Tenures," *AEJ*, May 9, 1846; Sherman Croswell and Richard Sutton, eds., *Debates and Proceedings in the New York State Convention, For the Revision of the Constitution* (Albany: Argus, 1846), 422, 802, 805.

2. Thorpe, *Constitutions*, 2054-55.

3. Croswell and Sutton, *Debates and Proceedings*, 64, 681-82, 802-3. See also *NYRS*, 2d ed. (1836), 1:714; New York, *Laws*, 10 sess. (1787), 415-16; McAdam, *Bench and Bar*, 1:466-67. Valentine Treadwell of Rensselaerville offered the "faithful servant" characterization of Harris in the form of a toast at the Anti-Rent Party's traditional July 4 rally at New Scotland, Albany County. See *Atlas*, July 23, 1846. In the fall Treadwell ran successfully for the assembly on the Anti-Rent and Whig tickets. See *Freeholder*, Sept. 16, 1846; *AEJ*, Oct. 4, 1846.

4. Croswell and Sutton, *Debates and Proceedings*, 803.

5. Ibid., 809, 811. The private roads amendment, which simply stated that "private roads may be opened in the manner prescribed by law," went into section 7 of the Bill of Rights; the Private Road Act of 1772, which had been struck down in 1843, went right back into *NYRS*, 4th ed., 2 vols. (1852), 1:1040.

6. "What Can be Done?," *Freeholder*, Oct. 7, 1846.

7. *AEJ*, Oct. 5, 1846; Glyndon G. Van Deusen, *Thurlow Weed: Wizard of the Lobby* (Boston: Little, Brown, 1947), 264.

8. *Freeholder*, Sept. 2, 1846.

9. Greeley to Weed, May 14, 1846, Weed Papers, UR; *Atlas*, July 23, 1846; *AEJ*, Sept. 24, 1846.

10. Robert J. Rayback, *Millard Fillmore: Biography of a President* (Buffalo: Buffalo Historical Society, 1959), 167–68; Hammond, *Political History*, 681–82; *AEJ*, Sept. 24-25, 1846; *Herald*, Sept. 25, 1846.

11. *NYEP*, Oct. 16, 1846; Young to Harris, Sept. 29, 1846, NYSL. For the confusion surrounding Young's pardon-pledge letter, see the various quotations and commentaries compiled in the *Atlas*, Nov. 2, 8, 12, 15, 1846. See also Nelson K. Wheeler to Azariah Flagg, Dec. 26, 1846, Flagg Papers, box 2, NYPL. By the time Young wrote the letter, Governor Wright already had pardoned Burrill, Knapp, Osterhout, and Tompkins—the four Delaware anti-renters convicted of violating the Armed and Disguised Act months before the shooting of Osman Steele. See *Freeholder*, Sept. 16, 1846; *Atlas*, Sept. 26, 1846.

12. Greeley to Weed, Sept. 28, 1846, Weed Papers, UR.

13. *Freeholder*, Oct. 14, 1846. For a sympathetic account of Devyr's attempt to stop the Harris juggernaut, see Henry Christman, *Tin Horns and Calico* (New York: Henry Holt, 1945), 261–68, 271–75.

14. *Freeholder*, Oct. 14, 1846; Hammond, *Political History*, 683–85. Young, mum to the last, neither accepted nor repudiated the Anti-Rent nomination. Gardiner declined it in a long letter that appeared in the Democratic press. See Gardiner to S. C. Grinnell et al., *NYEP*, Oct. 19, 1846. But see also Greeley's canny response in the *Tribune*, Oct. 21, 1846.

15. *AEJ*, Oct. 8, 1846; *Tribune*, Oct. 10, 15, 26, 29, 1846; *Courier and Enquirer*, Oct. 7, 14, 20, Nov. 14, 1846.

16. Livingston to William H. Averell, Oct. 8, 1846, quoted in Thomas Summerhill, "The Farmers' Republic: Agrarian Protest and the Capitalist Transformation of Upstate New York, 1840–1900" (Ph.D. diss., University of California, San Diego, 1993), 231–32; Greeley to Weed, Oct. 8, 1846, NYHS; Fish to Weed, Oct. 26, 1846; Fish to A. G. Johnson, Oct. 26, 1846, Fish Papers, DLC; *Tribune*, Oct. 29, Nov. 14, 1846.

17. Christman, *Tin Horns and Calico*, 272–75, 277–78; *Anti-Renter*, Oct. 31, 1846. See also *Atlas*, Oct. 14, 22, 1846 (promoting Shafer's candidacy on the Democratic ticket). Masquerier got 1,100 votes statewide; voters in the Anti-Rent counties supplied only 200 of them. See *AEJ*, Nov. 28, 1846.

18. *Freeholder*, Nov. 4, 1846; Greeley to Clay, Nov. 15, 1846, Clay Papers, DLC (m); Fish to Barnard, Nov. 26, 1846, Fish Papers, DLC. For the numbers, see "The Official Canvass," *Argus*, Dec. 4, 1846.

19. Fish to Barnard, Nov. 26, 1846, Fish Papers, DLC (Fish's emphasis).

20. *AEJ*, Nov. 4–7, 10, 13, 16, 28 (Weed's emphasis). The "Locofoco editors" to whom Weed referred were Edwin Croswell and his Hunker satellites. See *Argus*, Nov. 9, 18, 21, 1846. Equally self-serving radical Democrats claimed that Hunker treachery, not the Anti-Rent vote, was "*the* cause" of the Democratic debacle. See *Atlas*, Dec. 4, 5, 7, 10, 1846; John A. Garraty, *Silas Wright* (New York: Columbia University Press, 1949), 380–88. For a regression analysis that conclusively demonstrates the decisive impact of the Anti-Rent vote, see John F. Kirn Jr., "Elections, Roll Calls, and the Decline of the Second Party System in New York State, 1846–1853" (paper presented at the Social Science History Association meetings, 1995), table 1846.1. The best account of Congress's reconstruction of national

economic policy in 1846 is Charles Sellers, *James K. Polk, Continentalist, 1843–1846* (Princeton: Princeton University Press, 1966), 445–76.

21. *AEJ*, Dec. 30, 1846.

22. Johnson's authorship of the pardon proclamation is clear not only in the document's prose but also between the lines of his editorial in the *Freeholder*, Feb. 3, 1847.

23. Lincoln, *Governor Messages*, 4:363–80; *Argus*, Jan. 5, 1847. The pardon proclamation, which described manorial tenures as "inconvenient and injurious, unjust and oppressive," was printed in *AEJ*, Jan. 27, 1847. For the celebrations in Clinton Prison and the manor counties, see Christman, *Tin Horns and Calico*, 282–88. For typical complaints, see *NYEP*, Jan. 28, 1847; Barnard to Fish, Feb. 3, 1847, Fish Papers, DLC.

24. "LNY," *AEJ*, Jan. 12, 13, 16, Feb. 2, 1847; "Landlord and Tenant: Sketch of a Debate . . . on Mr. Allaben's resolution," *Argus*, Jan. 16, 1847. The committee did not report until April 30, ten days before the legislature adjourned; Allaben's motion to make the recommended title-test measure the special order for May 10 lost by a vote of 36-57. See *Report of the select committee on the subject of leasehold estates and the difficulties between landlord and tenant*, NYAD 162, 70 sess. (1847); "LNY," *AEJ*, May 8, 1847.

25. W. H. Seward to Francis Seward, Jan. 17, 1847, Frederick W. Seward, *Seward at Washington, as Senator and Secretary of State: A Memoir of His Life, With Selections from His Letters, 1846–1861* (New York: Derby and Miller, 1891), 34.

26. Albert Champlin Mayham, *The Anti-Rent War on Blenheim Hill* (Jefferson, N.Y.: Frederick L. Frazee, 1906), 74–76.

27. *Argus*, Aug. 18, 1845; James D. Livingston and Sherry H. Penny, "The Breakup of Livingston Manor," in *The Livingston Legacy: Three Centuries of American History*, ed. Richard T. Wiles (Annandale-on-Hudson, N.Y.: Bard College Office of Publications, 1987), 415–16; Alf Evers, *The Catskills: From Wilderness to Woodstock* (Garden City, N.Y.: Doubleday, 1972), 429–30; John Kiersted to Henry Overing, July 1, 1847, Kiersted Letters, NYSL.

28. "New York's Great Landowner, George Clarke," *Magazine of American History* 22 (1889): 246–49; David Maldwyn Ellis, *Landlords and Farmers in the Hudson-Mohawk Region, 1790–1860* (Ithaca: Cornell University Press, 1946), 187, 308–9; *Memorial of Stephen Van Rensselaer*, NYSD 47, 70 sess. (1847); *William P. Van Rensselaer v. Witbeck*, 4 How. Practice Rep. 381 (N.Y. Sup. Ct. 1850); *Van Rensselaer v. Dennison*, 8 Barb. 23 (N.Y. Sup. Ct. 1850).

29. "The Legislative Committees on the Subject of Landlord and Tenant," *Freeholder*, Mar. 11, 1846.

30. Calvin Pepper Jr., "To the Anti-Renters of Columbia County—Read This," ibid., July 22, 1846.

31. Calvin Pepper Jr., "Ex-Governor Seward's Speech Upon the Manor Titles," ibid., Sept. 16, 1846; Livingston and Penny, "Breakup of Livingston Manor," 419–20.

32. *AEJ*, Apr. 2, 24, 26, June 19, 1847.

33. *Tribune*, Apr. 9, 22, 28, May 6, 13, 1847 (Greeley's emphasis).

34. Ibid., Mar. 17, 1847 (Greeley's emphasis). It is likely that Greeley had been impressed by the Van Rensselaer brief in *Van Vechten v. Clute* (Albany Co. Circuit Ct., 1847), the test case Pepper filed and later abandoned. The brief provided satisfactory answers to all the pertinent allegations of fraud, including the William and Mary seal on the Queen Anne patent of 1704. See "Title of Van Rensselaer Estate," *AEJ*, Feb. 10, 1847.

35. *NYRS*, 2d ed. (1836), 2:221. See also the parent statute, which had fixed a forty-year limitation on the state's cause of action, in New York, *Laws*, 11 sess. (1788), 683–88. When the 1788 statute went into force, the people of New York were still receiving "rents and

profits" from Stephen Van Rensselaer III in the form of quitrents previously payable to the British crown. But the act authorized any person seised of land charged with an annual quitrent to commute the same by paying the state treasurer $1.50 for every 12.5¢ of annual rent. Van Rensselaer paid the required commutation fee on December 26, 1806, thereby extinguishing the people's cause of action under the second condition of the Quiet-Title Act. See *People v. Van Rensselaer*, 9 N.Y. 291, 326-27 (N.Y. Ct. Appeals 1853).

36. Chaplain W. Morrison, *Democratic Politics and Sectionalism: The Wilmot Proviso Controversy* (Chapel Hill: University of North Carolina Press, 1967), 13-51; Milo M. Quaife, ed., *The Diary of James K. Polk during His Presidency, 1845-1849*, 4 vols. (Chicago: A. C. McClurg, 1910), 2:75, 4:251. See also the contrasting, though not necessarily incompatible interpretations in Eric Foner, "The Wilmot Proviso Revisited," *JAH* 56 (1969): 262-79; Michael F. Holt, *The Political Crisis of the 1850s* (New York: John Wiley and Sons, 1978), 49-66.

37. *NYEP*, Sept. 28, 1846, Jan. 23, 1847; Wright to Dix, Jan. 19, 1847, Gillet, *Wright*, 1916-17.

38. *Argus*, Jan. 22, 1847 (Croswell's emphasis); *Atlas*, Feb. 3, 1847; Joseph G. Rayback, *Free Soil: The Election of 1848* (Lexington: University Press of Kentucky, 1970), 71. See also "Legislative Debates: Extension of Slavery," *Argus*, Jan. 19, 21, 1847. For the resolutions, see New York, *Laws*, 70 sess. (1847), 377.

39. Ira Harris, "Extension of Slavery: Remarks . . . on the Resolutions relative to the Extension of Slavery," *AEJ*, Jan. 27, 1847 (Harris's emphasis); *Tribune*, Feb. 16, Apr. 7, 1847; *Courier and Enquirer*, July 14, 30, Aug. 13, 1847.

40. Seward, *Works*, 3:97; Oliver Dyer, ed., *Phonographic Report of the Proceedings of the National Free Soil Convention at Buffalo, New York, August 9th and 10th, 1848* (Buffalo: G. H. Derby, 1848), 11; [Martin Van Buren et al.], "Address of the Democratic Members of the Legislature of the State of New York, April 12, 1848," in *The Writings and Speeches of Samuel J. Tilden*, ed. John Bigelow, 2 vols. (New York: Harper and Brothers, 1885), 2:569; *Tribune*, Mar. 4, 1847; *NYEP*, Jan. 7, Feb. 2, Nov. 8, 1847; James Willard Hurst, *Law and the Conditions of Freedom in the Nineteenth-Century United States* (Madison: University of Wisconsin Press, 1956), 25. For an especially discerning discussion of the free-soil argument that is punctuated with quotations drawn from New Yorkers in the 1847-48 period, see Eric Foner, *Free Soil, Free Labor, Free Men: The Ideology of the Republican Party before the Civil War* (New York: Oxford University Press, 1970), 11-72.

41. For an incisive treatment of the "constitutional utopians," see Robert M. Cover, *Justice Accused: Antislavery and the Judicial Process* (New Haven: Yale University Press, 1975), 154-58. Compare the argument set forth in Spooner's *The Unconstitutionality of Slavery* (Boston: B. Marsh, 1845) with John Bigelow's in "The Constitutionality of the Wilmot Proviso," *NYEP*, Aug. 18, 1847.

42. *Congressional Globe*, 29th Cong., 2d sess. (1847), 551-55; Herbert D. A. Donovan, *The Barnburners* (New York: New York University Press, 1925), 85-87; John Mayfield, *Rehearsal for Republicanism: Free Soil and the Politics of Antislavery* (Port Washington, N.Y.: Kennikat Press, 1980), 94-98. See also "Slavery Triumphs," *Tribune*, Mar. 4, 1847; "The 'Wilmot Proviso' and the Organ of the 'Secret Circular,'" *Argus*, Mar. 6, 1847. The Barnburner-dominated Free Soil Party did make overtures to the National Reformers in 1848. But every measure they promoted, including free 160-acre homesteads on the nation's public lands, had a prospective operation. See Rayback, *Free Soil*, 210, 220-22, 264-66.

43. *NYEP*, May 20, 24, 1847; *Argus*, May 24, June 8, 18, 1847; *AEJ*, May 19, 21, 31, June 8, 1847.

44. *NYEP*, Oct. 3, 1847; *AEJ*, Oct. 8, 1847; F. Seward, *Seward at Washington*, 55. At a subsequent Barnburner convention, held at Herkimer on October 26, New York Democrats were told "to vote as they must do when no regular nominations have been made." See O. C. Gardiner, "Herkimer Convention," in *The Great Issue . . . Being a Brief Historical Sketch of the Free Soil Question* (New York: Wm. C. Bryant, 1848), 50–55. Addison Gardiner, who defeated Fish in the 1846 lieutenant governor race, had resigned following his election to the Court of Appeals; Governor Young summoned the legislature for a special session in June to authorize the election of a successor. For the enabling act, see New York, *Laws*, 70 sess. (1847), 263.

45. *Freeholder*, Oct. 20, 27, 1847. Three weeks earlier, Assemblyman Allaben endorsed the land-limitation program that George Henry Evans had been promoting for years and Whig anti-renters had always opposed. See *Report of a majority of the committee on memorials for a limitation of the quantity of land that any individual may hereafter acquire in this State*, NYAD 203, 70 sess. (1847).

46. *Freeholder*, Oct. 27, Nov. 3, 10, 1847. Bouton took Johnson's name off the masthead on Jan. 19, 1848. For the allotment of counties to senate districts under the constitution of 1846, see Thorpe, *Constitutions*, 2656–58.

47. *AEJ*, Nov. 8, 1847; Barnard to Fish, Nov. 3, 1847; Fish to Barnard, Nov. 9, 1847, Fish Papers, DLC. Fish came closer to being nominated by the Anti-Rent Party than either he or Barnard had reason to know. Charles O. Shepherd, the Liberty nominee for lieutenant governor, won by a vote of 11-10 on the second ballot. See "The State Convention," *Freeholder*, Oct. 20, 1847. For the county-by-county returns for lieutenant governor and comptroller, see *AEJ*, Nov. 24, 1847; for a roster of the legislators-elect, see *Argus*, Nov. 11, 1847.

48. Lincoln, *Governor Messages*, 4:409–12.

49. *Tribune*, Jan. 5, 1848; *Freeholder*, Jan. 12, 1848; "LNY," *AEJ*, Jan. 13, 1848.

50. "LNY," *AEJ*, Mar. 4, 1848; *Report of the minority of the select committee on landlord and tenant*, NYAD 126, 71 sess. (1848), 4. For the majority report, see *AEJ*, Mar. 8, 1848. Myers attended the Herkimer Convention in 1847 and served on the committee charged with framing an address to the people. See Gardiner, *The Great Issue*, 49.

51. *Freeholder*, Mar. 29, Apr. 12, 1848; "LNY," *AEJ*, Mar. 30–31, Apr. 7, 10, 1848; Valentine Treadwell, "Speech . . . upon the passage of the Joint Resolution instructing the Attorney General to investigate the Manorial Titles," *Freeholder*, Apr. 19, 1848. The resolution is in New York, *Laws*, 71 sess. (1848), 582–83.

52. *Freeholder*, Mar. 8, 15, 1848.

53. For the act struck down in the unreported *Gilbert* case, see New York, *Laws*, 39 sess. (1816), 158–59; *NYRS*, 2d ed. (1836), 2:452–53.

54. *Taylor v. Porter*, 4 Hill 140, 143 (N.Y. Sup. Ct. 1843); *White v. White*, 5 Barb. 474, 485–86 (N.Y. Sup. Ct. 1849) (summarizing and explaining *Gilbert*). Mason's inference, though plausible, cannot be regarded as "irresistible." John Bigelow, writing while the constitutional convention was in session, urged the delegates to adopt language that would have expressly prohibited compensated takings for private use. None of the people's deputies offered such a motion. See "The Convention—Rights of the Citizen," *NYEP*, July 31, 1846.

55. *Freeholder*, May 10, 1848.

56. Ibid., Aug. 9, 30, 1848.

57. Donovan, *Barnburners*, 98–109; Van Deusen, *Weed*, 163–64; *Freeholder*, Oct. 4, 11, 1848; *Argus*, Nov. 21, 28, 1848; *Report of the Attorney General in answer to a resolution of the Senate on the subject of Manorial Lands*, NYSD 27, 74 sess. (1851), 1–2. For a biographical

sketch of Schoolcraft, who became Weed's "closest advisor" during the 1850s, see Hendrik Booraem V, *The Formation of the Republican Party in New York: Politics and Conscience in the Antebellum North* (New York: New York University Press, 1983), 31, 96-97.

58. *Freeholder*, Nov. 29, 1848; Allan Nevins, *Hamilton Fish* (New York: Dodd and Mead, 1936), 29-35; Van Deusen, *Weed*, 165-66; *Herald*, Apr. 24, 1852.

CHAPTER TWELVE

1. "The Pending Issue," *Freeholder*, Jan. 17, 1849.

2. "A Word of Advice to Tenants," ibid., Apr. 17, 1850.

3. *Hay v. Cohoes Co.*, 3 Barb. 42, 47 (N.Y. Sup. Ct. 1848); *Emory v. Conner*, 3 N.Y. 511, 517 (N.Y. Ct. Appeals 1850). See also Edward S. Corwin, "The Extension of Judicial Review in New York, 1783-1905," *Michigan Law Review* 15 (1917): 281-313; Morton J. Horwitz, *The Transformation of American Law, 1780-1860* (Cambridge: Harvard University Press, 1977), 256-61.

4. Marvin Meyers, *The Jacksonian Persuasion: Politics and Belief*, 2d ed. (Stanford: Stanford University Press, 1960), 233-37, 253-75; James A. Henretta, "The Slow Triumph of Liberal Individualism: Law and Politics in New York, 1780-1860," in *American Chameleon: Individualism in Trans-National Context*, ed. Richard O. Curry and Lawrence B. Goodhart (Kent: Kent State University Press, 1991), 87-106; Michael F. Holt, "Winding Roads to Recovery: The Whig Party from 1844 to 1848," in *Essays on Antebellum Politics, 1840-1860*, ed. Stephen E. Maizlish and John J. Kushma (College Station: Texas A&M University Press, 1982), 153-65; Merrill D. Peterson, *The Great Triumvirate: Webster, Clay, and Calhoun* (New York: Oxford University Press, 1987), 384-85, 431-41; Douglass C. North, *The Economic Growth of the United States, 1790-1860* (New York: W. W. Norton, 1966), 83, 88-89, 206-12.

5. "A New Project," *Freeholder*, Mar. 20, 1850.

6. *Overba[u]gh v. Patrie*, 8 Barb. 28 (N.Y. Sup. Ct. 1850) (hereinafter cited as *Overbaugh*); "Important Decision—Overbaugh v. Patrie," *Freeholder*, Mar. 6, 1850.

7. Richard H. Levet, *Ambrose L. (Aqua Fortis) Jordan, Lawyer* (New York: Vantage Press, 1973), 13, 19-21, 40-76, 112-37; Proctor, "Albany Bar," 143.

8. Blackstone, *Commentaries*, 2:42.

9. For the rival theories, see *Report of the select committee on so much of the Governor's message as relates to the difficulties existing between the proprietors of certain leasehold estates and their tenants* (hereinafter cited as *Tilden Report*), NYAD 156, 69 sess. (1846), 26-27; *Report of the minority of the select committee on so much of the Governor's message as relates to leasehold estates* (hereinafter cited as *Spencer Report*), NYSD 92, 69 sess. (1846), 16-17. For the Quiet-Title Act, see *NYRS*, 2d ed. (1836), 2:221.

10. Sherman Croswell and Richard Sutton, eds., *Debates and Proceedings in the New York State Convention, For the Revision of the Constitution* (Albany: Argus, 1846), 514-15.

11. Jordan to A. H. Greene, Sept. 11, 1848, quoted in Levet, *Jordan*, 169; *Report of the Attorney General in answer to a resolution of the Senate on the subject of Manorial Lands* (hereinafter cited as *Chatfield Report No. 2*), NYSD 27, 74 sess. (1851), 1-2; *Freeholder*, June 7, July 5, Sept. 20, 27, 1848. For the dismissal, see "Legal Proceedings," ibid., Apr. 18, 1849.

12. *Chatfield Report No. 2*, 2-5; David Maldwyn Ellis, *Landlords and Farmers in the Hudson-Mohawk Region, 1790-1860* (Ithaca: Cornell University Press, 1946), 297-98; Jordan to Schoolcraft, *AEJ*, Sept. 28, 1849. See also Jordan's complaints about the "disposition

materially to impair the rights of parties by varying the remedies retrospectively" in Croswell and Sutton, *Debates and Proceedings in the New York Convention*, 634-35.

13. "Quarter Sales," *Freeholder*, Oct. 20, 1847. For the quotation, see *Livingston v. Stickles*, 7 Hill 253, 255 (N.Y. Ct. Errors 1843) (hereinafter cited as *Stickles*). Oliver Barbour's report of *Overbaugh* did not include an abstract of the lawyers' briefs. My summary of Stevens's argument is based on Taber's reply. See Azor Taber, *Report of the Argument . . . in the Cause of Overbaugh and others vs. Patrie, decided in the Supreme Court, in the February term, 1850* (Albany: Weed, Parsons, 1850).

14. *Jackson* ex dem. *Lewis & Wife v. Schutz*, 18 Johns. 174, 182, 184 (N.Y. Sup. Ct. 1820) (hereinafter cited as *Schutz*).

15. Taber, *Report of the Argument*, 27-28, 42, 44-46. For the impulse to fuse *Schutz* with the other cases in string citations, see *Stickles*, 255; *Duer Report*, 6; *Tilden Report*, 27-28; George Babcock, "The Manorial Question: Remarks . . . in the Senate on the motion to recommit the bill for the relief of tenants," *AEJ*, Apr. 19, 1850.

16. See the discussion in chapter 1 at notes 50-55.

17. Daniel Dewey Barnard, "The Anti-Rent Movement and Outbreak in New York," *Whig Review* 2 (1845): 588; *Schutz*, 186.

18. *Tilden Report*, 28; Taber, *Report of the Argument*, 45.

19. *Overbaugh*, 39-40. The court's condition-subsequent language came directly from counsel's brief. See Taber, *Report of the Argument*, 17.

20. *Freeholder*, Mar. 6, Apr. 10, 1850; Anson Bingham and Andrew J. Colvin, *A Treatise on Rents, Real and Personal Covenants, and Conditions* (Albany: W. G. Little, 1857), discussed below at notes 49-50. For the quotation, see Colvin, "Remarks . . . delivered at the Anti-Rent Celebration, Berne, July 4, 1848," *Freeholder*, July 12, 1848.

21. *Freeholder*, Apr. 24, 1850.

22. DeAlva Alexander, *A Political History of the State of New York*, vol. 2, *1839-1861* (New York: Henry Holt, 1906), 149-50; John Mayfield, *Rehearsal for Republicanism: Free Soil and the Politics of Antislavery* (Port Washington, N.Y.: Kennikat Press, 1980), 141-46. For a roster of the legislators-elect, see *Argus*, Nov. 20, 1849. Democratic and Whig candidates won equal numbers of the statewide offices.

23. *AEJ*, Sept. 26, 28, Oct. 19, 31, 1849; *Atlas*, Oct. 19, 20, 30, 1849; *Freeholder*, Oct. 2, 31, 1849. See also "Review of the Past," ibid., May 15, 1850. For the impact of the tenant vote, see the returns for the statewide offices in *Argus*, Nov. 22, 1849.

24. *Report of the Attorney General in answer to a Senate resolution of the 8th of January* (hereinafter cited as *Chatfield Report No. 1*), NYSD 26, 73 sess. (1850), 2-3.

25. "LNY," *AEJ*, Jan. 7, 11, 14, 16, Feb. 14, 1850; *Report of the select committee upon petitions for relief of tenants holding lands under certain persons claiming manorial title in this State*, NYAD 80, 73 sess. (1850), 2. For Walworth's brief, framed for the January hearings on Johnson's senate bill, see *Argus*, Mar. 27, 1850. See also *Fletcher v. Peck*, 6 Cranch 87 (U.S. 1810).

26. "LNY," *AEJ*, Feb. 18, 21, 23, 25 (quotation) 1850; Thomas B. Carroll, "Relief under Manorial Titles: Speech . . . on the bill for the relief of tenants holding lands under perpetual leases in this State," ibid., Mar. 1, 1850.

27. "Tenants on Manor Lands: Sketch of the Debate . . . on the Bill for the Relief of Tenants holding Leases of Land under Manorial Titles," *AEJ*, Feb. 25, 1850; "LNY," *Argus*, Feb. 21, 1850; "LNY," *AEJ*, Feb. 23, 1850; *Report of a majority of the Judiciary Committee on the bill to settle the controversies existing between the State of New York and certain occupants and claimants of land and to confirm the title to said lands* (hereinafter cited as *Mann-Babcock Report*), NYSD 96, 73 sess. (1850), 2. For the political persuasions of Mann

and Babcock, respectively, see *Argus*, Oct. 29, 1849; Robert J. Rayback, *Millard Fillmore: Biography of a President* (Buffalo: Buffalo Historical Society, 1959), 283–86.

28. "LNY," *AEJ*, Mar. 13, 20, 22, 1850. For the bill, see *Mann-Babcock Report*, 19–22.

29. *Freeholder*, Mar. 20, 1850; *Mann-Babcock Report*, 2.

30. *Freeholder*, Mar. 20, 1850; "Sketch of the Debate in the Senate on the Manorial Title Bill [March 23]," *Argus*, Apr. 19, 1850.

31. "LNY," *Argus*, Mar. 25, 1850; Babcock, "The Manorial Question"; *Freeholder*, Apr. 3, 1850. Ten Democrats and eight Whigs voted to pass the Schoonmaker-Snyder substitute; four Democrats and four Whigs joined Babcock and Mann in voting nay.

32. "The Manorial Rent Question: Sketch of the Debate in the Assembly . . . on the Senate Bill for the Relief of Tenants," *Argus*, Apr. 12, 1850; Thorpe, *Constitutions*, 2659.

33. Joel B. Nott, "Leaseholds in Perpetuity: Speech . . . on the abolition of Leasehold Estates in perpetuity," *AEJ*, Mar. 16, 1850; "A Nott-Able Project," *Albany Express*, reprinted in *Freeholder*, Mar. 20, 1850; J[ohn] C. Spencer, "Leaseholds in Perpetuity," *Argus*, Mar. 18, 1850; J. B. Nott, "Lease-Hold Estates in Perpetuity," ibid., Mar. 21, 1850; J. C. Spencer, "Leasehold Estates in Perpetuity," ibid., Mar. 26, 1850; *Mann-Babcock Report*, 8–10. Nott, a veteran Anti-Rent leader, had once been the featured speaker at the traditional Independence Day rally in Berne. See *Freeholder*, July 12, 1848.

34. *YA*, July 26, 1845 (Evans's emphasis).

35. Elisha Hammond to C. F. Bouton, *Freeholder*, Aug. 30, 1848; "Patents in Schoharie County," ibid., Aug. 14, 1850. The distinction between conditions precedent and conditions subsequent had been a fixture in the Supreme Court's adjudication of private-land claims arising from cessions of territory since *United States v. Arredondo*, 6 Pet. 691, 745–46 (U.S. 1832).

36. For the state's argument, see Ambrose Jordan to A. J. TenBroek, *Freeholder*, Sept. 27, 1847.

37. *People v. Van Rensselaer*, 8 Barb. 189 (N.Y. Sup. Ct. 1850).

38. *Chatfield Report No. 2*, 2–4; *People v. Livingston*, 8 Barb. 253 (N.Y. Sup. Ct. 1850).

39. *People v. Clarke*, 10 Barb. 120, 155–56 (N.Y. Sup. Ct. 1851); *Chatfield Report No. 2*, 4–5; "Opinion of Judge Cady," *Freeholder*, Mar. 26, 1851. See also Edith M. Fox, *Land Speculation in the Mohawk Country* (Ithaca: Cornell University Press, 1949).

40. *Chatfield Report No. 1*, 3–7; *Chatfield Report No. 2*, 3.

41. *People v. Arnold* (arg.), 4 N.Y. 508, 509–10 (N.Y. Ct. Appeals 1851).

42. "Manor of Rensselaerwyck: Opinion of Judge Harris," *AEJ*, Sept. 11, 1852; *Tilden Report*, 22–23.

43. *People v. Van Rensselaer*, 9 N.Y. 291, 339 (N.Y. Ct. Appeals 1853).

44. Lincoln, *Governor Messages*, 4:727; Ellis, *Landlords and Farmers*, 304. For a splendid account of Clarke's operation in the 1850–70 period, see Thomas Summerhill, "Farming on Shares: Landlords, Tenants, and the Rise of the Hop and Dairy Economies in Central New York," *NYH* 76 (1995): 125–52.

45. *De Peyster v. Michael*, 6 N.Y. 467, 493 (hereinafter cited as *De Peyster*); *Overba[u]gh v. Patrie*, 6 N.Y. 510 (N.Y. Ct. Appeals 1852). Ruggles had become chief justice upon the resignation Greene Bronson. See *Argus*, Apr. 7, 1851.

46. *De Peyster*, 503. Ruggles's position on the Quia Emptores question did not sweep the field. Justice Hiram Denio later adopted the Pepper-Taber-Harris argument that the ancient statute came into force upon the British conquest of New Netherland in the 1660s. An eminent historian of New York land law agreed. See *Van Rensselaer v. Hays*, 19 N.Y. 68, 73–76 (N.Y. Ct. Appeals 1859); Robert Ludlow Fowler, *History of the Law of Real Property in New York* (New York: Baker, Voorhis, 1895), 29–34. Fowler's claim that *Hays* overruled *De*

Peyster on this point, however, may be dismissed as a flight of fancy. The question was not before the court in *Hays*; the precise moment when the right to subinfeudate ceased was of no concern to bench or bar after *De Peyster* came down and the relation of the parties on Rensselaerwyck became, as a matter of settled law, a rent charge rather than a rent service. See *Van Rensselaer v. Read*, 26 N.Y. 558, 563 (N.Y. Ct. Appeals 1863).

47. *De Peyster*, 505. Julius Goebel later argued, much as Emmot had in 1820, that not even the Act Concerning Tenures extinguished rent service on the great estates of eastern New York. Chief Justice Ruggles's claim that it did evoked an uncharacteristically gentle rebuke from Goebel. He called it "a strange conclusion." See Julius Goebel Jr. and Joseph M. Smith, *The Law Practice of Alexander Hamilton: Documents and Commentary*, 5 vols. (New York: Columbia University Press, 1964–81), 3:313. Goebel was probably right on all counts. What he never acknowledged, however, was the psychological obstacle that kept nineteenth-century judges from accepting the possibility that rent service still existed in New York State.

48. *De Peyster*, 497, 504, 508 (Ruggles's emphasis).

49. Bingham and Colvin, *A Treatise on Rents*, 1–4, 17–19, 29–31, 33, 35–53, 56–59, 66–77, 79–94, 180–265.

50. Ibid., 63.

51. Barnard, "The Anti-Rent Movement," 597; *YA*, July 26, 1845. The *Freeholder* put out its last paper on June 11, 1851.

52. David Murray, "The Antirent Episode in New York," in *Annual Report of the American Historical Association for the Year 1896*, 2 vols. (Washington, D.C.: Government Printing Office, 1897), 1:171; Ellis, *Landlords and Farmers*, 302–3, 309; "Van Rensselaer Mansion Sold," *Freeholder*, Aug. 7, 1850.

53. Arthur B. Gregg, *Old Hellebergh: Historical Sketches of the West Manor of Rensselaerwyck, Including an Account of the Anti-Rent Wars* (Altamont, N.Y.: Altamont Enterprise, 1936), 164; Simon W. Rosendale, "Closing Phases of the Manorial System in Albany," *Proceedings of the New York State Historical Association* 8 (1909): 238–39, 244–45; Nathaniel Bartlett Sylvester, *History of Rensselaer County, New York* (Philadelphia: Everts and Peck, 1880), 73. Following the adoption of the Field Code in 1848, New York civil procedure required process and pleadings to run in the name of "the real party at interest." As Church explained in an 1862 hearing, however, the indentures in Albany County "have been conditionally assigned, or rather . . . have been assigned under an agreement that I hold the residuary interest, after the debts still remaining are paid to the original parties." See *Report of the Committee of the Judiciary relative to Involuntary Servitude*, NYAD 237, 85 sess. (1862), 6–10; *Van Rensselaer v. Dennison*, 35 N.Y. 393, 402 (N.Y. Ct. Appeals 1866).

54. Ira Harris, "The Anti-Rent Question: Remarks . . . upon the Anti-Rent Question," *AEJ*, Feb. 10, 1846; *People v. Livingston*, 8 Barb. 253, 298–99 (N.Y. Sup. Ct. 1850). The third member of the panel was George Gould, a Troy attorney elected on the Know-Nothing ticket in 1855. He already had slammed the new Anti-Rent argument on circuit in *Main v. Feathers*, 21 Barb. 646 (N.Y. Sup. Ct. 1856); Gould's doctrinal analysis there, further elaborated in his separate opinion in *Van Rensselaer v. Smith*, 27 Barb. 104 (N.Y. Sup. Ct. 1858) (hereinafter cited as *Smith*), did not prevail in the Court of Appeals. The discussion that follows therefore focuses on Justice Wright's opinion, with which Harris concurred.

55. *Smith*, 172. For the statutes, see New York *Laws*, 10 sess. (1787), 415–16; 28 sess. (1805), 492–93; 69 sess. (1846), 369. See also *Van Rensselaer v. Snyder*, 13 N.Y. 299, 304 (N.Y. Ct. Appeals 1855). The obscure decision that precipitated the 1805 act was *Devisees of Van Rensselaer v. Executors of Platner*, 2 Johns. Cas. 24 (N.Y. Sup. Ct. 1800). Speaking through Chief Justice John Lansing, the court held that the devisees of John Van Rensselaer of Claverack could not bring an action at law, though they might in equity, to recover on rent

covenants in a lease in fee. Lansing conceded that an English statute passed in the reign of Henry VIII, a version of which the New York legislature enacted in 1788, authorized grantees of reversions to enforce covenants in conventional leases. In his view, however, the statute did not make a lease in fee assignable. The 1805 statute was designed to negate the court's decision:

> Whereas it hath been doubted whether the provisions contained in the [1788] act, entitled "An act to enable grantees of reversions to take advantage of the conditions to be performed by lessees," hereby intended to be amended, extend to any but assignees of reversions dependent on estates for life or years; and whereas leases or grants, in fee reserving rents, have long since been in use in this State, and to remove all doubts respecting the true construction of the aforesaid act, *Be it enacted . . .* that all the provisions of said act, and the remedies thereby given, shall be construed to extend as well to grants or leases in fee reserving rents, as to leases for life and years, any law, usage or custom to the contrary thereof notwithstanding.

For the origins of the 1788 act, which the New York legislature purported to amend in 1805, see the discussion in chapter 1 at note 45.

56. Bingham and Colvin, *A Treatise on Rents*, 29, 41.

57. Ibid., 44, 100–133, 171–76; *Smith* (arg.), 115–19, 123, 125. For the due process quotation, see *Report of the Committee on the Judiciary, on the act to amend the Revised Statutes, relative to "Proceedings for the recovery of rent, and of demised premises,"* NYSD 45, 83 sess. (1860), 6. The statutory construction maxim began its career in *Dash v. Van Kleeck*, 7 Johns. 477 (N.Y. Sup. Ct. 1811). Harris had invoked it in *Snyder v. Snyder*, 3 Barb. 621 (N.Y. Sup. Ct. 1848).

58. *Smith*, 175–76 (my emphasis). For a different view, chock-full of invective and imputations of corrupt motives, see Alexander G. Johnson, *A Chapter of History, or the Progress of Judicial Usurpation* (Troy: A. W. Scribner, 1863), 22–23. See also Henry Christman, *Tin Horns and Calico* (New York: Henry Holt, 1945), 294–95.

59. *Van Rensselaer v. Hays*, 19 N.Y. 68, 86, 97; *Van Rensselaer v. Ball*, 19 N.Y. 100, 105 (N.Y. Ct. Appeals 1859); *Westerfeldt v. Gregg*, 12 N.Y. 202, 212 (N.Y. Ct. Appeals 1854). See also Denio's concurring opinion, fusing the due process requirement with the prospectivity norm in legislation, in *Wynehamer v. People*, 13 N.Y. 378, 459 (N.Y. Ct. Appeals 1856).

60. *Hays*, 85.

61. *Ball*, 105–6.

62. The phrase "contagion of liberty" was coined and elaborated in Barnard Bailyn, *The Ideological Origins of the American Revolution* (Cambridge: Harvard University Press, 1967), 230–319. For a discerning treatment of both the Federalist impulse to counteract it and some long-term ramifications of their efforts, see Joyce Appleby, "The American Heritage: The Heirs and the Disinherited," *JAH* 74 (1987): 138–53.

63. *AEJ*, Apr. 15, 1859; *Atlas and Argus*, Apr. 17, 1859.

64. The number of leases in fee for Albany County has been calculated from data in *Spencer Report*, 10; Ellis, *Landlords and Farmers*, 309–10.

65. See the "Official Canvass of Votes . . . in the County of Albany," *AEJ*, Nov. 30, 1859.

CHAPTER THIRTEEN

1. For an especially poignant account of the ejectments, based in part on oral history, see Arthur B. Gregg, *Old Hellebergh: Historical Sketches of the West Manor of Rensselaerwyck, Including an Account of the Anti-Rent Wars* (Altamont, N.Y.: Altamont Enterprise, 1936).

2. New York, *Laws*, 85 sess. (1865), 1084.

3. *AEJ*, Feb. 18, 20, 22, 1860; *Atlas and Argus*, Feb. 20, 1863; Gregg, *Old Hellebergh*, 167. According to the reporter's statement of the facts in *Van Rensselaer v. Ball*, 19 N.Y. 100 (N.Y. Ct. Appeals 1859), Ball's father William had been the original grantee and Peter "had paid rent for his father" until his death "twelve or fourteen years before the trial" in 1857. The accumulated back rents on most Berne farms were substantially greater.

4. *Atlas and Argus*, Feb. 20, 1860.

5. *Report of the Committee on the Judiciary relative to Bills Proposing amendments to the Statutes as to Real Estate* (hereinafter cited as *Bingham Report*), NYAD 92, 83 sess. (1860), 5. See also Anson Bingham, "Speech . . . on the Law of Conveyance of Real Estate," *AEJ*, Mar. 29, 1860. For the introduction of the house bills, see *NYAJ*, 83 sess. (1860), 159. Colvin introduced comparable measures in the upper house on January 11 (modifying 1846 act) and January 28 (effectively repealing the 1805 act). See *NYSJ*, 83 sess. (1860), 59, 142.

6. John I. Slingerland, "Landlord and Tenant: Speech . . . in Assembly, March 13, 1860," *AEJ*, Apr. 9, 1860 (Slingerland's emphasis). All quotations and all emphasis in the five paragraphs that follow are from this document.

7. *Report of the Minority of the Committee on the Judiciary, on Bills Proposing amendments to the Revised Statutes, relative to Real Estate* (hereinafter cited as *Callicott Report*), NYAD 98, 83 sess. (1860), 7; "LNY," *AEJ*, Mar. 14, 1860. Jacques, Milliken, and Robinson were also on the Judiciary Committee yet did not sign either Bingham's majority report or Callicott's minority report. For a list of the committee members, see *NYAJ*, 83 sess. (1860), 67–69.

8. "LNY," *AEJ*, Mar. 14, 1860; *Callicott Report*, 8.

9. "LNY," *AEJ*, Mar. 14, 1860; *Callicott Report*, 8.

10. *NYAJ*, 83 sess. (1860), 857–58, 1013–16; "LNY," *AEJ*, Apr. 5, 1860; *NYSJ*, 83 sess. (1860), 748–49; New York, *Laws*, 83 sess. (1860), 675. The political parties took no stand on the Anti-Rent bill, and partisanship had no discernible effect on the outcome. Republicans cast 44 aye votes and 40 nay votes in the first assembly roll call on March 29; Democrats cast 10 ayes and 18 nays. The Finch substitute passed 19-6 in the senate. Ten Republicans and nine Democrats voted for it; all the nay votes were cast by Republicans.

11. *De Peyster v. Michael*, 6 N.Y. 467, 505 (N.Y. Ct. Appeals 1852) (hereinafter cited as *De Peyster*); New York, *Laws*, 10 sess. (1787), 415–16; 11 sess. (1788), 604; 28 sess. (1805), 492–93. See also the discussion in chapter 1 at notes 45–47 and in chapter 12 at note 55.

12. *Van Rensselaer v. Hays*, 19 N.Y. 68, 85 (N.Y. Ct. Appeals 1859).

13. For Church's financial embarrassments, see *Report of the Committee of the Judiciary, Relative to Involuntary Servitude* (hereinafter cited as *Church Testimony*), NYAD 237, 85 sess. (1862), 6–10. For biographical sketches of Hogeboom and Peckham, respectively, see Peyton F. Miller, *A Group of Great Lawyers of Columbia County, New York* (Hudson, N.Y.: De Vinne Press, 1904), 180–83; Proctor, "Albany Bar," 148–50. Peckham's son, Rufus Jr., also sat on the New York Supreme Court and the Court of Appeals before President Grover Cleveland appointed him to the Supreme Court of the United States. See also *De Peyster*, 470 (listing Hogeboom as counsel for the tenant-in-fee defendant).

14. *Main v. Green*, 32 Barb. 448, 453; *Van Rensselaer v. Secor*, 32 Barb. 469 (N.Y. Sup. Ct. 1860). George Gould, the third judge on the panel, wrote an overwrought concurring opinion after Oliver Barbour sent the reports to press. See 33 Barb. 136.

15. *Main*, 458–59 (Hogeboom's emphasis).

16. Ibid.

17. Ibid., 456–57; *Dash v. Van Kleeck*, 7 Johns. 477, 508–9 (N.Y. Sup. Ct. 1805); *Quacken-*

bush v. Danks, 1 Denio 128, 130–31 (N.Y. Sup. Ct. 1844); *Snyder v. Snyder*, 3 Barb. 621, 623–24 (N.Y. Sup. Ct. 1848); Theodore Sedgwick [Jr.], *A Treatise on the Rules which Govern the Interpretation and Application of Statutory and Constitutional Law* (New York: John S. Voorhies, 1857), 188–216. For Bingham's previous reliance on the canon, see the discussion in chapter 12 at note 57.

18. Edward S. Corwin, "The Basic Doctrine of American Constitutional Law," *Michigan Law Review* 12 (1914): 247–76.

19. *AEJ*, Oct. 3, 15, 1860.

20. *Argus*, May 26, 1865; *AEJ*, May 30, 1865; Simon W. Rosendale, "Closing Phases of the Manorial System in Albany," *Proceedings of the New York State Historical Association* 8 (1909): 239; *Church Testimony*, 9; *Van Rensselaer v. Barringer*, 39 N.Y. 9, 12, 16–17 (N.Y. Ct. Appeals 1868). See also *Van Rensselaer v. Read*, 26 N.Y. 558 (N.Y. Ct. Appeals 1863); *Van Rensselaer v. Slingerland*, 26 N.Y. 580 (N.Y. Ct. Appeals 1863).

21. *AEJ*, May 30–31, 1865; *Argus*, May 26, 1865.

22. *AEJ*, May 30–31, June 2–3, 1865; Gregg, *Old Hellebergh*, 168; Henry Pitt Phelps, *The Albany Hand-Book: A Strangers' Guide and Residents' Manual* (Albany: Brandow and Barton, 1884), 11.

23. *AEJ*, July 15, Aug. 13, 1865.

24. For a thoughtful discussion of "Anti-Rent today," focusing on memory and the use of historical symbols in political discourse, see Rachelle H. Saltzman, "Calico Indians and Pistol Pills: Traditional Drama, Historical Symbols, and Political Actions in Upstate New York," *New York Folklore* 20 (1994): 1–17. Many of the songs, which are sung every year at folk festivals in eastern New York, are printed in the appendix of Henry Christman, *Tin Horns and Calico* (New York: Henry Holt, 1945).

25. *Argus*, May 26, 1865.

26. *AEJ*, Sept. 11, 1844. For Church's road to bankruptcy, see Gregg, *Old Hellebergh*, 172–73.

27. Christman, *Tin Horns and Calico*, 301 (quoting *Troy News*).

28. Henry George, *Progress and Poverty: An Inquiry into the Cause of Industrial Depressions and of Increase of Want with Increase of Wealth*, 50th Anniversary Edition (New York: Robert Schalkenbach Foundation, 1930), 362.

29. "Anti-Rent State Convention," *Argus*, Feb. 10, 1845; Alexis de Tocqueville, *Democracy in America*, ed. Phillips Bradley, 2 vols. (New York: Alfred A. Knopf, 1945), 1:58; [C. F. Bouton], "Our Meetings and Our Prospect," *Freeholder*, July 19, 1948; [Minor Frink], "A Plain Talk with Landlords," ibid., Apr. 24, 1850.

30. For the logic and significance of the phrase "polity of courts and parties," see Stephen Skowronek, *Building a New American State: The Expansion of National Administrative Capacities, 1877–1920* (New York: Cambridge University Press, 1982), 5–35.

31. Lincoln to Albert G. Hodges, Apr. 4, 1864, *Collected Works of Abraham Lincoln*, ed. Roy P. Basler, 9 vols. (New Brunswick, N.J.: Rutgers University Press, 1953–55), 7:282.

32. *Albany Times-Union*, July 7, 1991 (clipping courtesy of Richard Hamm).

Index